©2015 Kitware, Inc. *(cover, preface, postface)*
©2015 Insight Software Consortium *(main text body)*
Published by Kitware, Inc. http://www.kitware.com

An electronic version of this document is available from http://itk.org.

This work is licensed under a Creative Commons Attribution 3.0 Unported License.

This project has been funded in whole or in part with Federal funds from the National Institutes of Health (NLM, NIDCR, NIMH, NEI, NINDS, NIDCD, NCI), the NSF, and the DoD (TATRC). Funding has primarily come under the direction of the National Library of Medicine, National Institutes of Health, under numerous contracts. Recently, the major revision to the toolkit, ITKv4, was made possible by NLM directed funds from the American Reinvestment and Recovery Act (ARRA).

All product names mentioned herein are the trademarks of their respective owners.

Document created with LaTeX, using CMake as configuration manager, with a Python script to extract examples from the ITK/Examples directory. All code in this document compiled at the time of publication.

Printed and produced in the United States of America.
ISBN 9781-930934-28-3

The ITK Software Guide
Book 2: Design and Functionality
Fourth Edition
Updated for ITK version 4.7

Hans J. Johnson, Matthew M. McCormick, Luis Ibáñez,
and the *Insight Software Consortium*

January 16, 2015

http://itk.org
Email: community@itk.org

The purpose of computing is Insight, not numbers.

Richard Hamming

ABOUT THE COVER

The cover image consists of a photograph of ABS plastic anatomical objects printed with a MakerBot Replicator 2X 3D printer. Mesh STL files were generated from the images with VTK.

Skull. Given that the origins of ITK are with the Visible Human Project, it is appropriate that the skull was derived from the Visible Woman dataset. The skull was segmented with ITK from the Visible Woman head CT images with simple thresholding[1].

Brain. The brain model was segmented with ITK as described in the open science publication:

> McCormick M, Liu X, Jomier J, Marion C and Ibanez L. ITK: enabling reproducible research and open science. Front. Neuroinform. 8:13. 2014. doi: 10.3389/fninf.2014.00013

---

[1] https://github.com/XiaoxiaoLiu/3D-printing

ABSTRACT

The Insight Toolkit (ITK) is an open-source software toolkit for performing registration and segmentation. *Segmentation* is the process of identifying and classifying data found in a digitally sampled representation. Typically the sampled representation is an image acquired from such medical instrumentation as CT or MRI scanners. *Registration* is the task of aligning or developing correspondences between data. For example, in the medical environment, a CT scan may be aligned with a MRI scan in order to combine the information contained in both.

ITK is a cross-platform software. It uses a build environment known as CMake to manage platform-specific project generation and compilation process in a platform-independent way. ITK is implemented in C++. ITK's implementation style employs generic programming, which involves the use of templates to generate, at compile-time, code that can be applied *generically* to any class or data-type that supports the operations used by the template. The use of C++ templating means that the code is highly efficient and many issues are discovered at compile-time, rather than at run-time during program execution. It also means that many of ITK's algorithms can be applied to arbitrary spatial dimensions and pixel types.

An automated wrapping system integrated with ITK generates an interface between C++ and a high-level programming language Python. This enables rapid prototyping and faster exploration of ideas by shortening the edit-compile-execute cycle. In addition to automated wrapping, the SimpleITK project provides a streamlined interface to ITK that is available for C++, Python, Java, CSharp, R, Tcl and Ruby.

Developers from around the world can use, debug, maintain, and extend the software because ITK is an open-source project. ITK uses a model of software development known as Extreme Programming. Extreme Programming collapses the usual software development methodology into a simultaneous iterative process of design-implement-test-release. The key features of Extreme Programming are communication and testing. Communication among the members of the ITK community is what helps manage the rapid evolution of the software. Testing is what keeps the software stable. An extensive testing process supported by the system known as CDash measures the quality of ITK code on a daily basis. The ITK Testing Dashboard is updated continuously, reflecting the quality of the code at any moment.

The most recent version of this document is available online at http://itk.org/ItkSoftwareGuide.pdf. This book is a guide to developing software with ITK; it is the second of two companion books. This book covers detailed design and functionality for reading and writing images, filtering, registration, segmentation, and performing statistical analysis. The first book covers building and installation, general architecture and design, as well as the process of contributing in the ITK community.

CONTRIBUTORS

The Insight Toolkit (ITK) has been created by the efforts of many talented individuals and prestigious organizations. It is also due in great part to the vision of the program established by Dr. Terry Yoo and Dr. Michael Ackerman at the National Library of Medicine.

This book lists a few of these contributors in the following paragraphs. Not all developers of ITK are credited here, so please visit the Web pages at http://itk.org/ITK/project/parti.html for the names of additional contributors, as well as checking the GIT source logs for code contributions.

The following is a brief description of the contributors to this software guide and their contributions.

Luis Ibáñez is principal author of this text. He assisted in the design and layout of the text, implemented the bulk of the LaTeX and CMake build process, and was responsible for the bulk of the content. He also developed most of the example code found in the `Insight/Examples` directory.

Will Schroeder helped design and establish the organization of this text and the `Insight/Examples` directory. He is principal content editor, and has authored several chapters.

Lydia Ng authored the description for the registration framework and its components, the section on the multiresolution framework, and the section on deformable registration methods. She also edited the section on the resampling image filter and the sections on various level set segmentation algorithms.

Joshua Cates authored the iterators chapter and the text and examples describing watershed segmentation. He also co-authored the level-set segmentation material.

Jisung Kim authored the chapter on the statistics framework.

Julien Jomier contributed the chapter on spatial objects and examples on model-based registration using spatial objects.

Karthik Krishnan reconfigured the process for automatically generating images from all the examples. Added a large number of new examples and updated the Filtering and Segmentation chapters for the second edition.

Stephen Aylward contributed material describing spatial objects and their application.

Tessa Sundaram contributed the section on deformable registration using the finite element method.

YinPeng Jin contributed the examples on hybrid segmentation methods.

Celina Imielinska authored the section describing the principles of hybrid segmentation methods.

Mark Foskey contributed the examples on the AutomaticTopologyMeshSource class.

Mathieu Malaterre contributed the entire section on the description and use of DICOM readers and writers based on the GDCM library. He also contributed an example on the use of the VTKImageIO class.

Gavin Baker contributed the section on how to write composite filters. Also known as minipipeline filters.

Since the software guide is generated in part from the ITK source code itself, many ITK developers have been involved in updating and extending the ITK documentation. These include **David Doria**, **Bradley Lowekamp, Mark Foskey, Gaëtan Lehmann, Andreas Schuh, Tom Vercauteren, Cory Quammen, Daniel Blezek, Paul Hughett, Matthew McCormick, Josh Cates, Arnaud Gelas, Jim Miller, Brad King, Gabe Hart, Hans Johnson**.

Hans Johnson, Kent Williams, Constantine Zakkaroff, Xiaoxiao Liu, Ali Ghayoor, and **Matthew McCormick** updated the documentation for the initial ITK Version 4 release.

Luis Ibáñez and **Sébastien Barré** designed the original Book 1 cover. **Matthew McCormick** and **Brad King** updated the code to produce the Book 1 cover for ITK 4 and VTK 6. **Xiaoxiao Liu, Bill Lorensen, Luis Ibáñez,**and **Matthew McCormick** created the 3D printed anatomical objects that were photographed by **Sébastien Barré** for the Book 2 cover. **Steve Jordan** designed the layout of the covers.

Lisa Avila, Hans Johnson, Matthew McCormick, Sandy McKenzie, Christopher Mullins, Katie Osterdahl, and **Michka Popoff** prepared the book for the 4.7 print release.

CONTENTS

LIST OF FIGURES

LIST OF TABLES

READING AND WRITING IMAGES

This chapter describes the toolkit architecture supporting reading and writing of images to files. ITK does not enforce any particular file format, instead, it provides a structure supporting a variety of formats that can be easily extended by the user as new formats become available.

We begin the chapter with some simple examples of file I/O.

1.1 Basic Example

The source code for this section can be found in the file
`ImageReadWrite.cxx`.

The classes responsible for reading and writing images are located at the beginning and end of the data processing pipeline. These classes are known as data sources (readers) and data sinks (writers). Generally speaking they are referred to as filters, although readers have no pipeline input and writers have no pipeline output.

The reading of images is managed by the class `itk::ImageFileReader` while writing is performed by the class `itk::ImageFileWriter`. These two classes are independent of any particular file format. The actual low level task of reading and writing specific file formats is done behind the scenes by a family of classes of type `itk::ImageIO`.

The first step for performing reading and writing is to include the following headers.

```
#include "itkImageFileReader.h"
#include "itkImageFileWriter.h"
```

Then, as usual, a decision must be made about the type of pixel used to represent the image processed by the pipeline. Note that when reading and writing images, the pixel type of the image **is not necessarily** the same as the pixel type stored in the file. Your choice of the pixel type (and hence template parameter) should be driven mainly by two considerations:

- It should be possible to cast the pixel type in the file to the pixel type you select. This casting will be performed using the standard C-language rules, so you will have to make sure that the conversion does not result in information being lost.

- The pixel type in memory should be appropriate to the type of processing you intend to apply on the images.

A typical selection for medical images is illustrated in the following lines.

```
typedef short         PixelType;
const  unsigned int  Dimension = 2;
typedef itk::Image< PixelType, Dimension >   ImageType;
```

Note that the dimension of the image in memory should match that of the image in the file. There are a couple of special cases in which this condition may be relaxed, but in general it is better to ensure that both dimensions match.

We can now instantiate the types of the reader and writer. These two classes are parameterized over the image type.

```
typedef itk::ImageFileReader< ImageType >   ReaderType;
typedef itk::ImageFileWriter< ImageType >   WriterType;
```

Then, we create one object of each type using the New() method and assign the result to a itk::SmartPointer.

```
ReaderType::Pointer reader = ReaderType::New();
WriterType::Pointer writer = WriterType::New();
```

The name of the file to be read or written is passed to the SetFileName() method.

```
reader->SetFileName( inputFilename  );
writer->SetFileName( outputFilename );
```

We can now connect these readers and writers to filters to create a pipeline. For example, we can create a short pipeline by passing the output of the reader directly to the input of the writer.

```
writer->SetInput( reader->GetOutput() );
```

At first glance this may look like a quite useless program, but it is actually implementing a powerful file format conversion tool! The execution of the pipeline is triggered by the invocation of the Update() methods in one of the final objects. In this case, the final data pipeline object is the writer. It is a wise practice of defensive programming to insert any Update() call inside a try/catch block in case exceptions are thrown during the execution of the pipeline.

```
try
  {
  writer->Update();
  }
catch( itk::ExceptionObject & err )
  {
  std::cerr << "ExceptionObject caught !" << std::endl;
  std::cerr << err << std::endl;
  return EXIT_FAILURE;
  }
```

Note that exceptions should only be caught by pieces of code that know what to do with them. In a typical application this catch block should probably reside in the GUI code. The action on the

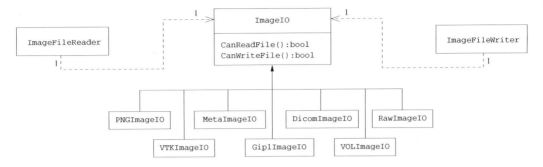

Figure 1.1: Collaboration diagram of the ImageIO classes.

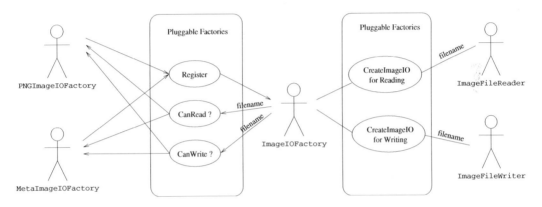

Figure 1.2: Use cases of ImageIO factories.

catch block could inform the user about the failure of the IO operation.

The IO architecture of the toolkit makes it possible to avoid explicit specification of the file format used to read or write images.[1] The object factory mechanism enables the ImageFileReader and ImageFileWriter to determine (at run-time) which file format it is working with. Typically, file formats are chosen based on the filename extension, but the architecture supports arbitrarily complex processes to determine whether a file can be read or written. Alternatively, the user can specify the data file format by explicit instantiation and assignment of the appropriate itk::ImageIO subclass.

For historical reasons and as a convenience to the user, the itk::ImageFileWriter also has a Write() method that is aliased to the Update() method. You can in principle use either of them but Update() is recommended since Write() may be deprecated in the future.

To better understand the IO architecture, please refer to Figures 1.1, 1.2, and 1.3.

The following section describes the internals of the IO architecture provided in the toolkit.

---

[1] In this example no file format is specified; this program can be used as a general file conversion utility.

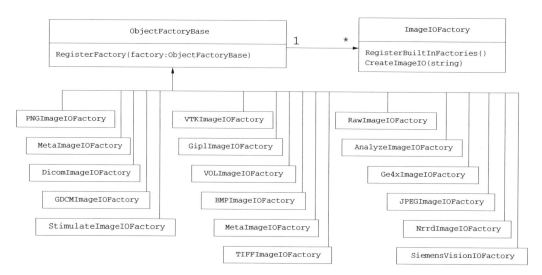

Figure 1.3: Class diagram of the ImageIO factories.

1.2   Pluggable Factories

The principle behind the input/output mechanism used in ITK is known as *pluggable-factories* [21]. This concept is illustrated in the UML diagram in Figure 1.1. From the user's point of view the objects responsible for reading and writing files are the `itk::ImageFileReader` and `itk::ImageFileWriter` classes. These two classes, however, are not aware of the details involved in reading or writing particular file formats like PNG or DICOM. What they do is dispatch the user's requests to a set of specific classes that are aware of the details of image file formats. These classes are the `itk::ImageIO` classes. The ITK delegation mechanism enables users to extend the number of supported file formats by just adding new classes to the ImageIO hierarchy.

Each instance of ImageFileReader and ImageFileWriter has a pointer to an ImageIO object. If this pointer is empty, it will be impossible to read or write an image and the image file reader/writer must determine which ImageIO class to use to perform IO operations. This is done basically by passing the filename to a centralized class, the `itk::ImageIOFactory` and asking it to identify any subclass of ImageIO capable of reading or writing the user-specified file. This is illustrated by the use cases on the right side of Figure 1.2. The ImageIOFactory acts here as a dispatcher that helps locate the actual IO factory classes corresponding to each file format.

Each class derived from ImageIO must provide an associated factory class capable of producing an instance of the ImageIO class. For example, for PNG files, there is a `itk::PNGImageIO` object that knows how to read this image files and there is a `itk::PNGImageIOFactory` class capable of constructing a PNGImageIO object and returning a pointer to it. Each time a new file format is added (i.e., a new ImageIO subclass is created), a factory must be implemented as a derived class of the ObjectFactoryBase class as illustrated in Figure 1.3.

For example, in order to read PNG files, a PNGImageIOFactory is created and registered with the central ImageIOFactory singleton[2] class as illustrated in the left side of Figure 1.2. When the ImageFileReader asks the ImageIOFactory for an ImageIO capable of reading the file identified with *filename* the ImageIOFactory will iterate over the list of registered factories and will ask each one of them if they know how to read the file. The factory that responds affirmatively will be used to create the specific ImageIO instance that will be returned to the ImageFileReader and used to perform the read operations.

In most cases the mechanism is transparent to the user who only interacts with the ImageFileReader and ImageFileWriter. It is possible, however, to explicitly select the type of ImageIO object to use. This is illustrated by the following example.

1.3   Using ImageIO Classes Explicitly

The source code for this section can be found in the file
`ImageReadExportVTK.cxx`.

In cases where the user knows what file format to use and wants to indicate this explicitly, a specific `itk::ImageIO` class can be instantiated and assigned to the image file reader or writer. This circumvents the `itk::ImageIOFactory` mechanism which tries to find the appropriate ImageIO class for performing the IO operations. Explicit selection of the ImageIO also allows the user to invoke specialized features of a particular class which may not be available from the general API provided by ImageIO.

The following example illustrates explicit instantiation of an IO class (in this case a VTK file format), setting its parameters and then connecting it to the `itk::ImageFileWriter`.

The example begins by including the appropriate headers.

```
#include "itkImageFileReader.h"
#include "itkImageFileWriter.h"
#include "itkVTKImageIO.h"
```

Then, as usual, we select the pixel types and the image dimension. Remember, if the file format represents pixels with a particular type, C-style casting will be performed to convert the data.

```
typedef unsigned short       PixelType;
const   unsigned int         Dimension = 2;
typedef itk::Image< PixelType, Dimension >   ImageType;
```

We can now instantiate the reader and writer. These two classes are parameterized over the image type. We instantiate the `itk::VTKImageIO` class as well. Note that the ImageIO objects are not templated.

```
typedef itk::ImageFileReader< ImageType >   ReaderType;
typedef itk::ImageFileWriter< ImageType >   WriterType;
typedef itk::VTKImageIO                      ImageIOType;
```

Then, we create one object of each type using the New() method and assigning the result to a `itk::SmartPointer`.

---

[2]*Singleton* means that there is only one instance of this class in a particular application

```
ReaderType::Pointer reader = ReaderType::New();
WriterType::Pointer writer = WriterType::New();
ImageIOType::Pointer vtkIO = ImageIOType::New();
```

The name of the file to be read or written is passed with the SetFileName() method.

```
reader->SetFileName( inputFilename );
writer->SetFileName( outputFilename );
```

We can now connect these readers and writers to filters in a pipeline. For example, we can create a short pipeline by passing the output of the reader directly to the input of the writer.

```
writer->SetInput( reader->GetOutput() );
```

Explicitly declaring the specific VTKImageIO allow users to invoke methods specific to a particular IO class. For example, the following line specifies to the writer to use ASCII format when writing the pixel data.

```
vtkIO->SetFileTypeToASCII();
```

The VTKImageIO object is then connected to the ImageFileWriter. This will short-circuit the action of the ImageIOFactory mechanism. The ImageFileWriter will not attempt to look for other ImageIO objects capable of performing the writing tasks. It will simply invoke the one provided by the user.

```
writer->SetImageIO( vtkIO );
```

Finally we invoke Update() on the ImageFileWriter and place this call inside a try/catch block in case any errors occur during the writing process.

```
try
  {
  writer->Update();
  }
catch( itk::ExceptionObject & err )
  {
  std::cerr << "ExceptionObject caught !" << std::endl;
  std::cerr << err << std::endl;
  return EXIT_FAILURE;
  }
```

Although this example only illustrates how to use an explicit ImageIO class with the Image-FileWriter, the same can be done with the ImageFileReader. The typical case in which this is done is when reading raw image files with the itk::RawImageIO object. The drawback of this approach is that the parameters of the image have to be explicitly written in the code. The direct use of raw files is **strongly discouraged** in medical imaging. It is always better to create a header for a raw file by using any of the file formats that combine a text header file and a raw binary file, like itk::MetaImageIO, itk::GiplImageIO and itk::VTKImageIO.

1.4   Reading and Writing RGB Images

The source code for this section can be found in the file
RGBImageReadWrite.cxx.

RGB images are commonly used for representing data acquired from cryogenic sections, optical microscopy and endoscopy. This example illustrates how to read and write RGB color images to and from a file. This requires the following headers as shown.

```
#include "itkRGBPixel.h"
#include "itkImage.h"
#include "itkImageFileReader.h"
#include "itkImageFileWriter.h"
```

The `itk::RGBPixel` class is templated over the type used to represent each one of the red, green and blue components. A typical instantiation of the RGB image class might be as follows.

```
typedef itk::RGBPixel< unsigned char >   PixelType;
typedef itk::Image< PixelType, 2 >        ImageType;
```

The image type is used as a template parameter to instantiate the reader and writer.

```
typedef itk::ImageFileReader< ImageType >  ReaderType;
typedef itk::ImageFileWriter< ImageType >  WriterType;

ReaderType::Pointer reader = ReaderType::New();
WriterType::Pointer writer = WriterType::New();
```

The filenames of the input and output files must be provided to the reader and writer respectively.

```
reader->SetFileName( inputFilename  );
writer->SetFileName( outputFilename );
```

Finally, execution of the pipeline can be triggered by invoking the Update() method in the writer.

```
writer->Update();
```

You may have noticed that apart from the declaration of the `PixelType` there is nothing in this code specific to RGB images. All the actions required to support color images are implemented internally in the `itk::ImageIO` objects.

1.5   Reading, Casting and Writing Images

The source code for this section can be found in the file
ImageReadCastWrite.cxx.

Given that ITK is based on the Generic Programming paradigm, most of the types are defined at compilation time. It is sometimes important to anticipate conversion between different types of images. The following example illustrates the common case of reading an image of one pixel type and writing it as a different pixel type. This process not only involves casting but also rescaling the image intensity since the dynamic range of the input and output pixel types can be quite different. The `itk::RescaleIntensityImageFilter` is used here to linearly rescale the image values.

The first step in this example is to include the appropriate headers.

```
#include "itkImageFileReader.h"
#include "itkImageFileWriter.h"
#include "itkRescaleIntensityImageFilter.h"
```

Then, as usual, a decision should be made about the pixel type that should be used to represent the images. Note that when reading an image, this pixel type **is not necessarily** the pixel type of the image stored in the file. Instead, it is the type that will be used to store the image as soon as it is read into memory.

```
typedef float              InputPixelType;
typedef unsigned char      OutputPixelType;
const   unsigned int       Dimension = 2;

typedef itk::Image< InputPixelType,  Dimension >    InputImageType;
typedef itk::Image< OutputPixelType, Dimension >    OutputImageType;
```

Note that the dimension of the image in memory should match the one of the image in the file. There are a couple of special cases in which this condition may be relaxed, but in general it is better to ensure that both dimensions match.

We can now instantiate the types of the reader and writer. These two classes are parameterized over the image type.

```
typedef itk::ImageFileReader< InputImageType  >  ReaderType;
typedef itk::ImageFileWriter< OutputImageType >  WriterType;
```

Below we instantiate the RescaleIntensityImageFilter class that will linearly scale the image intensities.

```
typedef itk::RescaleIntensityImageFilter<
                        InputImageType,
                        OutputImageType >    FilterType;
```

A filter object is constructed and the minimum and maximum values of the output are selected using the SetOutputMinimum() and SetOutputMaximum() methods.

```
FilterType::Pointer filter = FilterType::New();
filter->SetOutputMinimum(   0 );
filter->SetOutputMaximum( 255 );
```

Then, we create the reader and writer and connect the pipeline.

```
ReaderType::Pointer reader = ReaderType::New();
WriterType::Pointer writer = WriterType::New();

filter->SetInput( reader->GetOutput() );
writer->SetInput( filter->GetOutput() );
```

The name of the files to be read and written are passed with the SetFileName() method.

```
reader->SetFileName( inputFilename  );
writer->SetFileName( outputFilename );
```

Finally we trigger the execution of the pipeline with the Update() method on the writer. The output image will then be the scaled and cast version of the input image.

```
try
  {
  writer->Update();
  }
catch( itk::ExceptionObject & err )
  {
  std::cerr << "ExceptionObject caught !" << std::endl;
  std::cerr << err << std::endl;
  return EXIT_FAILURE;
  }
```

1.6   Extracting Regions

The source code for this section can be found in the file
ImageReadRegionOfInterestWrite.cxx.

This example should arguably be placed in the previous filtering chapter. However its usefulness for
typical IO operations makes it interesting to mention here. The purpose of this example is to read an
image, extract a subregion and write this subregion to a file. This is a common task when we want
to apply a computationally intensive method to the region of interest of an image.

As usual with ITK IO, we begin by including the appropriate header files.

```
#include "itkImageFileReader.h"
#include "itkImageFileWriter.h"
```

The itk::RegionOfInterestImageFilter is the filter used to extract a region from an image. Its
header is included below.

```
#include "itkRegionOfInterestImageFilter.h"
```

Image types are defined below.

```
typedef signed short        InputPixelType;
typedef signed short        OutputPixelType;
const   unsigned int        Dimension = 2;

typedef itk::Image< InputPixelType,  Dimension >   InputImageType;
typedef itk::Image< OutputPixelType, Dimension >   OutputImageType;
```

The types for the itk::ImageFileReader and itk::ImageFileWriter are instantiated using the
image types.

```
typedef itk::ImageFileReader< InputImageType  >  ReaderType;
typedef itk::ImageFileWriter< OutputImageType >  WriterType;
```

The RegionOfInterestImageFilter type is instantiated using the input and output image types. A filter
object is created with the New() method and assigned to a itk::SmartPointer.

```
typedef itk::RegionOfInterestImageFilter< InputImageType,
                                          OutputImageType > FilterType;

FilterType::Pointer filter = FilterType::New();
```

The RegionOfInterestImageFilter requires a region to be defined by the user. The region is specified by an itk::Index indicating the pixel where the region starts and an itk::Size indicating how many pixels the region has along each dimension. In this example, the specification of the region is taken from the command line arguments (this example assumes that a 2D image is being processed).

```
OutputImageType::IndexType start;
start[0] = atoi( argv[3] );
start[1] = atoi( argv[4] );

OutputImageType::SizeType size;
size[0] = atoi( argv[5] );
size[1] = atoi( argv[6] );
```

An itk::ImageRegion object is created and initialized with start and size obtained from the command line.

```
OutputImageType::RegionType desiredRegion;
desiredRegion.SetSize( size );
desiredRegion.SetIndex( start );
```

Then the region is passed to the filter using the SetRegionOfInterest() method.

```
filter->SetRegionOfInterest( desiredRegion );
```

Below, we create the reader and writer using the New() method and assign the result to a itk::SmartPointer.

```
ReaderType::Pointer reader = ReaderType::New();
WriterType::Pointer writer = WriterType::New();
```

The name of the file to be read or written is passed with the SetFileName() method.

```
reader->SetFileName( inputFilename  );
writer->SetFileName( outputFilename );
```

Below we connect the reader, filter and writer to form the data processing pipeline.

```
filter->SetInput( reader->GetOutput() );
writer->SetInput( filter->GetOutput() );
```

Finally we execute the pipeline by invoking Update() on the writer. The call is placed in a try/catch block in case exceptions are thrown.

```
try
  {
  writer->Update();
  }
catch( itk::ExceptionObject & err )
  {
  std::cerr << "ExceptionObject caught !" << std::endl;
  std::cerr << err << std::endl;
  return EXIT_FAILURE;
  }
```

1.7 Extracting Slices

The source code for this section can be found in the file
ImageReadExtractWrite.cxx.

This example illustrates the common task of extracting a 2D slice from a 3D volume. This is typically
used for display purposes and for expediting user feedback in interactive programs. Here we simply
read a 3D volume, extract one of its slices and save it as a 2D image. Note that caution should be
used when working with 2D slices from a 3D dataset, since for most image processing operations, the
application of a filter on an extracted slice is not equivalent to first applying the filter in the volume
and then extracting the slice.

In this example we start by including the appropriate header files.

```
#include "itkImageFileReader.h"
#include "itkImageFileWriter.h"
```

The filter used to extract a region from an image is the itk::ExtractImageFilter. Its header is
included below. This filter is capable of extracting $(N-1)$-dimensional images from N-dimensional
ones.

```
#include "itkExtractImageFilter.h"
```

Image types are defined below. Note that the input image type is $3D$ and the output image type is
$2D$.

```
typedef signed short          InputPixelType;
typedef signed short          OutputPixelType;

typedef itk::Image< InputPixelType,  3 >    InputImageType;
typedef itk::Image< OutputPixelType, 2 >    OutputImageType;
```

The types for the itk::ImageFileReader and itk::ImageFileWriter are instantiated using the
image types.

```
typedef itk::ImageFileReader< InputImageType  >   ReaderType;
typedef itk::ImageFileWriter< OutputImageType >   WriterType;
```

Below, we create the reader and writer using the New() method and assign the result to a
itk::SmartPointer.

```
ReaderType::Pointer reader = ReaderType::New();
WriterType::Pointer writer = WriterType::New();
```

The name of the file to be read or written is passed with the SetFileName() method.

```
reader->SetFileName( inputFilename  );
writer->SetFileName( outputFilename );
```

The ExtractImageFilter type is instantiated using the input and output image types. A filter object is
created with the New() method and assigned to a itk::SmartPointer.

```
typedef itk::ExtractImageFilter< InputImageType,
                                 OutputImageType > FilterType;
FilterType::Pointer filter = FilterType::New();
filter->InPlaceOn();
filter->SetDirectionCollapseToSubmatrix();
```

The ExtractImageFilter requires a region to be defined by the user. The region is specified by an itk::Index indicating the pixel where the region starts and an itk::Size indicating how many pixels the region has along each dimension. In order to extract a 2D image from a 3D data set, it is enough to set the size of the region to 0 in one dimension. This will indicate to ExtractImageFilter that a dimensional reduction has been specified. Here we take the region from the largest possible region of the input image. Note that UpdateOutputInformation() is being called first on the reader. This method updates the metadata in the output image without actually reading in the bulk-data.

```
reader->UpdateOutputInformation();
InputImageType::RegionType inputRegion =
       reader->GetOutput()->GetLargestPossibleRegion();
```

We take the size from the region and collapse the size in the Z component by setting its value to 0. This will indicate to the ExtractImageFilter that the output image should have a dimension less than the input image.

```
InputImageType::SizeType size = inputRegion.GetSize();
size[2] = 0;
```

Note that in this case we are extracting a Z slice, and for that reason, the dimension to be collapsed is the one with index 2. You may keep in mind the association of index components $\{X = 0, Y = 1, Z = 2\}$. If we were interested in extracting a slice perpendicular to the Y axis we would have set size[1]=0;.

Then, we take the index from the region and set its Z value to the slice number we want to extract. In this example we obtain the slice number from the command line arguments.

```
InputImageType::IndexType start = inputRegion.GetIndex();
const unsigned int sliceNumber = atoi( argv[3] );
start[2] = sliceNumber;
```

Finally, an itk::ImageRegion object is created and initialized with the start and size we just prepared using the slice information.

```
InputImageType::RegionType desiredRegion;
desiredRegion.SetSize( size );
desiredRegion.SetIndex( start );
```

Then the region is passed to the filter using the SetExtractionRegion() method.

```
filter->SetExtractionRegion( desiredRegion );
```

Below we connect the reader, filter and writer to form the data processing pipeline.

```
filter->SetInput( reader->GetOutput() );
writer->SetInput( filter->GetOutput() );
```

Finally we execute the pipeline by invoking Update() on the writer. The call is placed in a try/catch block in case exceptions are thrown.

```
try
  {
  writer->Update();
  }
catch( itk::ExceptionObject & err )
  {
  std::cerr << "ExceptionObject caught !" << std::endl;
  std::cerr << err << std::endl;
  return EXIT_FAILURE;
  }
```

1.8   Reading and Writing Vector Images

Images whose pixel type is a Vector, a CovariantVector, an Array, or a Complex are quite common in image processing. It is convenient then to describe rapidly how those images can be saved into files and how they can be read from those files later on.

1.8.1   The Minimal Example

The source code for this section can be found in the file
VectorImageReadWrite.cxx.

This example illustrates how to read and write an image of pixel type `itk::Vector`.

We should include the header files for the Image, the ImageFileReader and the ImageFileWriter.

```
#include "itkImage.h"
#include "itkImageFileReader.h"
#include "itkImageFileWriter.h"
```

Then we define the specific type of vector to be used as pixel type.

```
const unsigned int VectorDimension = 3;

typedef itk::Vector< float, VectorDimension >   PixelType;
```

We define the image dimension, and along with the pixel type we use it for fully instantiating the image type.

```
const unsigned int ImageDimension = 2;

typedef itk::Image< PixelType, ImageDimension > ImageType;
```

Having the image type at hand, we can instantiate the reader and writer types, and use them for creating one object of each type.

```
typedef itk::ImageFileReader< ImageType > ReaderType;
typedef itk::ImageFileWriter< ImageType > WriterType;

ReaderType::Pointer reader = ReaderType::New();
WriterType::Pointer writer = WriterType::New();
```

A filename must be provided to both the reader and the writer. In this particular case we take those filenames from the command line arguments.

```
reader->SetFileName( argv[1] );
writer->SetFileName( argv[2] );
```

This being a minimal example, we create a short pipeline where we simply connect the output of the reader to the input of the writer.

```
writer->SetInput( reader->GetOutput() );
```

The execution of this short pipeline is triggered by invoking the writer's `Update()` method. This invocation must be placed inside a `try/catch` block since its execution may result in exceptions being thrown.

```
try
  {
  writer->Update();
  }
catch( itk::ExceptionObject & err )
  {
  std::cerr << "ExceptionObject caught !" << std::endl;
  std::cerr << err << std::endl;
  return EXIT_FAILURE;
  }
```

Of course, you could envision the addition of filters in between the reader and the writer. Those filters could perform operations on the vector image.

1.8.2   Producing and Writing Covariant Images

The source code for this section can be found in the file
`CovariantVectorImageWrite.cxx`.

This example illustrates how to write an image whose pixel type is `CovariantVector`. For practical purposes all the content in this example is applicable to images of pixel type `itk::Vector`, `itk::Point` and `itk::FixedArray`. These pixel types are similar in that they are all arrays of fixed size in which the components have the same representational type.

In order to make this example a bit more interesting we setup a pipeline to read an image, compute its gradient and write the gradient to a file. Gradients are represented with `itk::CovariantVectors` as opposed to Vectors. In this way, gradients are transformed correctly under `itk::AffineTransforms` or in general, any transform having anisotropic scaling.

Let's start by including the relevant header files.

```
#include "itkImageFileReader.h"
#include "itkImageFileWriter.h"
```

We use the `itk::GradientRecursiveGaussianImageFilter` in order to compute the image gradient. The output of this filter is an image whose pixels are CovariantVectors.

```
#include "itkGradientRecursiveGaussianImageFilter.h"
```

We read an image of `signed short` pixels and compute the gradient to produce an image of CovariantVectors where each component is of type `float`.

```
typedef signed short          InputPixelType;
typedef float                 ComponentType;
const   unsigned int          Dimension = 2;

typedef itk::CovariantVector< ComponentType,
                              Dimension >     OutputPixelType;

typedef itk::Image< InputPixelType,  Dimension >   InputImageType;
typedef itk::Image< OutputPixelType, Dimension >   OutputImageType;
```

The `itk::ImageFileReader` and `itk::ImageFileWriter` are instantiated using the image types.

```
typedef itk::ImageFileReader< InputImageType  >  ReaderType;
typedef itk::ImageFileWriter< OutputImageType >  WriterType;
```

The GradientRecursiveGaussianImageFilter class is instantiated using the input and output image types. A filter object is created with the `New()` method and assigned to a `itk::SmartPointer`.

```
typedef itk::GradientRecursiveGaussianImageFilter<
                              InputImageType,
                              OutputImageType    > FilterType;

FilterType::Pointer filter = FilterType::New();
```

We select a value for the σ parameter of the GradientRecursiveGaussianImageFilter. Note that σ for this filter is specified in millimeters.

```
filter->SetSigma( 1.5 );        // Sigma in millimeters
```

Below, we create the reader and writer using the `New()` method and assign the result to a `itk::SmartPointer`.

```
ReaderType::Pointer reader = ReaderType::New();
WriterType::Pointer writer = WriterType::New();
```

The name of the file to be read or written is passed to the `SetFileName()` method.

```
reader->SetFileName( inputFilename  );
writer->SetFileName( outputFilename );
```

Below we connect the reader, filter and writer to form the data processing pipeline.

```
filter->SetInput( reader->GetOutput() );
writer->SetInput( filter->GetOutput() );
```

Finally we execute the pipeline by invoking `Update()` on the writer. The call is placed in a `try/catch` block in case exceptions are thrown.

```
try
  {
  writer->Update();
  }
catch( itk::ExceptionObject & err )
  {
  std::cerr << "ExceptionObject caught !" << std::endl;
  std::cerr << err << std::endl;
  return EXIT_FAILURE;
  }
```

1.8.3   Reading Covariant Images

Let's now take the image that we just created and read it into another program.

The source code for this section can be found in the file
CovariantVectorImageRead.cxx.

This example illustrates how to read an image whose pixel type is CovariantVector. For practical purposes this example is applicable to images of pixel type itk::Vector, itk::Point and itk::FixedArray. These pixel types are similar in that they are all arrays of fixed size in which the components have the same representation type.

In this example we are reading a gradient image from a file (written in the previous example) and computing its magnitude using the itk::VectorMagnitudeImageFilter. Note that this filter is different from the itk::GradientMagnitudeImageFilter which actually takes a scalar image as input and computes the magnitude of its gradient. The VectorMagnitudeImageFilter class takes an image of vector pixel type as input and computes pixel-wise the magnitude of each vector.

Let's start by including the relevant header files.

```
#include "itkImageFileReader.h"
#include "itkImageFileWriter.h"
#include "itkVectorMagnitudeImageFilter.h"
#include "itkRescaleIntensityImageFilter.h"
```

We read an image of itk::CovariantVector pixels and compute pixel magnitude to produce an image where each pixel is of type unsigned short. The components of the CovariantVector are selected to be float here. Notice that a renormalization is required in order to map the dynamic range of the magnitude values into the range of the output pixel type. The itk::RescaleIntensityImageFilter is used to achieve this.

```
typedef float                     ComponentType;
const   unsigned int              Dimension = 2;

typedef itk::CovariantVector< ComponentType,
                              Dimension   >      InputPixelType;

typedef float                                   MagnitudePixelType;
typedef unsigned short                          OutputPixelType;

typedef itk::Image< InputPixelType,     Dimension >    InputImageType;
typedef itk::Image< MagnitudePixelType, Dimension >    MagnitudeImageType;
typedef itk::Image< OutputPixelType,    Dimension >    OutputImageType;
```

The `itk::ImageFileReader` and `itk::ImageFileWriter` are instantiated using the image types.

```
typedef itk::ImageFileReader< InputImageType  >  ReaderType;
typedef itk::ImageFileWriter< OutputImageType >  WriterType;
```

The VectorMagnitudeImageFilter is instantiated using the input and output image types. A filter object is created with the `New()` method and assigned to a `itk::SmartPointer`.

```
typedef itk::VectorMagnitudeImageFilter<
                                 InputImageType,
                                 MagnitudeImageType   > FilterType;

FilterType::Pointer filter = FilterType::New();
```

The RescaleIntensityImageFilter class is instantiated next.

```
typedef itk::RescaleIntensityImageFilter<
                                 MagnitudeImageType,
                                 OutputImageType >      RescaleFilterType;

RescaleFilterType::Pointer  rescaler = RescaleFilterType::New();
```

In the following the minimum and maximum values for the output image are specified. Note the use of the `itk::NumericTraits` class which allows us to define a number of type-related constants in a generic way. The use of traits is a fundamental characteristic of generic programming [5, 1].

```
rescaler->SetOutputMinimum( itk::NumericTraits< OutputPixelType >::min() );
rescaler->SetOutputMaximum( itk::NumericTraits< OutputPixelType >::max() );
```

Below, we create the reader and writer using the `New()` method and assign the result to a `itk::SmartPointer`.

```
ReaderType::Pointer reader = ReaderType::New();
WriterType::Pointer writer = WriterType::New();
```

The name of the file to be read or written is passed with the `SetFileName()` method.

```
reader->SetFileName( inputFilename  );
writer->SetFileName( outputFilename );
```

Below we connect the reader, filter and writer to form the data processing pipeline.

```
filter->SetInput( reader->GetOutput() );
rescaler->SetInput( filter->GetOutput() );
writer->SetInput( rescaler->GetOutput() );
```

Finally we execute the pipeline by invoking `Update()` on the writer. The call is placed in a try/catch block in case exceptions are thrown.

```
try
  {
  writer->Update();
  }
catch( itk::ExceptionObject & err )
  {
  std::cerr << "ExceptionObject caught !" << std::endl;
  std::cerr << err << std::endl;
  return EXIT_FAILURE;
  }
```

1.9   Reading and Writing Complex Images

The source code for this section can be found in the file
`ComplexImageReadWrite.cxx`.

This example illustrates how to read and write an image of pixel type `std::complex`. The complex type is defined as an integral part of the C++ language. The characteristics of the type are specified in the C++ standard document in Chapter 26 "Numerics Library", page 565, in particular in section 26.2 [4].

We start by including the headers of the complex class, the image, and the reader and writer classes.

```
#include <complex>
#include "itkImage.h"
#include "itkImageFileReader.h"
#include "itkImageFileWriter.h"
```

The image dimension and pixel type must be declared. In this case we use the `std::complex<>` as the pixel type. Using the dimension and pixel type we proceed to instantiate the image type.

```
const unsigned int Dimension = 2;

typedef std::complex< float >                PixelType;
typedef itk::Image< PixelType, Dimension > ImageType;
```

The image file reader and writer types are instantiated using the image type. We can then create objects for both of them.

```
typedef itk::ImageFileReader< ImageType > ReaderType;
typedef itk::ImageFileWriter< ImageType > WriterType;

ReaderType::Pointer reader = ReaderType::New();
WriterType::Pointer writer = WriterType::New();
```

File names should be provided for both the reader and the writer. In this particular example we take those file names from the command line arguments.

```
reader->SetFileName( argv[1] );
writer->SetFileName( argv[2] );
```

Here we simply connect the output of the reader as input to the writer. This simple program could be used for converting complex images from one file format to another.

```
writer->SetInput( reader->GetOutput() );
```

The execution of this short pipeline is triggered by invoking the `Update()` method of the writer. This invocation must be placed inside a try/catch block since its execution may result in exceptions being thrown.

```
try
  {
  writer->Update();
  }
catch( itk::ExceptionObject & err )
  {
  std::cerr << "ExceptionObject caught !" << std::endl;
  std::cerr << err << std::endl;
  return EXIT_FAILURE;
  }
```

For a more interesting use of this code, you may want to add a filter in between the reader and the writer and perform any complex image to complex image operation. A practical application of this code is presented in section 2.10 in the context of Fourier analysis.

1.10 Extracting Components from Vector Images

The source code for this section can be found in the file
`CovariantVectorImageExtractComponent.cxx`.

This example illustrates how to read an image whose pixel type is `CovariantVector`, extract one of its components to form a scalar image and finally save this image into a file.

The `itk::VectorIndexSelectionCastImageFilter` is used to extract a scalar from the vector image. It is also possible to cast the component type when using this filter. It is the user's responsibility to make sure that the cast will not result in any information loss.

Let's start by including the relevant header files.

```
#include "itkImageFileReader.h"
#include "itkImageFileWriter.h"
#include "itkVectorIndexSelectionCastImageFilter.h"
#include "itkRescaleIntensityImageFilter.h"
```

We read an image of `itk::CovariantVector` pixels and extract one of its components to generate a scalar image of a consistent pixel type. Then, we rescale the intensities of this scalar image and write it as an image of unsigned short pixels.

```
typedef float                         ComponentType;
const   unsigned int                  Dimension = 2;

typedef itk::CovariantVector< ComponentType,
                              Dimension  >       InputPixelType;

typedef unsigned short                            OutputPixelType;

typedef itk::Image< InputPixelType,   Dimension >   InputImageType;
typedef itk::Image< ComponentType,    Dimension >   ComponentImageType;
typedef itk::Image< OutputPixelType,  Dimension >   OutputImageType;
```

The `itk::ImageFileReader` and `itk::ImageFileWriter` are instantiated using the image types.

```
typedef itk::ImageFileReader< InputImageType  >  ReaderType;
typedef itk::ImageFileWriter< OutputImageType >  WriterType;
```

The VectorIndexSelectionCastImageFilter is instantiated using the input and output image types. A filter object is created with the `New()` method and assigned to a `itk::SmartPointer`.

```
typedef itk::VectorIndexSelectionCastImageFilter<
                              InputImageType,
                              ComponentImageType  > FilterType;

FilterType::Pointer componentExtractor = FilterType::New();
```

The VectorIndexSelectionCastImageFilter class requires us to specify which of the vector components is to be extracted from the vector image. This is done with the `SetIndex()` method. In this example we obtain this value from the command line arguments.

```
componentExtractor->SetIndex( indexOfComponentToExtract );
```

The `itk::RescaleIntensityImageFilter` filter is instantiated here.

```
typedef itk::RescaleIntensityImageFilter<
                          ComponentImageType,
                          OutputImageType >      RescaleFilterType;

RescaleFilterType::Pointer  rescaler = RescaleFilterType::New();
```

The minimum and maximum values for the output image are specified in the following. Note the use of the `itk::NumericTraits` class which allows us to define a number of type-related constants in a generic way. The use of traits is a fundamental characteristic of generic programming [5, 1].

```
rescaler->SetOutputMinimum( itk::NumericTraits< OutputPixelType >::min() );
rescaler->SetOutputMaximum( itk::NumericTraits< OutputPixelType >::max() );
```

Below, we create the reader and writer using the `New()` method and assign the result to a `itk::SmartPointer`.

```
ReaderType::Pointer reader = ReaderType::New();
WriterType::Pointer writer = WriterType::New();
```

The name of the file to be read or written is passed to the `SetFileName()` method.

```
reader->SetFileName( inputFilename  );
writer->SetFileName( outputFilename );
```

Below we connect the reader, filter and writer to form the data processing pipeline.

```
componentExtractor->SetInput( reader->GetOutput() );
rescaler->SetInput( componentExtractor->GetOutput() );
writer->SetInput( rescaler->GetOutput() );
```

Finally we execute the pipeline by invoking `Update()` on the writer. The call is placed in a `try/catch` block in case exceptions are thrown.

```
try
  {
  writer->Update();
  }
catch( itk::ExceptionObject & err )
  {
  std::cerr << "ExceptionObject caught !" << std::endl;
  std::cerr << err << std::endl;
  return EXIT_FAILURE;
  }
```

1.11 Reading and Writing Image Series

It is still quite common to store 3D medical images in sets of files each one containing a single slice of a volume dataset. Those 2D files can be read as individual 2D images, or can be grouped together in order to reconstruct a 3D dataset. The same practice can be extended to higher dimensions, for example, for managing 4D datasets by using sets of files each one containing a 3D image. This practice is common in the domain of cardiac imaging, perfusion, functional MRI and PET. This section illustrates the functionalities available in ITK for dealing with reading and writing series of images.

1.11.1 Reading Image Series

The source code for this section can be found in the file
ImageSeriesReadWrite.cxx.

This example illustrates how to read a series of 2D slices from independent files in order to compose a volume. The class `itk::ImageSeriesReader` is used for this purpose. This class works in combination with a generator of filenames that will provide a list of files to be read. In this particular example we use the `itk::NumericSeriesFileNames` class as a filename generator. This generator uses a `printf` style of string format with a "`%d`" field that will be successively replaced by a number specified by the user. Here we will use a format like "`file%03d.png`" for reading PNG files named file001.png, file002.png, file003.png... and so on.

This requires the following headers as shown.

```
#include "itkImage.h"
#include "itkImageSeriesReader.h"
#include "itkImageFileWriter.h"
#include "itkNumericSeriesFileNames.h"
#include "itkPNGImageIO.h"
```

We start by defining the `PixelType` and `ImageType`.

```
typedef unsigned char                          PixelType;
const unsigned int Dimension = 3;

typedef itk::Image< PixelType, Dimension >  ImageType;
```

The image type is used as a template parameter to instantiate the reader and writer.

```
typedef itk::ImageSeriesReader< ImageType >  ReaderType;
typedef itk::ImageFileWriter<   ImageType >  WriterType;

ReaderType::Pointer reader = ReaderType::New();
WriterType::Pointer writer = WriterType::New();
```

Then, we declare the filename generator type and create one instance of it.

```
typedef itk::NumericSeriesFileNames    NameGeneratorType;

NameGeneratorType::Pointer nameGenerator = NameGeneratorType::New();
```

The filename generator requires us to provide a pattern of text for the filenames, and numbers for the initial value, last value and increment to be used for generating the names of the files.

```
nameGenerator->SetSeriesFormat( "vwe%03d.png" );

nameGenerator->SetStartIndex( first );
nameGenerator->SetEndIndex( last );
nameGenerator->SetIncrementIndex( 1 );
```

The ImageIO object that actually performs the read process is now connected to the ImageSeries-Reader. This is the safest way of making sure that we use an ImageIO object that is appropriate for the type of files that we want to read.

```
reader->SetImageIO( itk::PNGImageIO::New() );
```

The filenames of the input files must be provided to the reader, while the writer is instructed to write the same volume dataset in a single file.

```
reader->SetFileNames( nameGenerator->GetFileNames() );

writer->SetFileName( outputFilename );
```

We connect the output of the reader to the input of the writer.

```
writer->SetInput( reader->GetOutput() );
```

Finally, execution of the pipeline can be triggered by invoking the `Update()` method in the writer. This call must be placed in a `try/catch` block since exceptions be potentially be thrown in the process of reading or writing the images.

```
try
  {
  writer->Update();
  }
catch( itk::ExceptionObject & err )
  {
  std::cerr << "ExceptionObject caught !" << std::endl;
  std::cerr << err << std::endl;
  return EXIT_FAILURE;
  }
```

1.11.2 Writing Image Series

The source code for this section can be found in the file
ImageReadImageSeriesWrite.cxx.

This example illustrates how to save an image using the itk::ImageSeriesWriter. This class
enables the saving of a 3D volume as a set of files containing one 2D slice per file.

The type of the input image is declared here and it is used for declaring the type of the reader. This
will be a conventional 3D image reader.

```
typedef itk::Image< unsigned char, 3 >       ImageType;
typedef itk::ImageFileReader< ImageType >   ReaderType;
```

The reader object is constructed using the New() operator and assigning the result to a
SmartPointer. The filename of the 3D volume to be read is taken from the command line arguments and passed to the reader using the SetFileName() method.

```
ReaderType::Pointer reader = ReaderType::New();
reader->SetFileName( argv[1] );
```

The type of the series writer must be instantiated taking into account that the input file is a 3D volume
and the output files are 2D images. Additionally, the output of the reader is connected as input to the
writer.

```
typedef itk::Image< unsigned char, 2 >       Image2DType;

typedef itk::ImageSeriesWriter< ImageType, Image2DType > WriterType;

WriterType::Pointer writer = WriterType::New();

writer->SetInput( reader->GetOutput() );
```

The writer requires a list of filenames to be generated. This list can be produced with the help of the
itk::NumericSeriesFileNames class.

```
typedef itk::NumericSeriesFileNames     NameGeneratorType;

NameGeneratorType::Pointer nameGenerator = NameGeneratorType::New();
```

The NumericSeriesFileNames class requires an input string in order to have a template for generating the filenames of all the output slices. Here we compose this string using a prefix taken from the
command line arguments and adding the extension for PNG files.

```
std::string format = argv[2];
format += "%03d.";
format += argv[3];    // filename extension

nameGenerator->SetSeriesFormat( format.c_str() );
```

The input string is going to be used for generating filenames by setting the values of the first and last slice. This can be done by collecting information from the input image. Note that before attempting to take any image information from the reader, its execution must be triggered with the invocation of the `Update()` method, and since this invocation can potentially throw exceptions, it must be put inside a `try/catch` block.

```
try
  {
  reader->Update();
  }
catch( itk::ExceptionObject & excp )
  {
  std::cerr << "Exception thrown while reading the image" << std::endl;
  std::cerr << excp << std::endl;
  }
```

Now that the image has been read we can query its largest possible region and recover information about the number of pixels along every dimension.

```
ImageType::ConstPointer inputImage = reader->GetOutput();
ImageType::RegionType    region    = inputImage->GetLargestPossibleRegion();
ImageType::IndexType     start     = region.GetIndex();
ImageType::SizeType      size      = region.GetSize();
```

With this information we can find the number that will identify the first and last slices of the 3D data set. These numerical values are then passed to the filename generator object that will compose the names of the files where the slices are going to be stored.

```
const unsigned int firstSlice = start[2];
const unsigned int lastSlice  = start[2] + size[2] - 1;

nameGenerator->SetStartIndex( firstSlice );
nameGenerator->SetEndIndex( lastSlice );
nameGenerator->SetIncrementIndex( 1 );
```

The list of filenames is taken from the names generator and it is passed to the series writer.

```
writer->SetFileNames( nameGenerator->GetFileNames() );
```

Finally we trigger the execution of the pipeline with the `Update()` method on the writer. At this point the slices of the image will be saved in individual files containing a single slice per file. The filenames used for these slices are those produced by the filename generator.

```
try
  {
  writer->Update();
  }
catch( itk::ExceptionObject & excp )
  {
  std::cerr << "Exception thrown while reading the image" << std::endl;
  std::cerr << excp << std::endl;
  }
```

Note that by saving data into isolated slices we are losing information that may be significant for medical applications, such as the interslice spacing in millimeters.

1.11.3 Reading and Writing Series of RGB Images

The source code for this section can be found in the file
`RGBImageSeriesReadWrite.cxx`.

RGB images are commonly used for representing data acquired from cryogenic sections, optical microscopy and endoscopy. This example illustrates how to read RGB color images from a set of files containing individual 2D slices in order to compose a 3D color dataset. Then we will save it into a single 3D file, and finally save it again as a set of 2D slices with other names.

This requires the following headers as shown.

```
#include "itkRGBPixel.h"
#include "itkImage.h"
#include "itkImageSeriesReader.h"
#include "itkImageSeriesWriter.h"
#include "itkNumericSeriesFileNames.h"
#include "itkPNGImageIO.h"
```

The `itk::RGBPixel` class is templated over the type used to represent each one of the Red, Green and Blue components. A typical instantiation of the RGB image class might be as follows.

```
typedef itk::RGBPixel< unsigned char >        PixelType;
const unsigned int Dimension = 3;

typedef itk::Image< PixelType, Dimension >     ImageType;
```

The image type is used as a template parameter to instantiate the series reader and the volumetric writer.

```
typedef itk::ImageSeriesReader< ImageType >  SeriesReaderType;
typedef itk::ImageFileWriter<   ImageType >  WriterType;

SeriesReaderType::Pointer seriesReader = SeriesReaderType::New();
WriterType::Pointer       writer       = WriterType::New();
```

We use a NumericSeriesFileNames class in order to generate the filenames of the slices to be read. Later on in this example we will reuse this object in order to generate the filenames of the slices to be written.

```
typedef itk::NumericSeriesFileNames      NameGeneratorType;

NameGeneratorType::Pointer nameGenerator = NameGeneratorType::New();

nameGenerator->SetStartIndex( first );
nameGenerator->SetEndIndex( last );
nameGenerator->SetIncrementIndex( 1 );

nameGenerator->SetSeriesFormat( "vwe%03d.png" );
```

The ImageIO object that actually performs the read process is now connected to the ImageSeries-Reader.

```
seriesReader->SetImageIO( itk::PNGImageIO::New() );
```

The filenames of the input slices are taken from the names generator and passed to the series reader.

```
seriesReader->SetFileNames( nameGenerator->GetFileNames() );
```

The name of the volumetric output image is passed to the image writer, and we connect the output of the series reader to the input of the volumetric writer.

```
writer->SetFileName( outputFilename );

writer->SetInput( seriesReader->GetOutput() );
```

Finally, execution of the pipeline can be triggered by invoking the `Update()` method in the volumetric writer. This, of course, is done from inside a try/catch block.

```
try
  {
  writer->Update();
  }
catch( itk::ExceptionObject & excp )
  {
  std::cerr << "Error reading the series " << std::endl;
  std::cerr << excp << std::endl;
  }
```

We now proceed to save the same volumetric dataset as a set of slices. This is done only to illustrate the process for saving a volume as a series of 2D individual datasets. The type of the series writer must be instantiated taking into account that the input file is a 3D volume and the output files are 2D images. Additionally, the output of the series reader is connected as input to the series writer.

```
typedef itk::Image< PixelType, 2 >      Image2DType;

typedef itk::ImageSeriesWriter< ImageType, Image2DType > SeriesWriterType;

SeriesWriterType::Pointer seriesWriter = SeriesWriterType::New();

seriesWriter->SetInput( seriesReader->GetOutput() );
```

We now reuse the filename generator in order to produce the list of filenames for the output series. In this case we just need to modify the format of the filename generator. Then, we pass the list of output filenames to the series writer.

```
nameGenerator->SetSeriesFormat( "output%03d.png" );

seriesWriter->SetFileNames( nameGenerator->GetFileNames() );
```

Finally we trigger the execution of the series writer from inside a try/catch block.

```
try
  {
  seriesWriter->Update();
  }
catch( itk::ExceptionObject & excp )
  {
  std::cerr << "Error reading the series " << std::endl;
  std::cerr << excp << std::endl;
  }
```

You may have noticed that apart from the declaration of the PixelType there is nothing in this code that is specific to RGB images. All the actions required to support color images are implemented internally in the itk::ImageIO objects.

1.12 Reading and Writing DICOM Images

1.12.1 Foreword

With the introduction of computed tomography (CT) followed by other digital diagnostic imaging modalities such as MRI in the 1970's, and the increasing use of computers in clinical applications, the American College of Radiology (ACR)[3] and the National Electrical Manufacturers Association (NEMA)[4] recognized the need for a standard method for transferring images as well as associated information between devices manufactured from various vendors.

ACR and NEMA formed a joint committee to develop a standard for Digital Imaging and Communications in Medicine (DICOM). This standard was developed in liaison with other Standardization Organizations such as CEN TC251, JIRA including IEEE, HL7 and ANSI USA as reviewers.

DICOM is a comprehensive set of standards for handling, storing and transmitting information in medical imaging. The DICOM standard was developed based on the previous NEMA specification. The standard specifies a file format definition as well as a network communication protocol. DICOM was developed to enable integration of scanners, servers, workstations and network hardware from multiple vendors into an image archiving and communication system.

DICOM files consist of a header and a body of image data. The header contains standardized as well as free-form fields. The set of standardized fields is called the public DICOM dictionary, an instance of this dictionary is available in ITK in the file Insight/Utilities/gdcm/Dict/dicomV3.dic. The list of free-form fields is also called the *shadow dictionary*.

A single DICOM file can contain multiples frames, allowing storage of volumes or animations. Image data can be compressed using a large variety of standards, including JPEG (both lossy and

---

[3]http://www.acr.org
[4]http://www.nema.org

lossless), LZW (Lempel Ziv Welch), and RLE (Run-length encoding).

The DICOM Standard is an evolving standard and it is maintained in accordance with the Procedures of the DICOM Standards Committee. Proposals for enhancements are forthcoming from the DICOM Committee member organizations based on input from users of the Standard. These proposals are considered for inclusion in future editions of the Standard. A requirement in updating the Standard is to maintain effective compatibility with previous editions.

For a more detailed description of the DICOM standard see [44].

The following sections illustrate how to use the functionalities that ITK provides for reading and writing DICOM files. This is extremely important in the domain of medical imaging since most of the images that are acquired in a clinical setting are stored and transported using the DICOM standard.

DICOM functionalities in ITK are provided by the GDCM library. This open source library was developed by the CREATIS Team [5] at INSA-Lyon [7]. Although originally this library was distributed under a LGPL License[6], the CREATIS Team was lucid enough to understand the limitations of that license and agreed to adopt the more open BSD-like License[7]. This change in their licensing made possible to distribute GDCM along with ITK.

GDCM is now maintained by Mathieu Malaterre and the GDCM community. The version distributed with ITK gets updated with major releases of the GDCM library.

1.12.2 Reading and Writing a 2D Image

The source code for this section can be found in the file
DicomImageReadWrite.cxx.

This example illustrates how to read a single DICOM slice and write it back as another DICOM slice. In the process an intensity rescaling is also applied.

In order to read and write the slice we use the itk::GDCMImageIO class which encapsulates a connection to the underlying GDCM library. In this way we gain access from ITK to the DICOM functionalities offered by GDCM. The GDCMImageIO object is connected as the ImageIO object to be used by the itk::ImageFileWriter.

We should first include the following header files.

```
#include "itkImageFileReader.h"
#include "itkImageFileWriter.h"
#include "itkRescaleIntensityImageFilter.h"
#include "itkGDCMImageIO.h"
```

Then we declare the pixel type and image dimension, and use them for instantiating the image type to be read.

---

[5]http://www.creatis.insa-lyon.fr
[6]http://www.gnu.org/copyleft/lesser.html
[7]http://www.opensource.org/licenses/bsd-license.php

```
typedef signed short InputPixelType;
const unsigned int   InputDimension = 2;

typedef itk::Image< InputPixelType, InputDimension > InputImageType;
```

With the image type we can instantiate the type of the reader, create one, and set the filename of the image to be read.

```
typedef itk::ImageFileReader< InputImageType > ReaderType;

ReaderType::Pointer reader = ReaderType::New();
reader->SetFileName( argv[1] );
```

GDCMImageIO is an ImageIO class for reading and writing DICOM v3 and ACR/NEMA images. The GDCMImageIO object is constructed here and connected to the ImageFileReader.

```
typedef itk::GDCMImageIO             ImageIOType;

ImageIOType::Pointer gdcmImageIO = ImageIOType::New();

reader->SetImageIO( gdcmImageIO );
```

At this point we can trigger the reading process by invoking the Update() method. Since this reading process may eventually throw an exception, we place the invocation inside a try/catch block.

```
try
  {
  reader->Update();
  }
catch (itk::ExceptionObject & e)
  {
  std::cerr << "exception in file reader " << std::endl;
  std::cerr << e << std::endl;
  return EXIT_FAILURE;
  }
```

We now have the image in memory and can get access to it using the GetOutput() method of the reader. In the remainder of this current example, we focus on showing how to save this image again in DICOM format in a new file.

First, we must instantiate an ImageFileWriter type. Then, we construct one, set the filename to be used for writing, and connect the input image to be written. Since in this example we write the image in different ways, and in each case use a different writer, we enumerated the variable names of the writer objects as well as their types.

```
typedef itk::ImageFileWriter< InputImageType >  Writer1Type;

Writer1Type::Pointer writer1 = Writer1Type::New();

writer1->SetFileName( argv[2] );
writer1->SetInput( reader->GetOutput() );
```

We need to explicitly set the proper image IO (GDCMImageIO) to the writer filter since the input DICOM dictionary is being passed along the writing process. The dictionary contains all necessary information that a valid DICOM file should contain, like Patient Name, Patient ID, Institution Name, etc.

```
writer1->SetImageIO( gdcmImageIO );
```

The writing process is triggered by invoking the `Update()` method. Since this execution may result in exceptions being thrown we place the `Update()` call inside a `try/catch` block.

```
try
  {
  writer1->Update();
  }
catch (itk::ExceptionObject & e)
  {
  std::cerr << "exception in file writer " << std::endl;
  std::cerr << e << std::endl;
  return EXIT_FAILURE;
  }
```

We will now rescale the image using the RescaleIntensityImageFilter. For this purpose we use a better suited pixel type: `unsigned char` instead of `signed short`. The minimum and maximum values of the output image are explicitly defined in the rescaling filter.

```
typedef unsigned char WritePixelType;

typedef itk::Image< WritePixelType, 2 > WriteImageType;

typedef itk::RescaleIntensityImageFilter<
              InputImageType, WriteImageType > RescaleFilterType;

RescaleFilterType::Pointer rescaler = RescaleFilterType::New();

rescaler->SetOutputMinimum(   0 );
rescaler->SetOutputMaximum( 255 );
```

We create a second writer object that will save the rescaled image into a new file, which is not in DICOM format. This is done only for the sake of verifying the image against the one that will be saved in DICOM format later in this example.

```
typedef itk::ImageFileWriter< WriteImageType >  Writer2Type;

Writer2Type::Pointer writer2 = Writer2Type::New();

writer2->SetFileName( argv[3] );

rescaler->SetInput( reader->GetOutput() );
writer2->SetInput( rescaler->GetOutput() );
```

The writer can be executed by invoking the `Update()` method from inside a `try/catch` block.

We proceed now to save the same rescaled image into a file in DICOM format. For this purpose we just need to set up a `itk::ImageFileWriter` and pass to it the rescaled image as input.

```
typedef itk::ImageFileWriter< WriteImageType >  Writer3Type;

Writer3Type::Pointer writer3 = Writer3Type::New();

writer3->SetFileName( argv[4] );
writer3->SetInput( rescaler->GetOutput() );
```

We now need to explicitly set the proper image IO (GDCMImageIO), but also we must tell the ImageFileWriter to not use the MetaDataDictionary from the input but from the GDCMImageIO since this is the one that contains the DICOM specific information

The GDCMImageIO object will automatically detect the pixel type, in this case `unsigned char` and it will update the DICOM header information accordingly.

```
writer3->UseInputMetaDataDictionaryOff ();
writer3->SetImageIO( gdcmImageIO );
```

Finally we trigger the execution of the DICOM writer by invoking the Update() method from inside a try/catch block.

```
try
  {
  writer3->Update();
  }
catch (itk::ExceptionObject & e)
  {
  std::cerr << "Exception in file writer " << std::endl;
  std::cerr << e << std::endl;
  return EXIT_FAILURE;
  }
```

1.12.3   Reading a 2D DICOM Series and Writing a Volume

The source code for this section can be found in the file
DicomSeriesReadImageWrite2.cxx.

Probably the most common representation of datasets in clinical applications is the one that uses sets of DICOM slices in order to compose 3-dimensional images. This is the case for CT, MRI and PET scanners. It is very common therefore for image analysts to have to process volumetric images stored in a set of DICOM files belonging to a common DICOM series.

The following example illustrates how to use ITK functionalities in order to read a DICOM series into a volume and then save this volume in another file format.

The example begins by including the appropriate headers. In particular we will need the itk::GDCMImageIO object in order to have access to the capabilities of the GDCM library for reading DICOM files, and the itk::GDCMSeriesFileNames object for generating the lists of filenames identifying the slices of a common volumetric dataset.

```
#include "itkImage.h"
#include "itkGDCMImageIO.h"
#include "itkGDCMSeriesFileNames.h"
#include "itkImageSeriesReader.h"
#include "itkImageFileWriter.h"
```

We define the pixel type and dimension of the image to be read. In this particular case, the dimensionality of the image is 3, and we assume a `signed short` pixel type that is commonly used for X-Rays CT scanners.

The image orientation information contained in the direction cosines of the DICOM header are read in and passed correctly down the image processing pipeline.

```
typedef signed short     PixelType;
const unsigned int       Dimension = 3;

typedef itk::Image< PixelType, Dimension >          ImageType;
```

We use the image type for instantiating the type of the series reader and for constructing one object of its type.

```
typedef itk::ImageSeriesReader< ImageType >         ReaderType;
ReaderType::Pointer reader = ReaderType::New();
```

A GDCMImageIO object is created and connected to the reader. This object is the one that is aware of the internal intricacies of the DICOM format.

```
typedef itk::GDCMImageIO         ImageIOType;
ImageIOType::Pointer dicomIO = ImageIOType::New();

reader->SetImageIO( dicomIO );
```

Now we face one of the main challenges of the process of reading a DICOM series: to identify from a given directory the set of filenames that belong together to the same volumetric image. Fortunately for us, GDCM offers functionalities for solving this problem and we just need to invoke those functionalities through an ITK class that encapsulates a communication with GDCM classes. This ITK object is the GDCMSeriesFileNames. Conveniently, we only need to pass to this class the name of the directory where the DICOM slices are stored. This is done with the SetDirectory() method. The GDCMSeriesFileNames object will explore the directory and will generate a sequence of filenames for DICOM files for one study/series. In this example, we also call the SetUseSeriesDetails(true) function that tells the GDCMSeriesFileNames object to use additional DICOM information to distinguish unique volumes within the directory. This is useful, for example, if a DICOM device assigns the same SeriesID to a scout scan and its 3D volume; by using additional DICOM information the scout scan will not be included as part of the 3D volume. Note that SetUseSeriesDetails(true) must be called prior to calling SetDirectory(). By default SetUseSeriesDetails(true) will use the following DICOM tags to sub-refine a set of files into multiple series:

0020 0011 Series Number

0018 0024 Sequence Name

0018 0050 Slice Thickness

0028 0010 Rows

0028 0011 Columns

If this is not enough for your specific case you can always add some more restrictions using the AddSeriesRestriction() method. In this example we will use the DICOM Tag: 0008 0021 DA 1 Series Date, to sub-refine each series. The format for passing the argument is a string containing first the group then the element of the DICOM tag, separated by a pipe (|) sign.

```
typedef itk::GDCMSeriesFileNames NamesGeneratorType;
NamesGeneratorType::Pointer nameGenerator = NamesGeneratorType::New();

nameGenerator->SetUseSeriesDetails( true );
nameGenerator->AddSeriesRestriction("0008|0021" );

nameGenerator->SetDirectory( argv[1] );
```

The GDCMSeriesFileNames object first identifies the list of DICOM series present in the given directory. We receive that list in a reference to a container of strings and then we can do things like print out all the series identifiers that the generator had found. Since the process of finding the series identifiers can potentially throw exceptions, it is wise to put this code inside a try/catch block.

```
typedef std::vector< std::string >     SeriesIdContainer;

const SeriesIdContainer & seriesUID = nameGenerator->GetSeriesUIDs();

SeriesIdContainer::const_iterator seriesItr = seriesUID.begin();
SeriesIdContainer::const_iterator seriesEnd = seriesUID.end();
while( seriesItr != seriesEnd )
  {
  std::cout << seriesItr->c_str() << std::endl;
  ++seriesItr;
  }
```

Given that it is common to find multiple DICOM series in the same directory, we must tell the GDCM classes what specific series we want to read. In this example we do this by checking first if the user has provided a series identifier in the command line arguments. If no series identifier has been passed, then we simply use the first series found during the exploration of the directory.

```
std::string seriesIdentifier;

if( argc > 3 ) // If no optional series identifier
  {
  seriesIdentifier = argv[3];
  }
else
  {
  seriesIdentifier = seriesUID.begin()->c_str();
  }
```

We pass the series identifier to the name generator and ask for all the filenames associated to that series. This list is returned in a container of strings by the GetFileNames() method.

```
typedef std::vector< std::string >     FileNamesContainer;
FileNamesContainer fileNames;

fileNames = nameGenerator->GetFileNames( seriesIdentifier );
```

The list of filenames can now be passed to the itk::ImageSeriesReader using the SetFileNames() method.

```
reader->SetFileNames( fileNames );
```

Finally we can trigger the reading process by invoking the Update() method in the reader. This call as usual is placed inside a try/catch block.

```
try
  {
  reader->Update();
  }
catch (itk::ExceptionObject &ex)
  {
  std::cout << ex << std::endl;
  return EXIT_FAILURE;
  }
```

At this point, we have a volumetric image in memory that we can access by invoking the GetOutput() method of the reader.

We proceed now to save the volumetric image in another file, as specified by the user in the command line arguments of this program. Thanks to the ImageIO factory mechanism, only the filename extension is needed to identify the file format in this case.

```
typedef itk::ImageFileWriter< ImageType > WriterType;
WriterType::Pointer writer = WriterType::New();

writer->SetFileName( argv[2] );

writer->SetInput( reader->GetOutput() );
```

The process of writing the image is initiated by invoking the Update() method of the writer.

```
    writer->Update();
```

Note that in addition to writing the volumetric image to a file we could have used it as the input for any 3D processing pipeline. Keep in mind that DICOM is simply a file format and a network protocol. Once the image data has been loaded into memory, it behaves as any other volumetric dataset that you could have loaded from any other file format.

1.12.4   Reading a 2D DICOM Series and Writing a 2D DICOM Series

The source code for this section can be found in the file
DicomSeriesReadSeriesWrite.cxx.

This example illustrates how to read a DICOM series into a volume and then save this volume into another DICOM series using the exact same header information. It makes use of the GDCM library.

The main purpose of this example is to show how to properly propagate the DICOM specific information along the pipeline to be able to correctly write back the image using the information from the input DICOM files.

Please note that writing DICOM files is quite a delicate operation since we are dealing with a significant amount of patient specific data. It is your responsibility to verify that the DICOM headers generated from this code are not introducing risks in the diagnosis or treatment of patients. It is as well your responsibility to make sure that the privacy of the patient is respected when you process data sets that contain personal information. Privacy issues are regulated in the United States by the HIPAA norms[8]. You would probably find similar legislation in every country.

---

[8]The Health Insurance Portability and Accountability Act of 1996. http://www.cms.hhs.gov/hipaa/

When saving datasets in DICOM format it must be made clear whether these datasets have been processed in any way, and if so, you should inform the recipients of the data about the purpose and potential consequences of the processing. This is fundamental if the datasets are intended to be used for diagnosis, treatment or follow-up of patients. For example, the simple reduction of a dataset from a 16-bits/pixel to a 8-bits/pixel representation may make it impossible to detect certain pathologies and as a result will expose the patient to the risk of remaining untreated for a long period of time while her/his pathology progresses.

You are strongly encouraged to get familiar with the report on medical errors "To Err is Human", produced by the U.S. Institute of Medicine [32]. Raising awareness about the high frequency of medical errors is a first step in reducing their occurrence.

After all these warnings, let us now go back to the code and get familiar with the use of ITK and GDCM for writing DICOM Series. The first step that we must take is to include the header files of the relevant classes. We include the GDCMImageIO class, the GDCM filenames generator, as well as the series reader and writer.

```
#include "itkGDCMImageIO.h"
#include "itkGDCMSeriesFileNames.h"
#include "itkImageSeriesReader.h"
#include "itkImageSeriesWriter.h"
```

As a second step, we define the image type to be used in this example. This is done by explicitly selecting a pixel type and a dimension. Using the image type we can define the type of the series reader.

```
typedef signed short      PixelType;
const unsigned int        Dimension = 3;

typedef itk::Image< PixelType, Dimension >      ImageType;
typedef itk::ImageSeriesReader< ImageType >     ReaderType;
```

We also declare types for the `itk::GDCMImageIO` object that will actually read and write the DICOM images, and the `itk::GDCMSeriesFileNames` object that will generate and order all the filenames for the slices composing the volume dataset. Once we have the types, we proceed to create instances of both objects.

```
typedef itk::GDCMImageIO                        ImageIOType;
typedef itk::GDCMSeriesFileNames                NamesGeneratorType;

ImageIOType::Pointer gdcmIO = ImageIOType::New();
NamesGeneratorType::Pointer namesGenerator = NamesGeneratorType::New();
```

Just as the previous example, we get the DICOM filenames from the directory. Note however, that in this case we use the `SetInputDirectory()` method instead of the `SetDirectory()`. This is done because in the present case we will use the filenames generator for producing both the filenames for reading and the filenames for writing. Then, we invoke the `GetInputFileNames()` method in order to get the list of filenames to read.

```
namesGenerator->SetInputDirectory( argv[1] );

const ReaderType::FileNamesContainer & filenames =
                    namesGenerator->GetInputFileNames();
```

We construct one instance of the series reader object. Set the DICOM image IO object to be used with it, and set the list of filenames to read.

```
ReaderType::Pointer reader = ReaderType::New();

reader->SetImageIO( gdcmIO );
reader->SetFileNames( filenames );
```

We can trigger the reading process by calling the `Update()` method on the series reader. It is wise to put this invocation inside a `try/catch` block since the process may eventually throw exceptions.

```
    reader->Update();
```

At this point we have the volumetric data loaded in memory and we can access it by invoking the `GetOutput()` method in the reader.

Now we can prepare the process for writing the dataset. First, we take the name of the output directory from the command line arguments.

```
const char * outputDirectory = argv[2];
```

Second, we make sure the output directory exists, using the cross-platform tools: itksys::SystemTools. In this case we choose to create the directory if it does not exist yet.

```
itksys::SystemTools::MakeDirectory( outputDirectory );
```

We explicitly instantiate the image type to be used for writing, and use the image type for instantiating the type of the series writer.

```
typedef signed short    OutputPixelType;
const unsigned int      OutputDimension = 2;

typedef itk::Image< OutputPixelType, OutputDimension >    Image2DType;

typedef itk::ImageSeriesWriter<
                        ImageType, Image2DType >  SeriesWriterType;
```

We construct a series writer and connect to its input the output from the reader. Then we pass the GDCM image IO object in order to be able to write the images in DICOM format.

```
SeriesWriterType::Pointer seriesWriter = SeriesWriterType::New();

seriesWriter->SetInput( reader->GetOutput() );
seriesWriter->SetImageIO( gdcmIO );
```

It is time now to setup the GDCMSeriesFileNames to generate new filenames using another output directory. Then simply pass those newly generated files to the series writer.

```
namesGenerator->SetOutputDirectory( outputDirectory );

seriesWriter->SetFileNames( namesGenerator->GetOutputFileNames() );
```

The following line of code is extremely important for this process to work correctly. The line is taking the MetaDataDictionary from the input reader and passing it to the output writer. This step is important because the MetaDataDictionary contains all the entries of the input DICOM header.

```
seriesWriter->SetMetaDataDictionaryArray(
                    reader->GetMetaDataDictionaryArray() );
```

Finally we trigger the writing process by invoking the Update() method in the series writer. We place this call inside a try/catch block, in case any exception is thrown during the writing process.

```
try
  {
  seriesWriter->Update();
  }
catch( itk::ExceptionObject & excp )
  {
  std::cerr << "Exception thrown while writing the series " << std::endl;
  std::cerr << excp << std::endl;
  return EXIT_FAILURE;
  }
```

Please keep in mind that you should avoid generating DICOM files which have the appearance of being produced by a scanner. It should be clear from the directory or filenames that these data were the result of the execution of some sort of algorithm. This will prevent your dataset from being used as scanner data by accident.

1.12.5 Printing DICOM Tags From One Slice

The source code for this section can be found in the file
DicomImageReadPrintTags.cxx.

It is often valuable to be able to query the entries from the header of a DICOM file. This can be used for consistency checking, or simply for verifying that we have the correct dataset in our hands. This example illustrates how to read a DICOM file and then print out most of the DICOM header information. The binary fields of the DICOM header are skipped.

The headers of the main classes involved in this example are specified below. They include the image file reader, the GDCMImageIO object, the MetaDataDictionary and its entry element, the MetaDataObject.

```
#include "itkImageFileReader.h"
#include "itkGDCMImageIO.h"
#include "itkMetaDataObject.h"
```

We instantiate the type to be used for storing the image once it is read into memory.

```
typedef signed short        PixelType;
const unsigned int          Dimension = 2;

typedef itk::Image< PixelType, Dimension >        ImageType;
```

Using the image type as a template parameter we instantiate the type of the image file reader and construct one instance of it.

```
typedef itk::ImageFileReader< ImageType >        ReaderType;

ReaderType::Pointer reader = ReaderType::New();
```

The GDCM image IO type is declared and used for constructing one image IO object.

```
typedef itk::GDCMImageIO        ImageIOType;
ImageIOType::Pointer dicomIO = ImageIOType::New();
```

We pass to the reader the filename of the image to be read and connect the ImageIO object to it too.

```
reader->SetFileName( argv[1] );
reader->SetImageIO( dicomIO );
```

The reading process is triggered with a call to the `Update()` method. This call should be placed inside a `try/catch` block because its execution may result in exceptions being thrown.

```
reader->Update();
```

Now that the image has been read, we obtain the MetaDataDictionary from the ImageIO object using the `GetMetaDataDictionary()` method.

```
typedef itk::MetaDataDictionary   DictionaryType;

const  DictionaryType & dictionary = dicomIO->GetMetaDataDictionary();
```

Since we are interested only in the DICOM tags that can be expressed in strings, we declare a MetaDataObject suitable for managing strings.

```
typedef itk::MetaDataObject< std::string > MetaDataStringType;
```

We instantiate the iterators that will make possible to walk through all the entries of the MetaData-Dictionary.

```
DictionaryType::ConstIterator itr = dictionary.Begin();
DictionaryType::ConstIterator end = dictionary.End();
```

For each one of the entries in the dictionary, we check first if its element can be converted to a string, a `dynamic_cast` is used for this purpose.

```
while( itr != end )
  {
  itk::MetaDataObjectBase::Pointer  entry = itr->second;

  MetaDataStringType::Pointer entryvalue =
    dynamic_cast<MetaDataStringType *>( entry.GetPointer() );
```

For those entries that can be converted, we take their DICOM tag and pass it to the `GetLabelFromTag()` method of the GDCMImageIO class. This method checks the DICOM dictionary and returns the string label associated with the tag that we are providing in the `tagkey` variable. If the label is found, it is returned in `labelId` variable. The method itself returns false if the `tagkey` is not found in the dictionary. For example "0010|0010" in `tagkey` becomes "Patient's Name" in `labelId`.

```
if( entryvalue )
    {
    std::string tagkey   = itr->first;
    std::string labelId;
    bool found   = itk::GDCMImageIO::GetLabelFromTag( tagkey, labelId );
```

The actual value of the dictionary entry is obtained as a string with the `GetMetaDataObjectValue()`

method.

```
std::string tagvalue = entryvalue->GetMetaDataObjectValue();
```

At this point we can print out an entry by concatenating the DICOM Name or label, the numeric tag and its actual value.

```
if( found )
  {
  std::cout << "(" << tagkey << ") " << labelId;
  std::cout << " = " << tagvalue.c_str() << std::endl;
  }
```

Finally we just close the loop that will walk through all the Dictionary entries.

```
  ++itr;
  }
```

It is also possible to read a specific tag. In that case the string of the entry can be used for querying the MetaDataDictionary.

```
std::string entryId = "0010|0010";
  DictionaryType::ConstIterator tagItr = dictionary.Find( entryId );
```

If the entry is actually found in the Dictionary, then we can attempt to convert it to a string entry by using a dynamic_cast.

```
if( tagItr != end )
  {
  MetaDataStringType::ConstPointer entryvalue =
    dynamic_cast<const MetaDataStringType *>(
                        tagItr->second.GetPointer() );
```

If the dynamic cast succeeds, then we can print out the values of the label, the tag and the actual value.

```
  if( entryvalue )
    {
    std::string tagvalue = entryvalue->GetMetaDataObjectValue();
    std::cout << "Patient's Name (" << entryId << ") ";
    std::cout << " is: " << tagvalue.c_str() << std::endl;
    }
```

Another way to read a specific tag is to use the encapsulation above MetaDataDictionary. Note that this is stricly equivalent to the above code.

```
std::string tagkey = "0008|1050";
std::string labelId;
if( itk::GDCMImageIO::GetLabelFromTag( tagkey, labelId ) )
  {
  std::string value;
  std::cout << labelId << " (" << tagkey << "): ";
  if( dicomIO->GetValueFromTag(tagkey, value) )
    {
    std::cout << value;
    }
  else
    {
    std::cout << "(No Value Found in File)";
    }
  std::cout << std::endl;
  }
else
  {
  std::cerr << "Trying to access inexistant DICOM tag." << std::endl;
  }
```

For a full description of the DICOM dictionary please look at the file.

```
Insight/Utilities/gdcm/Dicts/dicomV3.dic
```

The following piece of code will print out the proper pixel type / component for instantiating an `itk::ImageFileReader` that can properly import the printed DICOM file.

```
itk::ImageIOBase::IOPixelType pixelType
                          = reader->GetImageIO()->GetPixelType();
itk::ImageIOBase::IOComponentType componentType
                          = reader->GetImageIO()->GetComponentType();
std::cout << "PixelType: " << reader->GetImageIO()
                ->GetPixelTypeAsString(pixelType) << std::endl;
std::cout << "Component Type: " << reader->GetImageIO()
                ->GetComponentTypeAsString(componentType) << std::endl;
```

1.12.6   Printing DICOM Tags From a Series

The source code for this section can be found in the file
`DicomSeriesReadPrintTags.cxx`.

This example illustrates how to read a DICOM series into a volume and then print most of the DICOM header information. The binary fields are skipped.

The header files for the series reader and the GDCM classes for image IO and name generation should be included first.

```
#include "itkImageSeriesReader.h"
#include "itkGDCMImageIO.h"
#include "itkGDCMSeriesFileNames.h"
```

Next, we instantiate the type to be used for storing the image once it is read into memory.

```
typedef signed short        PixelType;
const unsigned int          Dimension = 3;

typedef itk::Image< PixelType, Dimension >      ImageType;
```

We use the image type for instantiating the series reader type and then we construct one object of this class.

```
typedef itk::ImageSeriesReader< ImageType >      ReaderType;

ReaderType::Pointer reader = ReaderType::New();
```

A GDCMImageIO object is created and assigned to the reader.

```
typedef itk::GDCMImageIO        ImageIOType;

ImageIOType::Pointer dicomIO = ImageIOType::New();

reader->SetImageIO( dicomIO );
```

A GDCMSeriesFileNames is declared in order to generate the names of DICOM slices. We specify the directory with the `SetInputDirectory()` method and, in this case, take the directory name from the command line arguments. You could have obtained the directory name from a file dialog in a GUI.

```
typedef itk::GDCMSeriesFileNames        NamesGeneratorType;

NamesGeneratorType::Pointer nameGenerator = NamesGeneratorType::New();

nameGenerator->SetInputDirectory( argv[1] );
```

The list of files to read is obtained from the name generator by invoking the `GetInputFileNames()` method and receiving the results in a container of strings. The list of filenames is passed to the reader using the `SetFileNames()` method.

```
typedef std::vector<std::string>        FileNamesContainer;
FileNamesContainer fileNames = nameGenerator->GetInputFileNames();

reader->SetFileNames( fileNames );
```

We trigger the reader by invoking the `Update()` method. This invocation should normally be done inside a `try/catch` block given that it may eventually throw exceptions.

```
reader->Update();
```

ITK internally queries GDCM and obtains all the DICOM tags from the file headers. The tag values are stored in the `itk::MetaDataDictionary` which is a general-purpose container for {key,value} pairs. The Metadata dictionary can be recovered from any ImageIO class by invoking the `GetMetaDataDictionary()` method.

```
typedef itk::MetaDataDictionary        DictionaryType;

const DictionaryType & dictionary = dicomIO->GetMetaDataDictionary();
```

In this example, we are only interested in the DICOM tags that can be represented as strings. Therefore, we declare a `itk::MetaDataObject` of string type in order to receive those particular values.

```
typedef itk::MetaDataObject< std::string > MetaDataStringType;
```

The metadata dictionary is organized as a container with its corresponding iterators. We can therefore visit all its entries by first getting access to its `Begin()` and `End()` methods.

```
DictionaryType::ConstIterator itr = dictionary.Begin();
DictionaryType::ConstIterator end = dictionary.End();
```

We are now ready for walking through the list of DICOM tags. For this purpose we use the iterators that we just declared. At every entry we attempt to convert it into a string entry by using the `dynamic_cast` based on RTTI information[9]. The dictionary is organized like a `std::map` structure, so we should use the `first` and `second` members of every entry in order to get access to the {key,value} pairs.

```
while( itr != end )
  {
  itk::MetaDataObjectBase::Pointer  entry = itr->second;

  MetaDataStringType::Pointer entryvalue =
    dynamic_cast<MetaDataStringType *>( entry.GetPointer() );

  if( entryvalue )
    {
    std::string tagkey   = itr->first;
    std::string tagvalue = entryvalue->GetMetaDataObjectValue();
    std::cout << tagkey << " = " << tagvalue << std::endl;
    }

  ++itr;
  }
```

It is also possible to query for specific entries instead of reading all of them as we did above. In this case, the user must provide the tag identifier using the standard DICOM encoding. The identifier is stored in a string and used as key in the dictionary.

```
std::string entryId = "0010|0010";

DictionaryType::ConstIterator tagItr = dictionary.Find( entryId );

if( tagItr == end )
  {
  std::cerr << "Tag " << entryId;
  std::cerr << " not found in the DICOM header" << std::endl;
  return EXIT_FAILURE;
  }
```

Since the entry may or may not be of string type we must again use a `dynamic_cast` in order to attempt to convert it to a string dictionary entry. If the conversion is successful, we can then print out its content.

---

[9]Run Time Type Information

```
MetaDataStringType::ConstPointer entryvalue =
  dynamic_cast<const MetaDataStringType *>( tagItr->second.GetPointer() );

if( entryvalue )
  {
  std::string tagvalue = entryvalue->GetMetaDataObjectValue();
  std::cout << "Patient's Name (" << entryId << ") ";
  std::cout << " is: " << tagvalue << std::endl;
  }
else
  {
  std::cerr << "Entry was not of string type" << std::endl;
  return EXIT_FAILURE;
  }
```

This type of functionality will probably be more useful when provided through a graphical user interface. For a full description of the DICOM dictionary please look at the following file.

```
Insight/Utilities/gdcm/Dicts/dicomV3.dic
```

1.12.7 Changing a DICOM Header

The source code for this section can be found in the file
`DicomImageReadChangeHeaderWrite.cxx`.

This example illustrates how to read a single DICOM slice and write it back with some changed header information as another DICOM slice. Header Key/Value pairs can be specified on the command line. The keys are defined in the file

```
Insight/Utilities/gdcm/Dicts/dicomV3.dic.
```

Please note that modifying the content of a DICOM header is a very risky operation. The header contains fundamental information about the patient and therefore its consistency must be protected from any data corruption. Before attempting to modify the DICOM headers of your files, you must make sure that you have a very good reason for doing so, and that you can ensure that this information change will not result in a lower quality of health care being delivered to the patient.

We must start by including the relevant header files. Here we include the image reader, image writer, the image, the metadata dictionary and its entries, the metadata objects and the GDCMImageIO. The metadata dictionary is the data container that stores all the entries from the DICOM header once the DICOM image file is read into an ITK image.

```
#include "itkImageFileReader.h"
#include "itkImageFileWriter.h"
#include "itkImage.h"
#include "itkMetaDataObject.h"
#include "itkGDCMImageIO.h"
```

We declare the image type by selecting a particular pixel type and image dimension.

```
typedef signed short InputPixelType;
const unsigned int   Dimension = 2;
typedef itk::Image< InputPixelType, Dimension > InputImageType;
```

We instantiate the reader type by using the image type as template parameter. An instance of the reader is created and the file name to be read is taken from the command line arguments.

```
typedef itk::ImageFileReader< InputImageType > ReaderType;
ReaderType::Pointer reader = ReaderType::New();
reader->SetFileName( argv[1] );
```

The GDCMImageIO object is created in order to provide the services for reading and writing DICOM files. The newly created image IO class is connected to the reader.

```
typedef itk::GDCMImageIO              ImageIOType;
ImageIOType::Pointer gdcmImageIO = ImageIOType::New();
reader->SetImageIO( gdcmImageIO );
```

The reading of the image is triggered by invoking Update() in the reader.

```
reader->Update();
```

We take the metadata dictionary from the image that the reader had loaded in memory.

```
InputImageType::Pointer inputImage = reader->GetOutput();
typedef itk::MetaDataDictionary    DictionaryType;
DictionaryType & dictionary = inputImage->GetMetaDataDictionary();
```

Now we access the entries in the metadata dictionary, and for particular key values we assign a new content to the entry. This is done here by taking {key,value} pairs from the command line arguments. The relevant method is EncapsulateMetaData that takes the dictionary and for a given key provided by entryId, replaces the current value with the content of the value variable. This is repeated for every potential pair present in the command line arguments.

```
for (int i = 3; i < argc; i+=2)
  {
  std::string entryId( argv[i] );
  std::string value( argv[i+1] );
  itk::EncapsulateMetaData<std::string>( dictionary, entryId, value );
  }
```

Now that the dictionary has been updated, we proceed to save the image. This output image will have the modified data associated with its DICOM header.

Using the image type, we instantiate a writer type and construct a writer. A short pipeline between the reader and the writer is connected. The filename to write is taken from the command line arguments. The image IO object is connected to the writer.

```
typedef itk::ImageFileWriter< InputImageType >  Writer1Type;

Writer1Type::Pointer writer1 = Writer1Type::New();

writer1->SetInput( reader->GetOutput() );
writer1->SetFileName( argv[2] );
writer1->SetImageIO( gdcmImageIO );
```

Execution of the writer is triggered by invoking the Update() method.

```
writer1->Update();
```

Remember again, that modifying the header entries of a DICOM file involves very serious risks for patients and therefore must be done with extreme caution.

FILTERING

This chapter introduces the most commonly used filters found in the toolkit. Most of these filters are intended to process images. They will accept one or more images as input and will produce one or more images as output. ITK is based on a data pipeline architecture in which the output of one filter is passed as input to another filter. (See the Data Processing Pipeline section in Book 1 for more information.)

2.1 Thresholding

The thresholding operation is used to change or identify pixel values based on specifying one or more values (called the *threshold* value). The following sections describe how to perform thresholding operations using ITK.

2.1.1 Binary Thresholding

The source code for this section can be found in the file
BinaryThresholdImageFilter.cxx.

This example illustrates the use of the binary threshold image filter. This filter is used to transform an image into a binary image by changing the pixel values according to the rule illustrated in Figure 2.1. The user defines two thresholds—Upper and Lower—and two intensity values—Inside and Outside. For each pixel in the input image, the value of the pixel is compared with the lower and upper thresholds. If the pixel value is inside the range defined by [Lower, Upper] the output pixel is assigned the InsideValue. Otherwise the output pixels are assigned to the OutsideValue. Thresholding is commonly applied as the last operation of a segmentation pipeline.

The first step required to use the itk::BinaryThresholdImageFilter is to include its header file.

```
#include "itkBinaryThresholdImageFilter.h"
```

The next step is to decide which pixel types to use for the input and output images.

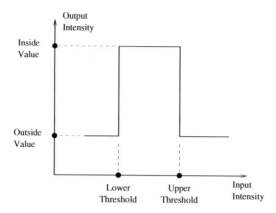

Figure 2.1: Transfer function of the BinaryThresholdImageFilter.

```
typedef  unsigned char  InputPixelType;
typedef  unsigned char  OutputPixelType;
```

The input and output image types are now defined using their respective pixel types and dimensions.

```
typedef itk::Image< InputPixelType,  2 >   InputImageType;
typedef itk::Image< OutputPixelType, 2 >   OutputImageType;
```

The filter type can be instantiated using the input and output image types defined above.

```
typedef itk::BinaryThresholdImageFilter<
            InputImageType, OutputImageType >  FilterType;
```

An `itk::ImageFileReader` class is also instantiated in order to read image data from a file. (See Section 1 on page 1 for more information about reading and writing data.)

```
typedef itk::ImageFileReader< InputImageType >  ReaderType;
```

An `itk::ImageFileWriter` is instantiated in order to write the output image to a file.

```
typedef itk::ImageFileWriter< OutputImageType >  WriterType;
```

Both the filter and the reader are created by invoking their `New()` methods and assigning the result to `itk::SmartPointers`.

```
ReaderType::Pointer reader = ReaderType::New();
FilterType::Pointer filter = FilterType::New();
```

The image obtained with the reader is passed as input to the BinaryThresholdImageFilter.

```
filter->SetInput( reader->GetOutput() );
```

The method `SetOutsideValue()` defines the intensity value to be assigned to those pixels whose intensities are outside the range defined by the lower and upper thresholds. The method `SetInsideValue()` defines the intensity value to be assigned to pixels with intensities falling inside the threshold range.

```
filter->SetOutsideValue( outsideValue );
filter->SetInsideValue(  insideValue  );
```

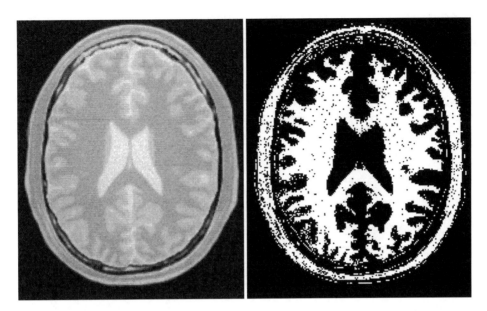

Figure 2.2: Effect of the BinaryThresholdImageFilter on a slice from a MRI proton density image of the brain.

The methods SetLowerThreshold() and SetUpperThreshold() define the range of the input image intensities that will be transformed into the InsideValue. Note that the lower and upper thresholds are values of the type of the input image pixels, while the inside and outside values are of the type of the output image pixels.

```
filter->SetLowerThreshold( lowerThreshold );
filter->SetUpperThreshold( upperThreshold );
```

The execution of the filter is triggered by invoking the Update() method. If the filter's output has been passed as input to subsequent filters, the Update() call on any downstream filters in the pipeline will indirectly trigger the update of this filter.

```
filter->Update();
```

Figure 2.2 illustrates the effect of this filter on a MRI proton density image of the brain. This figure shows the limitations of the filter for performing segmentation by itself. These limitations are particularly noticeable in noisy images and in images lacking spatial uniformity as is the case with MRI due to field bias.

The following classes provide similar functionality:

- itk::ThresholdImageFilter

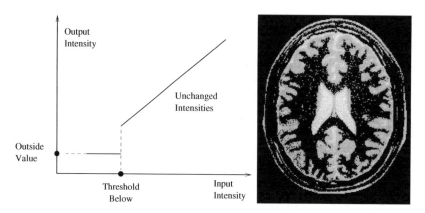

Figure 2.3: ThresholdImageFilter using the threshold-below mode.

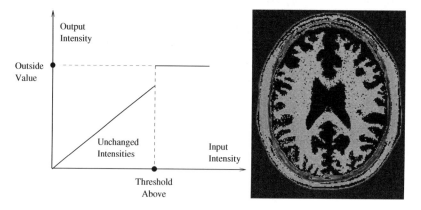

Figure 2.4: ThresholdImageFilter using the threshold-above mode.

2.1.2   General Thresholding

The source code for this section can be found in the file
ThresholdImageFilter.cxx.

This example illustrates the use of the itk::ThresholdImageFilter. This filter can be used to
transform the intensity levels of an image in three different ways.

- First, the user can define a single threshold. Any pixels with values below this threshold will
  be replaced by a user defined value, called here the OutsideValue. Pixels with values above
  the threshold remain unchanged. This type of thresholding is illustrated in Figure 2.3.

- Second, the user can define a particular threshold such that all the pixels with values above
  the threshold will be replaced by the OutsideValue. Pixels with values below the threshold
  remain unchanged. This is illustrated in Figure 2.4.

- Third, the user can provide two thresholds. All the pixels with intensity values inside the range

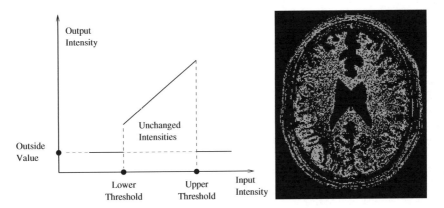

Figure 2.5: ThresholdImageFilter using the threshold-outside mode.

defined by the two thresholds will remain unchanged. Pixels with values outside this range will be assigned to the OutsideValue. This is illustrated in Figure 2.5.

The following methods choose among the three operating modes of the filter.

- ThresholdBelow()

- ThresholdAbove()

- ThresholdOutside()

The first step required to use this filter is to include its header file.

```
#include "itkThresholdImageFilter.h"
```

Then we must decide what pixel type to use for the image. This filter is templated over a single image type because the algorithm only modifies pixel values outside the specified range, passing the rest through unchanged.

```
typedef unsigned char PixelType;
```

The image is defined using the pixel type and the dimension.

```
typedef itk::Image< PixelType, 2 > ImageType;
```

The filter can be instantiated using the image type defined above.

```
typedef itk::ThresholdImageFilter< ImageType > FilterType;
```

An itk::ImageFileReader class is also instantiated in order to read image data from a file.

```
typedef itk::ImageFileReader< ImageType > ReaderType;
```

An itk::ImageFileWriter is instantiated in order to write the output image to a file.

```
typedef itk::ImageFileWriter< ImageType > WriterType;
```

Both the filter and the reader are created by invoking their New() methods and assigning the result to SmartPointers.

```
ReaderType::Pointer reader = ReaderType::New();
FilterType::Pointer filter = FilterType::New();
```

The image obtained with the reader is passed as input to the itk::ThresholdImageFilter.

```
filter->SetInput( reader->GetOutput() );
```

The method SetOutsideValue() defines the intensity value to be assigned to those pixels whose intensities are outside the range defined by the lower and upper thresholds.

```
filter->SetOutsideValue( 0 );
```

The method ThresholdBelow() defines the intensity value below which pixels of the input image will be changed to the OutsideValue.

```
filter->ThresholdBelow( 180 );
```

The filter is executed by invoking the Update() method. If the filter is part of a larger image processing pipeline, calling Update() on a downstream filter will also trigger update of this filter.

```
filter->Update();
```

The output of this example is shown in Figure 2.3. The second operating mode of the filter is now enabled by calling the method ThresholdAbove().

```
filter->ThresholdAbove( 180 );
filter->Update();
```

Updating the filter with this new setting produces the output shown in Figure 2.4. The third operating mode of the filter is enabled by calling ThresholdOutside().

```
filter->ThresholdOutside( 170,190 );
filter->Update();
```

The output of this third, "band-pass" thresholding mode is shown in Figure 2.5.

The examples in this section also illustrate the limitations of the thresholding filter for performing segmentation by itself. These limitations are particularly noticeable in noisy images and in images lacking spatial uniformity, as is the case with MRI due to field bias.

The following classes provide similar functionality:

- itk::BinaryThresholdImageFilter

2.2   Edge Detection

2.2.1   Canny Edge Detection

The source code for this section can be found in the file
CannyEdgeDetectionImageFilter.cxx.

This example introduces the use of the `itk::CannyEdgeDetectionImageFilter`. This filter is widely used for edge detection since it is the optimal solution satisfying the constraints of good sensitivity, localization and noise robustness.

The first step required for using this filter is to include its header file.

```
#include "itkCannyEdgeDetectionImageFilter.h"
```

This filter operates on images of pixel type `float`. It is then necessary to cast the type of the input images which are usually of integer type. The `itk::CastImageFilter` is used here for this purpose. Its image template parameters are defined for casting from the input type to the `float` type used for processing.

```
typedef itk::CastImageFilter< CharImageType, RealImageType>
                                              CastToRealFilterType;
```

The `itk::CannyEdgeDetectionImageFilter` is instantiated using the `float` image type.

2.3   Casting and Intensity Mapping

The filters discussed in this section perform pixel-wise intensity mappings. Casting is used to convert one pixel type to another, while intensity mappings also take into account the different intensity ranges of the pixel types.

2.3.1   Linear Mappings

The source code for this section can be found in the file `CastingImageFilters.cxx`.

Due to the use of Generic Programming in the toolkit, most types are resolved at compile-time. Few decisions regarding type conversion are left to run-time. It is up to the user to anticipate the pixel type-conversions required in the data pipeline. In medical imaging applications it is usually not desirable to use a general pixel type since this may result in the loss of valuable information.

This section introduces the mechanisms for explicit casting of images that flow through the pipeline. The following four filters are treated in this section: `itk::CastImageFilter`, `itk::RescaleIntensityImageFilter`, `itk::ShiftScaleImageFilter` and `itk::NormalizeImageFilter`. These filters are not directly related to each other except that they all modify pixel values. They are presented together here for the purpose of comparing their individual features.

The CastImageFilter is a very simple filter that acts pixel-wise on an input image, casting every pixel to the type of the output image. Note that this filter does not perform any arithmetic operation on the intensities. Applying CastImageFilter is equivalent to performing a `C-Style` cast on every pixel.

```
outputPixel = static_cast<OutputPixelType>( inputPixel )
```

The RescaleIntensityImageFilter linearly scales the pixel values in such a way that the minimum and maximum values of the input are mapped to minimum and maximum values provided by the user. This is a typical process for forcing the dynamic range of the image to fit within a particular scale and is common for image display. The linear transformation applied by this filter can be expressed as

$$outputPixel = (inputPixel - inpMin) \times \frac{(outMax - outMin)}{(inpMax - inpMin)} + outMin$$

.

The ShiftScaleImageFilter also applies a linear transformation to the intensities of the input image, but the transformation is specified by the user in the form of a multiplying factor and a value to be added. This can be expressed as

$$outputPixel = (inputPixel + Shift) \times Scale$$

.

The parameters of the linear transformation applied by the NormalizeImageFilter are computed internally such that the statistical distribution of gray levels in the output image have zero mean and a variance of one. This intensity correction is particularly useful in registration applications as a preprocessing step to the evaluation of mutual information metrics. The linear transformation of NormalizeImageFilter is given as

$$outputPixel = \frac{(inputPixel - mean)}{\sqrt{variance}}$$

.

As usual, the first step required to use these filters is to include their header files.

```
#include "itkCastImageFilter.h"
#include "itkRescaleIntensityImageFilter.h"
#include "itkNormalizeImageFilter.h"
```

Let's define pixel types for the input and output images.

```
typedef  unsigned char    InputPixelType;
typedef  float            OutputPixelType;
```

Then, the input and output image types are defined.

```
typedef itk::Image< InputPixelType,  3 >   InputImageType;
typedef itk::Image< OutputPixelType, 3 >   OutputImageType;
```

The filters are instantiated using the defined image types.

```
typedef itk::CastImageFilter<
        InputImageType, OutputImageType >  CastFilterType;

typedef itk::RescaleIntensityImageFilter<
        InputImageType, OutputImageType >  RescaleFilterType;

typedef itk::ShiftScaleImageFilter<
        InputImageType, OutputImageType >  ShiftScaleFilterType;

typedef itk::NormalizeImageFilter<
        InputImageType, OutputImageType >  NormalizeFilterType;
```

Object filters are created by invoking the New() method and assigning the result to
itk::SmartPointers.

```
CastFilterType::Pointer       castFilter      = CastFilterType::New();
RescaleFilterType::Pointer    rescaleFilter   = RescaleFilterType::New();
ShiftScaleFilterType::Pointer shiftFilter     = ShiftScaleFilterType::New();
NormalizeFilterType::Pointer  normalizeFilter = NormalizeFilterType::New();
```

The output of a reader filter (whose creation is not shown here) is now connected as input to the
various casting filters.

```
castFilter->SetInput(      reader->GetOutput() );
shiftFilter->SetInput(     reader->GetOutput() );
rescaleFilter->SetInput(   reader->GetOutput() );
normalizeFilter->SetInput( reader->GetOutput() );
```

Next we proceed to setup the parameters required by each filter. The CastImageFilter and the NormalizeImageFilter do not require any parameters. The RescaleIntensityImageFilter, on the other
hand, requires the user to provide the desired minimum and maximum pixel values of the output
image. This is done by using the SetOutputMinimum() and SetOutputMaximum() methods as
illustrated below.

```
rescaleFilter->SetOutputMinimum(  10 );
rescaleFilter->SetOutputMaximum( 250 );
```

The ShiftScaleImageFilter requires a multiplication factor (scale) and a post-scaling additive value
(shift). The methods SetScale() and SetShift() are used, respectively, to set these values.

```
shiftFilter->SetScale( 1.2 );
shiftFilter->SetShift( 25 );
```

Finally, the filters are executed by invoking the Update() method.

```
castFilter->Update();
shiftFilter->Update();
rescaleFilter->Update();
normalizeFilter->Update();
```

2.3.2   Non Linear Mappings

The following filter can be seen as a variant of the casting filters. Its main difference is the use of a
smooth and continuous transition function of non-linear form.

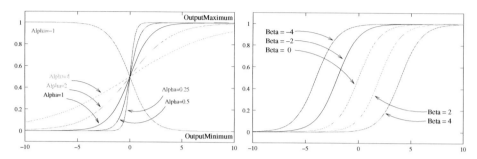

Figure 2.6: Effects of the various parameters in the SigmoidImageFilter. The alpha parameter defines the width of the intensity window. The beta parameter defines the center of the intensity window.

The source code for this section can be found in the file
`SigmoidImageFilter.cxx`.

The `itk::SigmoidImageFilter` is commonly used as an intensity transform. It maps a specific range of intensity values into a new intensity range by making a very smooth and continuous transition in the borders of the range. Sigmoids are widely used as a mechanism for focusing attention on a particular set of values and progressively attenuating the values outside that range. In order to extend the flexibility of the Sigmoid filter, its implementation in ITK includes four parameters that can be tuned to select its input and output intensity ranges. The following equation represents the Sigmoid intensity transformation, applied pixel-wise.

$$I' = (Max - Min) \cdot \frac{1}{\left(1 + e^{-\left(\frac{I-\beta}{\alpha}\right)}\right)} + Min \tag{2.1}$$

In the equation above, I is the intensity of the input pixel, I' the intensity of the output pixel, Min, Max are the minimum and maximum values of the output image, α defines the width of the input intensity range, and β defines the intensity around which the range is centered. Figure 2.6 illustrates the significance of each parameter.

This filter will work on images of any dimension and will take advantage of multiple processors when available.

The header file corresponding to this filter should be included first.

```
#include "itkSigmoidImageFilter.h"
```

Then pixel and image types for the filter input and output must be defined.

```
typedef    unsigned char  InputPixelType;
typedef    unsigned char  OutputPixelType;

typedef itk::Image< InputPixelType,  2 >   InputImageType;
typedef itk::Image< OutputPixelType, 2 >   OutputImageType;
```

Using the image types, we instantiate the filter type and create the filter object.

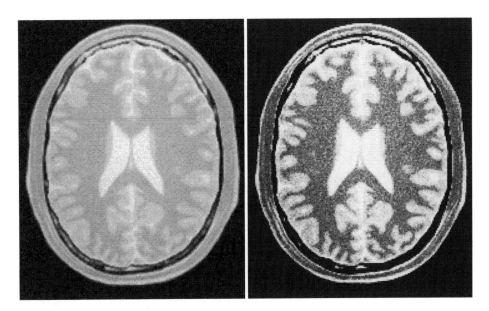

Figure 2.7: Effect of the Sigmoid filter on a slice from a MRI proton density brain image.

```
typedef itk::SigmoidImageFilter<
            InputImageType, OutputImageType > SigmoidFilterType;
SigmoidFilterType::Pointer sigmoidFilter = SigmoidFilterType::New();
```

The minimum and maximum values desired in the output are defined using the methods `SetOutputMinimum()` and `SetOutputMaximum()`.

```
sigmoidFilter->SetOutputMinimum(   outputMinimum );
sigmoidFilter->SetOutputMaximum(   outputMaximum );
```

The coefficients α and β are set with the methods `SetAlpha()` and `SetBeta()`. Note that α is proportional to the width of the input intensity window. As rule of thumb, we may say that the window is the interval $[-3\alpha, 3\alpha]$. The boundaries of the intensity window are not sharp. The α curve approaches its extrema smoothly, as shown in Figure 2.6. You may want to think about this in the same terms as when taking a range in a population of measures by defining an interval of $[-3\sigma, +3\sigma]$ around the population mean.

```
sigmoidFilter->SetAlpha(   alpha );
sigmoidFilter->SetBeta(   beta );
```

The input to the SigmoidImageFilter can be taken from any other filter, such as an image file reader, for example. The output can be passed down the pipeline to other filters, like an image file writer. An `Update()` call on any downstream filter will trigger the execution of the Sigmoid filter.

```
sigmoidFilter->SetInput( reader->GetOutput() );
writer->SetInput( sigmoidFilter->GetOutput() );
writer->Update();
```

Figure 2.7 illustrates the effect of this filter on a slice of MRI brain image using the following parameters.

- Minimum = 10

- Maximum = 240

- $\alpha = 10$

- $\beta = 170$

As can be seen from the figure, the intensities of the white matter were expanded in their dynamic range, while intensity values lower than $\beta - 3\alpha$ and higher than $\beta + 3\alpha$ became progressively mapped to the minimum and maximum output values. This is the way in which a Sigmoid can be used for performing smooth intensity windowing.

Note that both α and β can be positive and negative. A negative α will have the effect of *negating* the image. This is illustrated on the left side of Figure 2.6. An application of the Sigmoid filter as preprocessing for segmentation is presented in Section 4.3.1.

Sigmoid curves are common in the natural world. They represent the plot of sensitivity to a stimulus. They are also the integral curve of the Gaussian and, therefore, appear naturally as the response to signals whose distribution is Gaussian.

2.4   Gradients

Computation of gradients is a fairly common operation in image processing. The term "gradient" may refer in some contexts to the gradient vectors and in others to the magnitude of the gradient vectors. ITK filters attempt to reduce this ambiguity by including the *magnitude* term when appropriate. ITK provides filters for computing both the image of gradient vectors and the image of magnitudes.

2.4.1   Gradient Magnitude

The source code for this section can be found in the file
`GradientMagnitudeImageFilter.cxx`.

The magnitude of the image gradient is extensively used in image analysis, mainly to help in the determination of object contours and the separation of homogeneous regions. The `itk::GradientMagnitudeImageFilter` computes the magnitude of the image gradient at each pixel location using a simple finite differences approach. For example, in the case of *2D* the computation is equivalent to convolving the image with masks of type

-1	0	1

-1
0
1

then adding the sum of their squares and computing the square root of the sum.

This filter will work on images of any dimension thanks to the internal use of `itk::NeighborhoodIterator` and `itk::NeighborhoodOperator`.

The first step required to use this filter is to include its header file.

```
#include "itkGradientMagnitudeImageFilter.h"
```

Types should be chosen for the pixels of the input and output images.

```
typedef   float    InputPixelType;
typedef   float    OutputPixelType;
```

The input and output image types can be defined using the pixel types.

```
typedef itk::Image< InputPixelType,  2 >   InputImageType;
typedef itk::Image< OutputPixelType, 2 >   OutputImageType;
```

The type of the gradient magnitude filter is defined by the input image and the output image types.

```
typedef itk::GradientMagnitudeImageFilter<
            InputImageType, OutputImageType >  FilterType;
```

A filter object is created by invoking the `New()` method and assigning the result to a `itk::SmartPointer`.

```
FilterType::Pointer filter = FilterType::New();
```

The input image can be obtained from the output of another filter. Here, the source is an image reader.

```
filter->SetInput( reader->GetOutput() );
```

Finally, the filter is executed by invoking the `Update()` method.

```
filter->Update();
```

If the output of this filter has been connected to other filters in a pipeline, updating any of the downstream filters will also trigger an update of this filter. For example, the gradient magnitude filter may be connected to an image writer.

```
rescaler->SetInput( filter->GetOutput() );
writer->SetInput( rescaler->GetOutput() );
writer->Update();
```

Figure 2.8 illustrates the effect of the gradient magnitude filter on a MRI proton density image of the brain. The figure shows the sensitivity of this filter to noisy data.

Attention should be paid to the image type chosen to represent the output image since the dynamic range of the gradient magnitude image is usually smaller than the dynamic range of the input image. As always, there are exceptions to this rule, for example, synthetic images that contain high contrast objects.

This filter does not apply any smoothing to the image before computing the gradients. The results can therefore be very sensitive to noise and may not be the best choice for scale-space analysis.

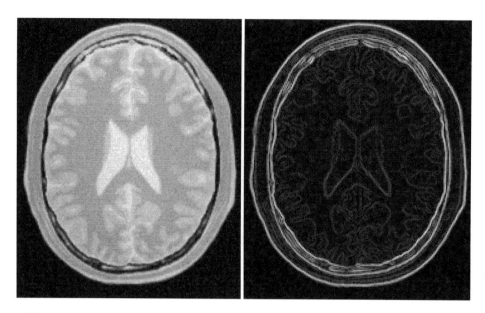

Figure 2.8: Effect of the GradientMagnitudeImageFilter on a slice from a MRI proton density image of the brain.

2.4.2   Gradient Magnitude With Smoothing

The source code for this section can be found in the file
`GradientMagnitudeRecursiveGaussianImageFilter.cxx`.

Differentiation is an ill-defined operation over digital data. In practice it is convenient to define a scale in which the differentiation should be performed. This is usually done by preprocessing the data with a smoothing filter. It has been shown that a Gaussian kernel is the most convenient choice for performing such smoothing. By choosing a particular value for the standard deviation (σ) of the Gaussian, an associated scale is selected that ignores high frequency content, commonly considered image noise.

The `itk::GradientMagnitudeRecursiveGaussianImageFilter` computes the magnitude of the image gradient at each pixel location. The computational process is equivalent to first smoothing the image by convolving it with a Gaussian kernel and then applying a differential operator. The user selects the value of σ.

Internally this is done by applying an IIR [1] filter that approximates a convolution with the derivative of the Gaussian kernel. Traditional convolution will produce a more accurate result, but the IIR approach is much faster, especially using large σs [16, 17].

GradientMagnitudeRecursiveGaussianImageFilter will work on images of any dimension by taking advantage of the natural separability of the Gaussian kernel and its derivatives.

The first step required to use this filter is to include its header file.

---

[1] Infinite Impulse Response

```
#include "itkGradientMagnitudeRecursiveGaussianImageFilter.h"
```

Types should be instantiated based on the pixels of the input and output images.

```
typedef    float     InputPixelType;
typedef    float     OutputPixelType;
```

With them, the input and output image types can be instantiated.

```
typedef itk::Image< InputPixelType,  2 >   InputImageType;
typedef itk::Image< OutputPixelType, 2 >   OutputImageType;
```

The filter type is now instantiated using both the input image and the output image types.

```
typedef itk::GradientMagnitudeRecursiveGaussianImageFilter<
                  InputImageType, OutputImageType > FilterType;
```

A filter object is created by invoking the `New()` method and assigning the result to a `itk::SmartPointer`.

```
FilterType::Pointer filter = FilterType::New();
```

The input image can be obtained from the output of another filter. Here, an image reader is used as source.

```
filter->SetInput( reader->GetOutput() );
```

The standard deviation of the Gaussian smoothing kernel is now set.

```
filter->SetSigma( sigma );
```

Finally the filter is executed by invoking the `Update()` method.

```
filter->Update();
```

If connected to other filters in a pipeline, this filter will automatically update when any downstream filters are updated. For example, we may connect this gradient magnitude filter to an image file writer and then update the writer.

```
rescaler->SetInput( filter->GetOutput() );
writer->SetInput( rescaler->GetOutput() );
writer->Update();
```

Figure 2.9 illustrates the effect of this filter on a MRI proton density image of the brain using σ values of 3 (left) and 5 (right). The figure shows how the sensitivity to noise can be regulated by selecting an appropriate σ. This type of scale-tunable filter is suitable for performing scale-space analysis.

Attention should be paid to the image type chosen to represent the output image since the dynamic range of the gradient magnitude image is usually smaller than the dynamic range of the input image.

2.4.3 Derivative Without Smoothing

The source code for this section can be found in the file
`DerivativeImageFilter.cxx`.

The `itk::DerivativeImageFilter` is used for computing the partial derivative of an image, the

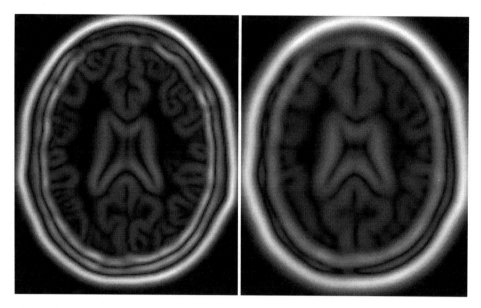

Figure 2.9: Effect of the GradientMagnitudeRecursiveGaussianImageFilter on a slice from a MRI proton density image of the brain.

derivative of an image along a particular axial direction.

The header file corresponding to this filter should be included first.

```
#include "itkDerivativeImageFilter.h"
```

Next, the pixel types for the input and output images must be defined and, with them, the image types can be instantiated. Note that it is important to select a signed type for the image, since the values of the derivatives will be positive as well as negative.

```
typedef   float   InputPixelType;
typedef   float   OutputPixelType;

const unsigned int Dimension = 2;

typedef itk::Image< InputPixelType,  Dimension >   InputImageType;
typedef itk::Image< OutputPixelType, Dimension >   OutputImageType;
```

Using the image types, it is now possible to define the filter type and create the filter object.

```
typedef itk::DerivativeImageFilter<
            InputImageType, OutputImageType >  FilterType;

FilterType::Pointer filter = FilterType::New();
```

The order of the derivative is selected with the SetOrder() method. The direction along which the derivative will be computed is selected with the SetDirection() method.

```
filter->SetOrder(     atoi( argv[4] ) );
filter->SetDirection( atoi( argv[5] ) );
```

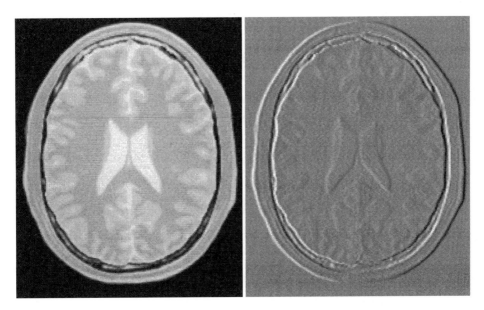

Figure 2.10: Effect of the Derivative filter on a slice from a MRI proton density brain image.

The input to the filter can be taken from any other filter, for example a reader. The output can be passed down the pipeline to other filters, for example, a writer. An Update() call on any downstream filter will trigger the execution of the derivative filter.

```
filter->SetInput( reader->GetOutput() );
writer->SetInput( filter->GetOutput() );
writer->Update();
```

Figure 2.10 illustrates the effect of the DerivativeImageFilter on a slice of MRI brain image. The derivative is taken along the *x* direction. The sensitivity to noise in the image is evident from this result.

2.5 Second Order Derivatives

2.5.1 Second Order Recursive Gaussian

The source code for this section can be found in the file
SecondDerivativeRecursiveGaussianImageFilter.cxx.

This example illustrates how to compute second derivatives of a 3D image using the
itk::RecursiveGaussianImageFilter.

It's good to be able to compute the raw derivative without any smoothing, but this can be problematic in a medical imaging scenario, when images will often have a certain amount of noise. It's almost always more desirable to include a smoothing step first, where an image is convolved with a Gaussian kernel in whichever directions the user desires a derivative. The nature of the Gaussian kernel makes it easy to combine these two steps into one, using an infinite impulse response (IIR) filter. In this example, all the second derivatives are computed independently in the same way, as if they were intended to be used for building the Hessian matrix of the image (a square matrix of second-order derivatives of an image, which is useful in many image processing techniques).

First, we will include the relevant header files: the itkRecursiveGaussianImageFilter, the image reader, writer, and duplicator.

```
#include "itkRecursiveGaussianImageFilter.h"
#include "itkImageFileReader.h"
#include "itkImageFileWriter.h"
#include "itkImageDuplicator.h"
#include <string>
```

Next, we declare our pixel type and output pixel type to be floats, and our image dimension to be 3.

```
typedef float            PixelType;
typedef float            OutputPixelType;

const unsigned int  Dimension = 3;
```

Using these definitions, define the image types, reader and writer types, and duplicator types, which are templated over the pixel types and dimension. Then, instantiate the reader, writer, and duplicator with the New() method.

```
typedef itk::Image< PixelType,         Dimension >  ImageType;
typedef itk::Image< OutputPixelType, Dimension >  OutputImageType;

typedef itk::ImageFileReader< ImageType       >  ReaderType;
typedef itk::ImageFileWriter< OutputImageType >  WriterType;

typedef itk::ImageDuplicator< OutputImageType >  DuplicatorType;

typedef itk::RecursiveGaussianImageFilter<
                              ImageType,
                              ImageType >  FilterType;

ReaderType::Pointer  reader   = ReaderType::New();
WriterType::Pointer  writer   = WriterType::New();

DuplicatorType::Pointer duplicator  = DuplicatorType::New();
```

Here we create three new filters. For each derivative we take, we will want to smooth in that direction first. So after the filters are created, each is given a dimension, and set to (in this example) the same sigma. Note that here, σ represents the standard deviation, whereas the itk::DiscreteGaussianImageFilter exposes the SetVariance method.

```
FilterType::Pointer ga = FilterType::New();
FilterType::Pointer gb = FilterType::New();
FilterType::Pointer gc = FilterType::New();

ga->SetDirection( 0 );
gb->SetDirection( 1 );
gc->SetDirection( 2 );

if( argc > 3 )
  {
  const float sigma = atof( argv[3] );
  ga->SetSigma( sigma );
  gb->SetSigma( sigma );
  gc->SetSigma( sigma );
  }
```

First we will compute the second derivative of the z-direction. In order to do this, we smooth in the x- and y- directions, and finally smooth and compute the derivative in the z-direction. Taking the zero-order derivative is equivalent to simply smoothing in that direction. This result is commonly notated I_{zz}.

```
ga->SetZeroOrder();
gb->SetZeroOrder();
gc->SetSecondOrder();

ImageType::Pointer inputImage = reader->GetOutput();

ga->SetInput( inputImage );
gb->SetInput( ga->GetOutput() );
gc->SetInput( gb->GetOutput() );

duplicator->SetInputImage( gc->GetOutput() );

gc->Update();
duplicator->Update();

ImageType::Pointer Izz = duplicator->GetModifiableOutput();
```

Recall that gc is the filter responsible for taking the second derivative. We can now take advantage of the pipeline architecture and, without much hassle, switch the direction of gc and gb, so that gc now takes the derivatives in the y-direction. Now we only need to call Update() on gc to re-run the entire pipeline from ga to gc, obtaining the second-order derivative in the y-direction, which is commonly notated I_{yy}.

```
gc->SetDirection( 1 ); // gc now works along Y
gb->SetDirection( 2 ); // gb now works along Z

gc->Update();
duplicator->Update();

ImageType::Pointer Iyy = duplicator->GetModifiableOutput();
```

Now we switch the directions of gc with that of ga in order to take the derivatives in the x-direction. This will give us I_{xx}.

```
gc->SetDirection( 0 );   // gc now works along X
ga->SetDirection( 1 );   // ga now works along Y

gc->Update();
duplicator->Update();

ImageType::Pointer Ixx = duplicator->GetModifiableOutput();
```

Now we can reset the directions to their original values, and compute first derivatives in different directions. Since we set both gb and gc to compute first derivatives, and ga to zero-order (which is only smoothing) we will obtain I_{yz}.

```
ga->SetDirection( 0 );
gb->SetDirection( 1 );
gc->SetDirection( 2 );

ga->SetZeroOrder();
gb->SetFirstOrder();
gc->SetFirstOrder();

gc->Update();
duplicator->Update();

ImageType::Pointer Iyz = duplicator->GetModifiableOutput();
```

Here is how you may easily obtain I_{xz}.

```
ga->SetDirection( 1 );
gb->SetDirection( 0 );
gc->SetDirection( 2 );

ga->SetZeroOrder();
gb->SetFirstOrder();
gc->SetFirstOrder();

gc->Update();
duplicator->Update();

ImageType::Pointer Ixz = duplicator->GetModifiableOutput();
```

For the sake of completeness, here is how you may compute I_{xz} and I_{xy}.

```
writer->SetInput( Ixz );
outputFileName = outputPrefix + "-Ixz.mhd";
writer->SetFileName( outputFileName.c_str() );
writer->Update();

ga->SetDirection( 2 );
gb->SetDirection( 0 );
gc->SetDirection( 1 );

ga->SetZeroOrder();
gb->SetFirstOrder();
gc->SetFirstOrder();

gc->Update();
duplicator->Update();

ImageType::Pointer Ixy = duplicator->GetModifiableOutput();

writer->SetInput( Ixy );
outputFileName = outputPrefix + "-Ixy.mhd";
writer->SetFileName( outputFileName.c_str() );
writer->Update();
```

2.5.2 Laplacian Filters

Laplacian Filter Recursive Gaussian

The source code for this section can be found in the file
LaplacianRecursiveGaussianImageFilter1.cxx.

This example illustrates how to use the itk::RecursiveGaussianImageFilter for computing the
Laplacian of a 2D image.

The first step required to use this filter is to include its header file.

```
#include "itkRecursiveGaussianImageFilter.h"
```

Types should be selected on the desired input and output pixel types.

```
typedef    float    InputPixelType;
typedef    float    OutputPixelType;
```

The input and output image types are instantiated using the pixel types.

```
typedef itk::Image< InputPixelType, 2 >  InputImageType;
typedef itk::Image< OutputPixelType, 2 >  OutputImageType;
```

The filter type is now instantiated using both the input image and the output image types.

```
typedef itk::RecursiveGaussianImageFilter<
                  InputImageType, OutputImageType >  FilterType;
```

This filter applies the approximation of the convolution along a single dimension. It is therefore necessary to concatenate several of these filters to produce smoothing in all directions. In this example,
we create a pair of filters since we are processing a 2D image. The filters are created by invoking the

New() method and assigning the result to a itk::SmartPointer.

We need two filters for computing the X component of the Laplacian and two other filters for computing the Y component.

```
FilterType::Pointer filterX1 = FilterType::New();
FilterType::Pointer filterY1 = FilterType::New();

FilterType::Pointer filterX2 = FilterType::New();
FilterType::Pointer filterY2 = FilterType::New();
```

Since each one of the newly created filters has the potential to perform filtering along any dimension, we have to restrict each one to a particular direction. This is done with the SetDirection() method.

```
filterX1->SetDirection( 0 );   // 0 --> X direction
filterY1->SetDirection( 1 );   // 1 --> Y direction

filterX2->SetDirection( 0 );   // 0 --> X direction
filterY2->SetDirection( 1 );   // 1 --> Y direction
```

The itk::RecursiveGaussianImageFilter can approximate the convolution with the Gaussian or with its first and second derivatives. We select one of these options by using the SetOrder() method. Note that the argument is an enum whose values can be ZeroOrder, FirstOrder and SecondOrder. For example, to compute the x partial derivative we should select FirstOrder for x and ZeroOrder for y. Here we want only to smooth in x and y, so we select ZeroOrder in both directions.

```
filterX1->SetOrder( FilterType::ZeroOrder );
filterY1->SetOrder( FilterType::SecondOrder );

filterX2->SetOrder( FilterType::SecondOrder );
filterY2->SetOrder( FilterType::ZeroOrder );
```

There are two typical ways of normalizing Gaussians depending on their application. For scale-space analysis it is desirable to use a normalization that will preserve the maximum value of the input. This normalization is represented by the following equation.

$$\frac{1}{\sigma\sqrt{2\pi}} \tag{2.2}$$

In applications that use the Gaussian as a solution of the diffusion equation it is desirable to use a normalization that preserves the integral of the signal. This last approach can be seen as a conservation of mass principle. This is represented by the following equation.

$$\frac{1}{\sigma^2\sqrt{2\pi}} \tag{2.3}$$

The itk::RecursiveGaussianImageFilter has a boolean flag that allows users to select between these two normalization options. Selection is done with the method SetNormalizeAcrossScale(). Enable this flag when analyzing an image across scale-space. In the current example, this setting has no impact because we are actually renormalizing the output to the dynamic range of the reader, so we simply disable the flag.

```
const bool normalizeAcrossScale = false;
filterX1->SetNormalizeAcrossScale( normalizeAcrossScale );
filterY1->SetNormalizeAcrossScale( normalizeAcrossScale );
filterX2->SetNormalizeAcrossScale( normalizeAcrossScale );
filterY2->SetNormalizeAcrossScale( normalizeAcrossScale );
```

The input image can be obtained from the output of another filter. Here, an image reader is used as the source. The image is passed to the x filter and then to the y filter. The reason for keeping these two filters separate is that it is usual in scale-space applications to compute not only the smoothing but also combinations of derivatives at different orders and smoothing. Some factorization is possible when separate filters are used to generate the intermediate results. Here this capability is less interesting, though, since we only want to smooth the image in all directions.

```
filterX1->SetInput( reader->GetOutput() );
filterY1->SetInput( filterX1->GetOutput() );

filterY2->SetInput( reader->GetOutput() );
filterX2->SetInput( filterY2->GetOutput() );
```

It is now time to select the σ of the Gaussian used to smooth the data. Note that σ must be passed to both filters and that sigma is considered to be in millimeters. That is, at the moment of applying the smoothing process, the filter will take into account the spacing values defined in the image.

```
filterX1->SetSigma( sigma );
filterY1->SetSigma( sigma );
filterX2->SetSigma( sigma );
filterY2->SetSigma( sigma );
```

Finally the two components of the Laplacian should be added together. The `itk::AddImageFilter` is used for this purpose.

```
typedef itk::AddImageFilter<
                OutputImageType,
                OutputImageType,
                OutputImageType > AddFilterType;

AddFilterType::Pointer addFilter = AddFilterType::New();

addFilter->SetInput1( filterY1->GetOutput() );
addFilter->SetInput2( filterX2->GetOutput() );
```

The filters are triggered by invoking `Update()` on the Add filter at the end of the pipeline.

```
try
  {
  addFilter->Update();
  }
catch( itk::ExceptionObject & err )
  {
  std::cout << "ExceptionObject caught !" << std::endl;
  std::cout << err << std::endl;
  return EXIT_FAILURE;
  }
```

The resulting image could be saved to a file using the `itk::ImageFileWriter` class.

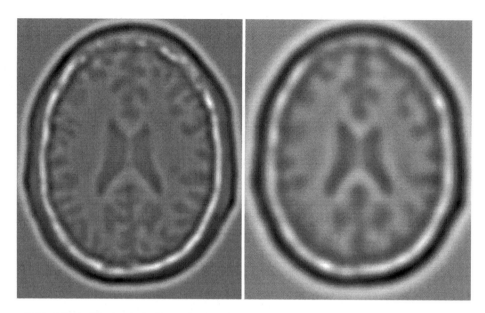

Figure 2.11: Effect of the LaplacianRecursiveGaussianImageFilter on a slice from a MRI proton density image of the brain.

```
typedef  float WritePixelType;

typedef itk::Image< WritePixelType, 2 >    WriteImageType;

typedef itk::ImageFileWriter< WriteImageType >  WriterType;

WriterType::Pointer writer = WriterType::New();

writer->SetInput( addFilter->GetOutput() );

writer->SetFileName( argv[2] );

writer->Update();
```

The source code for this section can be found in the file
`LaplacianRecursiveGaussianImageFilter2.cxx`.

The previous example showed how to use the `itk::RecursiveGaussianImageFilter` for computing the equivalent of a Laplacian of an image after smoothing with a Gaussian. The elements used in this previous example have been packaged together in the `itk::LaplacianRecursiveGaussianImageFilter` in order to simplify its usage. This current example shows how to use this convenience filter for achieving the same results as the previous example.

The first step required to use this filter is to include its header file.

```
#include "itkLaplacianRecursiveGaussianImageFilter.h"
```

Types should be selected on the desired input and output pixel types.

```
typedef   float   InputPixelType;
typedef   float   OutputPixelType;
```

The input and output image types are instantiated using the pixel types.

```
typedef itk::Image< InputPixelType,  2 >   InputImageType;
typedef itk::Image< OutputPixelType, 2 >   OutputImageType;
```

The filter type is now instantiated using both the input image and the output image types.

```
typedef itk::LaplacianRecursiveGaussianImageFilter<
                    InputImageType, OutputImageType >  FilterType;
```

This filter packages all the components illustrated in the previous example. The filter is created by invoking the New() method and assigning the result to a itk::SmartPointer.

```
FilterType::Pointer laplacian = FilterType::New();
```

The option for normalizing across scale space can also be selected in this filter.

```
laplacian->SetNormalizeAcrossScale( false );
```

The input image can be obtained from the output of another filter. Here, an image reader is used as the source.

```
laplacian->SetInput( reader->GetOutput() );
```

It is now time to select the σ of the Gaussian used to smooth the data. Note that σ must be passed to both filters and that sigma is considered to be in millimeters. That is, at the moment of applying the smoothing process, the filter will take into account the spacing values defined in the image.

```
laplacian->SetSigma( sigma );
```

Finally the pipeline is executed by invoking the Update() method.

```
try
  {
  laplacian->Update();
  }
catch( itk::ExceptionObject & err )
  {
  std::cout << "ExceptionObject caught !" << std::endl;
  std::cout << err << std::endl;
  return EXIT_FAILURE;
  }
```

2.6 Neighborhood Filters

The concept of locality is frequently encountered in image processing in the form of filters that compute every output pixel using information from a small region in the neighborhood of the input pixel. The classical form of these filters are the 3×3 filters in 2D images. Convolution masks based on these neighborhoods can perform diverse tasks ranging from noise reduction, to differential operations, to mathematical morphology.

The Insight toolkit implements an elegant approach to neighborhood-based image filtering. The input image is processed using a special iterator called the `itk::NeighborhoodIterator`. This iterator is capable of moving over all the pixels in an image and, for each position, it can address the pixels in a local neighborhood. Operators are defined that apply an algorithmic operation in the neighborhood of the input pixel to produce a value for the output pixel. The following section describes some of the more commonly used filters that take advantage of this construction. (See the Iterators chapter in Book 1 for more information.)

2.6.1   Mean Filter

The source code for this section can be found in the file
`MeanImageFilter.cxx`.

The `itk::MeanImageFilter` is commonly used for noise reduction. The filter computes the value of each output pixel by finding the statistical mean of the neighborhood of the corresponding input pixel. The following figure illustrates the local effect of the MeanImageFilter in a 2D case. The statistical mean of the neighborhood on the left is passed as the output value associated with the pixel at the center of the neighborhood.

28	26	50
27	25	29
25	30	32

$\longrightarrow$ 30.22 $\longrightarrow$ 30

Note that this algorithm is sensitive to the presence of outliers in the neighborhood. This filter will work on images of any dimension thanks to the internal use of `itk::SmartNeighborhoodIterator` and `itk::NeighborhoodOperator`. The size of the neighborhood over which the mean is computed can be set by the user.

The header file corresponding to this filter should be included first.

```
#include "itkMeanImageFilter.h"
```

Then the pixel types for input and output image must be defined and, with them, the image types can be instantiated.

```
typedef   unsigned char  InputPixelType;
typedef   unsigned char  OutputPixelType;

typedef itk::Image< InputPixelType,  2 >   InputImageType;
typedef itk::Image< OutputPixelType, 2 >   OutputImageType;
```

Using the image types it is now possible to instantiate the filter type and create the filter object.

```
typedef itk::MeanImageFilter<
          InputImageType, OutputImageType >  FilterType;

FilterType::Pointer filter = FilterType::New();
```

The size of the neighborhood is defined along every dimension by passing a `SizeType` object with

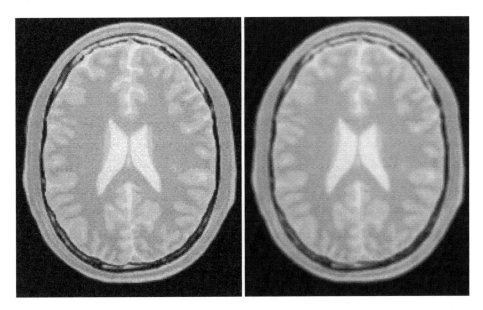

Figure 2.12: Effect of the MeanImageFilter on a slice from a MRI proton density brain image.

the corresponding values. The value on each dimension is used as the semi-size of a rectangular box. For example, in *2D* a size of 1,2 will result in a 3×5 neighborhood.

```
InputImageType::SizeType indexRadius;

indexRadius[0] = 1; // radius along x
indexRadius[1] = 1; // radius along y

filter->SetRadius( indexRadius );
```

The input to the filter can be taken from any other filter, for example a reader. The output can be passed down the pipeline to other filters, for example, a writer. An update call on any downstream filter will trigger the execution of the mean filter.

```
filter->SetInput( reader->GetOutput() );
writer->SetInput( filter->GetOutput() );
writer->Update();
```

Figure 2.12 illustrates the effect of this filter on a slice of MRI brain image using neighborhood radii of 1,1 which corresponds to a 3×3 classical neighborhood. It can be seen from this picture that edges are rapidly degraded by the diffusion of intensity values among neighbors.

2.6.2 Median Filter

The source code for this section can be found in the file
MedianImageFilter.cxx.

The `itk::MedianImageFilter` is commonly used as a robust approach for noise reduction. This filter is particularly efficient against *salt-and-pepper* noise. In other words, it is robust to the presence of gray-level outliers. MedianImageFilter computes the value of each output pixel as the statistical median of the neighborhood of values around the corresponding input pixel. The following figure illustrates the local effect of this filter in a *2D* case. The statistical median of the neighborhood on the left is passed as the output value associated with the pixel at the center of the neighborhood.

28	26	50
27	25	29
25	30	32

$\longrightarrow$ 28

This filter will work on images of any dimension thanks to the internal use of `itk::NeighborhoodIterator` and `itk::NeighborhoodOperator`. The size of the neighborhood over which the median is computed can be set by the user.

The header file corresponding to this filter should be included first.

```
#include "itkMedianImageFilter.h"
```

Then the pixel and image types of the input and output must be defined.

```
typedef   unsigned char   InputPixelType;
typedef   unsigned char   OutputPixelType;

typedef itk::Image< InputPixelType,  2 >   InputImageType;
typedef itk::Image< OutputPixelType, 2 >   OutputImageType;
```

Using the image types, it is now possible to define the filter type and create the filter object.

```
typedef itk::MedianImageFilter<
                InputImageType, OutputImageType >  FilterType;

FilterType::Pointer filter = FilterType::New();
```

The size of the neighborhood is defined along every dimension by passing a `SizeType` object with the corresponding values. The value on each dimension is used as the semi-size of a rectangular box. For example, in *2D* a size of 1,2 will result in a 3×5 neighborhood.

```
InputImageType::SizeType indexRadius;

indexRadius[0] = 1; // radius along x
indexRadius[1] = 1; // radius along y

filter->SetRadius( indexRadius );
```

The input to the filter can be taken from any other filter, for example a reader. The output can be passed down the pipeline to other filters, for example, a writer. An update call on any downstream filter will trigger the execution of the median filter.

```
filter->SetInput( reader->GetOutput() );
writer->SetInput( filter->GetOutput() );
writer->Update();
```

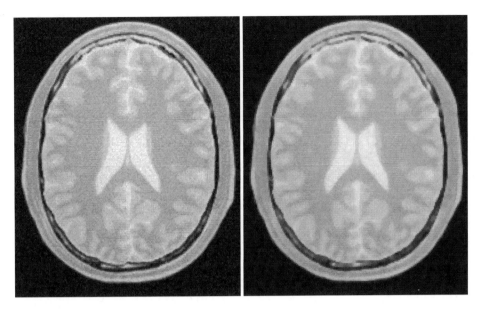

Figure 2.13: Effect of the MedianImageFilter on a slice from a MRI proton density brain image.

Figure 2.13 illustrates the effect of the MedianImageFilter filter on a slice of MRI brain image using a neighborhood radius of 1, 1, which corresponds to a 3×3 classical neighborhood. The filtered image demonstrates the moderate tendency of the median filter to preserve edges.

2.6.3 Mathematical Morphology

Mathematical morphology has proved to be a powerful resource for image processing and analysis [56]. ITK implements mathematical morphology filters using NeighborhoodIterators and `itk::NeighborhoodOperators`. The toolkit contains two types of image morphology algorithms: filters that operate on binary images and filters that operate on grayscale images.

Binary Filters

The source code for this section can be found in the file
`MathematicalMorphologyBinaryFilters.cxx`.

The following section illustrates the use of filters that perform basic mathematical morphology operations on binary images. The `itk::BinaryErodeImageFilter` and `itk::BinaryDilateImageFilter` are described here. The filter names clearly specify the type of image on which they operate. The header files required to construct a simple example of the use of the mathematical morphology filters are included below.

```
#include "itkBinaryErodeImageFilter.h"
#include "itkBinaryDilateImageFilter.h"
#include "itkBinaryBallStructuringElement.h"
```

The following code defines the input and output pixel types and their associated image types.

```
const unsigned int Dimension = 2;

typedef unsigned char    InputPixelType;
typedef unsigned char    OutputPixelType;

typedef itk::Image< InputPixelType,  Dimension >    InputImageType;
typedef itk::Image< OutputPixelType, Dimension >    OutputImageType;
```

Mathematical morphology operations are implemented by applying an operator over the neighborhood of each input pixel. The combination of the rule and the neighborhood is known as *structuring element*. Although some rules have become de facto standards for image processing, there is a good deal of freedom as to what kind of algorithmic rule should be applied to the neighborhood. The implementation in ITK follows the typical rule of minimum for erosion and maximum for dilation.

The structuring element is implemented as a NeighborhoodOperator. In particular, the default structuring element is the `itk::BinaryBallStructuringElement` class. This class is instantiated using the pixel type and dimension of the input image.

```
typedef itk::BinaryBallStructuringElement<
                    InputPixelType,
                    Dimension  >              StructuringElementType;
```

The structuring element type is then used along with the input and output image types for instantiating the type of the filters.

```
typedef itk::BinaryErodeImageFilter<
                        InputImageType,
                        OutputImageType,
                        StructuringElementType >  ErodeFilterType;

typedef itk::BinaryDilateImageFilter<
                        InputImageType,
                        OutputImageType,
                        StructuringElementType >  DilateFilterType;
```

The filters can now be created by invoking the New() method and assigning the result to `itk::SmartPointers`.

```
ErodeFilterType::Pointer  binaryErode  = ErodeFilterType::New();
DilateFilterType::Pointer binaryDilate = DilateFilterType::New();
```

The structuring element is not a reference counted class. Thus it is created as a C++ stack object instead of using New() and SmartPointers. The radius of the neighborhood associated with the structuring element is defined with the SetRadius() method and the CreateStructuringElement() method is invoked in order to initialize the operator. The resulting structuring element is passed to the mathematical morphology filter through the SetKernel() method, as illustrated below.

```
StructuringElementType  structuringElement;

structuringElement.SetRadius( 1 );  // 3x3 structuring element

structuringElement.CreateStructuringElement();

binaryErode->SetKernel( structuringElement );
binaryDilate->SetKernel( structuringElement );
```

A binary image is provided as input to the filters. This image might be, for example, the output of a binary threshold image filter.

```
thresholder->SetInput( reader->GetOutput() );

InputPixelType background =    0;
InputPixelType foreground = 255;

thresholder->SetOutsideValue( background );
thresholder->SetInsideValue( foreground );

thresholder->SetLowerThreshold( lowerThreshold );
thresholder->SetUpperThreshold( upperThreshold );

binaryErode->SetInput( thresholder->GetOutput() );
binaryDilate->SetInput( thresholder->GetOutput() );
```

The values that correspond to "objects" in the binary image are specified with the methods `SetErodeValue()` and `SetDilateValue()`. The value passed to these methods will be considered the value over which the dilation and erosion rules will apply.

```
binaryErode->SetErodeValue( foreground );
binaryDilate->SetDilateValue( foreground );
```

The filter is executed by invoking its `Update()` method, or by updating any downstream filter, such as an image writer.

```
writerDilation->SetInput( binaryDilate->GetOutput() );
writerDilation->Update();
```

Figure 2.14 illustrates the effect of the erosion and dilation filters on a binary image from a MRI brain slice. The figure shows how these operations can be used to remove spurious details from segmented images.

Grayscale Filters

The source code for this section can be found in the file `MathematicalMorphologyGrayscaleFilters.cxx`.

The following section illustrates the use of filters for performing basic mathematical morphology operations on grayscale images. The `itk::GrayscaleErodeImageFilter` and `itk::GrayscaleDilateImageFilter` are covered in this example. The filter names clearly specify the type of image on which they operate. The header files required for a simple example of the use of grayscale mathematical morphology filters are presented below.

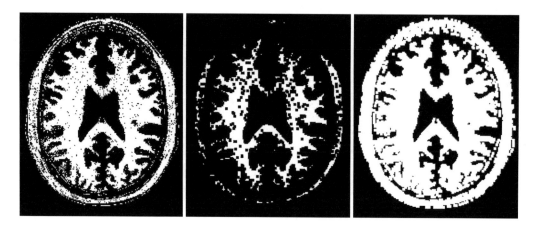

Figure 2.14: Effect of erosion and dilation in a binary image.

```
#include "itkGrayscaleErodeImageFilter.h"
#include "itkGrayscaleDilateImageFilter.h"
#include "itkBinaryBallStructuringElement.h"
```

The following code defines the input and output pixel types and their associated image types.

```
const unsigned int Dimension = 2;

typedef unsigned char    InputPixelType;
typedef unsigned char    OutputPixelType;

typedef itk::Image< InputPixelType,  Dimension >    InputImageType;
typedef itk::Image< OutputPixelType, Dimension >    OutputImageType;
```

Mathematical morphology operations are based on the application of an operator over a neighborhood of each input pixel. The combination of the rule and the neighborhood is known as *structuring element*. Although some rules have become the de facto standard in image processing there is a good deal of freedom as to what kind of algorithmic rule should be applied on the neighborhood. The implementation in ITK follows the typical rule of minimum for erosion and maximum for dilation.

The structuring element is implemented as a `itk::NeighborhoodOperator`. In particular, the default structuring element is the `itk::BinaryBallStructuringElement` class. This class is instantiated using the pixel type and dimension of the input image.

```
typedef itk::BinaryBallStructuringElement<
                  InputPixelType,
                  Dimension >          StructuringElementType;
```

The structuring element type is then used along with the input and output image types for instantiating the type of the filters.

```
typedef itk::GrayscaleErodeImageFilter<
                    InputImageType,
                    OutputImageType,
                    StructuringElementType >  ErodeFilterType;

typedef itk::GrayscaleDilateImageFilter<
                    InputImageType,
                    OutputImageType,
                    StructuringElementType >  DilateFilterType;
```

The filters can now be created by invoking the `New()` method and assigning the result to SmartPointers.

```
ErodeFilterType::Pointer  grayscaleErode  = ErodeFilterType::New();
DilateFilterType::Pointer grayscaleDilate = DilateFilterType::New();
```

The structuring element is not a reference counted class. Thus it is created as a C++ stack object instead of using `New()` and SmartPointers. The radius of the neighborhood associated with the structuring element is defined with the `SetRadius()` method and the `CreateStructuringElement()` method is invoked in order to initialize the operator. The resulting structuring element is passed to the mathematical morphology filter through the `SetKernel()` method, as illustrated below.

```
StructuringElementType  structuringElement;

structuringElement.SetRadius( 1 );  // 3x3 structuring element

structuringElement.CreateStructuringElement();

grayscaleErode->SetKernel( structuringElement );
grayscaleDilate->SetKernel( structuringElement );
```

A grayscale image is provided as input to the filters. This image might be, for example, the output of a reader.

```
grayscaleErode->SetInput( reader->GetOutput() );
grayscaleDilate->SetInput( reader->GetOutput() );
```

The filter is executed by invoking its `Update()` method, or by updating any downstream filter, such as an image writer.

```
writerDilation->SetInput( grayscaleDilate->GetOutput() );
writerDilation->Update();
```

Figure 2.15 illustrates the effect of the erosion and dilation filters on a binary image from a MRI brain slice. The figure shows how these operations can be used to remove spurious details from segmented images.

2.6.4 Voting Filters

Voting filters are quite a generic family of filters. In fact, both the Dilate and Erode filters from Mathematical Morphology are very particular cases of the broader family of voting filters. In a voting filter, the outcome of a pixel is decided by counting the number of pixels in its neighborhood and applying a rule to the result of that counting. For example, the typical implementation of erosion in

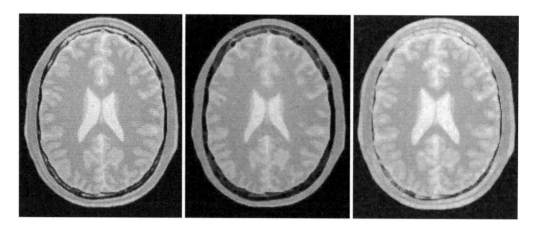

Figure 2.15: Effect of erosion and dilation in a grayscale image.

terms of a voting filter will be to label a foreground pixel as background if the number of background neighbors is greater than or equal to 1. In this context, you could imagine variations of erosion in which the count could be changed to require at least 3 foreground pixels in its neighborhood.

Binary Median Filter

One case of a voting filter is the BinaryMedianImageFilter. This filter is equivalent to applying a Median filter over a binary image. Having a binary image as input makes it possible to optimize the execution of the filter since there is no real need for sorting the pixels according to their frequency in the neighborhood.

The source code for this section can be found in the file
BinaryMedianImageFilter.cxx.

The itk::BinaryMedianImageFilter is commonly used as a robust approach for noise reduction. BinaryMedianImageFilter computes the value of each output pixel as the statistical median of the neighborhood of values around the corresponding input pixel. When the input images are binary, the implementation can be optimized by simply counting the number of pixels ON/OFF around the current pixel.

This filter will work on images of any dimension thanks to the internal use of itk::NeighborhoodIterator and itk::NeighborhoodOperator. The size of the neighborhood over which the median is computed can be set by the user.

The header file corresponding to this filter should be included first.

```
#include "itkBinaryMedianImageFilter.h"
```

Then the pixel and image types of the input and output must be defined.

```
typedef    unsigned char    InputPixelType;
typedef    unsigned char    OutputPixelType;


typedef itk::Image< InputPixelType,  2 >    InputImageType;
typedef itk::Image< OutputPixelType, 2 >    OutputImageType;
```

Using the image types, it is now possible to define the filter type and create the filter object.

```
typedef itk::BinaryMedianImageFilter<
               InputImageType, OutputImageType >  FilterType;


FilterType::Pointer filter = FilterType::New();
```

The size of the neighborhood is defined along every dimension by passing a `SizeType` object with the corresponding values. The value on each dimension is used as the semi-size of a rectangular box. For example, in $2D$ a size of $1, 2$ will result in a 3×5 neighborhood.

```
InputImageType::SizeType indexRadius;


indexRadius[0] = radiusX; // radius along x
indexRadius[1] = radiusY; // radius along y

filter->SetRadius( indexRadius );
```

The input to the filter can be taken from any other filter, for example a reader. The output can be passed down the pipeline to other filters, for example, a writer. An update call on any downstream filter will trigger the execution of the median filter.

```
filter->SetInput( reader->GetOutput() );
writer->SetInput( filter->GetOutput() );
writer->Update();
```

Figure 2.16 illustrates the effect of the BinaryMedianImageFilter filter on a slice of MRI brain image using a neighborhood radius of $2, 2$, which corresponds to a 5×5 classical neighborhood. The filtered image demonstrates the capability of this filter for reducing noise both in the background and foreground of the image, as well as smoothing the contours of the regions.

The typical effect of median filtration on a noisy digital image is a dramatic reduction in impulse noise spikes. The filter also tends to preserve brightness differences across signal steps, resulting in reduced blurring of regional boundaries. The filter also tends to preserve the positions of boundaries in an image.

Figure 2.17 below shows the effect of running the median filter with a 3x3 classical window size 1, 10 and 50 times. There is a tradeoff in noise reduction and the sharpness of the image when the window size is increased.

Hole Filling Filter

Another variation of voting filters is the Hole Filling filter. This filter converts background pixels into foreground only when the number of foreground pixels is a majority of the neighbors. By selecting the size of the majority, this filter can be tuned to fill in holes of different sizes. To be more precise, the effect of the filter is actually related to the curvature of the edge in which the pixel is located.

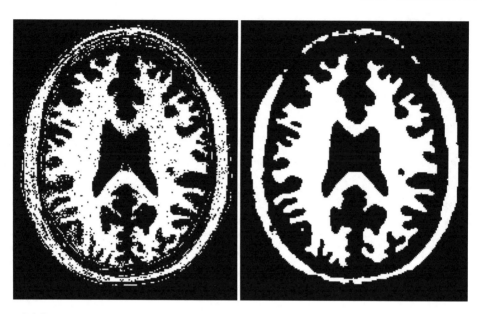

Figure 2.16: Effect of the BinaryMedianImageFilter on a slice from a MRI proton density brain image that has been thresholded in order to produce a binary image.

The source code for this section can be found in the file VotingBinaryHoleFillingImageFilter.cxx.

The itk::VotingBinaryHoleFillingImageFilter applies a voting operation in order to fill in cavities. This can be used for smoothing contours and for filling holes in binary images.

The header file corresponding to this filter should be included first.

```
#include "itkVotingBinaryHoleFillingImageFilter.h"
```

Then the pixel and image types of the input and output must be defined.

```
typedef    unsigned char  InputPixelType;
typedef    unsigned char  OutputPixelType;

typedef itk::Image< InputPixelType,  2 >   InputImageType;
typedef itk::Image< OutputPixelType, 2 >   OutputImageType;
```

Using the image types, it is now possible to define the filter type and create the filter object.

```
typedef itk::VotingBinaryHoleFillingImageFilter<
            InputImageType, OutputImageType >  FilterType;

FilterType::Pointer filter = FilterType::New();
```

The size of the neighborhood is defined along every dimension by passing a SizeType object with the corresponding values. The value on each dimension is used as the semi-size of a rectangular box. For example, in $2D$ a size of $1, 2$ will result in a 3×5 neighborhood.

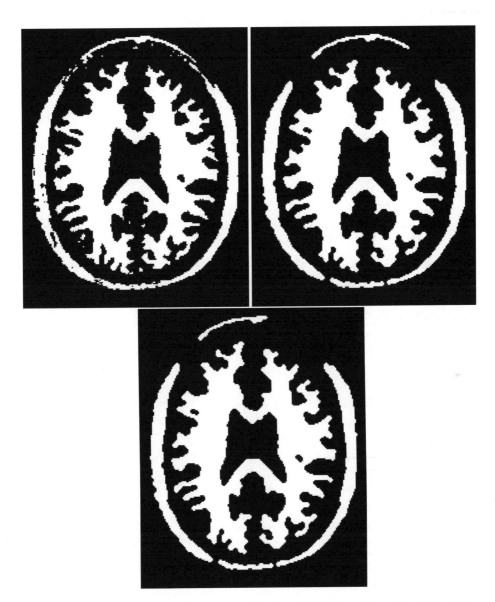

Figure 2.17: Effect of 1, 10 and 50 iterations of the BinaryMedianImageFilter using a 3x3 window.

```
InputImageType::SizeType indexRadius;

indexRadius[0] = radiusX; // radius along x
indexRadius[1] = radiusY; // radius along y

filter->SetRadius( indexRadius );
```

Since the filter is expecting a binary image as input, we must specify the levels that are going to be considered background and foreground. This is done with the `SetForegroundValue()` and `SetBackgroundValue()` methods.

```
filter->SetBackgroundValue(   0 );
filter->SetForegroundValue( 255 );
```

We must also specify the majority threshold that is going to be used as the decision criterion for converting a background pixel into a foreground pixel. The rule of conversion is that a background pixel will be converted into a foreground pixel if the number of foreground neighbors surpass the number of background neighbors by the majority value. For example, in a 2D image, with neighborhood of radius 1, the neighborhood will have size 3×3. If we set the majority value to 2, then we are requiring that the number of foreground neighbors should be at least (3x3 -1)/2 + majority. This is done with the `SetMajorityThreshold()` method.

```
filter->SetMajorityThreshold( 2 );
```

The input to the filter can be taken from any other filter, for example a reader. The output can be passed down the pipeline to other filters, for example, a writer. An update call on any downstream filter will trigger the execution of the median filter.

```
filter->SetInput( reader->GetOutput() );
writer->SetInput( filter->GetOutput() );
writer->Update();
```

Figure 2.18 illustrates the effect of the VotingBinaryHoleFillingImageFilter filter on a thresholded slice of MRI brain image using neighborhood radii of $1, 1, 2, 2$ and $3, 3$ that correspond respectively to neighborhoods of size $3 \times 3, 5 \times 5, 7 \times 7$. The filtered image demonstrates the capability of this filter for reducing noise both in the background and foreground of the image, as well as smoothing the contours of the regions.

Iterative Hole Filling Filter

The Hole Filling filter can be used in an iterative way, by applying it repeatedly until no pixel changes. In this context, the filter can be seen as a binary variation of a Level Set filter.

The source code for this section can be found in the file
VotingBinaryIterativeHoleFillingImageFilter.cxx.

The `itk::VotingBinaryIterativeHoleFillingImageFilter` applies a voting operation in order to fill in cavities. This can be used for smoothing contours and for filling holes in binary images. This filter runs a `itk::VotingBinaryHoleFillingImageFilter` internally until no pixels change or the maximum number of iterations has been reached.

The header file corresponding to this filter should be included first.

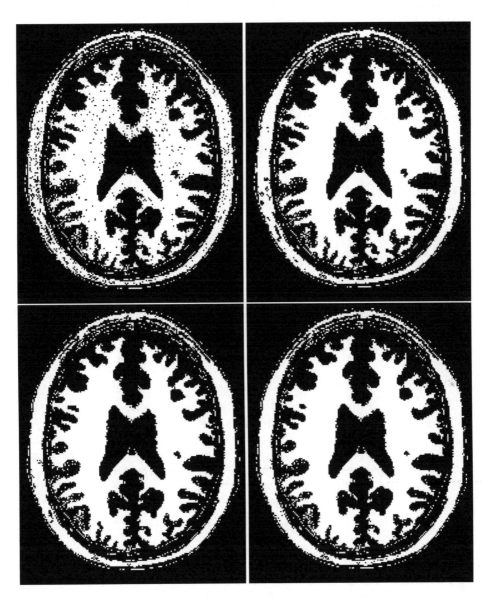

Figure 2.18: Effect of the VotingBinaryHoleFillingImageFilter on a slice from a MRI proton density brain image that has been thresholded in order to produce a binary image. The output images have used radius 1,2 and 3 respectively.

```
#include "itkVotingBinaryIterativeHoleFillingImageFilter.h"
```

Then the pixel and image types must be defined. Note that this filter requires the input and output images to be of the same type, therefore a single image type is required for the template instantiation.

```
typedef   unsigned char  PixelType;

typedef itk::Image< PixelType, 2 >   ImageType;
```

Using the image types, it is now possible to define the filter type and create the filter object.

```
typedef itk::VotingBinaryIterativeHoleFillingImageFilter<
                                    ImageType >  FilterType;

FilterType::Pointer filter = FilterType::New();
```

The size of the neighborhood is defined along every dimension by passing a `SizeType` object with the corresponding values. The value on each dimension is used as the semi-size of a rectangular box. For example, in 2D a size of 1,2 will result in a 3×5 neighborhood.

```
ImageType::SizeType indexRadius;

indexRadius[0] = radiusX; // radius along x
indexRadius[1] = radiusY; // radius along y

filter->SetRadius( indexRadius );
```

Since the filter is expecting a binary image as input, we must specify the levels that are going to be considered background and foreground. This is done with the `SetForegroundValue()` and `SetBackgroundValue()` methods.

```
filter->SetBackgroundValue(   0 );
filter->SetForegroundValue( 255 );
```

We must also specify the majority threshold that is going to be used as the decision criterion for converting a background pixel into a foreground pixel. The rule of conversion is that a background pixel will be converted into a foreground pixel if the number of foreground neighbors surpass the number of background neighbors by the majority value. For example, in a 2D image, with neighborhood of radius 1, the neighborhood will have size 3×3. If we set the majority value to 2, then we are requiring that the number of foreground neighbors should be at least (3x3 -1)/2 + majority. This is done with the `SetMajorityThreshold()` method.

```
filter->SetMajorityThreshold( 2 );
```

Finally we specify the maximum number of iterations for which this filter should run. The number of iterations will determine the maximum size of holes and cavities that this filter will be able to fill. The more iterations you run, the larger the cavities that will be filled in.

```
filter->SetMaximumNumberOfIterations( numberOfIterations );
```

The input to the filter can be taken from any other filter, for example a reader. The output can be passed down the pipeline to other filters, for example, a writer. An update call on any downstream filter will trigger the execution of the median filter.

```
filter->SetInput( reader->GetOutput() );
writer->SetInput( filter->GetOutput() );
writer->Update();
```

Figure 2.19 illustrates the effect of the VotingBinaryIterativeHoleFillingImageFilter filter on a thresholded slice of MRI brain image using neighborhood radii of 1, 1, 2, 2 and 3, 3 that correspond respectively to neighborhoods of size 3×3, 5×5, 7×7. The filtered image demonstrates the capability of this filter for reducing noise both in the background and foreground of the image, as well as smoothing the contours of the regions.

2.7 Smoothing Filters

Real image data has a level of uncertainty which is manifested in the variability of measures assigned to pixels. This uncertainty is usually interpreted as noise and considered an undesirable component of the image data. This section describes several methods that can be applied to reduce noise on images.

2.7.1 Blurring

Blurring is the traditional approach for removing noise from images. It is usually implemented in the form of a convolution with a kernel. The effect of blurring on the image spectrum is to attenuate high spatial frequencies. Different kernels attenuate frequencies in different ways. One of the most commonly used kernels is the Gaussian. Two implementations of Gaussian smoothing are available in the toolkit. The first one is based on a traditional convolution while the other is based on the application of IIR filters that approximate the convolution with a Gaussian [16, 17].

Discrete Gaussian

The source code for this section can be found in the file
`DiscreteGaussianImageFilter.cxx`.

The `itk::DiscreteGaussianImageFilter` computes the convolution of the input image with a Gaussian kernel. This is done in *ND* by taking advantage of the separability of the Gaussian kernel. A one-dimensional Gaussian function is discretized on a convolution kernel. The size of the kernel is extended until there are enough discrete points in the Gaussian to ensure that a user-provided maximum error is not exceeded. Since the size of the kernel is unknown a priori, it is necessary to impose a limit to its growth. The user can thus provide a value to be the maximum admissible size of the kernel. Discretization error is defined as the difference between the area under the discrete Gaussian curve (which has finite support) and the area under the continuous Gaussian.

Gaussian kernels in ITK are constructed according to the theory of Tony Lindeberg [35] so that smoothing and derivative operations commute before and after discretization. In other words, finite difference derivatives on an image *I* that has been smoothed by convolution with the Gaussian are equivalent to finite differences computed on *I* by convolving with a derivative of the Gaussian.

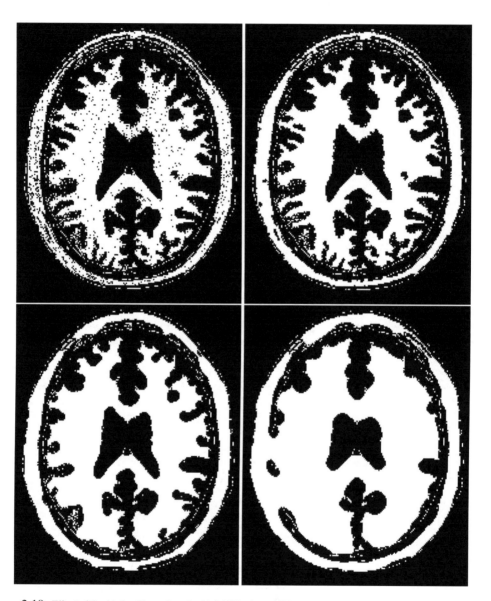

Figure 2.19: Effect of the VotingBinaryIterativeHoleFillingImageFilter on a slice from a MRI proton density brain image that has been thresholded in order to produce a binary image. The output images have used radius 1,2 and 3 respectively.

The first step required to use this filter is to include its header file. As with other examples, the includes here are truncated to those specific for this example.

```
#include "itkDiscreteGaussianImageFilter.h"
```

Types should be chosen for the pixels of the input and output images. Image types can be instantiated using the pixel type and dimension.

```
typedef   float     InputPixelType;
typedef   float     OutputPixelType;

typedef itk::Image< InputPixelType,  2 >   InputImageType;
typedef itk::Image< OutputPixelType, 2 >   OutputImageType;
```

The discrete Gaussian filter type is instantiated using the input and output image types. A corresponding filter object is created.

```
typedef itk::DiscreteGaussianImageFilter<
           InputImageType, OutputImageType >  FilterType;

FilterType::Pointer filter = FilterType::New();
```

The input image can be obtained from the output of another filter. Here, an image reader is used as its input.

```
filter->SetInput( reader->GetOutput() );
```

The filter requires the user to provide a value for the variance associated with the Gaussian kernel. The method `SetVariance()` is used for this purpose. The discrete Gaussian is constructed as a convolution kernel. The maximum kernel size can be set by the user. Note that the combination of variance and kernel-size values may result in a truncated Gaussian kernel.

```
filter->SetVariance( gaussianVariance );
filter->SetMaximumKernelWidth( maxKernelWidth );
```

Finally, the filter is executed by invoking the `Update()` method.

```
filter->Update();
```

If the output of this filter has been connected to other filters down the pipeline, updating any of the downstream filters will trigger the execution of this one. For example, a writer could be used after the filter.

```
rescaler->SetInput( filter->GetOutput() );
writer->SetInput( rescaler->GetOutput() );
writer->Update();
```

Figure 2.21 illustrates the effect of this filter on a MRI proton density image of the brain.

Note that large Gaussian variances will produce large convolution kernels and correspondingly longer computation times. Unless a high degree of accuracy is required, it may be more desirable to use the approximating `itk::RecursiveGaussianImageFilter` with large variances.

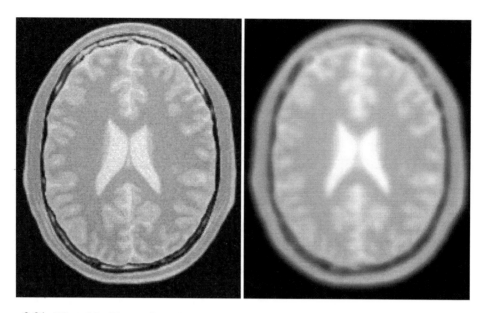

Figure 2.21: Effect of the DiscreteGaussianImageFilter on a slice from a MRI proton density image of the brain.

Binomial Blurring

The source code for this section can be found in the file
`BinomialBlurImageFilter.cxx`.

The `itk::BinomialBlurImageFilter` computes a nearest neighbor average along each dimension.
The process is repeated a number of times, as specified by the user. In principle, after a large number
of iterations the result will approach the convolution with a Gaussian.

The first step required to use this filter is to include its header file.

```
#include "itkBinomialBlurImageFilter.h"
```

Types should be chosen for the pixels of the input and output images. Image types can be instantiated
using the pixel type and dimension.

```
typedef    float      InputPixelType;
typedef    float      OutputPixelType;

typedef itk::Image< InputPixelType,  2 >   InputImageType;
typedef itk::Image< OutputPixelType, 2 >   OutputImageType;
```

The filter type is now instantiated using both the input image and the output image types. Then a
filter object is created.

```
typedef itk::BinomialBlurImageFilter<
                 InputImageType, OutputImageType >  FilterType;
FilterType::Pointer filter = FilterType::New();
```

The input image can be obtained from the output of another filter. Here, an image reader is used as

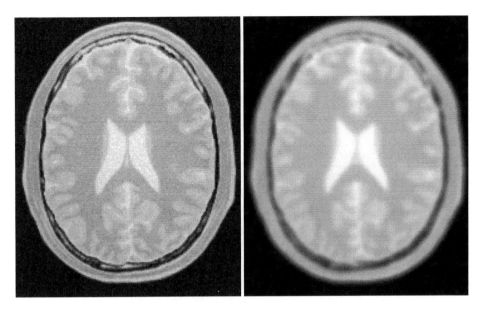

Figure 2.22: Effect of the BinomialBlurImageFilter on a slice from a MRI proton density image of the brain.

the source. The number of repetitions is set with the SetRepetitions() method. Computation time will increase linearly with the number of repetitions selected. Finally, the filter can be executed by calling the Update() method.

```
filter->SetInput( reader->GetOutput() );
filter->SetRepetitions( repetitions );
filter->Update();
```

Figure 2.22 illustrates the effect of this filter on a MRI proton density image of the brain.

Note that the standard deviation σ of the equivalent Gaussian is fixed. In the spatial spectrum, the effect of every iteration of this filter is like a multiplication with a sinus cardinal function.

Recursive Gaussian IIR

The source code for this section can be found in the file
SmoothingRecursiveGaussianImageFilter.cxx.

The classical method of smoothing an image by convolution with a Gaussian kernel has the drawback that it is slow when the standard deviation σ of the Gaussian is large. This is due to the larger size of the kernel, which results in a higher number of computations per pixel.

The itk::RecursiveGaussianImageFilter implements an approximation of convolution with the Gaussian and its derivatives by using IIR[2] filters. In practice this filter requires a constant number of operations for approximating the convolution, regardless of the σ value [16, 17].

---

[2]Infinite Impulse Response

The first step required to use this filter is to include its header file.

```
#include "itkRecursiveGaussianImageFilter.h"
```

Types should be selected on the desired input and output pixel types.

```
typedef    float    InputPixelType;
typedef    float    OutputPixelType;
```

The input and output image types are instantiated using the pixel types.

```
typedef itk::Image< InputPixelType,  2 >   InputImageType;
typedef itk::Image< OutputPixelType, 2 >   OutputImageType;
```

The filter type is now instantiated using both the input image and the output image types.

```
typedef itk::RecursiveGaussianImageFilter<
                      InputImageType, OutputImageType >  FilterType;
```

This filter applies the approximation of the convolution along a single dimension. It is therefore necessary to concatenate several of these filters to produce smoothing in all directions. In this example, we create a pair of filters since we are processing a 2D image. The filters are created by invoking the New() method and assigning the result to a itk::SmartPointer.

```
FilterType::Pointer filterX = FilterType::New();
FilterType::Pointer filterY = FilterType::New();
```

Since each one of the newly created filters has the potential to perform filtering along any dimension, we have to restrict each one to a particular direction. This is done with the SetDirection() method.

```
filterX->SetDirection( 0 );   // 0 --> X direction
filterY->SetDirection( 1 );   // 1 --> Y direction
```

The itk::RecursiveGaussianImageFilter can approximate the convolution with the Gaussian or with its first and second derivatives. We select one of these options by using the SetOrder() method. Note that the argument is an enum whose values can be ZeroOrder, FirstOrder and SecondOrder. For example, to compute the x partial derivative we should select FirstOrder for x and ZeroOrder for y. Here we want only to smooth in x and y, so we select ZeroOrder in both directions.

```
filterX->SetOrder( FilterType::ZeroOrder );
filterY->SetOrder( FilterType::ZeroOrder );
```

There are two typical ways of normalizing Gaussians depending on their application. For scale-space analysis it is desirable to use a normalization that will preserve the maximum value of the input. This normalization is represented by the following equation.

$$\frac{1}{\sigma\sqrt{2\pi}} \tag{2.4}$$

In applications that use the Gaussian as a solution of the diffusion equation it is desirable to use a normalization that preserve the integral of the signal. This last approach can be seen as a conservation of mass principle. This is represented by the following equation.

$$\frac{1}{\sigma^2 \sqrt{2\pi}} \qquad\qquad (2.5)$$

The `itk::RecursiveGaussianImageFilter` has a boolean flag that allows users to select between these two normalization options. Selection is done with the method `SetNormalizeAcrossScale()`. Enable this flag to analyzing an image across scale-space. In the current example, this setting has no impact because we are actually renormalizing the output to the dynamic range of the reader, so we simply disable the flag.

```
filterX->SetNormalizeAcrossScale( false );
filterY->SetNormalizeAcrossScale( false );
```

The input image can be obtained from the output of another filter. Here, an image reader is used as the source. The image is passed to the *x* filter and then to the *y* filter. The reason for keeping these two filters separate is that it is usual in scale-space applications to compute not only the smoothing but also combinations of derivatives at different orders and smoothing. Some factorization is possible when separate filters are used to generate the intermediate results. Here this capability is less interesting, though, since we only want to smooth the image in all directions.

```
filterX->SetInput( reader->GetOutput() );
filterY->SetInput( filterX->GetOutput() );
```

It is now time to select the σ of the Gaussian used to smooth the data. Note that σ must be passed to both filters and that sigma is considered to be in millimeters. That is, at the moment of applying the smoothing process, the filter will take into account the spacing values defined in the image.

```
filterX->SetSigma( sigma );
filterY->SetSigma( sigma );
```

Finally the pipeline is executed by invoking the `Update()` method.

```
filterY->Update();
```

Figure 2.23 illustrates the effect of this filter on a MRI proton density image of the brain using σ values of 3 (left) and 5 (right). The figure shows how the attenuation of noise can be regulated by selecting the appropriate standard deviation. This type of scale-tunable filter is suitable for performing scale-space analysis.

The RecursiveGaussianFilters can also be applied on multi-component images. For instance, the above filter could have applied with RGBPixel as the pixel type. Each component is then independently filtered. However the RescaleIntensityImageFilter will not work on RGBPixels since it does not mathematically make sense to rescale the output of multi-component images.

2.7.2 Local Blurring

In some cases it is desirable to compute smoothing in restricted regions of the image, or to do it using different parameters that are computed locally. The following sections describe options for applying local smoothing in images.

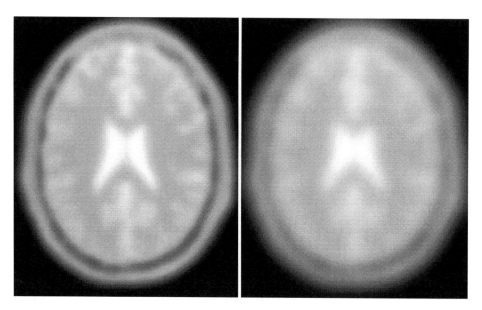

Figure 2.23: Effect of the SmoothingRecursiveGaussianImageFilter on a slice from a MRI proton density image of the brain.

Gaussian Blur Image Function

The source code for this section can be found in the file
`GaussianBlurImageFunction.cxx`.

2.7.3 Edge Preserving Smoothing

Introduction to Anisotropic Diffusion

The drawback of image denoising (smoothing) is that it tends to blur away the sharp boundaries in the image that help to distinguish between the larger-scale anatomical structures that one is trying to characterize (which also limits the size of the smoothing kernels in most applications). Even in cases where smoothing does not obliterate boundaries, it tends to distort the fine structure of the image and thereby changes subtle aspects of the anatomical shapes in question.

Perona and Malik [46] introduced an alternative to linear-filtering that they called *anisotropic diffusion*. Anisotropic diffusion is closely related to the earlier work of Grossberg [23], who used similar nonlinear diffusion processes to model human vision. The motivation for anisotropic diffusion (also called *nonuniform* or *variable conductance* diffusion) is that a Gaussian smoothed image is a single time slice of the solution to the heat equation, that has the original image as its initial conditions. Thus, the solution to

$$\frac{\partial g(x,y,t)}{\partial t} = \nabla \cdot \nabla g(x,y,t), \tag{2.6}$$

where $g(x,y,0) = f(x,y)$ is the input image, is $g(x,y,t) = G(\sqrt{2t}) \otimes f(x,y)$, where $G(\sigma)$ is a Gaussian with standard deviation σ.

Anisotropic diffusion includes a variable conductance term that, in turn, depends on the differential structure of the image. Thus, the variable conductance can be formulated to limit the smoothing at "edges" in images, as measured by high gradient magnitude, for example.

$$g_t = \nabla \cdot c(|\nabla g|)\nabla g, \qquad (2.7)$$

where, for notational convenience, we leave off the independent parameters of g and use the subscripts with respect to those parameters to indicate partial derivatives. The function $c(|\nabla g|)$ is a fuzzy cutoff that reduces the conductance at areas of large $|\nabla g|$, and can be any one of a number of functions. The literature has shown

$$c(|\nabla g|) = e^{-\frac{|\nabla g|^2}{2k^2}} \qquad (2.8)$$

to be quite effective. Notice that conductance term introduces a free parameter k, the *conductance parameter*, that controls the sensitivity of the process to edge contrast. Thus, anisotropic diffusion entails two free parameters: the conductance parameter, k, and the time parameter, t, that is analogous to σ, the effective width of the filter when using Gaussian kernels.

Equation 2.7 is a nonlinear partial differential equation that can be solved on a discrete grid using finite forward differences. Thus, the smoothed image is obtained only by an iterative process, not a convolution or non-stationary, linear filter. Typically, the number of iterations required for practical results are small, and large 2D images can be processed in several tens of seconds using carefully written code running on modern, general purpose, single-processor computers. The technique applies readily and effectively to 3D images, but requires more processing time.

In the early 1990's several research groups [22, 68] demonstrated the effectiveness of anisotropic diffusion on medical images. In a series of papers on the subject [72, 70, 71, 68, 69, 66], Whitaker described a detailed analytical and empirical analysis, introduced a smoothing term in the conductance that made the process more robust, invented a numerical scheme that virtually eliminated directional artifacts in the original algorithm, and generalized anisotropic diffusion to vector-valued images, an image processing technique that can be used on vector-valued medical data (such as the color cryosection data of the Visible Human Project).

For a vector-valued input $\vec{F} : U \mapsto \Re^m$ the process takes the form

$$\vec{F}_t = \nabla \cdot c(\mathcal{D}\vec{F})\vec{F}, \qquad (2.9)$$

where $\mathcal{D}\vec{F}$ is a *dissimilarity* measure of $\vec{F}$, a generalization of the gradient magnitude to vector-valued images, that can incorporate linear and nonlinear coordinate transformations on the range of $\vec{F}$. In this way, the smoothing of the multiple images associated with vector-valued data is coupled through the conductance term, that fuses the information in the different images. Thus vector-valued, nonlinear diffusion can combine low-level image features (e.g. edges) across all "channels" of a vector-valued image in order to preserve or enhance those features in all of image "channels".

Vector-valued anisotropic diffusion is useful for denoising data from devices that produce multiple values such as MRI or color photography. When performing nonlinear diffusion on a color image, the color channels are diffused separately, but linked through the conductance term. Vector-valued diffusion is also useful for processing registered data from different devices or for denoising higher-order geometric or statistical features from scalar-valued images [66, 73].

The output of anisotropic diffusion is an image or set of images that demonstrates reduced noise and texture but preserves, and can also enhance, edges. Such images are useful for a variety of processes including statistical classification, visualization, and geometric feature extraction. Previous work has shown [69] that anisotropic diffusion, over a wide range of conductance parameters, offers quantifiable advantages over linear filtering for edge detection in medical images.

Since the effectiveness of nonlinear diffusion was first demonstrated, numerous variations of this approach have surfaced in the literature [61]. These include alternatives for constructing dissimilarity measures [54], directional (i.e., tensor-valued) conductance terms [65, 3] and level set interpretations [67].

Gradient Anisotropic Diffusion

The source code for this section can be found in the file
`GradientAnisotropicDiffusionImageFilter.cxx`.

The `itk::GradientAnisotropicDiffusionImageFilter` implements an N-dimensional version of the classic Perona-Malik anisotropic diffusion equation for scalar-valued images [46].

The conductance term for this implementation is chosen as a function of the gradient magnitude of the image at each point, reducing the strength of diffusion at edge pixels.

$$C(\mathbf{x}) = e^{-(\frac{\|\nabla U(\mathbf{x})\|}{K})^2} \tag{2.10}$$

The numerical implementation of this equation is similar to that described in the Perona-Malik paper [46], but uses a more robust technique for gradient magnitude estimation and has been generalized to N-dimensions.

The first step required to use this filter is to include its header file.

```
#include "itkGradientAnisotropicDiffusionImageFilter.h"
```

Types should be selected based on the pixel types required for the input and output images. The image types are defined using the pixel type and the dimension.

```
typedef    float    InputPixelType;
typedef    float    OutputPixelType;

typedef itk::Image< InputPixelType,  2 >   InputImageType;
typedef itk::Image< OutputPixelType, 2 >   OutputImageType;
```

The filter type is now instantiated using both the input image and the output image types. The filter object is created by the `New()` method.

```
typedef itk::GradientAnisotropicDiffusionImageFilter<
            InputImageType, OutputImageType > FilterType;
FilterType::Pointer filter = FilterType::New();
```

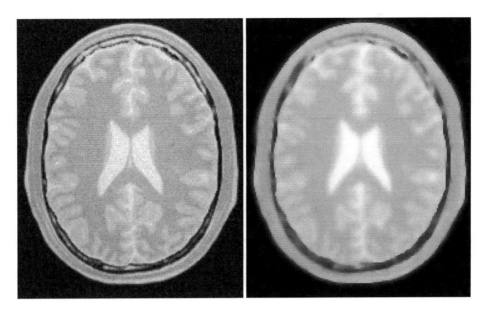

Figure 2.24: Effect of the GradientAnisotropicDiffusionImageFilter on a slice from a MRI Proton Density image of the brain.

The input image can be obtained from the output of another filter. Here, an image reader is used as source.

```
filter->SetInput( reader->GetOutput() );
```

This filter requires three parameters: the number of iterations to be performed, the time step and the conductance parameter used in the computation of the level set evolution. These parameters are set using the methods SetNumberOfIterations(), SetTimeStep() and SetConductanceParameter() respectively. The filter can be executed by invoking Update().

```
filter->SetNumberOfIterations( numberOfIterations );
filter->SetTimeStep( timeStep );
filter->SetConductanceParameter( conductance );

filter->Update();
```

Typical values for the time step are 0.25 in 2*D* images and 0.125 in 3*D* images. The number of iterations is typically set to 5; more iterations result in further smoothing and will increase the computing time linearly.

Figure 2.24 illustrates the effect of this filter on a MRI proton density image of the brain. In this example the filter was run with a time step of 0.25, and 5 iterations. The figure shows how homogeneous regions are smoothed and edges are preserved.

The following classes provide similar functionality:

- itk::BilateralImageFilter

- itk::CurvatureAnisotropicDiffusionImageFilter

- itk::CurvatureFlowImageFilter

Curvature Anisotropic Diffusion

The source code for this section can be found in the file
CurvatureAnisotropicDiffusionImageFilter.cxx.

The itk::CurvatureAnisotropicDiffusionImageFilter performs anisotropic diffusion on an
image using a modified curvature diffusion equation (MCDE).

MCDE does not exhibit the edge enhancing properties of classic anisotropic diffusion, which can
under certain conditions undergo a "negative" diffusion, which enhances the contrast of edges. Equations of the form of MCDE always undergo positive diffusion, with the conductance term only varying the strength of that diffusion.

Qualitatively, MCDE compares well with other non-linear diffusion techniques. It is less sensitive to
contrast than classic Perona-Malik style diffusion, and preserves finer detailed structures in images.
There is a potential speed trade-off for using this function in place of itkGradientNDAnisotropicDif-
fusionFunction. Each iteration of the solution takes roughly twice as long. Fewer iterations, however,
may be required to reach an acceptable solution.

The MCDE equation is given as:

$$f_t = |\nabla f| \nabla \cdot c(|\nabla f|) \frac{\nabla f}{|\nabla f|} \qquad (2.11)$$

where the conductance modified curvature term is

$$\nabla \cdot \frac{\nabla f}{|\nabla f|} \qquad (2.12)$$

The first step required for using this filter is to include its header file.

```
#include "itkCurvatureAnisotropicDiffusionImageFilter.h"
```

Types should be selected based on the pixel types required for the input and output images. The
image types are defined using the pixel type and the dimension.

```
typedef    float    InputPixelType;
typedef    float    OutputPixelType;

typedef itk::Image< InputPixelType,  2 >   InputImageType;
typedef itk::Image< OutputPixelType, 2 >   OutputImageType;
```

The filter type is now instantiated using both the input image and the output image types. The filter
object is created by the New() method.

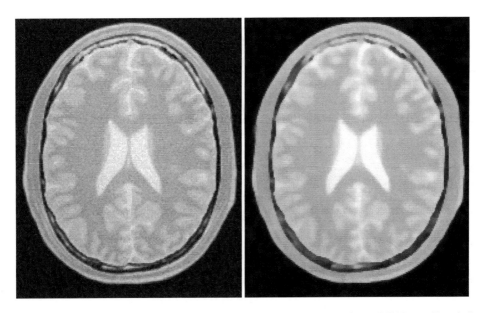

Figure 2.25: Effect of the CurvatureAnisotropicDiffusionImageFilter on a slice from a MRI Proton Density image of the brain.

```
typedef itk::CurvatureAnisotropicDiffusionImageFilter<
            InputImageType, OutputImageType > FilterType;

FilterType::Pointer filter = FilterType::New();
```

The input image can be obtained from the output of another filter. Here, an image reader is used as source.

```
filter->SetInput( reader->GetOutput() );
```

This filter requires three parameters: the number of iterations to be performed, the time step used in the computation of the level set evolution and the value of conductance. These parameters are set using the methods SetNumberOfIterations(), SetTimeStep() and SetConductance() respectively. The filter can be executed by invoking Update().

```
filter->SetNumberOfIterations( numberOfIterations );
filter->SetTimeStep( timeStep );
filter->SetConductanceParameter( conductance );
if (useImageSpacing)
  {
  filter->UseImageSpacingOn();
  }
filter->Update();
```

Typical values for the time step are 0.125 in $2D$ images and 0.0625 in $3D$ images. The number of iterations can be usually around 5, more iterations will result in further smoothing and will increase the computing time linearly. The conductance parameter is usually around 3.0.

Figure 2.25 illustrates the effect of this filter on a MRI proton density image of the brain. In this example the filter was run with a time step of 0.125, 5 iterations and a conductance value of 3.0. The figure shows how homogeneous regions are smoothed and edges are preserved.

The following classes provide similar functionality:

- `itk::BilateralImageFilter`

- `itk::CurvatureFlowImageFilter`

- `itk::GradientAnisotropicDiffusionImageFilter`

Curvature Flow

The source code for this section can be found in the file
`CurvatureFlowImageFilter.cxx`.

The `itk::CurvatureFlowImageFilter` performs edge-preserving smoothing in a similar fashion to the classical anisotropic diffusion. The filter uses a level set formulation where the iso-intensity contours in an image are viewed as level sets, where pixels of a particular intensity form one level set. The level set function is then evolved under the control of a diffusion equation where the speed is proportional to the curvature of the contour:

$$I_t = \kappa |\nabla I| \tag{2.13}$$

where κ is the curvature.

Areas of high curvature will diffuse faster than areas of low curvature. Hence, small jagged noise artifacts will disappear quickly, while large scale interfaces will be slow to evolve, thereby preserving sharp boundaries between objects. However, it should be noted that although the evolution at the boundary is slow, some diffusion will still occur. Thus, continual application of this curvature flow scheme will eventually result in the removal of information as each contour shrinks to a point and disappears.

The first step required to use this filter is to include its header file.

```
#include "itkCurvatureFlowImageFilter.h"
```

Types should be selected based on the pixel types required for the input and output images.

```
typedef    float    InputPixelType;
typedef    float    OutputPixelType;
```

With them, the input and output image types can be instantiated.

```
typedef itk::Image< InputPixelType,  2 >   InputImageType;
typedef itk::Image< OutputPixelType, 2 >   OutputImageType;
```

The CurvatureFlow filter type is now instantiated using both the input image and the output image types.

```
typedef itk::CurvatureFlowImageFilter<
                InputImageType, OutputImageType >  FilterType;
```

A filter object is created by invoking the `New()` method and assigning the result to a `itk::SmartPointer`.

```
FilterType::Pointer filter = FilterType::New();
```

The input image can be obtained from the output of another filter. Here, an image reader is used as source.

```
filter->SetInput( reader->GetOutput() );
```

The CurvatureFlow filter requires two parameters: the number of iterations to be performed and the time step used in the computation of the level set evolution. These two parameters are set using the methods `SetNumberOfIterations()` and `SetTimeStep()` respectively. Then the filter can be executed by invoking `Update()`.

```
filter->SetNumberOfIterations( numberOfIterations );
filter->SetTimeStep( timeStep );
filter->Update();
```

Typical values for the time step are 0.125 in $2D$ images and 0.0625 in $3D$ images. The number of iterations can be usually around 10, more iterations will result in further smoothing and will increase the computing time linearly. Edge-preserving behavior is not guaranteed by this filter. Some degradation will occur on the edges and will increase as the number of iterations is increased.

If the output of this filter has been connected to other filters down the pipeline, updating any of the downstream filters will trigger the execution of this one. For example, a writer filter could be used after the curvature flow filter.

```
rescaler->SetInput( filter->GetOutput() );
writer->SetInput( rescaler->GetOutput() );
writer->Update();
```

Figure 2.26 illustrates the effect of this filter on a MRI proton density image of the brain. In this example the filter was run with a time step of 0.25 and 10 iterations. The figure shows how homogeneous regions are smoothed and edges are preserved.

The following classes provide similar functionality:

- `itk::GradientAnisotropicDiffusionImageFilter`

- `itk::CurvatureAnisotropicDiffusionImageFilter`

- `itk::BilateralImageFilter`

MinMaxCurvature Flow

The source code for this section can be found in the file `MinMaxCurvatureFlowImageFilter.cxx`.

The MinMax curvature flow filter applies a variant of the curvature flow algorithm where diffusion

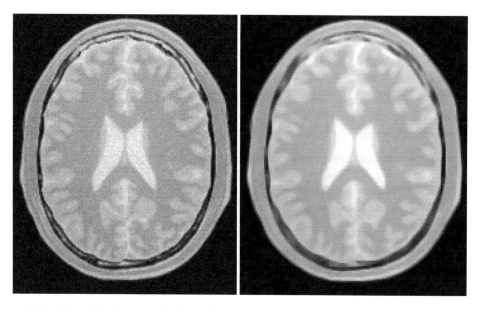

Figure 2.26: Effect of the CurvatureFlowImageFilter on a slice from a MRI proton density image of the brain.

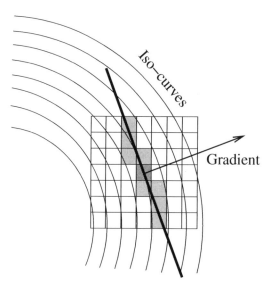

Figure 2.27: Elements involved in the computation of min-max curvature flow.

is turned on or off depending of the scale of the noise that one wants to remove. The evolution speed is switched between $min(\kappa,0)$ and $max(\kappa,0)$ such that:

$$I_t = F|\nabla I| \qquad (2.14)$$

where F is defined as

$$F = \begin{cases} max(\kappa,0) & : & Average < Threshold \\ min(\kappa,0) & : & Average \geq Threshold \end{cases} \qquad (2.15)$$

The *Average* is the average intensity computed over a neighborhood of a user-specified radius of the pixel. The choice of the radius governs the scale of the noise to be removed. The *Threshold* is calculated as the average of pixel intensities along the direction perpendicular to the gradient at the *extrema* of the local neighborhood.

A speed of $F = max(\kappa,0)$ will cause small dark regions in a predominantly light region to shrink. Conversely, a speed of $F = min(\kappa,0)$, will cause light regions in a predominantly dark region to shrink. Comparison between the neighborhood average and the threshold is used to select the the right speed function to use. This switching prevents the unwanted diffusion of the simple curvature flow method.

Figure 2.27 shows the main elements involved in the computation. The set of square pixels represent the neighborhood over which the average intensity is being computed. The gray pixels are those lying close to the direction perpendicular to the gradient. The pixels which intersect the neighborhood bounds are used to compute the threshold value in the equation above. The integer radius of the neighborhood is selected by the user.

The first step required to use the `itk::MinMaxCurvatureFlowImageFilter` is to include its header file.

```
#include "itkMinMaxCurvatureFlowImageFilter.h"
```

Types should be selected based on the pixel types required for the input and output images. The input and output image types are instantiated.

```
typedef    float      InputPixelType;
typedef    float      OutputPixelType;

typedef itk::Image< InputPixelType,  2 >   InputImageType;
typedef itk::Image< OutputPixelType, 2 >   OutputImageType;
```

The `itk::MinMaxCurvatureFlowImageFilter` type is now instantiated using both the input image and the output image types. The filter is then created using the `New()` method.

```
typedef itk::MinMaxCurvatureFlowImageFilter<
            InputImageType, OutputImageType >  FilterType;
FilterType::Pointer filter = FilterType::New();
```

The input image can be obtained from the output of another filter. Here, an image reader is used as source.

```
filter->SetInput( reader->GetOutput() );
```

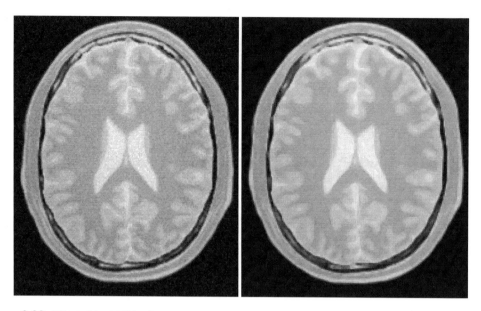

Figure 2.28: Effect of the MinMaxCurvatureFlowImageFilter on a slice from a MRI proton density image of the brain.

The `itk::MinMaxCurvatureFlowImageFilter` requires the two normal parameters of the CurvatureFlow image, the number of iterations to be performed and the time step used in the computation of the level set evolution. In addition, the radius of the neighborhood is also required. This last parameter is passed using the `SetStencilRadius()` method. Note that the radius is provided as an integer number since it is referring to a number of pixels from the center to the border of the neighborhood. Then the filter can be executed by invoking `Update()`.

```
filter->SetTimeStep( timeStep );
filter->SetNumberOfIterations( numberOfIterations );
filter->SetStencilRadius( radius );
filter->Update();
```

Typical values for the time step are 0.125 in 2D images and 0.0625 in 3D images. The number of iterations can be usually around 10, more iterations will result in further smoothing and will increase the computing time linearly. The radius of the stencil can be typically 1. The *edge-preserving* characteristic is not perfect on this filter. Some degradation will occur on the edges and will increase as the number of iterations is increased.

If the output of this filter has been connected to other filters down the pipeline, updating any of the downstream filters will trigger the execution of this one. For example, a writer filter can be used after the curvature flow filter.

```
rescaler->SetInput( filter->GetOutput() );
writer->SetInput( rescaler->GetOutput() );
writer->Update();
```

Figure 2.28 illustrates the effect of this filter on a MRI proton density image of the brain. In this example the filter was run with a time step of 0.125, 10 iterations and a radius of 1. The figure shows how homogeneous regions are smoothed and edges are preserved. Notice also, that the result in the figure has sharper edges than the same example using simple curvature flow in Figure 2.26.

The following classes provide similar functionality:

- itk::CurvatureFlowImageFilter

Bilateral Filter

The source code for this section can be found in the file
BilateralImageFilter.cxx.

The itk::BilateralImageFilter performs smoothing by using both domain and range neighborhoods. Pixels that are close to a pixel in the image domain and similar to a pixel in the image range are used to calculate the filtered value. Two Gaussian kernels (one in the image domain and one in the image range) are used to smooth the image. The result is an image that is smoothed in homogeneous regions yet has edges preserved. The result is similar to anisotropic diffusion but the implementation is non-iterative. Another benefit to bilateral filtering is that any distance metric can be used for kernel smoothing the image range. Bilateral filtering is capable of reducing the noise in an image by an order of magnitude while maintaining edges. The bilateral operator used here was described by Tomasi and Manduchi (*Bilateral Filtering for Gray and Color Images*. IEEE ICCV. 1998.)

The filtering operation can be described by the following equation

$$h(\mathbf{x}) = k(\mathbf{x})^{-1} \int_{\omega} f(\mathbf{w}) c(\mathbf{x}, \mathbf{w}) s(f(\mathbf{x}), f(\mathbf{w})) d\mathbf{w} \tag{2.16}$$

where $\mathbf{x}$ holds the coordinates of a *ND* point, $f(\mathbf{x})$ is the input image and $h(\mathbf{x})$ is the output image. The convolution kernels $c()$ and $s()$ are associated with the spatial and intensity domain respectively. The *ND* integral is computed over ω which is a neighborhood of the pixel located at $\mathbf{x}$. The normalization factor $k(\mathbf{x})$ is computed as

$$k(\mathbf{x}) = \int_{\omega} c(\mathbf{x}, \mathbf{w}) s(f(\mathbf{x}), f(\mathbf{w})) d\mathbf{w} \tag{2.17}$$

The default implementation of this filter uses Gaussian kernels for both $c()$ and $s()$. The c kernel can be described as

$$c(\mathbf{x}, \mathbf{w}) = e^{\left(\frac{\|\mathbf{x} - \mathbf{w}\|^2}{\sigma_c^2} \right)} \tag{2.18}$$

where σ_c is provided by the user and defines how close pixel neighbors should be in order to be considered for the computation of the output value. The *s* kernel is given by

$$s(f(\mathbf{x}), f(\mathbf{w})) = e^{(\frac{(f(\mathbf{x}) - f(\mathbf{w})^2}{\sigma_s^2})} \tag{2.19}$$

where σ_s is provided by the user and defines how close the neighbor's intensity be in order to be considered for the computation of the output value.

The first step required to use this filter is to include its header file.

```
#include "itkBilateralImageFilter.h"
```

The image types are instantiated using pixel type and dimension.

```
typedef    unsigned char   InputPixelType;
typedef    unsigned char   OutputPixelType;

typedef itk::Image< InputPixelType, 2 >   InputImageType;
typedef itk::Image< OutputPixelType, 2 >  OutputImageType;
```

The bilateral filter type is now instantiated using both the input image and the output image types and the filter object is created.

```
typedef itk::BilateralImageFilter<
            InputImageType, OutputImageType >  FilterType;
FilterType::Pointer filter = FilterType::New();
```

The input image can be obtained from the output of another filter. Here, an image reader is used as a source.

```
filter->SetInput( reader->GetOutput() );
```

The Bilateral filter requires two parameters. First, we must specify the standard deviation σ to be used for the Gaussian kernel on image intensities. Second, the set of σs to be used along each dimension in the space domain. This second parameter is supplied as an array of float or double values. The array dimension matches the image dimension. This mechanism makes it possible to enforce more coherence along some directions. For example, more smoothing can be done along the *X* direction than along the *Y* direction.

In the following code example, the σ values are taken from the command line. Note the use of ImageType::ImageDimension to get access to the image dimension at compile time.

```
const unsigned int Dimension = InputImageType::ImageDimension;
double domainSigmas[ Dimension ];
for(unsigned int i=0; i<Dimension; i++)
  {
  domainSigmas[i] = atof( argv[3] );
  }
const double rangeSigma = atof( argv[4] );
```

The filter parameters are set with the methods SetRangeSigma() and SetDomainSigma().

```
filter->SetDomainSigma( domainSigmas );
filter->SetRangeSigma(  rangeSigma  );
```

The output of the filter is connected here to a intensity rescaler filter and then to a writer. Invoking

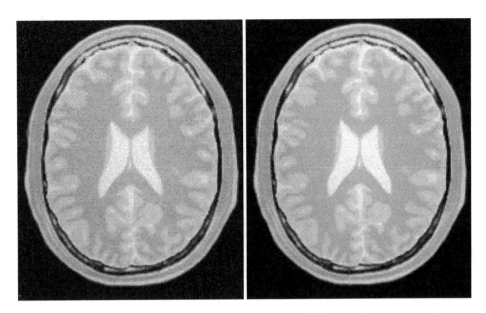

Figure 2.29: Effect of the BilaterallmageFilter on a slice from a MRI proton density image of the brain.

`Update()` on the writer triggers the execution of both filters.

```
rescaler->SetInput( filter->GetOutput() );
writer->SetInput( rescaler->GetOutput() );
writer->Update();
```

Figure 2.29 illustrates the effect of this filter on a MRI proton density image of the brain. In this example the filter was run with a range σ of 5.0 and a domain σ of 6.0. The figure shows how homogeneous regions are smoothed and edges are preserved.

The following classes provide similar functionality:

- `itk::GradientAnisotropicDiffusionImageFilter`

- `itk::CurvatureAnisotropicDiffusionImageFilter`

- `itk::CurvatureFlowImageFilter`

2.7.4   Edge Preserving Smoothing in Vector Images

Anisotropic diffusion can also be applied to images whose pixels are vectors. In this case the diffusion is computed independently for each vector component. The following classes implement versions of anisotropic diffusion on vector images.

Vector Gradient Anisotropic Diffusion

The source code for this section can be found in the file
VectorGradientAnisotropicDiffusionImageFilter.cxx.

The itk::VectorGradientAnisotropicDiffusionImageFilter implements an *N*-dimensional
version of the classic Perona-Malik anisotropic diffusion equation for vector-valued images. Typically in vector-valued diffusion, vector components are diffused independently of one another using
a conductance term that is linked across the components. The diffusion equation was illustrated in
2.7.3.

This filter is designed to process images of itk::Vector type. The code relies on various typedefs
and overloaded operators defined in itk::Vector. It is perfectly reasonable, however, to apply this
filter to images of other, user-defined types as long as the appropriate typedefs and operator overloads
are in place. As a general rule, follow the example of itk::Vector in defining your data types.

The first step required to use this filter is to include its header file.

```
#include "itkVectorGradientAnisotropicDiffusionImageFilter.h"
```

Types should be selected based on required pixel type for the input and output images. The image
types are defined using the pixel type and the dimension.

```
typedef float                          InputPixelType;
typedef itk::CovariantVector< float, 2 > VectorPixelType;
typedef itk::Image< InputPixelType,  2 > InputImageType;
typedef itk::Image< VectorPixelType, 2 > VectorImageType;
```

The filter type is now instantiated using both the input image and the output image types. The filter
object is created by the New() method.

```
typedef itk::VectorGradientAnisotropicDiffusionImageFilter<
                    VectorImageType, VectorImageType >  FilterType;
FilterType::Pointer filter = FilterType::New();
```

The input image can be obtained from the output of another filter. Here, an image reader is used as
source and its data is passed through a gradient filter in order to generate an image of vectors.

```
gradient->SetInput( reader->GetOutput() );
filter->SetInput( gradient->GetOutput() );
```

This filter requires two parameters: the number of iterations to be performed and the time step
used in the computation of the level set evolution. These parameters are set using the methods
SetNumberOfIterations() and SetTimeStep() respectively. The filter can be executed by invoking Update().

```
filter->SetNumberOfIterations( numberOfIterations );
filter->SetTimeStep( timeStep );
filter->SetConductanceParameter(1.0);
filter->Update();
```

Typical values for the time step are 0.125 in *2D* images and 0.0625 in *3D* images. The number of
iterations can be usually around 5, however more iterations will result in further smoothing and will
linearly increase the computing time.

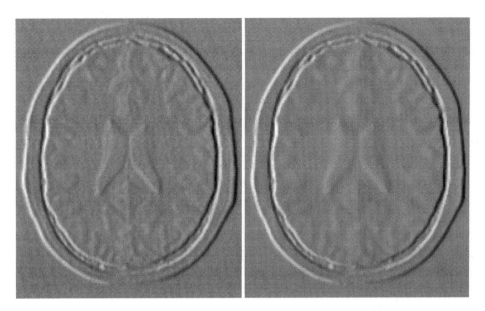

Figure 2.30: Effect of the VectorGradientAnisotropicDiffusionImageFilter on the X component of the gradient from a MRI proton density brain image.

Figure 2.30 illustrates the effect of this filter on a MRI proton density image of the brain. The images show the X component of the gradient before (left) and after (right) the application of the filter. In this example the filter was run with a time step of 0.25, and 5 iterations.

Vector Curvature Anisotropic Diffusion

The source code for this section can be found in the file
VectorCurvatureAnisotropicDiffusionImageFilter.cxx.

The itk::VectorCurvatureAnisotropicDiffusionImageFilter performs anisotropic diffusion on a vector image using a modified curvature diffusion equation (MCDE). The MCDE is the same described in 2.7.3.

Typically in vector-valued diffusion, vector components are diffused independently of one another using a conductance term that is linked across the components.

This filter is designed to process images of itk::Vector type. The code relies on various typedefs and overloaded operators defined in itk::Vector. It is perfectly reasonable, however, to apply this filter to images of other, user-defined types as long as the appropriate typedefs and operator overloads are in place. As a general rule, follow the example of the itk::Vector class in defining your data types.

The first step required to use this filter is to include its header file.

```
#include "itkVectorCurvatureAnisotropicDiffusionImageFilter.h"
```

Types should be selected based on required pixel type for the input and output images. The image types are defined using the pixel type and the dimension.

```
typedef float                          InputPixelType;
typedef itk::CovariantVector< float, 2 > VectorPixelType;
typedef itk::Image< InputPixelType,  2 > InputImageType;
typedef itk::Image< VectorPixelType, 2 > VectorImageType;
```

The filter type is now instantiated using both the input image and the output image types. The filter object is created by the New() method.

```
typedef itk::VectorCurvatureAnisotropicDiffusionImageFilter<
                    VectorImageType, VectorImageType >  FilterType;
FilterType::Pointer filter = FilterType::New();
```

The input image can be obtained from the output of another filter. Here, an image reader is used as source and its data is passed through a gradient filter in order to generate an image of vectors.

```
gradient->SetInput( reader->GetOutput() );
filter->SetInput( gradient->GetOutput() );
```

This filter requires two parameters: the number of iterations to be performed and the time step used in the computation of the level set evolution. These parameters are set using the methods SetNumberOfIterations() and SetTimeStep() respectively. The filter can be executed by invoking Update().

```
filter->SetNumberOfIterations( numberOfIterations );
filter->SetTimeStep( timeStep );
filter->SetConductanceParameter(1.0);
filter->Update();
```

Typical values for the time step are 0.125 in 2D images and 0.0625 in 3D images. The number of iterations can be usually around 5, however more iterations will result in further smoothing and will increase the computing time linearly.

Figure 2.31 illustrates the effect of this filter on a MRI proton density image of the brain. The images show the X component of the gradient before (left) and after (right) the application of the filter. In this example the filter was run with a time step of 0.25, and 5 iterations.

2.7.5   Edge Preserving Smoothing in Color Images

Gradient Anisotropic Diffusion

The source code for this section can be found in the file
RGBGradientAnisotropicDiffusionImageFilter.cxx.

The vector anisotropic diffusion approach applies to color images equally well. As in the vector case, each RGB component is diffused independently. The following example illustrates the use of the Vector curvature anisotropic diffusion filter on an image with itk::RGBPixel type.

The first step required to use this filter is to include its header file.

```
#include "itkVectorGradientAnisotropicDiffusionImageFilter.h"
```

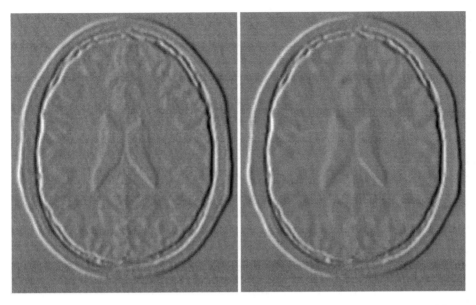

Figure 2.31: Effect of the VectorCurvatureAnisotropicDiffusionImageFilter on the X component of the gradient from a MRIproton density brain image.

Also the headers for Image and RGBPixel type are required.

```
#include "itkRGBPixel.h"
#include "itkImage.h"
```

It is desirable to perform the computation on the RGB image using float representation. However for input and output purposes unsigned char RGB components are commonly used. It is necessary to cast the type of color components along the pipeline before writing them to a file. The itk::VectorCastImageFilter is used to achieve this goal.

```
#include "itkImageFileReader.h"
#include "itkImageFileWriter.h"
#include "itkVectorCastImageFilter.h"
```

The image type is defined using the pixel type and the dimension.

```
typedef itk::RGBPixel< float >            InputPixelType;
typedef itk::Image< InputPixelType, 2 > InputImageType;
```

The filter type is now instantiated and a filter object is created by the New() method.

```
typedef itk::VectorGradientAnisotropicDiffusionImageFilter<
                 InputImageType, InputImageType >  FilterType;
FilterType::Pointer filter = FilterType::New();
```

The input image can be obtained from the output of another filter. Here, an image reader is used as source.

```
typedef itk::ImageFileReader< InputImageType >  ReaderType;
ReaderType::Pointer reader = ReaderType::New();
reader->SetFileName( argv[1] );
filter->SetInput( reader->GetOutput() );
```

This filter requires two parameters: the number of iterations to be performed and the time step used in the computation of the level set evolution. These parameters are set using the methods SetNumberOfIterations() and SetTimeStep() respectively. The filter can be executed by invoking Update().

```
filter->SetNumberOfIterations( numberOfIterations );
filter->SetTimeStep( timeStep );
filter->SetConductanceParameter(1.0);
filter->Update();
```

The filter output is now cast to unsigned char RGB components by using the itk::VectorCastImageFilter.

```
typedef itk::RGBPixel< unsigned char >  WritePixelType;
typedef itk::Image< WritePixelType, 2 > WriteImageType;
typedef itk::VectorCastImageFilter<
            InputImageType, WriteImageType > CasterType;
CasterType::Pointer caster = CasterType::New();
```

Finally, the writer type can be instantiated. One writer is created and connected to the output of the cast filter.

```
typedef itk::ImageFileWriter< WriteImageType >  WriterType;
WriterType::Pointer writer = WriterType::New();
caster->SetInput( filter->GetOutput() );
writer->SetInput( caster->GetOutput() );
writer->SetFileName( argv[2] );
writer->Update();
```

Figure 2.32 illustrates the effect of this filter on a RGB image from a cryogenic section of the Visible Woman data set. In this example the filter was run with a time step of 0.125, and 20 iterations. The input image has 570×670 pixels and the processing took 4 minutes on a Pentium 4 2GHz.

Curvature Anisotropic Diffusion

The source code for this section can be found in the file RGBCurvatureAnisotropicDiffusionImageFilter.cxx.

The vector anisotropic diffusion approach can be applied equally well to color images. As in the vector case, each RGB component is diffused independently. The following example illustrates the use of the itk::VectorCurvatureAnisotropicDiffusionImageFilter on an image with itk::RGBPixel type.

The first step required to use this filter is to include its header file.

```
#include "itkVectorCurvatureAnisotropicDiffusionImageFilter.h"
```

Also the headers for Image and RGBPixel type are required.

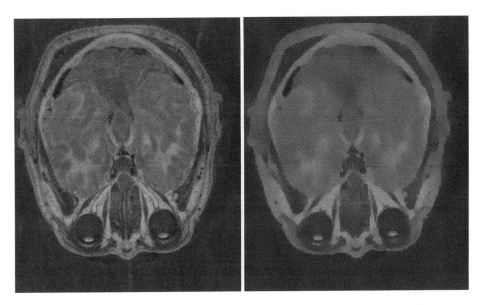

Figure 2.32: Effect of the VectorGradientAnisotropicDiffusionImageFilter on a RGB image from a cryogenic section of the Visible Woman data set.

```
#include "itkRGBPixel.h"
#include "itkImage.h"
```

It is desirable to perform the computation on the RGB image using `float` representation. However for input and output purposes `unsigned char` RGB components are commonly used. It is necessary to cast the type of color components in the pipeline before writing them to a file. The `itk::VectorCastImageFilter` is used to achieve this goal.

```
#include "itkImageFileReader.h"
#include "itkImageFileWriter.h"
#include "itkVectorCastImageFilter.h"
```

The image type is defined using the pixel type and the dimension.

```
typedef itk::RGBPixel< float >            InputPixelType;
typedef itk::Image< InputPixelType, 2 > InputImageType;
```

The filter type is now instantiated and a filter object is created by the `New()` method.

```
typedef itk::VectorCurvatureAnisotropicDiffusionImageFilter<
                    InputImageType, InputImageType >  FilterType;
FilterType::Pointer filter = FilterType::New();
```

The input image can be obtained from the output of another filter. Here, an image reader is used as a source.

```
typedef itk::ImageFileReader< InputImageType >  ReaderType;
ReaderType::Pointer reader = ReaderType::New();
reader->SetFileName( argv[1] );
filter->SetInput( reader->GetOutput() );
```

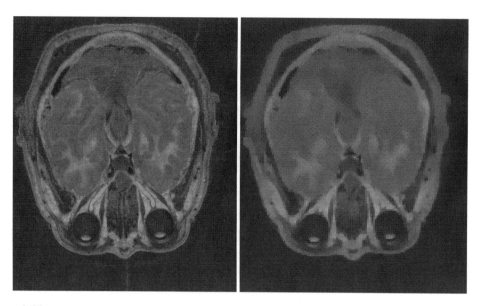

Figure 2.33: Effect of the VectorCurvatureAnisotropicDiffusionImageFilter on a RGB image from a cryogenic section of the Visible Woman data set.

This filter requires two parameters: the number of iterations to be performed and the time step used in the computation of the level set evolution. These parameters are set using the methods SetNumberOfIterations() and SetTimeStep() respectively. The filter can be executed by invoking Update().

```
filter->SetNumberOfIterations( numberOfIterations );
filter->SetTimeStep( timeStep );
filter->SetConductanceParameter(1.0);
filter->Update();
```

The filter output is now cast to unsigned char RGB components by using the itk::VectorCastImageFilter.

```
typedef itk::RGBPixel< unsigned char >  WritePixelType;
typedef itk::Image< WritePixelType, 2 > WriteImageType;
typedef itk::VectorCastImageFilter<
              InputImageType, WriteImageType >  CasterType;
CasterType::Pointer caster = CasterType::New();
```

Finally, the writer type can be instantiated. One writer is created and connected to the output of the cast filter.

```
typedef itk::ImageFileWriter< WriteImageType >  WriterType;
WriterType::Pointer writer = WriterType::New();
caster->SetInput( filter->GetOutput() );
writer->SetInput( caster->GetOutput() );
writer->SetFileName( argv[2] );
writer->Update();
```

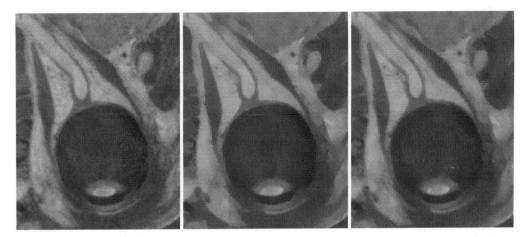

Figure 2.34: Comparison between the gradient (center) and curvature (right) Anisotropic Diffusion filters. Original image at left.

Figure 2.33 illustrates the effect of this filter on a RGB image from a cryogenic section of the Visible Woman data set. In this example the filter was run with a time step of 0.125, and 20 iterations. The input image has 570×670 pixels and the processing took 4 minutes on a Pentium 4 at 2GHz.

Figure 2.34 compares the effect of the gradient and curvature anisotropic diffusion filters on a small region of the same cryogenic slice used in Figure 2.33. The region used in this figure is only 127×162 pixels and took 14 seconds to compute on the same platform.

2.8   Distance Map

The source code for this section can be found in the file
DanielssonDistanceMapImageFilter.cxx.

This example illustrates the use of the itk::DanielssonDistanceMapImageFilter. This filter generates a distance map from the input image using the algorithm developed by Danielsson [13]. As secondary outputs, a Voronoi partition of the input elements is produced, as well as a vector image with the components of the distance vector to the closest point. The input to the map is assumed to be a set of points on the input image. The label of each group of pixels is assigned by the itk::ConnectedComponentImageFilter.

The first step required to use this filter is to include its header file.

```
#include "itkDanielssonDistanceMapImageFilter.h"
```

Then we must decide what pixel types to use for the input and output images. Since the output will contain distances measured in pixels, the pixel type should be able to represent at least the width of the image, or said in *N*-dimensional terms, the maximum extension along all the dimensions. The input, output (distance map), and voronoi partition image types are now defined using their respective

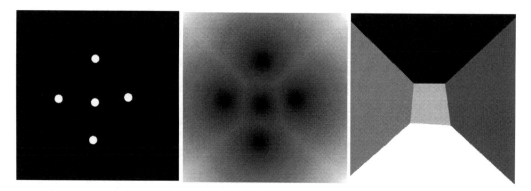

Figure 2.35: DanielssonDistanceMapImageFilter output. Set of pixels, distance map and Voronoi partition.

pixel type and dimension.

```
typedef  unsigned char                    InputPixelType;
typedef  unsigned short                    OutputPixelType;
typedef  unsigned char                     VoronoiPixelType;
typedef itk::Image< InputPixelType,  2 >  InputImageType;
typedef itk::Image< OutputPixelType,  2 >  OutputImageType;
typedef itk::Image< VoronoiPixelType, 2 > VoronoiImageType;
```

The filter type can be instantiated using the input and output image types defined above. A filter
object is created with the `New()` method.

```
typedef itk::DanielssonDistanceMapImageFilter<
              InputImageType, OutputImageType, VoronoiImageType >  FilterType;
FilterType::Pointer filter = FilterType::New();
```

The input to the filter is taken from a reader and its output is passed to a
`itk::RescaleIntensityImageFilter` and then to a writer. The scaler and writer are both
templated over the image type, so we instantiate a separate pipeline for the voronoi partition map
starting at the scaler.

```
labeler->SetInput(reader->GetOutput() );
filter->SetInput( labeler->GetOutput() );
scaler->SetInput( filter->GetOutput() );
writer->SetInput( scaler->GetOutput() );
```

The Voronoi map is obtained with the `GetVoronoiMap()` method. In the lines below we connect this
output to the intensity rescaler.

```
voronoiScaler->SetInput( filter->GetVoronoiMap() );
voronoiWriter->SetInput( voronoiScaler->GetOutput() );
```

Figure 2.35 illustrates the effect of this filter on a binary image with a set of points. The input image
is shown at the left, and the distance map at the center and the Voronoi partition at the right. This
filter computes distance maps in N-dimensions and is therefore capable of producing *N*-dimensional
Voronoi partitions.

The distance filter also produces an image of `itk::Offset` pixels representing the vectorial distance

to the closest object in the scene. The type of this output image is defined by the VectorImageType
trait of the filter type.

```
typedef FilterType::VectorImageType   OffsetImageType;
```

We can use this type for instantiating an `itk::ImageFileWriter` type and creating an object of
this class in the following lines.

```
typedef itk::ImageFileWriter< OffsetImageType >  WriterOffsetType;
WriterOffsetType::Pointer offsetWriter = WriterOffsetType::New();
```

The output of the distance filter can be connected as input to the writer.

```
offsetWriter->SetInput( filter->GetVectorDistanceMap() );
```

Execution of the writer is triggered by the invocation of the `Update()` method. Since this method
can potentially throw exceptions it must be placed in a `try/catch` block.

```
try
  {
  offsetWriter->Update();
  }
catch( itk::ExceptionObject & exp )
  {
  std::cerr << "Exception caught !" << std::endl;
  std::cerr <<      exp    << std::endl;
  }
```

Note that only the `itk::MetaImageIO` class supports reading and writing images of pixel type
`itk::Offset`.

The source code for this section can be found in the file
`SignedDanielssonDistanceMapImageFilter.cxx`.

This example illustrates the use of the `itk::SignedDanielssonDistanceMapImageFilter`. This
filter generates a distance map by running Danielsson distance map twice, once on the input image
and once on the flipped image.

The first step required to use this filter is to include its header file.

```
#include "itkSignedDanielssonDistanceMapImageFilter.h"
```

Then we must decide what pixel types to use for the input and output images. Since the output will
contain distances measured in pixels, the pixel type should be able to represent at least the width of
the image, or said in *N*-dimensional terms, the maximum extension along all the dimensions. The
input and output image types are now defined using their respective pixel type and dimension.

```
typedef  unsigned char   InputPixelType;
typedef  float           OutputPixelType;
typedef  unsigned short  VoronoiPixelType;
const unsigned int Dimension = 2;

typedef itk::Image< InputPixelType,   Dimension >  InputImageType;
typedef itk::Image< OutputPixelType,  Dimension >  OutputImageType;
typedef itk::Image< VoronoiPixelType, Dimension >  VoronoiImageType;
```

The only change with respect to the previous example is to replace the DanielssonDistanceMapIm-

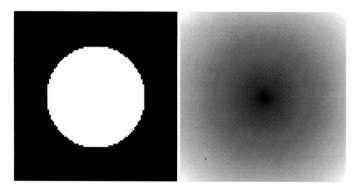

Figure 2.36: SignedDanielssonDistanceMapImageFilter applied on a binary circle image. The intensity has been rescaled for purposes of display.

ageFilter with the SignedDanielssonDistanceMapImageFilter.

```
typedef itk::SignedDanielssonDistanceMapImageFilter<
                              InputImageType,
                              OutputImageType,
                              VoronoiImageType > FilterType;

FilterType::Pointer filter = FilterType::New();
```

The distances inside the circle are defined to be negative, while the distances outside the circle are positive. To change the convention, use the `InsideIsPositive(bool)` function.

Figure 2.36 illustrates the effect of this filter. The input image and the distance map are shown.

2.9   Geometric Transformations

2.9.1   Filters You Should be Afraid to Use

2.9.2   Change Information Image Filter

This one is the scariest and most dangerous filter in the entire toolkit. You should not use this filter unless you are entirely certain that you know what you are doing. In fact if you decide to use this filter, you should write your code, then go for a long walk, get more coffee and ask yourself if you really needed to use this filter. If the answer is yes, then you should discuss this issue with someone you trust and get his/her opinion in writing. In general, if you need to use this filter, it means that you have a poor image provider that is putting your career at risk along with the life of any potential patient whose images you may end up processing.

2.9.3 Flip Image Filter

The source code for this section can be found in the file
FlipImageFilter.cxx.

The itk::FlipImageFilter is used for flipping the image content in any of the coordinate axes. This filter must be used with **EXTREME** caution. You probably don't want to appear in the news-papers as responsible for a surgery mistake in which a doctor extirpates the left kidney when he should have extracted the right one[3] . If that prospect doesn't scare you, maybe it is time for you to reconsider your career in medical image processing. Flipping effects which seem innocuous at first view may still have dangerous consequences. For example, flipping the cranio-caudal axis of a CT scan forces an observer to flip the left-right axis in order to make sense of the image.

The header file corresponding to this filter should be included first.

```
#include "itkFlipImageFilter.h"
```

Then the pixel types for input and output image must be defined and, with them, the image types can be instantiated.

```
typedef   unsigned char  PixelType;

typedef itk::Image< PixelType,  2 >   ImageType;
```

Using the image types it is now possible to instantiate the filter type and create the filter object.

```
typedef itk::FlipImageFilter< ImageType >  FilterType;

FilterType::Pointer filter = FilterType::New();
```

The axes to flip are specified in the form of an Array. In this case we take them from the command line arguments.

```
typedef FilterType::FlipAxesArrayType      FlipAxesArrayType;

FlipAxesArrayType flipArray;

flipArray[0] = atoi( argv[3] );
flipArray[1] = atoi( argv[4] );

filter->SetFlipAxes( flipArray );
```

The input to the filter can be taken from any other filter, for example a reader. The output can be passed down the pipeline to other filters, for example, a writer. Invoking Update() on any down-stream filter will trigger the execution of the FlipImage filter.

```
filter->SetInput( reader->GetOutput() );
writer->SetInput( filter->GetOutput() );
writer->Update();
```

Figure 2.37 illustrates the effect of this filter on a slice of an MRI brain image using a flip array $[0, 1]$ which means that the Y axis was flipped while the X axis was conserved.

---

[3]*Wrong side* surgery accounts for 2% of the reported medical errors in the United States. Trivial... but equally dangerous.

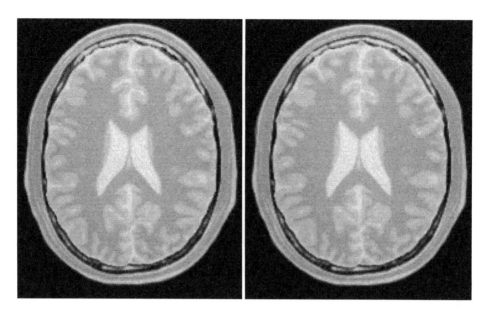

Figure 2.37: Effect of the FlipImageFilter on a slice from a MRI proton density brain image.

2.9.4   Resample Image Filter

Introduction

The source code for this section can be found in the file
ResampleImageFilter.cxx.

Resampling an image is a very important task in image analysis. It is especially important in the
frame of image registration. The itk::ResampleImageFilter implements image resampling
through the use of itk::Transforms. The inputs expected by this filter are an image, a transform and an interpolator. The space coordinates of the image are mapped through the transform in
order to generate a new image. The extent and spacing of the resulting image are selected by the
user. Resampling is performed in space coordinates, not pixel/grid coordinates. It is quite important
to ensure that image spacing is properly set on the images involved. The interpolator is required
since the mapping from one space to the other will often require evaluation of the intensity of the
image at non-grid positions.

The header file corresponding to this filter should be included first.

```
#include "itkResampleImageFilter.h"
```

The header files corresponding to the transform and interpolator must also be included.

```
#include "itkAffineTransform.h"
#include "itkNearestNeighborInterpolateImageFunction.h"
```

The dimension and pixel types for input and output image must be defined and with them the image types can be instantiated.

```
const unsigned int                      Dimension = 2;
typedef unsigned char                   InputPixelType;
typedef unsigned char                   OutputPixelType;
typedef itk::Image< InputPixelType,  Dimension > InputImageType;
typedef itk::Image< OutputPixelType, Dimension > OutputImageType;
```

Using the image and transform types it is now possible to instantiate the filter type and create the filter object.

```
typedef itk::ResampleImageFilter<InputImageType,OutputImageType> FilterType;
FilterType::Pointer filter = FilterType::New();
```

The transform type is typically defined using the image dimension and the type used for representing space coordinates.

```
typedef itk::AffineTransform< double, Dimension >  TransformType;
```

An instance of the transform object is instantiated and passed to the resample filter. By default, the parameters of the transform are set to represent the identity transform.

```
TransformType::Pointer transform = TransformType::New();
filter->SetTransform( transform );
```

The interpolator type is defined using the full image type and the type used for representing space coordinates.

```
typedef itk::NearestNeighborInterpolateImageFunction<
                    InputImageType, double >  InterpolatorType;
```

An instance of the interpolator object is instantiated and passed to the resample filter.

```
InterpolatorType::Pointer interpolator = InterpolatorType::New();
filter->SetInterpolator( interpolator );
```

Given that some pixels of the output image may end up being mapped outside the extent of the input image it is necessary to decide what values to assign to them. This is done by invoking the SetDefaultPixelValue() method.

```
filter->SetDefaultPixelValue( 0 );
```

The sampling grid of the output space is specified with the spacing along each dimension and the origin.

```
// pixel spacing in millimeters along X and Y
const double spacing[ Dimension ] = { 1.0, 1.0 };
filter->SetOutputSpacing( spacing );

// Physical space coordinate of origin for X and Y
const double origin[ Dimension ] = { 0.0, 0.0 };
filter->SetOutputOrigin( origin );

InputImageType::DirectionType direction;
direction.SetIdentity();
filter->SetOutputDirection( direction );
```

The extent of the sampling grid on the output image is defined by a SizeType and is set using the

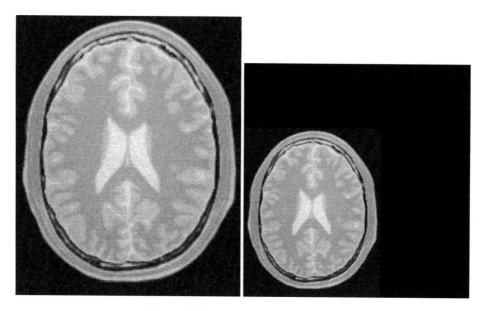

Figure 2.38: Effect of the resample filter.

SetSize() method.

```
InputImageType::SizeType   size;

size[0] = 300;  // number of pixels along X
size[1] = 300;  // number of pixels along Y

filter->SetSize( size );
```

The input to the filter can be taken from any other filter, for example a reader. The output can be passed down the pipeline to other filters, for example a writer. An update call on any downstream filter will trigger the execution of the resampling filter.

```
filter->SetInput( reader->GetOutput() );
writer->SetInput( filter->GetOutput() );
writer->Update();
```

Figure 2.38 illustrates the effect of this filter on a slice of MRI brain image using an affine transform containing an identity transform. Note that any analysis of the behavior of this filter must be done on the space coordinate system in millimeters, not with respect to the sampling grid in pixels. The figure shows the resulting image in the lower left quarter of the extent. This may seem odd if analyzed in terms of the image grid but is quite clear when seen with respect to space coordinates. Figure 2.38 is particularly misleading because the images are rescaled to fit nicely on the text of this book. Figure 2.39 clarifies the situation. It shows the two same images placed on an equally-scaled coordinate system. It becomes clear here that an identity transform is being used to map the image data, and that simply, we have requested to resample additional empty space around the image. The input image is 181×217 pixels in size and we have requested an output of 300×300 pixels. In this case, the input and output images both have spacing of $1mm \times 1mm$ and origin of $(0.0, 0.0)$.

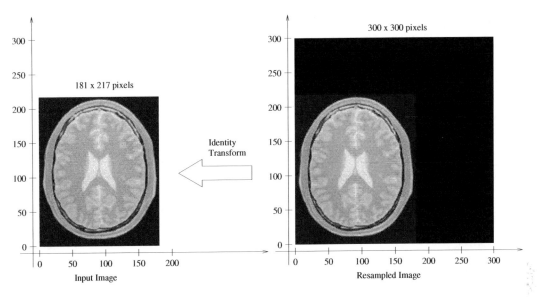

Figure 2.39: Analysis of the resample image done in a common coordinate system.

Let's now set values on the transform. Note that the supplied transform represents the mapping of points from the output space to the input space. The following code sets up a translation.

```
TransformType::OutputVectorType translation;
translation[0] = -30;  // X translation in millimeters
translation[1] = -50;  // Y translation in millimeters
transform->Translate( translation );
```

The output image resulting from the translation can be seen in Figure 2.40. Again, it is better to interpret the result in a common coordinate system as illustrated in Figure 2.41.

Probably the most important thing to keep in mind when resampling images is that the transform is used to map points from the **output** image space into the **input** image space. In this case, Figure 2.41 shows that the translation is applied to every point of the output image and the resulting position is used to read the intensity from the input image. In this way, the gray level of the point P in the output image is taken from the point $T(P)$ in the input image. Where T is the transformation. In the specific case of the Figure 2.41, the value of point $(105, 188)$ in the output image is taken from the point $(75, 138)$ of the input image because the transformation applied was a translation of $(-30, -50)$.

It is sometimes useful to intentionally set the default output value to a distinct gray value in order to highlight the mapping of the image borders. For example, the following code sets the default external value of 100. The result is shown in the right side of Figure 2.42.

```
filter->SetDefaultPixelValue( 100 );
```

With this change we can better appreciate the effect of the previous translation transform on the image resampling. Figure 2.42 illustrates how the point $(30, 50)$ of the output image gets its gray value from the point $(0, 0)$ of the input image.

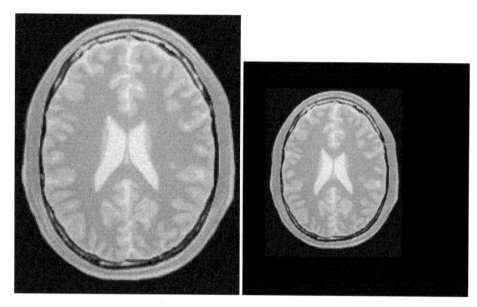

Figure 2.40: ResampleImageFilter with a translation by $(-30, -50)$.

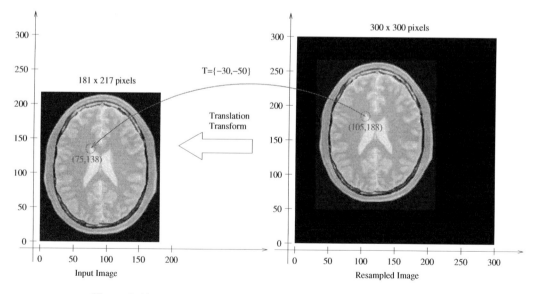

Figure 2.41: ResampleImageFilter. Analysis of a translation by $(-30, -50)$.

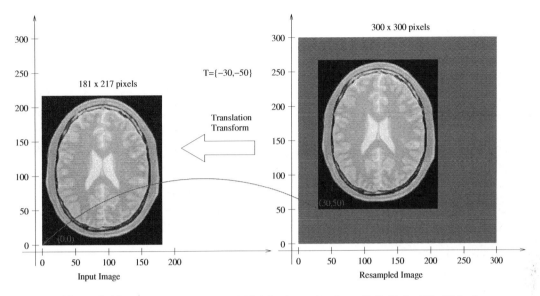

Figure 2.42: ResampleImageFilter highlighting image borders with SetDefaultPixelValue().

Importance of Spacing and Origin

The source code for this section can be found in the file
`ResampleImageFilter2.cxx`.

During the computation of the resampled image all the pixels in the output region are visited. This visit is performed using `ImageIterators` which walk in the integer grid-space of the image. For each pixel, we need to convert grid position to space coordinates using the image spacing and origin.

For example, the pixel of index $I = (20, 50)$ in an image of origin $O = (19.0, 29.0)$ and pixel spacing $S = (1.3, 1.5)$ corresponds to the spatial position

$$P[i] = I[i] \times S[i] + O[i] \tag{2.20}$$

which in this case leads to $P = (20 \times 1.3 + 19.0, 50 \times 1.5 + 29.0)$ and finally $P = (45.0, 104.0)$

The space coordinates of P are mapped using the transform T supplied to the `itk::ResampleImageFilter` in order to map the point P to the input image space point $Q = T(P)$.

The whole process is illustrated in Figure 2.43. In order to correctly interpret the process of the ResampleImageFilter you should be aware of the origin and spacing settings of both the input and output images.

In order to facilitate the interpretation of the transform we set the default pixel value to a value distinct from the image background.

```
filter->SetDefaultPixelValue( 50 );
```

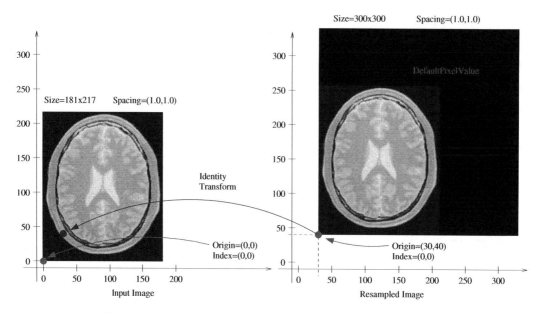

Figure 2.43: ResampleImageFilter selecting the origin of the output image.

Let's set up a uniform spacing for the output image.

```
// pixel spacing in millimeters along X & Y
const double spacing[ Dimension ] = { 1.0, 1.0 };
filter->SetOutputSpacing( spacing );
```

We will preserve the orientation of the input image by using the following call.

```
filter->SetOutputDirection( reader->GetOutput()->GetDirection() );
```

Additionally, we will specify a non-zero origin. Note that the values provided here will be those of the space coordinates for the pixel of index $(0,0)$.

```
// space coordinate of origin
const double origin[ Dimension ] = { 30.0, 40.0 };
filter->SetOutputOrigin( origin );
```

We set the transform to identity in order to better appreciate the effect of the origin selection.

```
transform->SetIdentity();
filter->SetTransform( transform );
```

The output resulting from these filter settings is analyzed in Figure 2.43.

In the figure, the output image point with index $I = (0,0)$ has space coordinates $P = (30,40)$. The identity transform maps this point to $Q = (30,40)$ in the input image space. Because the input image in this case happens to have spacing $(1.0, 1.0)$ and origin $(0.0, 0.0)$, the physical point $Q = (30,40)$ maps to the pixel with index $I = (30,40)$.

The code for a different selection of origin and image size is illustrated below. The resulting output

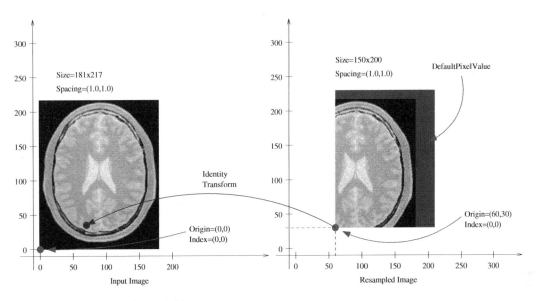

Figure 2.44: ResampleImageFilter origin in the output image.

is presented in Figure 2.44.

```
size[0] = 150;  // number of pixels along X
size[1] = 200;  // number of pixels along Y
filter->SetSize( size );
```

```
// space coordinate of origin
const double origin[ Dimension ] = { 60.0, 30.0 };
filter->SetOutputOrigin( origin );
```

The output image point with index $I = (0,0)$ now has space coordinates $P = (60,30)$. The identity transform maps this point to $Q = (60,30)$ in the input image space. Because the input image in this case happens to have spacing $(1.0, 1.0)$ and origin $(0.0, 0.0)$, the physical point $Q = (60,30)$ maps to the pixel with index $I = (60,30)$.

Let's now analyze the effect of a non-zero origin in the input image. Keeping the output image settings of the previous example, we modify only the origin values on the file header of the input image. The new origin assigned to the input image is $O = (50,70)$. An identity transform is still used as input for the ResampleImageFilter. The result of executing the filter with these parameters is presented in Figure 2.45.

The pixel with index $I = (56,120)$ on the output image has coordinates $P = (116,150)$ in physical space. The identity transform maps P to the point $Q = (116,150)$ on the input image space. The coordinates of Q are associated with the pixel of index $I = (66,80)$ on the input image.

Now consider the effect of the output spacing on the process of image resampling. In order to simplify the analysis, let's set the origin back to zero in both the input and output images.

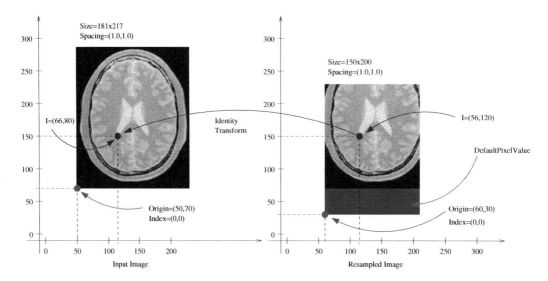

Figure 2.45: Effect of selecting the origin of the input image with ResampleImageFilter.

```
// space coordinate of origin
const double origin[ Dimension ] = { 0.0, 0.0 };
filter->SetOutputOrigin( origin );
```

We then specify a non-unit spacing for the output image.

```
// pixel spacing in millimeters
const double spacing[ Dimension ] = { 2.0, 3.0 };
filter->SetOutputSpacing( spacing );
```

Additionally, we reduce the output image extent, since the new pixels are now covering a larger area of 2.0mm × 3.0mm.

```
size[0] = 80;  // number of pixels along X
size[1] = 50;  // number of pixels along Y
filter->SetSize( size );
```

With these new parameters the physical extent of the output image is 160 millimeters by 150 millimeters.

Before attempting to analyze the effect of the resampling image filter it is important to make sure that the image viewer used to display the input and output images takes the spacing into account and appropriately scales the images on the screen. Please note that images in formats like PNG are not capable of representing origin and spacing. The toolkit assumes trivial default values for them. Figure 2.46 (center) illustrates the effect of using a naive viewer that does not take pixel spacing into account. A correct display is presented at the right in the same figure[4].

The filter output is analyzed in a common coordinate system with the input from Figure 2.47. In this figure, pixel $I = (33,27)$ of the output image is located at coordinates $P = (66.0, 81.0)$ of the physical

---

[4]A viewer is provided with ITK under the name of MetaImageViewer. This viewer takes into account pixel spacing.

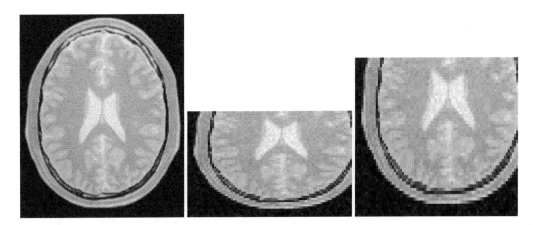

Figure 2.46: Resampling with different spacing seen by a naive viewer (center) and a correct viewer (right), input image (left).

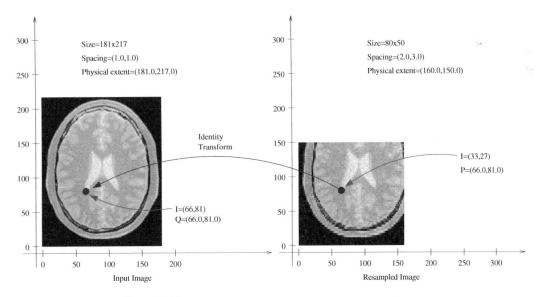

Figure 2.47: Effect of selecting the spacing on the output image.

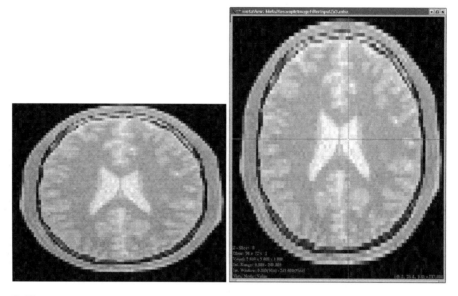

Figure 2.48: Input image with 2×3mm spacing as seen with a naive viewer (left) and a correct viewer (right).

space. The identity transform maps this point to $Q = (66.0, 81.0)$ in the input image physical space. The point Q is then associated to the pixel of index $I = (66, 81)$ on the input image, because this image has zero origin and unit spacing.

The input image spacing is also an important factor in the process of resampling an image. The following example illustrates the effect of non-unit pixel spacing on the input image. An input image similar to the those used in Figures 2.43 to 2.47 has been resampled to have pixel spacing of 2mm $\times$ 3mm. The input image is presented in Figure 2.48 as viewed with a naive image viewer (left) and with a correct image viewer (right).

The following code is used to transform this non-unit spacing input image into another non-unit spacing image located at a non-zero origin. The comparison between input and output in a common reference system is presented in figure 2.49.

Here we start by selecting the origin of the output image.

```
// space coordinate of origin
const double origin[ Dimension ] = { 25.0, 35.0 };
filter->SetOutputOrigin( origin );
```

We then select the number of pixels along each dimension.

```
size[0] = 40;  // number of pixels along X
size[1] = 45;  // number of pixels along Y
filter->SetSize( size );
```

Finally, we set the output pixel spacing.

```
const double spacing[ Dimension ] = { 4.0, 4.5 };
filter->SetOutputSpacing( spacing );
```

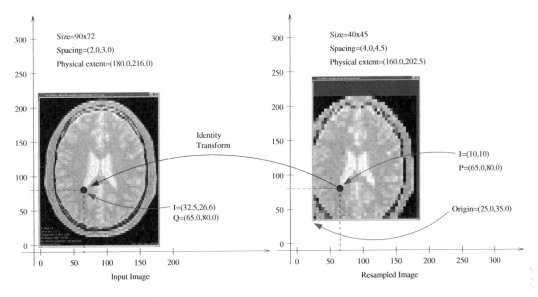

Figure 2.49: Effect of non-unit spacing on the input and output images.

Figure 2.49 shows the analysis of the filter output under these conditions. First, notice that the origin of the output image corresponds to the settings $O = (25.0, 35.0)$ millimeters, spacing $(4.0, 4.5)$ millimeters and size $(40, 45)$ pixels. With these parameters the pixel of index $I = (10, 10)$ in the output image is associated with the spatial point of coordinates $P = (10 \times 4.0 + 25.0, 10 \times 4.5 + 35.0)) = (65.0, 80.0)$. This point is mapped by the transform—identity in this particular case—to the point $Q = (65.0, 80.0)$ in the input image space. The point Q is then associated with the pixel of index $I = ((65.0 - 0.0)/2.0 - (80.0 - 0.0)/3.0) = (32.5, 26.6)$. Note that the index does not fall on a grid position. For this reason the value to be assigned to the output pixel is computed by interpolating values on the input image around the non-integer index $I = (32.5, 26.6)$.

Note also that the discretization of the image is more visible on the output presented on the right side of Figure 2.49 due to the choice of a low resolution—just 40×45 pixels.

A Complete Example

The source code for this section can be found in the file
ResampleImageFilter3.cxx.

Previous examples have described the basic principles behind the itk::ResampleImageFilter. Now it's time to have some fun with it.

Figure 2.51 illustrates the general case of the resampling process. The origin and spacing of the output image has been selected to be different from those of the input image. The circles represent the *center* of pixels. They are inscribed in a rectangle representing the *coverage* of this pixel. The spacing specifies the distance between pixel centers along every dimension.

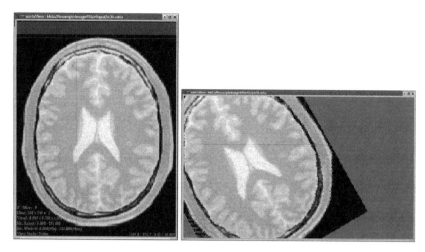

Figure 2.50: Effect of a rotation on the resampling filter. Input image at left, output image at right.

The transform applied is a rotation of 30 degrees. It is important to note here that the transform supplied to the `itk::ResampleImageFilter` is a *clockwise* rotation. This transform rotates the *coordinate system* of the output image 30 degrees clockwise. When the two images are relocated in a common coordinate system—as in Figure 2.51—the result is that the frame of the output image appears rotated 30 degrees *clockwise*. If the output image is seen with its coordinate system vertically aligned—as in Figure 2.50—the image content appears rotated 30 degrees *counter-clockwise*. Before continuing to read this section, you may want to meditate a bit on this fact while enjoying a cup of (Colombian) coffee.

The following code implements the conditions illustrated in Figure 2.51 with two differences: the output spacing is 40 times smaller and there are 40 times more pixels in both dimensions. Without these changes, few details will be recognizable in the images. Note that the spacing and origin of the input image should be prepared in advance by using other means since this filter cannot alter the actual content of the input image in any way.

In order to facilitate the interpretation of the transform we set the default pixel value to value be distinct from the image background.

```
filter->SetDefaultPixelValue( 100 );
```

The spacing is selected here to be 40 times smaller than the one illustrated in Figure 2.51.

```
double spacing[ Dimension ];
spacing[0] = 40.0 / 40.0; // pixel spacing in millimeters along X
spacing[1] = 30.0 / 40.0; // pixel spacing in millimeters along Y
filter->SetOutputSpacing( spacing );
```

We will preserve the orientation of the input image by using the following call.

```
filter->SetOutputDirection( reader->GetOutput()->GetDirection() );
```

Let us now set up the origin of the output image. Note that the values provided here will be those of

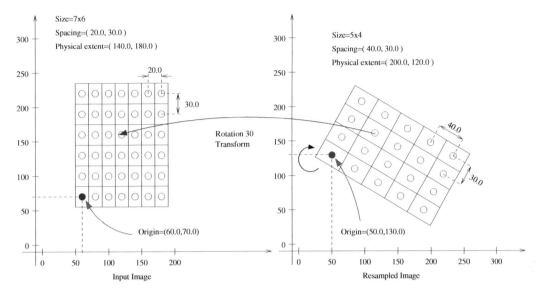

Figure 2.51: Input and output image placed in a common reference system.

the space coordinates for the output image pixel of index $(0,0)$.

```
double origin[ Dimension ];
origin[0] = 50.0; // X space coordinate of origin
origin[1] = 130.0; // Y space coordinate of origin
filter->SetOutputOrigin( origin );
```

The output image size is defined to be 40 times the one illustrated on the Figure 2.51.

```
InputImageType::SizeType   size;
size[0] = 5 * 40; // number of pixels along X
size[1] = 4 * 40; // number of pixels along Y
filter->SetSize( size );
```

Rotations are performed around the origin of physical coordinates—not the image origin nor the image center. Hence, the process of positioning the output image frame as it is shown in Figure 2.51 requires three steps. First, the image origin must be moved to the origin of the coordinate system. This is done by applying a translation equal to the negative values of the image origin.

```
TransformType::OutputVectorType translation1;
translation1[0] =   -origin[0];
translation1[1] =   -origin[1];
transform->Translate( translation1 );
```

In a second step, a rotation of 30 degrees is performed. In the `itk::AffineTransform`, angles are specified in *radians*. Also, a second boolean argument is used to specify if the current modification of the transform should be pre-composed or post-composed with the current transform content. In this case the argument is set to `false` to indicate that the rotation should be applied *after* the current transform content.

```
const double degreesToRadians = std::atan(1.0) / 45.0;
transform->Rotate2D( -30.0 * degreesToRadians, false );
```

The third and final step implies translating the image origin back to its previous location. This is be done by applying a translation equal to the origin values.

```
TransformType::OutputVectorType translation2;
translation2[0] =   origin[0];
translation2[1] =   origin[1];
transform->Translate( translation2, false );
filter->SetTransform( transform );
```

Figure 2.50 presents the actual input and output images of this example as shown by a correct viewer which takes spacing into account. Note the *clockwise* versus *counter-clockwise* effect discussed previously between the representation in Figure 2.51 and Figure 2.50.

As a final exercise, let's track the mapping of an individual pixel. Keep in mind that the transformation is initiated by walking through the pixels of the *output* image. This is the only way to ensure that the image will be generated without holes or redundant values. When you think about transformation it is always useful to analyze things from the output image towards the input image.

Let's take the pixel with index $I = (1,2)$ from the output image. The physical coordinates of this point in the output image reference system are $P = (1 \times 40.0 + 50.0, 2 \times 30.0 + 130.0) = (90.0, 190.0)$ millimeters.

This point P is now mapped through the `itk::AffineTransform` into the input image space. The operation subtracts the origin, applies a 30 degrees rotation and adds the origin back. Let's follow those steps. Subtracting the origin from P leads to $P1 = (40.0, 60.0)$, the rotation maps $P1$ to $P2 = (40.0 \times cos(30.0) + 60.0 \times sin(30.0), 40.0 \times sin(30.0) - 60.0 \times cos(30.0)) = (64.64, 31.96)$. Finally this point is translated back by the amount of the image origin. This moves $P2$ to $P3 = (114.64, 161.96)$.

The point $P3$ is now in the coordinate system of the input image. The pixel of the input image associated with this physical position is computed using the origin and spacing of the input image. $I = ((114.64 - 60.0)/20.0, (161 - 70.0)/30.0)$ which results in $I = (2.7, 3.0)$. Note that this is a non-grid position since the values are non-integers. This means that the gray value to be assigned to the output image pixel $I = (1,2)$ must be computed by interpolation of the input image values.

In this particular code the interpolator used is simply a `itk::NearestNeighborInterpolateImageFunction` which will assign the value of the closest pixel. This ends up being the pixel of index $I = (3,3)$ and can be seen from Figure 2.51.

Rotating an Image

The source code for this section can be found in the file `ResampleImageFilter4.cxx`.

The following example illustrates how to rotate an image around its center. In this particular case an `itk::AffineTransform` is used to map the input space into the output space.

The header of the affine transform is included below.

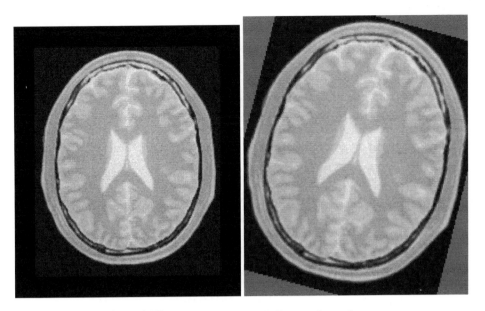

Figure 2.52: Effect of the resample filter rotating an image.

```
#include "itkAffineTransform.h"
```

The transform type is instantiated using the coordinate representation type and the space dimension. Then a transform object is constructed with the New() method and passed to a itk::SmartPointer.

```
typedef itk::AffineTransform< double, Dimension > TransformType;
TransformType::Pointer transform = TransformType::New();
```

The parameters of the output image are taken from the input image.

```
reader->Update();

const InputImageType * inputImage = reader->GetOutput();

const InputImageType::SpacingType & spacing = inputImage->GetSpacing();
const InputImageType::PointType & origin = inputImage->GetOrigin();
InputImageType::SizeType size =
    inputImage->GetLargestPossibleRegion().GetSize();

filter->SetOutputOrigin( origin );
filter->SetOutputSpacing( spacing );
filter->SetOutputDirection( inputImage->GetDirection() );
filter->SetSize( size );
```

Rotations are performed around the origin of physical coordinates—not the image origin nor the image center. Hence, the process of positioning the output image frame as it is shown in Figure 2.52 requires three steps. First, the image origin must be moved to the origin of the coordinate system. This is done by applying a translation equal to the negative values of the image origin.

```
TransformType::OutputVectorType translation1;

const double imageCenterX = origin[0] + spacing[0] * size[0] / 2.0;
const double imageCenterY = origin[1] + spacing[1] * size[1] / 2.0;

translation1[0] =    -imageCenterX;
translation1[1] =    -imageCenterY;

transform->Translate( translation1 );
```

In a second step, the rotation is specified using the method Rotate2D().

```
const double degreesToRadians = std::atan(1.0) / 45.0;
const double angle = angleInDegrees * degreesToRadians;
transform->Rotate2D( -angle, false );
```

The third and final step requires translating the image origin back to its previous location. This is be done by applying a translation equal to the origin values.

```
TransformType::OutputVectorType translation2;
translation2[0] =    imageCenterX;
translation2[1] =    imageCenterY;
transform->Translate( translation2, false );
filter->SetTransform( transform );
```

The output of the resampling filter is connected to a writer and the execution of the pipeline is triggered by a writer update.

```
try
  {
  writer->Update();
  }
catch( itk::ExceptionObject & excep )
  {
  std::cerr << "Exception caught !" << std::endl;
  std::cerr << excep << std::endl;
  }
```

Rotating and Scaling an Image

The source code for this section can be found in the file
ResampleImageFilter5.cxx.

This example illustrates the use of the itk::Similarity2DTransform. A similarity transform involves rotation, translation and scaling. Since the parameterization of rotations is difficult to get in a generic *ND* case, a particular implementation is available for *2D*.

The header file of the transform is included below.

```
#include "itkSimilarity2DTransform.h"
```

The transform type is instantiated using the coordinate representation type as the single template parameter.

```
typedef itk::Similarity2DTransform< double >  TransformType;
```

A transform object is constructed by calling New() and passing the result to a itk::SmartPointer.

```
TransformType::Pointer transform = TransformType::New();
```

The parameters of the output image are taken from the input image.

The Similarity2DTransform allows the user to select the center of rotation. This center is used for both rotation and scaling operations.

```
TransformType::InputPointType rotationCenter;
rotationCenter[0] = origin[0] + spacing[0] * size[0] / 2.0;
rotationCenter[1] = origin[1] + spacing[1] * size[1] / 2.0;
transform->SetCenter( rotationCenter );
```

The rotation is specified with the method SetAngle().

```
const double degreesToRadians = std::atan(1.0) / 45.0;
const double angle = angleInDegrees * degreesToRadians;
transform->SetAngle( angle );
```

The scale change is defined using the method SetScale().

```
transform->SetScale( scale );
```

A translation to be applied after the rotation and scaling can be specified with the method SetTranslation().

```
TransformType::OutputVectorType translation;

translation[0] =    13.0;
translation[1] =    17.0;

transform->SetTranslation( translation );

filter->SetTransform( transform );
```

Note that the order in which rotation, scaling and translation are defined is irrelevant in this transform. This is not the case in the Affine transform which is very generic and allows different combinations for initialization. In the Similarity2DTransform class the rotation and scaling will always be applied before the translation.

Figure 2.53 shows the effect of this rotation, translation and scaling on a slice of a brain MRI. The scale applied for producing this figure was 1.2 and the rotation angle was $10°$.

Resampling using a deformation field

The source code for this section can be found in the file WarpImageFilter1.cxx.

This example illustrates how to use the WarpImageFilter and a deformation field for resampling an image. This is typically done as the last step of a deformable registration algorithm.

```
#include "itkWarpImageFilter.h"
```

The deformation field is represented as an image of vector pixel types. The dimension of the vectors

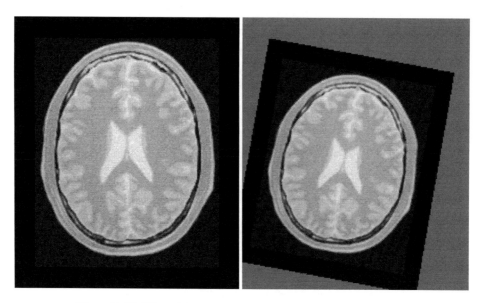

Figure 2.53: Effect of the resample filter rotating and scaling an image.

is the same as the dimension of the input image. Each vector in the deformation field represents the distance between a geometric point in the input space and a point in the output space such that:

$$p_{in} = p_{out} + \text{distance} \tag{2.21}$$

```
typedef float                                    VectorComponentType;
typedef itk::Vector< VectorComponentType, Dimension > VectorPixelType;
typedef itk::Image< VectorPixelType,  Dimension >    DisplacementFieldType;

typedef unsigned char                            PixelType;
typedef itk::Image< PixelType,  Dimension >   ImageType;
```

The field is read from a file, through a reader instantiated over the vector pixel types.

```
typedef   itk::ImageFileReader< DisplacementFieldType >  FieldReaderType;

FieldReaderType::Pointer fieldReader = FieldReaderType::New();
fieldReader->SetFileName( argv[2] );
fieldReader->Update();

DisplacementFieldType::ConstPointer deformationField =
                                    fieldReader->GetOutput();
```

The itk::WarpImageFilter is templated over the input image type, output image type and the deformation field type.

```
typedef itk::WarpImageFilter< ImageType,
                              ImageType,
                              DisplacementFieldType >  FilterType;

FilterType::Pointer filter = FilterType::New();
```

Typically the mapped position does not correspond to an integer pixel position in the input image. Interpolation via an image function is used to compute values at non-integer positions. This is done via the `SetInterpolator()` method.

```
typedef itk::LinearInterpolateImageFunction<
                    ImageType, double > InterpolatorType;

InterpolatorType::Pointer interpolator = InterpolatorType::New();

filter->SetInterpolator( interpolator );
```

The output image spacing and origin may be set via SetOutputSpacing(), SetOutputOrigin(). This is taken from the deformation field.

```
filter->SetOutputSpacing( deformationField->GetSpacing() );
filter->SetOutputOrigin(  deformationField->GetOrigin() );
filter->SetOutputDirection(  deformationField->GetDirection() );

filter->SetDisplacementField( deformationField );
```

Subsampling and image in the same space

The source code for this section can be found in the file
`SubsampleVolume.cxx`.

This example illustrates how to perform subsampling of a volume using ITK classes. In order to avoid aliasing artifacts, the volume must be processed by a low-pass filter before resampling. Here we use the `itk::RecursiveGaussianImageFilter` as a low-pass filter. The image is then resampled by using three different factors, one per dimension of the image.

The most important headers to include here are those corresponding to the resampling image filter, the transform, the interpolator and the smoothing filter.

```
#include "itkResampleImageFilter.h"
#include "itkIdentityTransform.h"
#include "itkRecursiveGaussianImageFilter.h"
```

We explicitly instantiate the pixel type and dimension of the input image, and the images that will be used internally for computing the resampling.

```
const      unsigned int   Dimension = 3;

typedef    unsigned char   InputPixelType;

typedef    float           InternalPixelType;
typedef    unsigned char   OutputPixelType;

typedef itk::Image< InputPixelType,    Dimension >   InputImageType;
typedef itk::Image< InternalPixelType, Dimension >   InternalImageType;
typedef itk::Image< OutputPixelType,   Dimension >   OutputImageType;
```

In this particular case we take the factors for resampling directly from the command line arguments.

```
const double factorX = atof( argv[3] );
const double factorY = atof( argv[4] );
const double factorZ = atof( argv[5] );
```

A casting filter is instantiated in order to convert the pixel type of the input image into the pixel type desired for computing the resampling.

```
typedef itk::CastImageFilter< InputImageType,
                              InternalImageType >   CastFilterType;

CastFilterType::Pointer caster = CastFilterType::New();

caster->SetInput( inputImage );
```

The smoothing filter of choice is the `RecursiveGaussianImageFilter`. We create three of them in order to have the freedom of performing smoothing with different sigma values along each dimension.

```
typedef itk::RecursiveGaussianImageFilter<
                              InternalImageType,
                              InternalImageType > GaussianFilterType;

GaussianFilterType::Pointer smootherX = GaussianFilterType::New();
GaussianFilterType::Pointer smootherY = GaussianFilterType::New();
GaussianFilterType::Pointer smootherZ = GaussianFilterType::New();
```

The smoothing filters are connected in a cascade in the pipeline.

```
smootherX->SetInput( caster->GetOutput() );
smootherY->SetInput( smootherX->GetOutput() );
smootherZ->SetInput( smootherY->GetOutput() );
```

The sigma values to use in the smoothing filters are computed based on the pixel spacing of the input image and the factors provided as arguments.

```
const InputImageType::SpacingType& inputSpacing = inputImage->GetSpacing();

const double sigmaX = inputSpacing[0] * factorX;
const double sigmaY = inputSpacing[1] * factorY;
const double sigmaZ = inputSpacing[2] * factorZ;

smootherX->SetSigma( sigmaX );
smootherY->SetSigma( sigmaY );
smootherZ->SetSigma( sigmaZ );
```

We instruct each one of the smoothing filters to act along a particular direction of the image, and set them to use normalization across scale space in order to account for the reduction of intensity that accompanies the diffusion process associated with the Gaussian smoothing.

```
smootherX->SetDirection( 0 );
smootherY->SetDirection( 1 );
smootherZ->SetDirection( 2 );

smootherX->SetNormalizeAcrossScale( false );
smootherY->SetNormalizeAcrossScale( false );
smootherZ->SetNormalizeAcrossScale( false );
```

The type of the resampling filter is instantiated using the internal image type and the output image type.

```
typedef itk::ResampleImageFilter<
              InternalImageType, OutputImageType > ResampleFilterType;

ResampleFilterType::Pointer resampler = ResampleFilterType::New();
```

Since the resampling is performed in the same physical extent of the input image, we select the IdentityTransform as the one to be used by the resampling filter.

```
typedef itk::IdentityTransform< double, Dimension > TransformType;

TransformType::Pointer transform = TransformType::New();
transform->SetIdentity();
resampler->SetTransform( transform );
```

The Linear interpolator is selected because it provides a good run-time performance. For applications that require better precision you may want to replace this interpolator with the itk::BSplineInterpolateImageFunction interpolator or with the itk::WindowedSincInterpolateImageFunction interpolator.

```
typedef itk::LinearInterpolateImageFunction<
                 InternalImageType, double > InterpolatorType;
InterpolatorType::Pointer interpolator = InterpolatorType::New();
resampler->SetInterpolator( interpolator );
```

The spacing to be used in the grid of the resampled image is computed using the input image spacing and the factors provided in the command line arguments.

```
OutputImageType::SpacingType spacing;

spacing[0] = inputSpacing[0] * factorX;
spacing[1] = inputSpacing[1] * factorY;
spacing[2] = inputSpacing[2] * factorZ;

resampler->SetOutputSpacing( spacing );
```

The origin and direction of the input image are both preserved and passed to the output image.

```
resampler->SetOutputOrigin( inputImage->GetOrigin() );
resampler->SetOutputDirection( inputImage->GetDirection() );
```

The number of pixels to use along each direction on the grid of the resampled image is computed using the number of pixels in the input image and the sampling factors.

```
InputImageType::SizeType    inputSize =
            inputImage->GetLargestPossibleRegion().GetSize();

typedef InputImageType::SizeType::SizeValueType SizeValueType;

InputImageType::SizeType    size;

size[0] = static_cast< SizeValueType >( inputSize[0] / factorX );
size[1] = static_cast< SizeValueType >( inputSize[1] / factorY );
size[2] = static_cast< SizeValueType >( inputSize[2] / factorZ );

resampler->SetSize( size );
```

Finally, the input to the resampler is taken from the output of the smoothing filter.

```
resampler->SetInput( smootherZ->GetOutput() );
```

At this point we can trigger the execution of the resampling by calling the Update() method, or we can choose to pass the output of the resampling filter to another section of pipeline, for example, an image writer.

Resampling an Anisotropic image to make it Isotropic

The source code for this section can be found in the file
ResampleVolumesToBeIsotropic.cxx.

It is unfortunate that it is still very common to find medical image datasets that have been acquired with large inter-slice spacings that result in voxels with anisotropic shapes. In many cases these voxels have ratios of $[1:5]$ or even $[1:10]$ between the resolution in the plane (x,y) and the resolution along the z axis. These datasets are close to **useless** for the purpose of computer-assisted image analysis. The abundance of datasets acquired with anisotropic voxel sizes bespeaks a dearth of understanding of the third dimension and its importance for medical image analysis in clinical settings and radiology reading rooms. Datasets acquired with large anisotropies bring with them the regressive message: *"I do not think 3D is informative"*. They stubbornly insist: *"all that you need to know, can be known by looking at individual slices, one by one"*. However, the fallacy of this statement is made evident by simply viewing the slices when reconstructed in any of the orthogonal planes. The rectangular pixel shape is ugly and distorted, and cripples any signal processing algorithm not designed specifically for this type of image.

Image analysts have a long educational battle to fight in the radiological setting in order to bring the message that 3D datasets acquired with anisotropies larger than $[1:2]$ are simply dismissive of the most fundamental concept of digital signal processing: The Shannon Sampling Theorem [58, 59].

Facing the inertia of many clinical imaging departments and their blithe insistence that these images are "good enough" for image processing, some image analysts have stoically tried to deal with these poor datasets. These image analysts usually proceed to subsample the high in-plane resolution and to super-sample the inter-slice resolution with the purpose of faking the type of dataset that they should have received in the first place: an **isotropic** dataset. This example is an illustration of how such an operation can be performed using the filters available in the Insight Toolkit.

Note that this example is not presented here as a *solution* to the problem of anisotropic datasets. On the contrary, this is simply a *dangerous palliative* which will only perpetuate the errant convictions of image acquisition departments. The real solution to the problem of the anisotropic dataset is to educate radiologists regarding the principles of image processing. If you really care about the technical decency of the medical image processing field, and you really care about providing your best effort to the patients who will receive health care directly or indirectly affected by your processed images, then it is your duty to reject anisotropic datasets and to patiently explain to your radiologist why anisotropic data are problematic for processing, and require crude workarounds which handicap your ability to draw accurate conclusions from the data and preclude his or her ability to provide quality care. Any barbarity such as a $[1:5]$ anisotropy ratio should be considered as a mere collection of slices, and not an authentic 3D dataset.

Please, before employing the techniques covered in this section, do kindly invite your fellow radiologist to see the dataset in an orthogonal slice. Magnify that image in a viewer without any linear interpolation until you see the daunting reality of the rectangular pixels. Let her/him know how absurd it is to process digital data which have been sampled at ratios of $[1 : 5]$ or $[1 : 10]$. Then, inform them that your only option is to throw away all that high in-plane resolution and to *make up* data between the slices in order to compensate for the low resolution. Only then will you be justified in using the following code.

Let's now move into the code. It is appropriate for you to experience guilt[5], because your use the code below is the evidence that we have lost one more battle on the quest for real 3D dataset processing.

This example performs subsampling on the in-plane resolution and performs super-sampling along the inter-slices resolution. The subsampling process requires that we preprocess the data with a smoothing filter in order to avoid the occurrence of aliasing effects due to overlap of the spectrum in the frequency domain [58, 59]. The smoothing is performed here using the `RecursiveGaussian` filter, because it provides a convenient run-time performance.

The first thing that you will need to do in order to resample this ugly anisotropic dataset is to include the header files for the `itk::ResampleImageFilter`, and the Gaussian smoothing filter.

```
#include "itkResampleImageFilter.h"
#include "itkRecursiveGaussianImageFilter.h"
```

The resampling filter will need a Transform in order to map point coordinates and will need an interpolator in order to compute intensity values for the new resampled image. In this particular case we use the `itk::IdentityTransform` because the image is going to be resampled by preserving the physical extent of the sampled region. The Linear interpolator is used as a common trade-off[6].

```
#include "itkIdentityTransform.h"
```

Note that, as part of the preprocessing of the image, in this example we are also rescaling the range of intensities. This operation has already been described as Intensity Windowing. In a real clinical application, this step requires careful consideration of the range of intensities that contain information about the anatomical structures that are of interest for the current clinical application. It practice you may want to remove this step of intensity rescaling.

```
#include "itkIntensityWindowingImageFilter.h"
```

We make explicit now our choices for the pixel type and dimension of the input image to be processed, as well as the pixel type that we intend to use for the internal computation during the smoothing and resampling.

---

[5]A feeling of regret or remorse for having committed some improper act; a recognition of one's own responsibility for doing something wrong.

[6]Although arguably we should use one type of interpolator for the in-plane subsampling process and another one for the inter-slice supersampling. But again, one should wonder why we apply any technical sophistication here, when we are covering up for an improper acquisition of medical data, trying to make it look as if it was correctly acquired.

```
const     unsigned int    Dimension = 3;

typedef   unsigned short  InputPixelType;
typedef   float           InternalPixelType;

typedef itk::Image< InputPixelType,    Dimension >  InputImageType;
typedef itk::Image< InternalPixelType, Dimension >  InternalImageType;
```

We instantiate the smoothing filter that will be used on the preprocessing for subsampling the in-plane resolution of the dataset.

```
typedef itk::RecursiveGaussianImageFilter<
                     InternalImageType,
                     InternalImageType > GaussianFilterType;
```

We create two instances of the smoothing filter: one will smooth along the *X* direction while the other will smooth along the *Y* direction. They are connected in a cascade in the pipeline, while taking their input from the intensity windowing filter. Note that you may want to skip the intensity windowing scale and simply take the input directly from the reader.

```
GaussianFilterType::Pointer smootherX = GaussianFilterType::New();
GaussianFilterType::Pointer smootherY = GaussianFilterType::New();

smootherX->SetInput( intensityWindowing->GetOutput() );
smootherY->SetInput( smootherX->GetOutput() );
```

We must now provide the settings for the resampling itself. This is done by searching for a value of isotropic resolution that will provide a trade-off between the evil of subsampling and the evil of supersampling. We advance here the conjecture that the geometrical mean between the in-plane and the inter-slice resolutions should be a convenient isotropic resolution to use. This conjecture is supported on nothing other than intuition and common sense. You can rightfully argue that this choice deserves a more technical consideration, but then, if you are so concerned about the technical integrity of the image sampling process, you should not be using this code, and should discuss these issues with the radiologist who acquired this ugly anisotropic dataset.

We take the image from the input and then request its array of pixel spacing values.

```
InputImageType::ConstPointer inputImage = reader->GetOutput();

const InputImageType::SpacingType& inputSpacing = inputImage->GetSpacing();
```

and apply our ad-hoc conjecture that the correct anisotropic resolution to use is the geometrical mean of the in-plane and inter-slice resolutions. Then set this spacing as the Sigma value to be used for the Gaussian smoothing at the preprocessing stage.

```
const double isoSpacing = std::sqrt( inputSpacing[2] * inputSpacing[0] );

smootherX->SetSigma( isoSpacing );
smootherY->SetSigma( isoSpacing );
```

We instruct the smoothing filters to act along the *X* and *Y* direction respectively.

```
smootherX->SetDirection( 0 );
smootherY->SetDirection( 1 );
```

Now that we have taken care of the smoothing in-plane, we proceed to instantiate the resampling filter that will reconstruct an isotropic image. We start by declaring the pixel type to be used as the output of this filter, then instantiate the image type and the type for the resampling filter. Finally we construct an instantiation of the filter.

```
typedef   unsigned char   OutputPixelType;

typedef itk::Image< OutputPixelType,   Dimension >   OutputImageType;

typedef itk::ResampleImageFilter<
            InternalImageType, OutputImageType >  ResampleFilterType;

ResampleFilterType::Pointer resampler = ResampleFilterType::New();
```

The resampling filter requires that we provide a Transform, which in this particular case can simply be an identity transform.

```
typedef itk::IdentityTransform< double, Dimension >  TransformType;

TransformType::Pointer transform = TransformType::New();
transform->SetIdentity();

resampler->SetTransform( transform );
```

The filter also requires an interpolator to be passed to it. In this case we chose to use a linear interpolator.

```
typedef itk::LinearInterpolateImageFunction<
                     InternalImageType, double >  InterpolatorType;

InterpolatorType::Pointer interpolator = InterpolatorType::New();

resampler->SetInterpolator( interpolator );
```

The pixel spacing of the resampled dataset is loaded in a SpacingType and passed to the resampling filter.

```
OutputImageType::SpacingType spacing;

spacing[0] = isoSpacing;
spacing[1] = isoSpacing;
spacing[2] = isoSpacing;

resampler->SetOutputSpacing( spacing );
```

The origin and orientation of the output image is maintained, since we decided to resample the image in the same physical extent of the input anisotropic image.

```
resampler->SetOutputOrigin( inputImage->GetOrigin() );
resampler->SetOutputDirection( inputImage->GetDirection() );
```

The number of pixels to use along each dimension in the grid of the resampled image is computed using the ratio between the pixel spacings of the input image and those of the output image. Note that the computation of the number of pixels along the Z direction is slightly different with the purpose of making sure that we don't attempt to compute pixels that are outside of the original anisotropic dataset.

```
InputImageType::SizeType    inputSize =
                 inputImage->GetLargestPossibleRegion().GetSize();

typedef InputImageType::SizeType::SizeValueType SizeValueType;

const double dx = inputSize[0] * inputSpacing[0] / isoSpacing;
const double dy = inputSize[1] * inputSpacing[1] / isoSpacing;

const double dz = (inputSize[2] - 1 ) * inputSpacing[2] / isoSpacing;
```

Finally the values are stored in a `SizeType` and passed to the resampling filter. Note that this process requires a casting since the computations are performed in `double`, while the elements of the `SizeType` are integers.

```
InputImageType::SizeType    size;

size[0] = static_cast<SizeValueType>( dx );
size[1] = static_cast<SizeValueType>( dy );
size[2] = static_cast<SizeValueType>( dz );

resampler->SetSize( size );
```

Our last action is to take the input for the resampling image filter from the output of the cascade of smoothing filters, and then to trigger the execution of the pipeline by invoking the `Update()` method on the resampling filter.

```
resampler->SetInput( smootherY->GetOutput() );

resampler->Update();
```

At this point we should take a moment in silence to reflect on the circumstances that have led us to accept this cover-up for the improper acquisition of medical data.

2.10   Frequency Domain

2.10.1   Computing a Fast Fourier Transform (FFT)

The source code for this section can be found in the file
`FFTImageFilter.cxx`.

In this section we assume that you are familiar with Spectral Analysis, in particular with the concepts of the Fourier Transform and the numerical implementation of the Fast Fourier transform. If you are not familiar with these concepts you may want to consult first any of the many available introductory books to spectral analysis [8, 9].

This example illustrates how to use the Fast Fourier Transform filter (FFT) for processing an image in the spectral domain. Given that FFT computation can be CPU intensive, there are multiple hardware specific implementations of FFT. It is convenient in many cases to delegate the actual computation of the transform to local available libraries. Particular examples of those libraries are fftw[7] and the VXL implementation of FFT. For this reason ITK provides a base abstract class that factorizes the interface to multiple specific implementations of FFT. This base class is the `itk::ForwardFFTImageFilter`, and two of its derived classes are `itk::VnlForwardFFTImageFilter` and `itk::FFTWRealToComplexConjugateImageFilter`.

A typical application that uses FFT will need to include the following header files.

```
#include "itkImage.h"
#include "itkVnlForwardFFTImageFilter.h"
#include "itkComplexToRealImageFilter.h"
#include "itkComplexToImaginaryImageFilter.h"
```

The first decision to make is related to the pixel type and dimension of the images on which we want to compute the Fourier transform.

```
typedef float  PixelType;
const unsigned int Dimension = 2;

typedef itk::Image< PixelType, Dimension > ImageType;
```

We use the same image type in order to instantiate the FFT filter, in this case the `itk::VnlForwardFFTImageFilter`. Once the filter type is instantiated, we can use it for creating one object by invoking the New() method and assigning the result to a SmartPointer.

```
typedef itk::VnlForwardFFTImageFilter< ImageType > FFTFilterType;

FFTFilterType::Pointer fftFilter = FFTFilterType::New();
```

The input to this filter can be taken from a reader, for example.

```
typedef itk::ImageFileReader< ImageType > ReaderType;
ReaderType::Pointer reader = ReaderType::New();
reader->SetFileName( argv[1] );

fftFilter->SetInput( reader->GetOutput() );
```

The execution of the filter can be triggered by invoking the Update() method. Since this invocation can eventually throw an exception, the call must be placed inside a try/catch block.

```
try
  {
  fftFilter->Update();
  }
catch( itk::ExceptionObject & excp )
  {
  std::cerr << "Error: " << std::endl;
  std::cerr << excp << std::endl;
  return EXIT_FAILURE;
  }
```

In general the output of the FFT filter will be a complex image. We can proceed to save this image in a file for further analysis. This can be done by simply instantiating an `itk::ImageFileWriter` using the trait of the output image from the FFT filter. We construct one instance of the writer and pass the output of the FFT filter as the input of the writer.

---

[7]http://www.fftw.org

```
typedef FFTFilterType::OutputImageType    ComplexImageType;

typedef itk::ImageFileWriter< ComplexImageType > ComplexWriterType;

ComplexWriterType::Pointer complexWriter = ComplexWriterType::New();
complexWriter->SetFileName( argv[4] );

complexWriter->SetInput( fftFilter->GetOutput() );
```

Finally we invoke the `Update()` method placed inside a try/catch block.

```
try
  {
  complexWriter->Update();
  }
catch( itk::ExceptionObject & excp )
  {
  std::cerr << "Error: " << std::endl;
  std::cerr << excp << std::endl;
  return EXIT_FAILURE;
  }
```

In addition to saving the complex image into a file, we could also extract its real and imaginary parts for further analysis. This can be done with the `itk::ComplexToRealImageFilter` and the `itk::ComplexToImaginaryImageFilter`.

We instantiate first the ImageFilter that will help us to extract the real part from the complex image. The `ComplexToRealImageFilter` takes as its first template parameter the type of the complex image and as its second template parameter it takes the type of the output image pixel. We create one instance of this filter and connect as its input the output of the FFT filter.

```
typedef itk::ComplexToRealImageFilter<
              ComplexImageType, ImageType > RealFilterType;

RealFilterType::Pointer realFilter = RealFilterType::New();

realFilter->SetInput( fftFilter->GetOutput() );
```

Since the range of intensities in the Fourier domain can be quite concentrated, it is convenient to rescale the image in order to visualize it. For this purpose we instantiate a `itk::RescaleIntensityImageFilter` that will rescale the intensities of the `real` image into a range suitable for writing in a file. We also set the minimum and maximum values of the output to the range of the pixel type used for writing.

```
typedef itk::RescaleIntensityImageFilter<
                       ImageType,
                       WriteImageType > RescaleFilterType;

RescaleFilterType::Pointer intensityRescaler = RescaleFilterType::New();

intensityRescaler->SetInput( realFilter->GetOutput() );

intensityRescaler->SetOutputMinimum(  0  );
intensityRescaler->SetOutputMaximum( 255 );
```

We can now instantiate the ImageFilter that will help us to extract the imaginary part from the complex image. The filter that we use here is the `itk::ComplexToImaginaryImageFilter`. It takes as first template parameter the type of the complex image and as second template parameter it takes the type of the output image pixel. An instance of the filter is created, and its input is connected to the output of the FFT filter.

```
typedef FFTFilterType::OutputImageType      ComplexImageType;

typedef itk::ComplexToImaginaryImageFilter<
                    ComplexImageType, ImageType > ImaginaryFilterType;

ImaginaryFilterType::Pointer imaginaryFilter = ImaginaryFilterType::New();

imaginaryFilter->SetInput( fftFilter->GetOutput() );
```

The Imaginary image can then be rescaled and saved into a file, just as we did with the Real part.

For the sake of illustrating the use of a `itk::ImageFileReader` on Complex images, here we instantiate a reader that will load the Complex image that we just saved. Note that nothing special is required in this case. The instantiation is done just the same as for any other type of image, which once again illustrates the power of Generic Programming.

```
typedef itk::ImageFileReader< ComplexImageType > ComplexReaderType;

ComplexReaderType::Pointer complexReader = ComplexReaderType::New();

complexReader->SetFileName( argv[4] );
complexReader->Update();
```

2.10.2   Filtering on the Frequency Domain

The source code for this section can be found in the file
`FFTImageFilterFourierDomainFiltering.cxx`.

One of the most common image processing operations performed in the Fourier Domain is the masking of the spectrum in order to eliminate a range of spatial frequencies from the input image. This operation is typically performed by taking the input image, computing its Fourier transform using a FFT filter, masking the resulting image in the Fourier domain with a mask, and finally taking the result of the masking and computing its inverse Fourier transform.

This typical process is illustrated in the example below.

We start by including the headers of the FFT filters and the Mask image filter. Note that we use two different types of FFT filters here. The first one expects as input an image of real pixel type (real in the sense of complex numbers) and produces as output a complex image. The second FFT filter expects as in put a complex image and produces a real image as output.

```
#include "itkVnlForwardFFTImageFilter.h"
#include "itkVnlInverseFFTImageFilter.h"
#include "itkMaskImageFilter.h"
```

The first decision to make is related to the pixel type and dimension of the images on which we want to compute the Fourier transform.

```
typedef float  InputPixelType;
const unsigned int Dimension = 2;

typedef itk::Image< InputPixelType, Dimension > InputImageType;
```

Then we select the pixel type to use for the mask image and instantiate the image type of the mask.

```
typedef unsigned char  MaskPixelType;

typedef itk::Image< MaskPixelType, Dimension > MaskImageType;
```

Both the input image and the mask image can be read from files or could be obtained as the output of a preprocessing pipeline. We omit here the details of reading the image since the process is quite standard.

Now the `itk::VnlForwardFFTImageFilter` can be instantiated. Like most ITK filters, the FFT filter is instantiated using the full image type. By not setting the output image type, we decide to use the default one provided by the filter. Using this type we construct one instance of the filter.

```
typedef itk::VnlForwardFFTImageFilter< InputImageType >  FFTFilterType;

FFTFilterType::Pointer fftFilter = FFTFilterType::New();

fftFilter->SetInput( inputReader->GetOutput() );
```

Since our purpose is to perform filtering in the frequency domain by altering the weights of the image spectrum, we need a filter that will mask the Fourier transform of the input image with a binary image. Note that the type of the spectral image is taken here from the traits of the FFT filter.

```
typedef FFTFilterType::OutputImageType     SpectralImageType;

typedef itk::MaskImageFilter< SpectralImageType,
                              MaskImageType,
                              SpectralImageType >  MaskFilterType;

MaskFilterType::Pointer maskFilter = MaskFilterType::New();
```

We connect the inputs to the mask filter by taking the outputs from the first FFT filter and from the reader of the Mask image.

```
maskFilter->SetInput1( fftFilter->GetOutput() );
maskFilter->SetInput2( maskReader->GetOutput() );
```

For the purpose of verifying the aspect of the spectrum after being filtered with the mask, we can write out the output of the Mask filter to a file.

```
typedef itk::ImageFileWriter< SpectralImageType > SpectralWriterType;
SpectralWriterType::Pointer spectralWriter = SpectralWriterType::New();
spectralWriter->SetFileName("filteredSpectrum.mhd");
spectralWriter->SetInput( maskFilter->GetOutput() );
spectralWriter->Update();
```

The output of the mask filter will contain the *filtered* spectrum of the input image. We must then apply an inverse Fourier transform on it in order to obtain the filtered version of the input image. For that purpose we create another instance of the FFT filter.

```
typedef itk::VnlInverseFFTImageFilter<
    SpectralImageType > IFFTFilterType;

IFFTFilterType::Pointer fftInverseFilter = IFFTFilterType::New();

fftInverseFilter->SetInput( maskFilter->GetOutput() );
```

The execution of the pipeline can be triggered by invoking the Update() method in this last filter. Since this invocation can eventually throw an exception, the call must be placed inside a try/catch block.

```
try
    {
    fftInverseFilter->Update();
    }
catch( itk::ExceptionObject & excp )
    {
    std::cerr << "Error: " << std::endl;
    std::cerr << excp << std::endl;
    return EXIT_FAILURE;
    }
```

The result of the filtering can now be saved into an image file, or be passed to a subsequent processing pipeline. Here we simply write it out to an image file.

```
typedef itk::ImageFileWriter< InputImageType > WriterType;
WriterType::Pointer writer = WriterType::New();
writer->SetFileName( argv[3] );
writer->SetInput( fftInverseFilter->GetOutput() );
```

Note that this example is just a minimal illustration of the multiple types of processing that are possible in the Fourier domain.

2.11 Extracting Surfaces

2.11.1 Surface extraction

The source code for this section can be found in the file
SurfaceExtraction.cxx.

Surface extraction has attracted continuous interest since the early days of image analysis, especially in the context of medical applications. Although it is commonly associated with image segmentation, surface extraction is not in itself a segmentation technique, instead it is a transformation that changes the way a segmentation is represented. In its most common form, isosurface extraction is the equivalent of image thresholding followed by surface extraction.

Probably the most widely known method of surface extraction is the *Marching Cubes* algorithm [37]. Although it has been followed by a number of variants [55], Marching Cubes has become an icon in medical image processing. The following example illustrates how to perform surface extraction in ITK using an algorithm similar to Marching Cubes [8].

---

[8] Note that the Marching Cubes algorithm is covered by a patent that expired on June 5th 2005.

The representation of unstructured data in ITK is done with the `itk::Mesh`. This class enables us to represent *N*-Dimensional grids of varied topology. It is natural for the filter that extracts surfaces from an image to produce a mesh as its output.

We initiate our example by including the header files of the surface extraction filter, the image and the mesh.

```
#include "itkBinaryMask3DMeshSource.h"
#include "itkImage.h"
```

We define then the pixel type and dimension of the image from which we are going to extract the surface.

```
const unsigned int Dimension = 3;
typedef unsigned char  PixelType;

typedef itk::Image< PixelType, Dimension >   ImageType;
```

With the same image type we instantiate the type of an ImageFileReader and construct one with the purpose of reading in the input image.

```
typedef itk::ImageFileReader< ImageType >   ReaderType;
ReaderType::Pointer reader = ReaderType::New();
reader->SetFileName( argv[1] );
```

The type of the `itk::Mesh` is instantiated by specifying the type to be associated with the pixel value of the Mesh nodes. This particular pixel type happens to be irrelevant for the purpose of extracting the surface.

```
typedef itk::Mesh<double>                          MeshType;
```

Having declared the Image and Mesh types we can now instantiate the surface extraction filter, and construct one by invoking its New() method.

```
typedef itk::BinaryMask3DMeshSource< ImageType, MeshType >   MeshSourceType;

MeshSourceType::Pointer meshSource = MeshSourceType::New();
```

In this example, the pixel value associated with the object to be extracted is read from the command line arguments and it is passed to the filter by using the SetObjectValue() method. Note that this is different from the traditional isovalue used in the Marching Cubes algorithm. In the case of the BinaryMask3DMeshSource filter, the object values define the membership of pixels to the object from which the surface will be extracted. In other words, the surface will be surrounding all pixels with value equal to the ObjectValue parameter.

```
const PixelType objectValue = static_cast<PixelType>( atof( argv[2] ) );

meshSource->SetObjectValue( objectValue );
```

The input to the surface extraction filter is taken from the output of the image reader.

```
meshSource->SetInput( reader->GetOutput() );
```

Finally we trigger the execution of the pipeline by invoking the Update() method. Given that the pipeline may throw an exception this call must be place inside a try/catch block.

```
try
  {
  meshSource->Update();
  }
catch( itk::ExceptionObject & exp )
  {
  std::cerr << "Exception thrown during Update() " << std::endl;
  std::cerr << exp << std::endl;
  return EXIT_FAILURE;
  }
```

We print out the number of nodes and cells in order to inspect the output mesh.

```
std::cout << "Nodes = " << meshSource->GetNumberOfNodes() << std::endl;
std::cout << "Cells = " << meshSource->GetNumberOfCells() << std::endl;
```

This resulting Mesh could be used as input for a deformable model segmentation algorithm, or it could be converted to a format suitable for visualization in an interactive application.

REGISTRATION

This chapter introduces ITK's capabilities for performing image registration. Image registration is the process of determining the spatial transform that maps points from one image to homologous points on a object in the second image. This concept is schematically represented in Figure 3.1. In ITK, registration is performed within a framework of pluggable components that can easily be

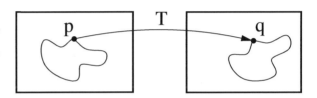

Figure 3.1: Image registration is the task of finding a spatial transform mapping one image into another.

interchanged. This flexibility means that a combinatorial variety of registration methods can be created, allowing users to pick and choose the right tools for their specific application.

3.1 Registration Framework

Let's begin with a simplified typical registration framework where its components and their interconnections are shown in Figure 3.2. The basic input data to the registration process are two images: one is defined as the *fixed* image $f(\mathbf{X})$ and the other as the *moving* image $m(\mathbf{X})$, where $\mathbf{X}$ represents a position in N-dimensional space. Registration is treated as an optimization problem with the goal of finding the spatial mapping that will bring the moving image into alignment with the fixed image.

The *transform* component $T(\mathbf{X})$ represents the spatial mapping of points from the fixed image space to points in the moving image space. The *interpolator* is used to evaluate moving image intensities at non-grid positions. The *metric* component $S(f, m \circ T)$ provides a measure of how well the fixed image is matched by the transformed moving image. This measure forms a quantitative criterion to be optimized by the *optimizer* over the search space defined by the parameters of the *transform*.

ITKv4 registration framework provides more flexibility to the above traditional registration concept. In this new framework, the registration computations can happen on a physical grid completely different than the fixed image domain having different sampling density. This "sampling domain" is considered as a new component in the registration framework known as **virtual image** that can be an arbitrary set of physical points, not necessarily a uniform grid of points.

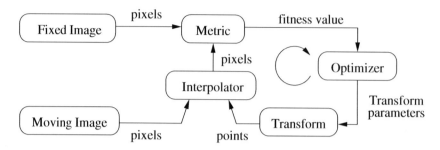

Figure 3.2: The basic components of a typical registration framework are two input images, a transform, a metric, an interpolator and an optimizer.

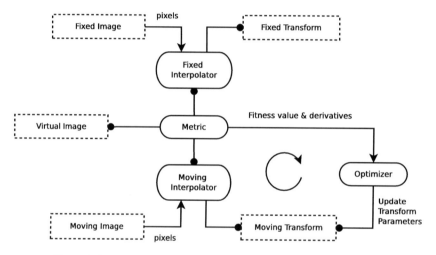

Figure 3.3: The basic components of the ITKv4 registration framework.

Various ITKv4 registration components are illustrated in Figure 3.3. Boxes with dashed borders show *data objects*, while those with solid borders show *process objects*.

The matching Metric class is a key component that controls most parts of the registration process since it handles fixed, moving and virtual images as well as fixed and moving transforms and interpolators.

Fixed and moving transforms and interpolators are used by the metric to evaluate the intensity values of the fixed and moving images at each physical point of the virtual space. Those intensity values are then used by the metric cost function to evaluate the fitness value and derivatives, which are passed to the optimizer that asks the moving transform to update its parameters based on the outputs of the cost function. Since the moving transform is shared between metric and optimizer, the above process will be repeated till the convergence criteria are met.

Later in section 3.3 you will get a better understanding of the behind-the-scenes processes of ITKv4 registration framework. First, we begin with some simple registration examples.

3.2 "Hello World" Registration

The source code for this section can be found in the file
`ImageRegistration1.cxx`.

This example illustrates the use of the image registration framework in Insight. It should be read as
a "Hello World" for ITK registration. Instead of means to an end, this example should be read as a
basic introduction to the elements typically involved when solving a problem of image registration.

A registration method requires the following set of components: two input images, a transform, a
metric and an optimizer. Some of these components are parameterized by the image type for which
the registration is intended. The following header files provide declarations of common types used
for these components.

```
#include "itkImageRegistrationMethodv4.h"
#include "itkTranslationTransform.h"
#include "itkMeanSquaresImageToImageMetricv4.h"
#include "itkRegularStepGradientDescentOptimizerv4.h"
```

The type of each registration component should be instantiated first. We start by selecting the image
dimension and the types to be used for representing image pixels.

```
const    unsigned int    Dimension = 2;
typedef  float           PixelType;
```

The types of the input images are instantiated by the following lines.

```
typedef itk::Image< PixelType, Dimension >  FixedImageType;
typedef itk::Image< PixelType, Dimension >  MovingImageType;
```

The transform that will map the fixed image space into the moving image space is defined below.

```
typedef itk::TranslationTransform< double, Dimension > TransformType;
```

An optimizer is required to explore the parameter space of the transform in search of optimal values
of the metric.

```
typedef itk::RegularStepGradientDescentOptimizerv4<double> OptimizerType;
```

The metric will compare how well the two images match each other. Metric types are usually templated over the image types as seen in the following type declaration.

```
typedef itk::MeanSquaresImageToImageMetricv4<
                        FixedImageType,
                        MovingImageType >   MetricType;
```

The registration method type is instantiated using the types of the fixed and moving images as well
as the output transform type. This class is responsible for interconnecting all the components that we
have described so far.

```
typedef itk::ImageRegistrationMethodv4<
                        FixedImageType,
                        MovingImageType,
                        TransformType  >  RegistrationType;
```

Each one of the registration components is created using its New() method and is assigned to its respective `itk::SmartPointer`.

```
MetricType::Pointer         metric       = MetricType::New();
OptimizerType::Pointer      optimizer    = OptimizerType::New();
RegistrationType::Pointer   registration = RegistrationType::New();
```

Each component is now connected to the instance of the registration method.

```
registration->SetMetric(      metric      );
registration->SetOptimizer(   optimizer   );
```

In this example the transform object does not need to be created and passed to the registration method like above since the registration filter will instantiate an internal transform object using the transform type that is passed to it as a template parameter.

Metric needs an interpolator to evaluate the intensities of the fixed and moving images at non-grid positions. The types of fixed and moving interpolators are declared here.

```
typedef itk::LinearInterpolateImageFunction<
                              FixedImageType,
                              double > FixedLinearInterpolatorType;

typedef itk::LinearInterpolateImageFunction<
                              MovingImageType,
                              double > MovingLinearInterpolatorType;
```

Then, fixed and moving interpolators are created and passed to the metric. Since linear interpolators are used as default, we could skip the following step in this example.

```
FixedLinearInterpolatorType::Pointer fixedInterpolator =
  FixedLinearInterpolatorType::New();
MovingLinearInterpolatorType::Pointer movingInterpolator =
  MovingLinearInterpolatorType::New();

metric->SetFixedInterpolator(  fixedInterpolator  );
metric->SetMovingInterpolator( movingInterpolator );
```

In this example, the fixed and moving images are read from files. This requires the `itk::ImageRegistrationMethodv4` to acquire its inputs from the output of the readers.

```
registration->SetFixedImage(    fixedImageReader->GetOutput()  );
registration->SetMovingImage(   movingImageReader->GetOutput() );
```

Now the registration process should be initialized. ITKv4 registration framework provides initial transforms for both fixed and moving images. These transforms can be used to setup an initial known correction of the misalignment between the virtual domain and fixed/moving image spaces. In this particular case, a translation transform is being used for initialization of the moving image space. The array of parameters for the initial moving transform is simply composed of the translation values along each dimension. Setting the values of the parameters to zero initializes the transform to an *Identity* transform. Note that the array constructor requires the number of elements to be passed as an argument.

```
TransformType::Pointer movingInitialTransform = TransformType::New();

TransformType::ParametersType initialParameters(
  movingInitialTransform->GetNumberOfParameters() );
initialParameters[0] = 0.0;  // Initial offset in mm along X
initialParameters[1] = 0.0;  // Initial offset in mm along Y

movingInitialTransform->SetParameters( initialParameters );

registration->SetMovingInitialTransform( movingInitialTransform );
```

In the registration filter this moving initial transform will be added to a composite transform that already includes an instantiation of the output optimizable transform; then, the resultant composite transform will be used by the optimizer to evaluate the metric values at each iteration.

Despite this, the fixed initial transform does not contribute to the optimization process. It is only used to access the fixed image from the virtual image space where the metric evaluation happens.

Virtual images are a new concept added to the ITKv4 registration framework, which potentially lets us to do the registration process in a physical domain totally different from the fixed and moving image domains. In fact, the region over which metric evaluation is performed is called virtual image domain. This domain defines the resolution at which the evaluation is performed, as well as the physical coordinate system.

The virtual reference domain is taken from the "virtual image" buffered region, and the input images should be accessed from this reference space using the fixed and moving initial transforms.

The legacy intuitive registration framework can be considered as a special case where the virtual domain is the same as the fixed image domain. As this case practically happens in most of the real life applications, the virtual image is set to be the same as the fixed image by default. However, the user can define the virtual domain differently than the fixed image domain by calling either SetVirtualDomain or SetVirtualDomainFromImage.

In this example, like the most examples of this chapter, the virtual image is considered the same as the fixed image. Since the registration process happens in the fixed image physical domain, the fixed initial transform maintains its default value of identity and does not need to be set.

However, a "Hello World!" example should show all the basics, so all the registration components are explicity set here.

In the next section of this chapter, you will get a better understanding from behind the scenes of the registration process when the initial fixed transform is not identity.

```
TransformType::Pointer    identityTransform = TransformType::New();
identityTransform->SetIdentity();

registration->SetFixedInitialTransform( identityTransform );
```

Note that the above process shows only one way of initializing the registration configuration. Another option is to initialize the output optimizable transform directly. In this approach, a transform object is created, initialized, and then passed to the registration method via SetInitialTransform(). This approach is shown in section 3.6.1.

At this point the registration method is ready for execution. The optimizer is the component that drives the execution of the registration. However, the ImageRegistrationMethodv4 class orchestrates the ensemble to make sure that everything is in place before control is passed to the optimizer.

It is usually desirable to fine tune the parameters of the optimizer. Each optimizer has particular parameters that must be interpreted in the context of the optimization strategy it implements. The optimizer used in this example is a variant of gradient descent that attempts to prevent it from taking steps that are too large. At each iteration, this optimizer will take a step along the direction of the `itk::ImageToImageMetricv4` derivative. Each time the direction of the derivative abruptly changes, the optimizer assumes that a local extrema has been passed and reacts by reducing the step length by a relaxation factor. The reducing factor should have a value between 0 and 1. This factor is set to 0.5 by default, and it can be changed to a different value via `SetRelaxationFactor()`. Also, the default value for the initial step length is 1, and this value can be changed manually with the method `SetLearningRate()`.

In addition to manual settings, the initial step size can also be estimated automatically, either at each iteration or only at the first iteration, by assigning a ScalesEstimator (as will be seen in later examples).

After several reductions of the step length, the optimizer may be moving in a very restricted area of the transform parameter space. By the method `SetMinimumStepLength()`, the user can define how small the step length should be to consider convergence to have been reached. This is equivalent to defining the precision with which the final transform should be known. User can also set some other stop criteria manually like maximum number of iterations.

In other gradient descent-based optimizers of the ITKv4 framework, such as `itk::GradientDescentLineSearchOptimizerv4` and `itk::ConjugateGradientLineSearchOptimizerv4`, the convergence criteria are set via `SetMinimumConvergenceValue()` which is computed based on the results of the last few iterations. The number of iterations involved in computations are defined by the convergence window size via `SetConvergenceWindowSize()` which is shown in later examples of this chapter.

Also note that unlike the previous versions, ITKv4 optimizers do not have a "maximize/minimize" option to modify the effect of the metric derivatives. Each assigned metric is assumed to return a parameter derivative result that "improves" the optimization.

```
optimizer->SetLearningRate( 4 );
optimizer->SetMinimumStepLength( 0.001 );
optimizer->SetRelaxationFactor( 0.5 );
```

In case the optimizer never succeeds reaching the desired precision tolerance, it is prudent to establish a limit on the number of iterations to be performed. This maximum number is defined with the method `SetNumberOfIterations()`.

```
optimizer->SetNumberOfIterations( 200 );
```

ITKv4 facilitates a multi-level registration framework whereby each stage is different in the resolution of its virtual space and the smoothness of the fixed and moving images. These criteria need to be defined before registration starts. Otherwise, the default values will be used. In this example, we run a simple registration in one level with no space shrinking or smoothing on the input data.

```
const unsigned int numberOfLevels = 1;

RegistrationType::ShrinkFactorsArrayType shrinkFactorsPerLevel;
shrinkFactorsPerLevel.SetSize( 1 );
shrinkFactorsPerLevel[0] = 1;

RegistrationType::SmoothingSigmasArrayType smoothingSigmasPerLevel;
smoothingSigmasPerLevel.SetSize( 1 );
smoothingSigmasPerLevel[0] = 0;

registration->SetNumberOfLevels ( numberOfLevels );
registration->SetSmoothingSigmasPerLevel( smoothingSigmasPerLevel );
registration->SetShrinkFactorsPerLevel( shrinkFactorsPerLevel );
```

The registration process is triggered by an invocation of the `Update()` method. If something goes wrong during the initialization or execution of the registration an exception will be thrown. We should therefore place the `Update()` method inside a `try/catch` block as illustrated in the following lines.

```
try
  {
  registration->Update();
  std::cout << "Optimizer stop condition: "
  << registration->GetOptimizer()->GetStopConditionDescription()
  << std::endl;
  }
catch( itk::ExceptionObject & err )
  {
  std::cerr << "ExceptionObject caught !" << std::endl;
  std::cerr << err << std::endl;
  return EXIT_FAILURE;
  }
```

In a real life application, you may attempt to recover from the error by taking more effective actions in the catch block. Here we are simply printing out a message and then terminating the execution of the program.

The result of the registration process is obtained using the `GetTransform()` method that returns a constant pointer to the output transform.

```
TransformType::ConstPointer transform = registration->GetTransform();
```

In the case of the `itk::TranslationTransform`, there is a straightforward interpretation of the parameters. Each element of the array corresponds to a translation along one spatial dimension.

```
TransformType::ParametersType finalParameters = transform->GetParameters();
const double TranslationAlongX = finalParameters[0];
const double TranslationAlongY = finalParameters[1];
```

The optimizer can be queried for the actual number of iterations performed to reach convergence. The `GetCurrentIteration()` method returns this value. A large number of iterations may be an indication that the learning rate has been set too small, which is undesirable since it results in long computational times.

```
const unsigned int numberOfIterations = optimizer->GetCurrentIteration();
```

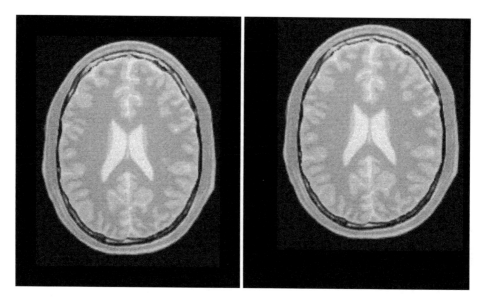

Figure 3.4: Fixed and Moving image provided as input to the registration method.

The value of the image metric corresponding to the last set of parameters can be obtained with the GetValue() method of the optimizer.

```
const double bestValue = optimizer->GetValue();
```

Let's execute this example over two of the images provided in Examples/Data:

- BrainProtonDensitySliceBorder20.png

- BrainProtonDensitySliceShifted13x17y.png

The second image is the result of intentionally translating the first image by $(13, 17)$ millimeters. Both images have unit-spacing and are shown in Figure 3.4. The registration takes 20 iterations and the resulting transform parameters are:

```
Translation X = 13.0012
Translation Y = 16.9999
```

As expected, these values match quite well the misalignment that we intentionally introduced in the moving image.

It is common, as the last step of a registration task, to use the resulting transform to map the moving image into the fixed image space.

Before the mapping process, notice that we have not used the direct initialization of the output transform in this example, so the parameters of the moving initial transform are not reflected in the output parameters of the registration filter. Hence, a composite transform is needed to concatenate both initial and output transforms together.

```
typedef itk::CompositeTransform<
                        double,
                        Dimension > CompositeTransformType;
CompositeTransformType::Pointer outputCompositeTransform =
  CompositeTransformType::New();
outputCompositeTransform->AddTransform( movingInitialTransform );
outputCompositeTransform->AddTransform(
  registration->GetModifiableTransform() );
```

Now the mapping process is easily done with the `itk::ResampleImageFilter`. Please refer to Section 2.9.4 for details on the use of this filter. First, a ResampleImageFilter type is instantiated using the image types. It is convenient to use the fixed image type as the output type since it is likely that the transformed moving image will be compared with the fixed image.

```
typedef itk::ResampleImageFilter<
                    MovingImageType,
                    FixedImageType >   ResampleFilterType;
```

A resampling filter is created and the moving image is connected as its input.

```
ResampleFilterType::Pointer resampler = ResampleFilterType::New();
resampler->SetInput( movingImageReader->GetOutput() );
```

The created output composite transform is also passed as input to the resampling filter.

```
resampler->SetTransform( outputCompositeTransform );
```

As described in Section 2.9.4, the ResampleImageFilter requires additional parameters to be specified, in particular, the spacing, origin and size of the output image. The default pixel value is also set to a distinct gray level in order to highlight the regions that are mapped outside of the moving image.

```
FixedImageType::Pointer fixedImage = fixedImageReader->GetOutput();
resampler->SetSize( fixedImage->GetLargestPossibleRegion().GetSize() );
resampler->SetOutputOrigin(  fixedImage->GetOrigin() );
resampler->SetOutputSpacing( fixedImage->GetSpacing() );
resampler->SetOutputDirection( fixedImage->GetDirection() );
resampler->SetDefaultPixelValue( 100 );
```

The output of the filter is passed to a writer that will store the image in a file. An `itk::CastImageFilter` is used to convert the pixel type of the resampled image to the final type used by the writer. The cast and writer filters are instantiated below.

```
typedef unsigned char                       OutputPixelType;

typedef itk::Image< OutputPixelType, Dimension > OutputImageType;

typedef itk::CastImageFilter<
                    FixedImageType,
                    OutputImageType >       CastFilterType;

typedef itk::ImageFileWriter< OutputImageType > WriterType;
```

The filters are created by invoking their `New()` method.

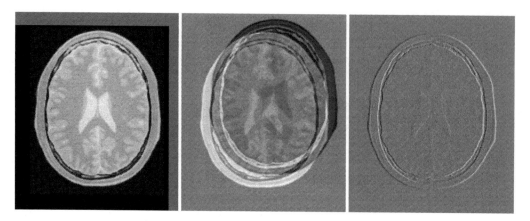

Figure 3.5: Mapped moving image and its difference with the fixed image before and after registration

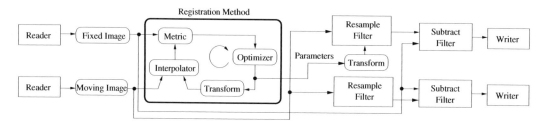

Figure 3.6: Pipeline structure of the registration example.

```
WriterType::Pointer       writer  =   WriterType::New();
CastFilterType::Pointer   caster  =   CastFilterType::New();
```

The filters are connected together and the Update() method of the writer is invoked in order to trigger the execution of the pipeline.

```
caster->SetInput( resampler->GetOutput() );
writer->SetInput( caster->GetOutput()   );
writer->Update();
```

The fixed image and the transformed moving image can easily be compared using the itk::SubtractImageFilter. This pixel-wise filter computes the difference between homologous pixels of its two input images.

```
typedef itk::SubtractImageFilter<
                            FixedImageType,
                            FixedImageType,
                            FixedImageType > DifferenceFilterType;

DifferenceFilterType::Pointer difference = DifferenceFilterType::New();

difference->SetInput1( fixedImageReader->GetOutput() );
difference->SetInput2( resampler->GetOutput() );
```

Note that the use of subtraction as a method for comparing the images is appropriate here because we chose to represent the images using a pixel type `float`. A different filter would have been used if the pixel type of the images were any of the unsigned integer types.

Since the differences between the two images may correspond to very low values of intensity, we rescale those intensities with a `itk::RescaleIntensityImageFilter` in order to make them more visible. This rescaling will also make it possible to visualize the negative values even if we save the difference image in a file format that only supports unsigned pixel values[1]. We also reduce the `DefaultPixelValue` to "1" in order to prevent that value from absorbing the dynamic range of the differences between the two images.

```
typedef itk::RescaleIntensityImageFilter<
                            FixedImageType,
                            OutputImageType >   RescalerType;

RescalerType::Pointer intensityRescaler = RescalerType::New();

intensityRescaler->SetInput( difference->GetOutput() );
intensityRescaler->SetOutputMinimum(   0 );
intensityRescaler->SetOutputMaximum( 255 );

resampler->SetDefaultPixelValue( 1 );
```

Its output can be passed to another writer.

```
WriterType::Pointer writer2 = WriterType::New();
writer2->SetInput( intensityRescaler->GetOutput() );
```

For the purpose of comparison, the difference between the fixed image and the moving image before registration can also be computed by simply setting the transform to an identity transform. Note that the resampling is still necessary because the moving image does not necessarily have the same spacing, origin and number of pixels as the fixed image. Therefore a pixel-by-pixel operation cannot in general be performed. The resampling process with an identity transform will ensure that we have a representation of the moving image in the grid of the fixed image.

```
resampler->SetTransform( identityTransform );
```

The complete pipeline structure of the current example is presented in Figure 3.6. The components of the registration method are depicted as well. Figure 3.5 (left) shows the result of resampling the moving image in order to map it onto the fixed image space. The top and right borders of the image appear in the gray level selected with the `SetDefaultPixelValue()` in the ResampleImageFilter. The center image shows the difference between the fixed image and the original moving image (i.e. the difference before the registration is performed). The right image shows the difference between the fixed image and the transformed moving image (i.e. after the registration has been performed). Both difference images have been rescaled in intensity in order to highlight those pixels where differences exist. Note that the final registration is still off by a fraction of a pixel, which causes bands around edges of anatomical structures to appear in the difference image. A perfect registration would have produced a null difference image.

It is always useful to keep in mind that registration is essentially an optimization problem. Figure

---

[1]This is the case of PNG, BMP, JPEG and TIFF among other common file formats.

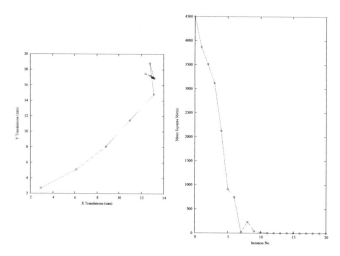

Figure 3.7: The sequence of translations and metric values at each iteration of the optimizer.

3.7 helps to reinforce this notion by showing the trace of translations and values of the image metric at each iteration of the optimizer. It can be seen from the top figure that the step length is reduced progressively as the optimizer gets closer to the metric extrema. The bottom plot clearly shows how the metric value decreases as the optimization advances. The log plot helps to highlight the normal oscillations of the optimizer around the extrema value.

In this section, we used a very simple example to introduce the basic components of a registration process in ITKv4. However, studying this example alone is not enough to start using the itk::ImageRegistrationMethodv4. In order to choose the best registration practice for a specific application, knowledge of other registration method instantiations and their capabilities are required. For example, direct initialization of the output optimizable transform is shown in section 3.6.1. This method can simplify the registration process in many cases. Also, multi-resolution and multistage registration approaches are illustrated in sections 3.7 and 3.8. These examples illustrate the flexibility in the usage of ITKv4 registration method framework that can help to provide faster and more reliable registration processes.

3.3   Features of the Registration Framework

This section presents internals of the registration process in ITKv4. Understanding what actually happens is necessary to have a correct interpretation of the results of a registration filter. It also helps to understand the most common difficulties that users encounter when they start using the ITKv4 registration framework:

- Registration is done in physical coordinates

- The direction of the transform maps from the space of the virtual image to that of the moving image

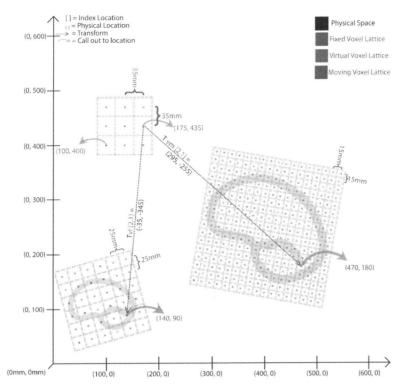

Figure 3.8: Different coordinate systems involved in the image registration process. Note that the transform being optimized is the one mapping from the physical space of the **virtual** image into the physical space of the **moving** image.

These two topics tend to create confusion because they are implemented in different ways in other systems, and community members tend to have different expectations regarding how registration should work in ITKv4. The situation is further complicated by the way most people describe image operations, as if they were manually performed on a continuous picture on a piece of paper.

These concepts are discussed in this section through a general example shown in Figure 3.8.

Recall that ITKv4 does the registration in "physical" space where fixed, moving and virtual images are placed. Also, note that the term of virtual image is deceptive here since it does not refer to any actual image. In fact, the virtual image defines the origin, direction and the spacing of a space lattice that holds the output resampled image of the registration process. The virtual pixel lattice is illustrated in green at the top left side of Figure 3.8.

As shown in this figure, generally there are two transforms involved in the registration process even though only one of them is being optimized. T_{vm} maps points from physical virtual space onto the physical space of the moving image, and in the same way T_{vf} finds homologous points between physical virtual space and the physical space of the fixed image. Note that only T_{vm} is optimized during the registration process. T_{vf} cannot be optimized. The fixed transform usually is an identity transform since the virtual image lattice is commonly defined as the fixed image lattice.

When the registration starts, the algorithm goes through each grid point of the virtual lattice in a raster sweep. At each point the fixed and moving transforms find coordinates of the homologous points in the fixed and moving image physical spaces, and interpolators are used to find the pixel intensities if mapped points are in non-grid positions. These intensity values are passed to a cost function to find the current metric value.

Note the direction of the mapping transforms here. For example, if you consider the T_{vm} transform, confusion often occurs since the transform shifts a virtual lattice point on the **positive** X direction. The visual effect of this mapping, once the moving image is resampled, is equivalent to manually shifting the moving image along the **negative** X direction. In the same way, when the T_{vm} transform applies a **clock-wise** rotation to the virtual space points, the visual effect of this mapping, once the moving image has been resampled, is equivalent to manually rotating the moving image **counter-clock-wise**. The same relationships also occur with the T_{vf} transform between the virtual space and the fixed image space.

This mapping direction is chosen because the moving image is resampled on the grid of the virtual image. In the resampling process, an algorithm iterates through every pixel of the output image and computes the intensity assigned to this pixel by mapping to its location in the moving image.

Instead, if we were to use the transform mapping coordinates from the moving image physical space into the virtual image physical space, then the resampling process would not guarantee that every pixel in the grid of the virtual image would receive one and only one value. In other words, the resampling would result in an image with holes and redundant or overlapping pixel values.

As seen in the previous examples, and as corroborated in the remaining examples in this chapter, the transform computed by the registration framework can be used directly in the resampling filter in order to map the moving image onto the discrete grid of the virtual image.

There are exceptional cases in which the transform desired is actually the inverse transform of the one computed by the ITK registration framework. Only those cases may require invoking the `GetInverse()` method that most transforms offer. Before attempting this, read the examples on resampling illustrated in section 2.9 in order to familiarize yourself with the correct interpretation of the transforms.

Now we come back to the situation illustrated in Figure 3.8. This figure shows the flexibility of the ITKv4 registration framework. We can register two images with different scales, sizes and resolutions. Also, we can create the output warped image with any desired size and resolution.

Nevertheless, note that the spatial transform computed during the registration process does not need to be concerned about a different number of pixels and different pixel sizes between fixed, moving and output images because the conversion from index space to the physical space implicitly takes care of the required scaling factor between the involved images.

One important consequence of this fact is that having the correct image origin, image pixel size, and image direction is fundamental for the success of the registration process in ITK, since we need this information to compute the exact location of each pixel lattice in the physical space; we must make sure that the correct values for the origin, spacing, and direction of all fixed, moving and virtual images are provided.

In this example, the spatial transform computed will **physically** map the brain from the moving image onto the virtual space and minimize its difference with the resampled brain from the fixed image into the virtual space. Fortunately in practice there is no need to resample the fixed image since the virtual image physical domain is often assumed to be the same as physical domain of the fixed image.

3.4 Monitoring Registration

The source code for this section can be found in the file
`ImageRegistration3.cxx`.

Given the numerous parameters involved in tuning a registration method for a particular application, it is not uncommon for a registration process to run for several minutes and still produce a useless result. To avoid this situation it is quite helpful to track the evolution of the registration as it progresses. The following section illustrates the mechanisms provided in ITK for monitoring the activity of the ImageRegistrationMethodv4 class.

Insight implements the *Observer/Command* design pattern [21]. The classes involved in this implementation are the `itk::Object`, `itk::Command` and `itk::EventObject` classes. The Object is the base class of most ITK objects. This class maintains a linked list of pointers to event observers. The role of observers is played by the Command class. Observers register themselves with an Object, declaring that they are interested in receiving notification when a particular event happens. A set of events is represented by the hierarchy of the Event class. Typical events are `Start`, `End`, `Progress` and `Iteration`.

Registration is controlled by an `itk::Optimizer`, which generally executes an iterative process. Most Optimizer classes invoke an `itk::IterationEvent` at the end of each iteration. When an event is invoked by an object, this object goes through its list of registered observers (Commands) and checks whether any one of them has expressed interest in the current event type. Whenever such an observer is found, its corresponding `Execute()` method is invoked. In this context, `Execute()` methods should be considered *callbacks*. As such, some of the common sense rules of callbacks should be respected. For example, `Execute()` methods should not perform heavy computational tasks. They are expected to execute rapidly, for example, printing out a message or updating a value in a GUI.

The following code illustrates a simple way of creating a Observer/Command to monitor a registration process. This new class derives from the Command class and provides a specific implementation of the `Execute()` method. First, the header file of the Command class must be included.

```
#include "itkCommand.h"
```

Our custom command class is called `CommandIterationUpdate`. It derives from the Command class and declares for convenience the types `Self` and `Superclass`. This facilitates the use of standard macros later in the class implementation.

```
class CommandIterationUpdate : public itk::Command
{
public:
  typedef  CommandIterationUpdate   Self;
  typedef  itk::Command             Superclass;
```

The following typedef declares the type of the SmartPointer capable of holding a reference to this object.

```
  typedef itk::SmartPointer<Self>  Pointer;
```

The `itkNewMacro` takes care of defining all the necessary code for the `New()` method. Those with curious minds are invited to see the details of the macro in the file `itkMacro.h` in the `Insight/Code/Common` directory.

```
  itkNewMacro( Self );
```

In order to ensure that the `New()` method is used to instantiate the class (and not the C++ `new` operator), the constructor is declared `protected`.

```
protected:
  CommandIterationUpdate() {};
```

Since this Command object will be observing the optimizer, the following typedefs are useful for converting pointers when the `Execute()` method is invoked. Note the use of `const` on the declaration of `OptimizerPointer`. This is relevant since, in this case, the observer is not intending to modify the optimizer in any way. A `const` interface ensures that all operations invoked on the optimizer are read-only.

```
  typedef itk::RegularStepGradientDescentOptimizerv4<double> OptimizerType;
  typedef const OptimizerType *                              OptimizerPointer;
```

ITK enforces const-correctness. There is hence a distinction between the `Execute()` method that can be invoked from a `const` object and the one that can be invoked from a non-`const` object. In this particular example the non-`const` version simply invoke the `const` version. In a more elaborate situation the implementation of both `Execute()` methods could be quite different. For example, you could imagine a non-`const` interaction in which the observer decides to stop the optimizer in response to a divergent behavior. A similar case could happen when a user is controlling the registration process from a GUI.

```
  void Execute(itk::Object *caller, const itk::EventObject & event)
    {
    Execute( (const itk::Object *)caller, event);
    }
```

Finally we get to the heart of the observer, the `Execute()` method. Two arguments are passed to this method. The first argument is the pointer to the object that invoked the event. The second argument is the event that was invoked.

```
  void Execute(const itk::Object * object, const itk::EventObject & event)
    {
```

Note that the first argument is a pointer to an Object even though the actual object invoking the event is probably a subclass of Object. In our case we know that the actual object is an optimizer. Thus we can perform a `dynamic_cast` to the real type of the object.

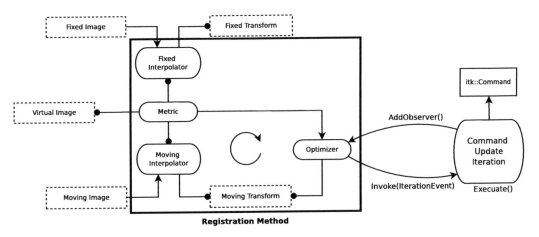

Figure 3.9: Interaction between the Command/Observer and the Registration Method.

```
OptimizerPointer optimizer =
                static_cast< OptimizerPointer >( object );
```

The next step is to verify that the event invoked is actually the one in which we are interested. This is checked using the RTTI[2] support. The CheckEvent() method allows us to compare the actual type of two events. In this case we compare the type of the received event with an IterationEvent. The comparison will return true if event is of type IterationEvent or derives from IterationEvent. If we find that the event is not of the expected type then the Execute() method of this command observer should return without any further action.

```
if( ! itk::IterationEvent().CheckEvent( &event ) )
  {
  return;
  }
```

If the event matches the type we are looking for, we are ready to query data from the optimizer. Here, for example, we get the current number of iterations, the current value of the cost function and the current position on the parameter space. All of these values are printed to the standard output. You could imagine more elaborate actions like updating a GUI or refreshing a visualization pipeline.

```
std::cout << optimizer->GetCurrentIteration() << " = ";
std::cout << optimizer->GetValue() << " : ";
std::cout << optimizer->GetCurrentPosition() << std::endl;
```

This concludes our implementation of a minimal Command class capable of observing our registration method. We can now move on to configuring the registration process.

Once all the registration components are in place we can create one instance of our observer. This is done with the standard New() method and assigned to a SmartPointer.

```
CommandIterationUpdate::Pointer observer = CommandIterationUpdate::New();
```

The newly created command is registered as observer on the optimizer, using the AddObserver()

---

[2]RTTI stands for: Run-Time Type Information

method. Note that the event type is provided as the first argument to this method. In order for the
RTTI mechanism to work correctly, a newly created event of the desired type must be passed as the
first argument. The second argument is simply the smart pointer to the observer. Figure 3.9 illustrates
the interaction between the Command/Observer class and the registration method.

```
optimizer->AddObserver( itk::IterationEvent(), observer );
```

At this point, we are ready to execute the registration. The typical call to Update() will do it. Note
again the use of the try/catch block around the Update() method in case an exception is thrown.

```
try
  {
  registration->Update();
  std::cout << "Optimizer stop condition: "
            << registration->GetOptimizer()->GetStopConditionDescription()
            << std::endl;
  }
catch( itk::ExceptionObject & err )
  {
  std::cout << "ExceptionObject caught !" << std::endl;
  std::cout << err << std::endl;
  return EXIT_FAILURE;
  }
```

The registration process is applied to the following images in Examples/Data:

- BrainProtonDensitySliceBorder20.png

- BrainProtonDensitySliceShifted13x17y.png

It produces the following output.

```
0 = 4499.45 : [2.9286959512455857, 2.7244705953923805]
1 = 3860.84 : [6.135143776902402, 5.115849348610004]
2 = 3508.02 : [8.822660051952475, 8.078492808653918]
3 = 3117.31 : [10.968558473732326, 11.454158663474674]
4 = 2125.43 : [13.105290365964755, 14.835634202454191]
5 = 911.308 : [12.75173580401588, 18.819978461140323]
6 = 741.417 : [13.139053510563274, 16.857840597942413]
7 = 16.8918 : [12.356787624301035, 17.480785285045815]
8 = 233.714 : [12.79212443526829, 17.234854683011704]
9 = 39.8027 : [13.167510875734614, 16.904574468172815]
10 = 16.5731 : [12.938831371165355, 17.005597654570586]
11 = 1.68763 : [13.063495692092735, 16.996443033457986]
12 = 1.79437 : [13.001061362657559, 16.999307384689935]
13 = 0.000762481 : [12.945418587211314, 17.0277701944711]
14 = 1.74802 : [12.974454390534774, 17.01621663980765]
15 = 0.430253 : [13.002439510423766, 17.002309966416835]
16 = 0.00531816 : [12.989877586882951, 16.99301810428082]
17 = 0.0721346 : [12.996759235073881, 16.996716492365685]
```

```
18 = 0.00996773 : [13.00288423694971, 17.00156618393022]
19 = 0.00516378 : [12.99928608126834, 17.000045636412015]
20 = 0.000228075 : [13.00123653240422, 16.999943471681494]
```

You can verify from the code in the Execute() method that the first column is the iteration number, the second column is the metric value and the third and fourth columns are the parameters of the transform, which is a *2D* translation transform in this case. By tracking these values as the registration progresses, you will be able to determine whether the optimizer is advancing in the right direction and whether the step-length is reasonable or not. That will allow you to interrupt the registration process and fine-tune parameters without having to wait until the optimizer stops by itself.

3.5   Multi-Modality Registration

Some of the most challenging cases of image registration arise when images of different modalities are involved. In such cases, metrics based on direct comparison of gray levels are not applicable. It has been extensively shown that metrics based on the evaluation of mutual information are well suited for overcoming the difficulties of multi-modality registration.

The concept of Mutual Information is derived from Information Theory and its application to image registration has been proposed in different forms by different groups [12, 38, 64]; a more detailed review can be found in [24, 47]. The Insight Toolkit currently provides two different implementations of Mutual Information metrics (see section 3.11 for details). The following example illustrates the practical use of one of these metrics.

3.5.1   Mattes Mutual Information

The source code for this section can be found in the file
ImageRegistration4.cxx.

In this example, we will solve a simple multi-modality problem using an implementation of mutual information. This implementation was published by Mattes *et. al* [41].

First, we include the header files of the components used in this example.

```
#include "itkImageRegistrationMethodv4.h"
#include "itkTranslationTransform.h"
#include "itkMattesMutualInformationImageToImageMetricv4.h"
#include "itkRegularStepGradientDescentOptimizerv4.h"
```

In this example the image types and all registration components, except the metric, are declared as in Section 3.2. The Mattes mutual information metric type is instantiated using the image types.

```
typedef itk::MattesMutualInformationImageToImageMetricv4<
    FixedImageType,
    MovingImageType > MetricType;
```

The metric is created using the New() method and then connected to the registration object.

```
MetricType::Pointer metric = MetricType::New();
registration->SetMetric( metric  );
```

The metric requires the user to specify the number of bins used to compute the entropy. In a typical application, 50 histogram bins are sufficient. Note however, that the number of bins may have
dramatic effects on the optimizer's behavior.

```
unsigned int numberOfBins = 24;

metric->SetNumberOfHistogramBins( numberOfBins );
```

To calculate the image gradients, an image gradient calculator based on ImageFunction is
used instead of image gradient filters. Image gradient methods are defined in the superclass
ImageToImageMetricv4.

```
metric->SetUseMovingImageGradientFilter( false );
metric->SetUseFixedImageGradientFilter( false );
```

Notice that in the ITKv4 registration framework, optimizers always try to minimize the cost function,
and the metrics always return a parameter and derivative result that improves the optimization, so
this metric computes the negative mutual information. The optimization parameters are tuned for
this example, so they are not exactly the same as the parameters used in Section 3.2.

```
optimizer->SetLearningRate( 8.00 );
optimizer->SetMinimumStepLength( 0.001 );
optimizer->SetNumberOfIterations( 200 );
optimizer->ReturnBestParametersAndValueOn();
```

Note that large values of the learning rate will make the optimizer unstable. Small values, on the other
hand, may result in the optimizer needing too many iterations in order to walk to the extrema of the
cost function. The easy way of fine tuning this parameter is to start with small values, probably
in the range of $\{1.0, 5.0\}$. Once the other registration parameters have been tuned for producing
convergence, you may want to revisit the learning rate and start increasing its value until you observe
that the optimization becomes unstable. The ideal value for this parameter is the one that results
in a minimum number of iterations while still keeping a stable path on the parametric space of the
optimization. Keep in mind that this parameter is a multiplicative factor applied on the gradient of
the metric. Therefore, its effect on the optimizer step length is proportional to the metric values
themselves. Metrics with large values will require you to use smaller values for the learning rate in
order to maintain a similar optimizer behavior.

Whenever the regular step gradient descent optimizer encounters change in the direction of movement in the parametric space, it reduces the size of the step length. The rate at which the step length
is reduced is controlled by a relaxation factor. The default value of the factor is 0.5. This value,
however may prove to be inadequate for noisy metrics since they tend to induce erratic movements
on the optimizers and therefore result in many directional changes. In those conditions, the optimizer
will rapidly shrink the step length while it is still too far from the location of the extrema in the cost
function. In this example we set the relaxation factor to a number higher than the default in order to
prevent the premature shrinkage of the step length.

```
optimizer->SetRelaxationFactor( 0.8 );
```

Instead of using the whole virtual domain (usually fixed image domain) for the registration, we can use a spatial sampled point set by supplying an arbitrary point list over which

to evaluate the metric. The point list is expected to be in the *fixed* image domain, and the points are transformed into the *virtual* domain internally as needed. The user can define the point set via `SetFixedSampledPointSet()`, and the point set is used by calling `SetUsedFixedSampledPointSet()`.

Also, instead of dealing with the metric directly, the user may define the sampling percentage and sampling strategy for the registration framework at each level. In this case, the registration filter manages the sampling operation over the fixed image space based on the input strategy (REGULAR, RANDOM) and passes the sampled point set to the metric internally.

```
RegistrationType::MetricSamplingStrategyType  samplingStrategy  =
  RegistrationType::RANDOM;
```

The number of spatial samples to be used depends on the content of the image. If the images are smooth and do not contain many details, the number of spatial samples can usually be as low as 1% of the total number of pixels in the fixed image. On the other hand, if the images are detailed, it may be necessary to use a much higher proportion, such as 20% to 50%. Increasing the number of samples improves the smoothness of the metric, and therefore helps when this metric is used in conjunction with optimizers that rely of the continuity of the metric values. The trade-off, of course, is that a larger number of samples results in longer computation times per every evaluation of the metric.

One mechanism for bringing the metric to its limit is to disable the sampling and use all the pixels present in the FixedImageRegion. This can be done with the `SetUseFixedSampledPointSet(false )` method. You may want to try this option only while you are fine tuning all other parameters of your registration. We don't use this method in this current example though.

It has been demonstrated empirically that the number of samples is not a critical parameter for the registration process. When you start fine tuning your own registration process, you should start using high values of number of samples, for example in the range of 20% to 50% of the number of pixels in the fixed image. Once you have succeeded to register your images you can then reduce the number of samples progressively until you find a good compromise on the time it takes to compute one evaluation of the metric. Note that it is not useful to have very fast evaluations of the metric if the noise in their values results in more iterations being required by the optimizer to converge. You must then study the behavior of the metric values as the iterations progress, just as illustrated in section 3.4.

```
double samplingPercentage = 0.20;
```

In ITKv4, a single virtual domain or spatial sample point set is used for the all iterations of the registration process. The use of a single sample set results in a smooth cost function that can improve the functionality of the optimizer.

```
registration->SetMetricSamplingStrategy( samplingStrategy );
registration->SetMetricSamplingPercentage( samplingPercentage );
```

Let's execute this example over two of the images provided in `Examples/Data`:

- `BrainT1SliceBorder20.png`

- `BrainProtonDensitySliceShifted13x17y.png`

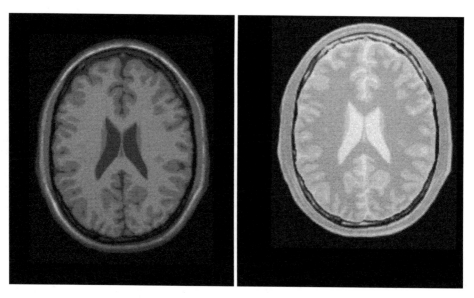

Figure 3.10: A T1 MRI (fixed image) and a proton density MRI (moving image) are provided as input to the registration method.

The second image is the result of intentionally translating the image `BrainProtonDensitySlice-Border20.png` by $(13, 17)$ millimeters. Both images have unit-spacing and are shown in Figure 3.10. The registration process converges after 46 iterations and produces the following results:

```
Translation X = 13.0204
Translation Y = 17.0006
```

These values are a very close match to the true misalignment introduced in the moving image.

The result of resampling the moving image is presented on the left of Figure 3.11. The center and right parts of the figure present a checkerboard composite of the fixed and moving images before and after registration respectively.

Figure 3.12 (upper-left) shows the sequence of translations followed by the optimizer as it searched the parameter space. The upper-right figure presents a closer look at the convergence basin for the last iterations of the optimizer. The bottom of the same figure shows the sequence of metric values computed as the optimizer searched the parameter space.

You must note however that there are a number of non-trivial issues involved in the fine tuning of parameters for the optimization. For example, the number of bins used in the estimation of Mutual Information has a dramatic effect on the performance of the optimizer. In order to illustrate this effect, the same example has been executed using a range of different values for the number of bins, from 10 to 30. If you repeat this experiment, you will notice that depending on the number of bins used, the optimizer's path may get trapped early on in local minima. Figure 3.13 shows the multiple paths that the optimizer took in the parametric space of the transform as a result of different selections

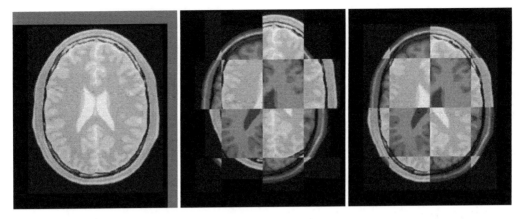

Figure 3.11: The mapped moving image (left) and the composition of fixed and moving images before (center) and after (right) registration with Mattes mutual information.

on the number of bins used by the Mattes Mutual Information metric. Note that many of the paths die in local minima instead of reaching the extrema value on the upper right corner.

Effects such as the one illustrated here highlight how useless is to compare different algorithms based on a non-exhaustive search of their parameter setting. It is quite difficult to be able to claim that a particular selection of parameters represent the best combination for running a particular algorithm. Therefore, when comparing the performance of two or more different algorithms, we are faced with the challenge of proving that none of the algorithms involved in the comparison are being run with a sub-optimal set of parameters.

The plots in Figures 3.12 and 3.13 were generated using Gnuplot[3]. The scripts used for this purpose are available in the ITKSoftwareGuide git repository under the directory

SoftwareGuide/Art.

Data for the plots were taken directly from the output that the Command/Observer in this example prints out to the console. The output was processed with the UNIX editor sed[4] in order to remove commas and brackets that were confusing for Gnuplot's parser. Both the shell script for running sed and for running Gnuplot are available in the directory indicated above. You may find useful to run them in order to verify the results presented here, and to eventually modify them for profiling your own registrations.

Open Science is not just an abstract concept. Open Science is something to be practiced every day with the simple gesture of sharing information with your peers, and by providing all the tools that they need for replicating the results that you are reporting. In Open Science, the only bad results are those that can not be replicated[5]. Science is dead when people blindly trust authorities [6] instead of verifying their statements by performing their own experiments [48, 49].

---

[3]http://www.gnuplot.info/

[4]http://www.gnu.org/software/sed/sed.html

[5]http://science.creativecommons.org/

[6]For example: Reviewers of Scientific Journals.

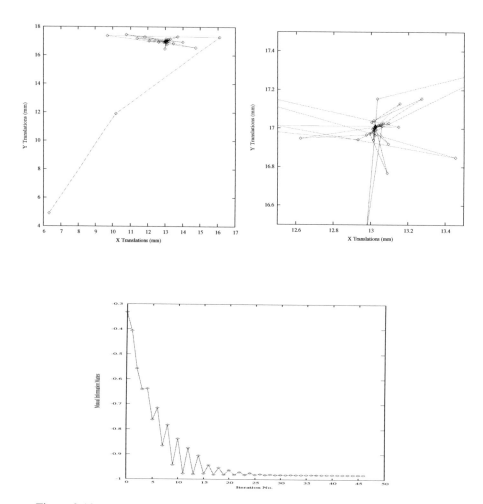

Figure 3.12: Sequence of translations and metric values at each iteration of the optimizer.

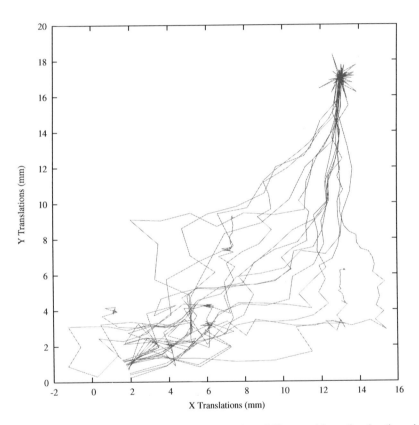

Figure 3.13: Sensitivity of the optimization path to the number of Bins used for estimating the value of Mutual Information with Mattes et al. approach.

3.6   Centered Transforms

The ITK image coordinate origin is typically located in one of the image corners (see the Defining Origin and Spacing section of Book 1 for details). This results in counter-intuitive transform behavior when rotations and scaling are involved. Users tend to assume that rotations and scaling are performed around a fixed point at the center of the image. In order to compensate for this difference in natural interpretation, the concept of *centered* transforms have been introduced into the toolkit. The following sections describe the main characteristics of such transforms.

The introduction of the centered transforms in the Insight Toolkit reflects the dynamic nature of a software library when it evolves in harmony with the requests of the community that it serves. This dynamism has, as everything else in real life, some advantages and some disadvantages. The main advantage is that when a need is identified by the users, it gets implemented in a matter of days or weeks. This capability for rapidly responding to the needs of a community is one of the major strengths of Open Source software. It has the additional safety that if the rest of the community does not wish to adopt a particular change, an isolated user can always implement that change in her local copy of the toolkit, since all the source code of ITK is available in a Apache 2.0 license[7] that does not restrict modification nor distribution of the code, and that does not impose the assimilation demands of viral licenses such as GPL[8].

The main disadvantage of dynamism, is of course, the fact that there is continuous change and a need for perpetual adaptation. The evolution of software occurs at different scales, some changes happen to evolve in localized regions of the code, while from time to time accommodations of a larger scale are needed. The need for continuous changes is addressed in Extreme Programming with the methodology of *Refactoring*. At any given point, the structure of the code may not project the organized and neatly distributed architecture that may have resulted from a monolithic and static design. There are, after all, good reasons why living beings can not have straight angles. What you are about to witness in this section is a clear example of the diversity of species that flourishes when evolution is in action [14].

3.6.1   Rigid Registration in 2D

The source code for this section can be found in the file
ImageRegistration5.cxx.

This example illustrates the use of the itk::CenteredRigid2DTransform for performing rigid registration in *2D*. The example code is for the most part identical to that presented in Section 3.2. The main difference is the use of the CenteredRigid2DTransform here instead of the itk::TranslationTransform.

In addition to the headers included in previous examples, the following header must also be included.

```
#include "itkCenteredRigid2DTransform.h"
```

The transform type is instantiated using the code below. The only template parameter for this class

---

[7]http://www.opensource.org/licenses/Apache-2.0
[8]http://www.gnu.org/copyleft/gpl.html

is the representation type of the space coordinates.

```
typedef itk::CenteredRigid2DTransform< double > TransformType;
```

In the Hello World! example, we used Fixed/Moving initial transforms to initialize the registration configuration. That approach was good to get an intuition of the registration method, specifically when we aim to run a multistage registration process, from which the output of each stage can be used to initialize the next registration stage.

To get a better underestanding of the registration process in such situations, consider an example of 3 stages registration process that is started using an initial moving transform (Γ_{mi}). Multiple stages are handled by linking multiple instantiations of the `itk::ImageRegistrationMethodv4` class. Inside the registration filter of the first stage, the initial moving transform is added to an internal composite transform along with an updatable identity transform (Γ_u). Although the whole composite transform is used for metric evaluation, only the Γ_u is set to be updated by the optimizer at each iteration. The Γ_u will be considered as the output transform of the current stage when the optimization process is converged. This implies that the output of this stage does not include the initialization parameters, so we need to concatenate the output and the initialization transform into a composite transform to be considered as the final transform of the first registration stage.

$$T_1(x) = \Gamma_{mi}(\Gamma_{stage_1}(x))$$

Consider that, as explained in section 3.3, the above transform is a mapping from the vitual domain (i.e. fixed image space, when no fixed initial transform) to the moving image space.

Then, the result transform of the first stage will be used as the initial moving transform for the second stage of the registration process, and this approach goes on until the last stage of the registration process.

At the end of the registration process, the Γ_{mi} and the outputs of each stage can be concatenated into a final composite transform that is considered to be the final output of the whole registration process.

$$I'_m(x) = I_m(\Gamma_{mi}(\Gamma_{stage_1}(\Gamma_{stage_2}(\Gamma_{stage_3}(x)))))$$

The above approach is especially useful if individual stages are characterized by different types of transforms, e.g. when we run a rigid registration process that is proceeded by an affine registration which is completed by a BSpline registration at the end.

In addition to the above method, there is also a direct initialization method in which the initial transform will be optimized directly. In this way the initial transform will be modified during the registration process, so it can be used as the final transform when the registration process is completed. This direct approach is conceptually close to what was happening in ITKv3 registration.

Using this method is very simple and efficient when we have only one level of registration, which is the case in this example. Also, a good application of this initialization method in a multi-stage scenario is when two consequent stages have the same transform types, or at least the initial parameters can easily be inferred from the result of the previous stage, such as when a translation transform is followed by a rigid transform.

The direct initialization approach is shown by the current example in which we try to initialize the parameters of the optimizable transform (Γ_u) directly.

For this purpose, first, the initial transform object is constructed below. This transform will be initialized, and its initial parameters will be used when the registration process starts.

```
TransformType::Pointer initialTransform = TransformType::New();
```

In this example, the input images are taken from readers. The code below updates the readers in order to ensure that the image parameters (size, origin and spacing) are valid when used to initialize the transform. We intend to use the center of the fixed image as the rotation center and then use the vector between the fixed image center and the moving image center as the initial translation to be applied after the rotation.

```
fixedImageReader->Update();
movingImageReader->Update();
```

The center of rotation is computed using the origin, size and spacing of the fixed image.

```
FixedImageType::Pointer fixedImage = fixedImageReader->GetOutput();

const SpacingType fixedSpacing = fixedImage->GetSpacing();
const OriginType  fixedOrigin  = fixedImage->GetOrigin();
const RegionType  fixedRegion  = fixedImage->GetLargestPossibleRegion();
const SizeType    fixedSize    = fixedRegion.GetSize();

TransformType::InputPointType centerFixed;

centerFixed[0] = fixedOrigin[0] + fixedSpacing[0] * fixedSize[0] / 2.0;
centerFixed[1] = fixedOrigin[1] + fixedSpacing[1] * fixedSize[1] / 2.0;
```

The center of the moving image is computed in a similar way.

```
MovingImageType::Pointer movingImage = movingImageReader->GetOutput();

const SpacingType movingSpacing = movingImage->GetSpacing();
const OriginType  movingOrigin  = movingImage->GetOrigin();
const RegionType  movingRegion  = movingImage->GetLargestPossibleRegion();
const SizeType    movingSize    = movingRegion.GetSize();

TransformType::InputPointType centerMoving;

centerMoving[0] = movingOrigin[0] + movingSpacing[0] * movingSize[0] / 2.0;
centerMoving[1] = movingOrigin[1] + movingSpacing[1] * movingSize[1] / 2.0;
```

Then, we initialize the transform by passing the center of the fixed image as the rotation center with the SetCenter() method. Also, the translation is set as the vector relating the center of the moving image to the center of the fixed image. This last vector is passed with the method SetTranslation().

```
initialTransform->SetCenter( centerFixed );
initialTransform->SetTranslation( centerMoving - centerFixed );
```

Let's finally initialize the rotation with a zero angle.

```
initialTransform->SetAngle( 0.0 );
```

Now the current parameters of the initial transform will be set to a registration method, so they can be assigned to the Γ_u directly. Note that you should not confuse the following function with the

`SetMoving(Fixed)InitialTransform()` methods that were used in Hello World! example.

```
registration->SetInitialTransform( initialTransform );
```

Keep in mind that the scale of units in rotation and translation is quite different. For example, here we know that the first element of the parameters array corresponds to the angle that is measured in radians, while the other parameters correspond to the translations and the center point coordinates that are measured in millimeters, so a naive application of gradient descent optimizer will not produce a smooth change of parameters, because a similar change of δ to each parameter will produce a different magnitude of impact on the transform. As the result, we need "parameter scales" to customize the learning rate for each parameter. We can take advantage of the scaling functionality provided by the optimizers.

In this example we use small factors in the scales associated with translations and the coordinates of the rotation center. However, for the transforms with larger parameters sets, it is not intuitive for a user to set the scales. Fortunately, a framework for automated estimation of parameter scales is provided by ITKv4 that will be discussed later in the example of section 3.8.

```
typedef OptimizerType::ScalesType        OptimizerScalesType;
OptimizerScalesType optimizerScales(
   initialTransform->GetNumberOfParameters() );
const double translationScale = 1.0 / 1000.0;

optimizerScales[0] = 1.0;
optimizerScales[1] = translationScale;
optimizerScales[2] = translationScale;
optimizerScales[3] = translationScale;
optimizerScales[4] = translationScale;

optimizer->SetScales( optimizerScales );
```

Next we set the normal parameters of the optimization method. In this case we are using an `itk::RegularStepGradientDescentOptimizerv4`. Below, we define the optimization parameters like the relaxation factor, learning rate (initial step length), minimal step length and number of iterations. These last two act as stopping criteria for the optimization.

```
double initialStepLength = 0.1;

optimizer->SetRelaxationFactor( 0.6 );
optimizer->SetLearningRate( initialStepLength );
optimizer->SetMinimumStepLength( 0.001 );
optimizer->SetNumberOfIterations( 200 );
```

Let's execute this example over two of the images provided in `Examples/Data`:

- `BrainProtonDensitySliceBorder20.png`

- `BrainProtonDensitySliceRotated10.png`

The second image is the result of intentionally rotating the first image by 10 degrees around the geometrical center of the image. Both images have unit-spacing and are shown in Figure 3.14. The registration takes 20 iterations and produces the results:

```
[0.17762, 110.489, 128.487, 0.00925022, 0.00140223]
```

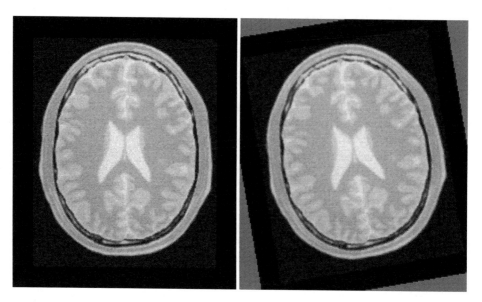

Figure 3.14: Fixed and moving images are provided as input to the registration method using the Centered-Rigid2D transform.

These results are interpreted as

- Angle = 0.17762 radians

- Center = (110.489, 128.487) millimeters

- Translation = (0.00925022, 0.00140223) millimeters

As expected, these values match the misalignment intentionally introduced into the moving image quite well, since 10 degrees is about 0.174532 radians.

Figure 3.15 shows from left to right the resampled moving image after registration, the difference between the fixed and moving images before registration, and the difference between the fixed and resampled moving image after registration. It can be seen from the last difference image that the rotational component has been solved but that a small centering misalignment persists.

Figure 3.16 shows plots of the main output parameters produced from the registration process. This includes the metric values at every iteration, the angle values at every iteration, and the translation components of the transform as the registration progresses.

Let's now consider the case in which rotations and translations are present in the initial registration, as in the following pair of images:

- `BrainProtonDensitySliceBorder20.png`

- `BrainProtonDensitySliceR10X13Y17.png`

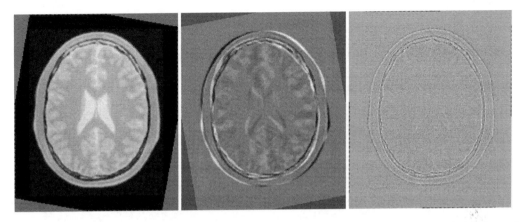

Figure 3.15: Resampled moving image (left). Differences between the fixed and moving images, before (center) and after (right) registration using the CenteredRigid2D transform.

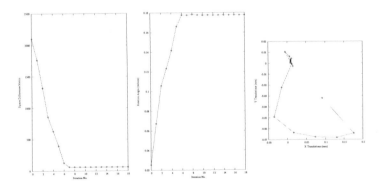

Figure 3.16: Metric values, rotation angle and translations during registration with the CenteredRigid2D transform.

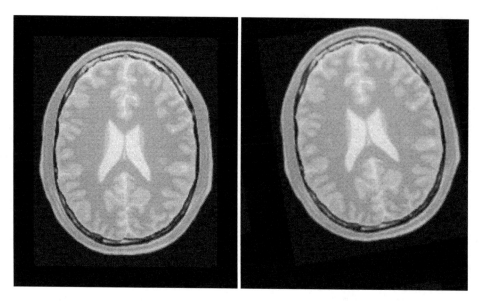

Figure 3.17: Fixed and moving images provided as input to the registration method using the CenteredRigid2D transform.

The second image is the result of intentionally rotating the first image by 10 degrees and then translating it 13*mm* in *X* and 17*mm* in *Y*. Both images have unit-spacing and are shown in Figure 3.17. In order to accelerate convergence it is convenient to use a larger step length as shown here.

```
optimizer->SetMaximumStepLength( 1.3 );
```

The registration now takes 35 iterations and produces the following results:

```
[0.174552, 110.041, 128.917, 12.9339, 15.9149]
```

These parameters are interpreted as

- Angle = 0.17452 radians

- Center = (110.041, 128.917) millimeters

- Translation = (12.9339, 15.9149) millimeters

These values approximately match the initial misalignment intentionally introduced into the moving image, since 10 degrees is about 0.174532 radians. The horizontal translation is well resolved while the vertical translation ends up being off by about one millimeter.

Figure 3.18 shows the output of the registration. The rightmost image of this figure shows the difference between the fixed image and the resampled moving image after registration.

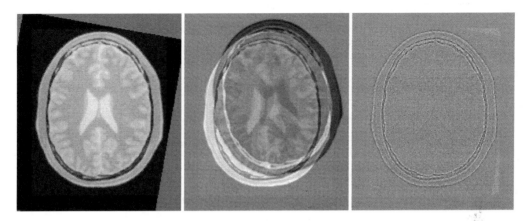

Figure 3.18: Resampled moving image (left). Differences between the fixed and moving images, before (center) and after (right) registration with the CenteredRigid2D transform.

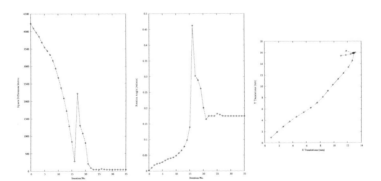

Figure 3.19: Metric values, rotation angle and translations during the registration using the CenteredRigid2D transform on an image with rotation and translation mis-registration.

Figure 3.19 shows plots of the main output registration parameters when the rotation and translations are combined. These results include the metric values at every iteration, the angle values at every iteration, and the translation components of the registration as the registration converges. It can be seen from the smoothness of these plots that a larger step length could have been supported easily by the optimizer. You may want to modify this value in order to get a better idea of how to tune the parameters.

3.6.2   Initializing with Image Moments

The source code for this section can be found in the file
ImageRegistration6.cxx.

This example illustrates the use of the itk::CenteredRigid2DTransform for performing registration. The example code is for the most part identical to the one presented in Section 3.6.1. Even though this current example is done in *2D*, the class itk::CenteredTransformInitializer is quite generic and could be used in other dimensions. The objective of the initializer class is to simplify the computation of the center of rotation and the translation required to initialize certain transforms such as the CenteredRigid2DTransform. The initializer accepts two images and a transform as inputs. The images are considered to be the fixed and moving images of the registration problem, while the transform is the one used to register the images.

The CenteredRigid2DTransform supports two modes of operation. In the first mode, the centers of the images are computed as space coordinates using the image origin, size and spacing. The center of the fixed image is assigned as the rotational center of the transform while the vector going from the fixed image center to the moving image center is passed as the initial translation of the transform. In the second mode, the image centers are not computed geometrically but by using the moments of the intensity gray levels. The center of mass of each image is computed using the helper class itk::ImageMomentsCalculator. The center of mass of the fixed image is passed as the rotational center of the transform while the vector going from the fixed image center of mass to the moving image center of mass is passed as the initial translation of the transform. This second mode of operation is quite convenient when the anatomical structures of interest are not centered in the image. In such cases the alignment of the centers of mass provides a better rough initial registration than the simple use of the geometrical centers. The validity of the initial registration should be questioned when the two images are acquired in different imaging modalities. In those cases, the center of mass of intensities in one modality does not necessarily match the center of mass of intensities in the other imaging modality.

The following are the most relevant headers in this example.

```
#include "itkCenteredRigid2DTransform.h"
#include "itkCenteredTransformInitializer.h"
```

The transform type is instantiated using the code below. The only template parameter of this class is the representation type of the space coordinates.

```
typedef itk::CenteredRigid2DTransform< double > TransformType;
```

Like the previous section, a direct initialization method is used here. The transform object is constructed below. This transform will be initialized, and its initial parameters will be considered as the parameters to be used when the registration process begins.

```
TransformType::Pointer   transform = TransformType::New();
```

The input images are taken from readers. It is not necessary to explicitly call `Update()` on the readers since the CenteredTransformInitializer class will do it as part of its initialization. The following code instantiates the initializer. This class is templated over the fixed and moving images type as well as the transform type. An initializer is then constructed by calling the `New()` method and assigning the result to a `itk::SmartPointer`.

```
typedef itk::CenteredTransformInitializer<
    TransformType,
    FixedImageType,
    MovingImageType > TransformInitializerType;

TransformInitializerType::Pointer initializer =
    TransformInitializerType::New();
```

The initializer is now connected to the transform and to the fixed and moving images.

```
initializer->SetTransform(   transform );
initializer->SetFixedImage(  fixedImageReader->GetOutput() );
initializer->SetMovingImage( movingImageReader->GetOutput() );
```

The use of the geometrical centers is selected by calling `GeometryOn()` while the use of center of mass is selected by calling `MomentsOn()`. Below we select the center of mass mode.

```
initializer->MomentsOn();
```

Finally, the computation of the center and translation is triggered by the `InitializeTransform()` method. The resulting values will be passed directly to the transform.

```
initializer->InitializeTransform();
```

The remaining parameters of the transform are initialized as before.

```
transform->SetAngle( 0.0 );
```

Now the initialized transform object will be set to the registration method, and the starting point of the registration is defined by its initial parameters.

If the `InPlaceOn()` method is called, this initialized transform will be the output transform object or "grafted" to the output. Otherwise, this "InitialTransform" will be deep-copied or "cloned" to the output.

```
registration->SetInitialTransform( transform );
registration->InPlaceOn();
```

Since the registration filter has `InPlace` set, the transform object is grafted to the output and is updated by the registration method.

Let's execute this example over some of the images provided in `Examples/Data`, for example:

- `BrainProtonDensitySliceBorder20.png`

- `BrainProtonDensitySliceR10X13Y17.png`

The second image is the result of intentionally rotating the first image by 10 degrees and shifting it 13mm in X and 17mm in Y. Both images have unit-spacing and are shown in Figure 3.14. The registration takes 22 iterations and produces:

```
[0.17429, 111.172, 131.563, 12.4582, 16.0724]
```

These parameters are interpreted as

- Angle = 0.17429 radians

- Center = $(111.172, 131.563)$ millimeters

- Translation = $(12.4582, 16.0724)$ millimeters

Note that the reported translation is not the translation of $(13, 17)$ that might be expected. The reason is that the five parameters of the CenteredRigid2DTransform are redundant. The actual movement in space is described by only 3 parameters. This means that there are infinite combinations of rotation center and translations that will represent the same actual movement in space. It is more illustrative in this case to take a look at the actual rotation matrix and offset resulting from the five parameters.

```
TransformType::MatrixType matrix = transform->GetMatrix();
TransformType::OffsetType offset = transform->GetOffset();

std::cout << "Matrix = " << std::endl << matrix << std::endl;
std::cout << "Offset = " << std::endl << offset << std::endl;
```

Which produces the following output.

```
Matrix =
0.98485 -0.173409
0.173409 0.98485

Offset =
[36.9567, -1.21272]
```

This output illustrates how counter-intuitive the mix of center of rotation and translations can be. Figure 3.20 will clarify this situation. The figure shows the original image on the left. A rotation of $10°$ around the center of the image is shown in the middle. The same rotation performed around the origin of coordinates is shown on the right. It can be seen here that changing the center of rotation introduces additional translations.

Let's analyze what happens to the center of the image that we just registered. Under the point of view of rotating $10°$ around the center and then applying a translation of $(13mm, 17mm)$. The image has a size of (221×257) pixels and unit spacing. Hence its center has coordinates $(110.5, 128.5)$. Since the rotation is done around this point, the center behaves as the fixed point of the transformation and

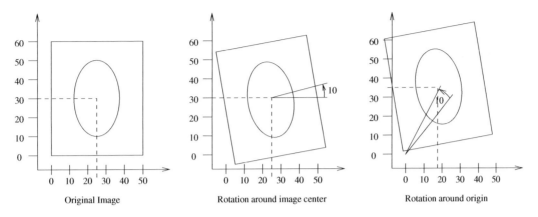

Figure 3.20: Effect of changing the center of rotation.

remains unchanged. Then with the $(13mm, 17mm)$ translation it is mapped to $(123.5, 145.5)$ which becomes its final position.

The matrix and offset that we obtained at the end of the registration indicate that this should be equivalent to a rotation of $10°$ around the origin, followed by a translation of $(36.95, -1.21)$. Let's compute this in detail. First the rotation of the image center by $10°$ around the origin will move the point to $(86.52, 147.97)$. Now, applying a translation of $(36.95, -1.21)$ maps this point to $(123.47, 146.76)$, which is close to the result of our previous computation.

It is unlikely that we could have chosen these translations as the initial guess, since we tend to think about images in a coordinate system whose origin is in the center of the image.

You may be wondering why the actual movement is represented by three parameters when we take the trouble of using five. In particular, why use a 5-dimensional optimizer space instead of a 3-dimensional one? The answer is that by using five parameters we have a much simpler way of initializing the transform with the rotation matrix and offset. Using the minimum three parameters it is not obvious how to determine what the initial rotation and translations should be.

Figure 3.22 shows the output of the registration. The image on the right of this figure shows the differences between the fixed image and the resampled moving image after registration.

Figure 3.23 plots the output parameters of the registration process. It includes the metric values at every iteration, the angle values at every iteration, and the values of the translation components as the registration progresses. Note that this is the complementary translation as used in the transform, not the actual total translation that is used in the transform offset. We could modify the observer to print the total offset instead of printing the array of parameters. Let's call that an exercise for the reader!

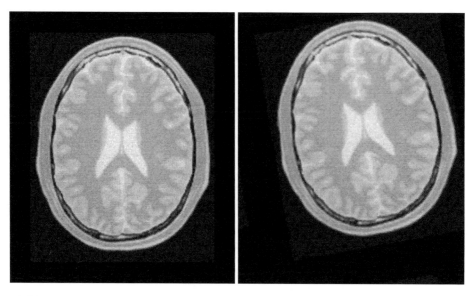

Figure 3.21: Fixed and moving images provided as input to the registration method using CenteredTransformInitializer.

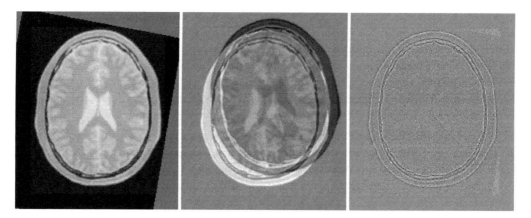

Figure 3.22: Resampled moving image (left). Differences between fixed and moving images, before registration
(center) and after registration (right) with the CenteredTransformInitializer.

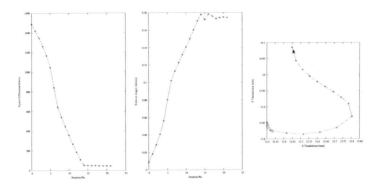

Figure 3.23: Plots of the Metric, rotation angle, center of rotation and translations during the registration using CenteredTransformInitializer.

3.6.3 Similarity Transform in 2D

The source code for this section can be found in the file
ImageRegistration7.cxx.

This example illustrates the use of the itk::CenteredSimilarity2DTransform class for performing registration in 2D. The example code is for the most part identical to the code presented in Section 3.6.2. The main difference is the use of itk::CenteredSimilarity2DTransform here rather than the itk::CenteredRigid2DTransform class.

A similarity transform can be seen as a composition of rotations, translations and uniform (isotropic) scaling. It preserves angles and maps lines into lines. This transform is implemented in the toolkit as deriving from a rigid 2D transform and with a scale parameter added.

When using this transform, attention should be paid to the fact that scaling and translations are not independent. In the same way that rotations can locally be seen as translations, scaling also results in local displacements. Scaling is performed in general with respect to the origin of coordinates. However, we already saw how ambiguous that could be in the case of rotations. For this reason, this transform also allows users to setup a specific center. This center is used both for rotation and scaling.

In addition to the headers included in previous examples, here the following header must be included.

```
#include "itkCenteredSimilarity2DTransform.h"
```

The Transform class is instantiated using the code below. The only template parameter of this class is the representation type of the space coordinates.

```
typedef itk::CenteredSimilarity2DTransform< double > TransformType;
```

As before, the transform object is constructed and initialized before it is passed to the registration filter.

```
TransformType::Pointer  transform = TransformType::New();
```

In this example, we again use the helper class `itk::CenteredTransformInitializer` to compute a reasonable value for the initial center of rotation and the translation.

```
typedef itk::CenteredTransformInitializer<
  TransformType,
  FixedImageType,
  MovingImageType > TransformInitializerType;

TransformInitializerType::Pointer initializer
                               = TransformInitializerType::New();

initializer->SetTransform( transform );

initializer->SetFixedImage( fixedImageReader->GetOutput() );
initializer->SetMovingImage( movingImageReader->GetOutput() );

initializer->MomentsOn();

initializer->InitializeTransform();
```

The remaining parameters of the transform are initialized below.

```
transform->SetScale( initialScale );
transform->SetAngle( initialAngle );
```

Now the initialized transform object will be set to the registration method, and its initial parameters are used to initialize the registration process.

Also, by calling the `InPlaceOn()` method, this initialized transform will be the output transform object or "grafted" to the output of the registration process.

```
registration->SetInitialTransform( transform );
registration->InPlaceOn();
```

Keeping in mind that the scale of units in scaling, rotation and translation are quite different, we take advantage of the scaling functionality provided by the optimizers. We know that the first element of the parameters array corresponds to the scale factor, the second corresponds to the angle, third and fourth are the center of rotation and fifth and sixth are the remaining translation. We use henceforth small factors in the scales associated with translations and the rotation center.

```
typedef OptimizerType::ScalesType         OptimizerScalesType;
OptimizerScalesType optimizerScales( transform->GetNumberOfParameters() );
const double translationScale = 1.0 / 100.0;

optimizerScales[0] = 10.0;
optimizerScales[1] = 1.0;
optimizerScales[2] =  translationScale;
optimizerScales[3] =  translationScale;
optimizerScales[4] =  translationScale;
optimizerScales[5] =  translationScale;

optimizer->SetScales( optimizerScales );
```

We also set the ordinary parameters of the optimization method. In this case we are using a `itk::RegularStepGradientDescentOptimizerv4`. Below we define the optimization parameters, i.e. initial learning rate (step length), minimal step length and number of iterations. The last two act as stopping criteria for the optimization.

```
optimizer->SetLearningRate( steplength );
optimizer->SetMinimumStepLength( 0.0001 );
optimizer->SetNumberOfIterations( 500 );
```

Let's execute this example over some of the images provided in Examples/Data, for example:

- BrainProtonDensitySliceBorder20.png

- BrainProtonDensitySliceR10X13Y17S12.png

The second image is the result of intentionally rotating the first image by 10 degrees, scaling by $1/1.2$ and then translating by $(-13, -17)$. Both images have unit-spacing and are shown in Figure 3.24. The registration takes 60 iterations and produces:

```
[0.833193, -0.174514, 111.025, 131.92, -12.7267, -12.757]
```

That are interpreted as

- Scale factor $= 0.833193$

- Angle $= -0.174514$ radians

- Center $= (111.025, 131.92)$ millimeters

- Translation $= (-12.7267, -12.757)$ millimeters

These values approximate the misalignment intentionally introduced into the moving image. Since 10 degrees is about 0.174532 radians.

Figure 3.25 shows the output of the registration. The right image shows the squared magnitude of pixel differences between the fixed image and the resampled moving image.

Figure 3.26 shows the plots of the main output parameters of the registration process. The metric values at every iteration are shown on the left. The rotation angle and scale factor values are shown in the two center plots while the translation components of the registration are presented in the plot on the right.

3.6.4   Rigid Transform in 3D

The source code for this section can be found in the file ImageRegistration8.cxx.

This example illustrates the use of the itk::VersorRigid3DTransform class for performing registration of two 3D images. The class itk::CenteredTransformInitializer is used to initialize the center and translation of the transform. The case of rigid registration of 3D images is probably one of the most common uses of image registration.

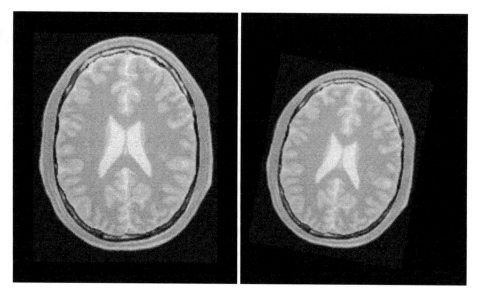

Figure 3.24: Fixed and Moving image provided as input to the registration method using the Similarity2D transform.

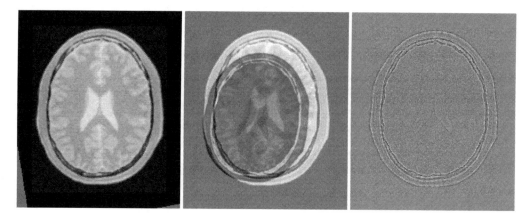

Figure 3.25: Resampled moving image (left). Differences between fixed and moving images, before (center) and after (right) registration with the Similarity2D transform.

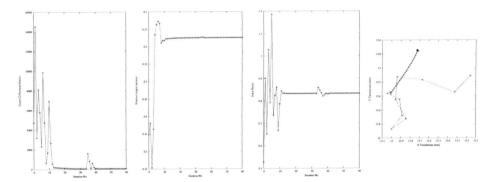

Figure 3.26: Plots of the Metric, rotation angle, scale factor, and translations during the registration using Similarity2D transform.

The following are the most relevant headers of this example.

```
#include "itkVersorRigid3DTransform.h"
#include "itkCenteredTransformInitializer.h"
```

The parameter space of the VersorRigid3DTransform is not a vector space, because addition is not a closed operation in the space of versor components. Hence, we need to use Versor composition operation to update the first three components of the parameter array (rotation parameters), and Vector addition for updating the last three components of the parameters array (translation parameters) [25, 28].

In the previous version of ITK, a special optimizer, itk::VersorRigid3DTransformOptimizer was needed for registration to deal with versor computations. Fortunately in ITKv4, the itk::RegularStepGradientDescentOptimizerv4 can be used for both vector and versor transform optimizations because, in the new registration framework, the task of updating parameters is delegated to the moving transform itself. The UpdateTransformParameters method is implemented in the itk::Transform class as a virtual function, and all the derived transform classes can have their own implementations of this function. Due to this fact, the updating function is re-implemented for versor transforms so it can handle versor composition of the rotation parameters.

```
#include "itkRegularStepGradientDescentOptimizerv4.h"
```

The Transform class is instantiated using the code below. The only template parameter to this class is the representation type of the space coordinates.

```
typedef itk::VersorRigid3DTransform< double > TransformType;
```

The initial transform object is constructed below. This transform will be initialized, and its initial parameters will be used when the registration process starts.

```
TransformType::Pointer  initialTransform = TransformType::New();
```

The input images are taken from readers. It is not necessary here to explicitly call Update() on the readers since the itk::CenteredTransformInitializer will do it as part of its computations. The following code instantiates the type of the initializer. This class is templated over the fixed and moving image types as well as the transform type. An initializer is then constructed by calling the New() method and assigning the result to a smart pointer.

```
typedef itk::CenteredTransformInitializer<
    TransformType,
    FixedImageType,
    MovingImageType >  TransformInitializerType;
TransformInitializerType::Pointer initializer =
    TransformInitializerType::New();
```

The initializer is now connected to the transform and to the fixed and moving images.

```
initializer->SetTransform(   initialTransform );
initializer->SetFixedImage(  fixedImageReader->GetOutput() );
initializer->SetMovingImage( movingImageReader->GetOutput() );
```

The use of the geometrical centers is selected by calling GeometryOn() while the use of center of mass is selected by calling MomentsOn(). Below we select the center of mass mode.

```
initializer->MomentsOn();
```

Finally, the computation of the center and translation is triggered by the InitializeTransform() method. The resulting values will be passed directly to the transform.

```
initializer->InitializeTransform();
```

The rotation part of the transform is initialized using a itk::Versor which is simply a unit quaternion. The VersorType can be obtained from the transform traits. The versor itself defines the type of the vector used to indicate the rotation axis. This trait can be extracted as VectorType. The following lines create a versor object and initialize its parameters by passing a rotation axis and an angle.

```
typedef TransformType::VersorType  VersorType;
typedef VersorType::VectorType     VectorType;
VersorType      rotation;
VectorType      axis;
axis[0] = 0.0;
axis[1] = 0.0;
axis[2] = 1.0;
const double angle = 0;
rotation.Set( axis, angle );
initialTransform->SetRotation( rotation );
```

Now the current initialized transform will be set to the registration method, so its initial parameters can be used to initialize the registration process.

```
registration->SetInitialTransform( initialTransform );
```

Let's execute this example over some of the images available in the following website

http://public.kitware.com/pub/itk/Data/BrainWeb.

Note that the images in this website are compressed in .tgz files. You should download these files and decompress them in your local system. After decompressing and extracting the files you could take a pair of volumes, for example the pair:

- `brainweb1e1a10f20.mha`

- `brainweb1e1a10f20Rot10Tx15.mha`

The second image is the result of intentionally rotating the first image by 10 degrees around the origin and shifting it 15*mm* in *X*.

Also, instead of doing the above steps manually, you can turn on the following flag in your build environment:

`ITK_USE_BRAINWEB_DATA`

Then, the above data will be loaded to your local ITK build directory.

The registration takes 21 iterations and produces:

```
[7.2295e-05, -7.20626e-05, -0.0872168, 2.64765, -17.4626, -0.00147153]
```

That are interpreted as

- Versor = $(7.2295e-05, -7.20626e-05, -0.0872168)$

- Translation = $(2.64765, -17.4626, -0.00147153)$ millimeters

This Versor is equivalent to a rotation of 9.98 degrees around the *Z* axis.

Note that the reported translation is not the translation of $(15.0, 0.0, 0.0)$ that we may be naively expecting. The reason is that the `VersorRigid3DTransform` is applying the rotation around the center found by the `CenteredTransformInitializer` and then adding the translation vector shown above.

It is more illustrative in this case to take a look at the actual rotation matrix and offset resulting from the 6 parameters.

```
TransformType::MatrixType matrix = finalTransform->GetMatrix();
TransformType::OffsetType offset = finalTransform->GetOffset();
std::cout << "Matrix = " << std::endl << matrix << std::endl;
std::cout << "Offset = " << std::endl << offset << std::endl;
```

The output of this print statements is

```
Matrix =
0.984786 0.173769 -0.000156187
-0.173769 0.984786 -0.000131469
0.000130965 0.000156609 1

Offset =
[-15, 0.0189186, -0.0305439]
```

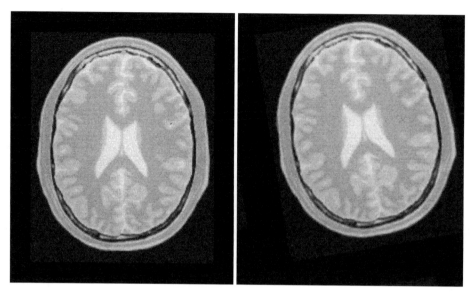

Figure 3.27: Fixed and moving image provided as input to the registration method using CenteredTransformInitializer.

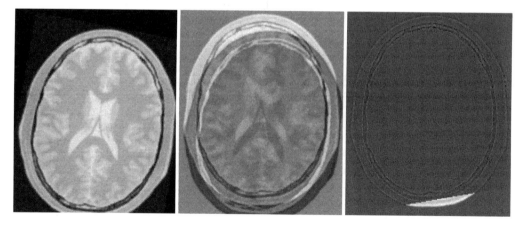

Figure 3.28: Resampled moving image (left). Differences between fixed and moving images, before (center)
and after (right) registration with the CenteredTransformInitializer.

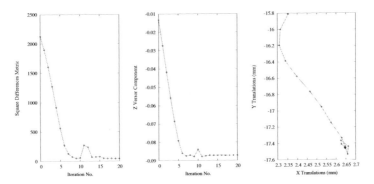

Figure 3.29: Plots of the metric, rotation angle, center of rotation and translations during the registration using CenteredTransformInitializer.

From the rotation matrix it is possible to deduce that the rotation is happening in the X,Y plane and that the angle is on the order of $\arcsin(0.173769)$ which is very close to 10 degrees, as we expected.

Figure 3.28 shows the output of the registration. The center image in this figure shows the differences between the fixed image and the resampled moving image before the registration. The image on the right side presents the difference between the fixed image and the resampled moving image after the registration has been performed. Note that these images are individual slices extracted from the actual volumes. For details, look at the source code of this example, where the ExtractImageFilter is used to extract a slice from the the center of each one of the volumes. One of the main purposes of this example is to illustrate that the toolkit can perform registration on images of any dimension. The only limitations are, as usual, the amount of memory available for the images and the amount of computation time that it will take to complete the optimization process.

Figure 3.29 shows the plots of the main output parameters of the registration process. The Z component of the versor is plotted as an indication of how the rotation progresses. The X,Y translation components of the registration are plotted at every iteration too.

Shell and Gnuplot scripts for generating the diagrams in Figure 3.29 are available in the ITKSoftwareGuide repository under the directory

SoftwareGuide/Art.

You are strongly encouraged to run the example code, since only in this way can you gain first-hand experience with the behavior of the registration process. Once again, this is a simple reflection of the philosophy that we put forward in this book:

If you can not replicate it, then it does not exist!

We have seen enough published papers with pretty pictures, presenting results that in practice are impossible to replicate. That is vanity, not science.

3.6.5   Centered Affine Transform

The source code for this section can be found in the file
`ImageRegistration9.cxx`.

This example illustrates the use of the `itk::AffineTransform` for performing registration in 2*D*.
The example code is, for the most part, identical to that in 3.6.2. The main difference is the use of
the AffineTransform here instead of the `itk::CenteredRigid2DTransform`. We will focus on the
most relevant changes in the current code and skip the basic elements already explained in previous
examples.

Let's start by including the header file of the AffineTransform.

```
#include "itkAffineTransform.h"
```

We then define the types of the images to be registered.

```
const     unsigned int    Dimension = 2;
typedef  float            PixelType;

typedef itk::Image< PixelType, Dimension >  FixedImageType;
typedef itk::Image< PixelType, Dimension >  MovingImageType;
```

The transform type is instantiated using the code below. The template parameters of this class are
the representation type of the space coordinates and the space dimension.

```
typedef itk::AffineTransform< double, Dimension  > TransformType;
```

The transform object is constructed below and is initialized before the registration process starts.

```
TransformType::Pointer  transform = TransformType::New();
```

In this example, we again use the `itk::CenteredTransformInitializer` helper class in order to
compute reasonable values for the initial center of rotation and the translations. The initializer is set
to use the center of mass of each image as the initial correspondence correction.

```
typedef itk::CenteredTransformInitializer<
  TransformType,
  FixedImageType,
  MovingImageType >  TransformInitializerType;
TransformInitializerType::Pointer initializer
  = TransformInitializerType::New();
initializer->SetTransform(   transform );
initializer->SetFixedImage(  fixedImageReader->GetOutput() );
initializer->SetMovingImage( movingImageReader->GetOutput() );
initializer->MomentsOn();
initializer->InitializeTransform();
```

Now we pass the transform object to the registration filter, and it will be grafted to the output transform of the registration filter by updating its parameters during the the registration process.

```
registration->SetInitialTransform( transform );
registration->InPlaceOn();
```

Keeping in mind that the scale of units in scaling, rotation and translation are quite different, we
take advantage of the scaling functionality provided by the optimizers. We know that the first $N \times N$

elements of the parameters array correspond to the rotation matrix factor, and the last N are the components of the translation to be applied after multiplication with the matrix is performed.

```
typedef OptimizerType::ScalesType        OptimizerScalesType;
OptimizerScalesType optimizerScales( transform->GetNumberOfParameters() );

optimizerScales[0] = 1.0;
optimizerScales[1] = 1.0;
optimizerScales[2] = 1.0;
optimizerScales[3] = 1.0;
optimizerScales[4] = translationScale;
optimizerScales[5] = translationScale;

optimizer->SetScales( optimizerScales );
```

We also set the usual parameters of the optimization method. In this case we are using an `itk::RegularStepGradientDescentOptimizerv4` as before. Below, we define the optimization parameters like learning rate (initial step length), minimum step length and number of iterations. These last two act as stopping criteria for the optimization.

```
optimizer->SetLearningRate( steplength );
optimizer->SetMinimumStepLength( 0.0001 );
optimizer->SetNumberOfIterations( maxNumberOfIterations );
```

Finally we trigger the execution of the registration method by calling the `Update()` method. The call is placed in a `try/catch` block in the case any exceptions are thrown.

```
try
  {
  registration->Update();
  std::cout << "Optimizer stop condition: "
            << registration->GetOptimizer()->GetStopConditionDescription()
            << std::endl;
  }
catch( itk::ExceptionObject & err )
  {
  std::cerr << "ExceptionObject caught !" << std::endl;
  std::cerr << err << std::endl;
  return EXIT_FAILURE;
  }
```

Once the optimization converges, we recover the parameters from the registration method. We can also recover the final value of the metric with the `GetValue()` method and the final number of iterations with the `GetCurrentIteration()` method.

```
const TransformType::ParametersType finalParameters =
  registration->GetOutput()->Get()->GetParameters();

const double finalRotationCenterX = transform->GetCenter()[0];
const double finalRotationCenterY = transform->GetCenter()[1];
const double finalTranslationX    = finalParameters[4];
const double finalTranslationY    = finalParameters[5];

const unsigned int numberOfIterations = optimizer->GetCurrentIteration();
const double bestValue = optimizer->GetValue();
```

Let's execute this example over two of the images provided in `Examples/Data`:

- `BrainProtonDensitySliceBorder20.png`

- `BrainProtonDensitySliceR10X13Y17.png`

The second image is the result of intentionally rotating the first image by 10 degrees and then translating by $(-13, -17)$. Both images have unit-spacing and are shown in Figure 3.30. We execute the code using the following parameters: step length=1.0, translation scale= 0.0001 and maximum number of iterations = 300. With these images and parameters the registration takes 92 iterations and produces

```
90   44.0851 [0.9849, -0.1729, 0.1725, 0.9848, 12.4541, 16.0759] AffineAngle: 9.9494
```

These results are interpreted as

- Iterations = 92

- Final Metric = 44.0386

- Center = $(111.204, 131.591)$ millimeters

- Translation = $(12.4542, 16.076)$ millimeters

- Affine scales = $(1.00014, .999732)$

The second component of the matrix values is usually associated with $\sin\theta$. We obtain the rotation through SVD of the affine matrix. The value is 9.9494 degrees, which is approximately the intentional misalignment of 10.0 degrees.

Figure 3.31 shows the output of the registration. The right most image of this figure shows the squared magnitude difference between the fixed image and the resampled moving image.

Figure 3.32 shows the plots of the main output parameters of the registration process. The metric values at every iteration are shown on the left plot. The angle values are shown on the middle plot, while the translation components of the registration are presented on the right plot. Note that the final total offset of the transform is to be computed as a combination of the shift due to rotation plus the explicit translation set on the transform.

3.7   Multi-Resolution Registration

Performing image registration using a multi-resolution approach is widely used to improve speed, accuracy and robustness. The basic idea is that registration is first performed at a coarse scale where the images have fewer pixels. The spatial mapping determined at the coarse level is then used to initialize registration at the next finer scale. This process is repeated until it reaches the finest possible scale. This coarse-to-fine strategy greatly improves the registration success rate and also increases robustness by eliminating local optima at coarser scales. Robustness can be improved even more by smoothing the images at coarse scales.

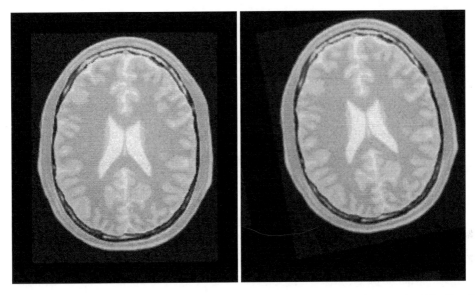

Figure 3.30: Fixed and moving images provided as input to the registration method using the AffineTransform.

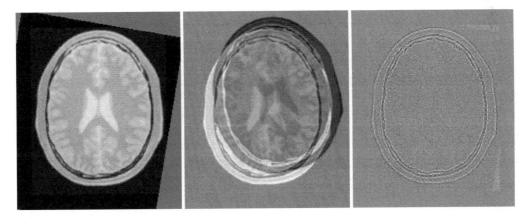

Figure 3.31: The resampled moving image (left), and the difference between the fixed and moving images before (center) and after (right) registration with the AffineTransform transform.

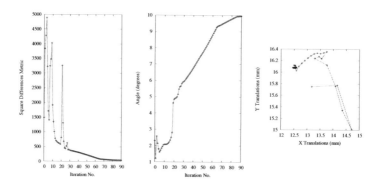

Figure 3.32: Metric values, rotation angle and translations during the registration using the AffineTransform transform.

In all previous examples we ran the registration process at a single resolution. However, the ITKv4 registration framework is structured to provide a multi-resolution registration method. For this purpose we only need to define the number of levels as well as the resolution and smoothness of the input images at each level. The registration filter smoothes and subsamples the images according to user-defined *ShrinkFactor* and *SmoothingSigma* vectors.

We now present the multi-resolution capabilities of the framework by way of an example.

3.7.1   Fundamentals

The source code for this section can be found in the file
`MultiResImageRegistration1.cxx`.

This example illustrates the use of the `itk::ImageRegistrationMethodv4` to solve a simple multi-modality registration problem by a multi-resolution approach. Since ITKv4 registration method is designed based on a multi-resolution structure, a separate set of classes are no longer required to run the registration process of this example.

This a great advantage over the previous versions of ITK, as in ITKv3 we had to use a different filter (`itk::MultiResolutionImageRegistrationMethod`) to run a multi-resolution process. Also, we had to use image pyramids filters (`itk::MultiResolutionPyramidImageFilter`) for creating the sequence of downsampled images. Hence, you can see how ITKv4 framework is more user-friendly in more complex situations.

To begin the example, we include the headers of the registration components we will use.

```
#include "itkImageRegistrationMethodv4.h"
#include "itkTranslationTransform.h"
#include "itkMattesMutualInformationImageToImageMetricv4.h"
#include "itkRegularStepGradientDescentOptimizerv4.h"
```

The ImageRegistrationMethodv4 solves a registration problem in a coarse-to-fine manner as illustrated in Figure 3.33. The registration is first performed at the coarsest level using the images at the

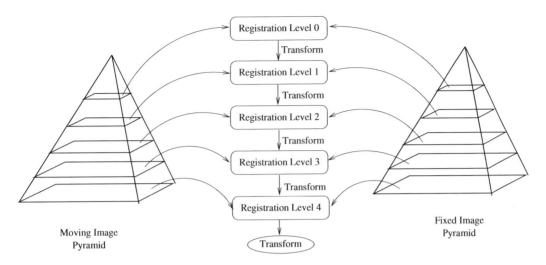

Figure 3.33: Conceptual representation of the multi-resolution registration process.

first level of the fixed and moving image pyramids. The transform parameters determined by the registration are then used to initialize the registration at the next finer level using images from the second level of the pyramids. This process is repeated as we work up to the finest level of image resolution.

In a typical registration scenario, a user will tweak component settings or even swap out components between multi-resolution levels. For example, when optimizing at a coarse resolution, it may be possible to take more aggressive step sizes and have a more relaxed convergence criterion.

Tweaking the components between resolution levels can be done using ITK's implementation of the *Command/Observer* design pattern. Before beginning registration at each resolution level, where ImageRegistrationMethodv4 invokes a `MultiResolutionIterationEvent()`. The registration components can be changed by implementing a `itk::Command` which responds to the event. A brief description of the interaction between events and commands was previously presented in Section 3.4.

We will illustrate this mechanism by changing the parameters of the optimizer between each resolution level by way of a simple interface command. First, we include the header file of the Command class.

```
#include "itkCommand.h"
```

Our new interface command class is called `RegistrationInterfaceCommand`. It derives from Command and is templated over the multi-resolution registration type.

```
template <typename TRegistration>
class RegistrationInterfaceCommand : public itk::Command
{
```

We then define `Self`, `Superclass`, `Pointer`, `New()` and a constructor in a similar fashion to the `CommandIterationUpdate` class in Section 3.4.

```
public:
  typedef  RegistrationInterfaceCommand   Self;
  typedef  itk::Command                   Superclass;
  typedef  itk::SmartPointer<Self>        Pointer;
  itkNewMacro( Self );

protected:
  RegistrationInterfaceCommand() {};
```

For convenience, we declare types useful for converting pointers in the `Execute()` method.

```
public:
  typedef  TRegistration        RegistrationType;
  typedef  RegistrationType * RegistrationPointer;
  typedef  itk::RegularStepGradientDescentOptimizerv4<double>  OptimizerType;
  typedef  OptimizerType * OptimizerPointer;
```

Two arguments are passed to the `Execute()` method: the first is the pointer to the object which invoked the event and the second is the event that was invoked.

```
  void Execute( itk::Object * object, const itk::EventObject & event)
    {
```

First we verify that the event invoked is of the right type, `itk::MultiResolutionIterationEvent()`. If not, we return without any further action.

```
    if( !(itk::MultiResolutionIterationEvent().CheckEvent( &event ) ) )
      {
      return;
      }
```

We then convert the input object pointer to a RegistrationPointer. Note that no error checking is done here to verify the `dynamic_cast` was successful since we know the actual object is a registration method. Then we ask for the optimizer object from the registration method.

```
    RegistrationPointer registration =
      static_cast<RegistrationPointer>( object );
    OptimizerPointer optimizer = static_cast< OptimizerPointer >(
        registration->GetModifiableOptimizer() );
```

If this is the first resolution level we set the learning rate (representing the first step size) and the minimum step length (representing the convergence criterion) to large values. At each subsequent resolution level, we will reduce the minimum step length by a factor of 5 in order to allow the optimizer to focus on progressively smaller regions. The learning rate is set up to the current step length. In this way, when the optimizer is reinitialized at the beginning of the registration process for the next level, the step length will simply start with the last value used for the previous level. This will guarantee the continuity of the path taken by the optimizer through the parameter space.

```
    if ( registration->GetCurrentLevel() == 0 )
      {
      optimizer->SetLearningRate( 16.00 );
      optimizer->SetMinimumStepLength( 2.5 );
      }
    else
      {
      optimizer->SetLearningRate( optimizer->GetCurrentStepLength() );
      optimizer->SetMinimumStepLength(
        optimizer->GetMinimumStepLength() * 0.2 );
      }
```

Another version of the Execute() method accepting a const input object is also required since this method is defined as pure virtual in the base class. This version simply returns without taking any action.

```
  void Execute(const itk::Object * , const itk::EventObject & )
    {
    return;
    }
};
```

The fixed and moving image types are defined as in previous examples. The downsampled images for different resolution levels are created internally by the registration method based on the values provided for *ShrinkFactor* and *SmoothingSigma* vectors.

The types for the registration components are then derived using the fixed and moving image type, as in previous examples.

To set the optimizer parameters, note that *LearningRate* and *MinimumStepLength* are set in the obsever at the begining of each resolution level. The other optimizer parameters are set as follows.

```
  optimizer->SetNumberOfIterations( 200 );
  optimizer->SetRelaxationFactor( 0.5 );
```

We set the number of multi-resolution levels to three and set the corresponding shrink factor and smoothing sigma values for each resolution level. Using smoothing in the subsampled images in low-resolution levels can avoid large fluctuations in the metric function, which prevents the optimizer from becoming trapped in local minima. In this simple example we have no smoothing, and we have used small shrinkings for the first two resolution levels.

```
const unsigned int numberOfLevels = 3;

RegistrationType::ShrinkFactorsArrayType shrinkFactorsPerLevel;
shrinkFactorsPerLevel.SetSize( 3 );
shrinkFactorsPerLevel[0] = 3;
shrinkFactorsPerLevel[1] = 2;
shrinkFactorsPerLevel[2] = 1;

RegistrationType::SmoothingSigmasArrayType smoothingSigmasPerLevel;
smoothingSigmasPerLevel.SetSize( 3 );
smoothingSigmasPerLevel[0] = 0;
smoothingSigmasPerLevel[1] = 0;
smoothingSigmasPerLevel[2] = 0;

registration->SetNumberOfLevels ( numberOfLevels );
registration->SetShrinkFactorsPerLevel( shrinkFactorsPerLevel );
registration->SetSmoothingSigmasPerLevel( smoothingSigmasPerLevel );
```

Once all the registration components are in place we can create an instance of our interface command and connect it to the registration object using the `AddObserver()` method.

```
typedef RegistrationInterfaceCommand<RegistrationType> CommandType;
CommandType::Pointer command = CommandType::New();

registration->AddObserver( itk::MultiResolutionIterationEvent(), command );
```

Then we trigger the registration process by calling `Update()`.

Let's execute this example using the following images

- BrainT1SliceBorder20.png

- BrainProtonDensitySliceShifted13x17y.png

The output produced by the execution of the method is

```
0    -0.316956    [11.4200, 11.2063]
1    -0.562048    [18.2938, 25.6545]
2    -0.407696    [11.3643, 21.6569]
3    -0.5702      [13.7244, 18.4274]
4    -0.803252    [11.1634, 15.3547]


0    -0.697586    [12.8778, 16.3846]
1    -0.901984    [13.1794, 18.3617]
2    -0.827423    [13.0545, 17.3695]
3    -0.92754     [12.8528, 16.3901]
4    -0.902671    [12.9426, 16.8819]
5    -0.941212    [13.1402, 17.3413]


0    -0.922239    [13.0364, 17.1138]
1    -0.930203    [12.9463, 16.8806]
```

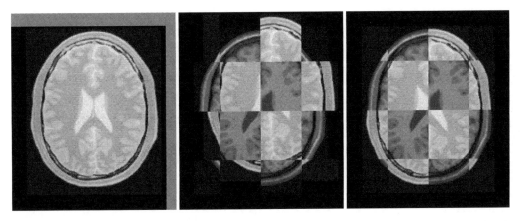

Figure 3.34: Mapped moving image (left) and composition of fixed and moving images before (center) and after (right) registration.

```
2   -0.930959    [13.0191, 16.9822]


Result =
Translation X = 13.0192
Translation Y = 16.9823
Iterations    = 4
Metric value  = -0.929237
```

These values are a close match to the true misalignment of $(13, 17)$ introduced in the moving image.

The result of resampling the moving image is presented in the left image of Figure 3.34. The center and right images of the figure depict a checkerboard composite of the fixed and moving images before and after registration.

Figure 3.35 (left) shows the sequence of translations followed by the optimizer as it searched the parameter space. The right side of the same figure shows the sequence of metric values computed as the optimizer searched the parameter space. From the trace, we can see that with the more aggressive optimization parameters we get quite close to the optimal value within 5 iterations with the remaining iterations just doing fine adjustments. It is interesting to compare these results with those of the single resolution example in Section 3.5.1, where 46 iterations were required as more conservative optimization parameters had to be used.

3.8 Multi-Stage Registration

In section 3.7 you noticed how to tweak component settings between multi-resolution levels and saw how it can benefit the registration process. That is, the matching metric gets close to the optimal value before final parameter adjustments in full resolution. This approach saves large amounts of

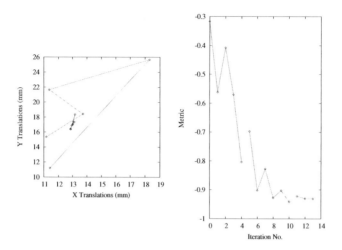

Figure 3.35: Sequence of translations and metric values at each iteration of the optimizer.

time in most practical cases, since fewer iterations are required at the full resolution level. This is helpful in cases like a deformable registration process on a large dataset, e.g. a high-resolution 3D image.

Another possible scheme is to apply a simple rigid transform for the initial coarse registration, then upgrade to an affine transform at the finer level. Finally, proceed to a deformable transform at the last level when we are close enough to the optimal value.

Fortunately, `itk::ImageRegistrationMethodv4` allows for multistage registration whereby each stage is characterized by possibly different transforms and different image metrics. As in the above situation, you may want to perform a linear registration followed by a deformable registration with both stages performed across multiple resolutions.

Multiple stages are handled by linking multiple instantiations of this class. An optional composite transform can be used as a container to concatenate the output transforms of multiple stages.

We now present the multistage capabilities of the framework by way of an example.

3.8.1 Fundamentals

The source code for this section can be found in the file
`MultiStageImageRegistration1.cxx`.

This example illustrates the use of more complex components of the registration framework. In particular, it introduces a multistage, multi-resolution approach to run a multi-modal registration process using two linear `itk::TranslationTransform` and `itk::AffineTransform`. Also, it shows the use of *Scale Estimators* for fine-tuning the scale parameters of the optimizer when an Affine transform is used. The `itk::RegistrationParameterScalesFromPhysicalShift` filter is used for automatic estimation of the parameters scales.

To begin the example, we include the headers of the registration components we will use.

```
#include "itkImageRegistrationMethodv4.h"

#include "itkMattesMutualInformationImageToImageMetricv4.h"

#include "itkRegularStepGradientDescentOptimizerv4.h"
#include "itkConjugateGradientLineSearchOptimizerv4.h"

#include "itkTranslationTransform.h"
#include "itkAffineTransform.h"
#include "itkCompositeTransform.h"
```

In a multistage scenario, each stage needs an individual instantiation of the itk::ImageRegistrationMethodv4, so each stage can possibly have a different transform, a different optimizer, and a different image metric and can be performed in multiple levels. The configuration of the registration method at each stage closely follows the procedure in the previous section.

In early stages we can use simpler transforms and more aggressive optimization parameters to take big steps toward the optimal value. Then, at the final stage we can have a more complex transform to do fine adjustments of the final parameters.

A possible scheme is to use a simple translation transform for initial coarse registration levels and upgrade to an affine transform at the finer level. Since we have two different types of transforms, we can use a multistage registration approach as shown in the current example.

First we need to configure the registration components of the initial stage. The instantiation of the transform type requires only the dimension of the space and the type used for representing space coordinates.

```
typedef itk::TranslationTransform< double, Dimension >    TTransformType;
```

The types of other registration components are defined here. itk::RegularStepGradientDescentOptimizerv4 is used as the optimizer of the first stage. Also, we use itk::MattesMutualInformationImageToImageMetricv4 as the metric since it is fitted for a multi-modal registration.

```
typedef itk::RegularStepGradientDescentOptimizerv4< double > TOptimizerType;
typedef itk::MattesMutualInformationImageToImageMetricv4<
   FixedImageType,
   MovingImageType > MetricType;
typedef itk::ImageRegistrationMethodv4<
   FixedImageType,
   MovingImageType,
   TTransformType >  TRegistrationType;
```

Then, all the components are instantiated using their New() method and connected to the registration object as in previous examples.

The output transform of the registration process will be constructed internally in the registration filter since the related *TransformType* is already passed to the registration method as a template parameter. However, we should provide an initial moving transform for the registration method if needed.

```
TTransformType::Pointer    movingInitTx  = TTransformType::New();
```

After setting the initial parameters, the initial transform can be passed to the registration filter by
SetMovingInitialTransform() method.

```
transRegistration->SetMovingInitialTransform( movingInitTx );
```

We can use a itk::CompositeTransform to stack all the output transforms resulted from multiple
stages. This composite transform should also hold the moving initial transform (if it exists) because
as explained in section 3.6.1, the output of each registration stage does not include the input initial
transform to that stage.

```
typedef itk::CompositeTransform< double,
                                 Dimension >  CompositeTransformType;
CompositeTransformType::Pointer  compositeTransform  =
                                 CompositeTransformType::New();
compositeTransform->AddTransform( movingInitTx );
```

In the case of this simple example, the first stage is run only in one level of registration at a coarse
resolution.

```
const unsigned int numberOfLevels1 = 1;

TRegistrationType::ShrinkFactorsArrayType shrinkFactorsPerLevel1;
shrinkFactorsPerLevel1.SetSize( numberOfLevels1 );
shrinkFactorsPerLevel1[0] = 3;

TRegistrationType::SmoothingSigmasArrayType smoothingSigmasPerLevel1;
smoothingSigmasPerLevel1.SetSize( numberOfLevels1 );
smoothingSigmasPerLevel1[0] = 2;

transRegistration->SetNumberOfLevels ( numberOfLevels1 );
transRegistration->SetShrinkFactorsPerLevel( shrinkFactorsPerLevel1 );
transRegistration->SetSmoothingSigmasPerLevel( smoothingSigmasPerLevel1 );
```

Also, for this initial stage we can use a more agressive parameter set for the optimizer by taking a
big step size and relaxing stop criteria.

```
transOptimizer->SetLearningRate( 16 );
transOptimizer->SetMinimumStepLength( 1.5 );
```

Once all the registration components are in place, we trigger the registration process by calling
Update() and add the result output transform to the final composite transform, so this composite
transform can be used to initialize the next registration stage.

```
try
  {
  transRegistration->Update();
  std::cout << "Optimizer stop condition: "
    << transRegistration->GetOptimizer()->GetStopConditionDescription()
    << std::endl;
  }
catch( itk::ExceptionObject & err )
  {
  std::cout << "ExceptionObject caught !" << std::endl;
  std::cout << err << std::endl;
  return EXIT_FAILURE;
  }

compositeTransform->AddTransform(
  transRegistration->GetModifiableTransform() );
```

Now we can upgrade to an Affine transform as the second stage of registration process. The Affine-Transform is a linear transformation that maps lines into lines. It can be used to represent translations, rotations, anisotropic scaling, shearing or any combination of them. Details about the affine transform can be seen in Section 3.9.16. The instantiation of the transform type requires only the dimension of the space and the type used for representing space coordinates.

```
typedef itk::AffineTransform< double, Dimension >       ATransformType;
```

We also use a different optimizer in configuration of the second stage while the metric is kept the same as before.

```
typedef itk::ConjugateGradientLineSearchOptimizerv4Template<
   double >          AOptimizerType;
typedef itk::ImageRegistrationMethodv4<
  FixedImageType,
  MovingImageType,
  ATransformType > ARegistrationType;
```

Again all the components are instantiated using their New() method and connected to the registration object like in previous stages.

The current stage can be initialized using the initial transform of the registration and the result transform of the previous stage, so that both are concatenated into the composite transform.

```
affineRegistration->SetMovingInitialTransform( compositeTransform );
```

In Section 3.6.2 we showed the importance of center of rotation in the registration process. In Affine transforms, the center of rotation is defined by the fixed parameters set, which are set by default to [0, 0]. However, consider a situation where the origin of the virtual space, in which the registration is run, is far away from the zero origin. In such cases, leaving the center of rotation as the default value can make the optimization process unstable. Therefore, we are always interested to set the center of rotation to the center of virtual space which is usually the fixed image space.

Note that either center of gravity or geometrical center can be used as the center of rotation. In this example center of rotation is set to the geometrical center of the fixed image. We could also use itk::ImageMomentsCalculator filter to compute the center of mass.

Based on the above discussion, the user must set the fixed parameters of the registration transform outside of the registraton method, so first we instantiate an object of the output transform type.

```
ATransformType::Pointer affineTx = ATransformType::New();
```

Then, we compute the physical center of the fixed image and set that as the center of the output
Affine transform.

```
typedef FixedImageType::SpacingType      SpacingType;
typedef FixedImageType::PointType        OriginType;
typedef FixedImageType::RegionType       RegionType;
typedef FixedImageType::SizeType         SizeType;

FixedImageType::Pointer fixedImage = fixedImageReader->GetOutput();

const SpacingType fixedSpacing = fixedImage->GetSpacing();
const OriginType  fixedOrigin  = fixedImage->GetOrigin();
const RegionType  fixedRegion  = fixedImage->GetLargestPossibleRegion();
const SizeType    fixedSize    = fixedRegion.GetSize();

ATransformType::InputPointType centerFixed;
centerFixed[0] =
   fixedOrigin[0] + fixedSpacing[0] * fixedSize[0] / 2.0;
centerFixed[1] =
   fixedOrigin[1] + fixedSpacing[1] * fixedSize[1] / 2.0;

const unsigned int numberOfFixedParameters =
   affineTx->GetFixedParameters().Size();
ATransformType::ParametersType fixedParameters( numberOfFixedParameters );
for (unsigned int i = 0; i < numberOfFixedParameters; ++i)
   {
   fixedParameters[i] = centerFixed[i];
   }
affineTx->SetFixedParameters( fixedParameters );
```

Then, the initialized output transform should be connected to the registration object by using
SetInitialTransform() method.

It is important to distinguish between the SetInitialTransform() and
SetMovingInitialTransform() that was used to initialize the registration stage based on
the results of the previous stages. You can assume that the first one is used for direct manipulation
of the optimizable transform in current registration process.

```
affineRegistration->SetInitialTransform( affineTx  );
```

The set of optimizable parameters in the Affine transform have different dynamic ranges. Typically
the parameters associated with the matrix have values around $[-1:1]$, although they are not restricted
to this interval. Parameters associated with translations, on the other hand, tend to have much higher
values, typically on the order of 10.0 to 100.0. This difference in dynamic range negatively affects
the performance of gradient descent optimizers. ITK provides some mechanisms to compensate for
such differences in values among the parameters when they are passed to the optimizer.

The first mechanism consists of providing an array of scale factors to the optimizer. These factors
re-normalize the gradient components before they are used to compute the step of the optimizer at the
current iteration. These scales are estimated by the user intuitively as shown in previous examples
of this chapter. In our particular case, a common choice for the scale parameters is to set all those

associated with the matrix coefficients to 1.0, that is, the first $N \times N$ factors. Then, we set the remaining scale factors to a small value.

Here the affine transform is represented by the matrix **M** and the vector **T**. The transformation of a point **P** into **P′** is expressed as

$$\begin{bmatrix} P'_x \\ P'_y \end{bmatrix} = \begin{bmatrix} M_{11} & M_{12} \\ M_{21} & M_{22} \end{bmatrix} \cdot \begin{bmatrix} P_x \\ P_y \end{bmatrix} + \begin{bmatrix} T_x \\ T_y \end{bmatrix} \tag{3.1}$$

Based on the above discussion, we need much smaller scales for translation parameters of vector **T** (T_x, T_y) compared to the parameters of matrix **M** $(M_{11}, M_{12}, M_{21}, M_{22})$. However, it is not easy to have an intuitive estimation of all parameter scales when we have to deal with a large paramter space.

Fortunately, ITKv4 provides a framework for automated parameter scaling. `itk::RegistrationParameterScalesEstimator` vastly reduces the difficulty of tuning parameters for different transform/metric combinations. Parameter scales are estimated by analyzing the result of a small parameter update on the change in the magnitude of physical space deformation induced by the transformation.

The impact from a unit change of a parameter may be defined in multiple ways, such as the maximum shift of voxels in index or physical space, or the average norm of transform Jacobian. Filters `itk::RegistrationParameterScalesFromPhysicalShift` and `itk::RegistrationParameterScalesFromIndexShift` use the first definition to estimate the scales, while the `itk::RegistrationParameterScalesFromJacobian` filter estimates scales based on the later definition. In all methods, the goal is to rescale the transform parameters such that a unit change of each *scaled parameter* will have the same impact on deformation.

In this example the first filter is chosen to estimate the parameter scales. The scales estimator will then be passed to optimizer.

```
typedef itk::RegistrationParameterScalesFromPhysicalShift<
  MetricType> ScalesEstimatorType;
ScalesEstimatorType::Pointer scalesEstimator =
  ScalesEstimatorType::New();
scalesEstimator->SetMetric( affineMetric );
scalesEstimator->SetTransformForward( true );

affineOptimizer->SetScalesEstimator( scalesEstimator );
```

The step length has to be proportional to the expected values of the parameters in the search space. Since the expected values of the matrix coefficients are around 1.0, the initial step of the optimization should be a small number compared to 1.0. As a guideline, it is useful to think of the matrix coefficients as combinations of $cos(\theta)$ and $sin(\theta)$. This leads to use values close to the expected rotation measured in radians. For example, a rotation of 1.0 degree is about 0.017 radians.

However, we need not worry about the above considerations. Thanks to the *ScalesEstimator*, the initial step size can also be estimated automatically, either at each iteration or only at the first iteration. In this example we choose to estimate learning rate once at the begining of the registration process.

```
affineOptimizer->SetDoEstimateLearningRateOnce( true );
affineOptimizer->SetDoEstimateLearningRateAtEachIteration( false );
```

At the second stage, we run two levels of registration, where the second level is run in full resolution in which we do the final adjustments of the output parameters.

```
const unsigned int numberOfLevels2 = 2;

ARegistrationType::ShrinkFactorsArrayType shrinkFactorsPerLevel2;
shrinkFactorsPerLevel2.SetSize( numberOfLevels2 );
shrinkFactorsPerLevel2[0] = 2;
shrinkFactorsPerLevel2[1] = 1;

ARegistrationType::SmoothingSigmasArrayType smoothingSigmasPerLevel2;
smoothingSigmasPerLevel2.SetSize( numberOfLevels2 );
smoothingSigmasPerLevel2[0] = 1;
smoothingSigmasPerLevel2[1] = 0;

affineRegistration->SetNumberOfLevels ( numberOfLevels2 );
affineRegistration->SetShrinkFactorsPerLevel( shrinkFactorsPerLevel2 );
affineRegistration->SetSmoothingSigmasPerLevel( smoothingSigmasPerLevel2 );
```

Finally we trigger the registration process by calling `Update()` and add the output transform of the last stage to the composite transform. This composite transform will be considered as the final transform of this multistage registration process and will be used by the resampler to resample the moving image in to the virtual domain space (fixed image space if there is no fixed initial transform).

```
try
  {
  affineRegistration->Update();
  std::cout << "Optimizer stop condition: "
    << affineRegistration->GetOptimizer()->GetStopConditionDescription()
    << std::endl;
  }
catch( itk::ExceptionObject & err )
  {
  std::cout << "ExceptionObject caught !" << std::endl;
  std::cout << err << std::endl;
  return EXIT_FAILURE;
  }

compositeTransform->AddTransform(
  affineRegistration->GetModifiableTransform() );
```

Let's execute this example using the following multi-modality images:

- BrainT1SliceBorder20.png

- BrainProtonDensitySliceR10X13Y17.png

The second image is the result of intentionally rotating the first image by 10 degrees and then translating by $(-13, -17)$. Both images have unit-spacing and are shown in Figure 3.36.

The registration converges after 5 iterations in the translation stage. Also, in the second stage, the registration converges after 46 iterations in the first level, and 6 iterations in the second level. The final results when printed as an array of parameters are:

```
Initial parameters of the registration process:
```

```
[3, 5]
```

```
Translation parameters after first registration stage:
[9.0346, 10.8303]
```

```
Affine parameters after second registration stage:
[0.9864, -0.1733, 0.1738, 0.9863, 0.9693, 0.1482]
```

As it can be seen, the translation parameters after the first stage compensate most of the offset between the fixed and moving images. When the images are close to each other, the affine registration is run for the rotation and the final match. By reordering the Affine array of parameters as coefficients of matrix $\mathbf{M}$ and vector $\mathbf{T}$ they can now be seen as

$$M = \begin{bmatrix} 0.9864 & -0.1733 \\ 0.1738 & 0.9863 \end{bmatrix} \text{ and } T = \begin{bmatrix} 0.9693 \\ 0.1482 \end{bmatrix} \tag{3.2}$$

In this form, it is easier to interpret the effect of the transform. The matrix $\mathbf{M}$ is responsible for scaling, rotation and shearing while $\mathbf{T}$ is responsible for translations.

The second component of the matrix values is usually associated with $\sin\theta$. We obtain the rotation through SVD of the affine matrix. The value is 9.975 degrees, which is approximately the intentional misalignment of 10.0 degrees.

Also, let's compute the total translation values resulting from initial transform, translation transform, and the Affine transform together.

In X direction:
$$3 + 9.0346 + 0.9693 = 13.0036 \tag{3.3}$$

In Y direction:
$$5 + 10.8303 + 0.1482 = 15.9785 \tag{3.4}$$

It can be seen that the translation values closely match the true misalignment introduced in the moving image.

It is important to note that once the images are registered at a sub-pixel level, any further improvement of the registration relies heavily on the quality of the interpolator. It may then be reasonable to use a coarse and fast interpolator in the lower resolution levels and switch to a high-quality but slow interpolator in the final resolution level. However, in this example we used a linear interpolator for all stages and different registration levels since it is so fast.

The result of resampling the moving image is presented in the left image of Figure 3.37. The center and right images of the figure depict a checkerboard composite of the fixed and moving images before and after registration.

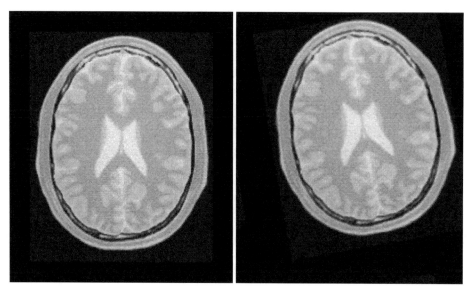

Figure 3.36: Fixed and moving images provided as input to the registration method using the AffineTransform.

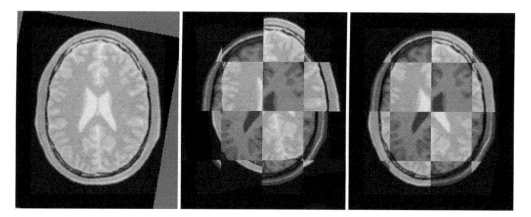

Figure 3.37: Mapped moving image (left) and composition of fixed and moving images before (center) and after (right) registration.

3.8.2   Cascaded Multistage Registration

The source code for this section can be found in the file
`MultiStageImageRegistration2.cxx`.

This examples shows how different stages can be cascaded together directly in a multistage registration process. The example code is, for the most part, identical to the previous multistage example. The main difference is that no initial transform is used, and the output of the first stage is directly linked to the second stage, and the whole registration process is triggered only once by calling `Update()` after the last stage stage.

We will focus on the most relevent changes in current code and skip all the similar parts already explained in the previous example.

Let's start by defining different types of the first stage.

```
typedef itk::TranslationTransform< double, Dimension >    TTransformType;
typedef itk::RegularStepGradientDescentOptimizerv4<double> TOptimizerType;
typedef itk::MattesMutualInformationImageToImageMetricv4<
   FixedImageType,
   MovingImageType >  MetricType;
typedef itk::ImageRegistrationMethodv4<
   FixedImageType,
   MovingImageType >  TRegistrationType;
```

Type definitions are the same as previous example with an important subtle change: the transform type is not passed to the registration method as a template parameter anymore. In this case, the registration filter will consider the transform base class `itk::Transform` as the type of its output transform.

Instead of passing the transform type, we create an explicit instantiation of the transform object outside of the registration filter, and connect that to the registration object using the `SetInitialTransform()` method. Also, by calling `InPlaceOn()` method, this transform object will be the output transform of the registration filter or will be grafted to the output.

```
TTransformType::Pointer translationTx = TTransformType::New();

transRegistration->SetInitialTransform( translationTx );
transRegistration->InPlaceOn();
```

Also, there is no initial transform defined for this example.

As in the previous example, the first stage is run using only one level of registration at a coarse resolution level. However, notice that we do not need to update the translation registration filter at this step since the output of this stage will be directly connected to the initial input of the next stage. Due to ITK's pipeline structure, when we call the `Update()` at the last stage, the first stage will be updated as well.

Now we upgrade to an Affine transform as the second stage of registration process, and as before, we initially define and instantiate different components of the current registration stage. We have used a new optimizer but the same metric in new configurations.

```
typedef itk::AffineTransform< double, Dimension > ATransformType;
typedef itk::ConjugateGradientLineSearchOptimizerv4Template<
  double > AOptimizerType;
typedef itk::ImageRegistrationMethodv4<
  FixedImageType,
  MovingImageType > ARegistrationType;
```

Again notice that *TransformType* is not passed to the type definition of the registration filter. It is important because when the registration filter considers transform base class `itk::Transform` as the type of its output transform, it prevents the type mismatch when the two stages are cascaded to each other.

Then, all components are instantiated using their `New()` method and connected to the registration object among the transform type. Despite the previous example, here we use the fixed image's center of mass to initialize the fixed parameters of the Affine transform. `itk::ImageMomentsCalculator` filter is used for this purpose.

```
typedef itk::ImageMomentsCalculator<
  FixedImageType > FixedImageCalculatorType;

FixedImageCalculatorType::Pointer fixedCalculator =
  FixedImageCalculatorType::New();
fixedCalculator->SetImage( fixedImage );
fixedCalculator->Compute();

FixedImageCalculatorType::VectorType fixedCenter =
  fixedCalculator->GetCenterOfGravity();
```

Then, we initialize the fixed parameters (center of rotation) in the Affine transform and connect that to the registration object.

```
ATransformType::Pointer    affineTx  = ATransformType::New();

const unsigned int numberOfFixedParameters =
                                affineTx->GetFixedParameters().Size();
ATransformType::ParametersType fixedParameters( numberOfFixedParameters );
for (unsigned int i = 0; i < numberOfFixedParameters; ++i)
    {
    fixedParameters[i] = fixedCenter[i];
    }
affineTx->SetFixedParameters( fixedParameters );

affineRegistration->SetInitialTransform( affineTx );
affineRegistration->InPlaceOn();
```

Now, the output of the first stage is wrapped through a `itk::DataObjectDecorator` and is passed to the input of the second stage as the moving initial transform via `SetMovingInitialTransformInput()` method. Note that this API has an "Input" word attached to the name of another initialization method `SetMovingInitialTransform()` that already has been used in previous example. This extension means that the following API expects a data object decorator type.

```
affineRegistration->SetMovingInitialTransformInput(
  transRegistration->GetTransformOutput() );
```

Second stage runs two levels of registration, where the second level is run in full resolution.

Once all the registration components are in place, finally we trigger the whole registration process, including two cascaded registration stages, by calling Update() on the registration filter of the last stage, which causes both stages be updated.

```
try
  {
  affineRegistration->Update();
  std::cout << "Optimizer stop condition: "
            << affineRegistration->
                          GetOptimizer()->GetStopConditionDescription()
            << std::endl;
  }
catch( itk::ExceptionObject & err )
  {
  std::cout << "ExceptionObject caught !" << std::endl;
  std::cout << err << std::endl;
  return EXIT_FAILURE;
  }
```

Finally, a composite transform is used to concatenate the results of all stages together, which will be considered as the final output of this multistage process and will be passed to the resampler to resample the moving image into the virtual domain space (fixed image space if there is no fixed initial transform).

```
typedef itk::CompositeTransform< double,
                        Dimension > CompositeTransformType;
CompositeTransformType::Pointer   compositeTransform  =
                              CompositeTransformType::New();
compositeTransform->AddTransform( translationTx );
compositeTransform->AddTransform( affineTx );
```

Let's execute this example using the same multi-modality images as before. The registration converges after 6 iterations in the first stage, also in 45 and 11 iterations corresponding to the first level and second level of the Affine stage. The final results when printed as an array of parameters are:

```
Translation parameters after first registration stage:
[11.600, 15.1814]

Affine parameters after second registration stage:
[0.9860, -0.1742, 0.1751, 0.9862, 0.9219, 0.8023]
```

Let's reorder the Affine array of parameters again as coefficients of matrix **M** and vector **T**. They can now be seen as

$$M = \begin{bmatrix} 0.9860 & -0.1742 \\ 0.1751 & 0.9862 \end{bmatrix} \text{ and } T = \begin{bmatrix} 0.9219 \\ 0.8023 \end{bmatrix} \tag{3.5}$$

10.02 degrees is the rotation value computed from the affine matrix parameters, which approximately equals the intentional misalignment.

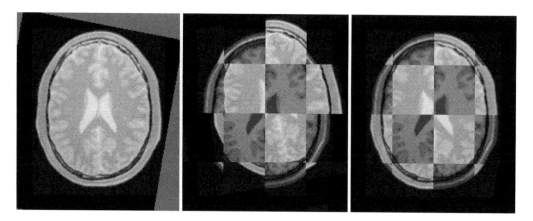

Figure 3.38: Mapped moving image (left) and composition of fixed and moving images before (center) and after (right) registration.

Also for the total translation value resulted from both transforms, we have:

In X direction:
$$11.6004 + 0.9219 = 12.5223 \tag{3.6}$$

In Y direction:
$$15.1814 + 0.8023 = 15.9837 \tag{3.7}$$

These results closely match the true misalignment introduced in the moving image.

The result of resampling the moving image is presented in the left image of Figure 3.38. The center and right images of the figure depict a checkerboard composite of the fixed and moving images before and after registration.

With the completion of these examples, we will now review the main features of the components forming the registration framework.

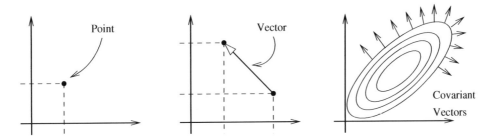

Figure 3.39: Geometric representation objects in ITK.

3.9   Transforms

In the Insight Toolkit, `itk::Transform` objects encapsulate the mapping of points and vectors from an input space to an output space. If a transform is invertible, back transform methods are also provided. Currently, ITK provides a variety of transforms from simple translation, rotation and scaling to general affine and kernel transforms. Note that, while in this section we discuss transforms in the context of registration, transforms are general and can be used for other applications. Some of the most commonly used transforms will be discussed in detail later. Let's begin by introducing the objects used in ITK for representing basic spatial concepts.

3.9.1   Geometrical Representation

ITK implements a consistent geometric representation of space. The characteristics of classes involved in this representation are summarized in Table 3.1. In this regard, ITK takes full advantage of the capabilities of Object Oriented programming and resists the temptation of using simple arrays of `float` or `double` in order to represent geometrical objects. The use of basic arrays would have blurred the important distinction between the different geometrical concepts and would have allowed for the innumerable conceptual and programming errors that result from using a vector where a point is needed or vice versa.

Additional uses of the `itk::Point`, `itk::Vector` and `itk::CovariantVector` classes have been discussed in the Data Representation chaper of Book 1. Each one of these classes behaves differently under spatial transformations. It is therefore quite important to keep their distinction clear. Figure 3.39 illustrates the differences between these concepts.

Transform classes provide different methods for mapping each one of the basic space-representation objects. Points, vectors and covariant vectors are transformed using the methods `TransformPoint()`, `TransformVector()` and `TransformCovariantVector()` respectively.

One of the classes that deserves further comments is the `itk::Vector`. This ITK class tends to be misinterpreted as a container of elements instead of a geometrical object. This is a common misconception originating from the colloquial use by computer scientists and software engineers of the term "Vector". The actual word "Vector" is relatively young. It was coined by William Hamilton in his book *"Elements of Quaternions"* published in 1886 (post-mortem)[25]. In the same

Class	Geometrical concept
itk::Point	Position in space. In *N*-dimensional space it is represented by an array of *N* numbers associated with space coordinates.
itk::Vector	Relative position between two points. In *N*-dimensional space it is represented by an array of *N* numbers, each one associated with the distance along a coordinate axis. Vectors do not have a position in space. A vector is defined as the subtraction of two points.
itk::CovariantVector	Orthogonal direction to a $(N-1)$-dimensional manifold in space. For example, in $3D$ it corresponds to the vector orthogonal to a surface. This is the appropriate class for representing gradients of functions. Covariant vectors do not have a position in space. Covariant vector should not be added to Points, nor to Vectors.

Table 3.1: Summary of objects representing geometrical concepts in ITK.

text Hamilton coined the terms: *"Scalar"*, *"Versor"* and *"Tensor"*. Although the modern term of *"Tensor"* is used in Calculus in a different sense of what Hamilton defined in his book at the time [18].

A *"Vector"* is, by definition, a mathematical object that embodies the concept of "direction in space". Strictly speaking, a Vector describes the relationship between two Points in space, and captures both their relative distance and orientation.

Computer scientists and software engineers misused the term vector in order to represent the concept of an "Indexed Set" [5]. Mechanical Engineers and Civil Engineers, who deal with the real world of physical objects will not commit this mistake and will keep the word *"Vector"* attached to a geometrical concept. Biologists, on the other hand, will associate *"Vector"* to a "vehicle" that allows them to direct something in a particular direction, for example, a virus that allows them to insert pieces of code into a DNA strand [36].

Textbooks in programming do not help to clarify those concepts and loosely use the term *"Vector"* for the purpose of representing an "enumerated set of common elements". STL follows this trend and continues using the word *"Vector"* in this manner [5, 1]. Linear algebra separates the *"Vector"* from its notion of geometric reality and makes it an abstract set of numbers with arithmetic operations associated.

For those of you who are looking for the *"Vector"* in the Software Engineering sense, please look at the itk::Array and itk::FixedArray classes that actually provide such functionalities. Additionally, the itk::VectorContainer and itk::MapContainer classes may be of interest too. These container classes are intended for algorithms which require insertion and deletion of elements, and those which may have large numbers of elements.

The Insight Toolkit deals with real objects that inhabit the physical space. This is particularly true in the context of the image registration framework. We chose to give the appropriate name to the mathematical objects that describe geometrical relationships in N-Dimensional space. It is for this reason that we explicitly make clear the distinction between Point, Vector and CovariantVector, despite the fact that most people would be happy with a simple use of `double[3]` for the three concepts and then will proceed to perform all sort of conceptually flawed operations such as

- Adding two Points

- Dividing a Point by a Scalar

- Adding a Covariant Vector to a Point

- Adding a Covariant Vector to a Vector

In order to enforce the correct use of the geometrical concepts in ITK we organized these classes in a hierarchy that supports reuse of code and compartmentalizes the behavior of the individual classes. The use of the `itk::FixedArray` as the base class of the `itk::Point`, the `itk::Vector` and the `itk::CovariantVector` was a design decision based on the decision to use the correct nomenclature.

An `itk::FixedArray` is an enumerated collection with a fixed number of elements. You can instantiate a fixed array of letters, or a fixed array of images, or a fixed array of transforms, or a fixed array of geometrical shapes. Therefore, the FixedArray only implements the functionality that is necessary to access those enumerated elements. No assumptions can be made at this point on any other operations required by the elements of the FixedArray, except that it will have a default constructor.

The `itk::Point` is a type that represents the spatial coordinates of a spatial location. Based on geometrical concepts we defined the valid operations of the Point class. In particular we made sure that no `operator+()` was defined between Points, and that no `operator*( scalar )` nor `operator/( scalar )` were defined for Points.

In other words, you can perform ITK operations such as:

- Vector = Point - Point

- Point += Vector

- Point -= Vector

- Point = BarycentricCombination(Point, Point)

and you cannot (because you **should not**) perform operations such as

- Point = Point * Scalar

- Point = Point + Point

- Point = Point / Scalar

The `itk::Vector` is, by Hamilton's definition, the subtraction between two points. Therefore a Vector must satisfy the following basic operations:

- Vector = Point - Point

- Point = Point + Vector

- Point = Point - Vector

- Vector = Vector + Vector

- Vector = Vector - Vector

An `itk::Vector` object is intended to be instantiated over elements that support mathematical operation such as addition, subtraction and multiplication by scalars.

3.9.2   Transform General Properties

Each transform class typically has several methods for setting its parameters. For example, `itk::Euler2DTransform` provides methods for specifying the offset, angle, and the entire rotation matrix. However, for use in the registration framework, the parameters are represented by a flat Array of doubles to facilitate communication with generic optimizers. In the case of the Euler2DTransform, the transform is also defined by three doubles: the first representing the angle, and the last two the offset. The flat array of parameters is defined using `SetParameters()`. A description of the parameters and their ordering is documented in the sections that follow.

In the context of registration, the transform parameters define the search space for optimizers. That is, the goal of the optimization is to find the set of parameters defining a transform that results in the best possible value of an image metric. The more parameters a transform has, the longer its computational time will be when used in a registration method since the dimension of the search space will be equal to the number of transform parameters.

Another requirement that the registration framework imposes on the transform classes is the computation of their Jacobians. In general, metrics require the knowledge of the Jacobian in order to compute Metric derivatives. The Jacobian is a matrix whose elements are the partial derivatives of the output point with respect to the array of parameters that defines the transform:[9]

$$
J = \begin{bmatrix}
\frac{\partial x_1}{\partial p_1} & \frac{\partial x_1}{\partial p_2} & \cdots & \frac{\partial x_1}{\partial p_m} \\
\frac{\partial x_2}{\partial p_1} & \frac{\partial x_2}{\partial p_2} & \cdots & \frac{\partial x_2}{\partial p_m} \\
\vdots & \vdots & \ddots & \vdots \\
\frac{\partial x_n}{\partial p_1} & \frac{\partial x_n}{\partial p_2} & \cdots & \frac{\partial x_n}{\partial p_m}
\end{bmatrix}
\tag{3.8}
$$

where $\{p_i\}$ are the transform parameters and $\{x_i\}$ are the coordinates of the output point. Within this framework, the Jacobian is represented by an `itk::Array2D` of doubles and is obtained from the transform by method `GetJacobian()`. The Jacobian can be interpreted as a matrix that indicates for a point in the input space how much its mapping on the output space will change as a response to a

---

[9]Note that the term *Jacobian* is also commonly used for the matrix representing the derivatives of output point coordinates with respect to input point coordinates. Sometimes the term is loosely used to refer to the determinant of such a matrix. [18]

Behavior	Number of Parameters	Parameter Ordering	Restrictions
Maps every point to itself, every vector to itself and every co-variant vector to it-self.	0	NA	Only defined when the in-put and output space has the same number of dimensions.

Table 3.2: Characteristics of the identity transform.

Behavior	Number of Parameters	Parameter Ordering	Restrictions
Represents a simple translation of points in the input space and has no effect on vec-tors or covariant vec-tors.	Same as the input space dimension.	The i-th parame-ter represents the translation in the i-th dimension.	Only defined when the input and output space have the same number of dimensions.

Table 3.3: Characteristics of the TranslationTransform class.

small variation in one of the transform parameters. Note that the values of the Jacobian matrix depend on the point in the input space. So actually the Jacobian can be noted as $J(\mathbf{X})$, where $\mathbf{X} = \{x_i\}$. The use of transform Jacobians enables the efficient computation of metric derivatives. When Jacobians are not available, metrics derivatives have to be computed using finite differences at a price of $2M$ evaluations of the metric value, where M is the number of transform parameters.

The following sections describe the main characteristics of the transform classes available in ITK.

3.9.3 Identity Transform

The identity transform `itk::IdentityTransform` is mainly used for debugging purposes. It is provided to methods that require a transform and in cases where we want to have the certainty that the transform will have no effect whatsoever in the outcome of the process. It is just a NULL operation. The main characteristics of the identity transform are summarized in Table 3.2

3.9.4 Translation Transform

The `itk::TranslationTransform` is probably the simplest yet one of the most useful transforma-tions. It maps all Points by adding a Vector to them. Vector and covariant vectors remain unchanged under this transformation since they are not associated with a particular position in space. Trans-

Behavior	Number of Parameters	Parameter Ordering	Restrictions
Points are transformed by multiplying each one of their coordinates by the corresponding scale factor for the dimension. Vectors are transformed as points. Covariant vectors are transformed by *dividing* their components by the scale factor in the corresponding dimension.	Same as the input space dimension.	The *i*-th parameter represents the scaling in the *i*-th dimension.	Only defined when the input and output space have the same number of dimensions.

Table 3.4: Characteristics of the ScaleTransform class.

lation is the best transform to use when starting a registration method. Before attempting to solve for rotations or scaling it is important to overlap the anatomical objects in both images as much as possible. This is done by resolving the translational misalignment between the images. Translations also have the advantage of being fast to compute and having parameters that are easy to interpret. The main characteristics of the translation transform are presented in Table 3.3.

3.9.5   Scale Transform

The itk::ScaleTransform represents a simple scaling of the vector space. Different scaling factors can be applied along each dimension. Points are transformed by multiplying each one of their coordinates by the corresponding scale factor for the dimension. Vectors are transformed in the same way as points. Covariant vectors, on the other hand, are transformed differently since anisotropic scaling does not preserve angles. Covariant vectors are transformed by *dividing* their components by the scale factor of the corresponding dimension. In this way, if a covariant vector was orthogonal to a vector, this orthogonality will be preserved after the transformation. The following equations summarize the effect of the transform on the basic geometric objects.

$$
\begin{array}{rclclcl}
\text{Point} & \mathbf{P}' & = & T(\mathbf{P}) & : & \mathbf{P}'_i & = & \mathbf{P}_i \cdot \mathbf{S}_i \\
\text{Vector} & \mathbf{V}' & = & T(\mathbf{V}) & : & \mathbf{V}'_i & = & \mathbf{V}_i \cdot \mathbf{S}_i \\
\text{Covariant Vector} & \mathbf{C}' & = & T(\mathbf{C}) & : & \mathbf{C}'_i & = & \mathbf{C}_i / \mathbf{S}_i
\end{array}
\tag{3.9}
$$

where $\mathbf{P}_i$, $\mathbf{V}_i$ and $\mathbf{C}_i$ are the point, vector and covariant vector i-th components while $\mathbf{S}_i$ is the scaling factor along dimension $i-th$. The following equation illustrates the effect of the scaling transform on a $3D$ point.

$$\begin{bmatrix} x' \\ y' \\ z' \end{bmatrix} = \begin{bmatrix} S_1 & 0 & 0 \\ 0 & S_2 & 0 \\ 0 & 0 & S_3 \end{bmatrix} \cdot \begin{bmatrix} x \\ y \\ z \end{bmatrix} \tag{3.10}$$

Scaling appears to be a simple transformation but there are actually a number of issues to keep in mind when using different scale factors along every dimension. There are subtle effects—for example, when computing image derivatives. Since derivatives are represented by covariant vectors, their values are not intuitively modified by scaling transforms.

One of the difficulties with managing scaling transforms in a registration process is that typical optimizers manage the parameter space as a vector space where addition is the basic operation. Scaling is better treated in the frame of a logarithmic space where additions result in regular multiplicative increments of the scale. Gradient descent optimizers have trouble updating step length, since the effect of an additive increment on a scale factor diminishes as the factor grows. In other words, a scale factor variation of $(1.0 + \varepsilon)$ is quite different from a scale variation of $(5.0 + \varepsilon)$.

Registrations involving scale transforms require careful monitoring of the optimizer parameters in order to keep it progressing at a stable pace. Note that some of the transforms discussed in following sections, for example, the AffineTransform, have hidden scaling parameters and are therefore subject to the same vulnerabilities of the ScaleTransform.

In cases involving misalignments with simultaneous translation, rotation and scaling components it may be desirable to solve for these components independently. The main characteristics of the scale transform are presented in Table 3.4.

3.9.6   Scale Logarithmic Transform

The `itk::ScaleLogarithmicTransform` is a simple variation of the `itk::ScaleTransform`. It is intended to improve the behavior of the scaling parameters when they are modified by optimizers. The difference between this transform and the ScaleTransform is that the parameter factors are passed here as logarithms. In this way, multiplicative variations in the scale become additive variations in the logarithm of the scaling factors.

3.9.7   Euler2DTransform

`itk::Euler2DTransform` implements a rigid transformation in $2D$. It is composed of a plane rotation and a two-dimensional translation. The rotation is applied first, followed by the translation. The following equation illustrates the effect of this transform on a $2D$ point,

$$\begin{bmatrix} x' \\ y' \end{bmatrix} = \begin{bmatrix} \cos\theta & -\sin\theta \\ \sin\theta & \cos\theta \end{bmatrix} \cdot \begin{bmatrix} x \\ y \end{bmatrix} + \begin{bmatrix} T_x \\ T_y \end{bmatrix} \tag{3.11}$$

where θ is the rotation angle and (T_x, T_y) are the components of the translation.

Behavior	Number of Parameters	Parameter Ordering	Restrictions
Points are transformed by multiplying each one of their coordinates by the corresponding scale factor for the dimension. Vectors are transformed as points. Covariant vectors are transformed by *dividing* their components by the scale factor in the corresponding dimension.	Same as the input space dimension.	The *i*-th parameter represents the scaling in the *i*-th dimension.	Only defined when the input and output space have the same number of dimensions. The difference between this transform and the ScaleTransform is that here the scaling factors are passed as logarithms, in this way their behavior is closer to the one of a Vector space.

Table 3.5: Characteristics of the ScaleLogarithmicTransform class.

Behavior	Number of Parameters	Parameter Ordering	Restrictions
Represents a 2D rotation and a 2D translation. Note that the translation component has no effect on the transformation of vectors and covariant vectors.	3	The first parameter is the angle in radians and the last two parameters are the translation in each dimension.	Only defined for two-dimensional input and output spaces.

Table 3.6: Characteristics of the Euler2DTransform class.

Behavior	Number of Parameters	Parameter Ordering	Restrictions
Represents a 2D rotation around a user-provided center followed by a 2D translation.	5	The first parameter is the angle in radians. Second and third are the center of rotation coordinates and the last two parameters are the translation in each dimension.	Only defined for two-dimensional input and output spaces.

Table 3.7: Characteristics of the CenteredRigid2DTransform class.

A challenging aspect of this transformation is the fact that translations and rotations do not form a vector space and cannot be managed as linearly independent parameters. Typical optimizers make the loose assumption that parameters exist in a vector space and rely on the step length to be small enough for this assumption to hold approximately.

In addition to the non-linearity of the parameter space, the most common difficulty found when using this transform is the difference in units used for rotations and translations. Rotations are measured in radians; hence, their values are in the range $[-\pi, \pi]$. Translations are measured in millimeters and their actual values vary depending on the image modality being considered. In practice, translations have values on the order of 10 to 100. This scale difference between the rotation and translation parameters is undesirable for gradient descent optimizers because they deviate from the trajectories of descent and make optimization slower and more unstable. In order to compensate for these differences, ITK optimizers accept an array of scale values that are used to normalize the parameter space.

Registrations involving angles and translations should take advantage of the scale normalization functionality in order to obtain the best performance out of the optimizers. The main characteristics of the Euler2DTransform class are presented in Table 3.6.

3.9.8 CenteredRigid2DTransform

itk::CenteredRigid2DTransform implements a rigid transformation in 2D. The main difference between this transform and the itk::Euler2DTransform is that here we can specify an arbitrary center of rotation, while the Euler2DTransform always uses the origin of the coordinate system as the center of rotation. This distinction is quite important in image registration since ITK images usually have their origin in the corner of the image rather than the middle. Rotational mis-registrations usually exist, however, as rotations around the center of the image, or at least as rotations around a point in the middle of the anatomical structure captured by the image. Using gradient descent optimizers, it is almost impossible to solve non-origin rotations using a transform with origin rotations since the deep basin of the real solution is usually located across a high ridge in the topography of the cost function.

In practice, the user must supply the center of rotation in the input space, the angle of rotation and a translation to be applied after the rotation. With these parameters, the transform initializes a rotation matrix and a translation vector that together perform the equivalent of translating the center of rotation to the origin of coordinates, rotating by the specified angle, translating back to the center of rotation and finally translating by the user-specified vector.

As with the Euler2DTransform, this transform suffers from the difference in units used for rotations and translations. Rotations are measured in radians; hence, their values are in the range $[-\pi, \pi]$. The center of rotation and the translations are measured in millimeters, and their actual values vary depending on the image modality being considered. Registrations involving angles and translations should take advantage of the scale normalization functionality of the optimizers in order to get the best performance out of them.

The following equation illustrates the effect of the transform on an input point (x, y) that maps to the output point (x', y'),

$$
\begin{bmatrix} x' \\ y' \end{bmatrix} = \begin{bmatrix} \cos\theta & -\sin\theta \\ \sin\theta & \cos\theta \end{bmatrix} \cdot \begin{bmatrix} x - C_x \\ y - C_y \end{bmatrix} + \begin{bmatrix} T_x + C_x \\ T_y + C_y \end{bmatrix}
\tag{3.12}
$$

where θ is the rotation angle, (C_x, C_y) are the coordinates of the rotation center and (T_x, T_y) are the components of the translation. Note that the center coordinates are subtracted before the rotation and added back after the rotation. The main features of the CenteredRigid2DTransform are presented in Table 3.7.

3.9.9   Similarity2DTransform

The itk::Similarity2DTransform can be seen as a rigid transform combined with an isotropic scaling factor. This transform preserves angles between lines. In its 2D implementation, the four parameters of this transformation combine the characteristics of the itk::ScaleTransform and itk::Euler2DTransform. In particular, those relating to the non-linearity of the parameter space and the non-uniformity of the measurement units. Gradient descent optimizers should be used with caution on such parameter spaces since the notions of gradient direction and step length are ill-defined.

The following equation illustrates the effect of the transform on an input point (x, y) that maps to the output point (x', y'),

$$
\begin{bmatrix} x' \\ y' \end{bmatrix} = \begin{bmatrix} \lambda & 0 \\ 0 & \lambda \end{bmatrix} \cdot \begin{bmatrix} \cos\theta & -\sin\theta \\ \sin\theta & \cos\theta \end{bmatrix} \cdot \begin{bmatrix} x - C_x \\ y - C_y \end{bmatrix} + \begin{bmatrix} T_x + C_x \\ T_y + C_y \end{bmatrix}
\tag{3.13}
$$

where λ is the scale factor, θ is the rotation angle, (C_x, C_y) are the coordinates of the rotation center and (T_x, T_y) are the components of the translation. Note that the center coordinates are subtracted

Behavior	Number of Parameters	Parameter Ordering	Restrictions
Represents a 2D rotation, homogeneous scaling and a 2D translation. Note that the translation component has no effect on the transformation of vectors and covariant vectors.	4	The first parameter is the scaling factor for all dimensions, the second is the angle in radians, and the last two parameters are the translations in (x, y) respectively.	Only defined for two-dimensional input and output spaces.

Table 3.8: Characteristics of the Similarity2DTransform class.

before the rotation and scaling, and they are added back afterwards. The main features of the Similarity2DTransform are presented in Table 3.8.

A possible approach for controlling optimization in the parameter space of this transform is to dynamically modify the array of scales passed to the optimizer. The effect produced by the parameter scaling can be used to steer the walk in the parameter space (by giving preference to some of the parameters over others). For example, perform some iterations updating only the rotation angle, then balance the array of scale factors in the optimizer and perform another set of iterations updating only the translations.

3.9.10 QuaternionRigidTransform

The `itk::QuaternionRigidTransform` class implements a rigid transformation in 3D space. The rotational part of the transform is represented using a quaternion while the translation is represented with a vector. Quaternions components do not form a vector space and hence raise the same concerns as the `itk::Similarity2DTransform` when used with gradient descent optimizers.

The `itk::QuaternionRigidTransformGradientDescentOptimizer` was introduced into the toolkit to address these concerns. This specialized optimizer implements a variation of a gradient descent algorithm adapted for a quaternion space. This class ensures that after advancing in any direction on the parameter space, the resulting set of transform parameters is mapped back into the permissible set of parameters. In practice, this comes down to normalizing the newly-computed quaternion to make sure that the transformation remains rigid and no scaling is applied. The main characteristics of the QuaternionRigidTransform are presented in Table 3.9.

The Quaternion rigid transform also accepts a user-defined center of rotation. In this way, the transform can easily be used for registering images where the rotation is mostly relative to the center of the image instead of one of the corners. The coordinates of this rotation center are not subject to

Behavior	Number of Parameters	Parameter Ordering	Restrictions
Represents a 3D rotation and a 3D translation. The rotation is specified as a quaternion, defined by a set of four numbers **q**. The relationship between quaternion and rotation about vector **n** by angle θ is as follows: $$\mathbf{q} = (\mathbf{n}\sin(\theta/2), \cos(\theta/2))$$ Note that if the quaternion is not of unit length, scaling will also result.	7	The first four parameters defines the quaternion and the last three parameters the translation in each dimension.	Only defined for three-dimensional input and output spaces.

Table 3.9: Characteristics of the QuaternionRigidTransform class.

optimization. They only participate in the computation of the mappings for Points and in the computation of the Jacobian. The transformations for Vectors and CovariantVector are not affected by the selection of the rotation center.

3.9.11 VersorTransform

By definition, a *Versor* is the rotational part of a Quaternion. It can also be defined as a *unit-quaternion* [25, 28]. Versors only have three independent components, since they are restricted to reside in the space of unit-quaternions. The implementation of versors in the toolkit uses a set of

Behavior	Number of Parameters	Parameter Ordering	Restrictions
Represents a 3D rotation. The rotation is specified by a versor or unit quaternion. The rotation is performed around a user-specified center of rotation.	3	The three parameters define the versor.	Only defined for three-dimensional input and output spaces.

Table 3.10: Characteristics of the Versor Transform

Behavior	Number of Parameters	Parameter Ordering	Restrictions
Represents a 3D rotation and a 3D translation. The rotation is specified by a versor or unit quaternion, while the translation is represented by a vector. Users can specify the coordinates of the center of rotation.	6	The first three parameters define the versor and the last three parameters the translation in each dimension.	Only defined for three-dimensional input and output spaces.

Table 3.11: Characteristics of the VersorRigid3DTransform class.

three numbers. These three numbers correspond to the first three components of a quaternion. The fourth component of the quaternion is computed internally such that the quaternion is of unit length. The main characteristics of the `itk::VersorTransform` are presented in Table 3.10.

This transform exclusively represents rotations in 3D. It is intended to rapidly solve the rotational component of a more general misalignment. The efficiency of this transform comes from using a parameter space of reduced dimensionality. Versors are the best possible representation for rotations in 3D space. Sequences of versors allow the creation of smooth rotational trajectories; for this reason, they behave stably under optimization methods.

The space formed by versor parameters is not a vector space. Standard gradient descent algorithms are not appropriate for exploring this parameter space. An optimizer specialized for the versor space is available in the toolkit under the name of `itk::VersorTransformOptimizer`. This optimizer implements versor derivatives as originally defined by Hamilton [25].

The center of rotation can be specified by the user with the `SetCenter()` method. The center is not part of the parameters to be optimized, therefore it remains the same during an optimization process. Its value is used during the computations for transforming Points and when computing the Jacobian.

3.9.12 VersorRigid3DTransform

The `itk::VersorRigid3DTransform` implements a rigid transformation in 3D space. It is a variant of the `itk::QuaternionRigidTransform` and the `itk::VersorTransform`. It can be seen as a `itk::VersorTransform` plus a translation defined by a vector. The advantage of this class with respect to the QuaternionRigidTransform is that it exposes only six parameters, three for the versor components and three for the translational components. This reduces the search space for the optimizer to six dimensions instead of the seven dimensional used by the QuaternionRigidTransform. This transform also allows the users to set a specific center of rotation. The center coordinates are

Behavior	Number of Parameters	Parameter Ordering	Restrictions
Represents a rigid rotation in 3D space. That is, a rotation followed by a 3D translation. The rotation is specified by three angles representing rotations to be applied around the X, Y and Z axes one after another. The translation part is represented by a Vector. Users can also specify the coordinates of the center of rotation.	6	The first three parameters are the rotation angles around X, Y and Z axes, and the last three parameters are the translations along each dimension.	Only defined for three-dimensional input and output spaces.

Table 3.12: Characteristics of the Euler3DTransform class.

not modified during the optimization performed in a registration process. The main features of this transform are summarized in Table 3.11. This transform is probably the best option to use when dealing with rigid transformations in 3D.

Given that the space of Versors is not a Vector space, typical gradient descent optimizers are not well suited for exploring the parametric space of this transform. The itk::VersorRigid3DTranformOptimizer has been introduced in the ITK toolkit with the purpose of providing an optimizer that is aware of the Versor space properties on the rotational part of this transform, as well as the Vector space properties on the translational part of the transform.

3.9.13 Euler3DTransform

The itk::Euler3DTransform implements a rigid transformation in 3D space. It can be seen as a rotation followed by a translation. This class exposes six parameters, three for the Euler angles that represent the rotation and three for the translational components. This transform also allows the users to set a specific center of rotation. The center coordinates are not modified during the optimization performed in a registration process. The main features of this transform are summarized in Table 3.12.

Three rotational parameters are non-linear and do not behave like Vector spaces. This must be taken into account when selecting an optimizer to work with this transform and when fine tuning the parameters of the optimizer. It is strongly recommended to use this transform by introducing very small variations on the rotational components. A small rotation will be in the range of 1 degree,

Behavior	Number of Parameters	Parameter Ordering	Restrictions
Represents a $3D$ rotation, a $3D$ translation and homogeneous scaling. The scaling factor is specified by a scalar, the rotation is specified by a versor, and the translation is represented by a vector. Users can also specify the coordinates of the center of rotation, which is the same center used for scaling.	7	The first three parameters define the Versor, the next three parameters the translation in each dimension, and the last parameter is the isotropic scaling factor.	Only defined for three-dimensional input and output spaces.

Table 3.13: Characteristics of the Similarity3DTransform class.

which in radians is approximately 0.01745.

You should not expect this transform to be able to compensate for large rotations just by being driven with the optimizer. In practice you must provide a reasonable initialization of the transform angles and only need to correct for residual rotations in the order of 10 or 20 degrees.

3.9.14   Similarity3DTransform

The `itk::Similarity3DTransform` implements a similarity transformation in $3D$ space. It can be seen as an homogeneous scaling followed by a `itk::VersorRigid3DTransform`. This class exposes seven parameters: one for the scaling factor, three for the versor components and three for the translational components. This transform also allows the user to set a specific center of rotation. The center coordinates are not modified during the optimization performed in a registration process. Both the rotation and scaling operations are performed with respect to the center of rotation. The main features of this transform are summarized in Table 3.13.

The scaling and rotational spaces are non-linear and do not behave like Vector spaces. This must be taken into account when selecting an optimizer to work with this transform and when fine tuning the parameters of the optimizer.

Behavior	**Number of Parameters**	**Parameter Ordering**	**Restrictions**
Represents a rigid 3D transformation followed by a perspective projection. The rotation is specified by a Versor, while the translation is represented by a Vector. Users can specify the coordinates of the center of rotation. They must specify a focal distance to be used for the perspective projection. The rotation center and the focal distance parameters are not modified during the optimization process.	6	The first three parameters define the Versor and the last three parameters the Translation in each dimension.	Only defined for three-dimensional input and two-dimensional output spaces. This is one of the few transforms where the input space has a different dimension from the output space.

Table 3.14: Characteristics of the Rigid3DPerspectiveTransform class.

Behavior	Number of Parameters	Parameter Ordering	Restrictions
Represents an affine transform composed of rotation, scaling, shearing and translation. The transform is specified by a $N \times N$ matrix and a $N \times 1$ vector where N is the space dimension.	$(N+1) \times N$	The first $N \times N$ parameters define the matrix in column-major order (where the column index varies the fastest). The last N parameters define the translations for each dimension.	Only defined when the input and output space have the same dimension.

Table 3.15: Characteristics of the AffineTransform class.

3.9.15 Rigid3DPerspectiveTransform

The `itk::Rigid3DPerspectiveTransform` implements a rigid transformation in $3D$ space followed by a perspective projection. This transform is intended to be used in $3D/2D$ registration problems where a 3D object is projected onto a 2D plane. This is the case in Fluoroscopic images used for image-guided intervention, and it is also the case for classical radiography. Users must provide a value for the focal distance to be used during the computation of the perspective transform. This transform also allows users to set a specific center of rotation. The center coordinates are not modified during the optimization performed in a registration process. The main features of this transform are summarized in Table 3.14. This transform is also used when creating Digitally Reconstructed Radiographs (DRRs).

The strategies for optimizing the parameters of this transform are the same ones used for optimizing the VersorRigid3DTransform. In particular, you can use the same VersorRigid3DTranformOptimizer in order to optimize the parameters of this class.

3.9.16 AffineTransform

The `itk::AffineTransform` is one of the most popular transformations used for image registration. Its main advantage comes from its representation as a linear transformation. The main features of this transform are presented in Table 3.15.

The set of AffineTransform coefficients can actually be represented in a vector space of dimension $(N+1) \times N$. This makes it possible for optimizers to be used appropriately on this search space. However, the high dimensionality of the search space also implies a high computational complexity of cost-function derivatives. The best compromise in the reduction of this computational time is to use the transform's Jacobian in combination with the image gradient for computing the cost-function derivatives.

The coefficients of the $N \times N$ matrix can represent rotations, anisotropic scaling and shearing. These coefficients are usually of a very different dynamic range compared to the translation coefficients. Coefficients in the matrix tend to be in the range $[-1 : 1]$, but are not restricted to this interval. Translation coefficients, on the other hand, can be on the order of 10 to 100, and are basically related to the image size and pixel spacing.

This difference in scale makes it necessary to take advantage of the functionality offered by the optimizers for rescaling the parameter space. This is particularly relevant for optimizers based on gradient descent approaches. This transform lets the user set an arbitrary center of rotation. The coordinates of the rotation center do not make part of the parameters array passed to the optimizer. Equation 3.14 illustrates the effect of applying the AffineTransform to a point in $3D$ space.

$$
\begin{bmatrix} x' \\ y' \\ z' \end{bmatrix} = \begin{bmatrix} M_{00} & M_{01} & M_{02} \\ M_{10} & M_{11} & M_{12} \\ M_{20} & M_{21} & M_{22} \end{bmatrix} \cdot \begin{bmatrix} x - C_x \\ y - C_y \\ z - C_z \end{bmatrix} + \begin{bmatrix} T_x + C_x \\ T_y + C_y \\ T_z + C_z \end{bmatrix} \tag{3.14}
$$

A registration based on the affine transform may be more effective when applied after simpler transformations have been used to remove the major components of misalignment. Otherwise it will incur an overwhelming computational cost. For example, using an affine transform, the first set of optimization iterations would typically focus on removing large translations. This task could instead be accomplished by a translation transform in a parameter space of size N instead of the $(N+1) \times N$ associated with the affine transform.

Tracking the evolution of a registration process that uses AffineTransforms can be challenging, since it is difficult to represent the coefficients in a meaningful way. A simple printout of the transform coefficients generally does not offer a clear picture of the current behavior and trend of the optimization. A better implementation uses the affine transform to deform a wire-frame cube which is shown in a $3D$ visualization display.

3.9.17 BSplineDeformableTransform

The `itk::BSplineDeformableTransform` is designed to be used for solving deformable registration problems. This transform is equivalent to generating a deformation field where a deformation vector is assigned to every point in space. The deformation vectors are computed using BSpline interpolation from the deformation values of points located in a coarse grid, which is usually referred to as the BSpline grid.

The BSplineDeformableTransform is not flexible enough to account for large rotations or shearing, or scaling differences. In order to compensate for this limitation, it provides the functionality of being composed with an arbitrary transform. This transform is known as the *Bulk* transform and it applied to points before they are mapped with the displacement field.

This transform does not provide functionality for mapping Vectors nor CovariantVectors—only Points can be mapped. This is because the variations of a vector under a deformable transform actually depend on the location of the vector in space. In other words, Vectors only make sense as

Behavior	Number of Parameters	Parameter Ordering	Restrictions
Represents a free-form deformation by providing a deformation field from the interpolation of deformations in a coarse grid.	$M \times N$	Where M is the number of nodes in the BSpline grid and N is the dimension of the space.	Only defined when the input and output space have the same dimension. This transform has the advantage of being able to compute deformable registration. It also has the disadvantage of a very high-dimensional parametric space, and therefore requiring long computation times.

Table 3.16: Characteristics of the BSplineDeformableTransform class.

the relative position between two points.

The BSplineDeformableTransform has a very large number of parameters and therefore is well suited for the `itk::LBFGSOptimizer` and `itk::LBFGSBOptimizer`. The use of this transform was proposed in the following papers [53, 40, 41].

3.9.18 KernelTransforms

Kernel Transforms are a set of Transforms that are also suitable for performing deformable registration. These transforms compute on-the-fly the displacements corresponding to a deformation field. The displacement values corresponding to every point in space are computed by interpolation from the vectors defined by a set of *Source Landmarks* and a set of *Target Landmarks*.

Several variations of these transforms are available in the toolkit. They differ in the type of interpolation kernel that is used when computing the deformation in a particular point of space. Note that these transforms are computationally expensive and that their numerical complexity is proportional to the number of landmarks and the space dimension.

The following is the list of Transforms based on the KernelTransform.

- `itk::ElasticBodySplineKernelTransform`

- `itk::ElasticBodyReciprocalSplineKernelTransform`

- `itk::ThinPlateSplineKernelTransform`

- `itk::ThinPlateR2LogRSplineKernelTransform`

- `itk::VolumeSplineKernelTransform`

Details about the mathematical background of these transform can be found in the paper by Davis *et. al* [15] and the papers by Rohr *et. al* [51, 52].

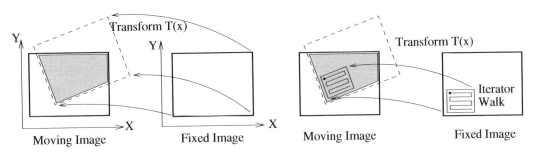

Figure 3.40: The moving image is mapped into the fixed image space under some spatial transformation. An iterator walks through the fixed image and its coordinates are mapped onto the moving image.

3.10 Interpolators

In the registration process, the metric typically compares intensity values in the fixed image against the corresponding values in the transformed moving image. When a point is mapped from one space to another by a transform, it will in general be mapped to a non-grid position. Therefore, interpolation is required to evaluate the image intensity at the mapped position.

Figure 3.40 (left) illustrates the mapping of the fixed image space onto the moving image space. The transform maps points from the fixed image coordinate system onto the moving image coordinate system. The figure highlights the region of overlap between the two images after the mapping. The right side illustrates how an iterator is used to walk through a region of the fixed image. Each one of the iterator positions is mapped by the transform onto the moving image space in order to find the homologous pixel.

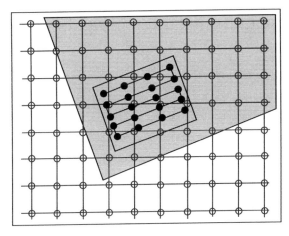

Figure 3.41: Grid positions of the fixed image map to non-grid positions of the moving image.

Figure 3.41 presents a detailed view of the mapping from the fixed image to the moving image. In general, the grid positions of the fixed image will not be mapped onto grid positions of the moving image. Interpolation is needed for estimating the intensity of the moving image at these non-grid positions. The service is provided in ITK by interpolator classes that can be plugged into the registration method.

The following interpolators are available:

- `itk::NearestNeighborInterpolateImageFunction`

- itk::LinearInterpolateImageFunction

- itk::BSplineInterpolateImageFunction

- itk::WindowedSincInterpolateImageFunction

In the context of registration, the interpolation method affects the smoothness of the optimization search space and the overall computation time. On the other hand, interpolations are executed thousands of times in a single optimization cycle. Hence, the user has to balance the simplicity of computation with the smoothness of the optimization when selecting the interpolation scheme.

The basic input to an itk::InterpolateImageFunction is the image to be interpolated. Once an image has been defined using SetInputImage(), a user can interpolate either at a point using Evaluate() or an index using EvaluateAtContinuousIndex().

Interpolators provide the method IsInsideBuffer() that tests whether a particular image index or a physical point falls inside the spatial domain for which image pixels exist.

3.10.1   Nearest Neighbor Interpolation

The itk::NearestNeighborInterpolateImageFunction simply uses the intensity of the nearest grid position. That is, it assumes that the image intensity is piecewise constant with jumps mid-way between grid positions. This interpolation scheme is cheap as it does not require any floating point computations.

3.10.2   Linear Interpolation

The itk::LinearInterpolateImageFunction assumes that intensity varies linearly between grid positions. Unlike nearest neighbor interpolation, the interpolated intensity is spatially continuous. However, the intensity gradient will be discontinuous at grid positions.

3.10.3   B-Spline Interpolation

The itk::BSplineInterpolateImageFunction represents the image intensity using B-spline basis functions. When an input image is first connected to the interpolator, B-spline coefficients are computed using recursive filtering (assuming mirror boundary conditions). Intensity at a non-grid position is computed by multiplying the B-spline coefficients with shifted B-spline kernels within a small support region of the requested position. Figure 3.42 illustrates on the left how the deformation values on the BSpline grid nodes are used for computing interpolated deformations in the rest of space. Note for example that when a cubic BSpline is used, the grid must have one extra node in one side of the image and two extra nodes on the other side, this along every dimension.

Currently, this interpolator supports splines of order 0 to 5. Using a spline of order 0 is almost identical to nearest neighbor interpolation; a spline of order 1 is exactly identical to linear interpo-

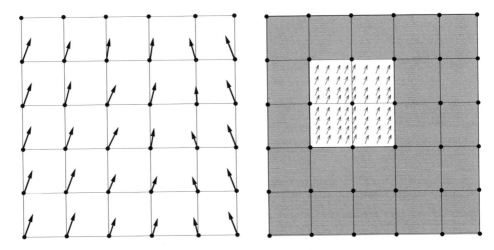

Figure 3.42: The left side illustrates the BSpline grid and the deformations that are known on those nodes. The right side illustrates the region where interpolation is possible when the BSpline is of cubic order. The small arrows represent deformation values that were interpolated from the grid deformations shown on the left side of the diagram.

lation. For splines of order greater than 1, both the interpolated value and its derivative are spatially continuous.

It is important to note that when using this scheme, the interpolated value may lie outside the range of input image intensities. This is especially important when handling unsigned data, as it is possible that the interpolated value is negative.

3.10.4 Windowed Sinc Interpolation

The `itk::WindowedSincInterpolateImageFunction` is the best possible interpolator for data that have been digitized in a discrete grid. This interpolator has been developed based on Fourier Analysis considerations. It is well known in signal processing that the process of sampling a spatial function using a periodic discrete grid results in a replication of the spectrum of that signal in the frequency domain.

The process of recovering the continuous signal from the discrete sampling is equivalent to the removal of the replicated spectra in the frequency domain. This can be done by multiplying the spectra with a box function that will set to zero all the frequencies above the highest frequency in the original signal. Multiplying the spectrum with a box function is equivalent to convolving the spatial discrete signal with a sinc function

$$sinc(x) = \sin(x)/x \qquad (3.15)$$

The sinc function has infinite support, which of course in practice can not really be implemented.

Therefore, the sinc is usually truncated by multiplying it with a Window function. The Windowed Sinc interpolator is the result of such an operation.

This interpolator presents a series of trade-offs in its utilization. Probably the most significant is that the larger the window, the more precise will be the resulting interpolation. However, large windows will also result in long computation times. Since the user can select the window size in this interpolator, it is up to the user to determine how much interpolation quality is required in her/his application and how much computation time can be justified. For details on the signal processing theory behind this interpolator, please refer to Meijering *et. al* [42].

The region of the image used for computing the interpolator is determined by the window *radius*. For example, in a 2D image where we want to interpolate the value at position (x, y) the following computation will be performed.

$$I(x,y) = \sum_{i=\lfloor x \rfloor + 1 - m}^{\lfloor x \rfloor + m} \sum_{j=\lfloor y \rfloor + 1 - m}^{\lfloor y \rfloor + m} I_{i,j} K(x-i) K(y-j) \tag{3.16}$$

where m is the *radius* of the window. Typically, values such as 3 or 4 are reasonable for the window radius. The function kernel $K(t)$ is composed by the *sinc* function and one of the windows listed above.

$$K(t) = w(t)\text{sinc}(t) = w(t)\frac{\sin(\pi t)}{\pi t} \tag{3.17}$$

Some of the windows that can be used with this interpolator are

Cosinus window
$$w(x) = \cos\left(\frac{\pi x}{2m}\right) \tag{3.18}$$

Hamming window
$$w(x) = 0.54 + 0.46\cos\left(\frac{\pi x}{m}\right) \tag{3.19}$$

Welch window
$$w(x) = 1 - \left(\frac{x^2}{m^2}\right) \tag{3.20}$$

Lancos window
$$w(x) = \text{sinc}\left(\frac{x}{m}\right) \tag{3.21}$$

Blackman window
$$w(x) = 0.42 + 0.5\cos\left(\frac{\pi x}{m}\right) + 0.08\cos\left(\frac{2\pi x}{m}\right) \tag{3.22}$$

The window functions listed above are available inside the itk::Function namespace. The conclusions of the referenced paper suggest to use the Welch, Cosine, Kaiser, and Lancos windows for m = 4,5. These are based on error in rotating medical images with respect to the linear interpolation method. In some cases the results achieve a 20-fold improvement in accuracy.

This filter can be used in the same way you would use any ImageInterpolationFunction. For instance, you can plug it into the ResampleImageFilter class. In order to instantiate the filter you must choose several template parameters.

```
typedef WindowedSincInterpolateImageFunction<
        TInputImage, VRadius, TWindowFunction,
        TBoundaryCondition, TCoordRep >    InterpolatorType;
```

TInputImage is the image type, as for any other interpolator.

VRadius is the radius of the kernel, i.e., the m from the formula above.

TWindowFunction is the window function object, which you can choose from about five different functions defined in this header. The default is the Hamming window, which is commonly used but not optimal according to the cited paper.

TBoundaryCondition is the boundary condition class used to determine the values of pixels that fall off the image boundary. This class has the same meaning here as in the itk::NeighborhoodIterator classes.

TCoordRep is again standard for interpolating functions, and should be float or double.

The WindowedSincInterpolateImageFunction is probably not the interpolator that you want to use for performing registration. Its computation burden makes it too expensive for this purpose. The best use of this interpolator is for the final resampling of the image, once the transform has been found using another less expensive interpolator in the registration process.

3.11   Metrics

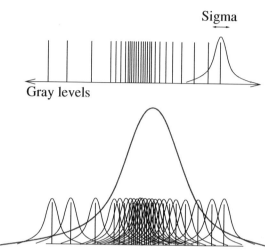

In ITK, `itk::ImageToImageMetricv4` objects quantitatively measure how well the transformed moving image fits the fixed image by comparing the gray-scale intensity of the images. These metrics are very flexible and can work with any transform or interpolation method and do not require reduction of the gray-scale images to sparse extracted information such as edges.

The metric component is perhaps the most critical element of the registration framework. The selection of which metric to use is highly dependent on the registration problem to be solved. For example, some metrics have a large capture range while others require initialization close to the optimal position. In addition, some metrics are only suitable for comparing images obtained from the same imaging modality, while others can handle inter-modality comparisons. Unfortunately, there are no clear-cut rules as to how to choose a metric.

Figure 3.43: In Parzen windowing, a continuous density function is constructed by superimposing kernel functions (Gaussian function in this case) centered on the intensity samples obtained from the image.

The matching Metric class controls most parts of the registration process since it handles fixed, moving and virtual images as well as fixed and moving transforms and interpolators. The method `GetValue()` can be used to evaluate the quantitative criterion at the transform parameters specified in the argument. Typically, the metric samples points within a defined region of the virtual lattice. For each point, the corresponding fixed and moving image positions are computed using the fixed initial transform and the moving transform with the specified parameters. Then, the fixed and moving interpolators are used to compute the fixed and moving image's intensities at the mapped positions. Details on this mapping are illustrated in Figures 3.40 and 3.41 assuming that virtual lattice is the same as the fixed image lattice, which is usually the case in practice.

The metrics also support region-based evaluation. The `SetFixedImageMask()` and `SetMovingImageMask()` methods may be used to restrict evaluation of the metric within a specified region. The masks may be of any type derived from `itk::SpatialObject`.

Besides the measure value, gradient-based optimization schemes also require derivatives of the measure with respect to each transform parameter. The methods `GetDerivatives()` and `GetValueAndDerivatives()` can be used to obtain the gradient information.

The following is the list of metrics currently available in ITKv4 registration framework:

- Mean squares
  `itk::MeanSquaresImageToImageMetricv4`

- Correlation
  `itk::CorrelationImageToImageMetricv4`

- Mutual information by Mattes
  `itk::MattesMutualInformationImageToImageMetricv4`

- Joint histogram mutual information
  `itk::JointHistogramMutualInformationHistogramImageToImageMetricv4`

- Demons metric
  `itk::DemonsImageToImageMetricv4`

- ANTS neighborhood correlation metric
  `itk::ANTSNeighborhoodCorrelationImageToImageMetricv4`

Also, in case you are interested in using the legacy ITK registration framework, the following is the list of metrics currently available in ITKv3:

- Mean squares
  `itk::MeanSquaresImageToImageMetric`

- Normalized correlation
  `itk::NormalizedCorrelationImageToImageMetric`

- Mean reciprocal squared difference
  `itk::MeanReciprocalSquareDifferenceImageToImageMetric`

- Mutual information by Viola and Wells
  `itk::MutualInformationImageToImageMetric`

- Mutual information by Mattes
  `itk::MattesMutualInformationImageToImageMetric`

- Kullback Liebler distance metric by Kullback and Liebler
  `itk::KullbackLeiblerCompareHistogramImageToImageMetric`

- Normalized mutual information
  `itk::NormalizedMutualInformationHistogramImageToImageMetric`

- Mean squares histogram
  `itk::MeanSquaresHistogramImageToImageMetric`

- Correlation coefficient histogram
  `itk::CorrelationCoefficientHistogramImageToImageMetric`

- Cardinality Match metric
  `itk::MatchCardinalityImageToImageMetric`

- Kappa Statistics metric
  `itk::KappaStatisticImageToImageMetric`

- Gradient Difference metric
  itk::GradientDifferenceImageToImageMetric

In the following sections, we describe the ITKv4 metric types in detail. You can check ITK descriptions in doxygen for details about ITKv3 metric classes.

For ease of notation, we will refer to the fixed image $f(\mathbf{X})$ and transformed moving image $(m \circ T(\mathbf{X}))$ as images A and B.

3.11.1 Mean Squares Metric

The itk::MeanSquaresImageToImageMetricv4 computes the mean squared pixel-wise difference in intensity between image A and B over a user defined region:

$$MS(A,B) = \frac{1}{N} \sum_{i=1}^{N} (A_i - B_i)^2 \qquad (3.23)$$

A_i is the i-th pixel of Image A
B_i is the i-th pixel of Image B
N is the number of pixels considered

The optimal value of the metric is zero. Poor matches between images A and B result in large values of the metric. This metric is simple to compute and has a relatively large capture radius.

This metric relies on the assumption that intensity representing the same homologous point must be the same in both images. Hence, its use is restricted to images of the same modality. Additionally, any linear changes in the intensity result in a poor match value.

Exploring a Metric

Getting familiar with the characteristics of the Metric as a cost function is fundamental in order to find the best way of setting up an optimization process that will use this metric for solving a registration problem. The following example illustrates a typical mechanism for studying the characteristics of a Metric. Although the example is using the Mean Squares metric, the same methodology can be applied to any of the other metrics available in the toolkit.

The source code for this section can be found in the file
MeanSquaresImageMetric1.cxx.

This example illustrates how to explore the domain of an image metric. This is a useful exercise before starting a registration process, since familiarity with the characteristics of the metric is fundamental for appropriate selection of the optimizer and its parameters used to drive the registration process. This process helps identify how noisy a metric may be in a given range of parameters, and it will also give an idea of the number of local minima or maxima in which an optimizer may get trapped while exploring the parametric space.

We start by including the headers of the basic components: Metric, Transform and Interpolator.

```
#include "itkMeanSquaresImageToImageMetricv4.h"
#include "itkTranslationTransform.h"
#include "itkNearestNeighborInterpolateImageFunction.h"
```

We define the dimension and pixel type of the images to be used in the evaluation of the Metric.

```
const       unsigned int    Dimension = 2;
typedef     float           PixelType;

typedef itk::Image< PixelType, Dimension >    ImageType;
```

The type of the Metric is instantiated and one is constructed. In this case we decided to use the same image type for both the fixed and the moving images.

```
typedef itk::MeanSquaresImageToImageMetricv4<
                    ImageType, ImageType >  MetricType;

MetricType::Pointer metric = MetricType::New();
```

We also instantiate the transform and interpolator types, and create objects of each class.

```
typedef itk::TranslationTransform< double, Dimension >  TransformType;

TransformType::Pointer transform = TransformType::New();


typedef itk::NearestNeighborInterpolateImageFunction<
                    ImageType, double >  InterpolatorType;

InterpolatorType::Pointer interpolator = InterpolatorType::New();
```

The classes required by the metric are connected to it. This includes the fixed and moving images, the interpolator and the transform.

```
metric->SetTransform( transform );
metric->SetMovingInterpolator( interpolator );

metric->SetFixedImage( fixedImage );
metric->SetMovingImage( movingImage );
```

Note that the SetTransform() method is equivalent to the SetMovingTransform() function. In this example there is no need to use the SetFixedTransform(), since the virtual domain is assumed to be the same as the fixed image domain set as following.

```
metric->SetVirtualDomainFromImage( fixedImage );
```

Finally we select a region of the parametric space to explore. In this case we are using a translation transform in 2D, so we simply select translations from a negative position to a positive position, in both x and y. For each one of those positions we invoke the GetValue() method of the Metric.

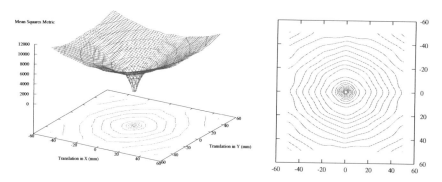

Figure 3.44: Plots of the Mean Squares Metric for an image compared to itself under multiple translations.

```
MetricType::MovingTransformParametersType displacement( Dimension );

const int rangex = 50;
const int rangey = 50;

for( int dx = -rangex; dx <= rangex; dx++ )
  {
  for( int dy = -rangey; dy <= rangey; dy++ )
    {
    displacement[0] = dx;
    displacement[1] = dy;
    metric->SetParameters( displacement );
    const double value = metric->GetValue();
    std::cout << dx << "   " << dy << "   " << value << std::endl;
    }
  }
```

Running this code using the image BrainProtonDensitySlice.png as both the fixed and the moving images results in the plot shown in Figure 3.44. From this figure, it can be seen that a gradient-based optimizer will be appropriate for finding the extrema of the Metric. It is also possible to estimate a good value for the step length of a gradient-descent optimizer.

This exercise of plotting the Metric is probably the best thing to do when a registration process is not converging and when it is unclear how to fine tune the different parameters involved in the registration. This includes the optimizer parameters, the metric parameters and even options such as preprocessing the image data with smoothing filters.

The shell and Gnuplot[10] scripts used for generating the graphics in Figure 3.44 are available in the directory

`ITKSoftwareGuide/SoftwareGuide/Art`

Of course, this plotting exercise becomes more challenging when the transform has more than three parameters, and when those parameters have very different value ranges. In those cases it is necessary to select only a key subset of parameters from the transform and to study the behavior of the metric

---

[10]http://www.gnuplot.info

when those parameters are varied.

3.11.2   Normalized Correlation Metric

The `itk::CorrelationImageToImageMetricv4` computes pixel-wise cross-correlation and normalizes it by the square root of the autocorrelation of the images:

$$NC(A,B) = -1 \times \frac{\sum_{i=1}^{N} (A_i \cdot B_i)}{\sqrt{\sum_{i=1}^{N} A_i^2 \cdot \sum_{i=1}^{N} B_i^2}} \tag{3.24}$$

A_i is the i-th pixel of Image A
B_i is the i-th pixel of Image B
N is the number of pixels considered

Note the -1 factor in the metric computation. This factor is used to make the metric be optimal when its minimum is reached. The optimal value of the metric is then minus one. Misalignment between the images results in small measure values. The use of this metric is limited to images obtained using the same imaging modality. The metric is insensitive to multiplicative factors between the two images. This metric produces a cost function with sharp peaks and well-defined minima. On the other hand, it has a relatively small capture radius.

3.11.3   Mutual Information Metric

The `itk::MattesMutualInformationImageToImageMetricv4` computes the mutual information between image A and image B. Mutual information (MI) measures how much information one random variable (image intensity in one image) tells about another random variable (image intensity in the other image). The major advantage of using MI is that the actual form of the dependency does not have to be specified. Therefore, complex mapping between two images can be modeled. This flexibility makes MI well suited as a criterion of multi-modality registration [47].

Mutual information is defined in terms of entropy. Let

$$H(A) = -\int p_A(a) \log p_A(a) \, da \tag{3.25}$$

be the entropy of random variable A, $H(B)$ the entropy of random variable B and

$$H(A,B) = \int p_{AB}(a,b) \log p_{AB}(a,b) \, da \, db \tag{3.26}$$

be the joint entropy of A and B. If A and B are independent, then

$$p_{AB}(a,b) = p_A(a) p_B(b) \tag{3.27}$$

and

$$H(A,B) = H(A) + H(B). \tag{3.28}$$

However, if there is any dependency, then

$$H(A,B) < H(A) + H(B). \tag{3.29}$$

The difference is called Mutual Information : $I(A,B)$

$$I(A,B) = H(A) + H(B) - H(A,B) \tag{3.30}$$

Parzen Windowing

In a typical registration problem, direct access to the marginal and joint probability densities is not available and hence the densities must be estimated from the image data. Parzen windows (also known as kernel density estimators) can be used for this purpose. In this scheme, the densities are constructed by taking intensity samples S from the image and super-positioning kernel functions $K(\cdot)$ centered on the elements of S as illustrated in Figure 3.43:

A variety of functions can be used as the smoothing kernel with the requirement that they are smooth, symmetric, have zero mean and integrate to one. For example, boxcar, Gaussian and B-spline functions are suitable candidates. A smoothing parameter is used to scale the kernel function. The larger the smoothing parameter, the wider the kernel function used and hence the smoother the density estimate. If the parameter is too large, features such as modes in the density will get smoothed out. On the other hand, if the smoothing parameter is too small, the resulting density may be too noisy. The estimation is given by the following equation.

$$p(a) \approx P^*(a) = \frac{1}{N} \sum_{s_j \in S} K(a - s_j) \tag{3.31}$$

Choosing the optimal smoothing parameter is a difficult research problem and beyond the scope of this software guide. Typically, the optimal value of the smoothing parameter will depend on the data and the number of samples used.

Mattes et al. Implementation

The implementation of mutual information metric available in ITKv4 follows the method specified by Mattes et al. in [40] and is implemented by the `itk::MattesMutualInformationImageToImageMetricv4` class.

In this implementation, only one set of intensity samples is drawn from the image. Using this set, the marginal and joint probability density function (PDF) is evaluated at discrete positions or bins uniformly spread within the dynamic range of the images. Entropy values are then computed by summing over the bins.

The number of spatial samples used is a ratio of the total number of samples and is set using the `SetMetricSamplingPercentage()` method directly from the registration framework `itk::ImageRegistrationMethodv4`. Also, The number of bins used to compute the entropy values is set in the metric class via the `SetNumberOfHistogramBins()` method.

Since the fixed image PDF does not contribute to the metric derivatives, it does not need to be smooth. Hence, a zero-order (boxcar) B-spline kernel is used for computing the PDF. On the other hand, to ensure smoothness, a third-order B-spline kernel is used to compute the moving image intensity PDF. The advantage of using a B-spline kernel over a Gaussian kernel is that the B-spline kernel has a finite support region. This is computationally attractive, as each intensity sample only affects a small number of bins and hence does not require a $N \times N$ loop to compute the metric value.

During the PDF calculations, the image intensity values are linearly scaled to have a minimum of zero and maximum of one. This rescaling means that a fixed B-spline kernel bandwidth of one can be used to handle image data with arbitrary magnitude and dynamic range.

3.11.4 Normalized Mutual Information Metric

Given two images, A and B, the normalized mutual information may be computed as

$$NMI(A,B) = 1 + \frac{I(A,B)}{H(A,B)} = \frac{H(A)+H(B)}{H(A,B)} \tag{3.32}$$

where the entropy of the images, $H(A)$, $H(B)$, the mutual information, $I(A,B)$ and the joint entropy $H(A,B)$ are computed as mentioned in 3.11.3. Details of the implementation may be found in [24].

3.11.5 Demons metric

The implementation of the `itk::DemonsImageToImageMetricv4` metric is taken from `itk::DemonsRegistrationFunction`.

The metric derivative can be calculated using image derivatives either from the fixed or moving images. The default is to use fixed-image gradients. See ObjectToObjectMetric::SetGradientSource to change this behavior.

An intensity threshold is used, below which image pixels are considered equal for the purpose of derivative calculation. The threshold can be changed by calling `SetIntensityDifferenceThreshold`.

Note that this metric supports only moving transforms with local support and with a number of local parameters that match the moving image dimension. In particular, it's meant to be used with `itk::DisplacementFieldTransform` and derived classes.

3.11.6 ANTS neighborhood correlation metric

The `itk::ANTSNeighborhoodCorrelationImageToImageMetricv4` metric computes normalized cross correlation using a small neighborhood for each voxel between two images, with speed optimizations for dense registration.

Around each voxel, the neighborhood is defined as a N-Dimensional rectangle centered at the voxel. The size of the rectangle is 2*radius+1. Normalized correlation between neighborhoods of the fixed image and the moving image are averaged over the whole image as the final metric. A radius less than 2 can be unstable. 2 is the default.

3.12 Optimizers

Optimization algorithms are encapsulated as `itk::ObjectToObjectOptimizer` objects within ITKv4. Optimizers are generic and can be used for applications other than registration. Within the registration framework, subclasses of `itk::SingleValuedNonLinearVnlOptimizerv4` are implemented as a wrap around already implemented vnl classes.

The basic input to an optimizer is a cost function or metric object. In the context of registration, `itk::ImageToImageMetricv4` classes provide this functionality. The metric is set using `SetInitialPosition()` and the optimization algorithm is invoked by `StartOptimization()`. Once the optimization has finished, the final parameters can be obtained using `GetCurrentPosition()`.

Some optimizers also allow rescaling of their individual parameters. This is convenient for normalizing parameter spaces where some parameters have different dynamic ranges. For example, the first parameter of `itk::Euler2DTransform` represents an angle while the last two parameters represent translations. A unit change in angle has a much greater impact on an image than a unit change in translation. This difference in scale appears as long narrow valleys in the search space making the optimization problem more difficult. Rescaling the translation parameters can help to fix this problem. Scales are represented as an `itk::Array` of doubles and set using `SetScales()`.

Estimating the scales parameters can also be done automatically using the `itk::OptimizerParameterScalesEstimatorTemplate` and its subclasses. The scales estimator object is then set to the optimizer via `SetScalesEstimator()`.

Despite the old version of ITK, there are only *Single Valued* types of optimizers available in ITKv4, which are suitable for dealing with cost functions that return a single value. These are indeed the most common type of cost functions, and are also known as *Single Valued* functions.

The types of single valued optimizers currently available in ITKv4 are:

- **Amoeba**: Nelder-Meade downhill simplex. This optimizer is actually implemented in the `vxl/vnl` numerics toolkit. The ITK class `itk::AmoebaOptimizerv4` is merely an adaptor class.

- **Gradient Descent**: Advances parameters in the direction of the gradient where the step size is governed by a learning rate (`itk::GradientDescentOptimizerv4`).

- **Gradient Descent Line Search**: Gradient descent with a golden section line search. `itk::GradientDescentLineSearchOptimizerv4` implements a simple gradient descent optimizer that is followed by a line search to find the best value for the learning rate.

- **Conjugate Gradient Descent Line Search**: Advances parameters in the direction of the Polak-Ribiere conjugate gradient where a line search is used to find the best value for the learning rate (`itk::ConjugateGradientLineSearchOptimizerv4`).

- **Quasi Newton**: Implements a Quasi-Newton optimizer with BFGS Hessian estimation. Second order approximation of the cost function is usually more efficient since it estimates the

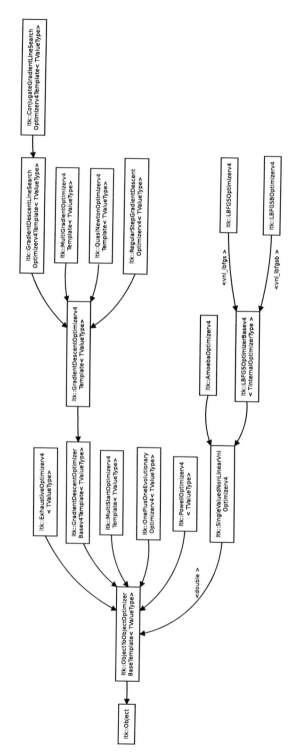

Figure 3.45: Class diagram of the optimizersv4 hierarchy.

descent or ascent direction more precisely. However, computation of Hessian is usually expensive or unavailable. Alternatively Quasi-Newton methods can estimate a Hessian from the gradients in previous steps. Here a specific Quasi-Newton method, BFGS, is used to compute the Quasi-Newton steps (`itk::QuasiNewtonOptimizerv4`).

- **LBFGS**: Limited memory Broyden, Fletcher, Goldfarb and Shannon minimization. It is an adaptor to an optimizer in `vnl` (`itk::LBFGSOptimizerv4`).

- **LBFGSB**: A modified version of the LBFGS optimizer that allows to specify bounds for the parameters in the search space. It is an adaptor to an optimizer in `netlib`. Details on this optimizer can be found in [10, 76] (`itk::LBFGSBOptimizerv4`).

- **One Plus One Evolutionary**: Strategy that simulates the biological evolution of a set of samples in the search space. This optimizer is mainly used in the process of bias correction of MRI images (`itk::OnePlusOneEvolutionaryOptimizerv4`). Details on this optimizer can be found in [60].

- **Regular Step Gradient Descent**: Advances parameters in the direction of the gradient where a bipartition scheme is used to compute the step size (`itk::RegularStepGradientDescentOptimizerv4`). This optimizer is also used for Versor transforms parameters, where the current rotation is composed with the gradient rotation to produce the new rotation versor. The translational part of the transform parameters are updated as usually done in a vector space. It follows the definition of versor gradients defined by Hamilton [25]

- **Powell Optimizer**: Powell optimization method. For an N-dimensional parameter space, each iteration minimizes(maximizes) the function in N (initially orthogonal) directions. This optimizer is described in [50]. (`itk::PowellOptimizerv4`).

- **Exhausive Optimizer**: Fully samples a grid on the parameteric space. This optimizer is equivalent to an exahaustive search in a discrete grid defined over the parametric space. The grid is centered on the initial position. The subdivisions of the grid along each one of the dimensions of the parametric space is defined by an array of number of steps (`itk::ExhaustiveOptimizerv4`).

Figure 3.45 illustrates the full class hierarchy of optimizers in ITK. Optimizers in the lower right corner are adaptor classes to optimizers existing in the `vxl/vnl` numerics toolkit. The optimizers interact with the `itk::CostFunction` class. In the registration framework this cost function is reimplemented in the form of ImageToImageMetric.

3.12.1 Registration using the One plus One Evolutionary Optimizer

The source code for this section can be found in the file
`ImageRegistration11.cxx`.

This example illustrates how to combine the MutualInformation metric with an Evolutionary algorithm for optimization. Evolutionary algorithms are naturally well-suited for optimizing the Mutual Information metric given its random and noisy behavior.

The structure of the example is almost identical to the one illustrated in ImageRegistration4. Therefore we focus here on the setup that is specifically required for the evolutionary optimizer.

```
#include "itkImageRegistrationMethodv4.h"
#include "itkTranslationTransform.h"
#include "itkMattesMutualInformationImageToImageMetricv4.h"
#include "itkOnePlusOneEvolutionaryOptimizerv4.h"
#include "itkNormalVariateGenerator.h"
```

In this example the image types and all registration components, except the metric, are declared as
in Section 3.2. The Mattes mutual information metric type is instantiated using the image types.

```
typedef itk::MattesMutualInformationImageToImageMetricv4<
                            FixedImageType,
                            MovingImageType >    MetricType;
```

The histogram bins metric parameter is set as follows.

```
metric->SetNumberOfHistogramBins( 20 );
```

As our previous discussion in section 3.5.1, only a subsample of the virtual domain is needed to
evaluate the metric. The number of spatial samples to be used depends on the content of the image,
and the user can define the sampling percentage and the way that sampling operation is managed
by the registration framework as follows. Sampling startegy can can be defined as *REGULAR* or
RANDOM, while the default value is *NONE*.

```
registration->SetMetricSamplingPercentage( samplingPercentage );

RegistrationType::MetricSamplingStrategyType  samplingStrategy  =
                                      RegistrationType::RANDOM;
registration->SetMetricSamplingStrategy( samplingStrategy );
```

Evolutionary algorithms are based on testing random variations of parameters. In order to support the
computation of random values, ITK provides a family of random number generators. In this example,
we use the itk::NormalVariateGenerator which generates values with a normal distribution.

```
typedef itk::Statistics::NormalVariateGenerator  GeneratorType;

GeneratorType::Pointer generator = GeneratorType::New();
```

The random number generator must be initialized with a seed.

```
generator->Initialize(12345);
```

Now we set the optimizer parameters.

```
optimizer->SetNormalVariateGenerator( generator );
optimizer->Initialize( 10 );
optimizer->SetEpsilon( 1.0 );
optimizer->SetMaximumIteration( 4000 );
```

This example is executed using the same multi-modality images as in the previous one. The registration converges after 24 iterations and produces the following results:

```
Translation X = 13.1719
Translation Y = 16.9006
```

These values are a very close match to the true misalignment introduced in the moving image.

3.12.2   Registration using masks constructed with Spatial objects

The source code for this section can be found in the file
ImageRegistration12.cxx.

This example illustrates the use SpatialObjects as masks for selecting the pixels that should contribute to the computation of Image Metrics. This example is almost identical to ImageRegistration6 with the exception that the SpatialObject masks are created and passed to the image metric.

The most important header in this example is the one corresponding to the itk::ImageMaskSpatialObject class.

```
#include "itkImageMaskSpatialObject.h"
```

Here we instantiate the type of the itk::ImageMaskSpatialObject using the same dimension of the images to be registered.

```
typedef itk::ImageMaskSpatialObject< Dimension >   MaskType;
```

Then we use the type for creating the spatial object mask that will restrict the registration to a reduced region of the image.

```
MaskType::Pointer  spatialObjectMask = MaskType::New();
```

The mask in this case is read from a binary file using the ImageFileReader instantiated for an unsigned char pixel type.

```
typedef itk::Image< unsigned char, Dimension >   ImageMaskType;
```

```
typedef itk::ImageFileReader< ImageMaskType >   MaskReaderType;
```

The reader is constructed and a filename is passed to it.

```
MaskReaderType::Pointer  maskReader = MaskReaderType::New();
```

```
maskReader->SetFileName( argv[3] );
```

As usual, the reader is triggered by invoking its Update() method. Since this may eventually throw an exception, the call must be placed in a try/catch block. Note that a full fledged application will place this try/catch block at a much higher level, probably under the control of the GUI.

```
try
  {
  maskReader->Update();
  }
catch( itk::ExceptionObject & err )
  {
  std::cerr << "ExceptionObject caught !" << std::endl;
  std::cerr << err << std::endl;
  return EXIT_FAILURE;
  }
```

The output of the mask reader is connected as input to the ImageMaskSpatialObject.

```
spatialObjectMask->SetImage( maskReader->GetOutput() );
```

Finally, the spatial object mask is passed to the image metric.

```
metric->SetFixedImageMask( spatialObjectMask );
```

Let's execute this example over some of the images provided in `Examples/Data`, for example:

- `BrainProtonDensitySliceBorder20.png`

- `BrainProtonDensitySliceR10X13Y17.png`

The second image is the result of intentionally rotating the first image by 10 degrees and shifting it 13mm in X and 17mm in Y. Both images have unit-spacing and are shown in Figure 3.14.

The registration converges after 23 iterations and produces the following results:

```
Angle (radians) 0.174407
Angle (degrees) 9.99281
Center X        = 111.172
Center Y        = 131.563
Translation X = 12.4584
Translation Y = 16.0726
```

These values are a very close match to the true misalignments introduced in the moving image.

Now we resample the moving image using the transform resulting from the registration process.

```
TransformType::MatrixType matrix = transform->GetMatrix();
TransformType::OffsetType offset = transform->GetOffset();

std::cout << "Matrix = " << std::endl << matrix << std::endl;
std::cout << "Offset = " << std::endl << offset << std::endl;
```

3.12.3   Rigid registrations incorporating prior knowledge

The source code for this section can be found in the file
`ImageRegistration13.cxx`.

This example illustrates how to do registration with a 2D Rigid Transform and with MutualInformation metric.

```
#include "itkMattesMutualInformationImageToImageMetricv4.h"
```

The CenteredRigid2DTransform applies a rigid transform in 2D space.

```
typedef itk::CenteredRigid2DTransform< double >  TransformType;

typedef itk::MattesMutualInformationImageToImageMetricv4<
                          FixedImageType,
                          MovingImageType >  MetricType;
```

```
metric->SetNumberOfHistogramBins( 20 );

double samplingPercentage = 0.20;
registration->SetMetricSamplingPercentage( samplingPercentage );

RegistrationType::MetricSamplingStrategyType  samplingStrategy =
                                     RegistrationType::RANDOM;
registration->SetMetricSamplingStrategy( samplingStrategy );
```

The `itk::CenteredRigid2DTransform` is initialized by 5 parameters, indicating the angle of rotation, the center coordinates and the translation to be applied after rotation. The initialization is done by the `itk::CenteredTransformInitializer`. The transform can operate in two modes, the first of which assumes that the anatomical objects to be registered are centered in their respective images. Hence the best initial guess for the registration is the one that superimposes those two centers. This second approach assumes that the moments of the anatomical objects are similar for both images and hence the best initial guess for registration is to superimpose both mass centers. The center of mass is computed from the moments obtained from the gray level values. Here we adopt the first approach. The `GeometryOn()` method toggles between the approaches.

```
typedef itk::CenteredTransformInitializer<
  TransformType,
  FixedImageType,
  MovingImageType > TransformInitializerType;
TransformInitializerType::Pointer initializer
  = TransformInitializerType::New();
initializer->SetTransform(   transform );

initializer->SetFixedImage(  fixedImageReader->GetOutput() );
initializer->SetMovingImage( movingImageReader->GetOutput() );
initializer->GeometryOn();
initializer->InitializeTransform();
```

The optimizer scales the metrics (the gradient in this case) by the scales during each iteration. Therefore, a large value of the center scale will prevent movement along the center during optimization. Here we assume that the fixed and moving images are likely to be related by a translation.

```
typedef OptimizerType::ScalesType          OptimizerScalesType;
OptimizerScalesType optimizerScales( transform->GetNumberOfParameters() );

const double translationScale = 1.0 / 128.0;
const double centerScale      = 1000.0; // prevents it from moving
                                        // during the optimization
optimizerScales[0] = 1.0;
optimizerScales[1] = centerScale;
optimizerScales[2] = centerScale;
optimizerScales[3] = translationScale;
optimizerScales[4] = translationScale;

optimizer->SetScales( optimizerScales );

optimizer->SetLearningRate( 0.5   );
optimizer->SetMinimumStepLength( 0.0001 );
optimizer->SetNumberOfIterations( 400 );
```

Let's execute this example over some of the images provided in `Examples/Data`, for example:

- BrainProtonDensitySlice.png

- BrainProtonDensitySliceR10X13Y17.png

The second image is the result of intentionally rotating the first image by 10 degrees and shifting it 13*mm* in *X* and 17*mm* in *Y*. Both images have unit-spacing and are shown in Figure 3.14. The example yielded the following results.

```
Angle (radians) 0.174585
Angle (degrees) 10.003
Center X      = 110
Center Y      = 128
Translation X = 13.09
Translation Y = 15.91
```

These values match the true misalignment introduced in the moving image.

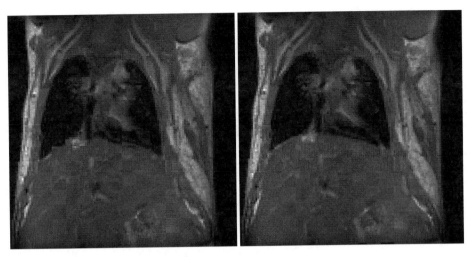

Figure 3.46: Checkerboard comparisons before and after FEM-based deformable registration.

3.13 Deformable Registration

3.13.1 FEM-Based Image Registration

The source code for this section can be found in the file
DeformableRegistration1.cxx.

The finite element (FEM) library within the Insight Toolkit can be used to solve deformable image registration problems. The first step in implementing a FEM-based registration is to include the appropriate header files.

```
#include "itkFEMRegistrationFilter.h"
```

Next, we use typedefs to instantiate all necessary classes. We define the image and element types we plan to use to solve a two-dimensional registration problem. We define multiple element types so that they can be used without recompiling the code.

```
typedef itk::Image<unsigned char, 2>                    DiskImageType;
typedef itk::Image<float, 2>                            ImageType;
typedef itk::fem::Element2DC0LinearQuadrilateralMembrane ElementType;
typedef itk::fem::Element2DC0LinearTriangularMembrane   ElementType2;
typedef itk::fem::FEMObject<2>                           FEMObjectType;
```

Note that in order to solve a three-dimensional registration problem, we would simply define 3D image and element types in lieu of those above. The following declarations could be used for a 3D problem:

```
typedef itk::Image<unsigned char, 3>                          fileImage3DType;
typedef itk::Image<float, 3>                                    Image3DType;
typedef itk::fem::Element3DC0LinearHexahedronMembrane    Element3DType;
typedef itk::fem::Element3DC0LinearTetrahedronMembrane   Element3DType2;
typedef itk::fem::FEMObject<3>                                FEMObject3DType;
```

Once all the necessary components have been instantiated, we can instantiate the `itk::FEMRegistrationFilter`, which depends on the image input and output types.

```
typedef itk::fem::FEMRegistrationFilter<ImageType,ImageType,FEMObjectType>
                                              RegistrationType;
```

In order to begin the registration, we declare an instance of the FEMRegistrationFilter and set its parameters. For simplicity, we will call it `registrationFilter`.

```
RegistrationType::Pointer registrationFilter = RegistrationType::New();
registrationFilter->SetMaxLevel(1);
registrationFilter->SetUseNormalizedGradient( true );
registrationFilter->ChooseMetric( 0 );

unsigned int maxiters = 20;
float        E = 100;
float        p = 1;
registrationFilter->SetElasticity(E, 0);
registrationFilter->SetRho(p, 0);
registrationFilter->SetGamma(1., 0);
registrationFilter->SetAlpha(1.);
registrationFilter->SetMaximumIterations( maxiters, 0 );
registrationFilter->SetMeshPixelsPerElementAtEachResolution(4, 0);
registrationFilter->SetWidthOfMetricRegion(1, 0);
registrationFilter->SetNumberOfIntegrationPoints(2, 0);
registrationFilter->SetDoLineSearchOnImageEnergy( 0 );
registrationFilter->SetTimeStep(1.);
registrationFilter->SetEmployRegridding(false);
registrationFilter->SetUseLandmarks(false);
```

In order to initialize the mesh of elements, we must first create "dummy" material and element objects and assign them to the registration filter. These objects are subsequently used to either read a predefined mesh from a file or generate a mesh using the software. The values assigned to the fields within the material object are arbitrary since they will be replaced with those specified earlier. Similarly, the element object will be replaced with those from the desired mesh.

```
// Create the material properties
itk::fem::MaterialLinearElasticity::Pointer m;
m = itk::fem::MaterialLinearElasticity::New();
m->SetGlobalNumber(0);
// Young's modulus of the membrane
m->SetYoungsModulus(registrationFilter->GetElasticity());
m->SetCrossSectionalArea(1.0);    // Cross-sectional area
m->SetThickness(1.0);             // Thickness
m->SetMomentOfInertia(1.0);       // Moment of inertia
m->SetPoissonsRatio(0.);          // Poisson's ratio -- DONT CHOOSE 1.0!!
m->SetDensityHeatProduct(1.0);    // Density-Heat capacity product

// Create the element type
ElementType::Pointer e1=ElementType::New();
e1->SetMaterial(m.GetPointer());
registrationFilter->SetElement(e1.GetPointer());
registrationFilter->SetMaterial(m);
```

Now we are ready to run the registration:

```
registrationFilter->RunRegistration();
```

To output the image resulting from the registration, we can call `GetWarpedImage()`. The image is written in floating point format.

```
itk::ImageFileWriter<ImageType>::Pointer warpedImageWriter;
warpedImageWriter = itk::ImageFileWriter<ImageType>::New();
warpedImageWriter->SetInput( registrationFilter->GetWarpedImage() );
warpedImageWriter->SetFileName("warpedMovingImage.mha");
try
{
  warpedImageWriter->Update();
}
catch( itk::ExceptionObject & excp )
{
  std::cerr << excp << std::endl;
  return EXIT_FAILURE;
}
```

We can also output the displacement field resulting from the registration; we can call `GetDisplacementField()` to get the multi-component image.

```
typedef itk::ImageFileWriter<RegistrationType::FieldType> DispWriterType;
DispWriterType::Pointer dispWriter = DispWriterType::New();
dispWriter->SetInput( registrationFilter->GetDisplacementField() );
dispWriter->SetFileName("displacement.mha");
try
{
  dispWriter->Update();
}
catch( itk::ExceptionObject & excp )
{
  std::cerr << excp << std::endl;
  return EXIT_FAILURE;
}
```

Figure 3.46 presents the results of the FEM-based deformable registration applied to two time-

separated slices of a living rat dataset. Checkerboard comparisons of the two images are shown
before registration (left) and after registration (right). Both images were acquired from the same
living rat, the first after inspiration of air into the lungs and the second after exhalation. Deformation
occurs due to the relaxation of the diaphragm and the intercostal muscles, both of which exert force
on the lung tissue and cause air to be expelled.

The following is a documented sample parameter file that can be used with this deformable registration example. This example demonstrates the setup of a basic registration problem that does not use
multi-resolution strategies. As a result, only one value for the parameters between (# of pixels
per element) and (maximum iterations) is necessary. In order to use a multi-resolution strategy, you would have to specify values for those parameters at each level of the pyramid.

```
% Configuration file #1 for DeformableRegistration1.cxx
%
% This example demonstrates the setup of a basic registration
% problem that does NOT use multi-resolution strategies.  As a
% result, only one value for the parameters between
% (# of pixels per element) and (maximum iterations) is necessary.
% If you were using multi-resolution, you would have to specify
% values for those parameters at each level of the pyramid.
%
% Note: the paths in the parameters assume you have the traditional
% ITK file hierarchy as shown below:
%
% ITK/Examples/RegistrationITKv4/DeformableRegistration1.cxx
% ITK/Examples/Data/RatLungSlice*
% ITK_Build_Dir/bin/DeformableRegistration1
%
% -------------------------------------------------------------
% Parameters for the single- or multi-resolution techniques
% -------------------------------------------------------------
1          % Number of levels in the multi-res pyramid (1 = single-res)
1          % Highest level to use in the pyramid
 1 1               % Scaling at lowest level of pyramid
 4                 % Number of pixels per element
 1.e4              % Elasticity (E)
 1.e4              % Density x capacity (RhoC)
 1                 % Image energy scaling (gamma) - sets gradient step size
 2                 % NumberOfIntegrationPoints
 1                 % WidthOfMetricRegion
 20                % MaximumIterations
% -----------------------------
% Parameters for the registration
% -----------------------------
0 0.99 % Similarity metric (0=mean sq, 1 = ncc, 2=pattern int, 3=MI, 5=demons)
1.0       % Alpha
0         % DescentDirection (1 = max, 0 = min)
0         % DoLineSearch (0=never, 1=always, 2=if needed)
1.e1      % TimeStep
```

```
0.5      % Landmark variance
0        % Employ regridding / enforce diffeomorphism ( >= 1 -> true)
% --------------------------------
% Information about the image inputs
% --------------------------------
128      % Nx (image x dimension)
128      % Ny (image y dimension)
0        % Nz (image z dimension - not used if 2D)
../../Insight/Examples/Data/RatLungSlice1.mha  % ReferenceFileName
../../Insight/Examples/Data/RatLungSlice2.mha  % TargetFileName
% ----------------------------------------------------------------
% The actions below depend on the values of the flags preceding them.
% For example, to write out the displacement fields, you have to set
% the value of WriteDisplacementField to 1.
% ----------------------------------------------------------------
0        % UseLandmarks? - read the file name below if this is true
-        % LandmarkFileName
./RatLung_result                          % ResultsFileName (prefix only)
1        % WriteDisplacementField?
./RatLung_disp                            % DisplacementsFileName (prefix only)
0        % ReadMeshFile?
-                                         % MeshFileName
END
```

3.13.2 BSplines Image Registration

The source code for this section can be found in the file
`DeformableRegistration4.cxx`.

This example illustrates the use of the `itk::BSplineTransform` class for performing registration of two *2D* images in an ITKv4 registration framework. Due to the large number of parameters of the BSpline transform, we will use a `itk::LBFGSOptimizerv4` instead of a simple steepest descent or a conjugate gradient descent optimizer.

The following are the most relevant headers to this example.

```
#include "itkBSplineTransform.h"
#include "itkLBFGSOptimizerv4.h"
```

The parameter space of the `BSplineTransform` is composed by the set of all the deformations associated with the nodes of the BSpline grid. This large number of parameters makes it possible to represent a wide variety of deformations, at the cost of requiring a significant amount of computation time.

We instantiate now the type of the `BSplineTransform` using as template parameters the type for coordinates representation, the dimension of the space, and the order of the BSpline.

```
const unsigned int SpaceDimension = ImageDimension;
const unsigned int SplineOrder = 3;
typedef double CoordinateRepType;

typedef itk::BSplineTransform<
                         CoordinateRepType,
                         SpaceDimension,
                         SplineOrder >           TransformType;
```

The transform object is constructed below.

```
TransformType::Pointer    transform   = TransformType::New();
```

Fixed parameters of the BSpline transform should be defined before the registration. These parameters define origin, dimension, direction and mesh size of the transform grid and are set based on specifications of the fixed image space lattice. We can use `itk::BSplineTransformInitializer` to initialize fixed parameters of a BSpline transform.

```
typedef itk::BSplineTransformInitializer<
  TransformType,
  FixedImageType> InitializerType;

InitializerType::Pointer transformInitializer = InitializerType::New();

unsigned int numberOfGridNodesInOneDimension = 8;

TransformType::MeshSizeType          meshSize;
meshSize.Fill( numberOfGridNodesInOneDimension - SplineOrder );

transformInitializer->SetTransform( transform );
transformInitializer->SetImage( fixedImage );
transformInitializer->SetTransformDomainMeshSize( meshSize );
transformInitializer->InitializeTransform();
```

After setting the fixed parameters of the transform, we set the initial transform to be an identity transform. It is like setting all the transform parameters to zero in created parameter space.

```
transform->SetIdentity();
```

Then, the initialized transform is connected to the registration object and is set to be optimized directly during the registration process.

Calling `InPlaceOn()` means that the current initialized transform will optimized directly and is grafted to the output, so it can be considered as the output transform object. Otherwise, the initial transform will be copied or "cloned" to the output transform object, and the copied object will be optimized during the registration process.

```
registration->SetInitialTransform( transform );
registration->InPlaceOn();
```

The `itk::RegistrationParameterScalesFromPhysicalShift` class is used to estimate the parameters scales before we set the optimizer.

```
typedef itk::RegistrationParameterScalesFromPhysicalShift<MetricType>
  ScalesEstimatorType;
ScalesEstimatorType::Pointer scalesEstimator = ScalesEstimatorType::New();
scalesEstimator->SetMetric( metric );
scalesEstimator->SetTransformForward( true );
scalesEstimator->SetSmallParameterVariation( 1.0 );
```

Now the scale estimator is passed to the `itk::LBFGSOptimizerv4`, and we set other parameters of the optimizer as well.

```
optimizer->SetGradientConvergenceTolerance( 5e-2 );
optimizer->SetLineSearchAccuracy( 1.2 );
optimizer->SetDefaultStepLength( 1.5 );
optimizer->TraceOn();
optimizer->SetMaximumNumberOfFunctionEvaluations( 1000 );
optimizer->SetScalesEstimator( scalesEstimator );
```

Let's execute this example using the rat lung images from the previous examples.

- `RatLungSlice1.mha`

- `RatLungSlice2.mha`

The *transform* object is updated during the registration process and is passed to the resampler to map the moving image space onto the fixed image space.

```
OptimizerType::ParametersType finalParameters = transform->GetParameters();
```

3.13.3 Level Set Motion for Deformable Registration

The source code for this section can be found in the file
`DeformableRegistration5.cxx`.

This example demonstrates how to use the level set motion to deformably register two images. The first step is to include the header files.

```
#include "itkLevelSetMotionRegistrationFilter.h"
#include "itkHistogramMatchingImageFilter.h"
#include "itkCastImageFilter.h"
#include "itkWarpImageFilter.h"
```

Second, we declare the types of the images.

```
const unsigned int Dimension = 2;
typedef unsigned short PixelType;

typedef itk::Image< PixelType, Dimension >  FixedImageType;
typedef itk::Image< PixelType, Dimension >  MovingImageType;
```

Image file readers are set up in a similar fashion to previous examples. To support the re-mapping of the moving image intensity, we declare an internal image type with a floating point pixel type and cast the input images to the internal image type.

```
typedef float                                              InternalPixelType;
typedef itk::Image< InternalPixelType, Dimension >  InternalImageType;
typedef itk::CastImageFilter< FixedImageType,
                              InternalImageType >    FixedImageCasterType;
typedef itk::CastImageFilter< MovingImageType,
                              InternalImageType >    MovingImageCasterType;

FixedImageCasterType::Pointer fixedImageCaster = FixedImageCasterType::New();
MovingImageCasterType::Pointer movingImageCaster
                               = MovingImageCasterType::New();

fixedImageCaster->SetInput( fixedImageReader->GetOutput() );
movingImageCaster->SetInput( movingImageReader->GetOutput() );
```

The level set motion algorithm relies on the assumption that pixels representing the same homologous point on an object have the same intensity on both the fixed and moving images to be registered. In this example, we will preprocess the moving image to match the intensity between the images using the `itk::HistogramMatchingImageFilter`.

The basic idea is to match the histograms of the two images at a user-specified number of quantile values. For robustness, the histograms are matched so that the background pixels are excluded from both histograms. For MR images, a simple procedure is to exclude all gray values smaller than the mean gray value of the image.

```
typedef itk::HistogramMatchingImageFilter<
                          InternalImageType,
                          InternalImageType >    MatchingFilterType;
MatchingFilterType::Pointer matcher = MatchingFilterType::New();
```

For this example, we set the moving image as the source or input image and the fixed image as the reference image.

```
matcher->SetInput( movingImageCaster->GetOutput() );
matcher->SetReferenceImage( fixedImageCaster->GetOutput() );
```

We then select the number of bins to represent the histograms and the number of points or quantile values where the histogram is to be matched.

```
matcher->SetNumberOfHistogramLevels( 1024 );
matcher->SetNumberOfMatchPoints( 7 );
```

Simple background extraction is done by thresholding at the mean intensity.

```
matcher->ThresholdAtMeanIntensityOn();
```

In the `itk::LevelSetMotionRegistrationFilter`, the deformation field is represented as an image whose pixels are floating point vectors.

```
typedef itk::Vector< float, Dimension >        VectorPixelType;
typedef itk::Image< VectorPixelType, Dimension >    DisplacementFieldType;
typedef itk::LevelSetMotionRegistrationFilter<
                          InternalImageType,
                          InternalImageType,
                          DisplacementFieldType> RegistrationFilterType;
RegistrationFilterType::Pointer filter = RegistrationFilterType::New();
```

The input fixed image is simply the output of the fixed image casting filter. The input moving image is the output of the histogram matching filter.

```
filter->SetFixedImage( fixedImageCaster->GetOutput() );
filter->SetMovingImage( matcher->GetOutput() );
```

The level set motion registration filter has two parameters: the number of iterations to be performed and the standard deviation of the Gaussian smoothing kernel to be applied to the image prior to calculating gradients.

```
filter->SetNumberOfIterations( 50 );
filter->SetGradientSmoothingStandardDeviations(4);
```

The registration algorithm is triggered by updating the filter. The filter output is the computed deformation field.

```
filter->Update();
```

The `itk::WarpImageFilter` can be used to warp the moving image with the output deformation field. Like the `itk::ResampleImageFilter`, the WarpImageFilter requires the specification of the input image to be resampled, an input image interpolator, and the output image spacing and origin.

```
typedef itk::WarpImageFilter<
                    MovingImageType,
                    MovingImageType,
                    DisplacementFieldType >     WarperType;
typedef itk::LinearInterpolateImageFunction<
                            MovingImageType,
                            double        >   InterpolatorType;
WarperType::Pointer warper = WarperType::New();
InterpolatorType::Pointer interpolator = InterpolatorType::New();
FixedImageType::Pointer fixedImage = fixedImageReader->GetOutput();

warper->SetInput( movingImageReader->GetOutput() );
warper->SetInterpolator( interpolator );
warper->SetOutputSpacing( fixedImage->GetSpacing() );
warper->SetOutputOrigin( fixedImage->GetOrigin() );
warper->SetOutputDirection( fixedImage->GetDirection() );
```

Unlike the ResampleImageFilter, the WarpImageFilter warps or transforms the input image with respect to the deformation field represented by an image of vectors. The resulting warped or resampled image is written to file as per previous examples.

```
warper->SetDisplacementField( filter->GetOutput() );
```

Let's execute this example using the rat lung data from the previous example. The associated data files can be found in `Examples/Data`:

- `RatLungSlice1.mha`

- `RatLungSlice2.mha`

The result of the demons-based deformable registration is presented in Figure 3.47. The checkerboard comparison shows that the algorithm was able to recover the misalignment due to expiration.

It may be also desirable to write the deformation field as an image of vectors. This can be done with

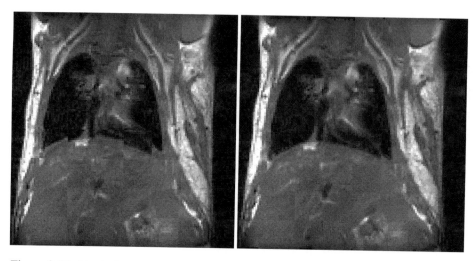

Figure 3.47: Checkerboard comparisons before and after demons-based deformable registration.

the following code.

```
typedef itk::ImageFileWriter< DisplacementFieldType > FieldWriterType;
FieldWriterType::Pointer fieldWriter = FieldWriterType::New();
fieldWriter->SetFileName( argv[4] );
fieldWriter->SetInput( filter->GetOutput() );

fieldWriter->Update();
```

Note that the file format used for writing the deformation field must be capable of representing multiple components per pixel. This is the case for the MetaImage and VTK file formats.

3.13.4 BSplines Multi-Grid Image Registration

The source code for this section can be found in the file
DeformableRegistration6.cxx.

This example illustrates the use of the itk::BSplineTransform class in a multi-resolution scheme. Here we run 3 levels of resolutions. The first level of registration is performed with the spline grid of low resolution. Then, a common practice is to increase the resolution of the B-spline mesh (or, analogously, the control point grid size) at each level.

For this purpose, we introduce the concept of transform adaptors. Each level of each stage is defined by a transform adaptor which describes how to adapt the transform to the current level by increasing the resolution from the previous level. Here, we used itk::BSplineTransformParametersAdaptor class to adapt the BSpline transform parameters at each resolution level. Note that for many transforms, such as affine, the concept of an adaptor may be nonsensical since the number of transform parameters does not change between resolution levels.

Since this example is quite similar to the previous example on the use of the BSplineTransform we omit most of the details already discussed and will focus on the aspects related to the multi-resolution approach.

We include the header files for the transform, optimizer and adaptor.

```
#include "itkBSplineTransform.h"
#include "itkLBFGSOptimizerv4.h"
#include "itkBSplineTransformParametersAdaptor.h"
```

We instantiate the type of the BSplineTransform using as template parameters the type for coordinates representation, the dimension of the space, and the order of the BSpline.

```
const unsigned int SpaceDimension = ImageDimension;
const unsigned int SplineOrder = 3;
typedef double CoordinateRepType;

typedef itk::BSplineTransform<
                    CoordinateRepType,
                    SpaceDimension,
                    SplineOrder >      TransformType;
```

We construct the transform object, initialize its parameters and connect that to the registration object.

```
TransformType::Pointer  outputBSplineTransform = TransformType::New();

// Initialize the fixed parameters of transform (grid size, etc).
//
typedef itk::BSplineTransformInitializer<
  TransformType,
  FixedImageType> InitializerType;

InitializerType::Pointer transformInitializer = InitializerType::New();

unsigned int numberOfGridNodesInOneDimension = 8;

TransformType::MeshSizeType           meshSize;
meshSize.Fill( numberOfGridNodesInOneDimension - SplineOrder );

transformInitializer->SetTransform( outputBSplineTransform );
transformInitializer->SetImage( fixedImage );
transformInitializer->SetTransformDomainMeshSize( meshSize );
transformInitializer->InitializeTransform();

// Set transform to identity
//
typedef TransformType::ParametersType      ParametersType;
const unsigned int numberOfParameters =
              outputBSplineTransform->GetNumberOfParameters();
ParametersType parameters( numberOfParameters );
parameters.Fill( 0.0 );
outputBSplineTransform->SetParameters( parameters );

registration->SetInitialTransform( outputBSplineTransform );
registration->InPlaceOn();
```

The registration process is run in three levels. The shrink factors and smoothing sigmas are set for each level.

```
const unsigned int numberOfLevels = 3;

RegistrationType::ShrinkFactorsArrayType shrinkFactorsPerLevel;
shrinkFactorsPerLevel.SetSize( numberOfLevels );
shrinkFactorsPerLevel[0] = 3;
shrinkFactorsPerLevel[1] = 2;
shrinkFactorsPerLevel[2] = 1;

RegistrationType::SmoothingSigmasArrayType smoothingSigmasPerLevel;
smoothingSigmasPerLevel.SetSize( numberOfLevels );
smoothingSigmasPerLevel[0] = 2;
smoothingSigmasPerLevel[1] = 1;
smoothingSigmasPerLevel[2] = 0;

registration->SetNumberOfLevels( numberOfLevels );
registration->SetSmoothingSigmasPerLevel( smoothingSigmasPerLevel );
registration->SetShrinkFactorsPerLevel( shrinkFactorsPerLevel );
```

Create the transform adaptors to modify the flexibility of the deformable transform for each level of this multi-resolution scheme.

```
RegistrationType::TransformParametersAdaptorsContainerType adaptors;

// First, get fixed image physical dimensions
TransformType::PhysicalDimensionsType          fixedPhysicalDimensions;
for( unsigned int i=0; i< SpaceDimension; i++ )
  {
  fixedPhysicalDimensions[i] = fixedImage->GetSpacing()[i] *
  static_cast<double>(
    fixedImage->GetLargestPossibleRegion().GetSize()[i] - 1 );
  }

// Create the transform adaptors specific to B-splines
for( unsigned int level = 0; level < numberOfLevels; level++ )
  {
  typedef itk::ShrinkImageFilter<
    FixedImageType,
    FixedImageType> ShrinkFilterType;
  ShrinkFilterType::Pointer shrinkFilter = ShrinkFilterType::New();
  shrinkFilter->SetShrinkFactors( shrinkFactorsPerLevel[level] );
  shrinkFilter->SetInput( fixedImage );
  shrinkFilter->Update();

  // A good heuristic is to double the b-spline mesh resolution at each level
  //
  TransformType::MeshSizeType requiredMeshSize;
  for( unsigned int d = 0; d < ImageDimension; d++ )
    {
    requiredMeshSize[d] = meshSize[d] << level;
    }

  typedef itk::BSplineTransformParametersAdaptor<TransformType>
    BSplineAdaptorType;
  BSplineAdaptorType::Pointer bsplineAdaptor = BSplineAdaptorType::New();
  bsplineAdaptor->SetTransform( outputBSplineTransform );
  bsplineAdaptor->SetRequiredTransformDomainMeshSize( requiredMeshSize );
  bsplineAdaptor->SetRequiredTransformDomainOrigin(
    shrinkFilter->GetOutput()->GetOrigin() );
  bsplineAdaptor->SetRequiredTransformDomainDirection(
    shrinkFilter->GetOutput()->GetDirection() );
  bsplineAdaptor->SetRequiredTransformDomainPhysicalDimensions(
    fixedPhysicalDimensions );

  adaptors.push_back( bsplineAdaptor.GetPointer() );
  }

registration->SetTransformParametersAdaptorsPerLevel( adaptors );
```

3.13.5 BSplines Multi-Grid Image Registration in 3D

The source code for this section can be found in the file
`DeformableRegistration7.cxx`.

This example illustrates the use of the `itk::BSplineTransform` class for performing registration
of two 3D images. The example code is for the most part identical to the code presented in Sec-

tion 3.13.4. The major difference is that in this example we set the image dimension to 3 and replace
the `itk::LBFGSOptimizerv4` optimizer with the `itk::LBFGSBOptimizerv4`. We made the modification because we found that LBFGS does not behave well when the starting position is at or close
to optimal; instead we used LBFGSB in unconstrained mode.

The following are the most relevant headers to this example.

```
#include "itkBSplineTransform.h"
#include "itkLBFGSBOptimizerv4.h"
```

The parameter space of the `BSplineTransform` is composed by the set of all the deformations
associated with the nodes of the BSpline grid. This large number of parameters enables it to represent
a wide variety of deformations, at the cost of requiring a significant amount of computation time.

We instantiate now the type of the `BSplineTransform` using as template parameters the type for
coordinates representation, the dimension of the space, and the order of the BSpline.

```
const unsigned int SpaceDimension = ImageDimension;
const unsigned int SplineOrder = 3;
typedef double CoordinateRepType;

typedef itk::BSplineTransform<
                    CoordinateRepType,
                    SpaceDimension,
                    SplineOrder >      TransformType;
```

The transform object is constructed, initialized like previous examples and passed to the registration
method.

```
TransformType::Pointer  outputBSplineTransform = TransformType::New();

registration->SetInitialTransform( outputBSplineTransform );
registration->InPlaceOn();
```

Next we set the parameters of the LBFGSB Optimizer. Note that this optimizer does not support
scales estimator and sets all the parameters scales to one. Also, we should set the boundary condition
for each variable, where `boundSelect[i]` can be set as:

UNBOUNDED, LOWERBOUNDED, BOTHBOUNDED, UPPERBOUNDED

```
const unsigned int numParameters =
  outputBSplineTransform->GetNumberOfParameters();
OptimizerType::BoundSelectionType boundSelect( numParameters );
OptimizerType::BoundValueType upperBound( numParameters );
OptimizerType::BoundValueType lowerBound( numParameters );

boundSelect.Fill( OptimizerType::UNBOUNDED );
upperBound.Fill( 0.0 );
lowerBound.Fill( 0.0 );

optimizer->SetBoundSelection( boundSelect );
optimizer->SetUpperBound( upperBound );
optimizer->SetLowerBound( lowerBound );

optimizer->SetCostFunctionConvergenceFactor( 1e+12 );
optimizer->SetGradientConvergenceTolerance( 1.0e-35 );
optimizer->SetNumberOfIterations( 500 );
optimizer->SetMaximumNumberOfFunctionEvaluations( 500 );
optimizer->SetMaximumNumberOfCorrections( 5 );
```

3.13.6 Image Warping with Kernel Splines

The source code for this section can be found in the file
LandmarkWarping2.cxx.

This example illustrates how to deform an image using a KernelBase spline and two sets of landmarks.

```
#include "itkVector.h"
#include "itkImage.h"
#include "itkLandmarkDisplacementFieldSource.h"
#include "itkImageFileReader.h"
#include "itkImageFileWriter.h"
#include "itkWarpImageFilter.h"
```

3.13.7 Image Warping with BSplines

The source code for this section can be found in the file
BSplineWarping1.cxx.

This example illustrates how to deform a 2D image using a BSplineTransform.

```
#include "itkImageFileReader.h"
#include "itkImageFileWriter.h"

#include "itkResampleImageFilter.h"

#include "itkBSplineTransform.h"
#include "itkTransformFileWriter.h"
```

First, we define the necessary types for the fixed and moving images and image readers.

```
const      unsigned int    ImageDimension = 2;

typedef    unsigned char                              PixelType;
typedef    itk::Image< PixelType, ImageDimension >  FixedImageType;
typedef    itk::Image< PixelType, ImageDimension >  MovingImageType;

typedef    itk::ImageFileReader< FixedImageType  >  FixedReaderType;
typedef    itk::ImageFileReader< MovingImageType >  MovingReaderType;

typedef    itk::ImageFileWriter< MovingImageType >  MovingWriterType;
```

Use the values from the fixed image to set the corresponding values in the resampler.

```
FixedImageType::SpacingType   fixedSpacing   = fixedImage->GetSpacing();
FixedImageType::PointType     fixedOrigin    = fixedImage->GetOrigin();
FixedImageType::DirectionType fixedDirection = fixedImage->GetDirection();

resampler->SetOutputSpacing( fixedSpacing );
resampler->SetOutputOrigin( fixedOrigin );
resampler->SetOutputDirection( fixedDirection );


FixedImageType::RegionType fixedRegion = fixedImage->GetBufferedRegion();
FixedImageType::SizeType   fixedSize =  fixedRegion.GetSize();
resampler->SetSize( fixedSize );
resampler->SetOutputStartIndex( fixedRegion.GetIndex() );


resampler->SetInput( movingReader->GetOutput() );

movingWriter->SetInput( resampler->GetOutput() );
```

We instantiate now the type of the BSplineTransform using as template parameters the type for coordinates representation, the dimension of the space, and the order of the B-spline.

```
const unsigned int SpaceDimension = ImageDimension;
const unsigned int SplineOrder = 3;
typedef double CoordinateRepType;

typedef itk::BSplineTransform<
                      CoordinateRepType,
                      SpaceDimension,
                      SplineOrder >      TransformType;

TransformType::Pointer bsplineTransform = TransformType::New();
```

Next, fill the parameters of the B-spline transform using values from the fixed image and mesh.

```
const unsigned int numberOfGridNodes = 7;

TransformType::PhysicalDimensionsType   fixedPhysicalDimensions;
TransformType::MeshSizeType             meshSize;

for( unsigned int i=0; i< SpaceDimension; i++ )
  {
  fixedPhysicalDimensions[i] = fixedSpacing[i] * static_cast<double>(
    fixedSize[i] - 1 );
  }
meshSize.Fill( numberOfGridNodes - SplineOrder );

bsplineTransform->SetTransformDomainOrigin( fixedOrigin );
bsplineTransform->SetTransformDomainPhysicalDimensions(
  fixedPhysicalDimensions );
bsplineTransform->SetTransformDomainMeshSize( meshSize );
bsplineTransform->SetTransformDomainDirection( fixedDirection );


typedef TransformType::ParametersType   ParametersType;
const unsigned int numberOfParameters =
          bsplineTransform->GetNumberOfParameters();

const unsigned int numberOfNodes = numberOfParameters / SpaceDimension;

ParametersType parameters( numberOfParameters );
```

The B-spline grid should now be fed with coefficients at each node. Since this is a two-dimensional grid, each node should receive two coefficients. Each coefficient pair is representing a displacement vector at this node. The coefficients can be passed to the B-spline in the form of an array where the first set of elements are the first component of the displacements for all the nodes, and the second set of elements is formed by the second component of the displacements for all the nodes.

In this example we read such displacements from a file, but for convenience we have written this file using the pairs of (x, y) displacement for every node. The elements read from the file should therefore be reorganized when assigned to the elements of the array. We do this by storing all the odd elements from the file in the first block of the array, and all the even elements from the file in the second block of the array. Finally the array is passed to the B-spline transform using the SetParameters().

```
std::ifstream infile;

infile.open( argv[1] );

for( unsigned int n=0; n < numberOfNodes; n++ )
  {
  infile >> parameters[n];
  infile >> parameters[n+numberOfNodes];
  }

infile.close();
```

Finally the array is passed to the B-spline transform using the SetParameters().

```
bsplineTransform->SetParameters( parameters );
```

At this point we are ready to use the transform as part of the resample filter. We trigger the execution of the pipeline by invoking `Update()` on the last filter of the pipeline, in this case writer.

```
resampler->SetTransform( bsplineTransform );

try
  {
  movingWriter->Update();
  }
catch( itk::ExceptionObject & excp )
  {
  std::cerr << "Exception thrown " << std::endl;
  std::cerr << excp << std::endl;
  return EXIT_FAILURE;
  }
```

3.14 Demons Deformable Registration

For the problem of intra-modality deformable registration, the Insight Toolkit provides an implementation of Thirion's "demons" algorithm [62, 63]. In this implementation, each image is viewed as a set of iso-intensity contours. The main idea is that a regular grid of forces deform an image by pushing the contours in the normal direction. The orientation and magnitude of the displacement is derived from the instantaneous optical flow equation:

$$\mathbf{D}(\mathbf{X}) \cdot \nabla \mathbf{f}(\mathbf{X}) = -\left(\mathbf{m}(\mathbf{X}) - \mathbf{f}(\mathbf{X})\right) \tag{3.33}$$

In the above equation, $f(\mathbf{X})$ is the fixed image, $m(\mathbf{X})$ is the moving image to be registered, and $\mathbf{D}(\mathbf{X})$ is the displacement or optical flow between the images. It is well known in optical flow literature that Equation 3.33 is insufficient to specify $\mathbf{D}(\mathbf{X})$ locally and is usually determined using some form of regularization. For registration, the projection of the vector on the direction of the intensity gradient is used:

$$\mathbf{D}(\mathbf{X}) = -\frac{\left(\mathbf{m}(\mathbf{X}) - \mathbf{f}(\mathbf{X})\right) \nabla \mathbf{f}(\mathbf{X})}{\|\nabla \mathbf{f}\|^2} \tag{3.34}$$

However, this equation becomes unstable for small values of the image gradient, resulting in large displacement values. To overcome this problem, Thirion re-normalizes the equation such that:

$$\mathbf{D}(\mathbf{X}) = -\frac{\left(\mathbf{m}(\mathbf{X}) - \mathbf{f}(\mathbf{X})\right) \nabla \mathbf{f}(\mathbf{X})}{\|\nabla \mathbf{f}\|^2 + \left(\mathbf{m}(\mathbf{X}) - \mathbf{f}(\mathbf{X})\right)^2 / \mathbf{K}} \tag{3.35}$$

Where K is a normalization factor that accounts for the units imbalance between intensities and gradients. This factor is computed as the mean squared value of the pixel spacings. The inclusion of K ensures the force computation is invariant to the pixel scaling of the images.

Starting with an initial deformation field $\mathbf{D}^0(\mathbf{X})$, the demons algorithm iteratively updates the field using Equation 3.35 such that the field at the N-th iteration is given by:

$$\mathbf{D}^N(\mathbf{X}) = \mathbf{D}^{N-1}(\mathbf{X}) - \frac{\left(\mathbf{m}(\mathbf{X} + \mathbf{D}^{N-1}(\mathbf{X})) - \mathbf{f}(\mathbf{X})\right) \nabla \mathbf{f}(\mathbf{X})}{\|\nabla \mathbf{f}\|^2 + \left(\mathbf{m}(\mathbf{X} + \mathbf{D}^{N-1}(\mathbf{X})) - \mathbf{f}(\mathbf{X})\right)^2} \tag{3.36}$$

Reconstruction of the deformation field is an ill-posed problem where matching the fixed and moving images has many solutions. For example, since each image pixel is free to move independently, it is possible that all pixels of one particular value in $m(\mathbf{X})$ could map to a single image pixel in $f(\mathbf{X})$ of the same value. The resulting deformation field may be unrealistic for real-world applications. An option to solve for the field uniquely is to enforce an elastic-like behavior, smoothing the deformation field with a Gaussian filter between iterations.

In ITK, the demons algorithm is implemented as part of the finite difference solver (FDS) framework and its use is demonstrated in the following example.

3.14.1   Asymmetrical Demons Deformable Registration

The source code for this section can be found in the file
DeformableRegistration2.cxx.

This example demonstrates how to use the "demons" algorithm to deformably register two images.
The first step is to include the header files.

```
#include "itkDemonsRegistrationFilter.h"
#include "itkHistogramMatchingImageFilter.h"
#include "itkCastImageFilter.h"
#include "itkWarpImageFilter.h"
```

Second, we declare the types of the images.

```
const unsigned int Dimension = 2;
typedef unsigned short PixelType;

typedef itk::Image< PixelType, Dimension >  FixedImageType;
typedef itk::Image< PixelType, Dimension >  MovingImageType;
```

Image file readers are set up in a similar fashion to previous examples. To support the re-mapping
of the moving image intensity, we declare an internal image type with a floating point pixel type and
cast the input images to the internal image type.

```
typedef float                                         InternalPixelType;
typedef itk::Image< InternalPixelType, Dimension > InternalImageType;
typedef itk::CastImageFilter< FixedImageType,
                              InternalImageType >  FixedImageCasterType;
typedef itk::CastImageFilter< MovingImageType,
                              InternalImageType >  MovingImageCasterType;

FixedImageCasterType::Pointer fixedImageCaster = FixedImageCasterType::New();
MovingImageCasterType::Pointer movingImageCaster
                                       = MovingImageCasterType::New();

fixedImageCaster->SetInput( fixedImageReader->GetOutput() );
movingImageCaster->SetInput( movingImageReader->GetOutput() );
```

The demons algorithm relies on the assumption that pixels representing the same homologous point
on an object have the same intensity on both the fixed and moving images to be registered. In this
example, we will preprocess the moving image to match the intensity between the images using the
itk::HistogramMatchingImageFilter.

The basic idea is to match the histograms of the two images at a user-specified number of quantile
values. For robustness, the histograms are matched so that the background pixels are excluded from
both histograms. For MR images, a simple procedure is to exclude all gray values that are smaller
than the mean gray value of the image.

```
typedef itk::HistogramMatchingImageFilter<
                              InternalImageType,
                              InternalImageType >  MatchingFilterType;
MatchingFilterType::Pointer matcher = MatchingFilterType::New();
```

For this example, we set the moving image as the source or input image and the fixed image as the reference image.

```
matcher->SetInput( movingImageCaster->GetOutput() );
matcher->SetReferenceImage( fixedImageCaster->GetOutput() );
```

We then select the number of bins to represent the histograms and the number of points or quantile values where the histogram is to be matched.

```
matcher->SetNumberOfHistogramLevels( 1024 );
matcher->SetNumberOfMatchPoints( 7 );
```

Simple background extraction is done by thresholding at the mean intensity.

```
matcher->ThresholdAtMeanIntensityOn();
```

In the `itk::DemonsRegistrationFilter`, the deformation field is represented as an image whose pixels are floating point vectors.

```
typedef itk::Vector< float, Dimension >            VectorPixelType;
typedef itk::Image< VectorPixelType, Dimension > DisplacementFieldType;
typedef itk::DemonsRegistrationFilter<
                        InternalImageType,
                        InternalImageType,
                        DisplacementFieldType> RegistrationFilterType;
RegistrationFilterType::Pointer filter = RegistrationFilterType::New();
```

The input fixed image is simply the output of the fixed image casting filter. The input moving image is the output of the histogram matching filter.

```
filter->SetFixedImage( fixedImageCaster->GetOutput() );
filter->SetMovingImage( matcher->GetOutput() );
```

The demons registration filter has two parameters: the number of iterations to be performed and the standard deviation of the Gaussian smoothing kernel to be applied to the deformation field after each iteration.

```
filter->SetNumberOfIterations( 50 );
filter->SetStandardDeviations( 1.0 );
```

The registration algorithm is triggered by updating the filter. The filter output is the computed deformation field.

```
filter->Update();
```

The `itk::WarpImageFilter` can be used to warp the moving image with the output deformation field. Like the `itk::ResampleImageFilter`, the WarpImageFilter requires the specification of the input image to be resampled, an input image interpolator, and the output image spacing and origin.

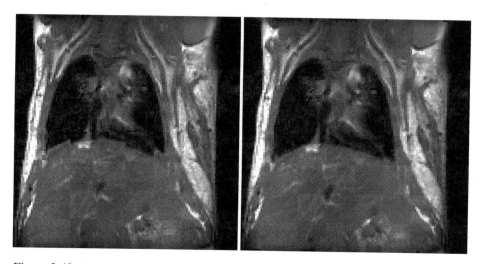

Figure 3.48: Checkerboard comparisons before and after demons-based deformable registration.

```
typedef itk::WarpImageFilter<
                    MovingImageType,
                    MovingImageType,
                    DisplacementFieldType  >      WarperType;
typedef itk::LinearInterpolateImageFunction<
                    MovingImageType,
                    double              >  InterpolatorType;
WarperType::Pointer warper = WarperType::New();
InterpolatorType::Pointer interpolator = InterpolatorType::New();
FixedImageType::Pointer fixedImage = fixedImageReader->GetOutput();

warper->SetInput( movingImageReader->GetOutput() );
warper->SetInterpolator( interpolator );
warper->SetOutputSpacing( fixedImage->GetSpacing() );
warper->SetOutputOrigin( fixedImage->GetOrigin() );
warper->SetOutputDirection( fixedImage->GetDirection() );
```

Unlike the ResampleImageFilter, the WarpImageFilter warps or transform the input image with respect to the deformation field represented by an image of vectors. The resulting warped or resampled image is written to file as per previous examples.

```
warper->SetDisplacementField( filter->GetOutput() );
```

Let's execute this example using the rat lung data from the previous example. The associated data files can be found in `Examples/Data`:

- `RatLungSlice1.mha`

- `RatLungSlice2.mha`

The result of the demons-based deformable registration is presented in Figure 3.48. The checkerboard comparison shows that the algorithm was able to recover the misalignment due to expiration.

It may be also desirable to write the deformation field as an image of vectors. This can be done with the following code.

```
typedef itk::ImageFileWriter< DisplacementFieldType > FieldWriterType;
FieldWriterType::Pointer fieldWriter = FieldWriterType::New();
fieldWriter->SetFileName( argv[4] );
fieldWriter->SetInput( filter->GetOutput() );

fieldWriter->Update();
```

Note that the file format used for writing the deformation field must be capable of representing multiple components per pixel. This is the case for the MetaImage and VTK file formats for example.

A variant of the force computation is also implemented in which the gradient of the deformed moving image is also involved. This provides a level of symmetry in the force calculation during one iteration of the PDE update. The equation used in this case is

$$\mathbf{D(X)} = -\frac{2\,(\mathbf{m(X)} - \mathbf{f(X)})\,(\nabla\mathbf{f(X)} + \nabla\mathbf{g(X)})}{\|\nabla\mathbf{f} + \nabla\mathbf{g}\|^2 + (\mathbf{m(X)} - \mathbf{f(X)})^2/\mathbf{K}} \tag{3.37}$$

The following example illustrates the use of this deformable registration method.

3.14.2 Symmetrical Demons Deformable Registration

The source code for this section can be found in the file
`DeformableRegistration3.cxx`.

This example demonstrates how to use a variant of the "demons" algorithm to deformably register two images. This variant uses a different formulation for computing the forces to be applied to the image in order to compute the deformation fields. The variant uses both the gradient of the fixed image and the gradient of the deformed moving image in order to compute the forces. This mechanism for computing the forces introduces a symmetry with respect to the choice of the fixed and moving images. This symmetry only holds during the computation of one iteration of the PDE updates. It is unlikely that total symmetry may be achieved by this mechanism for the entire registration process.

The first step for using this filter is to include the following header files.

```
#include "itkSymmetricForcesDemonsRegistrationFilter.h"
#include "itkHistogramMatchingImageFilter.h"
#include "itkCastImageFilter.h"
#include "itkWarpImageFilter.h"
```

Second, we declare the types of the images.

```
const unsigned int Dimension = 2;
typedef unsigned short PixelType;

typedef itk::Image< PixelType, Dimension >  FixedImageType;
typedef itk::Image< PixelType, Dimension >  MovingImageType;
```

Image file readers are set up in a similar fashion to previous examples. To support the re-mapping of the moving image intensity, we declare an internal image type with a floating point pixel type and cast the input images to the internal image type.

```
typedef float                                          InternalPixelType;
typedef itk::Image< InternalPixelType, Dimension > InternalImageType;
typedef itk::CastImageFilter< FixedImageType,
                              InternalImageType >  FixedImageCasterType;
typedef itk::CastImageFilter< MovingImageType,
                              InternalImageType >  MovingImageCasterType;

FixedImageCasterType::Pointer fixedImageCaster = FixedImageCasterType::New();
MovingImageCasterType::Pointer movingImageCaster
                                = MovingImageCasterType::New();

fixedImageCaster->SetInput( fixedImageReader->GetOutput() );
movingImageCaster->SetInput( movingImageReader->GetOutput() );
```

The demons algorithm relies on the assumption that pixels representing the same homologous point on an object have the same intensity on both the fixed and moving images to be registered. In this example, we will preprocess the moving image to match the intensity between the images using the itk::HistogramMatchingImageFilter.

The basic idea is to match the histograms of the two images at a user-specified number of quantile values. For robustness, the histograms are matched so that the background pixels are excluded from both histograms. For MR images, a simple procedure is to exclude all gray values that are smaller than the mean gray value of the image.

```
typedef itk::HistogramMatchingImageFilter<
                              InternalImageType,
                              InternalImageType >   MatchingFilterType;
MatchingFilterType::Pointer matcher = MatchingFilterType::New();
```

For this example, we set the moving image as the source or input image and the fixed image as the reference image.

```
matcher->SetInput( movingImageCaster->GetOutput() );
matcher->SetReferenceImage( fixedImageCaster->GetOutput() );
```

We then select the number of bins to represent the histograms and the number of points or quantile values where the histogram is to be matched.

```
matcher->SetNumberOfHistogramLevels( 1024 );
matcher->SetNumberOfMatchPoints( 7 );
```

Simple background extraction is done by thresholding at the mean intensity.

```
matcher->ThresholdAtMeanIntensityOn();
```

In the itk::SymmetricForcesDemonsRegistrationFilter, the deformation field is represented as an image whose pixels are floating point vectors.

```
typedef itk::Vector< float, Dimension >        VectorPixelType;
typedef itk::Image< VectorPixelType, Dimension >     DisplacementFieldType;
typedef itk::SymmetricForcesDemonsRegistrationFilter<
                              InternalImageType,
                              InternalImageType,
                              DisplacementFieldType> RegistrationFilterType;
RegistrationFilterType::Pointer filter = RegistrationFilterType::New();
```

The input fixed image is simply the output of the fixed image casting filter. The input moving image is the output of the histogram matching filter.

```
filter->SetFixedImage( fixedImageCaster->GetOutput() );
filter->SetMovingImage( matcher->GetOutput() );
```

The demons registration filter has two parameters: the number of iterations to be performed and the standard deviation of the Gaussian smoothing kernel to be applied to the deformation field after each iteration.

```
filter->SetNumberOfIterations( 50 );
filter->SetStandardDeviations( 1.0 );
```

The registration algorithm is triggered by updating the filter. The filter output is the computed deformation field.

```
filter->Update();
```

The `itk::WarpImageFilter` can be used to warp the moving image with the output deformation field. Like the `itk::ResampleImageFilter`, the WarpImageFilter requires the specification of the input image to be resampled, an input image interpolator, and the output image spacing and origin.

```
typedef itk::WarpImageFilter<
                      MovingImageType,
                      MovingImageType,
                      DisplacementFieldType >      WarperType;
typedef itk::LinearInterpolateImageFunction<
                      MovingImageType,
                      double        >  InterpolatorType;
WarperType::Pointer warper = WarperType::New();
InterpolatorType::Pointer interpolator = InterpolatorType::New();
FixedImageType::Pointer fixedImage = fixedImageReader->GetOutput();

warper->SetInput( movingImageReader->GetOutput() );
warper->SetInterpolator( interpolator );
warper->SetOutputSpacing( fixedImage->GetSpacing() );
warper->SetOutputOrigin( fixedImage->GetOrigin() );
warper->SetOutputDirection( fixedImage->GetDirection() );
```

Unlike the ResampleImageFilter, the WarpImageFilter warps or transforms the input image with respect to the deformation field represented by an image of vectors. The resulting warped or resampled image is written to file as per previous examples.

```
warper->SetDisplacementField( filter->GetOutput() );
```

Let's execute this example using the rat lung data from the previous example. The associated data files can be found in `Examples/Data`:

- `RatLungSlice1.mha`

- `RatLungSlice2.mha`

The result of the demons-based deformable registration is presented in Figure 3.49. The checkerboard comparison shows that the algorithm was able to recover the misalignment due to expiration.

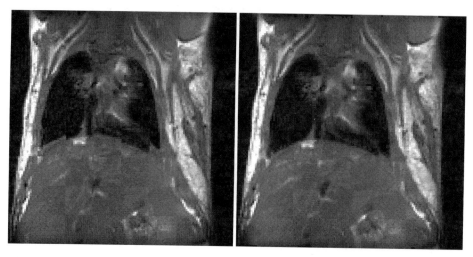

Figure 3.49: Checkerboard comparisons before and after demons-based deformable registration.

It may be also desirable to write the deformation field as an image of vectors. This can be done with the following code.

```
typedef itk::ImageFileWriter< DisplacementFieldType > FieldWriterType;

FieldWriterType::Pointer fieldWriter = FieldWriterType::New();
fieldWriter->SetFileName( argv[4] );
fieldWriter->SetInput( filter->GetOutput() );

fieldWriter->Update();
```

Note that the file format used for writing the deformation field must be capable of representing multiple components per pixel. This is the case for the MetaImage and VTK file formats for example.

3.15   Visualizing Deformation fields

Vector deformation fields may be visualized using ParaView. ParaView [26] is an open-source, multi-platform visualization application and uses the Visualization Toolkit as the data processing and rendering engine and has a user interface written using a unique blend of Tcl/Tk and C++. You may download it from http://paraview.org.

3.15.1   Visualizing 2D deformation fields

Let us visualize the deformation field obtained from Demons Registration algorithm generated from ITK/Examples/RegistrationITKv4/DeformableRegistration2.cxx.

Load the Deformation field in Paraview. (The deformation field must be capable of handling vector data, such as MetaImages). Paraview shows a color map of the magnitudes of the deformation fields as shown in 3.50.

Covert the deformation field to 3D vector data using a *Calculator*. The Calculator may be found in the *Filter* pull down menu. A screenshot of the calculator tab is shown in Figure 3.51. Although the deformation field is a 2D vector, we will generate a 3D vector with the third component set to 0 since Paraview generates glyphs only for 3D vectors. You may now apply a glyph of arrows to the resulting 3D vector field by using *Glyph* on the menu bar. The glyphs obtained will be very dense since a glyph is generated for each point in the data set. To better visualize the deformation field, you may adopt one of the following approaches.

Reduce the number of glyphs by reducing the number in *Max. Number of Glyphs* to a reasonable amount. This uniformly downsamples the number of glyphs. Alternatively, you may apply a *Threshold* filter to the *Magnitude* of the vector dataset and then glyph the vector data that lie above the threshold. This eliminates the smaller deformation fields that clutter the display. You may now reduce the number of glyphs to a reasonable value.

Figure 3.52 shows the vector field visualized using Paraview by thresholding the vector magnitudes by 2.1 and restricting the number of glyphs to 100.

3.15.2   Visualizing 3D deformation fields

Let us create a 3D deformation field. We will use Thin Plate Splines to warp a 3D dataset and create a deformation field. We will pick a set of point landmarks and translate them to provide a specification of correspondences at point landmarks. Note that the landmarks have been picked randomly for purposes of illustration and are not intended to portray a true deformation. The landmarks may be used to produce a deformation field in several ways. Most techniques minimize some regularizing functional representing the irregularity of the deformation field, which is usually some function of the spatial derivatives of the field. Here will we use *thin plate splines*. Thin plate splines minimize the regularizing functional

$$I[f(x,y)] = \iint (f_{xx}^2 + 2f_{xy}^2 + f_{yy}^2)dxdy \qquad (3.38)$$

where the subscripts denote partial derivatives of f.

We may now proceed as before to visualize the deformation field using Paraview as shown in Figure 3.53.

Let us register the deformed volumes generated by Thin plate warping in the previous example using DeformableRegistration4.cxx. Since ITK is in general N-dimensional, the only change in the example is to replace the `ImageDimension` by 3.

The registration method uses B-splines and an LBFGS optimizer. The trace in Table. 3.17 prints the trace of the optimizer through the search space.

Here $\|G\|$ is the norm of the gradient at the current estimate of the minimum, x. "Function Value" is the current value of the function, f(x).

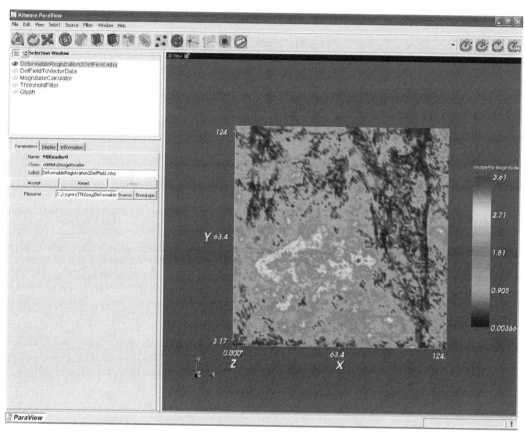

Figure 3.50: Deformation field magnitudes displayed using Paraview

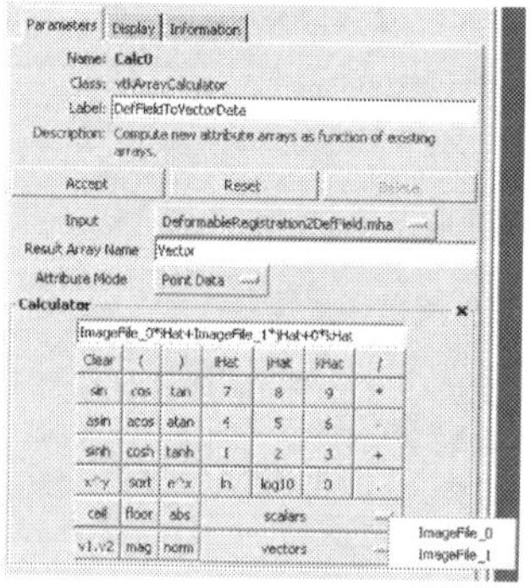

Figure 3.51: Calculators and filters may be used to compute the vector magnitude, compose vectors etc.

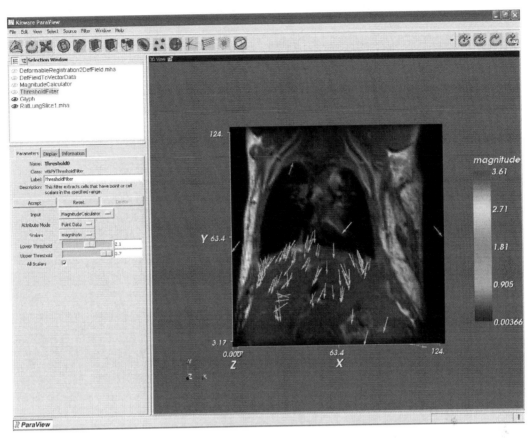

Figure 3.52: Deformation field visualized using Paraview after thresholding and subsampling.

Iteration	Function value	$\|G\|$	Step length
1	156.981	14.911	0.202
2	68.956	11.774	1.500
3	38.146	4.802	1.500
4	26.690	2.515	1.500
5	23.295	1.106	1.500
6	21.454	1.032	1.500
7	20.322	1.557	1.500
8	19.751	0.594	1.500

Table 3.17: LBFGS Optimizer trace.

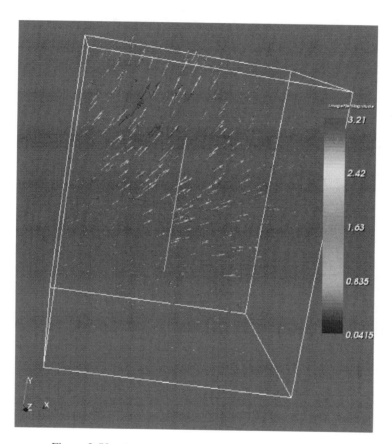

Figure 3.53: 3D Deformation field visualized using Paraview.

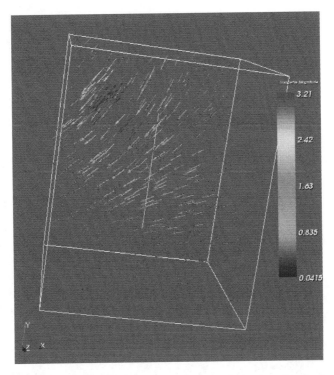

Figure 3.54: Resulting deformation field that maps the moving image to the fixed image.

The resulting deformation field that maps the moving to the fixed image is shown in 3.54. A difference image of two slices before and after registration is shown in 3.55. As can be seen from the figures, the deformation field is in close agreement to the one generated from the Thin plate spline warping.

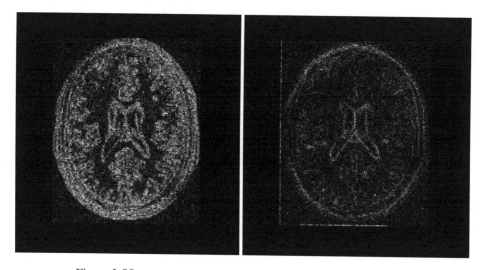

Figure 3.55: Difference image from a slice before and after registration.

3.16 Model Based Registration

This section introduces the concept of registering a geometrical model with an image. We refer to this concept as *model based registration* but this may not be the most widespread terminology. In this approach, a geometrical model is built first and a number of parameters are identified in the model. Variations of these parameters make it possible to adapt the model to the morphology of a particular patient. The task of registra-

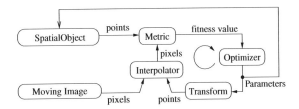

Figure 3.56: The basic components of model based registration are an image, a spatial object, a transform, a metric, an interpolator and an optimizer.

tion is then to find the optimal combination of model parameters that will make this model a good representation of the anatomical structures contained in an image.

For example, let's say that in the axial view of a brain image we can roughly approximate the skull with an ellipse. The ellipse becomes our simplified geometrical model, and registration is the task of finding the best center for the ellipse, the measures of its axis lengths and its orientation in the plane. This is illustrated in Figure 3.57. If we compare this approach with the image-to-image registration problem, we can see that the main difference here is that in addition to mapping the spatial position of the model, we can also customize internal parameters that change its shape.

Figure 3.56 illustrates the major components of the registration framework in ITK when a model-based registration problem is configured. The basic input data for the registration is provided by pixel data in an `itk::Image` and by geometrical data stored in a `itk::SpatialObject`. A metric has to be defined in order to evaluate the fitness between the model and the image. This fitness value can be improved by introducing variations in the spatial positioning of the SpatialObject and/or by changing its internal parameters. The search space for the optimizer is now the composition of the transform parameter and the shape internal parameters.

This same approach can be considered a segmentation technique, since once the model has been optimally superimposed on the image we could label pixels according to their associations with specific parts of the model. The applications of model to image registration/segmentation are endless. The main advantage of this approach is probably that, as opposed to image-to-image registration, it actually provides *Insight* into the anatomical structure contained in the image. The adapted model becomes a condensed representation of the essential elements of the anatomical structure.

ITK provides a hierarchy of classes intended to support the construction of shape models. This hierarchy has the SpatialObject as its base class. A number of basic functionalities are defined at this level, including the capacity to evaluate whether a given point is *inside* or *outside* of the model, form complex shapes by creating hierarchical conglomerates of basic shapes, and support basic spatial parameterizations like scale, orientation and position.

The following sections present examples of the typical uses of these powerful elements of the toolkit.

The source code for this section can be found in the file
`ModelToImageRegistration1.cxx`.

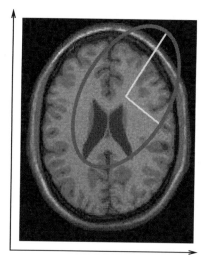
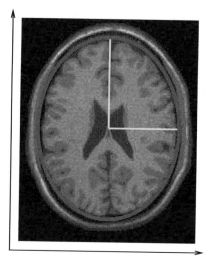

Model and Image Before Registration   Model and Image After Registration

Figure 3.57: Basic concept of Model-to-Image registration. A simplified geometrical model (ellipse) is registered against an anatomical structure (skull) by applying a spatial transform and modifying the model internal parameters. This image is not the result of an actual registration, it is shown here only with the purpose of illustrating the concept of model to image registration.

This example illustrates the use of the `itk::SpatialObject` as a component of the registration framework in order to perform model based registration. The current example creates a geometrical model composed of several ellipses. Then, it uses the model to produce a synthetic binary image of the ellipses. Next, it introduces perturbations on the position and shape of the model, and finally it uses the perturbed version as the input to a registration problem. A metric is defined to evaluate the fitness between the geometric model and the image.

Let's look first at the classes required to support SpatialObject. In this example we use the `itk::EllipseSpatialObject` as the basic shape components and we use the `itk::GroupSpatialObject` to group them together as a representation of a more complex shape. Their respective headers are included below.

```
#include "itkEllipseSpatialObject.h"
#include "itkGroupSpatialObject.h"
```

In order to generate the initial synthetic image of the ellipses, we use the `itk::SpatialObjectToImageFilter` that tests—for every pixel in the image—whether the pixel (and hence the spatial object) is *inside* or *outside* the geometric model.

```
#include "itkSpatialObjectToImageFilter.h"
```

A metric is defined to evaluate the fitness between the SpatialObject and the Image. The base class for this type of metric is the `itk::ImageToSpatialObjectMetric`, whose header is included below.

```
#include "itkImageToSpatialObjectMetric.h"
```

As in previous registration problems, we have to evaluate the image intensity in non-grid positions. The `itk::LinearInterpolateImageFunction` is used here for this purpose.

```
#include "itkLinearInterpolateImageFunction.h"
```

The SpatialObject is mapped from its own space into the image space by using a `itk::Transform`. In this example, we use the `itk::Euler2DTransform`.

```
#include "itkEuler2DTransform.h"
```

Registration is fundamentally an optimization problem. Here we include the optimizer used to search the parameter space and identify the best transformation that will map the shape model on top of the image. The optimizer used in this example is the `itk::OnePlusOneEvolutionaryOptimizer` that implements an evolutionary algorithm.

```
#include "itkOnePlusOneEvolutionaryOptimizer.h"
```

As in previous registration examples, it is important to track the evolution of the optimizer as it progresses through the parameter space. This is done by using the Command/Observer paradigm. The following lines of code implement the `itk::Command` observer that monitors the progress of the registration. The code is quite similar to what we have used in previous registration examples.

```
#include "itkCommand.h"
template < class TOptimizer >
class IterationCallback : public itk::Command
{
public:
  typedef IterationCallback             Self;
  typedef itk::Command                  Superclass;
  typedef itk::SmartPointer<Self>       Pointer;
  typedef itk::SmartPointer<const Self> ConstPointer;

  itkTypeMacro( IterationCallback, Superclass );
  itkNewMacro( Self );

  /** Type defining the optimizer. */
  typedef    TOptimizer     OptimizerType;

  /** Method to specify the optimizer. */
  void SetOptimizer( OptimizerType * optimizer )
    {
    m_Optimizer = optimizer;
    m_Optimizer->AddObserver( itk::IterationEvent(), this );
    }

  /** Execute method will print data at each iteration */
  void Execute(itk::Object *caller, const itk::EventObject & event)
    {
    Execute( (const itk::Object *)caller, event);
    }

  void Execute(const itk::Object *, const itk::EventObject & event)
    {
    if( typeid( event ) == typeid( itk::StartEvent ) )
      {
      std::cout << std::endl << "Position                Value";
      std::cout << std::endl << std::endl;
      }
    else if( typeid( event ) == typeid( itk::IterationEvent ) )
      {
      std::cout << m_Optimizer->GetCurrentIteration() << "   ";
      std::cout << m_Optimizer->GetValue() << "   ";
      std::cout << m_Optimizer->GetCurrentPosition() << std::endl;
      }
    else if( typeid( event ) == typeid( itk::EndEvent ) )
      {
      std::cout << std::endl << std::endl;
      std::cout << "After " << m_Optimizer->GetCurrentIteration();
      std::cout << "  iterations " << std::endl;
      std::cout << "Solution is    = " << m_Optimizer->GetCurrentPosition();
      std::cout << std::endl;
      }
    }
}
```

This command will be invoked at every iteration of the optimizer and will print out the current combination of transform parameters.

Consider now the most critical component of this new registration approach: the metric. This component evaluates the match between the SpatialObject and the Image. The smoothness and regularity of the metric determine the difficulty of the task assigned to the optimizer. In this case, we use a very robust optimizer that should be able to find its way even in the most discontinuous cost functions. The metric to be implemented should derive from the ImageToSpatialObjectMetric class.

The following code implements a simple metric that computes the sum of the pixels that are inside the spatial object. In fact, the metric maximum is obtained when the model and the image are aligned. The metric is templated over the type of the SpatialObject and the type of the Image.

```
template <typename TFixedImage, typename TMovingSpatialObject>
class SimpleImageToSpatialObjectMetric :
  public itk::ImageToSpatialObjectMetric<TFixedImage,TMovingSpatialObject>
{
```

The fundamental operation of the metric is its GetValue() method. It is in this method that the fitness value is computed. In our current example, the fitness is computed over the points of the SpatialObject. For each point, its coordinates are mapped through the transform into image space. The resulting point is used to evaluate the image and the resulting value is accumulated in a sum. Since we are not allowing scale changes, the optimal value of the sum will result when all the SpatialObject points are mapped on the white regions of the image. Note that the argument for the GetValue() method is the array of parameters of the transform.

```
MeasureType    GetValue( const ParametersType & parameters ) const
  {
    double value;
    this->m_Transform->SetParameters( parameters );

    value = 0;
    for(PointListType::const_iterator it = m_PointList.begin();
                                 it != m_PointList.end(); ++it)
      {
      PointType transformedPoint = this->m_Transform->TransformPoint(*it);
      if( this->m_Interpolator->IsInsideBuffer( transformedPoint ) )
        {
        value += this->m_Interpolator->Evaluate( transformedPoint );
        }
      }
    return value;
  }
```

Having defined all the registration components we are ready to put the pieces together and implement the registration process.

First we instantiate the GroupSpatialObject and EllipseSpatialObject. These two objects are parameterized by the dimension of the space. In our current example a 2D instantiation is created.

```
typedef itk::GroupSpatialObject< 2 >    GroupType;
typedef itk::EllipseSpatialObject< 2 >  EllipseType;
```

The image is instantiated in the following lines using the pixel type and the space dimension. This image uses a float pixel type since we plan to blur it in order to increase the capture radius of the optimizer. Images of real pixel type behave better under blurring than those of integer pixel type.

```
typedef itk::Image< float, 2 >    ImageType;
```

Here is where the fun begins! In the following lines we create the EllipseSpatialObjects using their

New() methods, and assigning the results to SmartPointers. These lines will create three ellipses.

```
EllipseType::Pointer ellipse1 = EllipseType::New();
EllipseType::Pointer ellipse2 = EllipseType::New();
EllipseType::Pointer ellipse3 = EllipseType::New();
```

Every class deriving from SpatialObject has particular parameters enabling the user to tailor its shape. In the case of the EllipseSpatialObject, SetRadius() is used to define the ellipse size. An additional SetRadius(Array) method allows the user to define the ellipse axes independently.

```
ellipse1->SetRadius( 10.0 );
ellipse2->SetRadius( 10.0 );
ellipse3->SetRadius( 10.0 );
```

The ellipses are created centered in space by default. We use the following lines of code to arrange the ellipses in a triangle. The spatial transform intrinsically associated with the object is accessed by the GetTransform() method. This transform can define a translation in space with the SetOffset() method. We take advantage of this feature to place the ellipses at particular points in space.

```
EllipseType::TransformType::OffsetType offset;
offset[ 0 ] = 100.0;
offset[ 1 ] =  40.0;

ellipse1->GetObjectToParentTransform()->SetOffset(offset);
ellipse1->ComputeObjectToWorldTransform();

offset[ 0 ] =  40.0;
offset[ 1 ] = 150.0;
ellipse2->GetObjectToParentTransform()->SetOffset(offset);
ellipse2->ComputeObjectToWorldTransform();

offset[ 0 ] = 150.0;
offset[ 1 ] = 150.0;
ellipse3->GetObjectToParentTransform()->SetOffset(offset);
ellipse3->ComputeObjectToWorldTransform();
```

Note that after a change has been made in the transform, the SpatialObject invokes the method ComputeGlobalTransform() in order to update its global transform. The reason for doing this is that SpatialObjects can be arranged in hierarchies. It is then possible to change the position of a set of spatial objects by moving the parent of the group.

Now we add the three EllipseSpatialObjects to a GroupSpatialObject that will be subsequently passed on to the registration method. The GroupSpatialObject facilitates the management of the three ellipses as a higher level structure representing a complex shape. Groups can be nested any number of levels in order to represent shapes with higher detail.

```
GroupType::Pointer group = GroupType::New();
group->AddSpatialObject( ellipse1 );
group->AddSpatialObject( ellipse2 );
group->AddSpatialObject( ellipse3 );
```

Having the geometric model ready, we proceed to generate the binary image representing the imprint of the space occupied by the ellipses. The SpatialObjectToImageFilter is used to that end. Note that this filter is instantiated over the spatial object used and the image type to be generated.

```
typedef itk::SpatialObjectToImageFilter< GroupType, ImageType >
  SpatialObjectToImageFilterType;
```

With the defined type, we construct a filter using the `New()` method. The newly created filter is assigned to a SmartPointer.

```
SpatialObjectToImageFilterType::Pointer imageFilter =
  SpatialObjectToImageFilterType::New();
```

The GroupSpatialObject is passed as input to the filter.

```
imageFilter->SetInput( group );
```

The `itk::SpatialObjectToImageFilter` acts as a resampling filter. Therefore it requires the user to define the size of the desired output image. This is specified with the `SetSize()` method.

```
ImageType::SizeType size;
size[ 0 ] = 200;
size[ 1 ] = 200;
imageFilter->SetSize( size );
```

Finally we trigger the execution of the filter by calling the `Update()` method.

```
imageFilter->Update();
```

In order to obtain a smoother metric, we blur the image using a `itk::DiscreteGaussianImageFilter`. This extends the capture radius of the metric and produce a more continuous cost function to optimize. The following lines instantiate the Gaussian filter and create one object of this type using the `New()` method.

```
typedef itk::DiscreteGaussianImageFilter< ImageType, ImageType >
  GaussianFilterType;
GaussianFilterType::Pointer  gaussianFilter =  GaussianFilterType::New();
```

The output of the SpatialObjectToImageFilter is connected as input to the DiscreteGaussianImage-Filter.

```
gaussianFilter->SetInput( imageFilter->GetOutput() );
```

The variance of the filter is defined as a large value in order to increase the capture radius. Finally the execution of the filter is triggered using the `Update()` method.

```
const double variance = 20;
gaussianFilter->SetVariance(variance);
gaussianFilter->Update();
```

Below we instantiate the type of the `itk::ImageToSpatialObjectRegistrationMethod` method and instantiate a registration object with the `New()` method. Note that the registration type is templated over the Image and the SpatialObject types. The spatial object in this case is the group of spatial objects.

```
typedef itk::ImageToSpatialObjectRegistrationMethod< ImageType, GroupType >
  RegistrationType;
RegistrationType::Pointer registration = RegistrationType::New();
```

Now we instantiate the metric that is templated over the image type and the spatial object type. As usual, the `New()` method is used to create an object.

```
typedef SimpleImageToSpatialObjectMetric< ImageType, GroupType > MetricType;
MetricType::Pointer metric = MetricType::New();
```

An interpolator will be needed to evaluate the image at non-grid positions. Here we instantiate a linear interpolator type.

```
typedef itk::LinearInterpolateImageFunction< ImageType, double >
  InterpolatorType;
InterpolatorType::Pointer interpolator = InterpolatorType::New();
```

The following lines instantiate the evolutionary optimizer.

```
typedef itk::OnePlusOneEvolutionaryOptimizer  OptimizerType;
OptimizerType::Pointer optimizer  = OptimizerType::New();
```

Next, we instantiate the transform class. In this case we use the Euler2DTransform that implements a rigid transform in 2D space.

```
typedef itk::Euler2DTransform<> TransformType;
TransformType::Pointer transform = TransformType::New();
```

Evolutionary algorithms are based on testing random variations of parameters. In order to support the computation of random values, ITK provides a family of random number generators. In this example, we use the `itk::NormalVariateGenerator` which generates values with a normal distribution.

```
itk::Statistics::NormalVariateGenerator::Pointer generator
  = itk::Statistics::NormalVariateGenerator::New();
```

The random number generator must be initialized with a seed.

```
generator->Initialize(12345);
```

The OnePlusOneEvolutionaryOptimizer is initialized by specifying the random number generator, the number of samples for the initial population and the maximum number of iterations.

```
optimizer->SetNormalVariateGenerator( generator );
optimizer->Initialize( 10 );
optimizer->SetMaximumIteration( 400 );
```

As in previous registration examples, we take care to normalize the dynamic range of the different transform parameters. In particular, the we must compensate for the ranges of the angle and translations of the Euler2DTransform. In order to achieve this goal, we provide an array of scales to the optimizer.

```
TransformType::ParametersType parametersScale;
parametersScale.set_size(3);
parametersScale[0] = 1000; // angle scale

for( unsigned int i=1; i<3; i++ )
  {
  parametersScale[i] = 2; // offset scale
  }
optimizer->SetScales( parametersScale );
```

Here we instantiate the Command object that will act as an observer of the registration method and print out parameters at each iteration. Earlier, we defined this command as a class templated over the optimizer type. Once it is created with the `New()` method, we connect the optimizer to the command.

```
typedef IterationCallback< OptimizerType >  IterationCallbackType;
IterationCallbackType::Pointer callback = IterationCallbackType::New();
callback->SetOptimizer( optimizer );
```

All the components are plugged into the ImageToSpatialObjectRegistrationMethod object. The typical `Set()` methods are used here. Note the use of the `SetMovingSpatialObject()` method for connecting the spatial object. We provide the blurred version of the original synthetic binary image as the input image.

```
registration->SetFixedImage( gaussianFilter->GetOutput() );
registration->SetMovingSpatialObject( group );
registration->SetTransform( transform );
registration->SetInterpolator( interpolator );
registration->SetOptimizer( optimizer );
registration->SetMetric( metric );
```

The initial set of transform parameters is passed to the registration method using the `SetInitialTransformParameters()` method. Note that since our original model is already registered with the synthetic image, we introduce an artificial mis-registration in order to initialize the optimization at some point away from the optimal value.

```
TransformType::ParametersType initialParameters(
    transform->GetNumberOfParameters() );

initialParameters[0] = 0.2;      // Angle
initialParameters[1] = 7.0;      // Offset X
initialParameters[2] = 6.0;      // Offset Y
registration->SetInitialTransformParameters(initialParameters);
```

Due to the character of the metric used to evaluate the fitness between the spatial object and the image, we must tell the optimizer that we are interested in finding the maximum value of the metric. Some metrics associate low numeric values with good matching, while others associate high numeric values with good matching. The `MaximizeOn()` and `MaximizeOff()` methods allow the user to deal with both types of metrics.

```
optimizer->MaximizeOn();
```

Finally, we trigger the execution of the registration process with the `Update()` method. We place this call in a `try/catch` block in case any exception is thrown during the process.

```
try
  {
  registration->Update();
  std::cout << "Optimizer stop condition: "
          << registration->GetOptimizer()->GetStopConditionDescription()
          << std::endl;
  }
catch( itk::ExceptionObject & exp )
  {
  std::cerr << "Exception caught ! " << std::endl;
  std::cerr << exp << std::endl;
  }
```

The set of transform parameters resulting from the registration can be recovered with the `GetLastTransformParameters()` method. This method returns the array of transform parame-

ters that should be interpreted according to the implementation of each transform. In our current
example, the Euler2DTransform has three parameters: the rotation angle, the translation in x and the
translation in y.

```
RegistrationType::ParametersType finalParameters
  = registration->GetLastTransformParameters();

std::cout << "Final Solution is : " << finalParameters << std::endl;
```

The results are presented in Figure 3.58. The left side shows the evolution of the angle parameter as
a function of iteration numbers, while the right side shows the (x, y) translation.

3.17   Point Set Registration

PointSet-to-PointSet registration is a common problem in medical image analysis. It usually arises
in cases where landmarks are extracted from images and are used for establishing the spatial correspondence between the images. This type of registration can be considered to be the simplest
case of feature-based registration. In general terms, feature-based registration is more efficient than
the intensity based method that we have presented so far. However, feature-base registration brings
the new problem of identifying and extracting the features from the images, which is not a minor
challenge.

The two most common scenarios in PointSet to PointSet registration are

- Two PointSets with the same number of points, and where each point in one set has a known
  correspondence to exactly one point in the second set.

- Two PointSets without known correspondences between the points of one set and the points of
  the other. In this case the PointSets may have different numbers of points.

The first case can be solved with a closed form solution when we are dealing with a Rigid or an Affine
Transform [27]. This is done in ITK with the class `itk::LandmarkBasedTransformInitializer`.
If we are interested in a deformable Transformation then the problem can be solved with the
`itk::KernelTransform` family of classes, which includes Thin Plate Splines among others [52].
In both circumstances, the availability o f correspondences between the points make possible to
apply a straight forward solution to the problem.

The classical algorithm for performing PointSet to PointSet registration is the Iterative Closest Point
(ICP) algorithm. The following examples illustrate how this can be used in ITK.

3.17.1   Point Set Registration in 2D

The source code for this section can be found in the file
`IterativeClosestPoint1.cxx`.

This example illustrates how to perform Iterative Closest Point (ICP) registration in ITK. The main
class featured in this section is the `itk::EuclideanDistancePointMetric`.

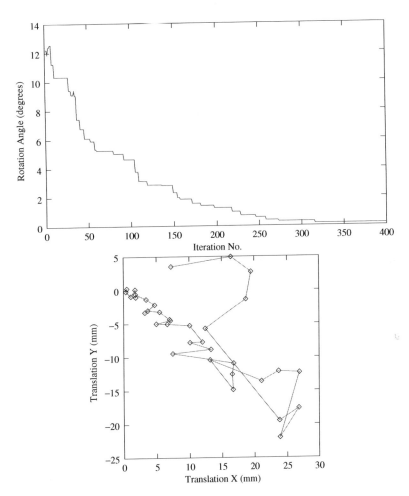

Figure 3.58: Plots of the angle and translation parameters for a registration process between an spatial object and an image.

The first step is to include the relevant headers.

```
#include "itkTranslationTransform.h"
#include "itkEuclideanDistancePointMetric.h"
#include "itkLevenbergMarquardtOptimizer.h"
#include "itkPointSetToPointSetRegistrationMethod.h"
```

Next, define the necessary types for the fixed and moving pointsets and point containers.

```
const unsigned int Dimension = 2;

typedef itk::PointSet< float, Dimension >   PointSetType;

PointSetType::Pointer fixedPointSet  = PointSetType::New();
PointSetType::Pointer movingPointSet = PointSetType::New();

typedef PointSetType::PointType       PointType;

typedef PointSetType::PointsContainer  PointsContainer;

PointsContainer::Pointer fixedPointContainer  = PointsContainer::New();
PointsContainer::Pointer movingPointContainer = PointsContainer::New();

PointType fixedPoint;
PointType movingPoint;
```

After the points are read in from files, set up the metric type.

```
typedef itk::EuclideanDistancePointMetric<
                            PointSetType,
                            PointSetType>
                                        MetricType;

MetricType::Pointer  metric = MetricType::New();
```

Now, setup the transform, optimizers, and registration method using the point set types defined earlier.

```
typedef itk::TranslationTransform< double, Dimension >        TransformType;

TransformType::Pointer transform = TransformType::New();


// Optimizer Type
typedef itk::LevenbergMarquardtOptimizer OptimizerType;

OptimizerType::Pointer      optimizer   = OptimizerType::New();
optimizer->SetUseCostFunctionGradient(false);

// Registration Method
typedef itk::PointSetToPointSetRegistrationMethod<
                                PointSetType,
                                PointSetType >
                                        RegistrationType;


RegistrationType::Pointer   registration = RegistrationType::New();

// Scale the translation components of the Transform in the Optimizer
OptimizerType::ScalesType scales( transform->GetNumberOfParameters() );
scales.Fill( 0.01 );
```

Next we setup the convergence criteria, and other properties required by the optimizer.

```
unsigned long   numberOfIterations =  100;
double          gradientTolerance  = 1e-5;   // convergence criterion
double          valueTolerance     = 1e-5;   // convergence criterion
double          epsilonFunction    = 1e-6;   // convergence criterion


optimizer->SetScales( scales );
optimizer->SetNumberOfIterations( numberOfIterations );
optimizer->SetValueTolerance( valueTolerance );
optimizer->SetGradientTolerance( gradientTolerance );
optimizer->SetEpsilonFunction( epsilonFunction );
```

In this case we start from an identity transform, but in reality the user will usually be able to provide a better guess than this.

```
transform->SetIdentity();
```

Finally, connect all the components required for the registration, and an observer.

```
registration->SetMetric(          metric       );
registration->SetOptimizer(       optimizer    );
registration->SetTransform(       transform    );
registration->SetFixedPointSet( fixedPointSet );
registration->SetMovingPointSet(  movingPointSet   );

// Connect an observer
CommandIterationUpdate::Pointer observer = CommandIterationUpdate::New();
optimizer->AddObserver( itk::IterationEvent(), observer );
```

3.17.2   Point Set Registration in 3D

The source code for this section can be found in the file
IterativeClosestPoint2.cxx.

This example illustrates how to perform Iterative Closest Point (ICP) registration in ITK using sets
of 3D points.

The first step is to include the relevant headers.

```
#include "itkEuler3DTransform.h"
#include "itkEuclideanDistancePointMetric.h"
#include "itkLevenbergMarquardtOptimizer.h"
#include "itkPointSetToPointSetRegistrationMethod.h"
#include <iostream>
#include <fstream>
```

First, define the necessary types for the moving and fixed point sets.

```
typedef itk::PointSet< float, Dimension >    PointSetType;

PointSetType::Pointer fixedPointSet  = PointSetType::New();
PointSetType::Pointer movingPointSet = PointSetType::New();

typedef PointSetType::PointType       PointType;

typedef PointSetType::PointsContainer  PointsContainer;

PointsContainer::Pointer fixedPointContainer  = PointsContainer::New();
PointsContainer::Pointer movingPointContainer = PointsContainer::New();

PointType fixedPoint;
PointType movingPoint;
```

After the points are read in from files, setup the metric to be used later by the registration.

```
typedef itk::EuclideanDistancePointMetric<
                            PointSetType,
                            PointSetType>
                                       MetricType;

MetricType::Pointer  metric = MetricType::New();
```

Next, setup the tranform, optimizers, and registration.

```
typedef itk::Euler3DTransform< double >        TransformType;

TransformType::Pointer transform = TransformType::New();


// Optimizer Type
typedef itk::LevenbergMarquardtOptimizer OptimizerType;

OptimizerType::Pointer        optimizer     = OptimizerType::New();
optimizer->SetUseCostFunctionGradient(false);

// Registration Method
typedef itk::PointSetToPointSetRegistrationMethod<
                                  PointSetType,
                                  PointSetType >
                                        RegistrationType;


RegistrationType::Pointer   registration   = RegistrationType::New();
```

Scale the translation components of the Transform in the Optimizer

```
OptimizerType::ScalesType scales( transform->GetNumberOfParameters() );
```

Next, set the scales and ranges for translations and rotations in the transform. Also, set the convergence criteria and number of iterations to be used by the optimizer.

```
const double translationScale = 1000.0;  // dynamic range of translations
const double rotationScale     =    1.0;  // dynamic range of rotations

scales[0] = 1.0 / rotationScale;
scales[1] = 1.0 / rotationScale;
scales[2] = 1.0 / rotationScale;
scales[3] = 1.0 / translationScale;
scales[4] = 1.0 / translationScale;
scales[5] = 1.0 / translationScale;

unsigned long   numberOfIterations = 2000;
double          gradientTolerance  = 1e-4;  // convergence criterion
double          valueTolerance     = 1e-4;  // convergence criterion
double          epsilonFunction    = 1e-5;  // convergence criterion

optimizer->SetScales( scales );
optimizer->SetNumberOfIterations( numberOfIterations );
optimizer->SetValueTolerance( valueTolerance );
optimizer->SetGradientTolerance( gradientTolerance );
optimizer->SetEpsilonFunction( epsilonFunction );
```

Here we start with an identity transform, although the user will usually be able to provide a better guess than this.

```
transform->SetIdentity();
```

Connect all the components required for the registration.

```
registration->SetMetric(        metric         );
registration->SetOptimizer(     optimizer      );
registration->SetTransform(     transform      );
registration->SetFixedPointSet( fixedPointSet );
registration->SetMovingPointSet(   movingPointSet   );
```

3.17.3   Point Set to Distance Map Metric

The source code for this section can be found in the file
IterativeClosestPoint3.cxx.

This example illustrates how to perform Iterative Closest Point (ICP) registration in ITK using a
DistanceMap in order to increase the performance. There is of course a trade-off between the time
needed for computing the DistanceMap and the time saved by its repeated use during the iterative
computation of the point-to-point distances. It is then necessary in practice to ponder both factors.

itk::EuclideanDistancePointMetric.

The first step is to include the relevant headers.

```
#include "itkTranslationTransform.h"
#include "itkEuclideanDistancePointMetric.h"
#include "itkLevenbergMarquardtOptimizer.h"
#include "itkPointSetToPointSetRegistrationMethod.h"
#include "itkDanielssonDistanceMapImageFilter.h"
#include "itkPointSetToImageFilter.h"
#include <iostream>
#include <fstream>
```

Next, define the necessary types for the fixed and moving point sets.

```
typedef itk::PointSet< float, Dimension >   PointSetType;

PointSetType::Pointer fixedPointSet  = PointSetType::New();
PointSetType::Pointer movingPointSet = PointSetType::New();

typedef PointSetType::PointType     PointType;

typedef PointSetType::PointsContainer  PointsContainer;

PointsContainer::Pointer fixedPointContainer  = PointsContainer::New();
PointsContainer::Pointer movingPointContainer = PointsContainer::New();

PointType fixedPoint;
PointType movingPoint;
```

Setup the metric, transform, optimizers and registration in a manner similar to the previous two
examples.

In the preparation of the distance map, we first need to map the fixed points into a binary image.

```
typedef itk::Image< unsigned char, Dimension > BinaryImageType;

typedef itk::PointSetToImageFilter<
                      PointSetType,
                      BinaryImageType> PointsToImageFilterType;

PointsToImageFilterType::Pointer
          pointsToImageFilter = PointsToImageFilterType::New();

pointsToImageFilter->SetInput( fixedPointSet );

BinaryImageType::SpacingType spacing;
spacing.Fill( 1.0 );

BinaryImageType::PointType origin;
origin.Fill( 0.0 );
```

Continue to prepare the distance map, in order to accelerate the distance computations.

```
pointsToImageFilter->SetSpacing( spacing );
pointsToImageFilter->SetOrigin( origin   );
pointsToImageFilter->Update();
BinaryImageType::Pointer binaryImage = pointsToImageFilter->GetOutput();

typedef itk::Image< unsigned short, Dimension > DistanceImageType;
typedef itk::DanielssonDistanceMapImageFilter<
          BinaryImageType, DistanceImageType> DistanceFilterType;

DistanceFilterType::Pointer distanceFilter = DistanceFilterType::New();
distanceFilter->SetInput( binaryImage );
distanceFilter->Update();
metric->SetDistanceMap( distanceFilter->GetOutput() );
```

3.18   Registration Troubleshooting

So you read the previous sections, you wrote the code, it compiles and links fine, but when you run it the registration results are not what you were expecting. In that case, this section is for you. This is a compilation of the most common problems that users face when performing image registration. It provides explanations on the potential sources of the problems, and advice on how to deal with those problems.

Most of the material in this section has been taken from frequently asked questions of the ITK users list.

3.18.1   Too many samples outside moving image buffer

http://public.kitware.com/pipermail/insight-users/2007-March/021442.html

This is a common error message in image registration.

It means that at the current iteration of the optimization, the two images as so off-registration that their spatial overlap is not large enough for bringing them back into registration.

The common causes of this problem are:

- Poor initialization: You must initialize the transform properly. Please familiarize yourself with the itk::CenteredTransformInitializer class.

- Optimizer steps too large. If you optimizer takes steps that are too large, it risks to become unstable and to send the images too far apart. You may want to start the optimizer with a maximum step length of 1.0, and only increase it once you have managed to fine tune all other registration parameters.

  Increasing the step length makes your program faster, but it also makes it more unstable.

- Poor set up of the transform parameters scaling. This is extremely critical in registration. You must make sure that you balance the relative difference of scale between the rotation parameters and the translation parameters.

  In typical medical datasets such as CT and MR, translations are measured in millimeters, and therefore are in the range of -100:100, while rotations are measured in radians, and therefore they tend to be in the range of -1:1.

  A rotation of 3 radians is catastrophic, while a translation of 3 millimeters is rather inoffensive. That difference in scale is the one that must be accounted for.

3.18.2   General heuristics for parameter fine-tunning

http://public.kitware.com/pipermail/insight-users/2007-March/021435.html

Here is some advice on how to fine tune the parameters of the registration process.

1) Set Maximum step length to 0.1 and do not change it until all other parameters are stable.

2) Set Minimum step length to 0.001 and do not change it.

You could interpret these two parameters as if their units were radians. So, 0.1 radian = 5.7 degrees.

3) Number of histogram bins:

First plot the histogram of your image using the example program in

Insight/Examples/Statistics/ImageHistogram2.cxx

In that program use first a large number of bins (for example 2000) and identify the different populations of intensity level and to what anatomical structures they correspond.

Once you identify the anatomical structures in the histogram, then rerun that same program with less and less number of bins, until you reach the minimun number of bins for which all the tissues that are important for your application, are still distinctly differentiated in the histogram. At that point, take that number of bins and us it for your Mutual Information metric.

4) Number of Samples: The trade-off with the number of samples is the following:

a) computation time of registration is linearly proportional to the number of samples b) the samples must be enough to significantly populate the joint histogram. c) Once the histogram is populated, there is not much use in adding more samples. Therefore do the following:

Plot the joint histogram of both images, using the number of bins that you selected in item (3). You can do this by modifying the code of the example:

Insight/Examples/Statistics/ ImageMutualInformation1.cxx you have to change the code to print out the values of the bins. Then use a plotting program such as gnuplot, or Matlab, or even Excel and look at the distribution. The number of samples to take must be enough for producing the same "appearance" of the joint histogram. As an arbitrary rule of thumb you may want to start using a high number of samples (80% - 100%). And do not change it until you have mastered the other parameters of the registration. Once you get your registration to converge you can revisit the number of samples and reduce it in order to make the registration run faster. You can simply reduce it until you find that the registration becomes unstable. That's your critical bound for the minimum number of samples. Take that number and multiply it by the magic number 1.5, to send it back to a stable region, or if your application is really critical, then use an even higher magic number x2.0.

This is just engineering: you figure out what is the minimal size of a piece of steel that will support a bridge, and then you enlarge it to keep it away from the critical value.

5) The MOST critical values of the registration process are the scaling parameters that define the proportions between the parameters of the transform. In your case, for an Affine Transform in 2D, you have 6 parameters. The first four are the ones of the Matrix, and the last two are the translation. The rotation matrix value must be in the ranges of radians which is typically [-1 to 1], while the translation values are in the ranges of millimeters (your image size units). You want to start by setting the scaling of the matrix parameters to 1.0, and the scaling of the Translation parameters to the holy esoteric values:

1.0 / (10.0 * pixelspacing[0] * imagesize[0]) 1.0 / (10.0 * pixelspacing[1] * imagesize[1])

This is telling the optimizer that you consider that rotating the image by 57 degrees is as "significant" as translating the image by half its physical extent.

Note that esoteric value has included the arbitrary number 10.0 in the denominator, for no other reason that we have been lucky when using that factor. This of course is just a superstition, so you should feel free to experiment with different values of this number.

Just keep in mind that what the optimizer will do is to "jump" in a parametric space of 6 dimensions, and that the component of the jump on every dimension will be proportional to 1/scaling factor * OptimizerStepLength. Since you set the optimizer Step Length to 0.1, the optimizer will start by exploring the rotations at jumps of about 5 degrees, which is a conservative rotation for most medical applications.

If you have reasons to think that your rotations are larger or smaller, then you should modify the scaling factor of the matrix parameters accordingly.

In the same way, if you think that 1/10 of the image size is too large as the first step for exploring the translations, then you should modify the scaling of translation parameters accordingly.

In order to drive all these you need to analyze the feedback that the observer is providing you. For example, plot the metric values, and plot the translation coordinates so that you can get a feeling of how the registration is behaving.

Note also that image registration is not a science. It is a pure engineerig practice, and therefore, there are no correct answers, nor "truths" to be found. It is all about how much quality you want, and how must computation time, and development time you are willing to pay for that quality. The "satisfying" answer for your specific application must be found by exploring the trade-offs between the different parameters that regulate the image registration process.

If you are proficient in VTK you may want to consider attaching some visualization to the Event observer, so that you can have a visual feedback on the progress of the registration. This is a lot more productive than trying to interpret the values printed out on the console by the observer.

SEGMENTATION

Segmentation of medical images is a challenging task. A myriad of different methods have been proposed and implemented in recent years. In spite of the huge effort invested in this problem, there is no single approach that can generally solve the problem of segmentation for the large variety of image modalities existing today.

The most effective segmentation algorithms are obtained by carefully customizing combinations of components. The parameters of these components are tuned for the characteristics of the image modality used as input and the features of the anatomical structure to be segmented.

The Insight Toolkit provides a basic set of algorithms that can be used to develop and customize a full segmentation application. Some of the most commonly used segmentation components are described in the following sections.

4.1 Region Growing

Region growing algorithms have proven to be an effective approach for image segmentation. The basic approach of a region growing algorithm is to start from a seed region (typically one or more pixels) that are considered to be inside the object to be segmented. The pixels neighboring this region are evaluated to determine if they should also be considered part of the object. If so, they are added to the region and the process continues as long as new pixels are added to the region. Region growing algorithms vary depending on the criteria used to decide whether a pixel should be included in the region or not, the type connectivity used to determine neighbors, and the strategy used to visit neighboring pixels.

Several implementations of region growing are available in ITK. This section describes some of the most commonly used.

4.1.1 Connected Threshold

A simple criterion for including pixels in a growing region is to evaluate intensity value inside a specific interval.

The source code for this section can be found in the file
`ConnectedThresholdImageFilter.cxx`.

The following example illustrates the use of the `itk::ConnectedThresholdImageFilter`. This filter uses the flood fill iterator. Most of the algorithmic complexity of a region growing method comes from visiting neighboring pixels. The flood fill iterator assumes this responsibility and greatly simplifies the implementation of the region growing algorithm. Thus the algorithm is left to establish a criterion to decide whether a particular pixel should be included in the current region or not.

The criterion used by the ConnectedThresholdImageFilter is based on an interval of intensity values provided by the user. Values of lower and upper threshold should be provided. The region-growing algorithm includes those pixels whose intensities are inside the interval.

$$I(\mathbf{X}) \in [\text{lower}, \text{upper}] \tag{4.1}$$

Let's look at the minimal code required to use this algorithm. First, the following header defining the ConnectedThresholdImageFilter class must be included.

```
#include "itkConnectedThresholdImageFilter.h"
```

Noise present in the image can reduce the capacity of this filter to grow large regions. When faced with noisy images, it is usually convenient to pre-process the image by using an edge-preserving smoothing filter. Any of the filters discussed in Section 2.7.3 could be used to this end. In this particular example we use the `itk::CurvatureFlowImageFilter`, so we need to include its header file.

```
#include "itkCurvatureFlowImageFilter.h"
```

We declare the image type based on a particular pixel type and dimension. In this case the `float` type is used for the pixels due to the requirements of the smoothing filter.

```
typedef   float            InternalPixelType;
const     unsigned int     Dimension = 2;
typedef itk::Image< InternalPixelType, Dimension >  InternalImageType;
```

The smoothing filter is instantiated using the image type as a template parameter.

```
typedef itk::CurvatureFlowImageFilter< InternalImageType, InternalImageType >
  CurvatureFlowImageFilterType;
```

Then the filter is created by invoking the `New()` method and assigning the result to a `itk::SmartPointer`.

```
CurvatureFlowImageFilterType::Pointer smoothing =
                     CurvatureFlowImageFilterType::New();
```

We now declare the type of the region growing filter. In this case it is the ConnectedThresholdImageFilter.

```
typedef itk::ConnectedThresholdImageFilter< InternalImageType,
                       InternalImageType > ConnectedFilterType;
```

Then we construct one filter of this class using the `New()` method.

```
ConnectedFilterType::Pointer connectedThreshold = ConnectedFilterType::New();
```

Now it is time to connect a simple, linear pipeline. A file reader is added at the beginning of the pipeline and a cast filter and writer are added at the end. The cast filter is required to convert `float` pixel types to integer types since only a few image file formats support `float` types.

```
smoothing->SetInput( reader->GetOutput() );
connectedThreshold->SetInput( smoothing->GetOutput() );
caster->SetInput( connectedThreshold->GetOutput() );
writer->SetInput( caster->GetOutput() );
```

The CurvatureFlowImageFilter requires a couple of parameters. The following are typical values for 2D images. However they may have to be adjusted depending on the amount of noise present in the input image.

```
smoothing->SetNumberOfIterations( 5 );
smoothing->SetTimeStep( 0.125 );
```

The ConnectedThresholdImageFilter has two main parameters to be defined. They are the lower and upper thresholds of the interval in which intensity values should fall in order to be included in the region. Setting these two values too close will not allow enough flexibility for the region to grow. Setting them too far apart will result in a region that engulfs the image.

```
connectedThreshold->SetLower(  lowerThreshold  );
connectedThreshold->SetUpper(  upperThreshold  );
```

The output of this filter is a binary image with zero-value pixels everywhere except on the extracted region. The intensity value set inside the region is selected with the method `SetReplaceValue()`.

```
connectedThreshold->SetReplaceValue( 255 );
```

The initialization of the algorithm requires the user to provide a seed point. It is convenient to select this point to be placed in a *typical* region of the anatomical structure to be segmented. The seed is passed in the form of a `itk::Index` to the `SetSeed()` method.

```
connectedThreshold->SetSeed( index );
```

The invocation of the `Update()` method on the writer triggers the execution of the pipeline. It is usually wise to put update calls in a `try/catch` block in case errors occur and exceptions are thrown.

```
try
  {
  writer->Update();
  }
catch( itk::ExceptionObject & excep )
  {
  std::cerr << "Exception caught !" << std::endl;
  std::cerr << excep << std::endl;
  }
```

Let's run this example using as input the image `BrainProtonDensitySlice.png` provided in the directory `Examples/Data`. We can easily segment the major anatomical structures by providing seeds in the appropriate locations and defining values for the lower and upper thresholds. Figure 4.1 illustrates several examples of segmentation. The parameters used are presented in Table 4.1.

Structure	Seed Index	Lower	Upper	Output Image
White matter	(60,116)	150	180	Second from left in Figure 4.1
Ventricle	(81,112)	210	250	Third from left in Figure 4.1
Gray matter	(107,69)	180	210	Fourth from left in Figure 4.1

Table 4.1: Parameters used for segmenting some brain structures shown in Figure 4.1 with the filter `itk::ConnectedThresholdImageFilter`.

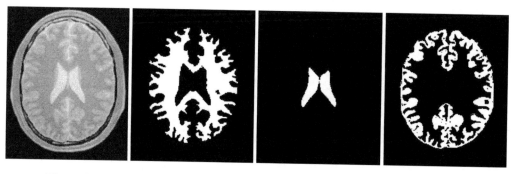

Figure 4.1: Segmentation results for the ConnectedThreshold filter for various seed points.

Notice that the gray matter is not being completely segmented. This illustrates the vulnerability of the region-growing methods when the anatomical structures to be segmented do not have a homogeneous statistical distribution over the image space. You may want to experiment with different values of the lower and upper thresholds to verify how the accepted region will extend.

Another option for segmenting regions is to take advantage of the functionality provided by the ConnectedThresholdImageFilter for managing multiple seeds. The seeds can be passed one-by-one to the filter using the `AddSeed()` method. You could imagine a user interface in which an operator clicks on multiple points of the object to be segmented and each selected point is passed as a seed to this filter.

4.1.2 Otsu Segmentation

Another criterion for classifying pixels is to minimize the error of misclassification. The goal is to find a threshold that classifies the image into two clusters such that we minimize the area under the histogram for one cluster that lies on the other cluster's side of the threshold. This is equivalent to minimizing the within class variance or equivalently maximizing the between class variance.

The source code for this section can be found in the file
`OtsuThresholdImageFilter.cxx`.

This example illustrates how to use the `itk::OtsuThresholdImageFilter`.

```
#include "itkOtsuThresholdImageFilter.h"
```

The next step is to decide which pixel types to use for the input and output images.

```
typedef  unsigned char  InputPixelType;
typedef  unsigned char  OutputPixelType;
```

The input and output image types are now defined using their respective pixel types and dimensions.

```
typedef itk::Image< InputPixelType,  2 >  InputImageType;
typedef itk::Image< OutputPixelType, 2 >  OutputImageType;
```

The filter type can be instantiated using the input and output image types defined above.

```
typedef itk::OtsuThresholdImageFilter<
             InputImageType, OutputImageType > FilterType;
```

An `itk::ImageFileReader` class is also instantiated in order to read image data from a file. (See Section 1 on page 1 for more information about reading and writing data.)

```
typedef itk::ImageFileReader< InputImageType >  ReaderType;
```

An `itk::ImageFileWriter` is instantiated in order to write the output image to a file.

```
typedef itk::ImageFileWriter< OutputImageType >  WriterType;
```

Both the filter and the reader are created by invoking their `New()` methods and assigning the result to `itk::SmartPointers`.

```
ReaderType::Pointer reader = ReaderType::New();
FilterType::Pointer filter = FilterType::New();
```

The image obtained with the reader is passed as input to the OtsuThresholdImageFilter.

```
filter->SetInput( reader->GetOutput() );
```

The method `SetOutsideValue()` defines the intensity value to be assigned to those pixels whose intensities are outside the range defined by the lower and upper thresholds. The method `SetInsideValue()` defines the intensity value to be assigned to pixels with intensities falling inside the threshold range.

```
filter->SetOutsideValue( outsideValue );
filter->SetInsideValue(  insideValue  );
```

The execution of the filter is triggered by invoking the `Update()` method. If the filter's output has been passed as input to subsequent filters, the `Update()` call on any downstream filters in the pipeline will indirectly trigger the update of this filter.

```
filter->Update();
```

We print out here the Threshold value that was computed internally by the filter. For this we invoke the `GetThreshold` method.

```
int threshold = filter->GetThreshold();
std::cout << "Threshold = " << threshold << std::endl;
```

Figure 4.2 illustrates the effect of this filter on a MRI proton density image of the brain. This figure shows the limitations of this filter for performing segmentation by itself. These limitations are particularly noticeable in noisy images and in images lacking spatial uniformity as is the case with MRI due to field bias.

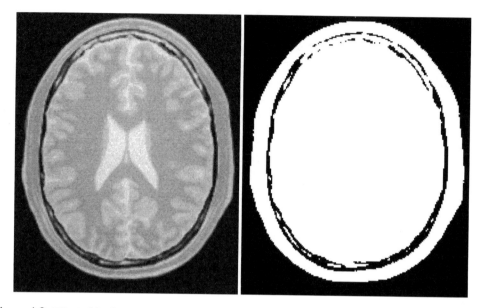

Figure 4.2: Effect of the OtsuThresholdImageFilter on a slice from a MRI proton density image of the brain.

The following classes provide similar functionality:

- itk::ThresholdImageFilter

The source code for this section can be found in the file
OtsuMultipleThresholdImageFilter.cxx.

This example illustrates how to use the itk::OtsuMultipleThresholdsCalculator.

```
#include "itkOtsuMultipleThresholdsCalculator.h"
```

OtsuMultipleThresholdsCalculator calculates thresholds for a given histogram so as to maximize the between-class variance. We use ScalarImageToHistogramGenerator to generate histograms. The histogram type defined by the generator is then used to instantiate the type of the Otsu threshold calculator.

```
typedef itk::Statistics::ScalarImageToHistogramGenerator<
                        InputImageType > ScalarImageToHistogramGeneratorType;

typedef ScalarImageToHistogramGeneratorType::HistogramType HistogramType;

typedef itk::OtsuMultipleThresholdsCalculator< HistogramType >
                                                        CalculatorType;
```

Once thresholds are computed we will use BinaryThresholdImageFilter to segment the input image into segments.

```
typedef itk::BinaryThresholdImageFilter<
InputImageType, OutputImageType > FilterType;
```

Create a histogram generator and calculator using the standard `New()` method.

```
ScalarImageToHistogramGeneratorType::Pointer scalarImageToHistogramGenerator
  = ScalarImageToHistogramGeneratorType::New();

CalculatorType::Pointer calculator = CalculatorType::New();
FilterType::Pointer filter = FilterType::New();
```

Set the following properties for the histogram generator and the calculators, in this case grabbing the number of thresholds from the command line.

```
scalarImageToHistogramGenerator->SetNumberOfBins( 128 );
calculator->SetNumberOfThresholds( atoi( argv[4] ) );
```

The pipeline will look as follows:

```
scalarImageToHistogramGenerator->SetInput( reader->GetOutput() );
calculator->SetInputHistogram(
                      scalarImageToHistogramGenerator->GetOutput() );
filter->SetInput( reader->GetOutput() );
writer->SetInput( filter->GetOutput() );
```

Thresholds are obtained using the `GetOutput` method.

```
const CalculatorType::OutputType &thresholdVector = calculator->GetOutput();
CalculatorType::OutputType::const_iterator itNum = thresholdVector.begin();
```

Threshold into separate segments and write out as binary images.

```
for(; itNum < thresholdVector.end(); itNum++)
  {
  std::cout << "OtsuThreshold["
            << (int)(itNum - thresholdVector.begin())
            << "] = "
            << static_cast<itk::NumericTraits<
                    CalculatorType::MeasurementType>::PrintType>(*itNum)
            << std::endl;
```

Also write out the image thresholded between the upper threshold and the max intensity.

```
upperThreshold = itk::NumericTraits<InputPixelType>::max();
filter->SetLowerThreshold( lowerThreshold );
filter->SetUpperThreshold( upperThreshold );
```

4.1.3 Neighborhood Connected

The source code for this section can be found in the file
`NeighborhoodConnectedImageFilter.cxx`.

The following example illustrates the use of the `itk::NeighborhoodConnectedImageFilter`. This filter is a close variant of the `itk::ConnectedThresholdImageFilter`. On one hand, the ConnectedThresholdImageFilter accepts a pixel in the region if its intensity is in the interval defined by two user-provided threshold values. The NeighborhoodConnectedImageFilter, on the other hand, will only accept a pixel if **all** its neighbors have intensities that fit in the interval. The size of the neighborhood to be considered around each pixel is defined by a user-provided integer radius.

The reason for considering the neighborhood intensities instead of only the current pixel intensity is that small structures are less likely to be accepted in the region. The operation of this filter is equivalent to applying the ConnectedThresholdImageFilter followed by mathematical morphology erosion using a structuring element of the same shape as the neighborhood provided to the NeighborhoodConnectedImageFilter.

```
#include "itkNeighborhoodConnectedImageFilter.h"
```

The `itk::CurvatureFlowImageFilter` is used here to smooth the image while preserving edges.

```
#include "itkCurvatureFlowImageFilter.h"
```

We now define the image type using a particular pixel type and image dimension. In this case the `float` type is used for the pixels due to the requirements of the smoothing filter.

```
typedef   float              InternalPixelType;
const     unsigned int    Dimension = 2;
typedef itk::Image< InternalPixelType, Dimension >  InternalImageType;
```

The smoothing filter type is instantiated using the image type as a template parameter.

```
typedef   itk::CurvatureFlowImageFilter<InternalImageType, InternalImageType>
  CurvatureFlowImageFilterType;
```

Then, the filter is created by invoking the `New()` method and assigning the result to a `itk::SmartPointer`.

```
CurvatureFlowImageFilterType::Pointer smoothing =
                    CurvatureFlowImageFilterType::New();
```

We now declare the type of the region growing filter. In this case it is the NeighborhoodConnectedImageFilter.

```
typedef itk::NeighborhoodConnectedImageFilter<InternalImageType,
                    InternalImageType > ConnectedFilterType;
```

One filter of this class is constructed using the `New()` method.

```
ConnectedFilterType::Pointer neighborhoodConnected
                              = ConnectedFilterType::New();
```

Now it is time to create a simple, linear data processing pipeline. A file reader is added at the beginning of the pipeline and a cast filter and writer are added at the end. The cast filter is required to convert `float` pixel types to integer types since only a few image file formats support `float` types.

```
smoothing->SetInput( reader->GetOutput() );
neighborhoodConnected->SetInput( smoothing->GetOutput() );
caster->SetInput( neighborhoodConnected->GetOutput() );
writer->SetInput( caster->GetOutput() );
```

The CurvatureFlowImageFilter requires a couple of parameters. The following are typical values for 2D images. However they may have to be adjusted depending on the amount of noise present in the input image.

```
smoothing->SetNumberOfIterations( 5 );
smoothing->SetTimeStep( 0.125 );
```

The NeighborhoodConnectedImageFilter requires that two main parameters are specified. They are the lower and upper thresholds of the interval in which intensity values must fall to be included in the region. Setting these two values too close will not allow enough flexibility for the region to grow. Setting them too far apart will result in a region that engulfs the image.

```
neighborhoodConnected->SetLower( lowerThreshold );
neighborhoodConnected->SetUpper( upperThreshold );
```

Here, we add the crucial parameter that defines the neighborhood size used to determine whether a pixel lies in the region. The larger the neighborhood, the more stable this filter will be against noise in the input image, but also the longer the computing time will be. Here we select a filter of radius 2 along each dimension. This results in a neighborhood of 5×5 pixels.

```
InternalImageType::SizeType   radius;

radius[0] = 2;   // two pixels along X
radius[1] = 2;   // two pixels along Y

neighborhoodConnected->SetRadius( radius );
```

As in the ConnectedThresholdImageFilter we must now provide the intensity value to be used for the output pixels accepted in the region and at least one seed point to define the initial region.

```
neighborhoodConnected->SetSeed( index );
neighborhoodConnected->SetReplaceValue( 255 );
```

The invocation of the Update() method on the writer triggers the execution of the pipeline. It is usually wise to put update calls in a try/catch block in case errors occur and exceptions are thrown.

```
try
  {
  writer->Update();
  }
catch( itk::ExceptionObject & excep )
  {
  std::cerr << "Exception caught !" << std::endl;
  std::cerr << excep << std::endl;
  }
```

Now we'll run this example using the image BrainProtonDensitySlice.png as input available from the directory Examples/Data. We can easily segment the major anatomical structures by providing seeds in the appropriate locations and defining values for the lower and upper thresholds. For example

Structure	Seed Index	Lower	Upper	Output Image
White matter	$(60, 116)$	150	180	Second from left in Figure 4.3
Ventricle	$(81, 112)$	210	250	Third from left in Figure 4.3
Gray matter	$(107, 69)$	180	210	Fourth from left in Figure 4.3

As with the ConnectedThresholdImageFilter, several seeds could be provided to the filter by using the AddSeed() method. Compare the output of Figure 4.3 with those of Figure 4.1 produced by the ConnectedThresholdImageFilter. You may want to play with the value of the neighborhood radius

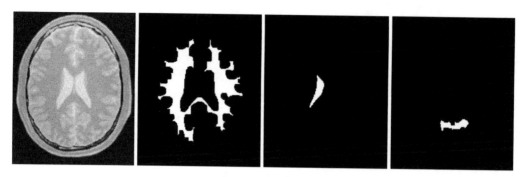

Figure 4.3: Segmentation results of the NeighborhoodConnectedImageFilter for various seed points.

and see how it affect the smoothness of the segmented object borders, the size of the segmented region and how much that costs in computing time.

4.1.4 Confidence Connected

The source code for this section can be found in the file
ConfidenceConnected.cxx.

The following example illustrates the use of the itk::ConfidenceConnectedImageFilter. The criterion used by the ConfidenceConnectedImageFilter is based on simple statistics of the current region. First, the algorithm computes the mean and standard deviation of intensity values for all the pixels currently included in the region. A user-provided factor is used to multiply the standard deviation and define a range around the mean. Neighbor pixels whose intensity values fall inside the range are accepted and included in the region. When no more neighbor pixels are found that satisfy the criterion, the algorithm is considered to have finished its first iteration. At that point, the mean and standard deviation of the intensity levels are recomputed using all the pixels currently included in the region. This mean and standard deviation defines a new intensity range that is used to visit current region neighbors and evaluate whether their intensity falls inside the range. This iterative process is repeated until no more pixels are added or the maximum number of iterations is reached. The following equation illustrates the inclusion criterion used by this filter,

$$I(\mathbf{X}) \in [m - f\sigma, m + f\sigma] \tag{4.2}$$

where m and σ are the mean and standard deviation of the region intensities, f is a factor defined by the user, $I()$ is the image and $\mathbf{X}$ is the position of the particular neighbor pixel being considered for inclusion in the region.

Let's look at the minimal code required to use this algorithm. First, the following header defining the itk::ConfidenceConnectedImageFilter class must be included.

```
#include "itkConfidenceConnectedImageFilter.h"
```

Noise present in the image can reduce the capacity of this filter to grow large regions. When faced with noisy images, it is usually convenient to pre-process the image by using an edge-preserving smoothing filter. Any of the filters discussed in Section 2.7.3 can be used to this end. In this particular example we use the `itk::CurvatureFlowImageFilter`, hence we need to include its header file.

```
#include "itkCurvatureFlowImageFilter.h"
```

We now define the image type using a pixel type and a particular dimension. In this case the `float` type is used for the pixels due to the requirements of the smoothing filter.

```
typedef   float           InternalPixelType;
const     unsigned int    Dimension = 2;
typedef itk::Image< InternalPixelType, Dimension >   InternalImageType;
```

The smoothing filter type is instantiated using the image type as a template parameter.

```
typedef itk::CurvatureFlowImageFilter< InternalImageType, InternalImageType >
    CurvatureFlowImageFilterType;
```

Next the filter is created by invoking the `New()` method and assigning the result to a `itk::SmartPointer`.

```
CurvatureFlowImageFilterType::Pointer smoothing =
                    CurvatureFlowImageFilterType::New();
```

We now declare the type of the region growing filter. In this case it is the ConfidenceConnectedImageFilter.

```
typedef itk::ConfidenceConnectedImageFilter<
            InternalImageType, InternalImageType> ConnectedFilterType;
```

Then, we construct one filter of this class using the `New()` method.

```
ConnectedFilterType::Pointer confidenceConnected
                            = ConnectedFilterType::New();
```

Now it is time to create a simple, linear pipeline. A file reader is added at the beginning of the pipeline and a cast filter and writer are added at the end. The cast filter is required here to convert `float` pixel types to integer types since only a few image file formats support `float` types.

```
smoothing->SetInput( reader->GetOutput() );
confidenceConnected->SetInput( smoothing->GetOutput() );
caster->SetInput( confidenceConnected->GetOutput() );
writer->SetInput( caster->GetOutput() );
```

The CurvatureFlowImageFilter requires two parameters. The following are typical values for $2D$ images. However they may have to be adjusted depending on the amount of noise present in the input image.

```
smoothing->SetNumberOfIterations( 5 );
smoothing->SetTimeStep( 0.125 );
```

The ConfidenceConnectedImageFilter requires two parameters. First, the factor f defines how large the range of intensities will be. Small values of the multiplier will restrict the inclusion of pixels to those having very similar intensities to those in the current region. Larger values of the multiplier will relax the accepting condition and will result in more generous growth of the region. Values that are too large will cause the region to grow into neighboring regions which may belong to separate anatomical structures. This is not desirable behavior.

```
confidenceConnected->SetMultiplier( 2.5 );
```

The number of iterations is specified based on the homogeneity of the intensities of the anatomical structure to be segmented. Highly homogeneous regions may only require a couple of iterations. Regions with ramp effects, like MRI images with inhomogeneous fields, may require more iterations. In practice, it seems to be more important to carefully select the multiplier factor than the number of iterations. However, keep in mind that there is no reason to assume that this algorithm should converge to a stable region. It is possible that by letting the algorithm run for more iterations the region will end up engulfing the entire image.

```
confidenceConnected->SetNumberOfIterations( 5 );
```

The output of this filter is a binary image with zero-value pixels everywhere except on the extracted region. The intensity value to be set inside the region is selected with the method SetReplaceValue().

```
confidenceConnected->SetReplaceValue( 255 );
```

The initialization of the algorithm requires the user to provide a seed point. It is convenient to select this point to be placed in a *typical* region of the anatomical structure to be segmented. A small neighborhood around the seed point will be used to compute the initial mean and standard deviation for the inclusion criterion. The seed is passed in the form of a itk::Index to the SetSeed() method.

```
confidenceConnected->SetSeed( index );
```

The size of the initial neighborhood around the seed is defined with the method SetInitialNeighborhoodRadius(). The neighborhood will be defined as an N-dimensional rectangular region with $2r + 1$ pixels on the side, where r is the value passed as initial neighborhood radius.

```
confidenceConnected->SetInitialNeighborhoodRadius( 2 );
```

The invocation of the Update() method on the writer triggers the execution of the pipeline. It is recommended to place update calls in a try/catch block in case errors occur and exceptions are thrown.

```
try
  {
  writer->Update();
  }
catch( itk::ExceptionObject & excep )
  {
  std::cerr << "Exception caught !" << std::endl;
  std::cerr << excep << std::endl;
  }
```

Let's now run this example using as input the image BrainProtonDensitySlice.png provided in the directory Examples/Data. We can easily segment the major anatomical structures by providing seeds in the appropriate locations. For example

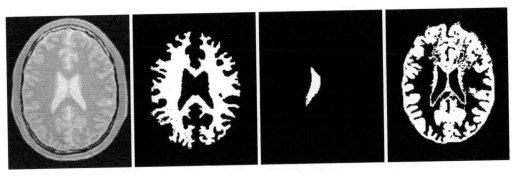

Figure 4.4: Segmentation results for the ConfidenceConnected filter for various seed points.

Structure	Seed Index	Output Image
White matter	(60,116)	Second from left in Figure 4.4
Ventricle	(81,112)	Third from left in Figure 4.4
Gray matter	(107,69)	Fourth from left in Figure 4.4

Note that the gray matter is not being completely segmented. This illustrates the vulnerability of the region growing methods when the anatomical structures to be segmented do not have a homogeneous statistical distribution over the image space. You may want to experiment with different numbers of iterations to verify how the accepted region will extend.

Application of the Confidence Connected filter on the Brain Web Data

This section shows some results obtained by applying the Confidence Connected filter on the Brain-Web database. The filter was applied on a $181 \times 217 \times 181$ crosssection of the *brainweb165a10f17* dataset. The data is a MR T1 acquisition, with an intensity non-uniformity of 20% and a slice thickness 1mm. The dataset may be obtained from http://www.bic.mni.mcgill.ca/brainweb/ or ftp://public.kitware.com/pub/itk/Data/BrainWeb/

The previous code was used in this example replacing the image dimension by 3. Gradient Anistropic diffusion was applied to smooth the image. The filter used 2 iterations, a time step of 0.05 and a conductance value of 3. The smoothed volume was then segmented using the Confidence Connected approach. Five seed points were used at coordinate locations (118,85,92), (63,87,94), (63,157,90), (111,188,90), (111,50,88). The ConfidenceConnnected filter used the parameters, a neighborhood radius of 2, 5 iterations and an f of 2.5 (the same as in the previous example). The results were then rendered using VolView.

Figure 4.5 shows the rendered volume. Figure 4.6 shows an axial, saggital and a coronal slice of the volume.

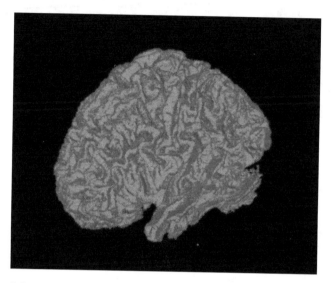

Figure 4.5: White matter segmented using Confidence Connected region growing.

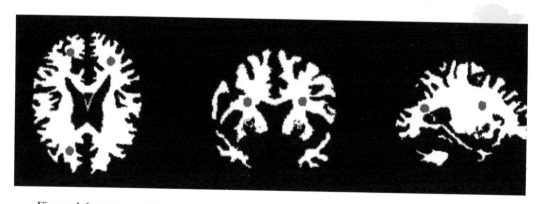

Figure 4.6: Axial, sagittal and coronal slice segmented using Confidence Connected region growing.

4.1.5 Isolated Connected

The source code for this section can be found in the file
IsolatedConnectedImageFilter.cxx.

The following example illustrates the use of the itk::IsolatedConnectedImageFilter. This
filter is a close variant of the itk::ConnectedThresholdImageFilter. In this filter two seeds and
a lower threshold are provided by the user. The filter will grow a region connected to the first seed
and **not connected** to the second one. In order to do this, the filter finds an intensity value that could
be used as upper threshold for the first seed. A binary search is used to find the value that separates
both seeds.

This example closely follows the previous ones. Only the relevant pieces of code are highlighted
here.

The header of the IsolatedConnectedImageFilter is included below.

```
#include "itkIsolatedConnectedImageFilter.h"
```

We define the image type using a pixel type and a particular dimension.

```
typedef  float           InternalPixelType;
const    unsigned int    Dimension = 2;
typedef itk::Image< InternalPixelType, Dimension >  InternalImageType;
```

The IsolatedConnectedImageFilter is instantiated in the lines below.

```
typedef itk::IsolatedConnectedImageFilter<InternalImageType,
                             InternalImageType> ConnectedFilterType;
```

One filter of this class is constructed using the New() method.

```
ConnectedFilterType::Pointer isolatedConnected = ConnectedFilterType::New();
```

Now it is time to connect the pipeline.

```
smoothing->SetInput( reader->GetOutput() );
isolatedConnected->SetInput( smoothing->GetOutput() );
caster->SetInput( isolatedConnected->GetOutput() );
writer->SetInput( caster->GetOutput() );
```

The IsolatedConnectedImageFilter expects the user to specify a threshold and two seeds. In this
example, we take all of them from the command line arguments.

```
isolatedConnected->SetLower( lowerThreshold );
isolatedConnected->AddSeed1( indexSeed1 );
isolatedConnected->AddSeed2( indexSeed2 );
```

As in the itk::ConnectedThresholdImageFilter we must now specify the intensity value to be
set on the output pixels and at least one seed point to define the initial region.

```
isolatedConnected->SetReplaceValue( 255 );
```

The invocation of the Update() method on the writer triggers the execution of the pipeline.

Adjacent Structures	Seed1	Seed2	Lower	Isolated value found
Gray matter vs White matter	$(61, 140)$	$(63, 43)$	150	183.31

Table 4.2: Parameters used for separating white matter from gray matter in Figure 4.7 using the IsolatedConnectedImageFilter.

```
try
  {
  writer->Update();
  }
catch( itk::ExceptionObject & excep )
  {
  std::cerr << "Exception caught !" << std::endl;
  std::cerr << excep << std::endl;
  }
```

The intensity value allowing us to separate both regions can be recovered with the method `GetIsolatedValue()`.

```
std::cout << "Isolated Value Found = ";
std::cout << isolatedConnected->GetIsolatedValue() << std::endl;
```

Let's now run this example using the image `BrainProtonDensitySlice.png` provided in the directory `Examples/Data`. We can easily segment the major anatomical structures by providing seed pairs in the appropriate locations and defining values for the lower threshold. It is important to keep in mind in this and the previous examples that the segmentation is being performed using the smoothed version of the image. The selection of threshold values should therefore be performed in the smoothed image since the distribution of intensities could be quite different from that of the input image. As a reminder of this fact, Figure 4.7 presents, from left to right, the input image and the result of smoothing with the `itk::CurvatureFlowImageFilter` followed by segmentation results.

This filter is intended to be used in cases where adjacent anatomical structures are difficult to separate. Selecting one seed in one structure and the other seed in the adjacent structure creates the appropriate setup for computing the threshold that will separate both structures. Table 4.2 presents the parameters used to obtain the images shown in Figure 4.7.

4.1.6 Confidence Connected in Vector Images

The source code for this section can be found in the file `VectorConfidenceConnected.cxx`.

This example illustrates the use of the confidence connected concept applied to images with vector pixel types. The confidence connected algorithm is implemented for vector images in the class `itk::VectorConfidenceConnected`. The basic difference between the scalar and vector version is that the vector version uses the covariance matrix instead of a variance, and a vector mean instead of a scalar mean. The membership of a vector pixel value to the region is measured using the Mahalanobis distance as implemented in the class `itk::Statistics::MahalanobisDistanceThresholdImageFunction`.

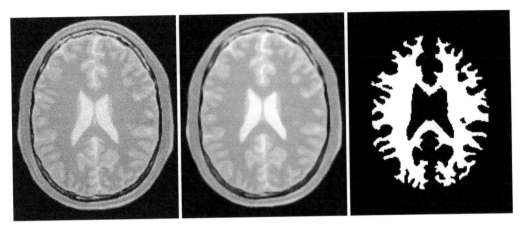

Figure 4.7: Segmentation results of the IsolatedConnectedImageFilter.

```
#include "itkVectorConfidenceConnectedImageFilter.h"
```

We now define the image type using a particular pixel type and dimension. In this case the float type is used for the pixels due to the requirements of the smoothing filter.

```
typedef   unsigned char                      PixelComponentType;
typedef   itk::RGBPixel< PixelComponentType >  InputPixelType;
const     unsigned int    Dimension = 2;
typedef itk::Image< InputPixelType, Dimension >  InputImageType;
```

We now declare the type of the region-growing filter.   In this case it is the itk::VectorConfidenceConnectedImageFilter.

```
typedef  itk::VectorConfidenceConnectedImageFilter< InputImageType,
                            OutputImageType > ConnectedFilterType;
```

Then, we construct one filter of this class using the New() method.

```
ConnectedFilterType::Pointer confidenceConnected
                                = ConnectedFilterType::New();
```

Next we create a simple, linear data processing pipeline.

```
confidenceConnected->SetInput( reader->GetOutput() );
writer->SetInput( confidenceConnected->GetOutput() );
```

The VectorConfidenceConnectedImageFilter requires two parameters. First, the multiplier factor f defines how large the range of intensities will be. Small values of the multiplier will restrict the inclusion of pixels to those having similar intensities to those already in the current region. Larger values of the multiplier relax the accepting condition and result in more generous growth of the region. Values that are too large will cause the region to grow into neighboring regions which may actually belong to separate anatomical structures.

```
confidenceConnected->SetMultiplier( multiplier );
```

The number of iterations is typically determined based on the homogeneity of the image intensity

representing the anatomical structure to be segmented. Highly homogeneous regions may only require a couple of iterations. Regions with ramp effects, like MRI images with inhomogeneous fields,
may require more iterations. In practice, it seems to be more relevant to carefully select the multiplier
factor than the number of iterations. However, keep in mind that there is no reason to assume that
this algorithm should converge to a stable region. It is possible that by letting the algorithm run for
more iterations the region will end up engulfing the entire image.

```
confidenceConnected->SetNumberOfIterations( iterations );
```

The output of this filter is a binary image with zero-value pixels everywhere except on the extracted region. The intensity value to be put inside the region is selected with the method
SetReplaceValue().

```
confidenceConnected->SetReplaceValue( 255 );
```

The initialization of the algorithm requires the user to provide a seed point. This point should be
placed in a *typical* region of the anatomical structure to be segmented. A small neighborhood around
the seed point will be used to compute the initial mean and standard deviation for the inclusion
criterion. The seed is passed in the form of a itk::Index to the SetSeed() method.

```
confidenceConnected->SetSeed( index );
```

The size of the initial neighborhood around the seed is defined with the method
SetInitialNeighborhoodRadius(). The neighborhood will be defined as an N-Dimensional rectangular region with $2r+1$ pixels on the side, where r is the value passed as initial neighborhood
radius.

```
confidenceConnected->SetInitialNeighborhoodRadius( 3 );
```

The invocation of the Update() method on the writer triggers the execution of the pipeline. It
is usually wise to put update calls in a try/catch block in case errors occur and exceptions are
thrown.

```
try
  {
  writer->Update();
  }
catch( itk::ExceptionObject & excep )
  {
  std::cerr << "Exception caught !" << std::endl;
  std::cerr << excep << std::endl;
  }
```

Now let's run this example using as input the image VisibleWomanEyeSlice.png provided in the
directory Examples/Data. We can easily segment the major anatomical structures by providing
seeds in the appropriate locations. For example,

Structure	Seed Index	Multiplier	Iterations	Output Image
Rectum	$(70, 120)$	7	1	Second from left in Figure 4.8
Rectum	$(23, 93)$	7	1	Third from left in Figure 4.8
Vitreo	$(66, 66)$	3	1	Fourth from left in Figure 4.8

The coloration of muscular tissue makes it easy to distinguish them from the surrounding anatomical

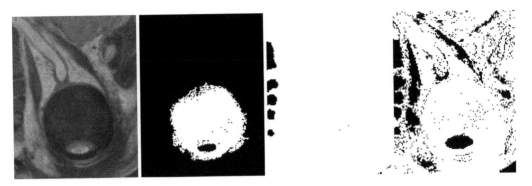

Figure 4.8: Segmentation results of the VectorConfidenceConnected filter for various seed points.

structures. The optic vitrea on the other hand has a coloration that is not very homogeneous inside the eyeball and does not facilitate a full segmentation based only on color.

The values of the final mean vector and covariance matrix used for the last iteration can be queried using the methods GetMean() and GetCovariance().

```
typedef ConnectedFilterType::MeanVectorType   MeanVectorType;

const MeanVectorType & mean = confidenceConnected->GetMean();

std::cout << "Mean vector = " << std::endl;
std::cout << mean << std::endl;

typedef ConnectedFilterType::CovarianceMatrixType   CovarianceMatrixType;

const CovarianceMatrixType & covariance
                           = confidenceConnected->GetCovariance();

std::cout << "Covariance matrix = " << std::endl;
std::cout << covariance << std::endl;
```

4.2 Segmentation Based on Watersheds

4.2.1 Overview

Watershed segmentation classifies pixels into regions using gradient descent on image features and analysis of weak points along region boundaries. Imagine water raining onto a landscape topology and flowing with gravity to collect in low basins. The size of those basins will grow with increasing amounts of precipitation until they spill into one another, causing small basins to merge together into larger basins. Regions (catchment basins) are formed by using local geometric structure to associate points in the image domain with local extrema in some feature measurement such as curvature or gradient magnitude. This technique is less sensitive to user-defined thresholds than classic region-growing methods, and may be better suited for fusing different types of features from different data sets. The watersheds technique is also more flexible in that it does not produce a single image

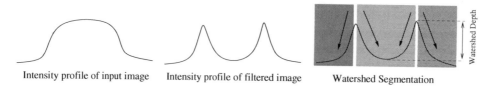

Intensity profile of input image   Intensity profile of filtered image   Watershed Segmentation

Figure 4.9: A fuzzy-valued boundary map, from an image or set of images, is segmented using local minima and catchment basins.

segmentation, but rather a hierarchy of segmentations from which a single region or set of regions can be extracted a-priori, using a threshold, or interactively, with the help of a graphical user interface [74, 75].

The strategy of watershed segmentation is to treat an image f as a height function, i.e., the surface formed by graphing f as a function of its independent parameters, $\vec{x} \in U$. The image f is often not the original input data, but is derived from that data through some filtering, graded (or fuzzy) feature extraction, or fusion of feature maps from different sources. The assumption is that higher values of f (or $-f$) indicate the presence of boundaries in the original data. Watersheds may therefore be considered as a final or intermediate step in a hybrid segmentation method, where the initial segmentation is the generation of the edge feature map.

Gradient descent associates regions with local minima of f (clearly interior points) using the watersheds of the graph of f, as in Figure 4.9. That is, a segment consists of all points in U whose paths of steepest descent on the graph of f terminate at the same minimum in f. Thus, there are as many segments in an image as there are minima in f. The segment boundaries are "ridges" [30, 31, 20] in the graph of f. In the 1D case ($U \subset \Re$), the watershed boundaries are the local maxima of f, and the results of the watershed segmentation is trivial. For higher-dimensional image domains, the watershed boundaries are not simply local phenomena; they depend on the shape of the entire watershed.

The drawback of watershed segmentation is that it produces a region for each local minimum—in practice too many regions—and an over segmentation results. To alleviate this, we can establish a minimum watershed depth. The watershed depth is the difference in height between the watershed minimum and the lowest boundary point. In other words, it is the maximum depth of water a region could hold without flowing into any of its neighbors. Thus, a watershed segmentation algorithm can sequentially combine watersheds whose depths fall below the minimum until all of the watersheds are of sufficient depth. This depth measurement can be combined with other saliency measurements, such as size. The result is a segmentation containing regions whose boundaries and size are significant. Because the merging process is sequential, it produces a hierarchy of regions, as shown in Figure 4.10. Previous work has shown the benefit of a user-assisted approach that provides a graphical interface to this hierarchy, so that a technician can quickly move from the small regions that lie within an area of interest to the union of regions that correspond to the anatomical structure [75].

There are two different algorithms commonly used to implement watersheds: top-down and bottom-up. The top-down, gradient descent strategy was chosen for ITK because we want to consider the output of multi-scale differential operators, and the f in question will therefore have floating point values. The bottom-up strategy starts with seeds at the local minima in the image and grows regions

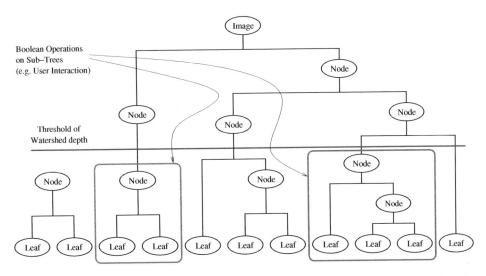

Figure 4.10: A watershed segmentation combined with a saliency measure (watershed depth) produces a hierarchy of regions. Structures can be derived from images by either thresholding the saliency measure or combining subtrees within the hierarchy.

outward and upward at discrete intensity levels (equivalent to a sequence of morphological operations and sometimes called *morphological watersheds* [56].) This limits the accuracy by enforcing a set of discrete gray levels on the image.

Figure 4.11 shows how the ITK image-to-image watersheds filter is constructed. The filter is actually a collection of smaller filters that modularize the several steps of the algorithm in a mini-pipeline. The segmenter object creates the initial segmentation via steepest descent from each pixel to local minima. Shallow background regions are removed (flattened) before segmentation using a simple minimum value threshold (this helps to minimize oversegmentation of the image). The initial segmentation is passed to a second sub-filter that generates a hierarchy of basins to a user-specified maximum watershed depth. The relabeler object at the end of the mini-pipeline uses the hierarchy

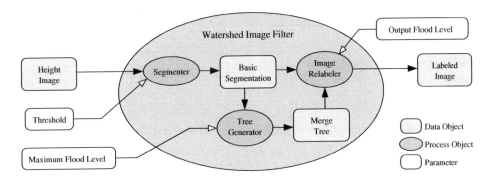

Figure 4.11: The construction of the Insight watersheds filter.

and the initial segmentation to produce an output image at any scale *below* the user-specified maximum. Data objects are cached in the mini-pipeline so that changing watershed depths only requires a (fast) relabeling of the basic segmentation. The three parameters that control the filter are shown in Figure 4.11 connected to their relevant processing stages.

4.2.2   Using the ITK Watershed Filter

The source code for this section can be found in the file
WatershedSegmentation1.cxx.

The following example illustrates how to preprocess and segment images using the itk::WatershedImageFilter. Note that the care with which the data are preprocessed will greatly affect the quality of your result. Typically, the best results are obtained by preprocessing the original image with an edge-preserving diffusion filter, such as one of the anisotropic diffusion filters, or the bilateral image filter. As noted in Section 4.2.1, the height function used as input should be created such that higher positive values correspond to object boundaries. A suitable height function for many applications can be generated as the gradient magnitude of the image to be segmented.

The   itk::VectorGradientMagnitudeAnisotropicDiffusionImageFilter class is used to smooth the image and the itk::VectorGradientMagnitudeImageFilter is used to generate the height function. We begin by including all preprocessing filter header files and the header file for the WatershedImageFilter. We use the vector versions of these filters because the input dataset is a color image.

```
#include "itkVectorGradientAnisotropicDiffusionImageFilter.h"
#include "itkVectorGradientMagnitudeImageFilter.h"
#include "itkWatershedImageFilter.h"
```

We now declare the image and pixel types to use for instantiation of the filters. All of these filters expect real-valued pixel types in order to work properly. The preprocessing stages are applied directly to the vector-valued data and the segmentation uses floating point scalar data. Images are converted from RGB pixel type to numerical vector type using itk::VectorCastImageFilter.

```
typedef itk::RGBPixel< unsigned char >        RGBPixelType;
typedef itk::Image< RGBPixelType, 2 >         RGBImageType;
typedef itk::Vector< float, 3 >               VectorPixelType;
typedef itk::Image< VectorPixelType, 2 >      VectorImageType;
typedef itk::Image< itk::IdentifierType, 2 >  LabeledImageType;
typedef itk::Image< float, 2 >                ScalarImageType;
```

The various image processing filters are declared using the types created above and eventually used in the pipeline.

```
typedef itk::ImageFileReader< RGBImageType >    FileReaderType;
typedef itk::VectorCastImageFilter< RGBImageType, VectorImageType >
                                                CastFilterType;
typedef itk::VectorGradientAnisotropicDiffusionImageFilter<
                     VectorImageType, VectorImageType >
                                                DiffusionFilterType;
typedef itk::VectorGradientMagnitudeImageFilter< VectorImageType >
                                                GradientMagnitudeFilterType;
typedef itk::WatershedImageFilter< ScalarImageType >
                                                WatershedFilterType;
```

Next we instantiate the filters and set their parameters. The first step in the image processing pipeline is diffusion of the color input image using an anisotropic diffusion filter. For this class of filters, the CFL condition requires that the time step be no more than 0.25 for two-dimensional images, and no more than 0.125 for three-dimensional images. The number of iterations and the conductance term will be taken from the command line. See Section 2.7.3 for more information on the ITK anisotropic diffusion filters.

```
DiffusionFilterType::Pointer diffusion = DiffusionFilterType::New();
diffusion->SetNumberOfIterations( atoi(argv[4]) );
diffusion->SetConductanceParameter( atof(argv[3]) );
diffusion->SetTimeStep(0.125);
```

The ITK gradient magnitude filter for vector-valued images can optionally take several parameters. Here we allow only enabling or disabling of principal component analysis.

```
GradientMagnitudeFilterType::Pointer
   gradient = GradientMagnitudeFilterType::New();
gradient->SetUsePrincipleComponents(atoi(argv[7]));
```

Finally we set up the watershed filter. There are two parameters. `Level` controls watershed depth, and `Threshold` controls the lower thresholding of the input. Both parameters are set as a percentage (0.0 - 1.0) of the maximum depth in the input image.

```
WatershedFilterType::Pointer watershed = WatershedFilterType::New();
watershed->SetLevel( atof(argv[6]) );
watershed->SetThreshold( atof(argv[5]) );
```

The output of WatershedImageFilter is an image of unsigned long integer labels, where a label denotes membership of a pixel in a particular segmented region. This format is not practical for visualization, so for the purposes of this example, we will convert it to RGB pixels. RGB images have the advantage that they can be saved as a simple png file and viewed using any standard image viewer software. The `itk::Functor::ScalarToRGBPixelFunctor` class is a special function object designed to hash a scalar value into an `itk::RGBPixel`. Plugging this functor into the `itk::UnaryFunctorImageFilter` creates an image filter which converts scalar images to RGB images.

```
typedef itk::Functor::ScalarToRGBPixelFunctor<unsigned long>
   ColorMapFunctorType;
typedef itk::UnaryFunctorImageFilter<LabeledImageType,
   RGBImageType, ColorMapFunctorType> ColorMapFilterType;
ColorMapFilterType::Pointer colormapper = ColorMapFilterType::New();
```

The filters are connected into a single pipeline, with readers and writers at each end.

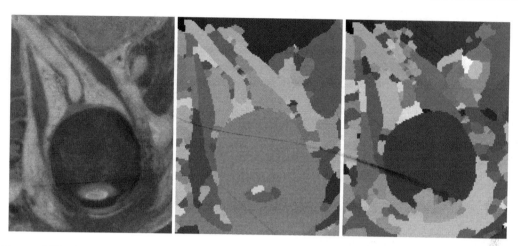

Figure 4.12: Segmented section of Visible Human female head and neck cryosection data. At left is the original image. The image in the middle was generated with parameters: conductance = 2.0, iterations = 10, threshold = 0.0, level = 0.05, principal components = on. The image on the right was generated with parameters: conductance = 2.0, iterations = 10, threshold = 0.001, level = 0.15, principal components = off.

```
caster->SetInput(reader->GetOutput());
diffusion->SetInput(caster->GetOutput());
gradient->SetInput(diffusion->GetOutput());
watershed->SetInput(gradient->GetOutput());
colormapper->SetInput(watershed->GetOutput());
writer->SetInput(colormapper->GetOutput());
```

Tuning the filter parameters for any particular application is a process of trial and error. The *threshold* parameter can be used to great effect in controlling oversegmentation of the image. Raising the threshold will generally reduce computation time and produce output with fewer and larger regions. The trick in tuning parameters is to consider the scale level of the objects that you are trying to segment in the image. The best time/quality trade-off will be achieved when the image is smoothed and thresholded to eliminate features just below the desired scale.

Figure 4.12 shows output from the example code. The input image is taken from the Visible Human female data around the right eye. The images on the right are colorized watershed segmentations with parameters set to capture objects such as the optic nerve and lateral rectus muscles, which can be seen just above and to the left and right of the eyeball. Note that a critical difference between the two segmentations is the mode of the gradient magnitude calculation.

A note on the computational complexity of the watershed algorithm is warranted. Most of the complexity of the ITK implementation lies in generating the hierarchy. Processing times for this stage are non-linear with respect to the number of catchment basins in the initial segmentation. This means that the amount of information contained in an image is more significant than the number of pixels in the image. A very large, but very flat input take less time to segment than a very small, but very detailed input.

4.3 Level Set Segmentation

The paradigm of the level set is that it is a numerical method for tracking the evolution of contours and surfaces. Instead of manipulating the contour directly, the contour is embedded as the zero level set of a higher dimensional function called the level-set function, $\psi(\mathbf{X}, \mathbf{t})$. The level-set function is then evolved under the control of a differential equation. At any time, the evolving contour can be obtained by extracting the zero level-set $\Gamma(\mathbf{X}, \mathbf{t}) = \{\psi(\mathbf{X}, \mathbf{t}) = \mathbf{0}\}$ from the output. The main advantages of using level sets is that arbitrarily complex shapes can be modeled and topological changes such as merging and splitting are handled implicitly.

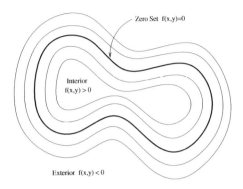

Figure 4.13: Concept of zero set in a level set.

Level sets can be used for image segmentation by using image-based features such as mean intensity, gradient and edges in the governing differential equation. In a typical approach, a contour is initialized by a user and is then evolved until it fits the form of an anatomical structure in the image. Many different implementations and variants of this basic concept have been published in the literature. An overview of the field has been made by Sethian [57].

The following sections introduce practical examples of some of the level set segmentation methods available in ITK. The remainder of this section describes features common to all of these filters except the itk::FastMarchingImageFilter, which is derived from a different code framework. Understanding these features will aid in using the filters more effectively.

Each filter makes use of a generic level-set equation to compute the update to the solution ψ of the partial differential equation.

$$\frac{d}{dt}\psi = -\alpha \mathbf{A}(\mathbf{x}) \cdot \nabla\psi - \beta P(\mathbf{x}) \,|\, \nabla\psi \,| + \gamma Z(\mathbf{x}) \kappa \,|\, \nabla\psi \,| \qquad (4.3)$$

where $\mathbf{A}$ is an advection term, P is a propagation (expansion) term, and Z is a spatial modifier term for the mean curvature κ. The scalar constants α, β, and γ weight the relative influence of each of the terms on the movement of the interface. A segmentation filter may use all of these terms in its calculations, or it may omit one or more terms. If a term is left out of the equation, then setting the corresponding scalar constant weighting will have no effect.

All of the level-set based segmentation filters *must* operate with floating point precision to produce valid results. The third, optional template parameter is the *numerical type* used for calculations and as the output image pixel type. The numerical type is float by default, but can be changed to double for extra precision. A user-defined, signed floating point type that defines all of the necessary arithmetic operators and has sufficient precision is also a valid choice. You should not use types such as int or unsigned char for the numerical parameter. If the input image pixel types do not match the numerical type, those inputs will be cast to an image of appropriate type when the

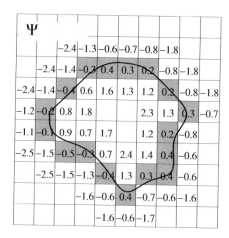

Figure 4.14: The implicit level set surface Γ is the black line superimposed over the image grid. The location of the surface is interpolated by the image pixel values. The grid pixels closest to the implicit surface are shown in gray.

filter is executed.

Most filters require two images as input, an initial model $\psi(\mathbf{X}, \mathbf{t} = \mathbf{0})$, and a *feature image*, which is either the image you wish to segment or some preprocessed version. You must specify the isovalue that represents the surface Γ in your initial model. The single image output of each filter is the function ψ at the final time step. It is important to note that the contour representing the surface Γ is the zero level-set of the output image, and not the isovalue you specified for the initial model. To represent Γ using the original isovalue, simply add that value back to the output.

The solution Γ is calculated to subpixel precision. The best discrete approximation of the surface is therefore the set of grid positions closest to the zero-crossings in the image, as shown in Figure 4.14. The itk::ZeroCrossingImageFilter operates by finding exactly those grid positions and can be used to extract the surface.

There are two important considerations when analyzing the processing time for any particular level-set segmentation task: the surface area of the evolving interface and the total distance that the surface must travel. Because the level-set equations are usually solved only at pixels near the surface (fast marching methods are an exception), the time taken at each iteration depends on the number of points on the surface. This means that as the surface grows, the solver will slow down proportionally. Because the surface must evolve slowly to prevent numerical instabilities in the solution, the distance the surface must travel in the image dictates the total number of iterations required.

Some level-set techniques are relatively insensitive to initial conditions and are therefore suitable for region-growing segmentation. Other techniques, such as the itk::LaplacianSegmentationLevelSetImageFilter, can easily become "stuck" on image features close to their initialization and should be used only when a reasonable prior segmentation is available as the initialization. For best efficiency, your initial model of the surface should be the best guess possible for the solution. When extending the example applications given here to higher

Figure 4.15: Collaboration diagram of the FastMarchingImageFilter applied to a segmentation task.

dimensional images, for example, you can improve results and dramatically decrease processing time by using a multi-scale approach. Start with a downsampled volume and work back to the full resolution using the results at each intermediate scale as the initialization for the next scale.

4.3.1 Fast Marching Segmentation

The source code for this section can be found in the file
FastMarchingImageFilter.cxx.

When the differential equation governing the level set evolution has a very simple form, a fast evolution algorithm called fast marching can be used.

The following example illustrates the use of the itk::FastMarchingImageFilter. This filter implements a fast marching solution to a simple level set evolution problem. In this example, the speed term used in the differential equation is expected to be provided by the user in the form of an image. This image is typically computed as a function of the gradient magnitude. Several mappings are popular in the literature, for example, the negative exponential $exp(-x)$ and the reciprocal $1/(1 + x)$. In the current example we decided to use a Sigmoid function since it offers a good number of control parameters that can be customized to shape a nice speed image.

The mapping should be done in such a way that the propagation speed of the front will be very low close to high image gradients while it will move rather fast in low gradient areas. This arrangement will make the contour propagate until it reaches the edges of anatomical structures in the image and then slow down in front of those edges. The output of the FastMarchingImageFilter is a *time-crossing map* that indicates, for each pixel, how much time it would take for the front to arrive at the pixel location.

The application of a threshold in the output image is then equivalent to taking a snapshot of the contour at a particular time during its evolution. It is expected that the contour will take a longer time to cross over the edges of a particular anatomical structure. This should result in large changes on the time-crossing map values close to the structure edges. Segmentation is performed with this filter by locating a time range in which the contour was contained for a long time in a region of the image space.

Figure 4.15 shows the major components involved in the application of the FastMarchingImageFilter to a segmentation task. It involves an initial stage of smoothing using the itk::CurvatureAnisotropicDiffusionImageFilter. The smoothed image is passed as the input to the itk::GradientMagnitudeRecursiveGaussianImageFilter and then to the itk::SigmoidImageFilter. Finally, the output of the FastMarchingImageFilter is passed to a itk::BinaryThresholdImageFilter in order to produce a binary mask representing the segmented object.

The code in the following example illustrates the typical setup of a pipeline for performing segmentation with fast marching. First, the input image is smoothed using an edge-preserving filter. Then the magnitude of its gradient is computed and passed to a sigmoid filter. The result of the sigmoid filter is the image potential that will be used to affect the speed term of the differential equation.

Let's start by including the following headers. First we include the header of the CurvatureAnisotropicDiffusionImageFilter that will be used for removing noise from the input image.

```
#include "itkCurvatureAnisotropicDiffusionImageFilter.h"
```

The headers of the GradientMagnitudeRecursiveGaussianImageFilter and SigmoidImageFilter are included below. Together, these two filters will produce the image potential for regulating the speed term in the differential equation describing the evolution of the level set.

```
#include "itkGradientMagnitudeRecursiveGaussianImageFilter.h"
#include "itkSigmoidImageFilter.h"
```

Of course, we will need the `itk::Image` class and the FastMarchingImageFilter class. Hence we include their headers.

```
#include "itkFastMarchingImageFilter.h"
```

The time-crossing map resulting from the FastMarchingImageFilter will be thresholded using the BinaryThresholdImageFilter. We include its header here.

```
#include "itkBinaryThresholdImageFilter.h"
```

Reading and writing images will be done with the `itk::ImageFileReader` and `itk::ImageFileWriter`.

```
#include "itkImageFileReader.h"
#include "itkImageFileWriter.h"
```

We now define the image type using a pixel type and a particular dimension. In this case the `float` type is used for the pixels due to the requirements of the smoothing filter.

```
typedef   float            InternalPixelType;
const      unsigned int      Dimension = 2;
typedef itk::Image< InternalPixelType, Dimension >  InternalImageType;
```

The output image, on the other hand, is declared to be binary.

```
typedef unsigned char                          OutputPixelType;
typedef itk::Image< OutputPixelType, Dimension > OutputImageType;
```

The type of the BinaryThresholdImageFilter filter is instantiated below using the internal image type and the output image type.

```
typedef itk::BinaryThresholdImageFilter< InternalImageType,
                  OutputImageType   >      ThresholdingFilterType;
ThresholdingFilterType::Pointer thresholder = ThresholdingFilterType::New();
```

The upper threshold passed to the BinaryThresholdImageFilter will define the time snapshot that we are taking from the time-crossing map. In an ideal application the user should be able to select this threshold interactively using visual feedback. Here, since it is a minimal example, the value is taken from the command line arguments.

```
thresholder->SetLowerThreshold(          0.0  );
thresholder->SetUpperThreshold( timeThreshold  );

thresholder->SetOutsideValue(  0  );
thresholder->SetInsideValue(  255 );
```

We instantiate reader and writer types in the following lines.

```
typedef  itk::ImageFileReader< InternalImageType > ReaderType;
typedef  itk::ImageFileWriter<  OutputImageType  > WriterType;
```

The CurvatureAnisotropicDiffusionImageFilter type is instantiated using the internal image type.

```
typedef   itk::CurvatureAnisotropicDiffusionImageFilter<
                    InternalImageType,
                    InternalImageType > SmoothingFilterType;
```

Then, the filter is created by invoking the New() method and assigning the result to a itk::SmartPointer.

```
SmoothingFilterType::Pointer smoothing = SmoothingFilterType::New();
```

The types of the GradientMagnitudeRecursiveGaussianImageFilter and SigmoidImageFilter are instantiated using the internal image type.

```
typedef   itk::GradientMagnitudeRecursiveGaussianImageFilter<
                    InternalImageType,
                    InternalImageType >  GradientFilterType;
typedef   itk::SigmoidImageFilter<
                    InternalImageType,
                    InternalImageType >  SigmoidFilterType;
```

The corresponding filter objects are instantiated with the New() method.

```
GradientFilterType::Pointer  gradientMagnitude = GradientFilterType::New();
SigmoidFilterType::Pointer sigmoid = SigmoidFilterType::New();
```

The minimum and maximum values of the SigmoidImageFilter output are defined with the methods SetOutputMinimum() and SetOutputMaximum(). In our case, we want these two values to be 0.0 and 1.0 respectively in order to get a nice speed image to feed to the FastMarchingImageFilter. Additional details on the use of the SigmoidImageFilter are presented in Section 2.3.2.

```
sigmoid->SetOutputMinimum(  0.0  );
sigmoid->SetOutputMaximum(  1.0  );
```

We now declare the type of the FastMarchingImageFilter.

```
typedef  itk::FastMarchingImageFilter< InternalImageType,
                    InternalImageType >   FastMarchingFilterType;
```

Then, we construct one filter of this class using the New() method.

```
FastMarchingFilterType::Pointer  fastMarching
                              = FastMarchingFilterType::New();
```

The filters are now connected in a pipeline shown in Figure 4.15 using the following lines.

```
smoothing->SetInput( reader->GetOutput() );
gradientMagnitude->SetInput( smoothing->GetOutput() );
sigmoid->SetInput( gradientMagnitude->GetOutput() );
fastMarching->SetInput( sigmoid->GetOutput() );
thresholder->SetInput( fastMarching->GetOutput() );
writer->SetInput( thresholder->GetOutput() );
```

The CurvatureAnisotropicDiffusionImageFilter class requires a couple of parameters to be defined. The following are typical values for $2D$ images. However they may have to be adjusted depending on the amount of noise present in the input image. This filter has been discussed in Section 2.7.3.

```
smoothing->SetTimeStep( 0.125 );
smoothing->SetNumberOfIterations( 5 );
smoothing->SetConductanceParameter( 9.0 );
```

The GradientMagnitudeRecursiveGaussianImageFilter performs the equivalent of a convolution with a Gaussian kernel followed by a derivative operator. The sigma of this Gaussian can be used to control the range of influence of the image edges. This filter has been discussed in Section 2.4.2.

```
gradientMagnitude->SetSigma( sigma );
```

The SigmoidImageFilter class requires two parameters to define the linear transformation to be applied to the sigmoid argument. These parameters are passed using the `SetAlpha()` and `SetBeta()` methods. In the context of this example, the parameters are used to intensify the differences between regions of low and high values in the speed image. In an ideal case, the speed value should be 1.0 in the homogeneous regions of anatomical structures and the value should decay rapidly to 0.0 around the edges of structures. The heuristic for finding the values is the following: From the gradient magnitude image, let's call $K1$ the minimum value along the contour of the anatomical structure to be segmented. Then, let's call $K2$ an average value of the gradient magnitude in the middle of the structure. These two values indicate the dynamic range that we want to map to the interval $[0:1]$ in the speed image. We want the sigmoid to map $K1$ to 0.0 and $K2$ to 1.0. Given that $K1$ is expected to be higher than $K2$ and we want to map those values to 0.0 and 1.0 respectively, we want to select a negative value for alpha so that the sigmoid function will also do an inverse intensity mapping. This mapping will produce a speed image such that the level set will march rapidly on the homogeneous region and will definitely stop on the contour. The suggested value for beta is $(K1 + K2)/2$ while the suggested value for alpha is $(K2 - K1)/6$, which must be a negative number. In our simple example the values are provided by the user from the command line arguments. The user can estimate these values by observing the gradient magnitude image.

```
sigmoid->SetAlpha( alpha );
sigmoid->SetBeta( beta );
```

The FastMarchingImageFilter requires the user to provide a seed point from which the contour will expand. The user can actually pass not only one seed point but a set of them. A good set of seed points increases the chances of segmenting a complex object without missing parts. The use of multiple seeds also helps to reduce the amount of time needed by the front to visit a whole object and hence reduces the risk of leaks on the edges of regions visited earlier. For example, when segmenting an elongated object, it is undesirable to place a single seed at one extreme of the object since the front will need a long time to propagate to the other end of the object. Placing several seeds along the axis of the object will probably be the best strategy to ensure that the entire object is captured early in the expansion of the front. One of the important properties of level sets is their natural ability to fuse several fronts implicitly without any extra bookkeeping. The use of multiple seeds takes good advantage of this property.

The seeds are passed stored in a container. The type of this container is defined as `NodeContainer` among the FastMarchingImageFilter traits.

```
typedef FastMarchingFilterType::NodeContainer       NodeContainer;
typedef FastMarchingFilterType::NodeType            NodeType;
NodeContainer::Pointer seeds = NodeContainer::New();
```

Nodes are created as stack variables and initialized with a value and an `itk::Index` position.

```
NodeType node;
const double seedValue = 0.0;

node.SetValue( seedValue );
node.SetIndex( seedPosition );
```

The list of nodes is initialized and then every node is inserted using the `InsertElement()`.

```
seeds->Initialize();
seeds->InsertElement( 0, node );
```

The set of seed nodes is now passed to the FastMarchingImageFilter with the method `SetTrialPoints()`.

```
fastMarching->SetTrialPoints( seeds );
```

The FastMarchingImageFilter requires the user to specify the size of the image to be produced as output. This is done using the `SetOutputSize()` method. Note that the size is obtained here from the output image of the smoothing filter. The size of this image is valid only after the `Update()` method of this filter has been called directly or indirectly.

```
fastMarching->SetOutputSize(
        reader->GetOutput()->GetBufferedRegion().GetSize() );
```

Since the front representing the contour will propagate continuously over time, it is desirable to stop the process once a certain time has been reached. This allows us to save computation time under the assumption that the region of interest has already been computed. The value for stopping the process is defined with the method `SetStoppingValue()`. In principle, the stopping value should be a little bit higher than the threshold value.

```
fastMarching->SetStoppingValue( stoppingTime );
```

The invocation of the `Update()` method on the writer triggers the execution of the pipeline. As usual, the call is placed in a `try/catch` block should any errors occur or exceptions be thrown.

Structure	Seed Index	σ	α	β	Threshold	Output Image from left
Left Ventricle	$(81, 114)$	1.0	-0.5	3.0	100	First
Right Ventricle	$(99, 114)$	1.0	-0.5	3.0	100	Second
White matter	$(56, 92)$	1.0	-0.3	2.0	200	Third
Gray matter	$(40, 90)$	0.5	-0.3	2.0	200	Fourth

Table 4.3: Parameters used for segmenting some brain structures shown in Figure 4.17 using the filter Fast-MarchingImageFilter. All of them used a stopping value of 100.

```
try
  {
  writer->Update();
  }
catch( itk::ExceptionObject & excep )
  {
  std::cerr << "Exception caught !" << std::endl;
  std::cerr << excep << std::endl;
  }
```

Now let's run this example using the input image `BrainProtonDensitySlice.png` provided in the directory `Examples/Data`. We can easily segment the major anatomical structures by providing seeds in the appropriate locations. The following table presents the parameters used for some structures.

Figure 4.16 presents the intermediate outputs of the pipeline illustrated in Figure 4.15. They are from left to right: the output of the anisotropic diffusion filter, the gradient magnitude of the smoothed image and the sigmoid of the gradient magnitude which is finally used as the speed image for the FastMarchingImageFilter.

Notice that the gray matter is not being completely segmented. This illustrates the vulnerability of the level set methods when the anatomical structures to be segmented do not occupy extended regions of the image. This is especially true when the width of the structure is comparable to the size of the attenuation bands generated by the gradient filter. A possible workaround for this limitation is to use multiple seeds distributed along the elongated object. However, note that white matter versus gray matter segmentation is not a trivial task, and may require a more elaborate approach than the one used in this basic example.

4.3.2 Shape Detection Segmentation

The source code for this section can be found in the file
`ShapeDetectionLevelSetFilter.cxx`.

The use of the `itk::ShapeDetectionLevelSetImageFilter` is illustrated in the following example. The implementation of this filter in ITK is based on the paper by Malladi et al [39]. In this implementation, the governing differential equation has an additional curvature-based term. This term acts as a smoothing term where areas of high curvature, assumed to be due to noise, are smoothed out. Scaling parameters are used to control the tradeoff between the expansion term and the smooth-

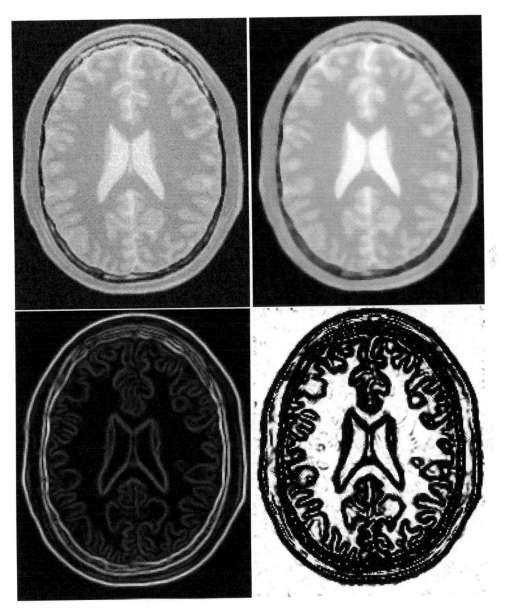

Figure 4.16: Images generated by the segmentation process based on the FastMarchingImageFilter. From left to right and top to bottom: input image to be segmented, image smoothed with an edge-preserving smoothing filter, gradient magnitude of the smoothed image, sigmoid of the gradient magnitude. This last image, the sigmoid, is used to compute the speed term for the front propagation.

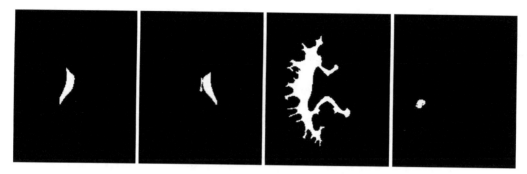

Figure 4.17: Images generated by the segmentation process based on the FastMarchingImageFilter. From left to right: segmentation of the left ventricle, segmentation of the right ventricle, segmentation of the white matter, attempt of segmentation of the gray matter.

ing term. One consequence of this additional curvature term is that the fast marching algorithm is no longer applicable, because the contour is no longer guaranteed to always be expanding. Instead, the level set function is updated iteratively.

The ShapeDetectionLevelSetImageFilter expects two inputs, the first being an initial Level Set in the form of an `itk::Image`, and the second being a feature image. For this algorithm, the feature image is an edge potential image that basically follows the same rules applicable to the speed image used for the FastMarchingImageFilter discussed in Section 4.3.1.

In this example we use an FastMarchingImageFilter to produce the initial level set as the distance function to a set of user-provided seeds. The FastMarchingImageFilter is run with a constant speed value which enables us to employ this filter as a distance map calculator.

Figure 4.18 shows the major components involved in the application of the ShapeDetection-LevelSetImageFilter to a segmentation task.   The first stage involves smoothing using the `itk::CurvatureAnisotropicDiffusionImageFilter`. The smoothed image is passed as the input for the `itk::GradientMagnitudeRecursiveGaussianImageFilter` and then to the `itk::SigmoidImageFilter` in order to produce the edge potential image. A set of user-provided seeds is passed to an FastMarchingImageFilter in order to compute the distance map. A constant value is subtracted from this map in order to obtain a level set in which the *zero set* represents the initial contour. This level set is also passed as input to the ShapeDetectionLevelSetImageFilter.

Finally, the level set at the output of the ShapeDetectionLevelSetImageFilter is passed to an Binary-ThresholdImageFilter in order to produce a binary mask representing the segmented object.

Let's start by including the headers of the main filters involved in the preprocessing.

```
#include "itkCurvatureAnisotropicDiffusionImageFilter.h"
#include "itkGradientMagnitudeRecursiveGaussianImageFilter.h"
#include "itkSigmoidImageFilter.h"
```

The edge potential map is generated using these filters as in the previous example.

We will need the Image class, the FastMarchingImageFilter class and the ShapeDetectionLevelSetImageFilter class. Hence we include their headers here.

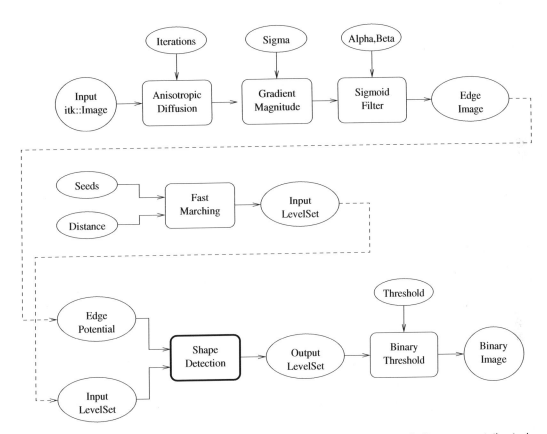

Figure 4.18: Collaboration diagram for the ShapeDetectionLevelSetImageFilter applied to a segmentation task.

```
#include "itkFastMarchingImageFilter.h"
#include "itkShapeDetectionLevelSetImageFilter.h"
```

The level set resulting from the ShapeDetectionLevelSetImageFilter will be thresholded at the zero level in order to get a binary image representing the segmented object. The BinaryThresholdImage-Filter is used for this purpose.

```
#include "itkBinaryThresholdImageFilter.h"
```

We now define the image type using a particular pixel type and a dimension. In this case the `float` type is used for the pixels due to the requirements of the smoothing filter.

```
typedef    float               InternalPixelType;
const      unsigned int     Dimension = 2;
typedef itk::Image< InternalPixelType, Dimension >  InternalImageType;
```

The output image, on the other hand, is declared to be binary.

```
typedef unsigned char                          OutputPixelType;
typedef itk::Image< OutputPixelType, Dimension > OutputImageType;
```

The type of the BinaryThresholdImageFilter filter is instantiated below using the internal image type and the output image type.

```
typedef itk::BinaryThresholdImageFilter< InternalImageType, OutputImageType >
    ThresholdingFilterType;
ThresholdingFilterType::Pointer thresholder = ThresholdingFilterType::New();
```

The upper threshold of the BinaryThresholdImageFilter is set to 0.0 in order to display the zero set of the resulting level set. The lower threshold is set to a large negative number in order to ensure that the interior of the segmented object will appear inside the binary region.

```
thresholder->SetLowerThreshold( -1000.0 );
thresholder->SetUpperThreshold(     0.0 );

thresholder->SetOutsideValue(  0  );
thresholder->SetInsideValue(  255 );
```

The CurvatureAnisotropicDiffusionImageFilter type is instantiated using the internal image type.

```
typedef    itk::CurvatureAnisotropicDiffusionImageFilter<
                    InternalImageType,
                    InternalImageType >  SmoothingFilterType;
```

The filter is instantiated by invoking the `New()` method and assigning the result to a `itk::SmartPointer`.

```
SmoothingFilterType::Pointer smoothing = SmoothingFilterType::New();
```

The types of the GradientMagnitudeRecursiveGaussianImageFilter and SigmoidImageFilter are instantiated using the internal image type.

```
typedef   itk::GradientMagnitudeRecursiveGaussianImageFilter<
                        InternalImageType,
                        InternalImageType >  GradientFilterType;

typedef   itk::SigmoidImageFilter<
                        InternalImageType,
                        InternalImageType >  SigmoidFilterType;
```

The corresponding filter objects are created with the method New().

```
GradientFilterType::Pointer  gradientMagnitude = GradientFilterType::New();
SigmoidFilterType::Pointer sigmoid = SigmoidFilterType::New();
```

The minimum and maximum values of the SigmoidImageFilter output are defined with the methods SetOutputMinimum() and SetOutputMaximum(). In our case, we want these two values to be 0.0 and 1.0 respectively in order to get a nice speed image to feed to the FastMarchingImageFilter. Additional details on the use of the SigmoidImageFilter are presented in Section 2.3.2.

```
sigmoid->SetOutputMinimum(  0.0  );
sigmoid->SetOutputMaximum(  1.0  );
```

We now declare the type of the FastMarchingImageFilter that will be used to generate the initial level set in the form of a distance map.

```
typedef  itk::FastMarchingImageFilter< InternalImageType, InternalImageType >
    FastMarchingFilterType;
```

Next we construct one filter of this class using the New() method.

```
FastMarchingFilterType::Pointer  fastMarching
                                     = FastMarchingFilterType::New();
```

In the following lines we instantiate the type of the ShapeDetectionLevelSetImageFilter and create an object of this type using the New() method.

```
typedef  itk::ShapeDetectionLevelSetImageFilter< InternalImageType,
                    InternalImageType >    ShapeDetectionFilterType;
ShapeDetectionFilterType::Pointer
    shapeDetection = ShapeDetectionFilterType::New();
```

The filters are now connected in a pipeline indicated in Figure 4.18 with the following code.

```
smoothing->SetInput( reader->GetOutput() );
gradientMagnitude->SetInput( smoothing->GetOutput() );
sigmoid->SetInput( gradientMagnitude->GetOutput() );

shapeDetection->SetInput( fastMarching->GetOutput() );
shapeDetection->SetFeatureImage( sigmoid->GetOutput() );

thresholder->SetInput( shapeDetection->GetOutput() );

writer->SetInput( thresholder->GetOutput() );
```

The CurvatureAnisotropicDiffusionImageFilter requires a couple of parameters to be defined. The following are typical values for 2D images. However they may have to be adjusted depending on the amount of noise present in the input image. This filter has been discussed in Section 2.7.3.

```
smoothing->SetTimeStep( 0.125 );
smoothing->SetNumberOfIterations( 5 );
smoothing->SetConductanceParameter( 9.0 );
```

The GradientMagnitudeRecursiveGaussianImageFilter performs the equivalent of a convolution with
a Gaussian kernel followed by a derivative operator. The sigma of this Gaussian can be used to
control the range of influence of the image edges. This filter has been discussed in Section 2.4.2.

```
gradientMagnitude->SetSigma( sigma );
```

The SigmoidImageFilter requires two parameters that define the linear transformation to be applied
to the sigmoid argument. These parameters have been discussed in Sections 2.3.2 and 4.3.1.

```
sigmoid->SetAlpha( alpha );
sigmoid->SetBeta( beta );
```

The FastMarchingImageFilter requires the user to provide a seed point from which the level set
will be generated. The user can actually pass not only one seed point but a set of them. Note the
FastMarchingImageFilter is used here only as a helper in the determination of an initial level set. We
could have used the `itk::DanielssonDistanceMapImageFilter` in the same way.

The seeds are stored in a container. The type of this container is defined as `NodeContainer` among
the FastMarchingImageFilter traits.

```
typedef FastMarchingFilterType::NodeContainer        NodeContainer;
typedef FastMarchingFilterType::NodeType             NodeType;
NodeContainer::Pointer seeds = NodeContainer::New();
```

Nodes are created as stack variables and initialized with a value and an `itk::Index` position. Note
that we assign the negative of the value of the user-provided distance to the unique node of the
seeds passed to the FastMarchingImageFilter. In this way, the value will increment as the front
is propagated, until it reaches the zero value corresponding to the contour. After this, the front will
continue propagating until it fills up the entire image. The initial distance is taken from the command
line arguments. The rule of thumb for the user is to select this value as the distance from the seed
points at which the initial contour should be.

```
NodeType node;
const double seedValue = - initialDistance;

node.SetValue( seedValue );
node.SetIndex( seedPosition );
```

The list of nodes is initialized and then every node is inserted using `InsertElement()`.

```
seeds->Initialize();
seeds->InsertElement( 0, node );
```

The set of seed nodes is now passed to the FastMarchingImageFilter with the method
`SetTrialPoints()`.

```
fastMarching->SetTrialPoints( seeds );
```

Since the FastMarchingImageFilter is used here only as a distance map generator, it does not require
a speed image as input. Instead, the constant value 1.0 is passed using the `SetSpeedConstant()`
method.

```
fastMarching->SetSpeedConstant( 1.0 );
```

The FastMarchingImageFilter requires the user to specify the size of the image to be produced as output. This is done using the `SetOutputSize()`. Note that the size is obtained here from the output image of the smoothing filter. The size of this image is valid only after the `Update()` methods of this filter have been called directly or indirectly.

```
fastMarching->SetOutputSize(
          reader->GetOutput()->GetBufferedRegion().GetSize() );
```

ShapeDetectionLevelSetImageFilter provides two parameters to control the competition between the propagation or expansion term and the curvature smoothing term. The methods `SetPropagationScaling()` and `SetCurvatureScaling()` defines the relative weighting between the two terms. In this example, we will set the propagation scaling to one and let the curvature scaling be an input argument. The larger the the curvature scaling parameter the smoother the resulting segmentation. However, the curvature scaling parameter should not be set too large, as it will draw the contour away from the shape boundaries.

```
shapeDetection->SetPropagationScaling( propagationScaling );
shapeDetection->SetCurvatureScaling( curvatureScaling );
```

Once activated, the level set evolution will stop if the convergence criteria or the maximum number of iterations is reached. The convergence criteria are defined in terms of the root mean squared (RMS) change in the level set function. The evolution is said to have converged if the RMS change is below a user-specified threshold. In a real application, it is desirable to couple the evolution of the zero set to a visualization module, allowing the user to follow the evolution of the zero set. With this feedback, the user may decide when to stop the algorithm before the zero set leaks through the regions of low gradient in the contour of the anatomical structure to be segmented.

```
shapeDetection->SetMaximumRMSError( 0.02 );
shapeDetection->SetNumberOfIterations( 800 );
```

The invocation of the `Update()` method on the writer triggers the execution of the pipeline. As usual, the call is placed in a `try/catch` block should any errors occur or exceptions be thrown.

```
try
  {
  writer->Update();
  }
catch( itk::ExceptionObject & excep )
  {
  std::cerr << "Exception caught !" << std::endl;
  std::cerr << excep << std::endl;
  }
```

Let's now run this example using as input the image `BrainProtonDensitySlice.png` provided in the directory `Examples/Data`. We can easily segment the major anatomical structures by providing seeds in the appropriate locations. Table 4.4 presents the parameters used for some structures. For all of the examples illustrated in this table, the propagation scaling was set to 1.0, and the curvature scaling set to 0.05.

Figure 4.19 presents the intermediate outputs of the pipeline illustrated in Figure 4.18. They are from left to right: the output of the anisotropic diffusion filter, the gradient magnitude of the smoothed

Structure	Seed Index	Distance	σ	α	β	Output Image
Left Ventricle	(81, 114)	5.0	1.0	-0.5	3.0	First in Figure 4.20
Right Ventricle	(99, 114)	5.0	1.0	-0.5	3.0	Second in Figure 4.20
White matter	(56, 92)	5.0	1.0	-0.3	2.0	Third in Figure 4.20
Gray matter	(40, 90)	5.0	0.5	-0.3	2.0	Fourth in Figure 4.20

Table 4.4: Parameters used for segmenting some brain structures shown in Figure 4.19 using the filter ShapeDetectionLevelSetFilter. All of them used a propagation scaling of 1.0 and curvature scaling of 0.05.

image and the sigmoid of the gradient magnitude which is finally used as the edge potential for the ShapeDetectionLevelSetImageFilter.

Notice that in Figure 4.20 the segmented shapes are rounder than in Figure 4.17 due to the effects of the curvature term in the driving equation. As with the previous example, segmentation of the gray matter is still problematic.

A larger number of iterations is required for segmenting large structures since it takes longer for the front to propagate and cover the structure. This drawback can be easily mitigated by setting many seed points in the initialization of the FastMarchingImageFilter. This will generate an initial level set much closer in shape to the object to be segmented and hence require fewer iterations to fill and reach the edges of the anatomical structure.

4.3.3 Geodesic Active Contours Segmentation

The source code for this section can be found in the file
`GeodesicActiveContourImageFilter.cxx`.

The use of the `itk::GeodesicActiveContourLevelSetImageFilter` is illustrated in the following example. The implementation of this filter in ITK is based on the paper by Caselles [11]. This implementation extends the functionality of the `itk::ShapeDetectionLevelSetImageFilter` by the addition of a third advection term which attracts the level set to the object boundaries.

GeodesicActiveContourLevelSetImageFilter expects two inputs. The first is an initial level set in the form of an `itk::Image`. The second input is a feature image. For this algorithm, the feature image is an edge potential image that basically follows the same rules used for the ShapeDetectionLevelSetImageFilter discussed in Section 4.3.2. The configuration of this example is quite similar to the example on the use of the ShapeDetectionLevelSetImageFilter. We omit most of the redundant description. A look at the code will reveal the great degree of similarity between both examples.

Figure 4.21 shows the major components involved in the application of the GeodesicActiveContourLevelSetImageFilter to a segmentation task. This pipeline is quite similar to the one used by the ShapeDetectionLevelSetImageFilter in section 4.3.2.

The pipeline involves a first stage of smoothing using the
`itk::CurvatureAnisotropicDiffusionImageFilter`.   The smoothed image is passed as the input to the `itk::GradientMagnitudeRecursiveGaussianImageFilter` and then to the

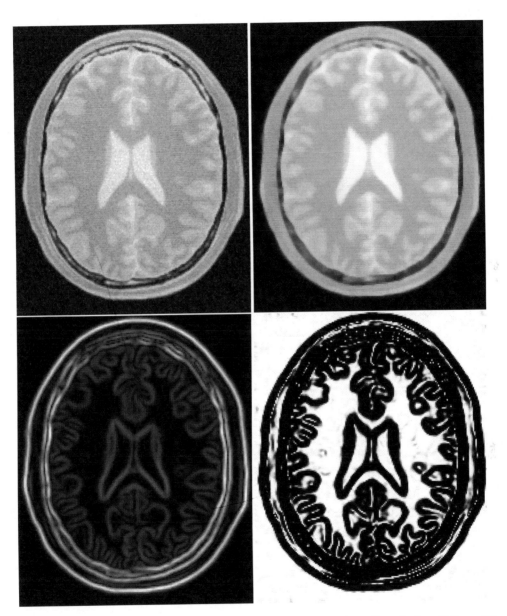

Figure 4.19: Images generated by the segmentation process based on the ShapeDetectionLevelSetImageFilter. From left to right and top to bottom: input image to be segmented, image smoothed with an edge-preserving smoothing filter, gradient magnitude of the smoothed image, sigmoid of the gradient magnitude. This last image, the sigmoid, is used to compute the speed term for the front propagation.

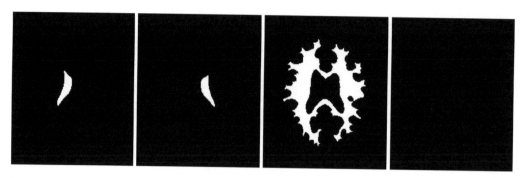

Figure 4.20: Images generated by the segmentation process based on the ShapeDetectionLevelSetImageFilter. From left to right: segmentation of the left ventricle, segmentation of the right ventricle, segmentation of the white matter, attempt of segmentation of the gray matter.

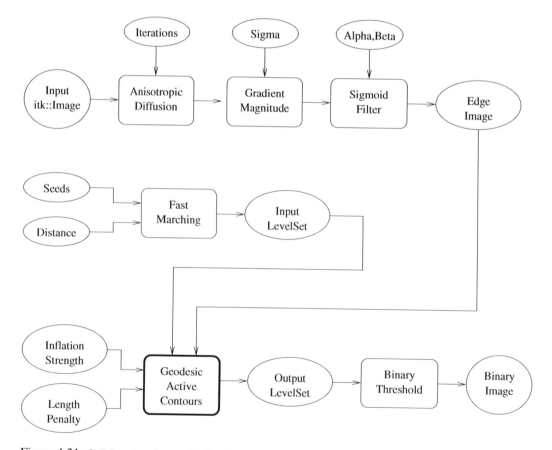

Figure 4.21: Collaboration diagram for the GeodesicActiveContourLevelSetImageFilter applied to a segmentation task.

`itk::SigmoidImageFilter` in order to produce the edge potential image. A set of user-provided seeds is passed to a `itk::FastMarchingImageFilter` in order to compute the distance map. A constant value is subtracted from this map in order to obtain a level set in which the *zero set* represents the initial contour. This level set is also passed as input to the GeodesicActiveContourLevelSetImageFilter.

Finally, the level set generated by the GeodesicActiveContourLevelSetImageFilter is passed to a `itk::BinaryThresholdImageFilter` in order to produce a binary mask representing the segmented object.

Let's start by including the headers of the main filters involved in the preprocessing.

```
#include "itkGeodesicActiveContourLevelSetImageFilter.h"
```

We now define the image type using a particular pixel type and dimension. In this case the `float` type is used for the pixels due to the requirements of the smoothing filter.

```
typedef    float              InternalPixelType;
const      unsigned int   Dimension = 2;
typedef itk::Image< InternalPixelType, Dimension >  InternalImageType;
```

In the following lines we instantiate the type of the GeodesicActiveContourLevelSetImageFilter and create an object of this type using the `New()` method.

```
typedef  itk::GeodesicActiveContourLevelSetImageFilter< InternalImageType,
            InternalImageType >    GeodesicActiveContourFilterType;
GeodesicActiveContourFilterType::Pointer geodesicActiveContour =
                          GeodesicActiveContourFilterType::New();
```

For the GeodesicActiveContourLevelSetImageFilter, scaling parameters are used to trade off between the propagation (inflation), the curvature (smoothing) and the advection terms. These parameters are set using methods `SetPropagationScaling()`, `SetCurvatureScaling()` and `SetAdvectionScaling()`. In this example, we will set the curvature and advection scales to one and let the propagation scale be a command-line argument.

```
geodesicActiveContour->SetPropagationScaling( propagationScaling );
geodesicActiveContour->SetCurvatureScaling( 1.0 );
geodesicActiveContour->SetAdvectionScaling( 1.0 );
```

The filters are now connected in a pipeline indicated in Figure 4.21 using the following lines:

```
smoothing->SetInput( reader->GetOutput() );
gradientMagnitude->SetInput( smoothing->GetOutput() );
sigmoid->SetInput( gradientMagnitude->GetOutput() );

geodesicActiveContour->SetInput(  fastMarching->GetOutput() );
geodesicActiveContour->SetFeatureImage( sigmoid->GetOutput() );

thresholder->SetInput( geodesicActiveContour->GetOutput() );
writer->SetInput( thresholder->GetOutput() );
```

The invocation of the `Update()` method on the writer triggers the execution of the pipeline. As usual, the call is placed in a `try/catch` block should any errors occur or exceptions be thrown.

Structure	Seed Index	Distance	σ	α	β	Propag.	Output Image
Left Ventricle	$(81, 114)$	5.0	1.0	-0.5	3.0	2.0	First
Right Ventricle	$(99, 114)$	5.0	1.0	-0.5	3.0	2.0	Second
White matter	$(56, 92)$	5.0	1.0	-0.3	2.0	10.0	Third
Gray matter	$(40, 90)$	5.0	0.5	-0.3	2.0	10.0	Fourth

Table 4.5: Parameters used for segmenting some brain structures shown in Figure 4.23 using the filter GeodesicActiveContourLevelSetImageFilter.

```
try
  {
  writer->Update();
  }
catch( itk::ExceptionObject & excep )
  {
  std::cerr << "Exception caught !" << std::endl;
  std::cerr << excep << std::endl;
  }
```

Let's now run this example using as input the image BrainProtonDensitySlice.png provided in the directory Examples/Data. We can easily segment the major anatomical structures by providing seeds in the appropriate locations. Table 4.5 presents the parameters used for some structures.

Figure 4.22 presents the intermediate outputs of the pipeline illustrated in Figure 4.21. They are from left to right: the output of the anisotropic diffusion filter, the gradient magnitude of the smoothed image and the sigmoid of the gradient magnitude which is finally used as the edge potential for the GeodesicActiveContourLevelSetImageFilter.

Segmentations of the main brain structures are presented in Figure 4.23. The results are quite similar to those obtained with the ShapeDetectionLevelSetImageFilter in Section 4.3.2.

Note that a relatively larger propagation scaling value was required to segment the white matter. This is due to two factors: the lower contrast at the border of the white matter and the complex shape of the structure. Unfortunately the optimal value of these scaling parameters can only be determined by experimentation. In a real application we could imagine an interactive mechanism by which a user supervises the contour evolution and adjusts these parameters accordingly.

4.3.4   Threshold Level Set Segmentation

The source code for this section can be found in the file
ThresholdSegmentationLevelSetImageFilter.cxx.

The itk::ThresholdSegmentationLevelSetImageFilter is an extension of the threshold connected-component segmentation to the level set framework. The goal is to define a range of intensity values that classify the tissue type of interest and then base the propagation term on the level set equation for that intensity range. Using the level set approach, the smoothness of the evolving surface can be constrained to prevent some of the "leaking" that is common in connected-component

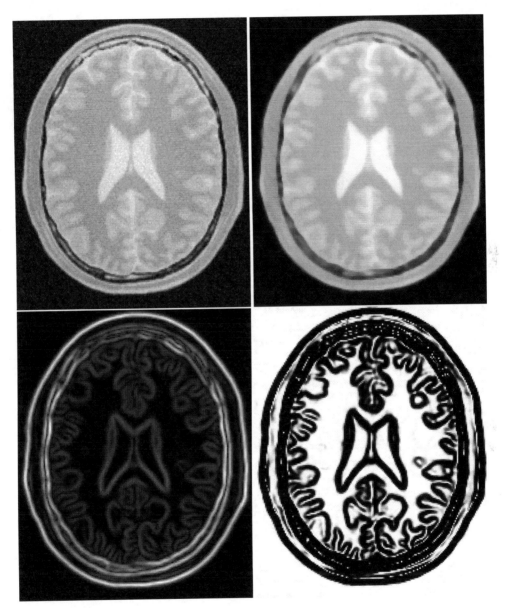

Figure 4.22: Images generated by the segmentation process based on the GeodesicActiveContourLevelSe-tImageFilter. From left to right and top to bottom: input image to be segmented, image smoothed with an edge-preserving smoothing filter, gradient magnitude of the smoothed image, sigmoid of the gradient magnitude. This last image, the sigmoid, is used to compute the speed term for the front propagation.

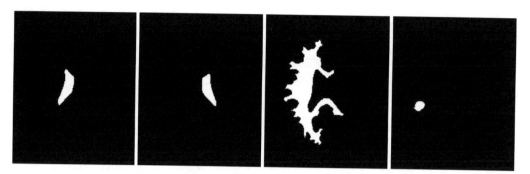

Figure 4.23: Images generated by the segmentation process based on the GeodesicActiveContourImageFilter. From left to right: segmentation of the left ventricle, segmentation of the right ventricle, segmentation of the white matter, attempt of segmentation of the gray matter.

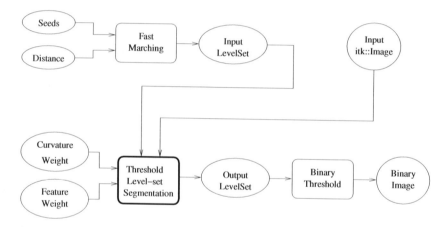

Figure 4.24: Collaboration diagram for the ThresholdSegmentationLevelSetImageFilter applied to a segmentation task.

schemes.

The propagation term P from Equation 4.3 is calculated from the FeatureImage input g with UpperThreshold U and LowerThreshold L according to the following formula.

$$P(\mathbf{x}) = \begin{cases} g(\mathbf{x}) - L & \text{if } g(\mathbf{x}) < (U - L)/2 + L \\ U - g(\mathbf{x}) & \text{otherwise} \end{cases} \qquad (4.4)$$

Figure 4.25 illustrates the propagation term function. Intensity values in g between L and H yield positive values in P, while outside intensities yield negative values in P.

The threshold segmentation filter expects two inputs. The first is an initial level set in the form of an itk::Image. The second input is the feature image g. For many applications, this filter requires little or no preprocessing of its input. Smoothing the input image is not usually required to produce

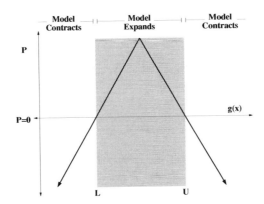

Figure 4.25: Propagation term for threshold-based level set segmentation. From Equation 4.4.

reasonable solutions, though it may still be warranted in some cases.

Figure 4.24 shows how the image processing pipeline is constructed. The initial surface is generated using the fast marching filter. The output of the segmentation filter is passed to a itk::BinaryThresholdImageFilter to create a binary representation of the segmented object. Let's start by including the appropriate header file.

```
#include "itkThresholdSegmentationLevelSetImageFilter.h"
```

We define the image type using a particular pixel type and dimension. In this case we will use 2D float images.

```
typedef   float          InternalPixelType;
const     unsigned int   Dimension = 2;
typedef itk::Image< InternalPixelType, Dimension >  InternalImageType;
```

The following lines instantiate a ThresholdSegmentationLevelSetImageFilter using the New() method.

```
typedef   itk::ThresholdSegmentationLevelSetImageFilter< InternalImageType,
   InternalImageType > ThresholdSegmentationLevelSetImageFilterType;
ThresholdSegmentationLevelSetImageFilterType::Pointer thresholdSegmentation =
   ThresholdSegmentationLevelSetImageFilterType::New();
```

For the ThresholdSegmentationLevelSetImageFilter, scaling parameters are used to balance the influence of the propagation (inflation) and the curvature (surface smoothing) terms from Equation 4.3. The advection term is not used in this filter. Set the terms with methods SetPropagationScaling() and SetCurvatureScaling(). Both terms are set to 1.0 in this example.

```
thresholdSegmentation->SetPropagationScaling( 1.0 );
if ( argc > 8 )
  {
  thresholdSegmentation->SetCurvatureScaling( atof(argv[8]) );
  }
else
  {
  thresholdSegmentation->SetCurvatureScaling( 1.0 );
  }
```

Structure	Seed Index	Lower	Upper	Output Image
White matter	$(60, 116)$	150	180	Second from left
Ventricle	$(81, 112)$	210	250	Third from left
Gray matter	$(107, 69)$	180	210	Fourth from left

Table 4.6: Segmentation results using the ThresholdSegmentationLevelSetImageFilter for various seed points. The resulting images are shown in Figure 4.26 .

The convergence criteria `MaximumRMSError` and `MaximumIterations` are set as in previous examples. We now set the upper and lower threshold values U and L, and the isosurface value to use in the initial model.

```
thresholdSegmentation->SetUpperThreshold( ::atof(argv[7]) );
thresholdSegmentation->SetLowerThreshold( ::atof(argv[6]) );
thresholdSegmentation->SetIsoSurfaceValue(0.0);
```

The filters are now connected in a pipeline indicated in Figure 4.24. Remember that before calling `Update()` on the file writer object, the fast marching filter must be initialized with the seed points and the output from the reader object. See previous examples and the source code for this section for details.

```
thresholdSegmentation->SetInput( fastMarching->GetOutput() );
thresholdSegmentation->SetFeatureImage( reader->GetOutput() );
thresholder->SetInput( thresholdSegmentation->GetOutput() );
writer->SetInput( thresholder->GetOutput() );
```

Invoking the `Update()` method on the writer triggers the execution of the pipeline. As usual, the call is placed in a `try/catch` block should any errors occur or exceptions be thrown.

```
try
  {
  reader->Update();
  const InternalImageType * inputImage = reader->GetOutput();
  fastMarching->SetOutputRegion( inputImage->GetBufferedRegion() );
  fastMarching->SetOutputSpacing( inputImage->GetSpacing() );
  fastMarching->SetOutputOrigin( inputImage->GetOrigin() );
  fastMarching->SetOutputDirection( inputImage->GetDirection() );
  writer->Update();
  }
catch( itk::ExceptionObject & excep )
  {
  std::cerr << "Exception caught !" << std::endl;
  std::cerr << excep << std::endl;
  }
```

Let's run this application with the same data and parameters as the example given for `itk::ConnectedThresholdImageFilter` in Section 4.1.1. We will use a value of 5 as the initial distance of the surface from the seed points. The algorithm is relatively insensitive to this initialization. Compare the results in Figure 4.26 with those in Figure 4.1. Notice how the smoothness constraint on the surface prevents leakage of the segmentation into both ventricles, but also localizes the segmentation to a smaller portion of the gray matter.

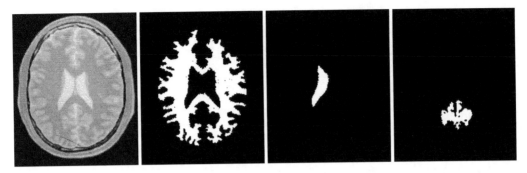

Figure 4.26: Images generated by the segmentation process based on the ThresholdSegmentationLevelSetImageFilter. From left to right: segmentation of the left ventricle, segmentation of the right ventricle, segmentation of the white matter, attempt of segmentation of the gray matter. The parameters used in this segmentations are presented in Table 4.6.

4.3.5 Canny-Edge Level Set Segmentation

The source code for this section can be found in the file
`CannySegmentationLevelSetImageFilter.cxx`.

The `itk::CannySegmentationLevelSetImageFilter` defines a speed term that minimizes distance to the Canny edges in an image. The initial level set model moves through a gradient advection field until it locks onto those edges. This filter is more suitable for refining existing segmentations than as a region-growing algorithm.

The two terms defined for the CannySegmentationLevelSetImageFilter are the advection term and the propagation term from Equation 4.3. The advection term is constructed by minimizing the squared distance transform from the Canny edges.

$$\min \int D^2 \Rightarrow D\nabla D \qquad (4.5)$$

where the distance transform D is calculated using a `itk::DanielssonDistanceMapImageFilter` applied to the output of the `itk::CannyEdgeDetectionImageFilter`.

For cases in which some surface expansion is to be allowed, a non-zero value may be set for the propagation term. The propagation term is simply D. As with all ITK level set segmentation filters, the curvature term controls the smoothness of the surface.

CannySegmentationLevelSetImageFilter expects two inputs. The first is an initial level set in the form of an `itk::Image`. The second input is the feature image g from which propagation and advection terms are calculated. It is generally a good idea to do some preprocessing of the feature image to remove noise.

Figure 4.27 shows how the image processing pipeline is constructed. We read two images: the image to segment and the image that contains the initial implicit surface. The goal is to refine the initial model from the second input and not to grow a new segmentation from seed points. The `feature`

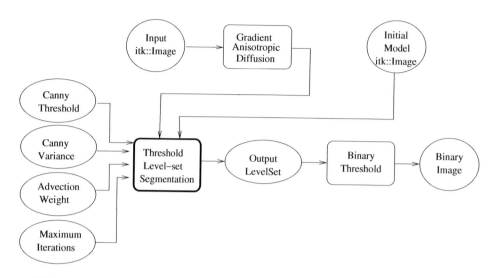

Figure 4.27: Collaboration diagram for the CannySegmentationLevelSetImageFilter applied to a segmentation task.

image is preprocessed with a few iterations of an anisotropic diffusion filter.

Let's start by including the appropriate header file.

```
#include "itkCannySegmentationLevelSetImageFilter.h"
#include "itkGradientAnisotropicDiffusionImageFilter.h"
```

We define the image type using a particular pixel type and dimension. In this case we will use 2D float images.

```
typedef   float            InternalPixelType;
const      unsigned int    Dimension = 2;
typedef itk::Image< InternalPixelType, Dimension >  InternalImageType;
```

The input image will be processed with a few iterations of feature-preserving diffusion. We create a filter and set the appropriate parameters.

```
typedef itk::GradientAnisotropicDiffusionImageFilter< InternalImageType,
  InternalImageType> DiffusionFilterType;
DiffusionFilterType::Pointer diffusion = DiffusionFilterType::New();
diffusion->SetNumberOfIterations(5);
diffusion->SetTimeStep(0.125);
diffusion->SetConductanceParameter(1.0);
```

The following lines define and instantiate a CannySegmentationLevelSetImageFilter.

```
typedef  itk::CannySegmentationLevelSetImageFilter< InternalImageType,
            InternalImageType > CannySegmentationLevelSetImageFilterType;
CannySegmentationLevelSetImageFilterType::Pointer cannySegmentation =
            CannySegmentationLevelSetImageFilterType::New();
```

As with the other ITK level set segmentation filters, the terms of the CannySegmentationLevelSetImageFilter level set equation can be weighted by scalars. For this application we will modify the relative weight of the advection term. The propagation and curvature term weights are set to their defaults of 0 and 1, respectively.

```
cannySegmentation->SetAdvectionScaling( ::atof(argv[6]) );
cannySegmentation->SetCurvatureScaling( 1.0 );
cannySegmentation->SetPropagationScaling( 0.0 );
```

The maximum number of iterations is specified from the command line. It may not be desirable in some applications to run the filter to convergence. Only a few iterations may be required.

```
cannySegmentation->SetMaximumRMSError( 0.01 );
cannySegmentation->SetNumberOfIterations( ::atoi(argv[8]) );
```

There are two important parameters in the CannySegmentationLevelSetImageFilter to control the behavior of the Canny edge detection. The *variance* parameter controls the amount of Gaussian smoothing on the input image. The *threshold* parameter indicates the lowest allowed value in the output image. Thresholding is used to suppress Canny edges whose gradient magnitudes fall below a certain value.

```
cannySegmentation->SetThreshold( ::atof(argv[4]) );
cannySegmentation->SetVariance(  ::atof(argv[5]) );
```

Finally, it is very important to specify the isovalue of the surface in the initial model input image. In a binary image, for example, the isosurface is found midway between the foreground and background values.

```
cannySegmentation->SetIsoSurfaceValue( ::atof(argv[7]) );
```

The filters are now connected in a pipeline indicated in Figure 4.27.

```
diffusion->SetInput( reader1->GetOutput() );
cannySegmentation->SetInput( reader2->GetOutput() );
cannySegmentation->SetFeatureImage( diffusion->GetOutput() );
thresholder->SetInput( cannySegmentation->GetOutput() );
writer->SetInput( thresholder->GetOutput() );
```

Invoking the Update() method on the writer triggers the execution of the pipeline. As usual, the call is placed in a try/catch block to handle any exceptions that may be thrown.

```
try
  {
  writer->Update();
  }
catch( itk::ExceptionObject & excep )
  {
  std::cerr << "Exception caught !" << std::endl;
  std::cerr << excep << std::endl;
  }
```

We can use this filter to make some subtle refinements to the ventricle segmentation from the previous example that used the itk::ThresholdSegmentationLevelSetImageFilter. The application was run using Examples/Data/BrainProtonDensitySlice.png and Examples/Data/VentricleModel.png as inputs, a threshold of 7.0, variance of 0.1, advection weight of 10.0, and an initial isosurface value of 127.5. One case was run for 15

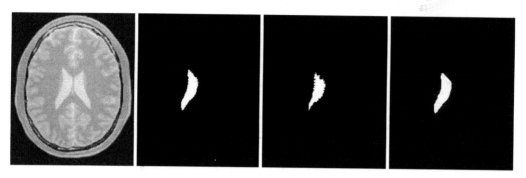

Figure 4.28: Results of applying the CannySegmentationLevelSetImageFilter to a prior ventricle segmentation. Shown from left to right are the original image, the prior segmentation of the ventricle from Figure 4.26, 15 iterations of the CannySegmentationLevelSetImageFilter, and the CannySegmentationLevelSetImageFilter run to convergence.

iterations and the second was run to convergence. Compare the results in the two rightmost images of Figure 4.28 with the ventricle segmentation from Figure 4.26 shown in the middle. Jagged edges are straightened and the small spur at the upper right-hand side of the mask has been removed.

The free parameters of this filter can be adjusted to achieve a wide range of shape variations from the original model. Finding the right parameters for your particular application is usually a process of trial and error. As with most ITK level set segmentation filters, examining the propagation (speed) and advection images can help the process of tuning parameters. These images are available using Set/Get methods from the filter after it has been updated.

In some cases it is interesting to take a direct look at the speed image used internally by this filter. This may help for setting the correct parameters for driving the segmentation. In order to obtain such speed image, the method GenerateSpeedImage() should be invoked first. Then we can recover the speed image with the GetSpeedImage() method as illustrated in the following lines.

```
cannySegmentation->GenerateSpeedImage();

typedef CannySegmentationLevelSetImageFilterType::SpeedImageType
                                                   SpeedImageType;
typedef itk::ImageFileWriter<SpeedImageType>        SpeedWriterType;
SpeedWriterType::Pointer speedWriter = SpeedWriterType::New();

speedWriter->SetInput( cannySegmentation->GetSpeedImage() );
```

4.3.6 Laplacian Level Set Segmentation

The source code for this section can be found in the file
LaplacianSegmentationLevelSetImageFilter.cxx.

The itk::LaplacianSegmentationLevelSetImageFilter defines a speed term based on second derivative features in the image. The speed term is calculated as the Laplacian of the image values. The goal is to attract the evolving level set surface to local zero-crossings in the Laplacian image.

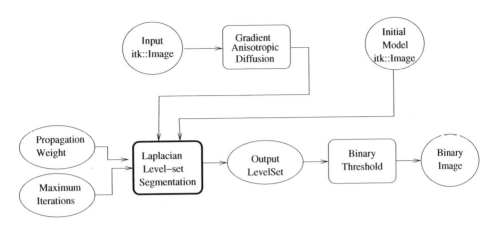

Figure 4.29: An image processing pipeline using LaplacianSegmentationLevelSetImageFilter for segmentation.

Like `itk::CannySegmentationLevelSetImageFilter`, this filter is more suitable for refining existing segmentations than as a stand-alone, region growing algorithm. It is possible to perform region growing segmentation, but be aware that the growing surface may tend to become "stuck" at local edges.

The propagation (speed) term for the LaplacianSegmentationLevelSetImageFilter is constructed by applying the `itk::LaplacianImageFilter` to the input feature image. One nice property of using the Laplacian is that there are no free parameters in the calculation.

LaplacianSegmentationLevelSetImageFilter expects two inputs. The first is an initial level set in the form of an `itk::Image`. The second input is the feature image g from which the propagation term is calculated (see Equation 4.3). Because the filter performs a second derivative calculation, it is generally a good idea to do some preprocessing of the feature image to remove noise.

Figure 4.29 shows how the image processing pipeline is constructed. We read two images: the image to segment and the image that contains the initial implicit surface. The goal is to refine the initial model from the second input to better match the structure represented by the initial implicit surface (a prior segmentation). The `feature` image is preprocessed using an anisotropic diffusion filter.

Let's start by including the appropriate header files.

```
#include "itkLaplacianSegmentationLevelSetImageFilter.h"
#include "itkGradientAnisotropicDiffusionImageFilter.h"
```

We define the image type using a particular pixel type and dimension. In this case we will use 2D `float` images.

```
typedef   float            InternalPixelType;
const     unsigned int     Dimension = 2;
typedef itk::Image< InternalPixelType, Dimension >  InternalImageType;
```

The input image will be processed with a few iterations of feature-preserving diffusion. We create a filter and set the parameters. The number of iterations and the conductance parameter are taken from the command line.

```
typedef itk::GradientAnisotropicDiffusionImageFilter< InternalImageType,
   InternalImageType> DiffusionFilterType;
DiffusionFilterType::Pointer diffusion = DiffusionFilterType::New();
diffusion->SetNumberOfIterations( atoi(argv[4]) );
diffusion->SetTimeStep(0.125);
diffusion->SetConductanceParameter( atof(argv[5]) );
```

The following lines define and instantiate a LaplacianSegmentationLevelSetImageFilter.

```
typedef itk::LaplacianSegmentationLevelSetImageFilter< InternalImageType,
        InternalImageType > LaplacianSegmentationLevelSetImageFilterType;
LaplacianSegmentationLevelSetImageFilterType::Pointer laplacianSegmentation
        = LaplacianSegmentationLevelSetImageFilterType::New();
```

As with the other ITK level set segmentation filters, the terms of the LaplacianSegmentationLevelSe-tImageFilter level set equation can be weighted by scalars. For this application we will modify the relative weight of the propagation term. The curvature term weight is set to its default of 1. The advection term is not used in this filter.

```
laplacianSegmentation->SetCurvatureScaling( 1.0 );
laplacianSegmentation->SetPropagationScaling( ::atof(argv[6]) );
```

The maximum number of iterations is set from the command line. It may not be desirable in some applications to run the filter to convergence. Only a few iterations may be required.

```
laplacianSegmentation->SetMaximumRMSError( 0.002 );
laplacianSegmentation->SetNumberOfIterations( ::atoi(argv[8]) );
```

Finally, it is very important to specify the isovalue of the surface in the initial model input image. In a binary image, for example, the isosurface is found midway between the foreground and background values.

```
laplacianSegmentation->SetIsoSurfaceValue( ::atof(argv[7]) );
```

The filters are now connected in a pipeline indicated in Figure 4.29.

```
diffusion->SetInput( reader1->GetOutput() );
laplacianSegmentation->SetInput( reader2->GetOutput() );
laplacianSegmentation->SetFeatureImage( diffusion->GetOutput() );
thresholder->SetInput( laplacianSegmentation->GetOutput() );
writer->SetInput( thresholder->GetOutput() );
```

Invoking the Update() method on the writer triggers the execution of the pipeline. As usual, the call is placed in a try/catch block to handle any exceptions that may be thrown.

```
try
  {
  writer->Update();
  }
catch( itk::ExceptionObject & excep )
  {
  std::cerr << "Exception caught !" << std::endl;
  std::cerr << excep << std::endl;
  }
```

We can use this filter to make some subtle refinements to the ventricle segmentation from the example using the filter   itk::ThresholdSegmentationLevelSetImageFilter.

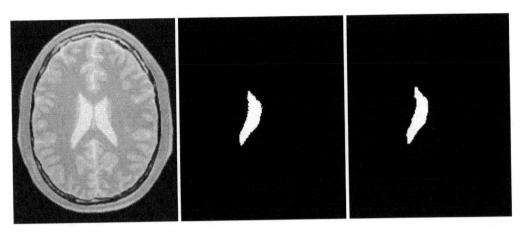

Figure 4.30: Results of applying LaplacianSegmentationLevelSetImageFilter to a prior ventricle segmentation. Shown from left to right are the original image, the prior segmentation of the ventricle from Figure 4.26, and the refinement of the prior using LaplacianSegmentationLevelSetImageFilter.

This application was run using `Examples/Data/BrainProtonDensitySlice.png` and `Examples/Data/VentricleModel.png` as inputs. We used 10 iterations of the diffusion filter with a conductance of 2.0. The propagation scaling was set to 1.0 and the filter was run until convergence. Compare the results in the rightmost images of Figure 4.30 with the ventricle segmentation from Figure 4.26 shown in the middle. Jagged edges are straightened and the small spur at the upper right-hand side of the mask has been removed.

4.3.7 Geodesic Active Contours Segmentation With Shape Guidance

The source code for this section can be found in the file
`GeodesicActiveContourShapePriorLevelSetImageFilter.cxx`.

In medical imaging applications, the general shape, location and orientation of an anatomical structure of interest is typically known *a priori*. This information can be used to aid the segmentation process especially when image contrast is low or when the object boundary is not distinct.

In [34], Leventon *et al.* extended the geodesic active contours method with an additional shape-influenced term in the driving PDE. The `itk::GeodesicActiveContourShapePriorLevelSetFilter` is a generalization of Leventon's approach and its use is illustrated in the following example.

To support shape-guidance, the generic level set equation (Eqn(4.3)) is extended to incorporate a shape guidance term:

$$\xi\left(\psi^*(\mathbf{x}) - \psi(\mathbf{x})\right) \tag{4.6}$$

where ψ^* is the signed distance function of the "best-fit" shape with respect to a shape model. The new term has the effect of driving the contour towards the best-fit shape. The scalar ξ weights the influence of the shape term in the overall evolution. In general, the best-fit shape is not known ahead of time and has to be iteratively estimated in conjunction with the contour evolution.

As with the `itk::GeodesicActiveContourLevelSetImageFilter`, the GeodesicActiveContour-ShapePriorLevelSetImageFilter expects two input images: the first is an initial level set and the second a feature image that represents the image edge potential. The configuration of this example is quite similar to the example in Section 4.3.3 and hence the description will focus on the new objects involved in the segmentation process as shown in Figure 4.31.

The process pipeline begins with centering the input image using the the `itk::ChangeInformationImageFilter` to simplify the estimation of the pose of the shape, to be explained later. The centered image is then smoothed using non-linear diffusion to remove noise and the gradient magnitude is computed from the smoothed image. For simplicity, this example uses the `itk::BoundedReciprocalImageFilter` to produce the edge potential image.

The `itk::FastMarchingImageFilter` creates an initial level set using three user specified seed positions and a initial contour radius. Three seeds are used in this example to facilitate the segmentation of long narrow objects in a smaller number of iterations. The output of the FastMarchingImageFilter is passed as the input to the GeodesicActiveContourShapePriorLevelSe-tImageFilter. At then end of the segmentation process, the output level set is passed to the `itk::BinaryThresholdImageFilter` to produce a binary mask representing the segmented object.

The remaining objects in Figure 4.31 are used for shape modeling and estimation. The `itk::PCAShapeSignedDistanceFunction` represents a statistical shape model defined by a mean signed distance and the first K principal components modes; while the `itk::Euler2DTransform` is used to represent the pose of the shape. In this implementation, the best-fit shape estimation problem is reformulated as a minimization problem where the `itk::ShapePriorMAPCostFunction` is the cost function to be optimized using the `itk::OnePlusOneEvolutionaryOptimizer`.

It should be noted that, although particular shape model, transform cost function, and optimizer are used in this example, the implementation is generic, allowing different instances of these components to be plugged in. This flexibility allows a user to tailor the behavior of the segmentation process to suit the circumstances of the targeted application.

Let's start the example by including the headers of the new filters involved in the segmentation.

```
#include "itkGeodesicActiveContourShapePriorLevelSetImageFilter.h"
#include "itkChangeInformationImageFilter.h"
#include "itkBoundedReciprocalImageFilter.h"
```

Next, we include the headers of the objects involved in shape modeling and estimation.

```
#include "itkPCAShapeSignedDistanceFunction.h"
#include "itkEuler2DTransform.h"
#include "itkOnePlusOneEvolutionaryOptimizer.h"
#include "itkNormalVariateGenerator.h"
#include "vnl/vnl_sample.h"
#include "itkNumericSeriesFileNames.h"
```

Given the numerous parameters involved in tuning this segmentation method it is not uncommon

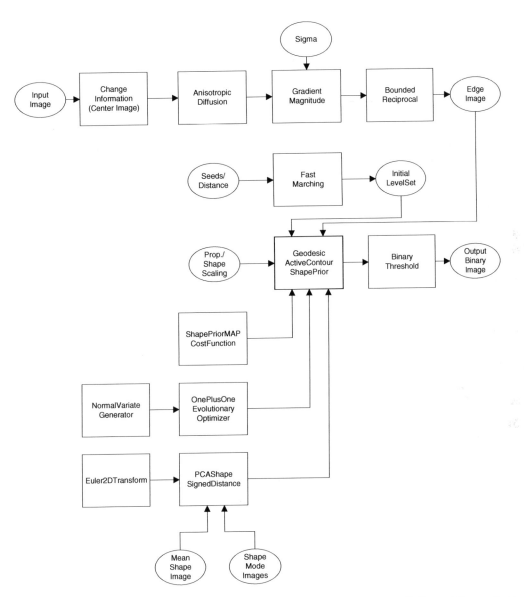

Figure 4.31: Collaboration diagram for the GeodesicActiveContourShapePriorLevelSetImageFilter applied to a segmentation task.

for a segmentation process to run for several minutes and still produce an unsatisfactory result. For debugging purposes it is quite helpful to track the evolution of the segmentation as it progresses. The following defines a custom `itk::Command` class for monitoring the RMS change and shape parameters at each iteration.

```
#include "itkCommand.h"

template<class TFilter>
class CommandIterationUpdate : public itk::Command
{
public:
  typedef CommandIterationUpdate   Self;
  typedef itk::Command             Superclass;
  typedef itk::SmartPointer<Self>  Pointer;
  itkNewMacro( Self );

protected:
  CommandIterationUpdate() {};

public:

  void Execute(itk::Object *caller, const itk::EventObject & event)
    {
    Execute( (const itk::Object *) caller, event);
    }

  void Execute(const itk::Object * object, const itk::EventObject & event)
    {
    const TFilter * filter = static_cast< const TFilter * >( object );
    if( typeid( event ) != typeid( itk::IterationEvent ) )
      { return; }

    std::cout << filter->GetElapsedIterations() << ": ";
    std::cout << filter->GetRMSChange() << " ";
    std::cout << filter->GetCurrentParameters() << std::endl;
    }
};
```

We define the image type using a particular pixel type and dimension. In this case we will use 2D `float` images.

```
typedef   float              InternalPixelType;
const     unsigned int       Dimension = 2;
typedef itk::Image< InternalPixelType, Dimension >  InternalImageType;
```

The following line instantiate a `itk::GeodesicActiveContourShapePriorLevelSetImageFilter` using the `New()` method.

```
typedef itk::GeodesicActiveContourShapePriorLevelSetImageFilter<
        InternalImageType, InternalImageType >
                                      GeodesicActiveContourFilterType;
GeodesicActiveContourFilterType::Pointer geodesicActiveContour =
                              GeodesicActiveContourFilterType::New();
```

The `itk::ChangeInformationImageFilter` is the first filter in the preprocessing stage and is used to force the image origin to the center of the image.

```
typedef itk::ChangeInformationImageFilter<
                        InternalImageType > CenterFilterType;


CenterFilterType::Pointer center = CenterFilterType::New();
center->CenterImageOn();
```

In this example, we will use the bounded reciprocal $1/(1+x)$ of the image gradient magnitude as the edge potential feature image.

```
typedef   itk::BoundedReciprocalImageFilter<
                        InternalImageType,
                        InternalImageType > ReciprocalFilterType;


ReciprocalFilterType::Pointer reciprocal = ReciprocalFilterType::New();
```

In the GeodesicActiveContourShapePriorLevelSetImageFilter, scaling parameters are used to trade off between the propagation (inflation), the curvature (smoothing), the advection, and the shape influence terms. These parameters are set using methods SetPropagationScaling(), SetCurvatureScaling(), SetAdvectionScaling() and SetShapePriorScaling(). In this example, we will set the curvature and advection scales to one and let the propagation and shape prior scale be command-line arguments.

```
geodesicActiveContour->SetPropagationScaling( propagationScaling );
geodesicActiveContour->SetShapePriorScaling( shapePriorScaling );
geodesicActiveContour->SetCurvatureScaling( 1.0 );
geodesicActiveContour->SetAdvectionScaling( 1.0 );
```

Each iteration, the current "best-fit" shape is estimated from the edge potential image and the current contour. To increase speed, only information within the sparse field layers of the current contour is used in the estimation. The default number of sparse field layers is the same as the ImageDimension which does not contain enough information to get a reliable best-fit shape estimate. Thus, we override the default and set the number of layers to 4.

```
geodesicActiveContour->SetNumberOfLayers( 4 );
```

The filters are then connected in a pipeline as illustrated in Figure 4.31.

```
center->SetInput( reader->GetOutput() );
smoothing->SetInput( center->GetOutput() );
gradientMagnitude->SetInput( smoothing->GetOutput() );
reciprocal->SetInput( gradientMagnitude->GetOutput() );

geodesicActiveContour->SetInput(  fastMarching->GetOutput() );
geodesicActiveContour->SetFeatureImage( reciprocal->GetOutput() );

thresholder->SetInput( geodesicActiveContour->GetOutput() );
writer->SetInput( thresholder->GetOutput() );
```

Next, we define the shape model. In this example, we use an implicit shape model based on the principal components such that:

$$\psi^*(\mathbf{x}) = \mu(\mathbf{x}) + \sum_k \alpha_k u_k(\mathbf{x}) \tag{4.7}$$

where $\mu(\mathbf{x})$ is the mean signed distance computed from training set of segmented objects and $u_k(\mathbf{x})$ are the first K principal components of the offset (signed distance - mean). The coefficients $\{\alpha_k\}$ form the set of *shape* parameters.

Given a set of training data, the `itk::ImagePCAShapeModelEstimator` can be used to obtain the mean and principal mode shape images required by PCAShapeSignedDistanceFunction.

```
typedef itk::PCAShapeSignedDistanceFunction<
                      double,
                      Dimension,
                      InternalImageType >     ShapeFunctionType;

ShapeFunctionType::Pointer shape = ShapeFunctionType::New();

shape->SetNumberOfPrincipalComponents( numberOfPCAModes );
```

In this example, we will read the mean shape and principal mode images from file. We will assume that the filenames of the mode images form a numeric series starting from index 0.

```
ReaderType::Pointer meanShapeReader = ReaderType::New();
meanShapeReader->SetFileName( argv[13] );
meanShapeReader->Update();

std::vector<InternalImageType::Pointer> shapeModeImages( numberOfPCAModes );

itk::NumericSeriesFileNames::Pointer fileNamesCreator =
        itk::NumericSeriesFileNames::New();

fileNamesCreator->SetStartIndex( 0 );
fileNamesCreator->SetEndIndex( numberOfPCAModes - 1 );
fileNamesCreator->SetSeriesFormat( argv[15] );
const std::vector<std::string> & shapeModeFileNames =
        fileNamesCreator->GetFileNames();

for ( unsigned int k = 0; k < numberOfPCAModes; k++ )
  {
  ReaderType::Pointer shapeModeReader = ReaderType::New();
  shapeModeReader->SetFileName( shapeModeFileNames[k].c_str() );
  shapeModeReader->Update();
  shapeModeImages[k] = shapeModeReader->GetOutput();
  }

shape->SetMeanImage( meanShapeReader->GetOutput() );
shape->SetPrincipalComponentImages( shapeModeImages );
```

Further we assume that the shape modes have been normalized by multiplying with the corresponding singular value. Hence, we can set the principal component standard deviations to all ones.

```
ShapeFunctionType::ParametersType pcaStandardDeviations( numberOfPCAModes );
pcaStandardDeviations.Fill( 1.0 );

shape->SetPrincipalComponentStandardDeviations( pcaStandardDeviations );
```

Next, we instantiate a `itk::Euler2DTransform` and connect it to the PCASignedDistanceFunction. The transform represent the pose of the shape. The parameters of the transform forms the set of *pose* parameters.

```
typedef itk::Euler2DTransform<double>    TransformType;
TransformType::Pointer transform = TransformType::New();

shape->SetTransform( transform );
```

Before updating the level set at each iteration, the parameters of the current best-fit shape is estimated by minimizing the `itk::ShapePriorMAPCostFunction`. The cost function is composed of four terms: contour fit, image fit, shape prior and pose prior. The user can specify the weights applied to each term.

```
typedef itk::ShapePriorMAPCostFunction<
                        InternalImageType,
                        InternalPixelType >   CostFunctionType;

CostFunctionType::Pointer costFunction = CostFunctionType::New();

CostFunctionType::WeightsType weights;
weights[0] = 1.0;  // weight for contour fit term
weights[1] = 20.0; // weight for image fit term
weights[2] = 1.0;  // weight for shape prior term
weights[3] = 1.0;  // weight for pose prior term

costFunction->SetWeights( weights );
```

Contour fit measures the likelihood of seeing the current evolving contour for a given set of shape/pose parameters. This is computed by counting the number of pixels inside the current contour but outside the current shape.

Image fit measures the likelihood of seeing certain image features for a given set of shape/pose parameters. This is computed by assuming that (1 - edge potential) approximates a zero-mean, unit variance Gaussian along the normal of the evolving contour. Image fit is then computed by computing the Laplacian goodness of fit of the Gaussian:

$$\sum \left(G(\psi(\mathbf{x})) - |1 - g(\mathbf{x})| \right)^2 \qquad (4.8)$$

where G is a zero-mean, unit variance Gaussian and g is the edge potential feature image.

The pose parameters are assumed to have a uniform distribution and hence do not contribute to the cost function. The shape parameters are assumed to have a Gaussian distribution. The parameters of the distribution are user-specified. Since we assumed the principal modes have already been normalized, we set the distribution to zero mean and unit variance.

```
CostFunctionType::ArrayType mean(   shape->GetNumberOfShapeParameters() );
CostFunctionType::ArrayType stddev( shape->GetNumberOfShapeParameters() );

mean.Fill( 0.0 );
stddev.Fill( 1.0 );
costFunction->SetShapeParameterMeans( mean );
costFunction->SetShapeParameterStandardDeviations( stddev );
```

In this example, we will use the `itk::OnePlusOneEvolutionaryOptimizer` to optimize the cost function.

```
typedef itk::OnePlusOneEvolutionaryOptimizer    OptimizerType;
OptimizerType::Pointer optimizer = OptimizerType::New();
```

The evolutionary optimization algorithm is based on testing random permutations of the parameters. As such, we need to provide the optimizer with a random number generator. In the following lines, we create a `itk::NormalVariateGenerator`, seed it, and connect it to the optimizer.

```
typedef itk::Statistics::NormalVariateGenerator GeneratorType;
GeneratorType::Pointer generator = GeneratorType::New();

generator->Initialize( 20020702 );

optimizer->SetNormalVariateGenerator( generator );
```

The cost function has $K + 3$ parameters. The first K parameters are the principal component multipliers, followed by the 2D rotation parameter (in radians) and the x- and y- translation parameters (in mm). We need to carefully scale the different types of parameters to compensate for the differences in the dynamic ranges of the parameters.

```
OptimizerType::ScalesType scales( shape->GetNumberOfParameters() );
scales.Fill( 1.0 );
for( unsigned int k = 0; k < numberOfPCAModes; k++ )
  {
  scales[k] = 20.0;  // scales for the pca mode multiplier
  }
scales[numberOfPCAModes] = 350.0;  // scale for 2D rotation
optimizer->SetScales( scales );
```

Next, we specify the initial radius, the shrink and grow mutation factors and termination criteria of the optimizer. Since the best-fit shape is re-estimated each iteration of the curve evolution, we do not need to spend too much time finding the true minimizing solution each time; we only need to head towards it. As such, we only require a small number of optimizer iterations.

```
double initRadius = 1.05;
double grow = 1.1;
double shrink = pow(grow, -0.25);
optimizer->Initialize(initRadius, grow, shrink);

optimizer->SetEpsilon(1.0e-6); // minimal search radius

optimizer->SetMaximumIteration(15);
```

Before starting the segmentation process we need to also supply the initial best-fit shape estimate. In this example, we start with the unrotated mean shape with the initial x- and y- translation specified through command-line arguments.

```
ShapeFunctionType::ParametersType parameters(
                          shape->GetNumberOfParameters() );
parameters.Fill( 0.0 );
parameters[numberOfPCAModes + 1] = atof( argv[16] ); // startX
parameters[numberOfPCAModes + 2] = atof( argv[17] ); // startY
```

Finally, we connect all the components to the filter and add our observer.

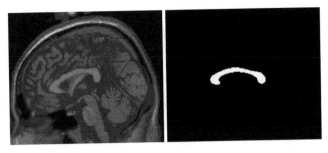

Figure 4.32: The input image to the GeodesicActiveContourShapePriorLevelSetImageFilter is a synthesized MR-T1 mid-sagittal slice (217 × 180 pixels, 1 × 1 mm spacing) of the brain (left) and the initial best-fit shape (right) chosen to roughly overlap the corpus callosum in the image to be segmented.

```
geodesicActiveContour->SetShapeFunction( shape );
geodesicActiveContour->SetCostFunction( costFunction );
geodesicActiveContour->SetOptimizer( optimizer );
geodesicActiveContour->SetInitialParameters( parameters );

typedef CommandIterationUpdate<GeodesicActiveContourFilterType> CommandType;
CommandType::Pointer observer = CommandType::New();
geodesicActiveContour->AddObserver( itk::IterationEvent(), observer );
```

The invocation of the Update() method on the writer triggers the execution of the pipeline. As usual, the call is placed in a try/catch block to handle exceptions should errors occur.

```
try
  {
  writer->Update();
  }
catch( itk::ExceptionObject & excep )
  {
  std::cerr << "Exception caught !" << std::endl;
  std::cerr << excep << std::endl;
  }
```

Deviating from previous examples, we will demonstrate this example using BrainMidSagittalSlice.png (Figure 4.32, left) from the Examples/Data directory. The aim here is to segment the corpus callosum from the image using a shape model defined by CorpusCallosumMeanShape.mha and the first three principal components CorpusCallosumMode0.mha, CorpusCallosumMode1.mha and CorpusCallosumMode12.mha. As shown in Figure 4.33, the first mode captures scaling, the second mode captures the shifting of mass between the rostrum and the splenium and the third mode captures the degree of curvature. Segmentation results with and without shape guidance are shown in Figure 4.34.

A sigma value of 1.0 was used to compute the image gradient and the propagation and shape prior scaling are respectively set to 0.5 and 0.02. An initial level set was created by placing one seed point in the rostrum $(60, 102)$, one in the splenium $(120, 85)$ and one centrally in the body $(88, 83)$ of the corpus callosum with an initial radius of 6 pixels at each seed position. The best-fit shape was initially placed with a translation of $(10, 0)$mm so that it roughly overlapped the corpus callosum in the image as shown in Figure 4.32 (right).

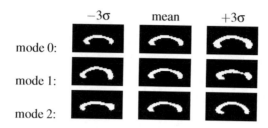

Figure 4.33: First three PCA modes of a low-resolution (58 × 31 pixels, 2 × 2 mm spacing) corpus callosum model used in the shape guided geodesic active contours example.

Figure 4.34: Corpus callosum segmentation using geodesic active contours without (left) and with (center) shape guidance. The image on the right represents the best-fit shape at the end of the segmentation process.

From Figure 4.34 it can be observed that without shape guidance (left), segmentation using geodesic active contour leaks in the regions where the corpus callosum blends into the surrounding brain tissues. With shape guidance (center), the segmentation is constrained by the global shape model to prevent leaking.

The final best-fit shape parameters after the segmentation process is:

```
Parameters: [-0.384988, -0.578738, 0.557793, 0.275202, 16.9992, 4.73473]
```

and is shown in Figure 4.34 (right). Note that a 0.28 radian (15.8 degree) rotation has been introduced to match the model to the corpus callosum in the image. Additionally, a negative weight for the first mode shrinks the size relative to the mean shape. A negative weight for the second mode shifts the mass to splenium, and a positive weight for the third mode increases the curvature. It can also be observed that the final segmentation is a combination of the best-fit shape with additional local deformation. The combination of both global and local shape allows the segmentation to capture fine details not represented in the shape model.

4.4 Feature Extraction

Extracting salient features from images is an important task on image processing. It is typically used for guiding segmentation methods, preparing data for registration methods, or as a mechanism for recognizing anatomical structures in images. The following section introduce some of the feature extraction methods available in ITK.

4.4.1 Hough Transform

The Hough transform is a widely used technique for detection of geometrical features in images. It is based on mapping the image into a parametric space in which it may be easier to identify if particular geometrical features are present in the image. The transformation is specific for each desired geometrical shape.

Line Extraction

The source code for this section can be found in the file
HoughTransform2DLinesImageFilter.cxx.

This example illustrates the use of the `itk::HoughTransform2DLinesImageFilter` to find straight lines in a 2-dimensional image.

First, we include the header files of the filter.

```
#include "itkHoughTransform2DLinesImageFilter.h"
```

Next, we declare the pixel type and image dimension and specify the image type to be used as input. We also specify the image type of the accumulator used in the Hough transform filter.

```
typedef   unsigned char   PixelType;
typedef   float           AccumulatorPixelType;
const     unsigned int    Dimension = 2;

typedef itk::Image< PixelType, Dimension >            ImageType;
typedef itk::Image< AccumulatorPixelType, Dimension > AccumulatorImageType;
```

We setup a reader to load the input image.

```
typedef itk::ImageFileReader< ImageType > ReaderType;
ReaderType::Pointer reader = ReaderType::New();

reader->SetFileName( argv[1] );
try
  {
  reader->Update();
  }
catch( itk::ExceptionObject & excep )
  {
  std::cerr << "Exception caught !" << std::endl;
  std::cerr << excep << std::endl;
  }
ImageType::Pointer localImage = reader->GetOutput();
```

Once the image is loaded, we apply a `itk::GradientMagnitudeImageFilter` to segment edges.
This casts the input image using a `itk::CastImageFilter`.

```
typedef itk::CastImageFilter< ImageType, AccumulatorImageType >
  CastingFilterType;
CastingFilterType::Pointer caster = CastingFilterType::New();

std::cout << "Applying gradient magnitude filter" << std::endl;

typedef itk::GradientMagnitudeImageFilter<AccumulatorImageType,
            AccumulatorImageType > GradientFilterType;
GradientFilterType::Pointer gradFilter = GradientFilterType::New();

caster->SetInput(localImage);
gradFilter->SetInput(caster->GetOutput());
gradFilter->Update();
```

The next step is to apply a threshold filter on the gradient magnitude image to keep only bright values.
Only pixels with a high value will be used by the Hough transform filter.

```
std::cout << "Thresholding" << std::endl;
typedef itk::ThresholdImageFilter<AccumulatorImageType> ThresholdFilterType;
ThresholdFilterType::Pointer threshFilter = ThresholdFilterType::New();

threshFilter->SetInput( gradFilter->GetOutput());
threshFilter->SetOutsideValue(0);
unsigned char threshBelow = 0;
unsigned char threshAbove = 255;
threshFilter->ThresholdOutside(threshBelow,threshAbove);
threshFilter->Update();
```

We create the HoughTransform2DLinesImageFilter based on the pixel type of the input image (the
resulting image from the ThresholdImageFilter).

```
std::cout << "Computing Hough Map" << std::endl;
typedef itk::HoughTransform2DLinesImageFilter<AccumulatorPixelType,
                        AccumulatorPixelType>  HoughTransformFilterType;

HoughTransformFilterType::Pointer houghFilter
                                = HoughTransformFilterType::New();
```

We set the input to the filter to be the output of the ThresholdImageFilter. We set also the number of lines we are looking for. Basically, the filter computes the Hough map, blurs it using a certain variance and finds maxima in the Hough map. After a maximum is found, the local neighborhood, a circle, is removed from the Hough map. SetDiscRadius() defines the radius of this disc.

The output of the filter is the accumulator.

```
houghFilter->SetInput(threshFilter->GetOutput());
houghFilter->SetNumberOfLines(atoi(argv[3]));

if(argc > 4 )
  {
  houghFilter->SetVariance(atof(argv[4]));
  }

if(argc > 5 )
  {
  houghFilter->SetDiscRadius(atof(argv[5]));
  }
houghFilter->Update();
AccumulatorImageType::Pointer localAccumulator = houghFilter->GetOutput();
```

We can also get the lines as `itk::LineSpatialObject`. The `GetLines()` function return a list of those.

```
HoughTransformFilterType::LinesListType lines;
lines = houghFilter->GetLines(atoi(argv[3]));
std::cout << "Found " << lines.size() << " line(s)." << std::endl;
```

We can then allocate an image to draw the resulting lines as binary objects.

```
typedef  unsigned char                   OutputPixelType;
typedef  itk::Image< OutputPixelType, Dimension > OutputImageType;

OutputImageType::Pointer  localOutputImage = OutputImageType::New();

OutputImageType::RegionType region(localImage->GetLargestPossibleRegion());
localOutputImage->SetRegions(region);
localOutputImage->CopyInformation(localImage);
localOutputImage->Allocate(true); // initialize buffer to zero
```

We iterate through the list of lines and we draw them.

```
typedef HoughTransformFilterType::LinesListType::const_iterator LineIterator;
LineIterator itLines = lines.begin();
while( itLines != lines.end() )
  {
```

We get the list of points which consists of two points to represent a straight line. Then, from these two points, we compute a fixed point u and a unit vector $\vec{v}$ to parameterize the line.

```
typedef HoughTransformFilterType::LineType::PointListType  PointListType;

PointListType                     pointsList = (*itLines)->GetPoints();
PointListType::const_iterator  itPoints = pointsList.begin();

double u[2];
u[0] = (*itPoints).GetPosition()[0];
u[1] = (*itPoints).GetPosition()[1];
itPoints++;
double v[2];
v[0] = u[0]-(*itPoints).GetPosition()[0];
v[1] = u[1]-(*itPoints).GetPosition()[1];

double norm = std::sqrt(v[0]*v[0]+v[1]*v[1]);
v[0] /= norm;
v[1] /= norm;
```

We draw a white pixels in the output image to represent the line.

```
ImageType::IndexType localIndex;
itk::Size<2> size = localOutputImage->GetLargestPossibleRegion().GetSize();
float diag = std::sqrt((float)( size[0]*size[0] + size[1]*size[1] ));

for(int i=static_cast<int>(-diag); i<static_cast<int>(diag); i++)
  {
  localIndex[0]=(long int)(u[0]+i*v[0]);
  localIndex[1]=(long int)(u[1]+i*v[1]);

  OutputImageType::RegionType outputRegion =
                  localOutputImage->GetLargestPossibleRegion();

  if( outputRegion.IsInside( localIndex ) )
    {
    localOutputImage->SetPixel( localIndex, 255 );
    }
  }
itLines++;
}
```

We setup a writer to write out the binary image created.

```
typedef itk::ImageFileWriter< OutputImageType > WriterType;
WriterType::Pointer writer = WriterType::New();
writer->SetFileName( argv[2] );
writer->SetInput( localOutputImage );

try
  {
  writer->Update();
  }
catch( itk::ExceptionObject & excep )
  {
  std::cerr << "Exception caught !" << std::endl;
  std::cerr << excep << std::endl;
  return EXIT_FAILURE;
  }
```

Circle Extraction

The source code for this section can be found in the file
`HoughTransform2DCirclesImageFilter.cxx`.

This example illustrates the use of the `itk::HoughTransform2DCirclesImageFilter` to find circles in a 2-dimensional image.

First, we include the header files of the filter.

```
#include "itkHoughTransform2DCirclesImageFilter.h"
```

Next, we declare the pixel type and image dimension and specify the image type to be used as input. We also specify the image type of the accumulator used in the Hough transform filter.

```
typedef   unsigned char   PixelType;
typedef   float           AccumulatorPixelType;
const     unsigned int    Dimension = 2;
typedef itk::Image< PixelType, Dimension >  ImageType;
ImageType::IndexType localIndex;
typedef itk::Image< AccumulatorPixelType, Dimension > AccumulatorImageType;
```

We setup a reader to load the input image.

```
typedef  itk::ImageFileReader< ImageType > ReaderType;
ReaderType::Pointer reader = ReaderType::New();
reader->SetFileName( argv[1] );
try
  {
  reader->Update();
  }
catch( itk::ExceptionObject & excep )
  {
  std::cerr << "Exception caught !" << std::endl;
  std::cerr << excep << std::endl;
  }
ImageType::Pointer localImage = reader->GetOutput();
```

We create the HoughTransform2DCirclesImageFilter based on the pixel type of the input image (the resulting image from the ThresholdImageFilter).

```
std::cout << "Computing Hough Map" << std::endl;

typedef itk::HoughTransform2DCirclesImageFilter<PixelType,
            AccumulatorPixelType> HoughTransformFilterType;
HoughTransformFilterType::Pointer houghFilter
                            = HoughTransformFilterType::New();
```

We set the input of the filter to be the output of the ImageFileReader. We set also the number of circles we are looking for. Basically, the filter computes the Hough map, blurs it using a certain variance and finds maxima in the Hough map. After a maximum is found, the local neighborhood, a circle, is removed from the Hough map. SetDiscRadiusRatio() defines the radius of this disc proportional to the radius of the disc found. The Hough map is computed by looking at the points above a certain threshold in the input image. Then, for each point, a Gaussian derivative function is computed to find the direction of the normal at that point. The standard deviation of the derivative function can be adjusted by SetSigmaGradient(). The accumulator is filled by drawing a line along the normal and the length of this line is defined by the minimum radius (SetMinimumRadius()) and the maximum radius (SetMaximumRadius()). Moreover, a sweep angle can be defined by SetSweepAngle() (default 0.0) to increase the accuracy of detection.

The output of the filter is the accumulator.

```
houghFilter->SetInput( reader->GetOutput() );

houghFilter->SetNumberOfCircles( atoi(argv[3]) );
houghFilter->SetMinimumRadius(   atof(argv[4]) );
houghFilter->SetMaximumRadius(   atof(argv[5]) );

if( argc > 6 )
  {
  houghFilter->SetSweepAngle( atof(argv[6]) );
  }
if( argc > 7 )
  {
  houghFilter->SetSigmaGradient( atoi(argv[7]) );
  }
if( argc > 8 )
  {
  houghFilter->SetVariance( atof(argv[8]) );
  }
if( argc > 9 )
  {
  houghFilter->SetDiscRadiusRatio( atof(argv[9]) );
  }

houghFilter->Update();
AccumulatorImageType::Pointer localAccumulator = houghFilter->GetOutput();
```

We can also get the circles as itk::EllipseSpatialObject. The GetCircles() function return a list of those.

```
HoughTransformFilterType::CirclesListType circles;
circles = houghFilter->GetCircles( atoi(argv[3]) );
std::cout << "Found " << circles.size() << " circle(s)." << std::endl;
```

We can then allocate an image to draw the resulting circles as binary objects.

```
typedef  unsigned char                               OutputPixelType;
typedef  itk::Image< OutputPixelType, Dimension > OutputImageType;

OutputImageType::Pointer  localOutputImage = OutputImageType::New();

OutputImageType::RegionType region;
region.SetSize(localImage->GetLargestPossibleRegion().GetSize());
region.SetIndex(localImage->GetLargestPossibleRegion().GetIndex());
localOutputImage->SetRegions( region );
localOutputImage->SetOrigin(localImage->GetOrigin());
localOutputImage->SetSpacing(localImage->GetSpacing());
localOutputImage->Allocate(true); // initializes buffer to zero
```

We iterate through the list of circles and we draw them.

```
typedef HoughTransformFilterType::CirclesListType CirclesListType;
CirclesListType::const_iterator itCircles = circles.begin();

while( itCircles != circles.end() )
  {
  std::cout << "Center: ";
  std::cout << (*itCircles)->GetObjectToParentTransform()->GetOffset()
            << std::endl;
  std::cout << "Radius: " << (*itCircles)->GetRadius()[0] << std::endl;
```

We draw white pixels in the output image to represent each circle.

```
for(double angle = 0;angle <= 2*vnl_math::pi; angle += vnl_math::pi/60.0 )
    {
    localIndex[0] =
        (long int)((*itCircles)->GetObjectToParentTransform()->GetOffset()[0]
                + (*itCircles)->GetRadius()[0]*std::cos(angle));
    localIndex[1] =
        (long int)((*itCircles)->GetObjectToParentTransform()->GetOffset()[1]
                + (*itCircles)->GetRadius()[0]*std::sin(angle));
    OutputImageType::RegionType outputRegion =
                        localOutputImage->GetLargestPossibleRegion();

    if( outputRegion.IsInside( localIndex ) )
      {
      localOutputImage->SetPixel( localIndex, 255 );
      }
    }
  itCircles++;
  }
```

We setup a writer to write out the binary image created.

```
typedef itk::ImageFileWriter< ImageType > WriterType;
WriterType::Pointer writer = WriterType::New();

writer->SetFileName( argv[2] );
writer->SetInput(localOutputImage );

try
  {
  writer->Update();
  }
catch( itk::ExceptionObject & excep )
  {
  std::cerr << "Exception caught !" << std::endl;
  std::cerr << excep << std::endl;
  }
```

STATISTICS

This chapter introduces the statistics functionalities in Insight. The statistics subsystem's primary purpose is to provide general capabilities for statistical pattern classification. However, its use is not limited for classification. Users might want to use data containers and algorithms in the statistics subsystem to perform other statistical analysis or to preprocess image data for other tasks.

The statistics subsystem mainly consists of three parts: data container classes, statistical algorithms, and the classification framework. In this chapter, we will discuss each major part in that order.

5.1 Data Containers

An `itk::Statistics::Sample` object is a data container of elements that we call *measurement vectors*. A measurement vector is an array of values (of the same type) measured on an object (In images, it can be a vector of the gray intensity value and/or the gradient value of a pixel). Strictly speaking from the design of the Sample class, a measurement vector can be any class derived from `itk::FixedArray`, including FixedArray itself.

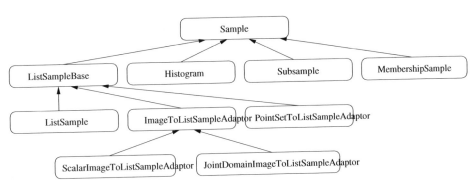

Figure 5.1: Sample class inheritance diagram.

5.1.1 Sample Interface

The source code for this section can be found in the file
ListSample.cxx.

This example illustrates the common interface of the Sample class in Insight.

Different subclasses of itk::Statistics::Sample expect different sets of template arguments. In this example, we use the itk::Statistics::ListSample class that requires the type of measurement vectors. The ListSample uses STL vector to store measurement vectors. This class conforms to the common interface of Sample. Most methods of the Sample class interface are for retrieving measurement vectors, the size of a container, and the total frequency. In this example, we will see those information retrieving methods in addition to methods specific to the ListSample class for data input.

To use the ListSample class, we include the header file for the class.

We need another header for measurement vectors. We are going to use the itk::Vector class which is a subclass of the itk::FixedArray class.

```
#include "itkListSample.h"
#include "itkVector.h"
```

The following code snippet defines the measurement vector type as a three component float itk::Vector. The MeasurementVectorType is the measurement vector type in the SampleType. An object is instantiated at the third line.

```
typedef itk::Vector< float, 3 > MeasurementVectorType;
typedef itk::Statistics::ListSample< MeasurementVectorType > SampleType;
SampleType::Pointer sample = SampleType::New();
```

In the above code snippet, the namespace specifier for ListSample is itk::Statistics:: instead of the usual namespace specifier for other ITK classes, itk::.

The newly instantiated object does not have any data in it. We have two different ways of storing data elements. The first method is using the PushBack method.

```
MeasurementVectorType mv;
mv[0] = 1.0;
mv[1] = 2.0;
mv[2] = 4.0;

sample->PushBack(mv);
```

The previous code increases the size of the container by one and stores mv as the first data element in it.

The other way to store data elements is calling the Resize method and then calling the SetMeasurementVector() method with a measurement vector. The following code snippet increases the size of the container to three and stores two measurement vectors at the second and the third slot. The measurement vector stored using the PushBack method above is still at the first slot.

```
sample->Resize(3);

mv[0] = 2.0;
mv[1] = 4.0;
mv[2] = 5.0;
sample->SetMeasurementVector(1, mv);

mv[0] = 3.0;
mv[1] = 8.0;
mv[2] = 6.0;
sample->SetMeasurementVector(2, mv);
```

We have seen how to create an ListSample object and store measurement vectors using the ListSample-specific interface. The following code shows the common interface of the Sample class. The Size method returns the number of measurement vectors in the sample. The primary data stored in Sample subclasses are measurement vectors. However, each measurement vector has its associated frequency of occurrence within the sample. For the ListSample and the adaptor classes (see Section 5.1.2), the frequency value is always one. itk::Statistics::Histogram can have a varying frequency (float type) for each measurement vector. We retrieve measurement vectors using the GetMeasurementVector(unsigned long instance identifier), and frequency using the GetFrequency(unsigned long instance identifier).

```
for ( unsigned long i = 0; i < sample->Size(); ++i )
  {
  std::cout << "id = " << i
            << "\t measurement vector = "
            << sample->GetMeasurementVector(i)
            << "\t frequency = "
            << sample->GetFrequency(i)
            << std::endl;
  }
```

The output should look like the following:

```
id = 0 measurement vector = 1 2 4 frequency = 1
id = 1 measurement vector = 2 4 5 frequency = 1
id = 2 measurement vector = 3 8 6 frequency = 1
```

We can get the same result with its iterator.

```
SampleType::Iterator iter = sample->Begin();

while( iter != sample->End() )
  {
  std::cout << "id = " << iter.GetInstanceIdentifier()
            << "\t measurement vector = "
            << iter.GetMeasurementVector()
            << "\t frequency = "
            << iter.GetFrequency()
            << std::endl;
  ++iter;
  }
```

The last method defined in the Sample class is the GetTotalFrequency() method that returns the sum of frequency values associated with every measurement vector in a container. In the case of

ListSample and the adaptor classes, the return value should be exactly the same as that of the `Size()` method, because the frequency values are always one for each measurement vector. However, for the `itk::Statistics::Histogram`, the frequency values can vary. Therefore, if we want to develop a general algorithm to calculate the sample mean, we must use the `GetTotalFrequency()` method instead of the `Size()` method.

```
std::cout << "Size = " << sample->Size() << std::endl;
std::cout << "Total frequency = "
          << sample->GetTotalFrequency() << std::endl;
```

5.1.2   Sample Adaptors

There are two adaptor classes that provide the common `itk::Statistics::Sample` interfaces for `itk::Image` and `itk::PointSet`, two fundamental data container classes found in ITK. The adaptor classes do not store any real data elements themselves.   These data come from the source data container plugged into them.   First, we will describe how to create an `itk::Statistics::ImageToListSampleAdaptor` and then an `itk::Statistics::PointSetToListSampleAdaptor` object.

ImageToListSampleAdaptor

The source code for this section can be found in the file
`ImageToListSampleAdaptor.cxx`.

This example shows how to instantiate an `itk::Statistics::ImageToListSampleAdaptor` object and plug-in an `itk::Image` object as the data source for the adaptor.

In this example, we use the ImageToListSampleAdaptor class that requires the input type of Image as the template argument. To users of the ImageToListSampleAdaptor, the pixels of the input image are treated as measurement vectors. The ImageToListSampleAdaptor is one of two adaptor classes among the subclasses of the `itk::Statistics::Sample`. That means an ImageToListSampleAdaptor object does not store any real data. The data comes from other ITK data container classes. In this case, an instance of the Image class is the source of the data.

To use an ImageToListSampleAdaptor object, include the header file for the class. Since we are using an adaptor, we also should include the header file for the Image class. For illustration, we use the `itk::RandomImageSource` that generates an image with random pixel values. So, we need to include the header file for this class. Another convenient filter is the `itk::ComposeImageFilter` which creates an image with pixels of array type from one or more input images composed of pixels of scalar type. Since an element of a Sample object is a measurement *vector*, you cannot plug in an image of scalar pixels. However, if we want to use an image of scalar pixels without the help from the ComposeImageFilter, we can use the `itk::Statistics::ScalarImageToListSampleAdaptor` class that is derived from the `itk::Statistics::ImageToListSampleAdaptor`. The usage of the ScalarImageToListSampleAdaptor is identical to that of the ImageToListSampleAdaptor.

```
#include "itkImageToListSampleAdaptor.h"
#include "itkImage.h"
#include "itkRandomImageSource.h"
#include "itkComposeImageFilter.h"
```

We assume you already know how to create an image. The following code snippet will create a 2D image of float pixels filled with random values.

```
typedef itk::Image<float,2> FloatImage2DType;

itk::RandomImageSource<FloatImage2DType>::Pointer random;
random = itk::RandomImageSource<FloatImage2DType>::New();

random->SetMin(    0.0 );
random->SetMax( 1000.0 );

typedef FloatImage2DType::SpacingValueType   SpacingValueType;
typedef FloatImage2DType::SizeValueType      SizeValueType;
typedef FloatImage2DType::PointValueType     PointValueType;

SizeValueType size[2] = {20, 20};
random->SetSize( size );

SpacingValueType spacing[2] = {0.7, 2.1};
random->SetSpacing( spacing );

PointValueType origin[2] = {15, 400};
random->SetOrigin( origin );
```

We now have an instance of Image and need to cast it to an Image object with an array pixel type (anything derived from the `itk::FixedArray` class such as `itk::Vector`, `itk::Point`, `itk::RGBPixel`, or `itk::CovariantVector`).

Since the image pixel type is `float` in this example, we will use a single element `float` FixedArray as our measurement vector type. And that will also be our pixel type for the cast filter.

```
typedef itk::FixedArray< float, 1 >             MeasurementVectorType;
typedef itk::Image< MeasurementVectorType, 2 > ArrayImageType;
typedef itk::ComposeImageFilter< FloatImage2DType, ArrayImageType >
                                                CasterType;

CasterType::Pointer caster = CasterType::New();
caster->SetInput( random->GetOutput() );
caster->Update();
```

Up to now, we have spent most of our time creating an image suitable for the adaptor. Actually, the hard part of this example is done. Now, we just define an adaptor with the image type and instantiate an object.

```
typedef itk::Statistics::ImageToListSampleAdaptor<
                                      ArrayImageType > SampleType;
SampleType::Pointer sample = SampleType::New();
```

The final task is to plug in the image object to the adaptor. After that, we can use the common methods and iterator interfaces shown in Section 5.1.1.

```
sample->SetImage( caster->GetOutput() );
```

If we are interested only in pixel values, the ScalarImageToListSampleAdaptor (scalar pixels) or the ImageToListSampleAdaptor (vector pixels) would be sufficient. However, if we want to perform some statistical analysis on spatial information (image index or pixel's physical location) and pixel values altogether, we want to have a measurement vector that consists of a pixel's value and physical position. In that case, we can use the itk::Statistics::JointDomainImageToListSampleAdaptor class. With this class, when we call the GetMeasurementVector() method, the returned measurement vector is composed of the physical coordinates and pixel values. The usage is almost the same as with Image-ToListSampleAdaptor. One important difference between JointDomainImageToListSampleAdaptor and the other two image adaptors is that the JointDomainImageToListSampleAdaptor has the SetNormalizationFactors() method. Each component of a measurement vector from the Joint-DomainImageToListSampleAdaptor is divided by the corresponding component value from the supplied normalization factors.

PointSetToListSampleAdaptor

The source code for this section can be found in the file
PointSetToListSampleAdaptor.cxx.

We will describe how to use itk::PointSet as a itk::Statistics::Sample using an adaptor in this example.

The itk::Statistics::PointSetToListSampleAdaptor class requires a PointSet as input. The PointSet class is an associative data container. Each point in a PointSet object can have an associated optional data value. For the statistics subsystem, the current implementation of PointSetToListSampleAdaptor takes only the point part into consideration. In other words, the measurement vectors from a PointSetToListSampleAdaptor object are points from the PointSet object that is plugged into the adaptor object.

To use an PointSetToListSampleAdaptor class, we include the header file for the class.

```
#include "itkPointSetToListSampleAdaptor.h"
```

Since we are using an adaptor, we also include the header file for the PointSet class.

```
#include "itkPointSet.h"
#include "itkVector.h"
```

Next we create a PointSet object. The following code snippet will create a PointSet object that stores points (its coordinate value type is float) in 3D space.

```
typedef itk::PointSet< short > PointSetType;
PointSetType::Pointer pointSet = PointSetType::New();
```

Note that the short type used in the declaration of PointSetType pertains to the pixel type associated with every point, not to the type used to represent point coordinates. If we want to change the type of the point in terms of the coordinate value and/or dimension, we have to modify the TMeshTraits (one of the optional template arguments for the PointSet class). The easiest way of creating a custom mesh traits instance is to specialize the existing itk::DefaultStaticMeshTraits. By specifying the TCoordRep template argument, we can change the coordinate value type of a point. By specifying the `VPointDimension` template argument, we can change the dimension of the point. As mentioned earlier, a `PointSetToListSampleAdaptor` object cares only about the points, and the type of measurement vectors is the type of points.

To make the example a little bit realistic, we add two points into the `pointSet`.

```
PointSetType::PointType point;
point[0] = 1.0;
point[1] = 2.0;
point[2] = 3.0;

pointSet->SetPoint( 0UL, point);

point[0] = 2.0;
point[1] = 4.0;
point[2] = 6.0;

pointSet->SetPoint( 1UL, point );
```

Now we have a PointSet object with two points in it. The PointSet is ready to be plugged into the adaptor. First, we create an instance of the PointSetToListSampleAdaptor class with the type of the input PointSet object.

```
typedef itk::Statistics::PointSetToListSampleAdaptor<
                                       PointSetType > SampleType;
SampleType::Pointer sample = SampleType::New();
```

Second, all we have to do is plug in the PointSet object to the adaptor. After that, we can use the common methods and iterator interfaces shown in Section 5.1.1.

```
sample->SetPointSet( pointSet );

SampleType::Iterator iter = sample->Begin();

while( iter != sample->End() )
  {
  std::cout << "id = " << iter.GetInstanceIdentifier()
            << "\t measurement vector = "
            << iter.GetMeasurementVector()
            << "\t frequency = "
            << iter.GetFrequency()
            << std::endl;
  ++iter;
  }
```

The source code for this section can be found in the file
`PointSetToAdaptor.cxx`.

We will describe how to use `itk::PointSet` as a `Sample` using an adaptor in this example.

`itk::Statistics::PointSetToListSampleAdaptor` class requires the type of input `itk::PointSet` object. The `itk::PointSet` class is an associative data container. Each point in a `PointSet` object can have its associated data value (optional). For the statistics subsystem, current implementation of `PointSetToListSampleAdaptor` takes only the point part into consideration. In other words, the measurement vectors from a `PointSetToListSampleAdaptor` object are points from the `PointSet` object that is plugged-into the adaptor object.

To use, an `itk::PointSetToListSampleAdaptor` object, we include the header file for the class.

```
#include "itkPointSetToListSampleAdaptor.h"
```

Since, we are using an adaptor, we also include the header file for the `itk::PointSet` class.

```
#include "itkPointSet.h"
```

We assume you already know how to create an `itk::PointSet` object. The following code snippet will create a 2D image of float pixels filled with random values.

```
typedef itk::PointSet<float,2> FloatPointSet2DType;

itk::RandomPointSetSource<FloatPointSet2DType>::Pointer random;
random = itk::RandomPointSetSource<FloatPointSet2DType>::New();
random->SetMin(0.0);
random->SetMax(1000.0);

unsigned long size[2] = {20, 20};
random->SetSize(size);
float spacing[2] = {0.7, 2.1};
random->SetSpacing( spacing );
float origin[2] = {15, 400};
random->SetOrigin( origin );
```

We now have an `itk::PointSet` object and need to cast it to an `itk::PointSet` object with array type (anything derived from the `itk::FixedArray` class) pixels.

Since, the `itk::PointSet` object's pixel type is float, We will use single element `float` `itk::FixedArray` as our measurement vector type. And that will also be our pixel type for the cast filter.

```
typedef itk::FixedArray< float, 1 >                    MeasurementVectorType;
typedef itk::PointSet< MeasurementVectorType, 2 > ArrayPointSetType;
typedef itk::ScalarToArrayCastPointSetFilter< FloatPointSet2DType,
                         ArrayPointSetType >    CasterType;

CasterType::Pointer caster = CasterType::New();
caster->SetInput( random->GetOutput() );
caster->Update();
```

Up to now, we spend most of time to prepare an `itk::PointSet` object suitable for the adaptor. Actually, the hard part of this example is done. Now, we must define an adaptor with the image type and instantiate an object.

```
typedef itk::Statistics::PointSetToListSampleAdaptor<
                         ArrayPointSetType > SampleType;
SampleType::Pointer sample = SampleType::New();
```

The final thing we have to is to plug-in the image object to the adaptor. After that, we can use the common methods and iterator interfaces shown in 5.1.1.

```
sample->SetPointSet( caster->GetOutput() );
```

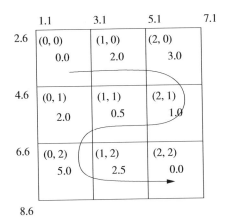

Figure 5.2: Conceptual histogram data structure.

5.1.3 Histogram

The source code for this section can be found in the file
Histogram.cxx.

This example shows how to create an `itk::Statistics::Histogram` object and use it.

We call an instance in a `Histogram` object a *bin*. The Histogram differs from
the `itk::Statistics::ListSample`, `itk::Statistics::ImageToListSampleAdaptor`, or
`itk::Statistics::PointSetToListSampleAdaptor` in significant ways. Histograms can have
a variable number of values (`float` type) for each measurement vector, while the three other classes
have a fixed value (one) for all measurement vectors. Also those array-type containers can have multiple instances (data elements) with identical measurement vector values. However, in a Histogram
object, there is one unique instance for any given measurement vector.

```
#include "itkHistogram.h"
#include "itkDenseFrequencyContainer2.h"
```

Here we create a histogram with dense frequency containers. In this example we will not have any
zero-frequency measurements, so the dense frequency container is the appropriate choice. If the
histogram is expected to have many empty (zero) bins, a sparse frequency container would be the
better option. Here we also set the size of the measurement vectors to be 2 components.

```
typedef float                                         MeasurementType;
typedef itk::Statistics::DenseFrequencyContainer2     FrequencyContainerType;
typedef FrequencyContainerType::AbsoluteFrequencyType FrequencyType;

const unsigned int numberOfComponents = 2;
typedef itk::Statistics::Histogram< MeasurementType,
  FrequencyContainerType > HistogramType;

HistogramType::Pointer histogram = HistogramType::New();
histogram->SetMeasurementVectorSize( numberOfComponents );
```

We initialize it as a 3×3 histogram with equal size intervals.

```
HistogramType::SizeType size( numberOfComponents );
size.Fill(3);
HistogramType::MeasurementVectorType lowerBound( numberOfComponents );
HistogramType::MeasurementVectorType upperBound( numberOfComponents );
lowerBound[0] = 1.1;
lowerBound[1] = 2.6;
upperBound[0] = 7.1;
upperBound[1] = 8.6;


histogram->Initialize(size, lowerBound, upperBound );
```

Now the histogram is ready for storing frequency values. We will fill each bin's frequency according to the Figure 5.2. There are three ways of accessing data elements in the histogram:

- using instance identifiers—just like any other Sample object;

- using n-dimensional indices—just like an Image object;

- using an iterator—just like any other Sample object.

In this example, the index $(0,0)$ refers the same bin as the instance identifier (0) refers to. The instance identifier of the index $(0, 1)$ is (3), $(0, 2)$ is (6), $(2, 2)$ is (8), and so on.

```
histogram->SetFrequency(0UL, static_cast<FrequencyType>(0.0));
histogram->SetFrequency(1UL, static_cast<FrequencyType>(2.0));
histogram->SetFrequency(2UL, static_cast<FrequencyType>(3.0));
histogram->SetFrequency(3UL, static_cast<FrequencyType>(2.0f));
histogram->SetFrequency(4UL, static_cast<FrequencyType>(0.5f));
histogram->SetFrequency(5UL, static_cast<FrequencyType>(1.0f));
histogram->SetFrequency(6UL, static_cast<FrequencyType>(5.0f));
histogram->SetFrequency(7UL, static_cast<FrequencyType>(2.5f));
histogram->SetFrequency(8UL, static_cast<FrequencyType>(0.0f));
```

Let us examine if the frequency is set correctly by calling the `GetFrequency(index)` method. We can use the `GetFrequency(instance identifier)` method for the same purpose.

```
HistogramType::IndexType index( numberOfComponents );
index[0] = 0;
index[1] = 2;
std::cout << "Frequency of the bin at index " << index
          << " is " << histogram->GetFrequency(index)
          << ", and the bin's instance identifier is "
          << histogram->GetInstanceIdentifier(index) << std::endl;
```

For test purposes, we create a measurement vector and an index that belongs to the center bin.

```
HistogramType::MeasurementVectorType mv( numberOfComponents );
mv[0] = 4.1;
mv[1] = 5.6;
index.Fill(1);
```

We retrieve the measurement vector at the index value $(1, 1)$, the center bin's measurement vector. The output is [4.1, 5.6].

```
std::cout << "Measurement vector at the center bin is "
          << histogram->GetMeasurementVector(index) << std::endl;
```

Since all the measurement vectors are unique in the Histogram class, we can determine the index from a measurement vector.

```
HistogramType::IndexType resultingIndex;
histogram->GetIndex(mv,resultingIndex);
std::cout << "Index of the measurement vector " << mv
          << " is " << resultingIndex << std::endl;
```

In a similar way, we can get the instance identifier from the index.

```
std::cout << "Instance identifier of index " << index
          << " is " << histogram->GetInstanceIdentifier(index)
          << std::endl;
```

If we want to check if an index is valid, we use the method `IsIndexOutOfBounds(index)`. The following code snippet fills the index variable with (100, 100). It is obviously not a valid index.

```
index.Fill(100);
if ( histogram->IsIndexOutOfBounds(index) )
  {
  std::cout << "Index " << index << " is out of bounds." << std::endl;
  }
```

The following code snippets show how to get the histogram size and frequency dimension.

```
std::cout << "Number of bins = " << histogram->Size()
          << " Total frequency = " << histogram->GetTotalFrequency()
          << " Dimension sizes = " << histogram->GetSize() << std::endl;
```

The Histogram class has a quantile calculation method, `Quantile(dimension, percent)`. The following code returns the 50th percentile along the first dimension. Note that the quantile calculation considers only one dimension.

```
std::cout << "50th percentile along the first dimension = "
          << histogram->Quantile(0, 0.5) << std::endl;
```

5.1.4 Subsample

The source code for this section can be found in the file
`Subsample.cxx`.

The `itk::Statistics::Subsample` is a derived sample. In other words, it requires another `itk::Statistics::Sample` object for storing measurement vectors. The Subsample class stores a subset of instance identifiers from another Sample object. *Any* Sample's subclass can be the source Sample object. You can create a Subsample object out of another Subsample object. The Subsample class is useful for storing classification results from a test Sample object or for just extracting some part of interest in a Sample object. Another good use of Subsample is sorting a Sample object. When we use an `itk::Image` object as the data source, we do not want to change the order of data elements in the image. However, we sometimes want to sort or select data elements according to their order. Statistics algorithms for this purpose accepts only Subsample objects as inputs. Changing the order in a Subsample object does not change the order of the source sample.

To use a Subsample object, we include the header files for the class itself and a Sample class. We will use the `itk::Statistics::ListSample` as the input sample.

```
#include "itkListSample.h"
#include "itkSubsample.h"
```

We need another header for measurement vectors. We are going to use the `itk::Vector` class in this example.

```
#include "itkVector.h"
```

The following code snippet will create a ListSample object with three-component float measurement vectors and put three measurement vectors into the list.

```
typedef itk::Vector< float, 3 > MeasurementVectorType;
typedef itk::Statistics::ListSample< MeasurementVectorType > SampleType;
SampleType::Pointer sample = SampleType::New();
MeasurementVectorType mv;
mv[0] = 1.0;
mv[1] = 2.0;
mv[2] = 4.0;

sample->PushBack(mv);

mv[0] = 2.0;
mv[1] = 4.0;
mv[2] = 5.0;
sample->PushBack(mv);

mv[0] = 3.0;
mv[1] = 8.0;
mv[2] = 6.0;
sample->PushBack(mv);
```

To create a Subsample instance, we define the type of the Subsample with the source sample type, in this case, the previously defined `SampleType`. As usual, after that, we call the `New()` method to create an instance. We must plug in the source sample, `sample`, using the `SetSample()` method. However, with regard to data elements, the Subsample is empty. We specify which data elements, among the data elements in the Sample object, are part of the Subsample. There are two ways of doing that. First, if we want to include every data element (instance) from the sample, we simply call the `InitializeWithAllInstances()` method like the following:

```
subsample->InitializeWithAllInstances();
```

This method is useful when we want to create a Subsample object for sorting all the data elements in a Sample object. However, in most cases, we want to include only a subset of a Sample object. For this purpose, we use the `AddInstance(instance identifier)` method in this example. In the following code snippet, we include only the first and last instance in our subsample object from the three instances of the Sample class.

```
typedef itk::Statistics::Subsample< SampleType > SubsampleType;
SubsampleType::Pointer subsample = SubsampleType::New();
subsample->SetSample( sample );

subsample->AddInstance( 0UL );
subsample->AddInstance( 2UL );
```

The Subsample is ready for use. The following code snippet shows how to use Iterator interfaces.

```
SubsampleType::Iterator iter = subsample->Begin();
while ( iter != subsample->End() )
   {
   std::cout << "instance identifier = " << iter.GetInstanceIdentifier()
             << "\t measurement vector = "
             << iter.GetMeasurementVector()
             << "\t frequency = "
             << iter.GetFrequency()
             << std::endl;
   ++iter;
   }
```

As mentioned earlier, the instances in a Subsample can be sorted without changing the order in the source Sample. For this purpose, the Subsample provides an additional instance indexing scheme. The indexing scheme is just like the instance identifiers for the Sample. The index is an integer value starting at 0, and the last value is one less than the number of all instances in a Subsample. The Swap(0, 1) method, for example, swaps two instance identifiers of the first data element and the second element in the Subsample. Internally, the Swap() method changes the instance identifiers in the first and second position. Using indices, we can print out the effects of the Swap() method. We use the GetMeasurementVectorByIndex(index) to get the measurement vector at the index position. However, if we want to use the common methods of Sample that accepts instance identifiers, we call them after we get the instance identifiers using GetInstanceIdentifier(index) method.

```
subsample->Swap(0, 1);

for ( int index = 0; index < subsample->Size(); ++index )
   {
   std::cout << "instance identifier = "
             << subsample->GetInstanceIdentifier(index)
             << "\t measurement vector = "
             << subsample->GetMeasurementVectorByIndex(index)
             << std::endl;
   }
```

Since we are using a ListSample object as the source sample, the following code snippet will return the same value (2) for the Size() and the GetTotalFrequency() methods. However, if we used a Histogram object as the source sample, the two return values might be different because a Histogram allows varying frequency values for each instance.

```
std::cout << "Size = " << subsample->Size() << std::endl;
std::cout << "Total frequency = "
          << subsample->GetTotalFrequency() << std::endl;
```

If we want to remove all instances that are associated with the Subsample, we call the Clear() method. After this invocation, the Size() and the GetTotalFrequency() methods return 0.

```
subsample->Clear();
std::cout << "Size = " << subsample->Size() << std::endl;
std::cout << "Total frequency = "
          << subsample->GetTotalFrequency() << std::endl;
```

5.1.5   MembershipSample

The source code for this section can be found in the file
MembershipSample.cxx.

The   itk::Statistics::MembershipSample   is   derived   from   the   class
itk::Statistics::Sample that associates a class label with each measurement vector.   It
needs another Sample object for storing measurement vectors. A MembershipSample object stores
a subset of instance identifiers from another Sample object. *Any* subclass of Sample can be the
source Sample object. The MembershipSample class is useful for storing classification results from
a test Sample object. The MembershipSample class can be considered as an associative container
that stores measurement vectors, frequency values, and *class labels*.

To use a MembershipSample object, we include the header files for the class itself and the Sample
class. We will use the itk::Statistics::ListSample as the input sample. We need another
header for measurement vectors. We are going to use the itk::Vector class which is a subclass of
the itk::FixedArray.

```
#include "itkListSample.h"
#include "itkMembershipSample.h"
#include "itkVector.h"
```

The following code snippet will create a ListSample object with three-component float measurement vectors and put three measurement vectors in the ListSample object.

```
typedef itk::Vector< float, 3 > MeasurementVectorType;
typedef itk::Statistics::ListSample< MeasurementVectorType > SampleType;
SampleType::Pointer sample = SampleType::New();
MeasurementVectorType mv;

mv[0] = 1.0;
mv[1] = 2.0;
mv[2] = 4.0;
sample->PushBack(mv);

mv[0] = 2.0;
mv[1] = 4.0;
mv[2] = 5.0;
sample->PushBack(mv);

mv[0] = 3.0;
mv[1] = 8.0;
mv[2] = 6.0;
sample->PushBack(mv);
```

To create a MembershipSample instance, we define the type of the MembershipSample using the
source sample type using the previously defined SampleType. As usual, after that, we call the
New() method to create an instance. We must plug in the source sample, Sample, using the

`SetSample()` method. We provide class labels for data instances in the Sample object using the `AddInstance()` method. As the required initialization step for the `membershipSample`, we must call the `SetNumberOfClasses()` method with the number of classes. We must add all instances in the source sample with their class labels. In the following code snippet, we set the first instance' class label to 0, the second to 0, the third (last) to 1. After this, the `membershipSample` has two `Subsample` objects. And the class labels for these two `Subsample` objects are 0 and 1. The 0 class `Subsample` object includes the first and second instances, and the 1 class includes the third instance.

```
typedef itk::Statistics::MembershipSample< SampleType >
  MembershipSampleType;

MembershipSampleType::Pointer membershipSample =
  MembershipSampleType::New();

membershipSample->SetSample(sample);
membershipSample->SetNumberOfClasses(2);

membershipSample->AddInstance(0U, 0UL );
membershipSample->AddInstance(0U, 1UL );
membershipSample->AddInstance(1U, 2UL );
```

The `Size()` and `GetTotalFrequency()` returns the same information that Sample does.

```
std::cout << "Total frequency = "
          << membershipSample->GetTotalFrequency() << std::endl;
```

The `membershipSample` is ready for use. The following code snippet shows how to use the `Iterator` interface. The MembershipSample's `Iterator` has an additional method that returns the class label (`GetClassLabel()`).

```
MembershipSampleType::ConstIterator iter = membershipSample->Begin();
while ( iter != membershipSample->End() )
  {
  std::cout << "instance identifier = " << iter.GetInstanceIdentifier()
            << "\t measurement vector = "
            << iter.GetMeasurementVector()
            << "\t frequency = "
            << iter.GetFrequency()
            << "\t class label = "
            << iter.GetClassLabel()
            << std::endl;
  ++iter;
  }
```

To see the numbers of instances in each class subsample, we use the `Size()` method of the `ClassSampleType` instance returned by the `GetClassSample(index)` method.

```
std::cout << "class label = 0 sample size = "
          << membershipSample->GetClassSample(0)->Size() << std::endl;
std::cout << "class label = 1 sample size = "
          << membershipSample->GetClassSample(1)->Size() << std::endl;
```

We call the `GetClassSample()` method to get the class subsample in the `membershipSample`. The `MembershipSampleType::ClassSampleType` is actually a specialization of the `itk::Statistics::Subsample`. We print out the instance identifiers, measurement vectors,

and frequency values that are part of the class. The output will be two lines for the two instances
that belong to the class 0.

```
MembershipSampleType::ClassSampleType::ConstPointer classSample =
                          membershipSample->GetClassSample( 0 );

MembershipSampleType::ClassSampleType::ConstIterator c_iter =
                                    classSample->Begin();

while ( c_iter != classSample->End() )
  {
  std::cout << "instance identifier = " << c_iter.GetInstanceIdentifier()
            << "\t measurement vector = "
            << c_iter.GetMeasurementVector()
            << "\t frequency = "
            << c_iter.GetFrequency() << std::endl;
  ++c_iter;
  }
```

5.1.6   MembershipSampleGenerator

The source code for this section can be found in the file
MembershipSampleGenerator.cxx.

To use, an MembershipSample object, we include the header files for the class itself and a Sample
class. We will use the ListSample as the input sample.

```
#include "itkListSample.h"
#include "itkMembershipSample.h"
```

We need another header for measurement vectors. We are going to use the itk::Vector class which
is a subclass of the itk::FixedArray in this example.

```
#include "itkVector.h"
```

The following code snippet will create a ListSample object with three-component float measurement vectors and put three measurement vectors in the ListSample object.

```
typedef itk::Vector< float, 3 > MeasurementVectorType;
typedef itk::Statistics::ListSample< MeasurementVectorType > SampleType;
SampleType::Pointer sample = SampleType::New();
MeasurementVectorType mv;

mv[0] = 1.0;
mv[1] = 2.0;
mv[2] = 4.0;
sample->PushBack(mv);

mv[0] = 2.0;
mv[1] = 4.0;
mv[2] = 5.0;
sample->PushBack(mv);

mv[0] = 3.0;
mv[1] = 8.0;
mv[2] = 6.0;
sample->PushBack(mv);
```

To create a MembershipSample instance, we define the type of the MembershipSample with the source sample type, in this case, previously defined SampleType. As usual, after that, we call New() method to instantiate an instance. We must plug in the source sample, sample object using the SetSample(source sample) method. However, in regard to **class labels**, the membershipSample is empty. We provide class labels for data instances in the sample object using the AddInstance(class label, instance identifier) method. As the required initialization step for the membershipSample, we must call the SetNumberOfClasses(number of classes) method with the number of classes. We must add all instances in the source sample with their class labels. In the following code snippet, we set the first instance class label to 0, the second to 0, the third (last) to 1. After this, the membershipSample has two Subclass objects. And the class labels for these two Subclass are 0 and 1. The **0** class Subsample object includes the first and second instances, and the **1** class includes the third instance.

```
typedef itk::Statistics::MembershipSample< SampleType >
  MembershipSampleType;

MembershipSampleType::Pointer membershipSample =
  MembershipSampleType::New();

membershipSample->SetSample(sample);
membershipSample->SetNumberOfClasses(2);

membershipSample->AddInstance(0U, 0UL );
membershipSample->AddInstance(0U, 1UL );
membershipSample->AddInstance(1U, 2UL );
```

The Size() and GetTotalFrequency() methods return the same values as the sample.

```
std::cout << "Size = " << membershipSample->Size() << std::endl;
std::cout << "Total frequency = "
          << membershipSample->GetTotalFrequency() << std::endl;
```

The membershipSample is ready for use. The following code snippet shows how to use Iterator interfaces. The MembershipSample Iterator has an additional method that returns the class label (GetClassLabel()).

```
MembershipSampleType::Iterator iter = membershipSample->Begin();
while ( iter != membershipSample->End() )
  {
  std::cout << "instance identifier = " << iter.GetInstanceIdentifier()
            << "\t measurement vector = "
            << iter.GetMeasurementVector()
            << "\t frequency = "
            << iter.GetFrequency()
            << "\t class label = "
            << iter.GetClassLabel()
            << std::endl;
  ++iter;
  }
```

To see the numbers of instances in each class subsample, we use the `GetClassSampleSize(class label)` method.

```
std::cout << "class label = 0 sample size = "
          << membershipSample->GetClassSampleSize(0) << std::endl;
std::cout << "class label = 1 sample size = "
          << membershipSample->GetClassSampleSize(0) << std::endl;
```

We call the `GetClassSample(class label)` method to get the class subsample in the `membershipSample`. The `MembershipSampleType::ClassSampleType` is actually an specialization of the `itk::Statistics::Subsample`. We print out the instance identifiers, measurement vectors, and frequency values that are part of the class. The output will be two lines for the two instances that belong to the class **0**.

```
MembershipSampleType::ClassSampleType::Pointer classSample =
  membershipSample->GetClassSample(0);
MembershipSampleType::ClassSampleType::Iterator c_iter =
  classSample->Begin();
while ( c_iter != classSample->End() )
  {
  std::cout << "instance identifier = " << c_iter.GetInstanceIdentifier()
            << "\t measurement vector = "
            << c_iter.GetMeasurementVector()
            << "\t frequency = "
            << c_iter.GetFrequency() << std::endl;
  ++c_iter;
  }
```

5.1.7   K-d Tree

The source code for this section can be found in the file
`KdTree.cxx`.

The `itk::Statistics::KdTree` implements a data structure that separates samples in a *k*-dimension space. The `std::vector` class is used here as the container for the measurement vectors from a sample.

```
#include "itkVector.h"
#include "itkListSample.h"
#include "itkWeightedCentroidKdTreeGenerator.h"
#include "itkEuclideanDistanceMetric.h"
```

We define the measurement vector type and instantiate a `itk::Statistics::ListSample` object, and then put 1000 measurement vectors in the object.

```
typedef itk::Vector< float, 2 > MeasurementVectorType;

typedef itk::Statistics::ListSample< MeasurementVectorType > SampleType;
SampleType::Pointer sample = SampleType::New();
sample->SetMeasurementVectorSize( 2 );

MeasurementVectorType mv;
for (unsigned int i = 0; i < 1000; ++i )
  {
  mv[0] = (float) i;
  mv[1] = (float) ((1000 - i) / 2 );
  sample->PushBack( mv );
  }
```

The following code snippet shows how to create two KdTree objects. The first object `itk::Statistics::KdTreeGenerator` has a minimal set of information (partition dimension, partition value, and pointers to the left and right child nodes). The second tree from the `itk::Statistics::WeightedCentroidKdTreeGenerator` has additional information such as the number of children under each node, and the vector sum of the measurement vectors belonging to children of a particular node. WeightedCentroidKdTreeGenerator and the resulting k-d tree structure were implemented based on the description given in the paper by Kanungo et al [29].

The instantiation and input variables are exactly the same for both tree generators. Using the `SetSample()` method we plug-in the source sample. The bucket size input specifies the limit on the maximum number of measurement vectors that can be stored in a terminal (leaf) node. A bigger bucket size results in a smaller number of nodes in a tree. It also affects the efficiency of search. With many small leaf nodes, we might experience slower search performance because of excessive boundary comparisons.

```
typedef itk::Statistics::KdTreeGenerator< SampleType > TreeGeneratorType;
TreeGeneratorType::Pointer treeGenerator = TreeGeneratorType::New();

treeGenerator->SetSample( sample );
treeGenerator->SetBucketSize( 16 );
treeGenerator->Update();

typedef itk::Statistics::WeightedCentroidKdTreeGenerator< SampleType >
  CentroidTreeGeneratorType;

CentroidTreeGeneratorType::Pointer centroidTreeGenerator =
                               CentroidTreeGeneratorType::New();

centroidTreeGenerator->SetSample( sample );
centroidTreeGenerator->SetBucketSize( 16 );
centroidTreeGenerator->Update();
```

After the generation step, we can get the pointer to the kd-tree from the generator by calling the

GetOutput() method. To traverse a kd-tree, we have to use the GetRoot() method. The method will return the root node of the tree. Every node in a tree can have its left and/or right child node. To get the child node, we call the Left() or the Right() method of a node (these methods do not belong to the kd-tree but to the nodes).

We can get other information about a node by calling the methods described below in addition to the child node pointers.

```
typedef TreeGeneratorType::KdTreeType TreeType;
typedef TreeType::KdTreeNodeType        NodeType;

TreeType::Pointer tree = treeGenerator->GetOutput();
TreeType::Pointer centroidTree = centroidTreeGenerator->GetOutput();

NodeType* root = tree->GetRoot();

if ( root->IsTerminal() )
  {
  std::cout << "Root node is a terminal node." << std::endl;
  }
else
  {
  std::cout << "Root node is not a terminal node." << std::endl;
  }

unsigned int partitionDimension;
float partitionValue;
root->GetParameters( partitionDimension, partitionValue);
std::cout << "Dimension chosen to split the space = "
          << partitionDimension << std::endl;
std::cout << "Split point on the partition dimension = "
          << partitionValue << std::endl;

std::cout << "Address of the left chile of the root node = "
          << root->Left() << std::endl;

std::cout << "Address of the right chile of the root node = "
          << root->Right() << std::endl;

root = centroidTree->GetRoot();
std::cout << "Number of the measurement vectors under the root node"
          << " in the tree hierarchy = " << root->Size() << std::endl;

NodeType::CentroidType centroid;
root->GetWeightedCentroid( centroid );
std::cout << "Sum of the measurement vectors under the root node = "
          << centroid << std::endl;

std::cout << "Number of the measurement vectors under the left child"
          << " of the root node = " << root->Left()->Size() << std::endl;
```

In the following code snippet, we query the three nearest neighbors of the queryPoint on the two tree. The results and procedures are exactly the same for both. First we define the point from which distances will be measured.

```
MeasurementVectorType queryPoint;
queryPoint[0] = 10.0;
queryPoint[1] = 7.0;
```

Then we instantiate the type of a distance metric, create an object of this type and set the origin of coordinates for measuring distances. The GetMeasurementVectorSize() method returns the length of each measurement vector stored in the sample.

```
typedef itk::Statistics::EuclideanDistanceMetric< MeasurementVectorType >
  DistanceMetricType;
DistanceMetricType::Pointer distanceMetric = DistanceMetricType::New();

DistanceMetricType::OriginType origin( 2 );
for ( unsigned int i = 0; i < sample->GetMeasurementVectorSize(); ++i )
  {
  origin[i] = queryPoint[i];
  }
distanceMetric->SetOrigin( origin );
```

We can now set the number of neighbors to be located and the point coordinates to be used as a reference system.

```
unsigned int numberOfNeighbors = 3;
TreeType::InstanceIdentifierVectorType neighbors;
tree->Search( queryPoint, numberOfNeighbors, neighbors);

std::cout <<
  "\n*** kd-tree knn search result using an Euclidean distance metric:"
  << std::endl
  << "query point = [" << queryPoint << "]" << std::endl
  << "k = " << numberOfNeighbors << std::endl;
std::cout << "measurement vector : distance from querry point " << std::endl;
std::vector<double> distances1 (numberOfNeighbors);
for ( unsigned int i = 0; i < numberOfNeighbors; ++i )
  {
  distances1[i] =  distanceMetric->Evaluate(
    tree->GetMeasurementVector( neighbors[i] ));
  std::cout << "[" << tree->GetMeasurementVector( neighbors[i] )
            << "] : "
            << distances1[i]
            << std::endl;
  }
```

Instead of using an Euclidean distance metric, Tree itself can also return the distance vector. Here we get the distance values from tree and compare them with previous values.

```
std::vector<double> distances2;
tree->Search( queryPoint, numberOfNeighbors, neighbors, distances2 );

std::cout << "\n*** kd-tree knn search result directly from tree:"
          << std::endl
          << "query point = [" << queryPoint << "]" << std::endl
          << "k = " << numberOfNeighbors << std::endl;
std::cout << "measurement vector : distance from querry point " << std::endl;
for ( unsigned int i = 0; i < numberOfNeighbors; ++i )
  {
  std::cout << "[" << tree->GetMeasurementVector( neighbors[i] )
            << "] : "
            << distances2[i]
            << std::endl;
  if ( distances2[i] != distances1[i] )
    {
    std::cerr << "Mismatched distance values by tree." << std::endl;
    return -1;
    }
  }
```

As previously indicated, the interface for finding nearest neighbors in the centroid tree is very similar.

```
std::vector<double> distances3;
centroidTree->Search(
  queryPoint, numberOfNeighbors, neighbors, distances3 );

centroidTree->Search( queryPoint, numberOfNeighbors, neighbors );
std::cout << "\n*** Weighted centroid kd-tree knn search result:"
          << std::endl
          << "query point = [" << queryPoint << "]" << std::endl
          << "k = " << numberOfNeighbors << std::endl;
std::cout << "measurement vector : distance_by_distMetric : distance_by_tree"
          << std::endl;
std::vector<double> distances4 (numberOfNeighbors);
for ( unsigned int i = 0; i < numberOfNeighbors; ++i )
  {
  distances4[i] = distanceMetric->Evaluate(
    centroidTree->GetMeasurementVector( neighbors[i]));
  std::cout << "[" << centroidTree->GetMeasurementVector( neighbors[i] )
            << "]            :            "
            << distances4[i]
            << "            :            "
            << distances3[i]
            << std::endl;
  if ( distances2[i] != distances1[i] )
    {
    std::cerr << "Mismatched distance values by centroid tree." << std::endl;
    return -1;
    }
  }
```

KdTree also supports searching points within a hyper-spherical kernel. We specify the radius and call the Search() method. In the case of the KdTree, this is done with the following lines of code.

```
double radius = 437.0;

tree->Search( queryPoint, radius, neighbors );

std::cout << "\nSearching points within a hyper-spherical kernel:"
          << std::endl;
std::cout << "*** kd-tree radius search result:" << std::endl
          << "query point = [" << queryPoint << "]" << std::endl
          << "search radius = " << radius << std::endl;
std::cout << "measurement vector : distance" << std::endl;
for ( unsigned int i = 0; i < neighbors.size(); ++i )
  {
  std::cout << "[" << tree->GetMeasurementVector( neighbors[i] )
            << "] : "
            << distanceMetric->Evaluate(
                 tree->GetMeasurementVector( neighbors[i]))
            << std::endl;
  }
```

In the case of the centroid KdTree, the `Search()` method is used as illustrated by the following code.

```
centroidTree->Search( queryPoint, radius, neighbors );
std::cout << "\n*** Weighted centroid kd-tree radius search result:"
          << std::endl
          << "query point = [" << queryPoint << "]" << std::endl
          << "search radius = " << radius << std::endl;
std::cout << "measurement vector : distance" << std::endl;
for ( unsigned int i = 0; i < neighbors.size(); ++i )
  {
  std::cout << "[" << centroidTree->GetMeasurementVector( neighbors[i] )
            << "] : "
            << distanceMetric->Evaluate(
                 centroidTree->GetMeasurementVector( neighbors[i]))
            << std::endl;
  }
```

5.2   Algorithms and Functions

In the previous section, we described the data containers in the ITK statistics subsystem. We also need data processing algorithms and statistical functions to conduct statistical analysis or statistical classification using these containers. Here we define an algorithm to be an operation over a set of measurement vectors in a sample. A function is an operation over individual measurement vectors. For example, if we implement a class (itk::Statistics::EuclideanDistance) to calculate the Euclidean distance between two measurement vectors, we call it a function, while if we implemented a class (itk::Statistics::MeanCalculator) to calculate the mean of a sample, we call it an algorithm.

5.2.1   Sample Statistics

We will show how to get sample statistics such as means and covariance from the (itk::Statistics::Sample) classes. Statistics can tells us characteristics of a sample. Such sample statistics are very important for statistical classification. When we know the form of the sample distributions and their parameters (statistics), we can conduct Bayesian classification. In ITK, sample mean and covariance calculation algorithms are implemented. Each algorithm also has its weighted version (see Section 5.2.1). The weighted versions are used in the expectation-maximization parameter estimation process.

Mean and Covariance

The source code for this section can be found in the file
SampleStatistics.cxx.

We include the header file for the itk::Vector class that will be our measurement vector template in this example.

```
#include "itkVector.h"
```

We will use the itk::Statistics::ListSample as our sample template. We include the header for the class too.

```
#include "itkListSample.h"
```

The following headers are for sample statistics algorithms.

```
#include "itkMeanSampleFilter.h"
#include "itkCovarianceSampleFilter.h"
```

The following code snippet will create a ListSample object with three-component float measurement vectors and put five measurement vectors in the ListSample object.

```
const unsigned int MeasurementVectorLength = 3;
typedef itk::Vector< float, MeasurementVectorLength > MeasurementVectorType;
typedef itk::Statistics::ListSample< MeasurementVectorType > SampleType;
SampleType::Pointer sample = SampleType::New();
sample->SetMeasurementVectorSize( MeasurementVectorLength );
MeasurementVectorType mv;
mv[0] = 1.0;
mv[1] = 2.0;
mv[2] = 4.0;

sample->PushBack( mv );

mv[0] = 2.0;
mv[1] = 4.0;
mv[2] = 5.0;
sample->PushBack( mv );

mv[0] = 3.0;
mv[1] = 8.0;
mv[2] = 6.0;
sample->PushBack( mv );

mv[0] = 2.0;
mv[1] = 7.0;
mv[2] = 4.0;
sample->PushBack( mv );

mv[0] = 3.0;
mv[1] = 2.0;
mv[2] = 7.0;
sample->PushBack( mv );
```

To calculate the mean (vector) of a sample, we instantiate the itk::Statistics::MeanSampleFilter class that implements the mean algorithm and plug in the sample using the SetInputSample(sample*) method. By calling the Update() method, we run the algorithm. We get the mean vector using the GetMean() method. The output from the GetOutput() method is the pointer to the mean vector.

```
typedef itk::Statistics::MeanSampleFilter< SampleType > MeanAlgorithmType;

MeanAlgorithmType::Pointer meanAlgorithm = MeanAlgorithmType::New();

meanAlgorithm->SetInput( sample );
meanAlgorithm->Update();

std::cout << "Sample mean = " << meanAlgorithm->GetMean() << std::endl;
```

The covariance calculation algorithm will also calculate the mean while performing the covariance matrix calculation. The mean can be accessed using the GetMean() method while the covariance can be accessed using the GetCovarianceMatrix() method.

```
typedef itk::Statistics::CovarianceSampleFilter< SampleType >
  CovarianceAlgorithmType;
CovarianceAlgorithmType::Pointer covarianceAlgorithm =
  CovarianceAlgorithmType::New();

covarianceAlgorithm->SetInput( sample );
covarianceAlgorithm->Update();

std::cout << "Mean = " << std::endl;
std::cout << covarianceAlgorithm->GetMean() << std::endl;

std::cout << "Covariance = " << std::endl;
std::cout << covarianceAlgorithm->GetCovarianceMatrix() << std::endl;
```

Weighted Mean and Covariance

The source code for this section can be found in the file
WeightedSampleStatistics.cxx.

We include the header file for the itk::Vector class that will be our measurement vector template
in this example.

```
#include "itkVector.h"
```

We will use the itk::Statistics::ListSample as our sample template. We include the header
for the class too.

```
#include "itkListSample.h"
```

The following headers are for the weighted covariance algorithms.

```
#include "itkWeightedMeanSampleFilter.h"
#include "itkWeightedCovarianceSampleFilter.h"
```

The following code snippet will create a ListSample instance with three-component float measurement vectors and put five measurement vectors in the ListSample object.

```
typedef itk::Statistics::ListSample< MeasurementVectorType > SampleType;
SampleType::Pointer sample = SampleType::New();
sample->SetMeasurementVectorSize( 3 );
MeasurementVectorType mv;
mv[0] = 1.0;
mv[1] = 2.0;
mv[2] = 4.0;

sample->PushBack( mv );

mv[0] = 2.0;
mv[1] = 4.0;
mv[2] = 5.0;
sample->PushBack( mv );

mv[0] = 3.0;
mv[1] = 8.0;
mv[2] = 6.0;
sample->PushBack( mv );

mv[0] = 2.0;
mv[1] = 7.0;
mv[2] = 4.0;
sample->PushBack( mv );

mv[0] = 3.0;
mv[1] = 2.0;
mv[2] = 7.0;
sample->PushBack( mv );
```

Robust versions of covariance algorithms require weight values for measurement vectors. We have two ways of providing weight values for the weighted mean and weighted covariance algorithms.

The first method is to plug in an array of weight values. The size of the weight value array should be equal to that of the measurement vectors. In both algorithms, we use the SetWeights(weights).

```
typedef itk::Statistics::WeightedMeanSampleFilter< SampleType >
  WeightedMeanAlgorithmType;

WeightedMeanAlgorithmType::WeightArrayType weightArray( sample->Size() );
weightArray.Fill( 0.5 );
weightArray[2] = 0.01;
weightArray[4] = 0.01;

WeightedMeanAlgorithmType::Pointer weightedMeanAlgorithm =
                                    WeightedMeanAlgorithmType::New();

weightedMeanAlgorithm->SetInput( sample );
weightedMeanAlgorithm->SetWeights( weightArray );
weightedMeanAlgorithm->Update();

std::cout << "Sample weighted mean = "
          << weightedMeanAlgorithm->GetMean() << std::endl;

typedef itk::Statistics::WeightedCovarianceSampleFilter< SampleType >
                                    WeightedCovarianceAlgorithmType;

WeightedCovarianceAlgorithmType::Pointer weightedCovarianceAlgorithm =
                              WeightedCovarianceAlgorithmType::New();

weightedCovarianceAlgorithm->SetInput( sample );
weightedCovarianceAlgorithm->SetWeights( weightArray );
weightedCovarianceAlgorithm->Update();

std::cout << "Sample weighted covariance = " << std::endl;
std::cout << weightedCovarianceAlgorithm->GetCovarianceMatrix() << std::endl;
```

The second method for computing weighted statistics is to plug-in a function that returns a weight value that is usually a function of each measurement vector. Since the `weightedMeanAlgorithm` and `weightedCovarianceAlgorithm` already have the input sample plugged in, we only need to call the `SetWeightingFunction(weights)` method.

```
ExampleWeightFunction::Pointer weightFunction = ExampleWeightFunction::New();

weightedMeanAlgorithm->SetWeightingFunction( weightFunction );
weightedMeanAlgorithm->Update();

std::cout << "Sample weighted mean = "
          << weightedMeanAlgorithm->GetMean() << std::endl;

weightedCovarianceAlgorithm->SetWeightingFunction( weightFunction );
weightedCovarianceAlgorithm->Update();

std::cout << "Sample weighted covariance = " << std::endl;
std::cout << weightedCovarianceAlgorithm->GetCovarianceMatrix();

std::cout << "Sample weighted mean (from WeightedCovarainceSampleFilter) = "
          << std::endl << weightedCovarianceAlgorithm->GetMean()
          << std::endl;
```

5.2.2 Sample Generation

SampleToHistogramFilter

The source code for this section can be found in the file
SampleToHistogramFilter.cxx.

Sometimes we want to work with a histogram instead of a list of measurement vectors (e.g.
itk::Statistics::ListSample, itk::Statistics::ImageToListSampleAdaptor,
or itk::Statistics::PointSetToListSample) to use less memory or to
perform a particular type od analysis. In such cases, we can import data
from a sample type to a itk::Statistics::Histogram object using the
itk::Statistics::SampleToHistogramFiler.

We use a ListSample object as the input for the filter. We include the header files for the ListSample
and Histogram classes, as well as the filter.

```
#include "itkListSample.h"
#include "itkHistogram.h"
#include "itkSampleToHistogramFilter.h"
```

We need another header for the type of the measurement vectors. We are going to use the
itk::Vector class which is a subclass of the itk::FixedArray in this example.

```
#include "itkVector.h"
```

The following code snippet creates a ListSample object with two-component int measurement vectors and put the measurement vectors: [1,1] - 1 time, [2,2] - 2 times, [3,3] - 3 times, [4,4] - 4 times,
[5,5] - 5 times into the listSample.

```
typedef int MeasurementType;
const unsigned int MeasurementVectorLength = 2;
typedef itk::Vector< MeasurementType , MeasurementVectorLength >
                                               MeasurementVectorType;

typedef itk::Statistics::ListSample< MeasurementVectorType > ListSampleType;
ListSampleType::Pointer listSample = ListSampleType::New();
listSample->SetMeasurementVectorSize( MeasurementVectorLength );

MeasurementVectorType mv;
for ( unsigned int i = 1; i < 6; i++ )
  {
  for ( unsigned int j = 0; j < 2; j++ )
    {
    mv[j] = ( MeasurementType ) i;
    }
  for ( unsigned int j = 0; j < i; j++ )
    {
    listSample->PushBack(mv);
    }
  }
```

Here, we set up the size and bound of the output histogram.

```
typedef float HistogramMeasurementType;
const unsigned int numberOfComponents = 2;
typedef itk::Statistics::Histogram< HistogramMeasurementType >
  HistogramType;

HistogramType::SizeType size( numberOfComponents );
size.Fill(5);

HistogramType::MeasurementVectorType lowerBound( numberOfComponents );
HistogramType::MeasurementVectorType upperBound( numberOfComponents );

lowerBound[0] = 0.5;
lowerBound[1] = 0.5;

upperBound[0] = 5.5;
upperBound[1] = 5.5;
```

Now, we set up the `SampleToHistogramFilter` object by passing `listSample` as the input and initializing the histogram size and bounds with the `SetHistogramSize()`, `SetHistogramBinMinimum()`, and `SetHistogramBinMaximum()` methods. We execute the filter by calling the `Update()` method.

```
typedef itk::Statistics::SampleToHistogramFilter< ListSampleType,
                       HistogramType > FilterType;
FilterType::Pointer filter = FilterType::New();

filter->SetInput( listSample );
filter->SetHistogramSize( size );
filter->SetHistogramBinMinimum( lowerBound );
filter->SetHistogramBinMaximum( upperBound );
filter->Update();
```

The `Size()` and `GetTotalFrequency()` methods return the same values as the `sample` does.

```
const HistogramType* histogram = filter->GetOutput();

HistogramType::ConstIterator iter = histogram->Begin();
while ( iter != histogram->End() )
  {
  std::cout << "Measurement vectors = " << iter.GetMeasurementVector()
          << " frequency = " << iter.GetFrequency() << std::endl;
  ++iter;
  }

std::cout << "Size = " << histogram->Size() << std::endl;
std::cout << "Total frequency = "
          << histogram->GetTotalFrequency() << std::endl;
```

NeighborhoodSampler

The source code for this section can be found in the file
`NeighborhoodSampler.cxx`.

When we want to create an `itk::Statistics::Subsample` object that includes only the measurement vectors within a radius from a center in a sample, we can use

the   itk::Statistics::NeighborhoodSampler.   In this example, we will use the
itk::Statistics::ListSample as the input sample.

We include the header files for the ListSample and the NeighborhoodSampler classes.

```
#include "itkListSample.h"
#include "itkNeighborhoodSampler.h"
```

We need another header for measurement vectors. We are going to use the itk::Vector class which
is a subclass of the itk::FixedArray.

```
#include "itkVector.h"
```

The following code snippet will create a ListSample object with two-component int measurement
vectors and put the measurement vectors: [1,1] - 1 time, [2,2] - 2 times, [3,3] - 3 times, [4,4] - 4
times, [5,5] - 5 times into the listSample.

```
typedef int MeasurementType;
const unsigned int MeasurementVectorLength = 2;
typedef itk::Vector< MeasurementType , MeasurementVectorLength >
                                              MeasurementVectorType;
typedef itk::Statistics::ListSample< MeasurementVectorType > SampleType;
SampleType::Pointer sample = SampleType::New();
sample->SetMeasurementVectorSize( MeasurementVectorLength );

MeasurementVectorType mv;
for ( unsigned int i = 1; i < 6; i++ )
  {
  for ( unsigned int j = 0; j < 2; j++ )
    {
    mv[j] = ( MeasurementType ) i;
    }
  for ( unsigned int j = 0; j < i; j++ )
    {
    sample->PushBack(mv);
    }
  }
```

We plug-in the sample to the NeighborhoodSampler using the SetInputSample(sample*). The
two required inputs for the NeighborhoodSampler are a center and a radius. We set these two inputs using the SetCenter(center vector*) and the SetRadius(double*) methods respectively.
And then we call the Update() method to generate the Subsample object. This sampling procedure subsamples measurement vectors within a hyper-spherical kernel that has the center and radius
specified.

```
typedef itk::Statistics::NeighborhoodSampler< SampleType > SamplerType;
SamplerType::Pointer sampler = SamplerType::New();

sampler->SetInputSample( sample );
SamplerType::CenterType center( MeasurementVectorLength );
center[0] = 3;
center[1] = 3;
double radius = 1.5;
sampler->SetCenter( &center );
sampler->SetRadius( &radius );
sampler->Update();

SamplerType::OutputType::Pointer output = sampler->GetOutput();
```

The `SamplerType::OutputType` is in fact `itk::Statistics::Subsample`. The following code prints out the resampled measurement vectors.

```
SamplerType::OutputType::Iterator iter = output->Begin();
while ( iter != output->End() )
  {
  std::cout << "instance identifier = " << iter.GetInstanceIdentifier()
            << "\t measurement vector = "
            << iter.GetMeasurementVector()
            << "\t frequency = "
            << iter.GetFrequency() << std::endl;
  ++iter;
  }
```

5.2.3 Sample Sorting

The source code for this section can be found in the file
SampleSorting.cxx.

Sometimes we want to sort the measurement vectors in a sample. The sorted vectors may reveal some characteristics of the sample. The *insert sort*, the *heap sort*, and the *introspective sort* algorithms [43] for samples are implemented in ITK. To learn pros and cons of each algorithm, please refer to [19]. ITK also offers the *quick select* algorithm.

Among the subclasses of the `itk::Statistics::Sample`, only the class `itk::Statistics::Subsample` allows users to change the order of the measurement vector. Therefore, we must create a Subsample to do any sorting or selecting.

We include the header files for the `itk::Statistics::ListSample` and the `Subsample` classes.

```
#include "itkListSample.h"
```

The sorting and selecting related functions are in the include file itkStatisticsAlgorithm.h. Note that all functions in this file are in the `itk::Statistics::Algorithm` namespace.

```
#include "itkStatisticsAlgorithm.h"
```

We need another header for measurement vectors. We are going to use the `itk::Vector` class which is a subclass of the `itk::FixedArray` in this example.

We define the types of the measurement vectors, the sample, and the subsample.

```
#include "itkVector.h"
```

We define two functions for convenience. The first one clears the content of the subsample and fill it with the measurement vectors from the sample.

```
void initializeSubsample(SubsampleType* subsample, SampleType* sample)
{
  subsample->Clear();
  subsample->SetSample(sample);
  subsample->InitializeWithAllInstances();
}
```

The second one prints out the content of the subsample using the Subsample's iterator interface.

```
void printSubsample(SubsampleType* subsample, const char* header)
{
  std::cout << std::endl;
  std::cout << header << std::endl;
  SubsampleType::Iterator iter = subsample->Begin();
  while ( iter != subsample->End() )
    {
    std::cout << "instance identifier = " << iter.GetInstanceIdentifier()
              << " \t measurement vector = "
              << iter.GetMeasurementVector()
              << std::endl;
    ++iter;
    }
}
```

The following code snippet will create a ListSample object with two-component int measurement vectors and put the measurement vectors: [5,5] - 5 times, [4,4] - 4 times, [3,3] - 3 times, [2,2] - 2 times,[1,1] - 1 time into the sample.

```
SampleType::Pointer sample = SampleType::New();

MeasurementVectorType mv;
for ( unsigned int i = 5; i > 0; --i )
  {
  for (unsigned int j = 0; j < 2; j++ )
    {
    mv[j] = ( MeasurementType ) i;
    }
  for ( unsigned int j = 0; j < i; j++ )
    {
    sample->PushBack(mv);
    }
  }
```

We create a Subsample object and plug-in the sample.

```
SubsampleType::Pointer subsample = SubsampleType::New();
subsample->SetSample(sample);
initializeSubsample(subsample, sample);
printSubsample(subsample, "Unsorted");
```

The common parameters to all the algorithms are the Subsample object (subsample), the dimension (activeDimension) that will be considered for the sorting or selecting (only the component belonging to the dimension of the measurement vectors will be considered), the beginning index, and the ending index of the measurement vectors in the subsample. The sorting or selecting algorithms are applied only to the range specified by the beginning index and the ending index. The ending index should be the actual last index plus one.

The itk::InsertSort function does not require any other optional arguments. The following function call will sort the all measurement vectors in the subsample. The beginning index is 0, and the ending index is the number of the measurement vectors in the subsample.

```
int activeDimension = 0;
itk::Statistics::Algorithm::InsertSort< SubsampleType >( subsample,
                        activeDimension, 0, subsample->Size() );
printSubsample(subsample, "InsertSort");
```

We sort the subsample using the heap sort algorithm. The arguments are identical to those of the insert sort.

```
initializeSubsample(subsample, sample);
itk::Statistics::Algorithm::HeapSort< SubsampleType >( subsample,
                        activeDimension, 0, subsample->Size() );
printSubsample(subsample, "HeapSort");
```

The introspective sort algorithm needs an additional argument that specifies when to stop the introspective sort loop and sort the fragment of the sample using the heap sort algorithm. Since we set the threshold value as 16, when the sort loop reach the point where the number of measurement vectors in a sort loop is not greater than 16, it will sort that fragment using the insert sort algorithm.

```
initializeSubsample(subsample, sample);
itk::Statistics::Algorithm::IntrospectiveSort< SubsampleType >
                    ( subsample, activeDimension, 0, subsample->Size(), 16 );
printSubsample(subsample, "IntrospectiveSort");
```

We query the median of the measurements along the activeDimension. The last argument tells the algorithm that we want to get the subsample->Size()/2-th element along the activeDimension. The quick select algorithm changes the order of the measurement vectors.

```
initializeSubsample(subsample, sample);
SubsampleType::MeasurementType median =
        itk::Statistics::Algorithm::QuickSelect< SubsampleType >( subsample,
                                    activeDimension,
                                    0, subsample->Size(),
                                    subsample->Size()/2 );
std::cout << std::endl;
std::cout << "Quick Select: median = " << median << std::endl;
```

5.2.4   Probability Density Functions

The probability density function (PDF) for a specific distribution returns the probability density for a measurement vector. To get the probability density from a PDF, we use the Evaluate(input) method. PDFs for different distributions require different sets of distribution parameters. Before calling the Evaluate() method, make sure to set the proper values for the distribution parameters.

Gaussian Distribution

The source code for this section can be found in the file
`GaussianMembershipFunction.cxx`.

The Gaussian probability density function `itk::Statistics::GaussianMembershipFunction`
requires two distribution parameters—the mean vector and the covariance matrix.

We include the header files for the class and the `itk::Vector`.

```
#include "itkVector.h"
#include "itkGaussianMembershipFunction.h"
```

We define the type of the measurement vector that will be input to the Gaussian membership function.

```
typedef itk::Vector< float, 2 > MeasurementVectorType;
```

The instantiation of the function is done through the usual `New()` method and a smart pointer.

```
typedef itk::Statistics::GaussianMembershipFunction< MeasurementVectorType >
  DensityFunctionType;
DensityFunctionType::Pointer densityFunction = DensityFunctionType::New();
```

The length of the measurement vectors in the membership function, in this case a
vector of length 2, is specified using the `SetMeasurementVectorSize()` method.

```
densityFunction->SetMeasurementVectorSize( 2 );
```

We create the two distribution parameters and set them. The mean is [0, 0], and the covariance matrix
is a 2 x 2 matrix:

$$\begin{pmatrix} 4 & 0 \\ 0 & 4 \end{pmatrix}$$

We obtain the probability density for the measurement vector: [0, 0] using the
`Evaluate(measurement vector)` method and print it out.

```
DensityFunctionType::MeanVectorType mean( 2 );
mean.Fill( 0.0 );

DensityFunctionType::CovarianceMatrixType cov;
cov.SetSize( 2, 2 );
cov.SetIdentity();
cov *= 4;

densityFunction->SetMean( mean );
densityFunction->SetCovariance( cov );

MeasurementVectorType mv;
mv.Fill( 0 );

std::cout << densityFunction->Evaluate( mv ) << std::endl;
```

5.2.5   Distance Metric

Euclidean Distance

The source code for this section can be found in the file
EuclideanDistanceMetric.cxx.

The Euclidean distance function (itk::Statistics::EuclideanDistanceMetric requires as
template parameter the type of the measurement vector. We can use this function for any subclass of
the itk::FixedArray. As a subclass of the itk::Statistics::DistanceMetric, it has two basic methods, the SetOrigin(measurement vector) and the Evaluate(measurement vector).
The Evaluate() method returns the distance between its argument (a measurement vector) and the
measurement vector set by the SetOrigin() method.

In addition to the two methods, EuclideanDistanceMetric has two more methods that return the
distance of two measurements — Evaluate(measurement vector, measurement vector) and
the coordinate distance between two measurements (not vectors) — Evaluate(measurement,
measurement). The argument type of the latter method is the type of the component of the measurement vector.

We include the header files for the class and the itk::Vector.

```
#include "itkVector.h"
#include "itkArray.h"
#include "itkEuclideanDistanceMetric.h"
```

We define the type of the measurement vector that will be input of the Euclidean distance function.
As a result, the measurement type is float.

```
typedef itk::Array< float > MeasurementVectorType;
```

The instantiation of the function is done through the usual New() method and a smart pointer.

```
typedef itk::Statistics::EuclideanDistanceMetric< MeasurementVectorType >
  DistanceMetricType;
DistanceMetricType::Pointer distanceMetric = DistanceMetricType::New();
```

We create three measurement vectors, the originPoint, the queryPointA, and the queryPointB.
The type of the originPoint is fixed in the itk::Statistics::DistanceMetric
base class as itk::Vector< double, length of the measurement vector of the each
distance metric instance>.

The Distance metric does not know about the length of the measurement vectors. We must set it
explicitly using the SetMeasurementVectorSize() method.

```
DistanceMetricType::OriginType originPoint( 2 );
MeasurementVectorType queryPointA( 2 );
MeasurementVectorType queryPointB( 2 );

originPoint[0] = 0;
originPoint[1] = 0;

queryPointA[0] = 2;
queryPointA[1] = 2;

queryPointB[0] = 3;
queryPointB[1] = 3;
```

In the following code snippet, we show the uses of the three different `Evaluate()` methods.

```
distanceMetric->SetOrigin( originPoint );
std::cout << "Euclidean distance between the origin and the query point A = "
          << distanceMetric->Evaluate( queryPointA )
          << std::endl;

std::cout << "Euclidean distance between the two query points (A and B) = "
          << distanceMetric->Evaluate( queryPointA, queryPointB )
          << std::endl;

std::cout << "Coordinate distance between "
          << "the first components of the two query points = "
          << distanceMetric->Evaluate( queryPointA[0], queryPointB[0] )
          << std::endl;
```

5.2.6 Decision Rules

A decision rule is a function that returns the index of one data element in a vector of data elements. The index returned depends on the internal logic of each decision rule. The decision rule is an essential part of the ITK statistical classification framework. The scores from a set of membership functions (e.g. probability density functions, distance metrics) are compared by a decision rule and a class label is assigned based on the output of the decision rule. The common interface is very simple. Any decision rule class must implement the `Evaluate()` method. In addition to this method, certain decision rule class can have additional method that accepts prior knowledge about the decision task. The `itk::MaximumRatioDecisionRule` is an example of such a class.

The argument type for the `Evaluate()` method is `std::vector< double >`. The decision rule classes are part of the `itk` namespace instead of `itk::Statistics` namespace.

For a project that uses a decision rule, it must link the `itkCommon` library. Decision rules are not templated classes.

Maximum Decision Rule

The source code for this section can be found in the file
`MaximumDecisionRule.cxx`.

The `itk::MaximumDecisionRule` returns the index of the largest discriminant score among the discriminant scores in the vector of discriminant scores that is the input argument of the `Evaluate()` method.

To begin the example, we include the header files for the class and the MaximumDecisionRule. We also include the header file for the `std::vector` class that will be the container for the discriminant scores.

```
#include "itkMaximumDecisionRule.h"
#include <vector>
```

The instantiation of the function is done through the usual `New()` method and a smart pointer.

```
typedef itk::Statistics::MaximumDecisionRule DecisionRuleType;
DecisionRuleType::Pointer decisionRule = DecisionRuleType::New();
```

We create the discriminant score vector and fill it with three values.   The `Evaluate(` `discriminantScores` `)` will return 2 because the third value is the largest value.

```
DecisionRuleType::MembershipVectorType discriminantScores;
discriminantScores.push_back( 0.1 );
discriminantScores.push_back( 0.3 );
discriminantScores.push_back( 0.6 );

std::cout << "MaximumDecisionRule: The index of the chosen = "
          << decisionRule->Evaluate( discriminantScores )
          << std::endl;
```

Minimum Decision Rule

The source code for this section can be found in the file `MinimumDecisionRule.cxx`.

The `Evaluate()` method of the `itk::MinimumDecisionRule` returns the index of the smallest discriminant score among the vector of discriminant scores that it receives as input.

To begin this example, we include the class header file. We also include the header file for the `std::vector` class that will be the container for the discriminant scores.

```
#include "itkMinimumDecisionRule.h"
#include <vector>
```

The instantiation of the function is done through the usual `New()` method and a smart pointer.

```
typedef itk::Statistics::MinimumDecisionRule DecisionRuleType;
DecisionRuleType::Pointer decisionRule = DecisionRuleType::New();
```

We create the discriminant score vector and fill it with three values.   The call `Evaluate(` `discriminantScores` `)` will return 0 because the first value is the smallest value.

```
DecisionRuleType::MembershipVectorType discriminantScores;
discriminantScores.push_back( 0.1 );
discriminantScores.push_back( 0.3 );
discriminantScores.push_back( 0.6 );

std::cout << "MinimumDecisionRule: The index of the chosen = "
          << decisionRule->Evaluate( discriminantScores )
          << std::endl;
```

Maximum Ratio Decision Rule

The source code for this section can be found in the file
`MaximumRatioDecisionRule.cxx`.

MaximumRatioDecisionRule returns the class label using a Bayesian style decision rule. The discriminant scores are evaluated in the context of class priors. If the discriminant scores are actual conditional probabilites (likelihoods) and the class priors are actual a priori class probabilities, then this decision rule operates as Bayes rule, returning the class i if

$$p(x|i)p(i) > p(x|j)p(j) \tag{5.1}$$

for all class j. The discriminant scores and priors are not required to be true probabilities.

This class is named the MaximumRatioDecisionRule as it can be implemented as returning the class i if

$$\frac{p(x|i)}{p(x|j)} > \frac{p(j)}{p(i)} \tag{5.2}$$

for all class j.

We include the header files for the class as well as the header file for the `std::vector` class that will be the container for the discriminant scores.

```
#include "itkMaximumRatioDecisionRule.h"
#include <vector>
```

The instantiation of the function is done through the usual `New()` method and a smart pointer.

```
typedef itk::Statistics::MaximumRatioDecisionRule DecisionRuleType;
DecisionRuleType::Pointer decisionRule = DecisionRuleType::New();
```

We create the discriminant score vector and fill it with three values. We also create a vector (aPrioris) for the *a priori* values. The `Evaluate( discriminantScores )` will return 1.

```
DecisionRuleType::MembershipVectorType discriminantScores;
discriminantScores.push_back( 0.1 );
discriminantScores.push_back( 0.3 );
discriminantScores.push_back( 0.6 );

DecisionRuleType::PriorProbabilityVectorType aPrioris;
aPrioris.push_back( 0.1 );
aPrioris.push_back( 0.8 );
aPrioris.push_back( 0.1 );

decisionRule->SetPriorProbabilities( aPrioris );
std::cout << "MaximumRatioDecisionRule: The index of the chosen = "
          << decisionRule->Evaluate( discriminantScores )
          << std::endl;
```

5.2.7   Random Variable Generation

A random variable generation class returns a variate when the `GetVariate()` method is called. When we repeatedly call the method for "enough" times, the set of variates we will get follows the distribution form of the random variable generation class.

Normal (Gaussian) Distribution

The source code for this section can be found in the file
`NormalVariateGenerator.cxx`.

The `itk::Statistics::NormalVariateGenerator` generates random variables according to the standard normal distribution (mean = 0, standard deviation = 1).

To use the class in a project, we must link the `itkStatistics` library to the project.

To begin the example we include the header file for the class.

```
#include "itkNormalVariateGenerator.h"
```

The NormalVariateGenerator is a non-templated class. We simply call the `New()` method to create an instance. Then, we provide the seed value using the `Initialize(seed value)`.

```
typedef itk::Statistics::NormalVariateGenerator GeneratorType;
GeneratorType::Pointer generator = GeneratorType::New();
generator->Initialize( (int) 2003 );

for ( unsigned int i = 0; i < 50; ++i )
  {
  std::cout << i << " : \t" << generator->GetVariate() << std::endl;
  }
```

5.3 Statistics applied to Images

5.3.1 Image Histograms

Scalar Image Histogram with Adaptor

The source code for this section can be found in the file
`ImageHistogram1.cxx`.

This example shows how to compute the histogram of a scalar image. Since the
statistics framework classes operate on Samples and ListOfSamples, we need to introduce a class that will make the image look like a list of samples. This class is the
`itk::Statistics::ImageToListSampleAdaptor`. Once we have connected this adaptor to an
image, we can proceed to use the `itk::Statistics::SampleToHistogramFilter` in order to
compute the histogram of the image.

First, we need to include the headers for the `itk::Statistics::ImageToListSampleAdaptor`
and the `itk::Image` classes.

```
#include "itkImageToListSampleAdaptor.h"
#include "itkImage.h"
```

Now we include the headers for the `Histogram`, the `SampleToHistogramFilter`, and the reader
that we will use for reading the image from a file.

```
#include "itkImageFileReader.h"
#include "itkHistogram.h"
#include "itkSampleToHistogramFilter.h"
```

The image type must be defined using the typical pair of pixel type and dimension specification.

```
typedef unsigned char        PixelType;
const unsigned int           Dimension = 2;

typedef itk::Image<PixelType, Dimension > ImageType;
```

Using the same image type we instantiate the type of the image reader that will provide the image
source for our example.

```
typedef itk::ImageFileReader< ImageType > ReaderType;

ReaderType::Pointer reader = ReaderType::New();

reader->SetFileName( argv[1] );
```

Now we introduce the central piece of this example, which is the use of the adaptor that will present
the `itk::Image` as if it was a list of samples. We instantiate the type of the adaptor by using the
actual image type. Then construct the adaptor by invoking its `New()` method and assigning the result
to the corresponding smart pointer. Finally we connect the output of the image reader to the input of
the adaptor.

```
typedef itk::Statistics::ImageToListSampleAdaptor< ImageType >    AdaptorType;

AdaptorType::Pointer adaptor = AdaptorType::New();

adaptor->SetImage( reader->GetOutput() );
```

You must keep in mind that adaptors are not pipeline objects. This means that they do not propagate update calls. It is therefore your responsibility to make sure that you invoke the Update() method of the reader before you attempt to use the output of the adaptor. As usual, this must be done inside a try/catch block because the read operation can potentially throw exceptions.

```
try
  {
  reader->Update();
  }
catch( itk::ExceptionObject & excp )
  {
  std::cerr << "Problem reading image file : " << argv[1] << std::endl;
  std::cerr << excp << std::endl;
  return -1;
  }
```

At this point, we are ready for instantiating the type of the histogram filter. We must first declare the type of histogram we wish to use. The adaptor type is also used as template parameter of the filter. Having instantiated this type, we proceed to create one filter by invoking its New() method.

```
typedef PixelType HistogramMeasurementType;
typedef itk::Statistics::Histogram< HistogramMeasurementType >
  HistogramType;
typedef itk::Statistics::SampleToHistogramFilter<
                                          AdaptorType,
                                          HistogramType>
                                          FilterType;

FilterType::Pointer filter = FilterType::New();
```

We define now the characteristics of the Histogram that we want to compute. This typically includes the size of each one of the component, but given that in this simple example we are dealing with a scalar image, then our histogram will have a single component. For the sake of generality, however, we use the HistogramType as defined inside of the Generator type. We define also the marginal scale factor that will control the precision used when assigning values to histogram bins. Finally we invoke the Update() method in the filter.

```
const unsigned int numberOfComponents = 1;
HistogramType::SizeType size( numberOfComponents );
size.Fill( 255 );

filter->SetInput( adaptor );
filter->SetHistogramSize( size );
filter->SetMarginalScale( 10 );

HistogramType::MeasurementVectorType min( numberOfComponents );
HistogramType::MeasurementVectorType max( numberOfComponents );

min.Fill( 0 );
max.Fill( 255 );

filter->SetHistogramBinMinimum( min );
filter->SetHistogramBinMaximum( max );

filter->Update();
```

Now we are ready for using the image histogram for any further processing. The histogram is obtained from the filter by invoking the `GetOutput()` method.

```
HistogramType::ConstPointer histogram = filter->GetOutput();
```

In this current example we simply print out the frequency values of all the bins in the image histogram.

```
const unsigned int histogramSize = histogram->Size();

std::cout << "Histogram size " << histogramSize << std::endl;

for( unsigned int bin=0; bin < histogramSize; bin++ )
  {
  std::cout << "bin = " << bin << " frequency = ";
  std::cout << histogram->GetFrequency( bin, 0 ) <<std::endl;
  }
```

Scalar Image Histogram with Generator

The source code for this section can be found in the file
`ImageHistogram2.cxx`.

From the previous example you will have noticed that there is a significant number of operations to perform to compute the simple histogram of a scalar image. Given that this is a relatively common operation, it is convenient to encapsulate many of these operations in a single helper class.

The `itk::Statistics::ScalarImageToHistogramGenerator` is the result of such encapsulation. This example illustrates how to compute the histogram of a scalar image using this helper class.

We should first include the header of the histogram generator and the image class.

```
#include "itkScalarImageToHistogramGenerator.h"
#include "itkImage.h"
```

The image type must be defined using the typical pair of pixel type and dimension specification.

```
typedef unsigned char       PixelType;
const unsigned int          Dimension = 2;

typedef itk::Image<PixelType, Dimension > ImageType;
```

We use now the image type in order to instantiate the type of the corresponding histogram generator class, and invoke its New() method in order to construct one.

```
typedef itk::Statistics::ScalarImageToHistogramGenerator<
                         ImageType >   HistogramGeneratorType;

HistogramGeneratorType::Pointer histogramGenerator =
                               HistogramGeneratorType::New();
```

The image to be passed as input to the histogram generator is taken in this case from the output of an image reader.

```
histogramGenerator->SetInput(  reader->GetOutput() );
```

We define also the typical parameters that specify the characteristics of the histogram to be computed.

```
histogramGenerator->SetNumberOfBins( 256 );
histogramGenerator->SetMarginalScale( 10.0 );

histogramGenerator->SetHistogramMin(  -0.5 );
histogramGenerator->SetHistogramMax( 255.5 );
```

Finally we trigger the computation of the histogram by invoking the Compute() method of the generator. Note again, that a generator is not a pipeline object and therefore it is up to you to make sure that the filters providing the input image have been updated.

```
histogramGenerator->Compute();
```

The resulting histogram can be obtained from the generator by invoking its GetOutput() method. It is also convenient to get the Histogram type from the traits of the generator type itself as shown in the code below.

```
typedef HistogramGeneratorType::HistogramType  HistogramType;

const HistogramType * histogram = histogramGenerator->GetOutput();
```

In this case we simply print out the frequency values of the histogram. These values can be accessed by using iterators.

```
HistogramType::ConstIterator itr = histogram->Begin();
HistogramType::ConstIterator end = histogram->End();

unsigned int binNumber = 0;
while( itr != end )
  {
  std::cout << "bin = " << binNumber << " frequency = ";
  std::cout << itr.GetFrequency() << std::endl;
  ++itr;
  ++binNumber;
  }
```

Color Image Histogram with Generator

The source code for this section can be found in the file
ImageHistogram3.cxx.

By now, you are probably thinking that the statistics framework in ITK is too complex for simply computing histograms from images. Here we illustrate that the benefit for this complexity is the power that these methods provide for dealing with more complex and realistic uses of image statistics than the trivial 256-bin histogram of 8-bit images that most software packages provide. One of such cases is the computation of histograms from multi-component images such as Vector images and color images.

This example shows how to compute the histogram of an RGB image by using the helper class ImageToHistogramFilter. In this first example we compute the histogram of each channel independently.

We start by including the header of the itk::Statistics::ImageToHistogramFilter, as well as the headers for the image class and the RGBPixel class.

```
#include "itkImageToHistogramFilter.h"
#include "itkImage.h"
#include "itkRGBPixel.h"
```

The type of the RGB image is defined by first instantiating a RGBPixel and then using the image dimension specification.

```
typedef unsigned char                            PixelComponentType;

typedef itk::RGBPixel< PixelComponentType >  RGBPixelType;

const unsigned int                           Dimension = 2;

typedef itk::Image< RGBPixelType, Dimension > RGBImageType;
```

Using the RGB image type we can instantiate the type of the corresponding histogram filter and construct one filter by invoking its New() method.

```
typedef itk::Statistics::ImageToHistogramFilter<
                    RGBImageType >   HistogramFilterType;

HistogramFilterType::Pointer histogramFilter =
                              HistogramFilterType::New();
```

The parameters of the histogram must be defined now. Probably the most important one is the arrangement of histogram bins. This is provided to the histogram through a size array. The type of the array can be taken from the traits of the HistogramFilterType type. We create one instance of the size object and fill in its content. In this particular case, the three components of the size array will correspond to the number of bins used for each one of the RGB components in the color image. The following lines show how to define a histogram on the red component of the image while disregarding the green and blue components.

```
typedef HistogramFilterType::HistogramSizeType   SizeType;

SizeType size( 3 );

size[0] = 255;        // number of bins for the Red    channel
size[1] =   1;        // number of bins for the Green channel
size[2] =   1;        // number of bins for the Blue   channel

histogramFilter->SetHistogramSize( size );
```

The marginal scale must be defined in the filter. This will determine the precision in the assignment of values to the histogram bins.

```
histogramFilter->SetMarginalScale( 10.0 );
```

Finally, we must specify the upper and lower bounds for the histogram. This can either be done manually using the SetHistogramBinMinimum() and SetHistogramBinMaximum() methods or it can be done automatically by calling SetHistogramAutoMinimumMaximum(true). Here we use the manual method.

```
HistogramFilterType::HistogramMeasurementVectorType lowerBound( 3 );
HistogramFilterType::HistogramMeasurementVectorType upperBound( 3 );

lowerBound[0] = 0;
lowerBound[1] = 0;
lowerBound[2] = 0;
upperBound[0] = 256;
upperBound[1] = 256;
upperBound[2] = 256;

histogramFilter->SetHistogramBinMinimum( lowerBound );
histogramFilter->SetHistogramBinMaximum( upperBound );
```

The input of the filter is taken from an image reader, and the computation of the histogram is triggered by invoking the Update() method of the filter.

```
histogramFilter->SetInput(  reader->GetOutput()  );

histogramFilter->Update();
```

We can now access the results of the histogram computation by declaring a pointer to histogram and getting its value from the filter using the GetOutput() method. Note that here we use a const HistogramType pointer instead of a const smart pointer because we are sure that the filter is not going to be destroyed while we access the values of the histogram. Depending on what you are doing, it may be safer to assign the histogram to a const smart pointer as shown in previous examples.

```
typedef HistogramFilterType::HistogramType  HistogramType;

const HistogramType * histogram = histogramFilter->GetOutput();
```

Just for the sake of exercising the experimental method [49], we verify that the resulting histogram actually have the size that we requested when we configured the filter. This can be done by invoking the Size() method of the histogram and printing out the result.

```
const unsigned int histogramSize = histogram->Size();

std::cout << "Histogram size " << histogramSize << std::endl;
```

Strictly speaking, the histogram computed here is the joint histogram of the three RGB components. However, given that we set the resolution of the green and blue channels to be just one bin, the histogram is in practice representing just the red channel. In the general case, we can alway access the frequency of a particular channel in a joint histogram, thanks to the fact that the histogram class offers a GetFrequency() method that accepts a channel as argument. This is illustrated in the following lines of code.

```
unsigned int channel = 0;  // red channel

std::cout << "Histogram of the red component" << std::endl;

for( unsigned int bin=0; bin < histogramSize; bin++ )
  {
  std::cout << "bin = " << bin << " frequency = ";
  std::cout << histogram->GetFrequency( bin, channel ) << std::endl;
  }
```

In order to reinforce the concepts presented above, we modify now the setup of the histogram filter in order to compute the histogram of the green channel instead of the red one. This is done by simply changing the number of bins desired on each channel and invoking the computation of the filter again by calling the Update() method.

```
size[0] =   1; // number of bins for the Red   channel
size[1] = 255; // number of bins for the Green channel
size[2] =   1; // number of bins for the Blue  channel

histogramFilter->SetHistogramSize( size );

histogramFilter->Update();
```

The result can be verified now by setting the desired channel to green and invoking the GetFrequency() method.

```
channel = 1;  // green channel

std::cout << "Histogram of the green component" << std::endl;

for( unsigned int bin=0; bin < histogramSize; bin++ )
  {
  std::cout << "bin = " << bin << " frequency = ";
  std::cout << histogram->GetFrequency( bin, channel ) << std::endl;
  }
```

To finalize the example, we do the same computation for the case of the blue channel.

```
size[0] =   1; // number of bins for the Red   channel
size[1] =   1; // number of bins for the Green channel
size[2] = 255; // number of bins for the Blue  channel

histogramFilter->SetHistogramSize( size );

histogramFilter->Update();
```

and verify the output.

```
channel = 2;  // blue channel

std::cout << "Histogram of the blue component" << std::endl;

for( unsigned int bin=0; bin < histogramSize; bin++ )
  {
  std::cout << "bin = " << bin << " frequency = ";
  std::cout << histogram->GetFrequency( bin, channel ) << std::endl;
  }
```

Color Image Histogram Writing

The source code for this section can be found in the file
`ImageHistogram4.cxx`.

The statistics framework in ITK has been designed for managing multi-variate statistics in a natural way. The `itk::Statistics::Histogram` class reflects this concept clearly since it is a N-variable joint histogram. This nature of the Histogram class is exploited in the following example in order to build the joint histogram of a color image encoded in RGB values.

Note that the same treatment could be applied further to any vector image thanks to the generic programming approach used in the implementation of the statistical framework.

The most relevant class in this example is the `itk::Statistics::ImageToHistogramFilter`. This class will take care of adapting the `itk::Image` to a list of samples and then to a histogram filter. The user is only bound to provide the desired resolution on the histogram bins for each one of the image components.

In this example we compute the joint histogram of the three channels of an RGB image. Our output histogram will be equivalent to a 3D array of bins. This histogram could be used further for feeding a segmentation method based on statistical pattern recognition. Such method was actually used during the generation of the image in the cover of the Software Guide.

The first step is to include the header files for the histogram filter, the RGB pixel type and the Image.

```
#include "itkImageToHistogramFilter.h"
#include "itkImage.h"
#include "itkRGBPixel.h"
```

We declare now the type used for the components of the RGB pixel, instantiate the type of the RGBPixel and instantiate the image type.

```
typedef unsigned char                       PixelComponentType;

typedef itk::RGBPixel< PixelComponentType >  RGBPixelType;

const unsigned int                          Dimension = 2;

typedef itk::Image< RGBPixelType, Dimension > RGBImageType;
```

Using the type of the color image, and in general of any vector image, we can now instantiate the type of the histogram filter class. We then use that type for constructing an instance of the filter by invoking its New() method and assigning the result to a smart pointer.

```
typedef itk::Statistics::ImageToHistogramFilter<
                    RGBImageType >   HistogramFilterType;

HistogramFilterType::Pointer histogramFilter =
                            HistogramFilterType::New();
```

The resolution at which the statistics of each one of the color component will be evaluated is defined by setting the number of bins along every component in the joint histogram. For this purpose we take the HistogramSizeType trait from the filter and use it to instantiate a size variable. We set in this variable the number of bins to use for each component of the color image.

```
typedef HistogramFilterType::HistogramSizeType   SizeType;

SizeType size(3);

size[0] = 256;  // number of bins for the Red   channel
size[1] = 256;  // number of bins for the Green channel
size[2] = 256;  // number of bins for the Blue  channel

histogramFilter->SetHistogramSize( size );
```

Finally, we must specify the upper and lower bounds for the histogram using the SetHistogramBinMinimum() and SetHistogramBinMaximum() methods.

```
typedef HistogramFilterType::HistogramMeasurementVectorType
    HistogramMeasurementVectorType;

HistogramMeasurementVectorType binMinimum( 3 );
HistogramMeasurementVectorType binMaximum( 3 );

binMinimum[0] = -0.5;
binMinimum[1] = -0.5;
binMinimum[2] = -0.5;

binMaximum[0] = 255.5;
binMaximum[1] = 255.5;
binMaximum[2] = 255.5;

histogramFilter->SetHistogramBinMinimum( binMinimum );
histogramFilter->SetHistogramBinMaximum( binMaximum );
```

The input to the histogram filter is taken from the output of an image reader. Of course, the output of any filter producing an RGB image could have been used instead of a reader.

```
histogramFilter->SetInput(  reader->GetOutput()  );
```

The marginal scale is defined in the histogram filter. This value will define the precision in the assignment of values to the histogram bins.

```
histogramFilter->SetMarginalScale( 10.0 );
```

Finally, the computation of the histogram is triggered by invoking the Update() method of the filter.

```
histogramFilter->Update();
```

At this point, we can recover the histogram by calling the `GetOutput()` method of the filter. The result is assigned to a variable that is instantiated using the `HistogramType` trait of the filter type.

```
typedef HistogramFilterType::HistogramType  HistogramType;

const HistogramType * histogram = histogramFilter->GetOutput();
```

We can verify that the computed histogram has the requested size by invoking its `Size()` method.

```
const unsigned int histogramSize = histogram->Size();

std::cout << "Histogram size " << histogramSize << std::endl;
```

The values of the histogram can now be saved into a file by walking through all of the histogram bins and pushing them into a std::ofstream.

```
std::ofstream histogramFile;
histogramFile.open( argv[2] );

HistogramType::ConstIterator itr = histogram->Begin();
HistogramType::ConstIterator end = histogram->End();

typedef HistogramType::AbsoluteFrequencyType AbsoluteFrequencyType;

while( itr != end )
  {
  const AbsoluteFrequencyType frequency = itr.GetFrequency();
  histogramFile.write( (const char *)(&frequency), sizeof(frequency) );

  if (frequency != 0)
    {
    HistogramType::IndexType index;
    index = histogram->GetIndex(itr.GetInstanceIdentifier());
    std::cout << "Index = " << index << ", Frequency = " << frequency
              << std::endl;
    }
  ++itr;
  }

histogramFile.close();
```

Note that here the histogram is saved as a block of memory in a raw file. At this point you can use visualization software in order to explore the histogram in a display that would be equivalent to a scatter plot of the RGB components of the input color image.

5.3.2   Image Information Theory

Many concepts from Information Theory have been used successfully in the domain of image processing. This section introduces some of such concepts and illustrates how the statistical framework in ITK can be used for computing measures that have some relevance in terms of Information Theory [58, 59, 33].

Computing Image Entropy

The concept of Entropy has been introduced into image processing as a crude mapping from its application in Communications. The notions of Information Theory can be deceiving and misleading when applied to images because their language from Communication Theory does not necessarily map to what people in the Imaging Community use.

For example, it is commonly said that

"The Entropy of an image is a measure of the amount of information contained in an image".

This statement is fundamentally **incorrect**.

The way the notion of Entropy is commonly measured in images is by first assuming that the spatial location of a pixel in an image is irrelevant! That is, we simply take the statistical distribution of the pixel values as it can be evaluated in a histogram and from that histogram we estimate the frequency of the value associated to each bin. In other words, we simply assume that the image is a set of pixels that are passing through a channel, just as things are commonly considered for communication purposes.

Once the frequency of every pixel value has been estimated, Information Theory defines that the amount of uncertainty that an observer will lose by taking one pixel and finding its real value to be the one associated with the i-th bin of the histogram, is given by $-\log_2(p_i)$, where p_i is the frequency in that histogram bin. Since a reduction in uncertainty is equivalent to an increase in the amount of information in the observer, we conclude that measuring one pixel and finding its level to be in the i-th bin results in an acquisition of $-\log_2(p_i)$ bits of information[1].

Since we could have picked any pixel at random, our chances of picking the ones that are associated to the i-th histogram bin are given by p_i. Therefore, the expected reduction in uncertainty that we can get from measuring the value of one pixel is given by

$$H = -\sum_i p_i \cdot \log_2(p_i) \tag{5.3}$$

This quantity H is what is usually defined as the *Entropy of the Image*. It would be more accurate to call it the Entropy of the random variable associated to the intensity value of *one* pixel. The fact that H is unrelated to the spatial arrangement of the pixels in an image shows how little of the real *Image Information H* actually represents. The Entropy of an image, as measured above, is only a crude indication of how the intensity values are spread in the dynamic range of intensities. For example, an image with maximum entropy will be the one that has a large dynamic range and every value in that range is equally probable.

The common convention of H as a representation of image information has terribly undermined the enormous potential on the application of Information Theory to image processing and analysis.

---

[1]Note that **bit** is the unit of amount of information. Our modern culture has vulgarized the bit and its multiples, the Byte, KiloByte, MegaByte, GigaByte and so on as simple measures of the amount of RAM memory and capacity of a hard drive in a computer. In that sense, a confusion is created between the encoding of a piece of data and its actual amount of information. For example a file composed of one million letters will take one million bytes in a hard disk, but it does not necessarily have one million bytes of information, since in many cases parts of the file can be predicted from others. This is the reason why data compression can manage to compact files.

The real concepts of Information Theory would require that we define the amount of information in an image based on our expectations and prior knowledge from that image. In particular, the *Amount of Information* provided by an image should measure the number of features that we are not able to predict based on our prior knowledge about that image. For example, if we know that we are going to analyze a CT scan of the abdomen of an adult human male in the age range of 40 to 45, there is already a good deal that we could predict about the content of that image. The real amount of information in the image is the representation of the features in the image that we could not predict from knowing that it is a CT scan from a human adult male.

The application of Information Theory to image analysis is still in its early infancy and it is an exciting and promising field to be explored further. All that being said, let's now look closer at how the concept of Entropy (which is not the amount of information in an image) can be measured with the ITK statistics framework.

The source code for this section can be found in the file
ImageEntropy1.cxx.

This example shows how to compute the entropy of an image. More formally this should be said : The reduction in uncertainty gained when we measure the intensity of *one* randomly selected pixel in this image, given that we already know the statistical distribution of the image intensity values.

In practice it is almost never possible to know the real statistical distribution of intensities and we are forced to estimate it from the evaluation of the histogram from one or several images of similar nature. We can use the counts in histogram bins in order to compute frequencies and then consider those frequencies to be estimations of the probablility of a new value to belong to the intensity range of that bin.

Since the first stage in estimating the entropy of an image is to compute its histogram, we must start by including the headers of the classes that will perform such a computation. In this case, we are going to use a scalar image as input, therefore we need the itk::Statistics::ScalarImageToHistogramGenerator class, as well as the image class.

```
#include "itkScalarImageToHistogramGenerator.h"
#include "itkImage.h"
```

The pixel type and dimension of the image are explicitly declared and then used for instantiating the image type.

```
typedef unsigned char       PixelType;
const   unsigned int        Dimension = 3;

typedef itk::Image< PixelType, Dimension > ImageType;
```

The image type is used as template parameter for instantiating the histogram generator.

```
typedef itk::Statistics::ScalarImageToHistogramGenerator<
                           ImageType >   HistogramGeneratorType;

HistogramGeneratorType::Pointer histogramGenerator =
                           HistogramGeneratorType::New();
```

The parameters of the desired histogram are defined, including the number of bins and the marginal scale. For convenience in this example, we read the number of bins from the command line arguments. In this way we can easily experiment with different values for the number of bins and see how that choice affects the computation of the entropy.

```
const unsigned int numberOfHistogramBins = atoi( argv[2] );

histogramGenerator->SetNumberOfBins( numberOfHistogramBins );
histogramGenerator->SetMarginalScale( 10.0 );
```

We can then connect as input the output image from a reader and trigger the histogram computation by invoking the `Compute()` method in the generator.

```
histogramGenerator->SetInput( reader->GetOutput() );

histogramGenerator->Compute();
```

The resulting histogram can be recovered from the generator by using the `GetOutput()` method. A histogram class can be declared using the `HistogramType` trait from the generator.

```
typedef HistogramGeneratorType::HistogramType  HistogramType;

const HistogramType * histogram = histogramGenerator->GetOutput();
```

We proceed now to compute the *estimation* of entropy given the histogram. The first conceptual jump to be done here is to assume that the histogram, which is the simple count of frequency of occurrence for the gray scale values of the image pixels, can be normalized in order to estimate the probability density function **PDF** of the actual statistical distribution of pixel values.

First we declare an iterator that will visit all the bins in the histogram. Then we obtain the total number of counts using the `GetTotalFrequency()` method, and we initialize the entropy variable to zero.

```
HistogramType::ConstIterator itr = histogram->Begin();
HistogramType::ConstIterator end = histogram->End();

double Sum = histogram->GetTotalFrequency();

double Entropy = 0.0;
```

We start now visiting every bin and estimating the probability of a pixel to have a value in the range of that bin. The base 2 logarithm of that probability is computed, and then weighted by the probability in order to compute the expected amount of information for any given pixel. Note that a minimum value is imposed for the probability in order to avoid computing logarithms of zeros.

Note that the $\log(2)$ factor is used to convert the natural logarithm in to a logarithm of base 2, and makes it possible to report the entropy in its natural unit: the bit.

```
while( itr != end )
  {
  const double probability = itr.GetFrequency() / Sum;

  if( probability > 0.99 / Sum )
    {
    Entropy += - probability * std::log( probability ) / std::log( 2.0 );
    }
  ++itr;
  }
```

The result of this sum is considered to be our estimation of the image entropy. Note that the Entropy value will change depending on the number of histogram bins that we use for computing the histogram. This is particularly important when dealing with images whose pixel values have dynamic ranges so large that our number of bins will always underestimate the variability of the data.

```
std::cout << "Image entropy = " << Entropy << " bits " << std::endl;
```

As an illustration, the application of this program to the image

- Examples/Data/BrainProtonDensitySlice.png

results in the following values of entropy for different values of number of histogram bins.

Number of Histogram Bins	16	32	64	128	255
Estimated Entropy (bits)	3.02	3.98	4.92	5.89	6.88

This table highlights the importance of carefully considering the characteristics of the histograms used for estimating Information Theory measures such as the entropy.

Computing Images Mutual Information

The source code for this section can be found in the file
ImageMutualInformation1.cxx.

This example illustrates how to compute the Mutual Information between two images using classes from the Statistics framework. Note that you could also use for this purpose the ImageMetrics designed for the image registration framework.

For example, you could use:

- itk::MutualInformationImageToImageMetric

- itk::MattesMutualInformationImageToImageMetric

- itk::MutualInformationHistogramImageToImageMetric

- itk::MutualInformationImageToImageMetric

- itk::NormalizedMutualInformationHistogramImageToImageMetric

- itk::KullbackLeiblerCompareHistogramImageToImageMetric

Mutual Information as computed in this example, and as commonly used in the context of image registration provides a measure of how much uncertainty on the value of a pixel in one image is reduced by measuring the homologous pixel in the other image. Note that Mutual Information as used here does not measure the amount of information that one image provides on the other image;

this would require us to take into account the spatial structures in the images as well as the semantics of the image context in terms of an observer.

This implies that there is still an enormous unexploited potential on the use of the Mutual Information concept in the domain of medical images, among the most interesting of which is the semantic description of image in terms of anatomical structures.

In this particular example we make use of classes from the Statistics framework in order to compute the measure of Mutual Information between two images. We assume that both images have the same number of pixels along every dimension and that they have the same origin and spacing. Therefore the pixels from one image are perfectly aligned with those of the other image.

We must start by including the header files of the image, histogram filter, reader and Join image filter. We will read both images and use the Join image filter in order to compose an image of two components using the information of each one of the input images in one component. This is the natural way of using the Statistics framework in ITK given that the fundamental statistical classes are expecting to receive multi-valued measures.

```
#include "itkImage.h"
#include "itkImageFileReader.h"
#include "itkJoinImageFilter.h"
#include "itkImageToHistogramFilter.h"
```

We define the pixel type and dimension of the images to be read.

```
typedef unsigned char                          PixelComponentType;
const unsigned int                             Dimension = 2;

typedef itk::Image< PixelComponentType, Dimension >    ImageType;
```

Using the image type we proceed to instantiate the readers for both input images. Then, we take their filenames from the command line arguments.

```
typedef itk::ImageFileReader< ImageType >              ReaderType;

ReaderType::Pointer reader1 = ReaderType::New();
ReaderType::Pointer reader2 = ReaderType::New();

reader1->SetFileName( argv[1] );
reader2->SetFileName( argv[2] );
```

Using the itk::JoinImageFilter we use the two input images and put them together in an image of two components.

```
typedef itk::JoinImageFilter< ImageType, ImageType >   JoinFilterType;

JoinFilterType::Pointer joinFilter = JoinFilterType::New();

joinFilter->SetInput1( reader1->GetOutput() );
joinFilter->SetInput2( reader2->GetOutput() );
```

At this point we trigger the execution of the pipeline by invoking the Update() method on the Join filter. We must put the call inside a try/catch block because the Update() call may potentially result in exceptions being thrown.

```
try
  {
  joinFilter->Update();
  }
catch( itk::ExceptionObject & excp )
  {
  std::cerr << excp << std::endl;
  return -1;
  }
```

We now prepare the types to be used for the computation of the joint histogram. For this purpose,
we take the type of the image resulting from the JoinImageFilter and use it as template argument of
the itk::ImageToHistogramFilter. We then construct one by invoking the New() method.

```
typedef JoinFilterType::OutputImageType                     VectorImageType;

typedef itk::Statistics::ImageToHistogramFilter<
                               VectorImageType >  HistogramFilterType;

HistogramFilterType::Pointer histogramFilter = HistogramFilterType::New();
```

We pass the multiple-component image as input to the histogram filter, and setup the marginal scale
value that will define the precision to be used for classifying values into the histogram bins.

```
histogramFilter->SetInput(  joinFilter->GetOutput()  );

histogramFilter->SetMarginalScale( 10.0 );
```

We must now define the number of bins to use for each one of the components in the joint image.
For this purpose we take the HistogramSizeType from the traits of the histogram filter type.

```
typedef HistogramFilterType::HistogramSizeType   HistogramSizeType;

HistogramSizeType size( 2 );

size[0] = 255;  // number of bins for the first  channel
size[1] = 255;  // number of bins for the second channel

histogramFilter->SetHistogramSize( size );
```

Finally, we must specify the upper and lower bounds for the histogram using the
SetHistogramBinMinimum() and SetHistogramBinMaximum() methods. The Update() method
is then called in order to trigger the computation of the histogram.

```
typedef HistogramFilterType::HistogramMeasurementVectorType
  HistogramMeasurementVectorType;

HistogramMeasurementVectorType binMinimum( 3 );
HistogramMeasurementVectorType binMaximum( 3 );

binMinimum[0] = -0.5;
binMinimum[1] = -0.5;
binMinimum[2] = -0.5;

binMaximum[0] = 255.5;
binMaximum[1] = 255.5;
binMaximum[2] = 255.5;

histogramFilter->SetHistogramBinMinimum( binMinimum );
histogramFilter->SetHistogramBinMaximum( binMaximum );

histogramFilter->Update();
```

The histogram can be recovered from the filter by creating a variable with the histogram type taken from the filter traits.

```
typedef HistogramFilterType::HistogramType  HistogramType;

const HistogramType * histogram = histogramFilter->GetOutput();
```

We now walk over all the bins of the joint histogram and compute their contribution to the value of the joint entropy. For this purpose we use histogram iterators, and the Begin() and End() methods. Since the values returned from the histogram are measuring frequency we must convert them to an estimation of probability by dividing them over the total sum of frequencies returned by the GetTotalFrequency() method.

```
HistogramType::ConstIterator itr = histogram->Begin();
HistogramType::ConstIterator end = histogram->End();

const double Sum = histogram->GetTotalFrequency();
```

We initialize to zero the variable to use for accumulating the value of the joint entropy, and then use the iterator for visiting all the bins of the joint histogram. For every bin we compute their contribution to the reduction of uncertainty. Note that in order to avoid logarithmic operations on zero values, we skip over those bins that have less than one count. The entropy contribution must be computed using logarithms in base two in order to express entropy in **bits**.

```
double JointEntropy = 0.0;

while( itr != end )
  {
  const double count = itr.GetFrequency();
  if( count > 0.0 )
    {
    const double probability = count / Sum;
    JointEntropy +=
      - probability * std::log( probability ) / std::log( 2.0 );
    }
  ++itr;
  }
```

Now that we have the value of the joint entropy we can proceed to estimate the values of the entropies for each image independently. This can be done by simply changing the number of bins and then recomputing the histogram.

```
size[0] = 255;  // number of bins for the first  channel
size[1] =   1;  // number of bins for the second channel

histogramFilter->SetHistogramSize( size );
histogramFilter->Update();
```

We initialize to zero another variable in order to start accumulating the entropy contributions from every bin.

```
itr = histogram->Begin();
end = histogram->End();

double Entropy1 = 0.0;

while( itr != end )
  {
  const double count = itr.GetFrequency();
  if( count > 0.0 )
    {
    const double probability = count / Sum;
    Entropy1 += - probability * std::log( probability ) / std::log( 2.0 );
    }
  ++itr;
  }
```

The same process is used for computing the entropy of the other component, simply by swapping the number of bins in the histogram.

```
size[0] =   1;  // number of bins for the first channel
size[1] = 255;  // number of bins for the second channel

histogramFilter->SetHistogramSize( size );
histogramFilter->Update();
```

The entropy is computed in a similar manner, just by visiting all the bins on the histogram and accumulating their entropy contributions.

```
itr = histogram->Begin();
end = histogram->End();

double Entropy2 = 0.0;

while( itr != end )
  {
  const double count = itr.GetFrequency();
  if( count > 0.0 )
    {
    const double probability = count / Sum;
    Entropy2 += - probability * std::log( probability ) / std::log( 2.0 );
    }
  ++itr;
  }
```

At this point we can compute any of the popular measures of Mutual Information. For example

```
double MutualInformation = Entropy1 + Entropy2 - JointEntropy;
```

or Normalized Mutual Information, where the value of Mutual Information is divided by the mean entropy of the input images.

```
double NormalizedMutualInformation1 =
            2.0 * MutualInformation / ( Entropy1 + Entropy2 );
```

A second form of Normalized Mutual Information has been defined as the mean entropy of the two images divided by their joint entropy.

```
double NormalizedMutualInformation2 = ( Entropy1 + Entropy2 ) / JointEntropy;
```

You probably will find very interesting how the value of Mutual Information is strongly dependent on the number of bins over which the histogram is defined.

5.4 Classification

In statistical classification, each object is represented by d features (a measurement vector), and the goal of classification becomes finding compact and disjoint regions (decision regions[19]) for classes in a d-dimensional feature space. Such decision regions are defined by decision rules that are known or can be trained. The simplest configuration of a classification consists of a decision rule and multiple membership functions; each membership function represents a class. Figure 5.3 illustrates this general framework.

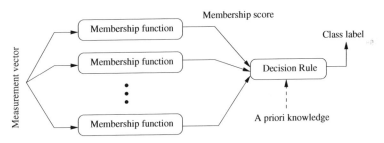

Figure 5.3: Simple conceptual classifier.

This framework closely follows that of Duda and Hart[19]. The classification process can be described as follows:

1. A measurement vector is input to each membership function.

2. Membership functions feed the membership scores to the decision rule.

3. A decision rule compares the membership scores and returns a class label.

This simple configuration can be used to formulated various classification tasks by using different membership functions and incorporating task specific requirements and prior knowledge into the

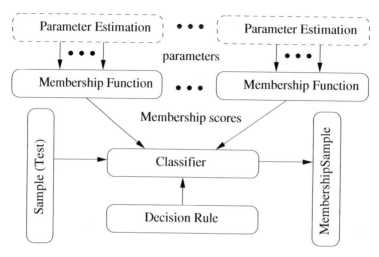

Figure 5.4: Statistical classification framework.

decision rule. For example, instead of using probability density functions as membership functions, through distance functions and a minimum value decision rule (which assigns a class from the distance function that returns the smallest value) users can achieve a least squared error classifier. As another example, users can add a rejection scheme to the decision rule so that even in a situation where the membership scores suggest a "winner", a measurement vector can be flagged as ill-defined. Such a rejection scheme can avoid risks of assigning a class label without a proper win margin.

5.4.1   k-d Tree Based k-Means Clustering

The source code for this section can be found in the file
KdTreeBasedKMeansClustering.cxx.

K-means clustering is a popular clustering algorithm because it is simple and usually converges to a reasonable solution. The k-means algorithm works as follows:

1. Obtains the initial k means input from the user.

2. Assigns each measurement vector in a sample container to its closest mean among the k number of means (i.e., update the membership of each measurement vectors to the nearest of the k clusters).

3. Calculates each cluster's mean from the newly assigned measurement vectors (updates the centroid (mean) of k clusters).

4. Repeats step 2 and step 3 until it meets the termination criteria.

The most common termination criterion is that if there is no measurement vector that changes its cluster membership from the previous iteration, then the algorithm stops.

The `itk::Statistics::KdTreeBasedKmeansEstimator` is a variation of this logic. The k-means clustering algorithm is computationally very expensive because it has to recalculate the mean at each iteration. To update the mean values, we have to calculate the distance between k means and each and every measurement vector. To reduce the computational burden, the KdTreeBasedKmeansEstimator uses a special data structure: the k-d tree (`itk::Statistics::KdTree`) with additional information. The additional information includes the number and the vector sum of measurement vectors under each node under the tree architecture.

With such additional information and the k-d tree data structure, we can reduce the computational cost of the distance calculation and means. Instead of calculating each measurement vector and k means, we can simply compare each node of the k-d tree and the k means. This idea of utilizing a k-d tree can be found in multiple articles [2] [45] [29]. Our implementation of this scheme follows the article by the Kanungo et al [29].

We use the `itk::Statistics::ListSample` as the input sample, the `itk::Vector` as the measurement vector. The following code snippet includes their header files.

```
#include "itkVector.h"
#include "itkListSample.h"
```

Since our k-means algorithm requires a `itk::Statistics::KdTree` object as an input, we include the KdTree class header file. As mentioned above, we need a k-d tree with the vector sum and the number of measurement vectors. Therefore we use the `itk::Statistics::WeightedCentroidKdTreeGenerator` instead of the `itk::Statistics::KdTreeGenerator` that generate a k-d tree without such additional information.

```
#include "itkKdTree.h"
#include "itkWeightedCentroidKdTreeGenerator.h"
```

The KdTreeBasedKmeansEstimator class is the implementation of the k-means algorithm. It does not create k clusters. Instead, it returns the mean estimates for the k clusters.

```
#include "itkKdTreeBasedKmeansEstimator.h"
```

To generate the clusters, we must create k instances of `itk::Statistics::DistanceToCentroidMembershipFunction` function as the membership functions for each cluster and plug that—along with a sample— into an `itk::Statistics::SampleClassifierFilter` object to get a `itk::Statistics::MembershipSample` that stores pairs of measurement vectors and their associated class labels (k labels).

```
#include "itkMinimumDecisionRule.h"
#include "itkSampleClassifierFilter.h"
```

We will fill the sample with random variables from two normal distribution using the `itk::Statistics::NormalVariateGenerator`.

```
#include "itkNormalVariateGenerator.h"
```

Since the `NormalVariateGenerator` class only supports 1-D, we define our measurement vector type as one component vector. We then, create a `ListSample` object for data inputs. Each measure-

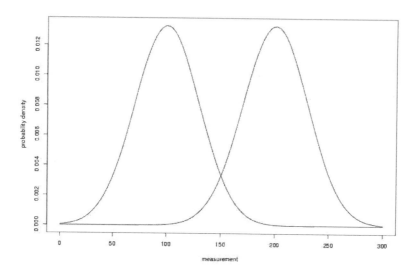

Figure 5.5: Two normal distributions' probability density plot (The means are 100 and 200, and the standard deviation is 30)

ment vector is of length 1. We set this using the `SetMeasurementVectorSize()` method.

```
typedef itk::Vector< double, 1 > MeasurementVectorType;
typedef itk::Statistics::ListSample< MeasurementVectorType > SampleType;
SampleType::Pointer sample = SampleType::New();
sample->SetMeasurementVectorSize( 1 );
```

The following code snippet creates a NormalVariateGenerator object. Since the random variable generator returns values according to the standard normal distribution (The mean is zero, and the standard deviation is one), before pushing random values into the `sample`, we change the mean and standard deviation. We want two normal (Gaussian) distribution data. We have two for loops. Each for loop uses different mean and standard deviation. Before we fill the `sample` with the second distribution data, we call `Initialize(random seed)` method, to recreate the pool of random variables in the `normalGenerator`.

To see the probability density plots from the two distribution, refer to the Figure 5.5.

```
typedef itk::Statistics::NormalVariateGenerator NormalGeneratorType;
NormalGeneratorType::Pointer normalGenerator = NormalGeneratorType::New();

normalGenerator->Initialize( 101 );

MeasurementVectorType mv;
double mean = 100;
double standardDeviation = 30;
for ( unsigned int i = 0; i < 100; ++i )
  {
  mv[0] = ( normalGenerator->GetVariate() * standardDeviation ) + mean;
  sample->PushBack( mv );
  }

normalGenerator->Initialize( 3024 );
mean = 200;
standardDeviation = 30;
for ( unsigned int i = 0; i < 100; ++i )
  {
  mv[0] = ( normalGenerator->GetVariate() * standardDeviation ) + mean;
  sample->PushBack( mv );
  }
```

We create a k-d tree. To see the details on the k-d tree generation, see the Section 5.1.7.

```
typedef itk::Statistics::WeightedCentroidKdTreeGenerator< SampleType >
  TreeGeneratorType;
TreeGeneratorType::Pointer treeGenerator = TreeGeneratorType::New();

treeGenerator->SetSample( sample );
treeGenerator->SetBucketSize( 16 );
treeGenerator->Update();
```

Once we have the k-d tree, it is a simple procedure to produce k mean estimates.

We create the KdTreeBasedKmeansEstimator. Then, we provide the initial mean values using the SetParameters(). Since we are dealing with two normal distribution in a 1-D space, the size of the mean value array is two. The first element is the first mean value, and the second is the second mean value. If we used two normal distributions in a 2-D space, the size of array would be four, and the first two elements would be the two components of the first normal distribution's mean vector. We plug-in the k-d tree using the SetKdTree().

The remaining two methods specify the termination condition. The estimation process stops when the number of iterations reaches the maximum iteration value set by the SetMaximumIteration(), or the distances between the newly calculated mean (centroid) values and previous ones are within the threshold set by the SetCentroidPositionChangesThreshold(). The final step is to call the StartOptimization() method.

The for loop will print out the mean estimates from the estimation process.

```
typedef TreeGeneratorType::KdTreeType TreeType;
typedef itk::Statistics::KdTreeBasedKmeansEstimator< TreeType >
                            EstimatorType;
EstimatorType::Pointer estimator = EstimatorType::New();

EstimatorType::ParametersType initialMeans(2);
initialMeans[0] = 0.0;
initialMeans[1] = 0.0;

estimator->SetParameters( initialMeans );
estimator->SetKdTree( treeGenerator->GetOutput() );
estimator->SetMaximumIteration( 200 );
estimator->SetCentroidPositionChangesThreshold(0.0);
estimator->StartOptimization();

EstimatorType::ParametersType estimatedMeans = estimator->GetParameters();

for ( unsigned int i = 0; i < 2; ++i )
  {
  std::cout << "cluster[" << i << "] " << std::endl;
  std::cout << "    estimated mean : " << estimatedMeans[i] << std::endl;
  }
```

If we are only interested in finding the mean estimates, we might stop. However, to illustrate how a classifier can be formed using the statistical classification framework. We go a little bit further in this example.

Since the k-means algorithm is an minimum distance classifier using the estimated k means and the measurement vectors. We use the DistanceToCentroidMembershipFunction class as membership functions. Our choice for the decision rule is the itk::Statistics::MinimumDecisionRule that returns the index of the membership functions that have the smallest value for a measurement vector.

After creating a SampleClassifier filter object and a MinimumDecisionRule object, we plug-in the decisionRule and the sample to the classifier filter. Then, we must specify the number of classes that will be considered using the SetNumberOfClasses() method.

The remainder of the following code snippet shows how to use user-specified class labels. The classification result will be stored in a MembershipSample object, and for each measurement vector, its class label will be one of the two class labels, 100 and 200 (unsigned int).

```
typedef itk::Statistics::DistanceToCentroidMembershipFunction<
                              MeasurementVectorType > MembershipFunctionType;
typedef itk::Statistics::MinimumDecisionRule         DecisionRuleType;
DecisionRuleType::Pointer decisionRule = DecisionRuleType::New();

typedef itk::Statistics::SampleClassifierFilter< SampleType > ClassifierType;
ClassifierType::Pointer classifier = ClassifierType::New();

classifier->SetDecisionRule( decisionRule );
classifier->SetInput( sample );
classifier->SetNumberOfClasses( 2 );

typedef ClassifierType::ClassLabelVectorObjectType
                              ClassLabelVectorObjectType;
typedef ClassifierType::ClassLabelVectorType ClassLabelVectorType;
typedef ClassifierType::ClassLabelType       ClassLabelType;

ClassLabelVectorObjectType::Pointer classLabelsObject =
   ClassLabelVectorObjectType::New();
ClassLabelVectorType& classLabelsVector = classLabelsObject->Get();

ClassLabelType class1 = 200;
classLabelsVector.push_back( class1 );
ClassLabelType class2 = 100;
classLabelsVector.push_back( class2 );

classifier->SetClassLabels( classLabelsObject );
```

The classifier is almost ready to do the classification process except that it needs two membership functions that represents two clusters respectively.

In this example, the two clusters are modeled by two Euclidean distance functions. The distance function (model) has only one parameter, its mean (centroid) set by the SetCentroid() method. To plug-in two distance functions, we create a MembershipFunctionVectorObject that contains a MembershipFunctionVector with two components and add it using the SetMembershipFunctions method. Then invocation of the Update() method will perform the classification.

```
typedef ClassifierType::MembershipFunctionVectorObjectType
  MembershipFunctionVectorObjectType;
typedef ClassifierType::MembershipFunctionVectorType
  MembershipFunctionVectorType;

MembershipFunctionVectorObjectType::Pointer membershipFunctionVectorObject =
  MembershipFunctionVectorObjectType::New();
MembershipFunctionVectorType& membershipFunctionVector =
  membershipFunctionVectorObject->Get();

int index = 0;
for ( unsigned int i = 0; i < 2; i++ )
  {
  MembershipFunctionType::Pointer membershipFunction
                               = MembershipFunctionType::New();
  MembershipFunctionType::CentroidType centroid(
                            sample->GetMeasurementVectorSize() );
  for ( unsigned int j = 0; j < sample->GetMeasurementVectorSize(); j++ )
    {
    centroid[j] = estimatedMeans[index++];
    }
  membershipFunction->SetCentroid( centroid );
  membershipFunctionVector.push_back( membershipFunction.GetPointer() );
  }
classifier->SetMembershipFunctions( membershipFunctionVectorObject );

classifier->Update();
```

The following code snippet prints out the measurement vectors and their class labels in the `sample`.

```
const ClassifierType::MembershipSampleType* membershipSample =
  classifier->GetOutput();
ClassifierType::MembershipSampleType::ConstIterator iter
                                    = membershipSample->Begin();

while ( iter != membershipSample->End() )
  {
  std::cout << "measurement vector = " << iter.GetMeasurementVector()
            << " class label = " << iter.GetClassLabel()
            << std::endl;
  ++iter;
  }
```

5.4.2   K-Means Classification

The source code for this section can be found in the file
`ScalarImageKmeansClassifier.cxx`.

This example shows how to use the KMeans model for classifying the pixel of a scalar image.

The `itk::Statistics::ScalarImageKmeansImageFilter` is used for taking a scalar image and applying the K-Means algorithm in order to define classes that represents statistical distributions of intensity values in the pixels. The classes are then used in this filter for generating a labeled image where every pixel is assigned to one of the classes.

```
#include "itkImage.h"
#include "itkImageFileReader.h"
#include "itkImageFileWriter.h"
#include "itkScalarImageKmeansImageFilter.h"
```

First we define the pixel type and dimension of the image that we intend to classify. With this image type we can also declare the `itk::ImageFileReader` needed for reading the input image, create one and set its input filename.

```
typedef signed short        PixelType;
const unsigned int          Dimension = 2;

typedef itk::Image<PixelType, Dimension > ImageType;

typedef itk::ImageFileReader< ImageType > ReaderType;
ReaderType::Pointer reader = ReaderType::New();
reader->SetFileName( inputImageFileName );
```

With the `ImageType` we instantiate the type of the `itk::ScalarImageKmeansImageFilter` that will compute the K-Means model and then classify the image pixels.

```
typedef itk::ScalarImageKmeansImageFilter< ImageType > KMeansFilterType;

KMeansFilterType::Pointer kmeansFilter = KMeansFilterType::New();

kmeansFilter->SetInput( reader->GetOutput() );

const unsigned int numberOfInitialClasses = atoi( argv[4] );
```

In general the classification will produce as output an image whose pixel values are integers associated to the labels of the classes. Since typically these integers will be generated in order (0,1,2,...N), the output image will tend to look very dark when displayed with naive viewers. It is therefore convenient to have the option of spreading the label values over the dynamic range of the output image pixel type. When this is done, the dynamic range of the pixels is divided by the number of classes in order to define the increment between labels. For example, an output image of 8 bits will have a dynamic range of [0:256], and when it is used for holding four classes, the non-contiguous labels will be (0,64,128,192). The selection of the mode to use is done with the method `SetUseNonContiguousLabels()`.

```
const unsigned int useNonContiguousLabels = atoi( argv[3] );

kmeansFilter->SetUseNonContiguousLabels( useNonContiguousLabels );
```

For each one of the classes we must provide a tentative initial value for the mean of the class. Given that this is a scalar image, each one of the means is simply a scalar value. Note however that in a general case of K-Means, the input image would be a vector image and therefore the means will be vectors of the same dimension as the image pixels.

```
for( unsigned k=0; k < numberOfInitialClasses; k++ )
  {
  const double userProvidedInitialMean = atof( argv[k+argoffset] );
  kmeansFilter->AddClassWithInitialMean( userProvidedInitialMean );
  }
```

The `itk::ScalarImageKmeansImageFilter` is predefined for producing an 8 bits scalar image as output. This output image contains labels associated to each one of the classes in the K-Means algorithm. In the following lines we use the `OutputImageType` in order to instantiate the type of a `itk::ImageFileWriter`. Then create one, and connect it to the output of the classification filter.

```
typedef KMeansFilterType::OutputImageType  OutputImageType;

typedef itk::ImageFileWriter< OutputImageType > WriterType;

WriterType::Pointer writer = WriterType::New();

writer->SetInput( kmeansFilter->GetOutput() );

writer->SetFileName( outputImageFileName );
```

We are now ready for triggering the execution of the pipeline. This is done by simply invoking the `Update()` method in the writer. This call will propagate the update request to the reader and then to the classifier.

```
try
  {
  writer->Update();
  }
catch( itk::ExceptionObject & excp )
  {
  std::cerr << "Problem encountered while writing ";
  std::cerr << " image file : " << argv[2] << std::endl;
  std::cerr << excp << std::endl;
  return EXIT_FAILURE;
  }
```

At this point the classification is done, the labeled image is saved in a file, and we can take a look at the means that were found as a result of the model estimation performed inside the classifier filter.

```
KMeansFilterType::ParametersType estimatedMeans =
                                  kmeansFilter->GetFinalMeans();

const unsigned int numberOfClasses = estimatedMeans.Size();

for ( unsigned int i = 0; i < numberOfClasses; ++i )
  {
  std::cout << "cluster[" << i << "] ";
  std::cout << "    estimated mean : " << estimatedMeans[i] << std::endl;
  }
```

Figure 5.6 illustrates the effect of this filter with three classes. The means were estimated by ScalarImageKmeansModelEstimator.cxx.

5.4.3 Bayesian Plug-In Classifier

The source code for this section can be found in the file
BayesianPluginClassifier.cxx.

In this example, we present a system that places measurement vectors into two Gaussian classes. The Figure 5.7 shows all the components of the classifier system and the data flow. This system dif-

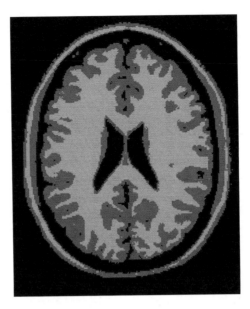

Figure 5.6: Effect of the KMeans classifier on a T1 slice of the brain.

fers with the previous k-means clustering algorithms in several ways. The biggest difference is that this classifier uses the `itk::Statistics::GaussianDensityFunctions` as membership functions instead of the `itk::Statistics::DistanceToCentroidMembershipFunction`. Since the membership function is different, the membership function requires a different set of parameters, mean vectors and covariance matrices. We choose the `itk::Statistics::CovarianceSampleFilter` (sample covariance) for the estimation algorithms of the two parameters. If we want a more robust estimation algorithm, we can replace this estimation algorithm with more alternatives without changing other components in the classifier system.

It is a bad idea to use the same sample for test and training (parameter estimation) of the parameters. However, for simplicity, in this example, we use a sample for test and training.

We use the `itk::Statistics::ListSample` as the sample (test and training). The `itk::Vector` is our measurement vector class. To store measurement vectors into two separate sample containers, we use the `itk::Statistics::Subsample` objects.

```
#include "itkVector.h"
#include "itkListSample.h"
#include "itkSubsample.h"
```

The following file provides us the parameter estimation algorithm.

```
#include "itkCovarianceSampleFilter.h"
```

The following files define the components required by ITK statistical classification framework: the decision rule, the membership function, and the classifier.

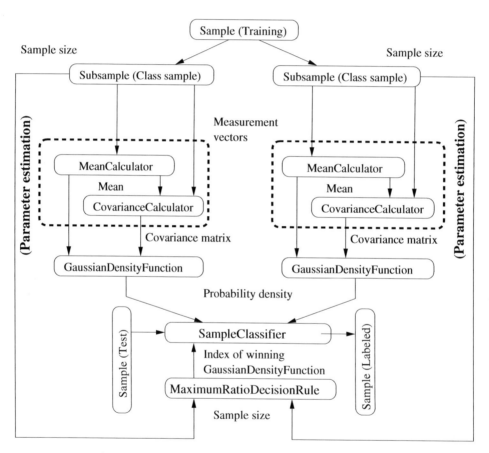

Figure 5.7: Bayesian plug-in classifier for two Gaussian classes.

```
#include "itkMaximumRatioDecisionRule.h"
#include "itkGaussianMembershipFunction.h"
#include "itkSampleClassifierFilter.h"
```

We will fill the sample with random variables from two normal distribution using the itk::Statistics::NormalVariateGenerator.

```
#include "itkNormalVariateGenerator.h"
```

Since the NormalVariateGenerator class only supports 1-D, we define our measurement vector type as a one component vector. We then, create a ListSample object for data inputs.

We also create two Subsample objects that will store the measurement vectors in `sample` into two separate sample containers. Each Subsample object stores only the measurement vectors belonging to a single class. This class sample will be used by the parameter estimation algorithms.

```
const unsigned int measurementVectorLength = 1;
typedef itk::Vector< double, measurementVectorLength > MeasurementVectorType;
typedef itk::Statistics::ListSample< MeasurementVectorType > SampleType;
SampleType::Pointer sample = SampleType::New();
// length of measurement vectors in the sample.
sample->SetMeasurementVectorSize( measurementVectorLength );

typedef itk::Statistics::Subsample< SampleType > ClassSampleType;
std::vector< ClassSampleType::Pointer > classSamples;
for ( unsigned int i = 0; i < 2; ++i )
  {
  classSamples.push_back( ClassSampleType::New() );
  classSamples[i]->SetSample( sample );
  }
```

The following code snippet creates a NormalVariateGenerator object. Since the random variable generator returns values according to the standard normal distribution (the mean is zero, and the standard deviation is one) before pushing random values into the `sample`, we change the mean and standard deviation. We want two normal (Gaussian) distribution data. We have two for loops. Each for loop uses different mean and standard deviation. Before we fill the `sample` with the second distribution data, we call `Initialize(random seed)` method, to recreate the pool of random variables in the `normalGenerator`. In the second for loop, we fill the two class samples with measurement vectors using the `AddInstance()` method.

To see the probability density plots from the two distributions, refer to Figure 5.5.

```
typedef itk::Statistics::NormalVariateGenerator NormalGeneratorType;
NormalGeneratorType::Pointer normalGenerator = NormalGeneratorType::New();

normalGenerator->Initialize( 101 );

MeasurementVectorType mv;
double mean = 100;
double standardDeviation = 30;
SampleType::InstanceIdentifier id = 0UL;
for ( unsigned int i = 0; i < 100; ++i )
  {
  mv.Fill( (normalGenerator->GetVariate() * standardDeviation ) + mean);
  sample->PushBack( mv );
  classSamples[0]->AddInstance( id );
  ++id;
  }

normalGenerator->Initialize( 3024 );
mean = 200;
standardDeviation = 30;
for ( unsigned int i = 0; i < 100; ++i )
  {
  mv.Fill( (normalGenerator->GetVariate() * standardDeviation ) + mean);
  sample->PushBack( mv );
  classSamples[1]->AddInstance( id );
  ++id;
  }
```

In the following code snippet, notice that the template argument for the CovarianceCalculator is
ClassSampleType (i.e., type of Subsample) instead of SampleType (i.e., type of ListSample). This
is because the parameter estimation algorithms are applied to the class sample.

```
typedef itk::Statistics::CovarianceSampleFilter< ClassSampleType >
  CovarianceEstimatorType;

std::vector< CovarianceEstimatorType::Pointer > covarianceEstimators;

for ( unsigned int i = 0; i < 2; ++i )
  {
  covarianceEstimators.push_back( CovarianceEstimatorType::New() );
  covarianceEstimators[i]->SetInput( classSamples[i] );
  covarianceEstimators[i]->Update();
  }
```

We print out the estimated parameters.

```
for ( unsigned int i = 0; i < 2; ++i )
  {
  std::cout << "class[" << i << "] " << std::endl;
  std::cout << "    estimated mean : "
            << covarianceEstimators[i]->GetMean()
            << "    covariance matrix : "
            << covarianceEstimators[i]->GetCovarianceMatrix() << std::endl;
  }
```

After creating a SampleClassifier object and a MaximumRatioDecisionRule object, we plug in the
decisionRule and the sample to the classifier. Then, we specify the number of classes that will be

considered using the `SetNumberOfClasses()` method.

The MaximumRatioDecisionRule requires a vector of *a priori* probability values. Such *a priori* probability will be the $P(\omega_i)$ of the following variation of the Bayes decision rule:

$$\text{Decide } \omega_i \text{ if } \frac{p(\vec{x}|\omega_i)}{p(\vec{x}|\omega_j)} > \frac{P(\omega_j)}{P(\omega_i)} \text{ for all } j \neq i \qquad (5.4)$$

The remainder of the code snippet shows how to use user-specified class labels. The classification result will be stored in a MembershipSample object, and for each measurement vector, its class label will be one of the two class labels, 100 and 200 (`unsigned int`).

```
typedef itk::Statistics::GaussianMembershipFunction< MeasurementVectorType >
                                          MembershipFunctionType;
typedef itk::Statistics::MaximumRatioDecisionRule DecisionRuleType;
DecisionRuleType::Pointer decisionRule = DecisionRuleType::New();

DecisionRuleType::PriorProbabilityVectorType aPrioris;
aPrioris.push_back( (double)classSamples[0]->GetTotalFrequency()
                / (double)sample->GetTotalFrequency() );
aPrioris.push_back( (double)classSamples[1]->GetTotalFrequency()
                / (double)sample->GetTotalFrequency() );
decisionRule->SetPriorProbabilities( aPrioris );

typedef itk::Statistics::SampleClassifierFilter< SampleType > ClassifierType;
ClassifierType::Pointer classifier = ClassifierType::New();

classifier->SetDecisionRule( decisionRule);
classifier->SetInput( sample );
classifier->SetNumberOfClasses( 2 );

typedef ClassifierType::ClassLabelVectorObjectType
                                    ClassLabelVectorObjectType;
typedef ClassifierType::ClassLabelVectorType ClassLabelVectorType;

ClassLabelVectorObjectType::Pointer classLabelVectorObject =
   ClassLabelVectorObjectType::New();
ClassLabelVectorType classLabelVector = classLabelVectorObject->Get();

ClassifierType::ClassLabelType class1 = 100;
classLabelVector.push_back( class1 );
ClassifierType::ClassLabelType class2 = 200;
classLabelVector.push_back( class2 );

classLabelVectorObject->Set( classLabelVector );
classifier->SetClassLabels( classLabelVectorObject );
```

The `classifier` is almost ready to perform the classification except that it needs two membership functions that represent the two clusters.

In this example, we can imagine that the two clusters are modeled by two Gaussian distribution functions. The distribution functions have two parameters, the mean, set by the `SetMean()` method, and the covariance, set by the `SetCovariance()` method. To plug-in two distribution functions, we create a new instance of MembershipFunctionVectorObjectType and populate its internal vector with new instances of MembershipFunction (i.e. GaussianMembershipFunction). This is done by calling the `Get()` method of `membershipFunctionVectorObject` to get the internal vector, populating this vector with two new membership functions and then calling `membershipFunctionVectorObject->Set( membershipFunctionVector )`. Finally, the invocation of the `Update()` method will perform the classification.

```
typedef ClassifierType::MembershipFunctionVectorObjectType
  MembershipFunctionVectorObjectType;
typedef ClassifierType::MembershipFunctionVectorType
  MembershipFunctionVectorType;

MembershipFunctionVectorObjectType::Pointer membershipFunctionVectorObject =
  MembershipFunctionVectorObjectType::New();
MembershipFunctionVectorType membershipFunctionVector =
  membershipFunctionVectorObject->Get();

for ( unsigned int i = 0; i < 2; i++ )
  {
  MembershipFunctionType::Pointer membershipFunction =
    MembershipFunctionType::New();
  membershipFunction->SetMean( covarianceEstimators[i]->GetMean() );
  membershipFunction->SetCovariance(
    covarianceEstimators[i]->GetCovarianceMatrix() );
  membershipFunctionVector.push_back( membershipFunction.GetPointer() );
  }
membershipFunctionVectorObject->Set( membershipFunctionVector );
classifier->SetMembershipFunctions( membershipFunctionVectorObject );

classifier->Update();
```

The following code snippet prints out pairs of a measurement vector and its class label in the `sample`.

```
const ClassifierType::MembershipSampleType* membershipSample
  = classifier->GetOutput();
ClassifierType::MembershipSampleType::ConstIterator iter
  = membershipSample->Begin();

while ( iter != membershipSample->End() )
  {
  std::cout << "measurement vector = " << iter.GetMeasurementVector()
            << " class label = " << iter.GetClassLabel() << std::endl;
  ++iter;
  }
```

5.4.4 Expectation Maximization Mixture Model Estimation

The source code for this section can be found in the file
`ExpectationMaximizationMixtureModelEstimator.cxx`.

In this example, we present an implementation of the expectation maximization (EM) process to generates parameter estimates for a two Gaussian component mixture model.

The Bayesian plug-in classifier example (see Section 5.4.3) used two Gaussian probability density functions (PDF) to model two Gaussian distribution classes (two models for two class). However, in some cases, we want to model a distribution as a mixture of several different distributions. Therefore, the probability density function ($p(x)$) of a mixture model can be stated as follows :

$$p(x) = \sum_{i=0}^{c} \alpha_i f_i(x) \tag{5.5}$$

where i is the index of the component, c is the number of components, α_i is the proportion of the component, and f_i is the probability density function of the component.

Now the task is to find the parameters(the component PDF's parameters and the proportion values) to maximize the likelihood of the parameters. If we know which component a measurement vector belongs to, the solutions to this problem is easy to solve. However, we don't know the membership of each measurement vector. Therefore, we use the expectation of membership instead of the exact membership. The EM process splits into two steps:

1. E step: calculate the expected membership values for each measurement vector to each classes.

2. M step: find the next parameter sets that maximize the likelihood with the expected membership values and the current set of parameters.

The E step is basically a step that calculates the *a posteriori* probability for each measurement vector.

The M step is dependent on the type of each PDF. Most of distributions belonging to exponential family such as Poisson, Binomial, Exponential, and Normal distributions have analytical solutions for updating the parameter set. The `itk::Statistics::ExpectationMaximizationMixtureModelEstimator` class assumes that such type of components.

In the following example we use the `itk::Statistics::ListSample` as the sample (test and training). The `itk::Vector::`is our measurement vector class. To store measurement vectors into two separate sample container, we use the `itk::Statistics::Subsample` objects.

```
#include "itkVector.h"
#include "itkListSample.h"
```

The following two files provides us the parameter estimation algorithms.

```
#include "itkGaussianMixtureModelComponent.h"
#include "itkExpectationMaximizationMixtureModelEstimator.h"
```

We will fill the sample with random variables from two normal distribution using the `itk::Statistics::NormalVariateGenerator`.

```
#include "itkNormalVariateGenerator.h"
```

Since the NormalVariateGenerator class only supports 1-D, we define our measurement vector type as a one component vector. We then, create a ListSample object for data inputs.

We also create two Subsample objects that will store the measurement vectors in the `sample` into two separate sample containers. Each Subsample object stores only the measurement vectors belonging to a single class. This *class sample* will be used by the parameter estimation algorithms.

```
unsigned int numberOfClasses = 2;
typedef itk::Vector< double, 1 > MeasurementVectorType;
typedef itk::Statistics::ListSample< MeasurementVectorType > SampleType;
SampleType::Pointer sample = SampleType::New();
sample->SetMeasurementVectorSize( 1 ); // length of measurement vectors
                                       // in the sample.
```

The following code snippet creates a NormalVariateGenerator object. Since the random variable generator returns values according to the standard normal distribution (the mean is zero, and the standard deviation is one) before pushing random values into the sample, we change the mean and standard deviation. We want two normal (Gaussian) distribution data. We have two for loops. Each for loop uses different mean and standard deviation. Before we fill the sample with the second distribution data, we call Initialize() method to recreate the pool of random variables in the normalGenerator. In the second for loop, we fill the two class samples with measurement vectors using the AddInstance() method.

To see the probability density plots from the two distribution, refer to Figure 5.5.

```
typedef itk::Statistics::NormalVariateGenerator NormalGeneratorType;
NormalGeneratorType::Pointer normalGenerator = NormalGeneratorType::New();

normalGenerator->Initialize( 101 );

MeasurementVectorType mv;
double mean = 100;
double standardDeviation = 30;
for ( unsigned int i = 0; i < 100; ++i )
  {
  mv[0] = ( normalGenerator->GetVariate() * standardDeviation ) + mean;
  sample->PushBack( mv );
  }


normalGenerator->Initialize( 3024 );
mean = 200;
standardDeviation = 30;
for ( unsigned int i = 0; i < 100; ++i )
  {
  mv[0] = ( normalGenerator->GetVariate() * standardDeviation ) + mean;
  sample->PushBack( mv );
  }
```

In the following code snippet notice that the template argument for the MeanCalculator and CovarianceCalculator is ClassSampleType (i.e., type of Subsample) instead of SampleType (i.e., type of ListSample). This is because the parameter estimation algorithms are applied to the class sample.

```
typedef itk::Array< double > ParametersType;
ParametersType params( 2 );

std::vector< ParametersType > initialParameters( numberOfClasses );
params[0] = 110.0;
params[1] = 800.0;
initialParameters[0] = params;

params[0] = 210.0;
params[1] = 850.0;
initialParameters[1] = params;

typedef itk::Statistics::GaussianMixtureModelComponent< SampleType >
  ComponentType;

std::vector< ComponentType::Pointer > components;
for ( unsigned int i = 0; i < numberOfClasses; i++ )
  {
  components.push_back( ComponentType::New() );
  (components[i])->SetSample( sample );
  (components[i])->SetParameters( initialParameters[i] );
  }
```

We run the estimator.

```
typedef itk::Statistics::ExpectationMaximizationMixtureModelEstimator<
                        SampleType > EstimatorType;
EstimatorType::Pointer estimator = EstimatorType::New();

estimator->SetSample( sample );
estimator->SetMaximumIteration( 200 );

itk::Array< double > initialProportions(numberOfClasses);
initialProportions[0] = 0.5;
initialProportions[1] = 0.5;

estimator->SetInitialProportions( initialProportions );

for ( unsigned int i = 0; i < numberOfClasses; i++)
  {
  estimator->AddComponent( (ComponentType::Superclass*)
                        (components[i]).GetPointer() );

  }

estimator->Update();
```

We then print out the estimated parameters.

```
for ( unsigned int i = 0; i < numberOfClasses; i++ )
  {
  std::cout << "Cluster[" << i << "]" << std::endl;
  std::cout << "    Parameters:" << std::endl;
  std::cout << "         " << (components[i])->GetFullParameters()
            << std::endl;
  std::cout << "    Proportion: ";
  std::cout << "         " << estimator->GetProportions()[i] << std::endl;
  }
```

5.4.5 Classification using Markov Random Field

Markov Random Fields are probabilistic models that use the correlation between pixels in a neighborhood to decide the object region. The itk::Statistics::MRFImageFilter uses the maximum a posteriori (MAP) estimates for modeling the MRF. The object traverses the data set and uses the model generated by the Mahalanobis distance classifier to gets the the distance between each pixel in the data set to a set of known classes, updates the distances by evaluating the influence of its neighboring pixels (based on a MRF model) and finally, classifies each pixel to the class which has the minimum distance to that pixel (taking the neighborhood influence under consideration). The energy function minimization is done using the iterated conditional modes (ICM) algorithm [6].

The source code for this section can be found in the file
ScalarImageMarkovRandomField1.cxx.

This example shows how to use the Markov Random Field approach for classifying the pixel of a scalar image.

The itk::Statistics::MRFImageFilter is used for refining an initial classification by introducing the spatial coherence of the labels. The user should provide two images as input. The first image is the one to be classified while the second image is an image of labels representing an initial classification.

The following headers are related to reading input images, writing the output image, and making the necessary conversions between scalar and vector images.

```
#include "itkImage.h"
#include "itkImageFileReader.h"
#include "itkImageFileWriter.h"
#include "itkComposeImageFilter.h"
```

The following headers are related to the statistical classification classes.

```
#include "itkMRFImageFilter.h"
#include "itkDistanceToCentroidMembershipFunction.h"
#include "itkMinimumDecisionRule.h"
```

First we define the pixel type and dimension of the image that we intend to classify. With this image type we can also declare the itk::ImageFileReader needed for reading the input image, create one and set its input filename. In this particular case we choose to use signed short as pixel type, which is typical for MicroMRI and CT data sets.

```
typedef signed short        PixelType;
const unsigned int          Dimension = 2;

typedef itk::Image<PixelType, Dimension > ImageType;

typedef itk::ImageFileReader< ImageType > ReaderType;
ReaderType::Pointer reader = ReaderType::New();
reader->SetFileName( inputImageFileName );
```

As a second step we define the pixel type and dimension of the image of labels that provides the initial classification of the pixels from the first image. This initial labeled image can be the output of a K-Means method like the one illustrated in section 5.4.2.

```
typedef unsigned char          LabelPixelType;

typedef itk::Image<LabelPixelType, Dimension > LabelImageType;

typedef itk::ImageFileReader< LabelImageType > LabelReaderType;
LabelReaderType::Pointer labelReader = LabelReaderType::New();
labelReader->SetFileName( inputLabelImageFileName );
```

Since the Markov Random Field algorithm is defined in general for images whose pixels have multiple components, that is, images of vector type, we must adapt our scalar image in order to satisfy the interface expected by the MRFImageFilter. We do this by using the itk::ComposeImageFilter. With this filter we will present our scalar image as a vector image whose vector pixels contain a single component.

```
typedef itk::FixedArray<LabelPixelType,1>  ArrayPixelType;

typedef itk::Image< ArrayPixelType, Dimension > ArrayImageType;

typedef itk::ComposeImageFilter<
                ImageType, ArrayImageType > ScalarToArrayFilterType;

ScalarToArrayFilterType::Pointer
   scalarToArrayFilter = ScalarToArrayFilterType::New();
scalarToArrayFilter->SetInput( reader->GetOutput() );
```

With the input image type ImageType and labeled image type LabelImageType we instantiate the type of the itk::MRFImageFilter that will apply the Markov Random Field algorithm in order to refine the pixel classification.

```
typedef itk::MRFImageFilter< ArrayImageType, LabelImageType > MRFFilterType;

MRFFilterType::Pointer mrfFilter = MRFFilterType::New();

mrfFilter->SetInput( scalarToArrayFilter->GetOutput() );
```

We set now some of the parameters for the MRF filter. In particular, the number of classes to be used during the classification, the maximum number of iterations to be run in this filter and the error tolerance that will be used as a criterion for convergence.

```
mrfFilter->SetNumberOfClasses( numberOfClasses );
mrfFilter->SetMaximumNumberOfIterations( numberOfIterations );
mrfFilter->SetErrorTolerance( 1e-7 );
```

The smoothing factor represents the tradeoff between fidelity to the observed image and the smoothness of the segmented image. Typical smoothing factors have values between 1 5. This factor will multiply the weights that define the influence of neighbors on the classification of a given pixel. The higher the value, the more uniform will be the regions resulting from the classification refinement.

```
mrfFilter->SetSmoothingFactor( smoothingFactor );
```

Given that the MRF filter need to continually relabel the pixels, it needs access to a set of membership functions that will measure to what degree every pixel belongs to a particular class. The classification is performed by the itk::ImageClassifierBase class, that is instantiated using the type of the input vector image and the type of the labeled image.

```
typedef itk::ImageClassifierBase<
                        ArrayImageType,
                        LabelImageType >   SupervisedClassifierType;

SupervisedClassifierType::Pointer classifier =
                        SupervisedClassifierType::New();
```

The classifier need a decision rule to be set by the user. Note that we must use `GetPointer()` in the call of the `SetDecisionRule()` method because we are passing a SmartPointer, and smart pointer cannot perform polymorphism, we must then extract the raw pointer that is associated to the smart pointer. This extraction is done with the GetPointer() method.

```
typedef itk::Statistics::MinimumDecisionRule DecisionRuleType;

DecisionRuleType::Pointer  classifierDecisionRule = DecisionRuleType::New();

classifier->SetDecisionRule( classifierDecisionRule.GetPointer() );
```

We now instantiate the membership functions. In this case we use the `itk::Statistics::DistanceToCentroidMembershipFunction` class templated over the pixel type of the vector image, that in our example happens to be a vector of dimension 1.

```
typedef itk::Statistics::DistanceToCentroidMembershipFunction<
                        ArrayPixelType >
                        MembershipFunctionType;

typedef MembershipFunctionType::Pointer MembershipFunctionPointer;


double meanDistance = 0;
MembershipFunctionType::CentroidType centroid(1);
for( unsigned int i=0; i < numberOfClasses; i++ )
  {
  MembershipFunctionPointer membershipFunction =
                        MembershipFunctionType::New();

  centroid[0] = atof( argv[i+numberOfArgumentsBeforeMeans] );

  membershipFunction->SetCentroid( centroid );

  classifier->AddMembershipFunction( membershipFunction );
  meanDistance += static_cast< double > (centroid[0]);
  }
if (numberOfClasses > 0)
  {
  meanDistance /= numberOfClasses;
  }
else
  {
  std::cerr << "ERROR: numberOfClasses is 0" << std::endl;
  return EXIT_FAILURE;
  }
```

We set the Smoothing factor. This factor will multiply the weights that define the influence of neighbors on the classification of a given pixel. The higher the value, the more uniform will be the regions resulting from the classification refinement.

```
mrfFilter->SetSmoothingFactor( smoothingFactor );
```

and we set the neighborhood radius that will define the size of the clique to be used in the computation of the neighbors' influence in the classification of any given pixel. Note that despite the fact that we call this a radius, it is actually the half size of an hypercube. That is, the actual region of influence will not be circular but rather an N-Dimensional box. For example, a neighborhood radius of 2 in a 3D image will result in a clique of size 5x5x5 pixels, and a radius of 1 will result in a clique of size 3x3x3 pixels.

```
mrfFilter->SetNeighborhoodRadius( 1 );
```

We should now set the weights used for the neighbors. This is done by passing an array of values that contains the linear sequence of weights for the neighbors. For example, in a neighborhood of size 3x3x3, we should provide a linear array of 9 weight values. The values are packaged in a std::vector and are supposed to be double. The following lines illustrate a typical set of values for a 3x3x3 neighborhood. The array is arranged and then passed to the filter by using the method SetMRFNeighborhoodWeight().

```
std::vector< double > weights;
weights.push_back(1.5);
weights.push_back(2.0);
weights.push_back(1.5);
weights.push_back(2.0);
weights.push_back(0.0); // This is the central pixel
weights.push_back(2.0);
weights.push_back(1.5);
weights.push_back(2.0);
weights.push_back(1.5);
```

We now scale weights so that the smoothing function and the image fidelity functions have comparable value. This is necessary since the label image and the input image can have different dynamic ranges. The fidelity function is usually computed using a distance function, such as the itk::DistanceToCentroidMembershipFunction or one of the other membership functions. They tend to have values in the order of the means specified.

```
double totalWeight = 0;
for(std::vector< double >::const_iterator wcIt = weights.begin();
    wcIt != weights.end(); ++wcIt )
  {
  totalWeight += *wcIt;
  }
for(std::vector< double >::iterator wIt = weights.begin();
    wIt != weights.end(); ++wIt )
  {
  *wIt = static_cast< double > ( (*wIt) * meanDistance / (2 * totalWeight));
  }

mrfFilter->SetMRFNeighborhoodWeight( weights );
```

Finally, the classifier class is connected to the Markof Random Fields filter.

```
mrfFilter->SetClassifier( classifier );
```

The output image produced by the itk::MRFImageFilter has the same pixel type as the labeled

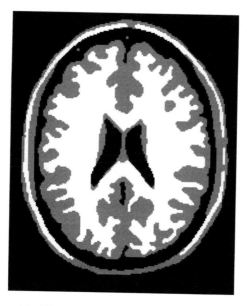

Figure 5.8: Effect of the MRF filter on a T1 slice of the brain.

input image. In the following lines we use the `OutputImageType` in order to instantiate the type of
a `itk::ImageFileWriter`. Then create one, and connect it to the output of the classification filter
after passing it through an intensity rescaler to rescale it to an 8 bit dynamic range

```
typedef MRFFilterType::OutputImageType  OutputImageType;

typedef itk::ImageFileWriter< OutputImageType > WriterType;

WriterType::Pointer writer = WriterType::New();

writer->SetInput( intensityRescaler->GetOutput() );

writer->SetFileName( outputImageFileName );
```

We are now ready for triggering the execution of the pipeline. This is done by simply invoking the
`Update()` method in the writer. This call will propagate the update request to the reader and then to
the MRF filter.

```
try
  {
  writer->Update();
  }
catch( itk::ExceptionObject & excp )
  {
  std::cerr << "Problem encountered while writing ";
  std::cerr << " image file : " << argv[2] << std::endl;
  std::cerr << excp << std::endl;
  return EXIT_FAILURE;
  }
```

Figure 5.8 illustrates the effect of this filter with three classes. In this example the filter was run with a smoothing factor of 3. The labeled image was produced by ScalarImageKmeansClassifier.cxx and the means were estimated by ScalarImageKmeansModelEstimator.cxx.

BIBLIOGRAPHY

[1] A. Alexandrescu. *Modern C++ Design: Generic Programming and Design Patterns Applied.* Professional Computing Series. Addison-Wesley, 2001. 1.8.3, 1.10, 3.9.1

[2] K. Alsabti, S. Ranka, and V. Singh. An efficient k-means clustering algorithm. In *First Workshop on High-Performance Data Mining*, 1998. 5.4.1

[3] L. Alvarez and J.-M. Morel. *A Morphological Approach To Multiscale Analysis: From Principles to Equations*, pages 229–254. Kluwer Academic Publishers, 1994. 2.7.3

[4] ANSI-ISO. *Programming Languages - C++*. American National Standards Institue, 1998. 1.9

[5] M. H. Austern. *Generic Programming and the STL:*. Professional Computing Series. Addison-Wesley, 1999. 1.8.3, 1.10, 3.9.1

[6] J. Besag. On the statistical analysis of dirty pictures. *J. Royal Statist. Soc. B.*, 48:259–302, 1986. 5.4.5

[7] Eric Boix, Mathieu Malaterre, Benoit Regrain, and Jean-Pierre Roux. *The GDCM Library.* CNRS, INSERM, INSA Lyon, UCB Lyon, http://www.creatis.insa-lyon.fr/Public/Gdcm/. 1.12.1

[8] R. N. Bracewell. *The Fourier Transform and its Applications*. McGraw-Hill, 1999. 2.10.1

[9] R. N. Bracewell. *Fourier Analysis and Imaging*. Plenum US, 2004. 2.10.1

[10] R. H. Byrd, P. Lu, and J. Nocedal. A limited memory algorithm for bound constrained optimization. *SIAM Journal on Scientific and Statistical Computing*, 16(5):1190–1208, 1995. 3.12

[11] V. Caselles, R. Kimmel, and G. Sapiro. Geodesic active contours. *International Journal on Computer Vision*, 22(1):61–97, 1997. 4.3.3

[12] A. Collignon, F. Maes, D. Delaere, D. Vandermeulen, P. Suetens, and G. Marchal. Automated multimodality image registration based on information theory. In *Information Processing in Medical Imaging 1995*, pages 263–274. Kluwer Academic Publishers, Dordrecht, The Netherlands, 1995. 3.5

[13] P. E. Danielsson. Euclidean distance mapping. *Computer Graphics and Image Processing*, 14:227–248, 1980. 2.8

[14] C. Darwin. *On the Origin of Species.* http://www.gutenberg.org, sixth edition, 1999. 3.6

[15] M. H. Davis, A. Khotanzad, D. P. Flamig, and S. E. Harms. A physics-based coordinate transformation for 3-d image matching. *IEEE Transactions on Medical Imaging*, 16(3), June 1997. 3.9.18

[16] R. Deriche. Fast algorithms for low level vision. *IEEE Transactions on Pattern Analysis and Machine Intelligence*, 12(1):78–87, 1990. 2.4.2, 2.7.1, 2.7.1

[17] R. Deriche. Recursively implementing the gaussian and its derivatives. Technical Report 1893, Unite de recherche INRIA Sophia-Antipolis, avril 1993. Research Repport. 2.4.2, 2.7.1, 2.7.1

[18] C. Dodson and T. Poston. *Tensor Geometry: The Geometric Viewpoint and its Uses.* Springer, 1997. 3.9.1, 9

[19] Richard O. Duda, Peter E. Hart, and David G. Stork. *Pattern classification.* A Wiley-Interscience Publication, second edition, 2000. 5.2.3, 5.4, 5.4

[20] David Eberly. *Ridges in Image and Data Analysis.* Kluwer Academic Publishers, Dordrecht, 1996. 4.2.1

[21] E. Gamma, R. Helm, R. Johnson, and J. Vlissides. *Design Patterns, Elements of Reusable Object-Oriented Software.* Professional Computing Series. Addison-Wesley, 1995. 1.2, 3.4

[22] G. Gerig, O. Kübler, R. Kikinis, and F. A. Jolesz. Nonlinear anisotropic filtering of MRI data. *IEEE Transactions on Medical Imaging*, 11(2):221–232, June 1992. 2.7.3

[23] Stephen Grossberg. Neural dynamics of brightness perception: Features, boundaries, diffusion, and resonance. *Perception and Psychophysics*, 36(5):428–456, 1984. 2.7.3

[24] J. Hajnal, D. J. Hawkes, and D. Hill. *Medical Image Registration.* CRC Press, 2001. 3.5, 3.11.4

[25] W. R. Hamilton. *Elements of Quaternions.* Chelsea Publishing Company, 1969. 3.6.4, 3.9.1, 3.9.11, 3.12

[26] A. Hendersen. *The Paraview Guide.* Kitware, Inc, 2004. 3.15

[27] B. K. Horn. Closed-form solution of absolute orientation using unit quaternions. *Journal of the Optical Society of America*, 4:629–642, April 1987. 3.17

[28] C. J. Joly. *A Manual of Quaternions.* MacMillan and Co. Limited, 1905. 3.6.4, 3.9.11

[29] Tapas Kanungo, David M. Mount, Nathan S. Netanyahu, Christine Piatko, Ruth Silverman, and Angela Y. Wu. An efficient k-means clustering algorithm: Analysis and implementation. 5.1.7, 5.4.1

[30] J. Koënderink and A. van Doorn. The Structure of Two-Dimensional Scalar Fields with Applications to Vision. *Biol. Cybernetics*, 33:151–158, 1979. 4.2.1

[31] J. Koenderink and A. van Doorn. Local features of smooth shapes: Ridges and courses. *SPIE Proc. Geometric Methods in Computer Vision II*, 2031:2–13, 1993. 4.2.1

[32] L. Kohn, J. Corrigan, and M.Donaldson, editors. *To Err is Human: Building a safer health system*. National Academy Press, 2001. 1.12.4

[33] S. Kullback. *Information Theory and Statistics*. Dover Publications, 1997. 5.3.2

[34] M. Leventon, W. Grimson, and O. Faugeras. Statistical shape influence in geodesic active contours. In *Proc. IEEE Conference on Computer Vision and Pattern Recognition (CVPR)*, volume 1, pages 316–323, 2000. 4.3.7

[35] T. Lindeberg. *Scale-Space Theory in Computer Science*. Kluwer Academic Publishers, 1994. 2.7.1

[36] H. Lodish, A. Berk, S. Zipursky, P. Matsudaira, D. Baltimore, and J. Darnell. *Molecular Cell Biology*. W. H. Freeman and Company, 2000. 3.9.1

[37] W. E. Lorensen and H. E. Cline. Marching cubes: A high resolution 3d surface construction algorithm. *Computer Graphics*, 21(4):163–169, July 1987. 2.11.1

[38] F. Maes, A. Collignon, D. Meulen, G. Marchal, and P. Suetens. Multi-modality image registration by maximization of mutual information. *IEEE Trans. on Med. Imaging*, 16:187–198, 1997. 3.5

[39] R. Malladi, J. A. Sethian, and B. C. Vermuri. Shape modeling with front propagation: A level set approach. *IEEE Trans. on Pattern Analysis and Machine Intelligence*, 17(2):158–174, 1995. 4.3.2

[40] D. Mattes, D. R. Haynor, H. Vesselle, T. K. Lewellen, and W. Eubank. Non-rigid multimodality image registration. In *Medical Imaging 2001: Image Processing*, pages 1609–1620, 2001. 3.9.17, 3.11.3

[41] D. Mattes, D. R. Haynor, H. Vesselle, T. K. Lewellen, and W. Eubank. PET-CT image registration in the chest using free-form deformations. *IEEE Trans. on Medical Imaging*, 22(1):120–128, January 2003. 3.5.1, 3.9.17

[42] E. H. Meijering, W. J. Niessen, J. P. Pluim, and M. A. Viergever. Quantitative comparison of sinc-approximating kernels for medical image interpolation. In W. M. Wells, A. Colchester, and S. Delp, editors, *MICCAI'98 First International Conference on Medical Image Computing and Computer-Assisted Intervention*, Lecture Notes in Computer Science, pages 972–980. Springer Verlag, September 1999. 3.10.4

[43] David R. Musser. Introspective sorting and selection algorithms. *Software–Practice and Experience*, 8:983–993, 1997. 5.2.3

[44] NEMA. The dicom standard. Technical report, NEMA, http://medial.nema.org/, 2013. 1.12.1

[45] Dan Pelleg and Andrew Moore. Accelerating exact k -means algorithms with geometric reasoning. In *Fifth ACM SIGKDD International Conference On Knowledge Discovery and Data Mining*, pages 277–281, 1999. 5.4.1

[46] P. Perona and J. Malik. Scale-space and edge detection using anisotropic diffusion. *IEEE Transactions on Pattern Analysis Machine Intelligence*, 12:629–639, 1990. 2.7.3, 2.7.3, 2.7.3

[47] J. P. Pluim, J. B. A. Maintz, and M. A. Viergever. Mutual-Information-Based Registration of Medical Images: A Survey. *IEEE Transactions on Medical Imaging*, 22(8):986–1004, August 2003. 3.5, 3.11.3

[48] K. Popper. *Open Society and Its Enemies*. Princenton University Press, 1971. 3.5.1

[49] K. Popper. *The Logic of Scientific Discovery*. Routledge, 2002. 3.5.1, 5.3.1

[50] W. H. Press, B. P. Flannery, S. A. Teukolsky, and W. T. Vetterling. *Numerical Recipes in C*. Cambridge University Press, second edition, 1992. 3.12

[51] K. Rohr, M. Fornefett, and H. S. Stiehl. Approximating thin-plate splines for elastric registration: Integration of landmark errors and orientation attributes. In A. Kuba, M. Samal, and A. Todd-Pkropek, editors, *Information Processing in Medical Imaging 1999 (IPMI'99)*, pages 252–265. Springer, 1999. 3.9.18

[52] K. Rohr, H. S. Stiehl, R. Sprengel, T. M. Buzug, J. Weese, and M. H Kuhn. Landmark-based elastic registration using approximating thin-plate splines. *IEEE Transactions on Medical Imaging*, 20(6):526–534, June 1997. 3.9.18, 3.17

[53] D. Rueckert, L. I. Sonoda, C. Hayes, D. L. G. Hill, M. O. Leach, and D. J. Hawkes. Nonrigid registration using free-form deformations: Application to breast mr images. *IEEE Transaction on Medical Imaging*, 18(8):712–721, 1999. 3.9.17

[54] G. Sapiro and D. Ringach. Anisotropic diffusion of multivalued images with applications to color filtering. *IEEE Trans. on Image Processing*, 5:1582–1586, 1996. 2.7.3

[55] W. Schroeder, K. Martin, and B. Lorensen. *The Visualization Toolkit, An Object Oriented Approach to 3D Graphics*. Kitware Inc, 1998. 2.11.1

[56] J. P. Serra. *Image Analysis and Mathematical Morphology*. Academic Press Inc., 1982. 2.6.3, 4.2.1

[57] J.A. Sethian. *Level Set Methods and Fast Marching Methods*. Cambridge University Press, 1996. 4.3

[58] C. E. Shannon. A mathematical theory of communication. *Bell System Technical Journal*, 27:379–423, July 1948. 2.9.4, 5.3.2

[59] C. E. Shannon and W. Weaver. *The Mathematical Theory of Communication*. University of Illinois Press, 1948. 2.9.4, 5.3.2

[60] M. Styner, C. Brehbuhler, G. Szekely, and G. Gerig. Parametric estimate of intensity homogeneities applied to MRI. *IEEE Trans. Medical Imaging*, 19(3):153–165, March 2000. 3.12

[61] Baart M. ter Haar Romeny, editor. *Geometry-Driven Diffusion in Computer Vision*. Kluwer Academic Publishers, 1994. 2.7.3

[62] J. P. Thirion. Fast non-rigid matching of 3D medical image. Technical report, Research Report RR-2547, Epidure Project, INRIA Sophia, May 1995. 3.14

[63] J.-P. Thirion. Image matching as a diffusion process: an analogy with maxwell's demons. *Medical Image Analysis*, 2(3):243–260, 1998. 3.14

[64] P. Viola and W. M. Wells III. Alignment by maximization of mutual information. *IJCV*, 24(2):137–154, 1997. 3.5

[65] J. Weickert, B.M. ter Haar Romeny, and M.A. Viergever. Conservative image transformations with restoration and scale-space properties. In *Proc. 1996 IEEE International Conference on Image Processing (ICIP-96, Lausanne, Sept. 16-19, 1996)*, pages 465–468, 1996. 2.7.3

[66] R. T. Whitaker and G. Gerig. *Vector-Valued Diffusion*, pages 93–134. Kluwer Academic Publishers, 1994. 2.7.3, 2.7.3

[67] R. T. Whitaker and X. Xue. Variable-Conductance, Level-Set Curvature for Image Processing. In *International Conference on Image Processing*, pages 142–145. IEEE, 2001. 2.7.3

[68] Ross T. Whitaker. Characterizing first and second order patches using geometry-limited diffusion. In *Information Processing in Medical Imaging 1993 (IPMI'93)*, pages 149–167, 1993. 2.7.3

[69] Ross T. Whitaker. *Geometry-Limited Diffusion*. PhD thesis, The University of North Carolina, Chapel Hill, North Carolina 27599-3175, 1993. 2.7.3, 2.7.3

[70] Ross T. Whitaker. Geometry-limited diffusion in the characterization of geometric patches in images. *Computer Vision, Graphics, and Image Processing: Image Understanding*, 57(1):111–120, January 1993. 2.7.3

[71] Ross T. Whitaker and Stephen M. Pizer. Geometry-based image segmentation using anisotropic diffusion. In Ying-Lie O, A. Toet, H.J.A.M Heijmans, D.H. Foster, and P. Meer, editors, *Shape in Picture: The mathematical description of shape in greylevel images*. Springer Verlag, Heidelberg, 1993. 2.7.3

[72] Ross T. Whitaker and Stephen M. Pizer. A multi-scale approach to nonuniform diffusion. *Computer Vision, Graphics, and Image Processing: Image Understanding*, 57(1):99–110, January 1993. 2.7.3

[73] Terry S. Yoo and James M. Coggins. Using statistical pattern recognition techniques to control variable conductance diffusion. In *Information Processing in Medical Imaging 1993 (IPMI'93)*, pages 459–471, 1993. 2.7.3

[74] T.S. Yoo, U. Neumann, H. Fuchs, S.M. Pizer, T. Cullip, J. Rhoades, and R.T. Whitaker. Direct visualization of volume data. *IEEE Computer Graphics and Applications*, 12(4):63–71, 1992. 4.2.1

[75] T.S. Yoo, S.M. Pizer, H. Fuchs, T. Cullip, J. Rhoades, and R. Whitaker. Achieving direct volume visualization with interactive semantic region selection. In *Information Processing in Medical Images*. Springer Verlag, 1991. 4.2.1, 4.2.1

[76] C. Zhu, R. H. Byrd, and J. Nocedal. L-bfgs-b: Algorithm 778: L-bfgs-b, fortran routines for large scale bound constrained optimization. *ACM Transactions on Mathematical Software*, 23(4):550–560, November 1997. 3.12

INDEX